21830

D1626267

IMI: information service

The

ADVERTISING

BOOK

The ADVERTISING BOOK

THE HISTORY OF ADVERTISING IN IRELAND

Hugh Oram

BOOKS

First published 1986 by
MO Books, 12 Magennis Place,
Dublin 2.

Copyright © Hugh Oram, 1986. All rights reserved.

British Library Cataloguing in Publication Data

Oram, Hugh
The History of Advertising in Ireland
The Advertising Book
1.Advertising-Ireland-History
I. Title
659.1'09415   HF5813.173
ISBN 0-9509184-3-1

Colour separations by Colour Repro Ltd.
Origination by Design & Art Facilities Ltd., Dublin
Typeset by Phototype-Set Ltd., Dublin
Indices typeset by Computer Graphics Ltd., Dublin
Printed and bound in Ireland by Mount Salus Press Ltd., Dublin

Foreword

Advertising is a comparatively new phenomenon in Ireland. It may have been big business in both America and Britain a century ago, but only since the establishment of the Irish Free State, with the consequent development of local commerce and industry, has advertising become a serious pursuit, relieved by flashes of humour. In this volume, I have tried to paint a portrait of the advertising industry in Ireland in its many stages of development, from the comparative lack of commercial and creative sophistication in earlier eras through to today's highly complex, computer-biased industry. Advertising has grown in strength and diversity in company with the numerous developments in the media scene, particularly since the arrival of Irish television.

In telling this quite fascinating history, I have been very dependent on the personal reminiscences of many people who have worked in the industry. Sadly, much historical material relating to advertising has been thrown out. Storage space is an expensive commodity and with the many moves of premises in recent years of both advertisers and advertising agencies, much archive material has been destroyed. I hope that this volume, compiled with the generous help of numerous advertising people, whose assistance is acknowledged elsewhere, will help to fill this gap. Also I hope that this book will help to encourage further studies of what is after all the most persuasive of industries in modern Ireland.

Hugh Oram
Dublin, November, 1986

A word of thanks

Many people have helped in the preparation of this book. First and most importantly, I should like to thank my wife Bernadette for her endless patience and her wise counsels; making the book would not have been possible without her help. Derek Garvey, my publisher, is thanked for his limitless energy and enthusiasm throughout the project. François Bonal of Épernay, France is thanked for his constant encouragement. Brian Kelly helped much with Northern Ireland coverage. The staff of Design & Art Facilities, who prepared the layout, as well as Robert Ballagh, who designed and illustrated the cover, are thanked, as is Rory O'Neill of Phototype-Set. The under-named contributed most generously with their time and in many cases, with visual and other material.

Michael Algar (Irish Film Board);
John Allen (Cara magazine, Aer Lingus);
Colin Anderson, Belfast;
Arnotts: *Bill Kelly, Michael Nesbitt, Ronnie Nesbitt;*
Eamonn Andrews;
Terry Balfe;
Bank of Ireland: *Gerry Murphy, Tony Hurst, Pat White;*
Cecil Barror;
Tom Behan (Ireland of the Welcomes);
Cecil Bell (W & C McDonnell);
Johnny van Belle;
Bill Bergin;
Bord Bainne: *Maura Hussey, Noel Lawlor, Pat McDonagh;*
Marie-Claire Bardoz (Musée de la Publicité, Paris);
Des Bingham (RMB, Belfast);
Dick Birchall (The Birchall Co);
Colm Brangan;
Brindley Advertising: *Basil Brindley, Berenice Brindley, Donald Brindley, Eileen Byrne, Michael McCabe;*
Seamus de Burca;
Business & Finance (*Hugh Hogan, Tom Lockhart);*
Harry Byers (Byers Advertising);
Brendan Byrne;
Des Byrne (Behaviour & Attitudes);
Esther and Frankie Byrne;
Ciaran Breathnach (Avondale Recording Studios);
David Burke (Tuam Herald);
Dermod Cafferky;
late Jack Cairns;
Noelle Campbell-Sharp;
Michael Carr;

Ed Carrigan;

P. J. Carroll & Co: *Gerry Kiernan, John Kiely, John Lepere, Von O'Toole*;

Colman Cassidy (Sunday Press);

Jim Caulfield (ESB);

late W. P. "Bill" Cavanagh (Association of Advertisers in Ireland);

CDP: *Bob Milne, Brendan O Broin, Peter O'Keeffe*;

Central Statistics Office, Dublin;

Frank Chambers;

Mrs Rita Childers;

CP&A: *Carmel Bruce, Cecil Dick*;

Maurice Clarke-Barry;

Pat Cleary (Clare Champion);

Derek Cobbe (Longford News);

Jim Cogan;

College of Commerce, Rathmines, Dublin: *Michael Hayes, Maureen Holland*;

Mary Colley (Anois);

Michael Colley (Murray Consultants);

Pan Collins;

Earl Connolly (Limerick Leader);

Paddy Considine (Adsell);

Eamon Cooke (Radio Dublin);

Vincent Corcoran;

Cork Examiner: *George Crosbie, Ted Crosbie, Catherine Lingwood, Joe O'Grady*;

Creative Film & Video: *John Devis, Pat Devlin*;

Brian Cronin & Associates: *Ronan Callan, Brian Cronin, Frank Loughrey, Ian Fox, Willie O'Toole*;

Colm Cronin;

Jack Cronin;

CRP: *Chris O'Kelly, Brian Stokes*;

Frank Cullen (National Newspapers of Ireland);

Michael Cullen (Marketing Opinion);

J. P. Cusack (Connacht Tribune);

Rena Dardis;

Dave Dark (McConnell's, Belfast);

Jack Davis (Meath Chronicle);

Gerald Davis (Davis Gallery);

Kingsley Dempsey (Parker Advertising);

Maymay Dignam;

Joe Dillon;

Luke Dillon-Mahon;

Domas: *Eoghan Plunkett, Joe Tiernan*;

Raymond Donnellan (Galway Advertiser);

Dermot Doolin (Irish Actors' Equity);

Downtown Radio, Newtownards: *Kieran Boyle, Ivan Tinman*;

Brian Doyle, Dublin;

John Doyle, Dingle;
Eddie Dunne;
Gregory Dunne (Leitrim Observer);
Easons: *Thurlo Butterly, Harold Clarke;*
Tommy Ellis (Tommy Ellis Recording Studios);
Bert van Emden;
Evening Herald: *Valerie McGrath, Joan Tighe;*
Fergus Farrell (Tara Publishing);
Pat Farrell, Galway;
Alex Findlater;
Peter Finnegan;
Denis Fitzgibbon (Toyota);
Frank Fitzpatrick (PF Marketing);
Clifton Flewitt (Irish Railway Records' Society);
Karen Flynn (Coca-Cola Ireland);
Fergus Flynn (Cinema & General Publicity);
Aubrey Fogarty Associates: *Aubrey Fogarty, Stuart Fogarty, Noel Johnson;*
Brendan Foreman (Abbey Theatre);
Jan de Fouw;
Rowel Friers;
Jim Furlong;
George Gaffney (Gaffney McHugh);
Finn Gallen (IDA);
George Gamlin, Honolulu;
Nuala Gardner;
Arthur Garrett;
Denis Garvey (Janus Advertising);
Eamonn Geraghty;
Goodalls of Ireland: *Mark Dorman, Aidan Flynn, N. J. McCarthy;*
late George Gracie;
Martin Giblin (T. P. Whelehan Son & Co);
Ida Grehan;
Terry Gogan;
Brian Halford;
John Hamilton (Southern Star);
Fred Hayden (Association of Advertisers in Ireland);
Jarlath Hayes;
P. J. Hennelly (Connaught Telegraph);
Mike Hogan (Q102 Radio);
Hunter Advertising: *Gareth Oldham, Robin Moore;*
John Hunter;
Irish Distillers: *Des Heather, John Young;*
Irish International: *Paddy Harte, John Conway, Finbar Costello;*
Irish Press: *Liam Flynn, Alan Maxwell;*
Irish Shell: *Ruth McDonnell, Noel Tierney;*
Jemma Publications: *John Caughey, Ian Collie, Frank Grennan,*

David Luke, John Mannion;
Trevor Jacobs (Arks);
Margaret Jennings;
Johnson Bros: *Terence C. Johnson, Brendan McDonald;*
John Kerry Keane (Kilkenny People);
Mrs Jean Keegan;
Con Kelleher;
Padraig Kennelly (Kerry's Eye);
Anthony Kennedy;
Ray Kennedy;
Colum Kenny (NIHE);
Michael B. Kenny;
Stuart M. Kenny (Kenny's Advertising);
Kerryman: *Bryan Cunningham, Sean Colgan;*
Cecil King (Donegal Democrat);
Billy King;
Jim King (Dublin Corporation public relations);
Cor Klaasen;
Gordon Lambert;
Basil Lapworth;
Mrs Cecily Leonard;
Hugh Leonard;
Nicholas Leonard;
Pat Liddy;
Bob Loughan (More O'Ferrall/Adshel);
Peter J. Lyons;
Brigid Lynch;
Mrs. Carmel Lynch;
Dara O Loingsigh;
Joe Lynch;
Frank Madden (Today's Grocer);
Gordon Magee (Morton Newspapers);
late Leo Maguire;
late Bill Maguire;
late Tommy Mangan;
David Markey (Irish Farmers' Monthly, New Hibernia);
Gene Martin;
Anton Mazer;
Brendan McCabe (Independent Newspapers);
Keith McCarthy-Morrogh (Baileys);
Norman McConnell;
McConnell's Advertising: *Catherine Donnelly, John Fanning, Maura Fox, Seamus Holden, John C. McConnell, Brendan Redmond, Vi Smith, Mike Tobin, Anne Wemyss;*
Fergus McDermott (Gilbey's of Ireland Sales);
Patricia McDonald (Brown Thomas);
Gabriel McDowell (John McMahon & Partners);

R. L. McDowell;
Jack McGouran (Quest PR);
Gerry McGuinness (Sunday World);
Neil McIvor (IDA);
Ted McLaughlin (Health Education Bureau);
Rex McKane (Belfast Progressive Advertising);
Kevin McSharry (Advertising Statistics Ireland);
Belinda Moller (Dublin Coca-Cola exhibition, 1986);
Shane Molloy (Lever Bros);
Jack Mooney;
Jim Moraghan (Institute of Public Administration);
Seamus Morahan (Leinster Leader);
Danny Moroney;
Paul Moy;
MRBI (*Annette Farrell, Jack Jones*);
Fred Mullen;
Brian Murphy (Diners Club);
Gerry Murphy (Irish Trade & Technical Publications);
Ken Murphy;
Sean Murray (Alfred Bird & Sons Ireland);
Michael Mullins (Esso);
Munster Express: *J. J. Walsh, Kieran Walsh;*
Paul Myers (Javelin);
National Library, Dublin;
Nenagh Heritage Centre: *Donal Murphy, Mary Rohan;*
Newspaper Library, Colindale, London;
Noelle Nathan (Irish Hospitals' Trust);
Fiona Nichol (Forman Dove Public Relations);
Jim Nolan (Institute of Advertising Practitioners in Ireland);
Yvonne Nolan;
Gerry O'Boyce (Irish Farmers' Journal);
Clare O'Brien London;
Jim O'Brien Senior (Display Contracts/Riverside Centre);
Diarmuid O Broin (Irish Management Institute);
Joe O'Byrne (O'Byrne Associates);
Manus O'Callaghan (Southern Advertising);
Sandra O'Callaghan (Image);
Enda O'Coineen (Afloat);
Don O'Connell (Doherty Advertising);
Kevin O'Doherty (Advertising Standards Authority);
Fred O'Donovan;
Niall O'Flynn (Player-Wills);
Willie O'Hanlon (Anglo-Celt);
O'Keeffes Advertising: *Noel Cautley, Marion O'Reilly;*
O'Kennedy Brindley: *Bill Davis, Iain MacCarthaigh, Michael McGovern, Pat O'Rorke;*
Desmond O'Kennedy;

Niel O'Kennedy;
Liam O'Leary Film Archives;
Des O'Meara (Des O'Meara & Partners);
Kitty O'Neill;
Michael O'Reilly;
Patsy O'Shannon;
Niall O'Sullivan (O'Connor O'Sullivan Advertising);
Outdoor Advertising Services: *Donal Bruton, Vincent Whelan;*
Peter Owens Advertising: *Kevin Casey, Breda O'Kennedy, Eddie O'Mahony, Peter Owens;*
Padbury Advertising: *Bob Nealon, Seamus Dignam;*
Pan International (Patricia Croke);
Helen Park (Brooke Bond Oxo);
Mrs Eileen Petrie (Modern Display Artists);
Fintan Power, Waterford;
Mrs Albert Price;
Conor Quinn (QMP);
RTE: *Brelda Baum, Colm Brophy, Aidan Burns, Gay Byrne, Michael Carroll, Paddy Clarke, Robert K. Gahan, Larry Gogan, Deirdre Henchy, Val Joyce, Cathal McCabe, Edward F. MacSweeney, Mike Murphy, Joan Newman, Bill O'Donovan, Dominic O'Reilly, Síle O'Sullivan, Eilis Pearse, Brian Pierce, Peadar Pierce, Richard Pine, Kieran Sheedy, Noel Shiels, Willie Styles;*
Pat Ryan (Nenagh Guardian);
Pat Ryan (Pat Ryan Associates);
"Russ" Russell (Windmill Lane);
John Roycroft;
Bernard Share;
Frank Sheerin;
Mary Sherry (Bovril Ireland);
Basil Singleton;
Liam de Siún (Bray Local Broadcasting);
Patricia Slevin;
Mrs Brendan Smith (Beryl Fagan);
Mr and Mrs Derek Snow;
Eimar Spillane;
Terry Spillane;
Mrs. Eileen Stapleton;
Patrick J. Stephenson (James H. North & Co);
Sunday Tribune *(Vincent Browne, Barry Connolly);*
Sunshine Radio: *Robbie Robinson, Stella Robinson;*
Superquinn: *Celine Murphy, Feargal Quinn;*
Martin Swords (Gallaher Dublin);
Harry Thuillier;
The Irish Times: *Jim Cooke, John Gibson, Noel Hayden, Tony Lennon, Major T. B. McDowell, Brenda McNiff, Ted Mullen, Louis O'Neill, Seamus O'Neill, Pat Ruane, Wally Sullivan, John Vincent.*
Jim Tobin (KMMD);

Jonathan Torrie (L & N Supermarkets, Waterford);
Joan Trimble (Impartial Reporter);
Martyn Turner;
Ken Tyrrell;
Robert Tate (Londonderry Sentinel);
Ulster Television: *Jim Creagh, Ken Hamilton, Ray Kennedy;*
Felipe Urrea (Shelbourne Hotel, Dublin);
Joan Walker;
late Capt Oliver Walsh;
Peter Walsh (Guinness);
Bill Walshe (The Innovation Group);
T. P. Whelehan;
Eamonn Williams;
Wilson Hartnell: *Mike Curley, Mary Finan, Ken Grace, Brian Martin, Murrough MacDevitt, Michael Maughan, Gerry McMahon, Eamonn Moore; Sean O Bradaigh, Isobel Rankine, Agnes Russell, Una O'Mahony;*
Stanley Wilson (Bord Failte)
Gunther Wulff;
J. N. Young;
John Young (Young Advertising);
Commandant Peter Young (Defence Forces).

For Bernadette

Contents

CHAPTER I

Introduction
Footprints in time

ADVERTISING IN IRELAND has been a serious business for most of this century, but very serious indeed since the start of television in Ireland, Ulster Television in 1959 and Telefis Eireann just over two years later. But the enormous impact of advertising through the new medium of television should not overlay the earlier stages of advertising in Ireland, where technical advances have gone hand in hand with a growing awareness of the benefits of advertising. Developments in the media have encouraged more sophisticated advertising. As recently as the early years of the 20th century, Irish commercial concerns were being admonished for having a very reactionary view of advertising, seeing it as distasteful and unnecessary. Now, most Irish advertisers have the American view, that successful advertising is a vital part of the infra-structure of the consumer society, that without advertising, brands and products cannot survive.

Goods and services have always needed to be sold; perhaps the very first advertiser to discover this most basic truth of advertising was a prostitute in ancient Greece, the best part of 5,000 years ago. She had her sales message stencilled on the soles of her sandals: "Follow Me". That same basic principle has been used by every advertiser since. Such is the scale of change in the advertising business that for the next 3,000 years, little happened on the advertising front. Not until the heyday of

Tradesmens' signs used in ancient Pompeii, 2,000 years ago.

1

the Roman Empire did advertising start to become recognisable as a modern commercial art form. Many tradesmen in ancient Rome, with no media in which to advertise — newspapers were 1,600 years in the future — resorted to shop-side advertising; for instance, the red and white barber's pole had its origins in Roman times, as did the bunch of grapes outside the wine shop. Signs outside shops told potential customers walking along the paved ways of Rome, Londininium and other towns and cities of the empire what they could buy inside. After the town of Pompeii, near present day Naples, was destroyed by the eruption of Vesuvius in AD 79, vestiges of advertising were left, buried for future generations under lava and volcanic dust. Outdoor posters advertising the town's whorehouses were found generations later; in generations to come, will remnants be found of present day television advertising, the odd video cassette, perhaps?

After the death of the Roman Empire, advertising was but one of the facets of contemporary life that went into hibernation for hundreds of years. As Europe progressed through the Dark Ages, little urban development took place. Advertising is synonymous with urban rather than rural societies because it needs clusters of people who can buy the advertised goods and services. All through the Middle Ages, the town crier was the main means of advertising shops and services in sufficiently developed towns. From the 12th century onwards, as Dublin and Cork began to expand, so too did the services of the town criers. But it was all very primitive and the further development of advertising had to await a new technological breakthrough — the invention of printing and the start of newspaper publishing.

Even after the first newspapers started up in Ireland, the concept of using them for conveying advertisements was slow to catch on. The first newspaper in Ireland was published in Cork in 1649, but technical developments in the industry inevitably concentrated the newspaper industry in the political and economic powerhouse of Ireland, Dublin. For the first few decades, newspaper advertising was slow to catch on; for instance, from the time Dublin had its first regularly published newspaper, about 1670, until the time that a Dublin newspaper (Faulkner's Dublin Journal) started using primitive woodcuts to illustrate advertisements represented the passing of some 55 years. Throughout the 18th century, newspapers took a passive attitude to advertising, waiting for it to come in, rather than going out after it with aggressive selling techniques, as is the modern case.

Again, economic reasons explained the low key rôle played by advertising. In many cases, one or two members of a family ran a newspaper; even though much of the editorial content was filched from London newspapers, the sheer manual work of hand setting the type and physically printing those early newspapers did not leave much time or energy for the advertising side. In the typical case of Limerick newspaper publisher John Ferrar, founder of the Limerick Chronicle, he had to do everything in his tiny shop cum workshop.

Streetscape in medieval Ireland; the array of bleeding bowls advertises the barber's stall.

18th century shopfront, with large windows used for display purposes.

Advertisements were brought by the populace to the counter: there was no question of Ferrar employing someone on the advertising side. This passive tradition, which existed in many other countries with extensive newspaper publishing industries, lasted until well into this present century.

For much of the 19th century, the impetus behind many newspapers was political: newspapers were founded to support the nationalist cause in varying degrees. Parnell was closely involved in the setting up of the *Drogheda Independent* just over a century ago, just as Davitt and his Land League movement provided a great thrust for the *Western People* when it was set up at the same time. Even with the lifting of Government taxes on both cover sales and advertisements in the 1850s, the drive to start new titles came from certain political involvements, while the economic rationale came largely from the promise of revenue from subscribers.

Through the 19th century, the North of Ireland was in the economic ascendant: hundreds of thousands of country people were pouring into Belfast to man the new linen mills and many other new factories and industries, like the tobacco factory of Gallahers and the shipyard of Harland and Wolff. The concentration of people into the new Belfast created Ireland's first and only taste of the same type of industrial revolution that was forged simultaneously in Britain. With this rapid expansion of Belfast, a huge new market was created.

Many of the advertising techniques widely used in 19th century Ireland are still used today, albeit in modified form. Signs outside pubs drew customers' attention to the pleasures within: the signs were a throwback to Roman times, while their modern counterparts, often in neon, continue the tradition. Other 19th century traditions continue in refined form: throughout that century and well into this, the pawnbroker played a pivotal role in the economy. Goods that were pledged at the sign of the three golden balls on Monday were redeemed (hopefully) in time for the next weekend. Today, Access and Visa provide the credit, without which the modern consumer society would grind to a halt.

Throughout the 19th century, the idea of advertising agencies in Ireland scarcely caught on. Those few firms that did exist in the last century derived much of their income from commission: on behalf of private individuals and firms, they placed advertisements in daily and weekly newspapers, extracting their commission in the process. The very first firm to do this was Johnstons, based at Eden Quay, set up in 1819, which was the forerunner of Easons and hence Easons Advertising agency. For much of the 19th century, the firm derived much of its advertising income from placing clients' copy in newspapers. As the century wore on, what became the firm of Easons in 1886 started to develop another profitable line — the placing of advertising at railway stations as the railway network was developed throughout Ireland. At the height of the railway "boom", there were

Early illustration: 1769 advertisement for sailing ship service between Galway and America.

Clock maker's advertisement, Limerick, 1760s.

Patent medicines, Limerick, 1766. Virgin's milk, an excellent cosmetic, cost 1s 7d.

The Old Eftablifhed TOBACCO·
and SNUFF Manufactory.

JOHN RYAN refpectfully informs his Friends
and the Publick, that he has REMOVED his
Manufactory to GEORGE's-QUAY, where Bufi-
nefs will be continued in the fame extenfive manner
as hitherto.
   N. B. His Country Cuftomers will be directed
from his former Shop.
                              Limerick, July 2, 1800.

Limerick, 1800.

OLD MALT WHISKEY, WINE, TEA, &c. &c.

A. KELLY,
No. 71, GRAFTON-STREET,

Has arrived to him, a choice Collection of GREEN and
BLACK TEA.
   Great allowance made on taking a quantity.
He has some of the OLDEST and NICEST FLAVORED
MALT WHISKEY in the Kingdom,
   Also, Old JAMAICA PINE APPLE RUM,
FRENCH BRANDY,
HOLLAND GENEVA,
And a great variety of PRIME OLD WINES,
Which he will dispose of, on the most reasonable and
liberal terms.
   Wanted a young Man, who understands the Grocery,
Wine and Spirit Business.

A tea and wine
merchant advertises,
Dublin, 1816.

Lottery advertisement,
Dublin, 1816.

EARLIEST INTELLIGENCE.

STATE LOTTERY
Begins Drawing   16.

SCHEME.

TICKETS and SHARES
Are on Sale at
THE LUCKY HORSE SHOE OFFICES
36, College Green, and 2, Capel Street.

CONTRACTOR & STOCK-BROKER.

800 stations scattered throughout the island. Even advertisements as part of the process of raising capital for new railway companies provided substantial extra income for newspapers in Ireland.

Like most other economic innovations over the last century, progress in Irish advertising was sparked off by developments in London. In turn, the advertising business in London developed in tandem with that in New York. Technically, the London advertising business was well advanced by the late 19th century and many of the modern advertising concepts, particularly on the creative side, began in London 100 years ago. Even the modern concept of account executives began there at that time; London advertising agencies were fortunate, because so many British firms were early converts to the idea of advertising. Mass budget, mass media campaigns for a host of consumer products became the norm in the late Victorian era, when the free market economy enjoyed untramelled freedom. Advertisers then did not have to worry themselves about a host of Government imposed rules and regulations. Advertising Standards' authorities were unimaginable in those days and with that lack of commercial and creative restriction, British advertising flourished. Much of the "noise" in modern advertising was supplied from the United States of America. While London led in technical advance, New York was to the forefront in bringing the latest sales techniques and the concept of aggressive marketing to the world of advertising.

It may seem a little surprising now, but communications then were still so embryonic that the arrival of London and New York advertising techniques into the Irish economy was slow indeed. The letter was still the main means of communication; by early this century, the telephone started to come into use. Oceanic cables were one fast means of communicating from one continent to the next, but if you went to America from Cobh, it took a week or more depending on the weather. The first aeroplane only took to the air, in America, some 80 years ago.

Just as the Irish political movements of the 19th century provided the impetus for many new newspapers around the country, so too did the political happenings of the early 20th century fuel the progress of Irish advertising. The foundation of McConnell's, today Ireland's largest advertising agency, in 1916, has a strangely appropriate historical symmetry. The arrival of McConnell's coincided with the arrival in Dublin of motor taxis: that new departure in Dublin public transport provided the new advertising firm with its very first account. The development of railways in Ireland from the 1850s onward had heightened population mobility: people could now travel fairly easily. With the advent of the train, seaside resorts such as Bray came into being. But with the growing popularity of the motor car from the early 1900s, shopping patterns began to change and advertising was given a boost. No longer did people just rely on their local shopkeepers: residents of the affluent district of Dalkey, for instance, could now travel by motor car, train or tram into the centre of Dublin and sample the shopping delights of a then elegant Grafton Street. Trams also provided a magnificent mobile advertising medium.

With the creation of the Irish Free State, an impetus was given to local manufacturing. With the arrival in power of Fianna Fail at the beginning of the 1930s, the urgency to set up local industries became paramount. British companies that had previously sold directly into the Irish market now had to set up subsidiary factories in Ireland. Not only was employment created, but Dublin advertising agencies suddenly found that many new accounts were created, as these new local industries started to help their own efforts to compete in Ireland through local advertising. A consciousness of the benefits of advertising percolated throughout Irish business on a wide scale, for the very first time. Northern Ireland, on the other hand, remained part of the UK; because it stayed a branch economy, there was little incentive for local advertising. To this day, the turnover of the Belfast advertising agency world lags far behind that of Dublin.

The Emergency, when many consumer goods were in such short supply that advertising was pointless, was a hiatus in the advertising industry. However, it saw the start of much socialising in the industry, through the AP Club and resuscitated Publicity Club. After the war, recovery began in the world economy; so too did a degree of recovery take place in Ireland. Its economy trundled from the late 1940s into the 1950s without any exciting gains being made: a stasis was achieved behind the high tariff barrier. Emigration and heavy unemployment ensured that the stagnation did not lift. Cultural influences from outside helped break the mould and in the process, change the life of the nation. As a reflection of those changes in society, with Ireland becoming far more urbanised, there was a vast quickening in the process of advertising. Undoubtedly, the biggest single factor for change has been the arrival of television. Up to the early 1950s, Irish society had not changed dramatically in many respects for two centuries. Ireland remained a largely agricultural economy, with a traditional family structure; the powerful influence of the Church provided the "cement" in the social structure. Ireland, culturally and socially, remained deeply conservative. The media remained set in its ways; true, an Irish radio service had started back in 1926, but it too had a deeply conservative and very formalised programme structure. Those were the days when practically everyone could come home for lunch; the working and social patterns and rituals of the week remained immutable for most people. Friday night was Amami night for most girls, while Saturdays were partially marked out for many people by two long-running advertisement campaigns, one for Lemon's Sweets, the other for O'Dearest mattresses.

Continental influences played their part, too. The commercial radio stations that were so prominent on the Continent in the 1930s gave a little nudge to the development of Ireland's radio service supported by

False teeth by royal appointment-advertisement in an 1860 edition of the Westmeath Independent.

Dundalk Democrat, **January 8, 1870.**

5

PHOSPHO-PERUVIAN GUANO.

MESSRS. PURDON, SOLE AGENTS FOR IRELAND,

BEG to state that the Company from whom they hold the Agency are not, nor ever were, in any way connected with the party advertising for Agents throughout Ireland for the sale of a so-called Phospho-Peruvian Guano.

Messrs. PURDON caution parties against being led into the supposition that it is the same Guano which is supplied through them, and which has produced such good results, as may be seen by reference to numerous testimonials and experiences, which may be had on application. They are now prepared to execute any orders with which they may be favoured, either from their Stores in Dublin or Liverpool, and which shall have their best attention.

ALL THE BAGS ARE BRANDED, PHOSPHO-PERUVIAN GUANO COMPANY.

This year's Importation has been analysed by Dr. Apjohn, Professor of Chemistry in Trinity College, and the Royal Agricultural Society. He says :—

" This is an admirable Manure; it includes, in abundant quantity, the constituents essential for promoting the production and growth of both green and cereal crops."

Office and Stores—23, BACHELOR'S-WALK, DUBLIN.

IMPORTANT TO AGRICULTURISTS.

THE DUBLIN MANURE COMPANY beg to direct special attention to their POTATOE MANURE, the application of which has been proved by numerous trials to greatly diminish the tendency of the Potatoe to disease, and to promote a luxuriant growth of this valuable crop.

The DUBLIN MANURE COMPANY use the raw materials which Ireland so abundantly affords for the manufacture of every kind of artificial manure. Consumers of such articles are, therefore, enabled to save 10 per cent. by purchasing from an Irish Company, as at least that amount is expended on freight and expenses chargeable on English manufactured manures.

The Company manufacture the following Manures, which they guarantee of the best description :—

TURNIP MANURE, &c.

	Per ton.
	£ s. d.
Vitriolised Bone Manure for Turnips	7 0 0
Urate for Mangels, Carrots, Cabbages and Rape	7 0 0
Potatoe, Corn, and Grass Manure	7 0 0
Mineral Superphosphate of Lime	6 0 0
Blood Manure	6 0 0
Crushed Bones	7 10 0
Sulphuric Acid (Oil of Vitriol)	9 0 0

Delivered free to Railways and Canals in Dublin.

From 7 cwt. to 8 cwt. without farm-yard manure, or 6 cwt. with farm-yard manure, will be a sufficient dressing for an Irish acre.

Analyses, testimonials in favor of, and directions for mode of using these Manures, may be had on application at the Office, 20, Usher's-quay.

JOSEPH WONFOR, F.C.S.S.L.D., Manager.

A reduction to very large consumers.

Manure for sale, 1860.

Jaunting car for sale, Wicklow, 1870.

FOR SALE,

ONE NEW JAUNTING CAR of the most modern style, built of the very best materials, Blue Cloth Cushions, &c., price £20

ONE SECOND-HAND DITTO, built by Magill, price £16.

ONE SECOND-HAND DITTO, by Nugent.

ONE SECOND-HAND TAX-CART, Whitechapel style, £12.

ONE EXCELLENT GIG, £9.

ONE SET OF BRASS MOUNTED SINGLE HARNESS, only £4 10s.

JOHN OAKES, COACH AND HARNESS MAKER, WICKLOW.

advertising. The Continent also played a formative design role in Irish advertising. That we were susceptible to Continental design influences could be seen in the Bovril building at Ringsend, later a snooker hall, but in its heyday one of the most elegant commercial premises in the city of Dublin. Its Art Deco theme could be found echoed in such creations as the Mick McQuaid tobacco stand at the 1946 Dublin Horse Show. The arrival of a veritable school of Dutch artists in the early 1950s had very beneficial effects on Irish advertising design and on the education for that design.

With the arrival of Ulster Television in late 1959, the modern consumer society came to Northern Ireland with a dramatic underlining. Once UTV went on the air, it was inevitable that pressure would build up fast for a television service in Dublin. Just over two years later, that service became a reality. Suddenly, advertisers had a brand new medium that could sell more persuasively than any previous means of advertising.

In many respects, Irish advertising did not come of age until the start of Telefis Eireann on January 1, 1962. True, many consumer brands had been on the Irish market since the previous century — Denny's bacon since 1820, Bird's Custard since 1837 and Bovril since 1886 — but their marketing was sedate, discreet almost. Media opportunities were limited. Advertisers could use newspapers — on the newspaper owners' terms — or the sponsored radio programmes of Radio Eireann, or outdoor posters with a little bus advertising thrown in, but that was it. Television became the most influential means of selling goods and because of that, advertisers soon took to it eagerly. Numerous success stories of products enjoying record sales thanks to television advertising encouraged the whole process. The extraordinary year-by-year rise in advertising revenue by the Irish television service, first Telefis Eireann, then Radio Telefis Eireann, is sufficient testimony to the power of the medium.

During the 19th century, when large display advertising started for specific brands in Irish newspapers and to a much lesser extent, magazines, most of those advertisements were created and placed by London advertising agencies. Similarly, when Telefis Eireann started, many of the commercial influences came from outside the country. When ITV started in London in 1955, American TV people had a heavy influence in the UK commercials' production industry. When TE started, many of the firms producing commercials for the new channel were offshoots of English firms. Locally owned commercials' production facilities barely existed. The changeover was smooth: within a few years, the industry came to depend more and more on local talent, a process completed with the unionisation of the production sector in 1974. By strange coincidence, just as unionisation came in, much of the great socialising in the industry, enjoyed through the 1940s, 1950s and 1960s, came to a permanent halt. The recession which started in 1973/74, and which has continued until now, seemingly without end, has meant much tighter operations in a far slimmer advertising industry.

While TV commercials' production has become more inward looking — some critics say it misses the leavening provided by outside directors — marketing has become much more internationalised. One of the most momentous steps in recent Irish history came in 1973 when Ireland joined the European Economic Community. The "siege" mentality of the tariff barrier era finally went, after 40 years. Also vanishing was the optimism, the buoyancy that characterised the Irish advertising industry, as well as Irish society, in the 1960s. Then there was a hope that the country was moving forward to permanently better times; this hope was reflected in the creative standards of that era.

The creation of the EEC has had many dramatic economic effects in Ireland; gone are the old barriers. The markets of mainland Europe are now as near in psychological terms as the British market, once the main outlet for most Irish exports. This opening up of the Irish marketplace has meant a loosening up of parochial attitudes in marketing: brand managers are now commonplace with many Irish firms and the concept of brand structures, and the paraphernalia they entail, have become everyday topics in the industry. In branding consumer products and services, brand managers are happy to take ideas from everywhere, but in practice the new ideas that influence Irish advertising and marketing practice, with the development of strong branding techniques, still tend to come from either Britain or the USA.

'Internationalisation' is a word often bandied about in local advertising and marketing circles: the great takeovers of the Dublin advertising agencies in recent years are often cited. However, although all but one of the big Dublin agencies have been taken over by international groups, the reality is that the foreign ownership of Irish agencies is controlled, by and large, from London. Irish advertising may be becoming more international in its outlook, but much control has slipped back to London, which is where we all came in, when so much advertising in Ireland during the 19th century was placed from London. Internationalism at creative level means, more often than not, that a local voice-over is added to a TV commercial made in London. Newspapers have adapted to change, with colour becoming more important. Outdoor, one of the oldest media, since posters have been printed and pasted up in Ireland since the late 17th century, flourishes today in many forms that would have been unrecognisable even 20 years ago, such as the city centre electronic displays.

On a much larger scale, the entry of Ireland into the EEC 13 years ago coincided almost exactly with the advent of computerisation in the advertising industry. With six television channels available over a large part of the country, the business of media planning has developed into computerised high technology. Backing all this up is an insistence on

World War I
advertisement published
in some Dublin
newspapers, 1916.

Trousers for sale, 1870.

TO THE NOBILITY, GENTRY AND CLERGY OF IRELAND.

54, Dame-street, Dublin.

We respectfully direct attention to our Establishment, and solicit the favour of an inspection of our Stock (which is at all times carefully selected), when next in this City. As Tailors, we believe we are perfectly conversant with the *best and most approved methods of Cutting*; we are particularly careful in our Measurements; *we pay close attention to the directions of Gentlemen ordering*, and the result is that we have succeeded in producing WELL FITTING Garments without subjecting our patrons to the annoyance consequent on inability or inattention, and have thereby secured the confidence of the public.

KENNY & OWENS,
TAILORS AND TROUSERS MAKERS,
54, DAME STREET,
DUBLIN.
INTRODUCERS OF THE
SCOTCH ANGOLA TROUSERS,
16s.
(*Thoroughly Shrunk*.)

A Bovril advertisement used in Ireland and Britain in the late 19th century, showing an apparent product endorsement by the Pope.

research that never existed in the old days. Product and campaign concepts are endlessly tested before, during and after; advertisers not unnaturally, want to know whether their new brands are going to work. The growing competition in the consumer marketplace, with declining or at best, static incomes and a multiplicity of brands, means that the "window" for successful new product launches is becoming ever smaller. In the old days, hunch and intuition were valuable tools in planning assaults on the marketplace: now, it all has to be preplanned, by computer. With this insistence on research and planning before, during and after, the spontaneity may have gone out of advertising, the creative heads may feel that their rôle is being downgraded.

Still, advertising is perhaps the best yardstick by which changing social values may be measured. Advertisements are often the best benchmark of an era: if many advertisements of the present day are dull, mechanistic and sometimes brutal, they are merely reflecting the tempo of the age. One welcome advance in the last few years has been accepted, rather belatedly in some quarters. In the old fashioned patriarchal society, mother stayed at home and minded both children and house. Her basic rôle had changed little over hundreds of years. With the rush of change in recent years, many women, particularly younger single women, are of at least equal economic status to the male sex. The growing liberation of women — still far from complete — has been largely reflected within the advertising industry. At most levels of advertising and marketing, except the top, women are on equal terms with men. The advertising industry, in the structure of its employment, realised the changing place of women in society, probably quicker than most other sectors.

Just as most, if not all, advertisers are reflecting the different structures of society in their advertising, so too are larger concepts changing. One Dublin advertising man remarked recently that the whole structure of advertising will have to change: a small percentage of the world's population is being urged, through advertising, to consume more and more. Most of the world's population does not have disposable income. Such is the pace of change in the world today and so fast are communications that no-one is remote from the most distant happenings or trends: we are all becoming more rather than less interconnected. Advertising is becoming more rather than less technologically exciting, because the pace of change is so much quicker. Older media are responding: colour is becoming far more commonplace in newspaper publishing now than even half a decade ago. The next major media step will be the arrival of satellite broadcasting; not only will it help change structures of advertising, but also social and cultural values, as Ireland in the EEC moves inexorably towards becoming part of the United States of Europe, a province in a continent. Satellite television will leave its footprints across the face of Irish society, just as that ancient Greek lady left her sales message in the sand.

CHAPTER TWO

ADVERTISERS AND AGENCIES

Turn of the Century
1879-1929

"Alas, my poor brother".

BOVRIL ADVERTISEMENT, 1896

HE ELEGANT FIGURE of Henry Crawford Hartnell, complete with wing collar, dark overcoat, bowler hat and rolled umbrella epitomised the new commercial spirit that was abroad in Dublin towards the end of the 19th century. Branded goods as we know them today were just starting to develop and these new goods, as well as many new services, such as the trams running to the city centre from the outlying suburbs, all required advertising. In 1879, Hartnell founded what many regarded as the forerunner of the modern Irish advertising agency, Wilson Hartnell and Company.

Wilson Hartnell (the Wilson came from Hartnell's partner in the venture, a Dublin Corporation engineer who returned to City Hall after three years) was set up in Dame Street, Dublin. In line with the developing business of advertising agents in England and the United States of America, Wilson Hartnell was really a press agent, like Eason's advertising department, buying space in the newspapers and selling it, for a profit, to individuals and firms who wanted to advertise. A description of early American advertising agencies by Stephen Fox in his book, *The Mirror Makers,* applies with equal force to the new press agencies just starting in Dublin, Wilson Hartnell & Co, shortly afterwards followed by O'Keeffes (started by F. B. O'Keeffe in D'Olier Street), Kenny's and Parker's. The advertising agency of the period conducted its affairs from one room, says Fox. A prospective

An agricultural machinery advertisement, late 19th century.
Photograph: Nenagh Heritage Centre.

Henry Crawford
Hartnell, co-founder of
Wilson Hartnell in 1879.

Advertisement for
Dublin-made ink, used
in national newspapers,
1925.

ASK YOUR STATIONER FOR :—
Draper's Dichroic Ink. The Best Black Ink Known.
AN IRISH INK MADE IN DUBLIN FOR
MORE THAN THREE-QUARTERS OF A CENTURY
Praised and Used by Pitman.
FLOWS FREELY FROM THE PEN.
NEVER THICKENS OR DEPOSITS.
DOES NOT CORRODE STEEL PENS.

"customer" (they were not called "clients" until several decades later), climbed the stairs and found himself right in the middle of the agency, with no railings or counters to detain him. In one corner of the room sat the boss, whose name the firm bore. In another corner sat the estimate man, who quoted rates and expenses, with his heavy scrapbooks at a slanted top desk. A bookkeeper stood by his upright station, with the copying press and office safe close at hand. Finally, a checking clerk and an office boy attended to their miscellaneous tasks. No telephones or typewriters intruded on the sounds of scratching pens and riffling papers.

At the rear of the office, separated by a low partition, were rows and rows of cubbyholes filled with periodicals, like the reading room of a public library. This collection, smelling agreeably of newsprint and printer's ink, enabled the advertising agent to claim that he kept regularly on file all the leading newspapers and magazines. The office staff of five was considered adequate for all but the largest agencies. There were no copywriters, art directors, account executives or marketing executives. In Mr Hartnell's office, the gas lighting would flare on dark days; otherwise the only sound to deface the near silence was the ticking of the wall clock. The telephone was 20 years away from being in widespread use, so all the business of Wilson Hartnell & Co was done by customers calling in to the agency in Commercial Buildings, or else when the staid Mr Hartnell walked just a few paces down Dame Street for morning coffee or lunch in the old Jury's hotel. Amid the heavy panelling of Jury's dining room, surrounded by sycophantic waistcoated waiters, Mr Hartnell would conduct his business at a measured and careful pace.

Advertising in Ireland was very discreet then. A Dublin dental surgeon, Frederick D. Davies, of 27 Westmoreland Street, placed a series of advertisements in the daily newspapers of the capital at the time that Hartnell was setting up his agency. The dentist's advertisements read: "Painless dentistry by the aid of laughing gas and ether spray." Patients could then have false teeth fitted, made from incorruptible mineral, from just one tooth to a complete set mounted on gum-coloured India rubber suction plates. The dentist used 4" double column semi-display advertisements. The copyline concluded with a real knock-out: "Guaranteed to restore articulation and mastication."

As Hartnell's agency developed, he obtained the Irish placing rights for some major British brands. Big London accounts like those for Nestlé and Mazawattee tea were handled for the Irish market by Wilson Hartnell. Three times a year, Mr Hartnell would leave his office, complete with portmanteau, hail a hansom cab to go as far as the North Wall terminal and take the ship to England. Three times a year, he came home from London with copy and space orders for these big English brands, which kept his firm going nicely. Eleven years after setting up the firm, he expanded into the publishing business by

The Big Toffee Rush of 1927

Never was there such a rush for toffee as since "Sunny Smile" was invented. Its delicious flavour has won everybody's favour. People who never eat toffee before are eating it now, and the others are eating more than ever. "Sunny Smile" is as pure and good as it tastes, and everybody who eats it can win a handsome prize in our competition.

FREE MOTOR CAR
MOTORBIKE, CYCLES, SELF-FILLING FOUNTAIN PENS, ETC.

All you have to do is to collect the wrappers from "Sunny Smile" Toffee and send them in to the manufacturers: Lamb Bros. (Dublin), Ltd., Inchicore, Dublin. You can get a leaflet describing the whole scheme from your confectioner to-day. Everybody has an equal chance to win one of the big prizes, and each person who sends in even one thousand wrappers will get a handsome propelling pencil, while those who send in 5,000 will be given a beautiful, self-filling fountain pen. Start collecting to-day and ask your friends to collect for you also.

SUNNY SMILE
Rich Cream **TOFFEE**

Made by LAMB BROS., Dublin, Limited, Inchicore, Co. Dublin.

Window sticker used by the old Rathdowney brewery in the Midlands about 70 years ago; it was printed by McCaw, Stevenson and Orr, Belfast.

Meehan's of Abbeyleix dates back to 1724; this advertisement was used in local newspapers early this century.

Sunny Smile toffee advertisement, 1927.

IRD'S CUSTARD POWDER provides not only Delicious Custard (not possessing a variety of delightful Dishes from the Recipes accompanying each Packet.

NO EGGS! NO RISK!!

Specially handy for Use in Seasons. So Cool and Refreshing with Fruits.

Bird's custard is one of the oldest convenience food brands in existence; it was launched in 1837 and sold in Ireland soon afterwards. The above advertisement for Bird's custard was used in 1895; the brand has been advertised constantly for the past 100 years.

Late 19th century Cork grocery store advertisement.

JOSHUA J. KEMP,
TEA IMPORTER,
WHOLESALE & FAMILY GROCER,
Purveyor and Contractor to the Army and Public Institutions,
32, GREAT GEORGE'S ST., CORK.

GROCERIES.

Tea.
Coffee.
Sugar, Lump.
  „   Crushed.
  „   Scale.
Barley, Pearl.
  „   Scotch.
Raisins.
Pepper, Black.
  „   White.
Mustard.
Starch.
Soda, Washing.
  „   Bread.
Rice.
Spices.
Currants.
Split Peas.
Nutmegs.
Marmalade.
Jams.
Currie Powder.
Pickles.
Sauces.
Corn Flour.
Arrowroot.
Cocoa.

SUNDRIES.

Biscuits.
Bath Brick.
Blacking.
Blue.
Candles, all kinds.
Soap, all kinds.
Black Lead.
Matches.
Vinegar.
Soft Soap.
Paper, all kinds
Paper Bags.
Knife Polish.
Plate Powder.
Salad Oil.
Salt.
Magnesia, Jennings'.
Flour.
Meal.
Silver Sand.
Bacon.
Hams.
Cheese.
Lard.
Tobacco.
Cigars.
Pipes.
Porter.
Ale.

launching the *Lady of the House* magazine, a monthly publication of feminine and general interest, described as an uncommonly beautiful production. He was following the American example; in the USA the development of magazine publishing and advertising was closely entwined. Hartnell launched the magazine in conjunction with Adam Findlater of the famous grocery firm; later, Hartnell assumed complete control.

As he was starting up, Hartnell had one or two other rivals in the business, most notably Easons, which had imposing premises at the corner of Sackville Street and Middle Abbey Street. It had been founded in 1819 as J. K. Johnson & Co, at Eden Quay, went bankrupt in 1850 and was bought over by W. H. Smith, the English newsagents. In the 1850s, the firm brought over a man from Manchester called Charles Eason to manage the Dublin branch and in 1886, he bought out the company from W. H. Smith when the latter man was made

Secretary of State for Ireland and renamed it "Easons". Most of Eason's advertising business in the latter part of the 19th century came from placing linage advertisements on behalf of clients, mostly individuals rather than commercial organisations, in the Dublin and provincial newspapers. But Easons was building up its railway advertising, selling the rights to advertise at nearly 800 railway stations the length and breadth of Ireland. By the 1880s, the railway network in Ireland had reached its zenith, so this side of Eason's business prospered. By 1900, half of the net profits of Eason's advertising business came from railway advertising. In 1888, John H. Parker set up a placement agency in Dame Street, not far from Wilson Hartnell. Before setting up his own firm, Parker had worked for W. H. Smith, the newsagents, in London and on his return to Dublin, for Easons and for the advertisement department of the old *Dublin Daily Express*. The year he started his firm, Parker acquired the account for placing recruitment advertising for St Patrick's Hospital; 98 years later, that account is still with J. H. Parker & Co, surely the longest period of time an account has stayed with one agency in Ireland.

About 1892, another present day advertising agency of repute was founded, just across the road from Amiens Street railway station, now known as Connolly Station. Young Kevin J. Kenny began his advertising career by selling the advertisement space for Arthur Griffith's newspaper, *The Nation*. Then he decided to set up his own business in Amiens Street. For a while, he described his firm, located in a double-fronted shop, as "the Kevin J. Kenny Multum in Parvo Advertising Agency". Up to the turn of the century, until it began to handle advertisement accounts in the modern way, much of its business consisted of placing personal advertisements in the press. Kenny also followed Hartnell's example by publishing magazines as well; in Kenny's case, they were publications for the school teaching profession. American advertising was far ahead. For instance, in 1892, New York agencies started using powerful electric lights to project advertisements onto clouds.

The development of advertising in the British market started to have an effect in Ireland, then very much part of the UK domestic market. In 1886, there were 17 advertising agents in London, while by 1896, there were 83, an enormous increase. Already, agencies in London had grown from being mere means of placing advertisements to providing a full service. By 1889, such companies as Cadburys, Liebig (meat extracts) and Rowntrees were employing advertising agents. In 1888, Mather and Crowther, one of the most successful London agencies, was turning over £20,000 a year and employing about 100 people.

Between 1884 and 1904, Mather and Crowther was recorded as having just one Irish account — Bushmills whiskey, one of the very first Irish-based accounts to go to a top London agency. A handful of other brands handled by Mather and Crowther then, have also

In 1892, Coca-Cola had a total yearly advertising budget of $12,000, spent mainly on point of sale material at American soda fountains. By the early 1900s, sheet music, as in this illustration, was being used to promote the brand.

CHAUFFEURS' OUTFITS

READY FOR SERVICE.

Chauffeurs' Smart Dark Blue, Green or Grey Liveries, with livery buttons, **55/-** and **65/-** each.

Chauffeurs' Caps to match liveries, **7/6** and **8/6** each.

Chauffeurs' Oxford Grey Frieze Overcoats, warmly lined, livery buttons, **48/-** each.

Chauffeurs' Overcoats in Dark Blue or Green, **65/-** each.

Chauffeurs' Driving Gloves, **9/6** and **12/6** each.

Chauffeurs' Leggings, **8/6**, **10/6**, **12/6**, **16/6**, **18/6**.

Illustrations and Price List on application.

PIM BROS., LTD.,

South Gt. George's St., DUBLIN.

Chauffeur's uniforms were advertised by Pim Bros of South Great George's Street, Dublin, in 1911, just as motoring was starting to catch on in Ireland.
Photograph: Wheels and Deals/Gill & Macmillan.

14

continued as top names: Dewar's whisky and H. Samuel watches. Other of its accounts have long since vanished, like the one for John Noble Knock-About Frocks.

An English soap maker called A & F Pears bought a portrait painted by the artist John Everett Millais. It showed his grandson blowing bubbles; the painting was sold to the *Illustrated London News*, from whom Pears bought the work. The soap firm saw it as the ideal advertisement for their products and by 1887, the Pears' soap "Bubbles" advertisement had achieved a tremendous popularity that was to last well into the 20th century.

Thomas Smith, a former railway porter who at one stage lost his life savings, founded his London agency in 1878, the year before Wilson Hartnell came into being. By the 1890s, the T. B. Smith agency was employing around 50 people and had huge departments for drawing and writing advertisements and making the subsequent blocks. The idea of the service agency was well established in London by about 1890. At one stage, Smith's claimed to have 620 clients, although many were very small accounts.

Sandwich board man in Portarlington, early this century.

In America, too, the industry was growing fast. Claude C. Hopkins, described as the "highest paid advertising man the world has ever known", whose house had a half mile of flower gardens, worked for the Lord & Thomas agency in Chicago. For Quaker Oats, he changed the name of the firm's Wheat Berries' product to Puffed Wheat, with a premium price, to pay for the advertising budget. The advertisement copy said that the Puffed Wheat had been "shot from guns". In the campaign run in magazines such as *Ladies Home Journal*, coupons offered consumers a free pack of the cereal. Hopkins devised the first campaign for Pepsodent toothpaste and concentrated on its ability to remove plaque. Hopkins bought a stake in the product and eventually made a million dollars from the American enthusiasm for dental hygiene.

In Britain, branding was widely introduced for the first time into many product areas, from household commodities to food and patent medicines. Initially, such basic products as sauces and meat extracts were advertised as branded products using newspapers, magazines and outdoor posters, then the only medium for colour. In the 1880s, rising incomes were reflected in advertising for furniture on credit terms and ready to wear mens' clothing. By 1889, Beechams, makers of the famous pills, was spending £99,000 a year on advertising, while Pears' soap was spending similar amounts at this period. Yet Wills, the cigarette manufacturers, only spent £2,400 on advertising in 1880. Retailers, too, started to advertise seriously. Robinson and Cleaver, the once famous Belfast department store, started advertising by using small one shilling classifieds. By the turn of the century, its advertising budget was £500 a month.

Thomas Lipton, whose grocery shops were once so well-known in Ireland, was heavily into advertising a century ago. He had advertising

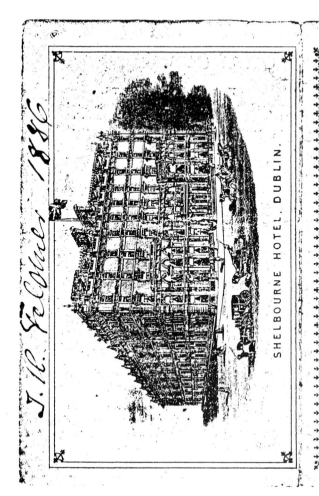

J. R. Février 1886

SHELBOURNE HOTEL, DUBLIN.

THE

Shelbourne Hotel,

DUBLIN,

JURY & COTTON, *Proprietors.*

The Hotel is situated in the most fashionable part of the City. Its aspect is southerly and from each window a splendid view of the Dublin and Wicklow Mountains is obtained, whilst it has the advantage of possessing, for the use of its visitors, the large and beautifully laid out pleasure grounds of St. Stephen's-green. As respects the Railways, the situation is also more central than that of any other Hotel in Dublin.

The Hotel contains on the ground floor a magnificent Coffee Room, a Ladies' Coffee Room, a Table d'Hote Room, a Ladies' Drawing Room and a General Reading Room. There are also a Smoking Room, a Billiard Room, a Hairdressing Room, and a Telegraph Office. In addition to these, there are one hundred and fifty Bed Rooms, twenty-four Sitting Rooms, Bath Rooms, and first-class arrangements for the comfort of families.

An Hydraulic Elevator to facilitate the access of the upper floor.

Applications to be made to the Manager.

Above and opposite:

The Shelbourne Hotel reopened in 1867 after extensive rebuilding; later, its owners produced this brochure to advertise the premises.

leaflets dropped from balloons to draw shoppers to his stores; imitation £1 notes that entitled shoppers to discounts were also heavily used. One of his best stunts was carried out at Christmas, 1881. He announced that he had brought over from America the world's largest cheese. Gold coins were pressed into it and the cheese was put on display. On Christmas Eve, the cheese was cut up into small pieces. So many customers turned up that police had to control the crowds.

In Ireland, advertising was much more discreet. The Guinness brewery spent its minute advertising budget just on showcards and mirrors, which were displayed in pubs that offered the stout on draught. A typical Guinness showcard, printed in 1873, showed an architectural drawing of the brewery at St James's Gate and not even a line of copy, just the name of the firm. In total contrast, big American advertising campaigns, like the one for Pepsodent, seem remarkably modern in their unrestrained enthusiasm after nearly a century. However, even a hundred years ago, purity was used in Ireland to sell ale: O'Connell's Dublin Ales announced to the public that they were brewed only from malt and hops. The product's pureness could not be questioned. In Manchester, pointed out the brewery with some glee, "thousands of people have been treated for arsenical poisoning from drinking adulterated beer". Ireland became one of the first countries in the world to produce margarine. By 1886, the McDonnell's butter factory at Thomas Street, Limerick (the firm is now W & C McDonnell of Drogheda) had margarine production in full swing. The substance had been invented in France in 1869 by Hippolyte Mège-Mouriés, who named it after the Greek word for pearls, margarites.

Many British food brands were launched in the 1880s and were backed by extensive advertising, which included Ireland. All-Irish products were scarce. In 1881, Rowntree's Gum Pastilles went on sale for the first time. They were sold loose to shops in big wooden boxes; the shopkeepers then sold them in bags to customers for one penny an ounce. By 1885, the new product had become so popular, in both Britain and Ireland, that Rowntrees was producing four tons of gum pastilles a week. The average wage in the Rowntree factory was £1 a week.

TARIFF OF CHARGES.

APARTMENTS.

Sitting Rooms	from 6s. to 15s. a day.
Bedrooms	from 3s. to 5s.
Do. (large, and with 2 Beds)	from 5s. to 6s.
Whole Suites for Families ...	from 13s. to 30s.

An additional charge of 1s. 6d. is made for each Supplementary Bed.

ATTENDANCE.

Each Person	... 1s. 6d. a day.

An additional charge of 25 per cent. is made, the meals being served in the apartments.

BREAKFAST.

From	2s. to 3s. 6d. each.

LUNCHEONS.

From	2s. upwards.

DINNERS.

Table d'Hote at 7 o'clock every day	... 5s. 0d. each.
Private Dinners	from 4s. 6d. „
Dinner off the Joint	from 3s. 0d. „

TEA.

One Cup of Tea	6d. each.
Plain Tea	2s. „

SERVANTS.

Board	5s. a day.
Bed	2s. „

FIRES AND LIGHTS.

Sitting Room Fire, per day, ...	... 2s od.
Bedroom Fires, from	... 1s. od.
Gas in Sitting Room, per night	... 1s. 6d.

BATHS.

Large Hot Bath	... 1s. 6d.
„ Cold Bath	... 1s. od.
Shower Bath	... 1s. od.
Hip Bath...	... 0s. 6d.
Sponge Bath	... 0s. 6d.

DOGS.

Are not allowed in the Apartment.

Charge for Food, each	2s. 6d. a day.

SPECIAL TERMS FOR FAMILIES FOR PROLONGED RESIDENCE. BOARD ARRANGEMENTS DURING THE WINTER MONTHS.

Visitors occupying Apartments, intending to leave the Hotel must give notice before 4 o'clock, otherwise they will be charged for the day.

It is particularly requested that no Money be paid without a Bill or receipt.

The Proprietors will not be responsible for any articles of value that may be lost in the Hotel, unless given in charge of the Manager and a receipt taken.

Any complaints against Servants should be made to the Manager at once.

Messrs. JURY and COTTON, being their own Shippers of Wine, have a great stock of First-class CLARETS and HOCK, which they can offer at greatly reduced wholesale prices.

YOU CANNOT BE SURE THAT IT IS

GALLAHER'S
TWO FLAKES
TOBACCO

YOU ARE BUYING UNLESS YOU INSIST ON GETTING IT
IN THEIR 1, 2, OR 4oz. DECORATED TINS,
SECURED BY PATENT BAND.

Gallaher's tobacco
advertisement, Belfast
Evening Telegraph,
January 1, 1900.

Jacob's Christmas price
list, 1891.

Doan's kidney pills,
1923.

Have you suspected
Your Kidneys?

"Every Picture tells a Story."

THERE are two ways to tell whether you have weak kidneys. The first is through the pains in the back and other outward signs. The second is by examining the urine.

If backache, recurring headaches, or a fretful, nervous, tired condition makes you suspect some kidney disorder, watch the urine. Look for any of the following signs: Too frequent or too few calls to urinate. Too much or too little flow each time. Too dark or too pale in colour. Scalding and painful when passing. Sandy, gritty or cloudy settlings. Bad odour, etc.

Doan's Backache Kidney Pills correct and regulate the kidney secretions, stimulate and strengthen weak kidneys and thereby permanently relieve urinary disorder, backache, rheumatic pain, nervousness, dizziness, gravel and other results of kidney weakness. Your own neighbours recommend Doan's.

A Cookstown Man
On 20th April, 1909, Mr. T. Shirlow, Dunmore, Lissan, Cookstown, said:—"About six years ago I noticed the kidney excretions were disordered. They were red in colour, thick, and painful, and left a sediment. Severe backache quite crippled me, my limbs swelled, and my face was badly puffed.

"I had been over a year at home when I used Doan's Backache Kidney Pills. As I kept on with the pills I grew stronger daily, and I have been well now for four years."

Thirteen years later, Mr. Shirlow said:—"I have never lost a day's work from my old complaint since Doan's Pills cured me.

(Signed) T. Shirlow."

Ask distinctly for Doan's, the 'Pills Mr. Shirlow recommends. Sold throughout Ireland, 2/9 a box.

DOAN'S
Backache Kidney Pills.

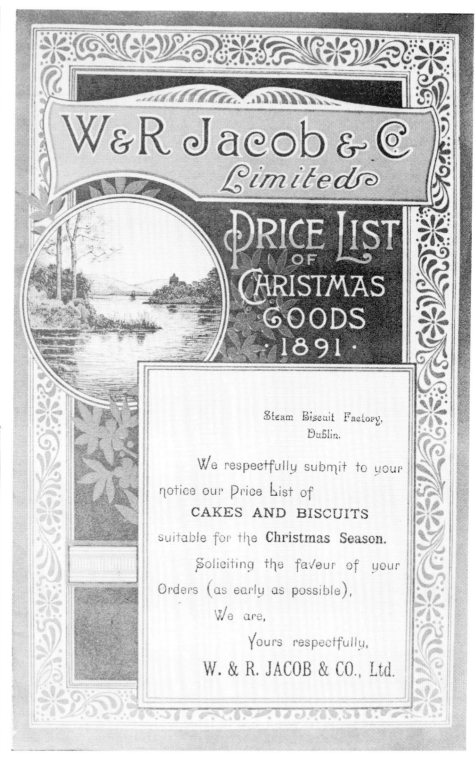

W & R Jacob & Co
Limited

PRICE LIST
OF
CHRISTMAS
GOODS
· 1891 ·

Steam Biscuit Factory,
Dublin.

We respectfully submit to your
notice our Price List of
CAKES AND BISCUITS
suitable for the **Christmas Season.**
Soliciting the favour of your
Orders (as early as possible),
We are,
Yours respectfully,
W. & R. JACOB & CO., Ltd.

Charlie McConnell (centre) and American periodical artist Herbert Gaffran watch Gordon Brewster, Independent Newspapers' staff artist, at work in 1924.

A cycle shop in Carlow, photographed in the early 1920s.

WOLSELEY CARS

Immediate Delivery
FOR
Holidays.
ALSO
Demonstration Car £199

NEW PRICES:

11/22 h.p. 2 and 4 seater popular models   £215
11/22 h.p. 2 and 4 seater de luxe model   £250
11/22 Saloon de luxe - - - £300

4 Wheel Brakes In Popular Models £10 extra

GRAFTON MOTOR CO., GRAFTON STREET, DUBLIN

Car advertisement 1927.

19

BEST BREAD BAKED

JOHNSTON
MOONEY AND
O'BRIEN, Ltd.

BALL'S BRIDGE BAKERY
DUBLIN

Telephone: Dublin 148

Johnston, Mooney and
O'Brien advertisement,
Dublin Evening Mail,
1923.

Holloway's pills
advertisement which
ran in the provincial
press in the last
century.

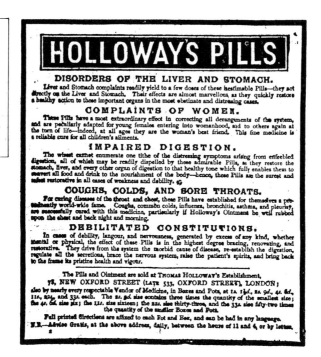

HOLLOWAY'S PILLS.

DISORDERS OF THE LIVER AND STOMACH.

Liver and Stomach complaints readily yield to a few doses of these inestimable Pills—they act directly on the Liver and Stomach. Their effects are almost marvellous, as they quickly restore a healthy action to those important organs in the most obstinate and distressing cases.

COMPLAINTS OF WOMEN.

These Pills have a most extraordinary effect in correcting all derangements of the system, and are peculiarly adapted for young females entering into womanhood, aid to others again at the turn of life—indeed, at all ages they are the woman's best friend. This fine medicine is a reliable cure for all children's ailments.

IMPAIRED DIGESTION.

The wisest cannot enumerate one tithe of the distressing symptoms arising from enfeebled digestion, all of which may be readily dispelled by these admirable Pills, as they restore the stomach, liver, and every other organ of digestion to that healthy tone which fully enables them to convert all food and drink to the nourishment of the body—hence, these Pills are the surest and safest restorative in all cases of weakness and debility.

COUGHS, COLDS, AND SORE THROATS.

For curing diseases of the throat and chest, these Pills have established for themselves a preeminently world-wide fame. Coughs, common colds, influenza, bronchitis, asthma, and pleurisy, are successfully cured with this medicine, particularly if Holloway's Ointment be well rubbed upon the chest and back night and morning.

DEBILITATED CONSTITUTIONS.

In cases of debility, langour, and nervousness, generated by excess of any kind, whether mental or physical, the effect of these Pills is in the highest degree bracing, renovating, and restorative. They drive from the system the morbid cause of disease, re-establish the digestion, regulate all the secretions, brace the nervous system, raise the patient's spirits, and bring back to the frame its pristine health and vigour.

The Pills and Ointment are sold at THOMAS HOLLOWAY'S Establishment,
78, NEW OXFORD STREET (LATE 533, OXFORD STREET), LONDON;
also by nearly every respectable Vendor of Medicine, in Boxes and Pots, at 1s. 1½d., 2s. 9d., 4s. 6d., 11s., 22s., and 33s. each. The 2s. 9d. size contains three times the quantity of the smallest size; the 4s. 6d. size six; the 11s. size sixteen; the 22s. size thirty-three, and the 33s. size fifty-two times the quantity of the smaller Boxes and Pots.

Full printed directions are affixed to each Pot and Box, and can be had in any language.
N.B.—Advice Gratis, at the above address, daily, between the hours of 11 and 4, or by letter.

Haybarn advertisement,
1896.
*Photograph: Nenagh Heritage
Centre.*

A. & J. MAIN AND CO.
LIMITED

HAY BARNS.
SEASON, 1896.

Many Hundreds Erected during Past Seasons.

11, Leinster-street, Dublin.
W. B. GILCHRIST, Manager for Ireland.

Terry's was one of the first firms to introduce branded eating chocolate, in the 1880s, although it did not introduce its pioneering boxed chocolate assortments for another 20 years.

In America, too, advertising was really coming into its own. J. Walter Thompson's forte was selling advertising into magazines, a previously neglected field. He joined a one-man placing agency, run by William J. Carlton, eventually buying it out in 1878 for the sum of $500, plus $800 for the office furniture. He renamed the agency after himself. He expanded rapidly in the magazine advertising field and when firms like Kodak and Prudential Insurance placed their accounts with J. Walter Thompson, he created the position of account executive. The next development in American advertising was the arrival of the copywriter. As late as 1892, no American agency had a full-time copywriter. Charles Austin Bates, a copy ace, was able to claim in 1895 that he was the best-known advertising man in America, earning over $20,000 a year and spending $10,000 advertising himself. The trend spread; copywriters joined agencies to take over a task previously reserved for the advertisers themselves. American advertising was starting to come of age.

American railway companies, which had previously only advertised local timetables in area newspapers, began to run big campaigns once they expanded and needed to attract inter-State passengers. The Pennsylvania and Union Pacific Railroads each budgeted over $200,000 a year on advertising, mainly in magazines. In the USA in the

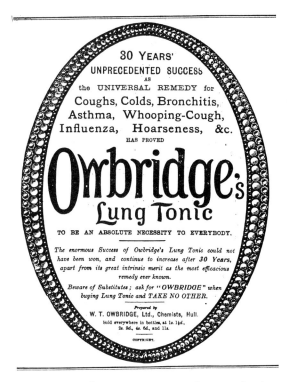

30 YEARS'
UNPRECEDENTED SUCCESS
AS
the UNIVERSAL REMEDY for
Coughs, Colds, Bronchitis,
Asthma, Whooping-Cough,
Influenza, Hoarseness, &c.
HAS PROVED

Owbridge's
Lung Tonic

TO BE AN ABSOLUTE NECESSITY TO EVERYBODY.

*The enormous Success of Owbridge's Lung Tonic could not
have been won, and continue to increase after 30 Years,
apart from its great intrinsic merit as the most efficacious
remedy ever known.*

*Beware of Substitutes; ask for " OWBRIDGE" when
buying Lung Tonic and TAKE NO OTHER.*

Prepared by
W. T. OWBRIDGE, Ltd., Chemists, Hull.
Sold everywhere in bottles, at 1s. 1½d.,
2s. 9d., 4s. 6d., and 11s.

COPYRIGHT.

1905 advertisement for Owbridge's lung tonic, used in the Irish Independent.

1890s, it became routine for any new product to be launched with heavy advertising. Such brands came on the market as Kodak cameras ("You press the button, we do the rest"), Coca-Cola (first sold in Atlanta in 1886), Campbell's Soups and Ingersoll watches. In 1898 came a revolution in the American food industry: the National Biscuit Company decided to launch a pre-packaged biscuit; before, biscuits had been sold loose from the barrel. $100,000 was spent in the initial advertising for the new brand. Here in Ireland, such mass advertising was anathema to nearly all firms. Jacob's Biscuits, for instance, relied mainly on showcards, including those of the famous "Marie" girl, placed over the racks of tins filled with appetising assortments of biscuits. Elaborate letterheads and full colour lists for the firm's shopkeeper customers completed the Jacob's advertising spend.

In comparison with Ireland's tiny advertising spending, in the late 1890s, total expenditure on advertising in America had grown to $500 million a year, 3.2 per cent of the gross national product. The largest American agency was Ayers, with 160 employees and a turnover of over $2 million. Advertising in America had reached respectability. One popular preacher of the time, Russell Conwell, even approved of advertising religion, quoting Christ, who said: "Let your light so shine before men, that they may see your good works."

In Drogheda in 1882, Peter Lyons founded his famous bakery. Initially, the bakery was behind the marvellously old fashioned shop in West Street, all marble counters, mirrors and high shelves for the

Sean Lynch, who founded Lynch Advertising in 1919.

21

Pim Brothers' department store in South Great George's Street, Dublin; it was acquired about 1843 and as it was rebuilt and expanded during the late 19th century, its wares were increasingly advertised.
Photograph: Irish Builder.

bread, but before many years had passed, in 1905, the bakery had to be moved to its present site in Stockwell Street because the business had grown so much. Undoubtedly, much of his success was due to product quality, but also to advertising. Strangely, all the bakeries in the town — there were about six major ones then — used to group their advertisements together in the weekly *Drogheda Independent*. There was less amicable rivalry, too. Another Drogheda bakery owner, Joe Shiels, used to paint his horse-drawn vans in almost the same livery as that used by Peter Lyons. In retaliation, the latter baker ran competitions in the local paper asking customers to write in why Shiels was copying Lyons, without naming the rival bakery! It was a popular pastime for newspaper readers in and around Drogheda, for Peter Lyons used to get many replies to his strange advertisements. Another Drogheda bakery, Tighe's, was into well thought out advertising slogans long before they came into popular use in Ireland: "Health is wealth — there's a wealth of health in Tighe's bread." In the mid-1880s, another new bakery product soon gained instant acceptance by the public, despite a lack of advertising. Jacob's the biscuit makers had been set up in Waterford in 1851. In the earlier years of the 19th century, a Quaker called Isaac Jacob ran a small bakery in Waterford to bake bread and sea biscuits. In 1851, one of his young sons, William Beale Jacob, went to England to have a look at the new fancy biscuit making industry. On his return home, he immediately set up the present day biscuit firm, together with his brother Robert. By 1853,

Spectacles advertisement, Dublin Evening Mail, **February 1, 1925.**

Elvery advertisement, 1923.

Opposite page:
Adam F. Torrie from Scotland set up his first grocery shop in Cork in 1886, when he was just 19. Soon afterwards, he expanded to Waterford. This year, the L & N Tea Company, now known as L & N Superstores, celebrates the centenary of its foundation. Items being sold this year at 1886 prices include a pint of Guinness for 2p. The photograph shows one of the earliest shops in the group.

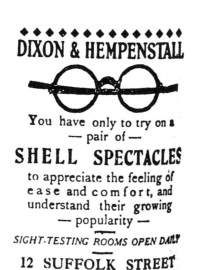

◆ ◆ ◆ ◆ ◆ ◆ ◆ ◆ ◆ ◆ ◆
DIXON & HEMPENSTALL

You have only to try on a
— pair of —
SHELL SPECTACLES
to appreciate the feeling of
ease and comfort, and
understand their growing
— popularity —

SIGHT-TESTING ROOMS OPEN DAILY

12 SUFFOLK STREET
◆ ◆ ◆ ◆ ◆ ◆ ◆ ◆ ◆ ◆ ◆ ◆ ◆

J. W. ELVERY & CO., Ltd.
WATERPROOFERS AND SPORT
OUTFTTERS

TENNIS,
CRICKET,
CROQUET,
LAWN BOWLS,
ETC.

All Sport
Requisites
AT THE

DUBLIN,
CORK,
LONDON.

the success of the operation meant that the Jacob's had to transfer production to Dublin. Its total sales that year amounted to £4,653. The firm overcame various tragedies as it grew; in 1861, Robert Jacob died by drowning. William Frederick Bewley, of the Dublin Quaker family, was then admitted as a partner.

In 1880, the factory was gutted by fire. The replacement factory remained a landmark in Bishop Street in south Dublin city for some 90 years. From the new factory in 1885, the Jacobs launched their new product line, cream crackers. George N. Jacob had been inspired by the American plain cracker and devised a similar product for the family firm in Dublin. For over a century now, its recipe has remained largely unchanged. In 1985, the product, in its centenary year, was treated in new product launch fashion. Sales, which had been dipping in recent

RAILWAYS.
GREAT SOUTHERN RAILWAYS.
INTERNATIONAL RUGBY FOOTBALL.
IRELAND v. SCOTLAND,
AT
LANSDOWNE ROAD, DUBLIN.
CHEAP TRIP TO DUBLIN.
On SATURDAY, 28th FEBRUARY, 1925.
SPECIAL EXPRESS TRAIN
Will run as under:

Great Southern Railways' advertisement for cheap railway excursions to rugby international, 1925.

Opposite page: This Arnott's advertisement appeared in an 1887 volume of cartoons published by the *Weekly Freeman's Journal*.

years, resumed their upward growth. Many of the other grocery brands that are equally famous today were launched at about the same time as Jacob's cream crackers.

By the 1880s, Crosse and Blackwell had about 30 varieties of soup on sale in glass jars and tins. The American Henry Heinz brought samples of his wares to London in 1886, such lines as Heinz Ideal Sauce and Heinz horse radish; before long, they started to infiltrate the Irish market. In 1885, Abram Lyle began to use the term "Golden Syrup" on his tins of treacle, together with the lion and bees trade mark and the legend "Out of the strong came forth sweetness." Camp coffee, whose Irish equivalent is Irel, was first formulated in 1885, for Gordon Highlander soldiers going to India. Bovril was brought to this part of the world from Canada in 1886. The most famous of its early advertisements, run in 1896, showed a bull looking at a jar of Bovril and saying: "Alas, my poor brother."

After all these new convenience foods, it was hardly surprising that Andrew's Liver Salts were formulated, being put on sale for the first time in 1894, in penny packs. In America, by the end of the century, patent medicine advertising was billing $75 million a year. Readers of newspapers and large circulation magazines were promised cures for everything from arthritis to sexual problems, as well as the odd bout of catarrh. Perhaps the best-known such product was Lydia Pinkham's Vegetable Compound, which promised cures for female complaints; once when the advertising budget was slashed, annual sales fell from $260,000 to $58,000.

1895 was a momentous year, although it may not have seemed so at the time, for certain modern inventions came on the market, having a profound effect, in due course, on the pattern of modern life and on the advertising industry. First of all, the Westminster Parliament made it legal to drive a car, in Ireland, as well as in Britain, without a man in front waving a flag. The infant car industry was given an enormous impetus. Secondly, the Lumiere Brothers in Paris showed the world's first moving picture films; the invention came to Dublin just six months later. Thirdly, the razor blade was invented.

As the century turned, from 19th to 20th, developments in the media and in advertising reflected the increasing speed of change in Irish economic life. In the media, the biggest single development in the early years of this century in Ireland was the launch of the new look *Irish Independent* in 1905. Its bright new broadsheet format mirrored the new London newspapers, such as the *Daily Mail* and the *Daily Express*. The new style of newspaper offered by William Martin Murphy appealed to the conservative advertisers of Ireland. He was also the first to offer certified circulation figures, a practice then taken up in London. Before long, Murphy had a dynamic new advertisement manager, Tom Grehan, who helped consolidate this revolution in newspaper advertising.

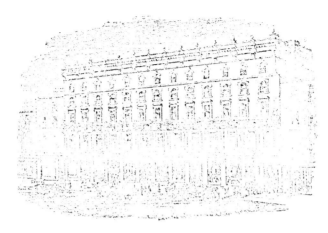

ARNOTT & COMPANY, DUBLIN, Ltd.,

Manufacturers and Warehousemen.

Tailoring and Ready-made Department.

Under the supervision of a first-class Cutter.

An immense variety of materials to select from, comprising the finest productions of the Home and Continental Markets, including all the most approved makes of Irish Tweeds, Serges, &c.

Costume and Dressmaking Department.

Considerably improved and enlarged.

Ladies will find the utmost attention paid to their Orders, which will be executed by our own workpeople on the premises.

Perfect Fit and Fashionable Finish Guaranteed in every instance.

GENERAL HOUSE-FURNISHERS, CARPET, CURTAIN, AND BEDDING MANUFACTURERS,

11, 12, 13, 14 & 15 HENRY-STREET.

ADVERTISING
In the Telephone Directory

FOR TERMS AND PARTICULARS OF
HEAVY TYPE ENTRIES
IN THE ALPHABETICAL LISTS,
ENTRIES IN CLASSIFIED LIST, AND
DISPLAY ADVERTISEMENTS,
Or ARTISTIC INSETS IN COLOUR

Apply to Sole Advertisement Contractors :—

McCONNELL'S
Advertising Service,
PUBLICITY HOUSE, DUBLIN.

Phone : Dublin 3215.   Telegrams : ADCRAFT, DUBLIN.

In the 1920s, McConnell's was the advertisement contractor for the Irish Free State telephone directory. This house advertisement appeared in the 1923 directory.

Albert Price was one of the best-known figures in the Irish advertising business. A native of Liverpool, he joined Clarke's, the Liverpool tobacco and snuff makers, in 1917, starting in the advertising department

Another revolution was becoming noticeable in the early years of the century-transport. William Martin Murphy, owner of Independent Newspapers and chairman of the Dublin United Tramways' Company, took credit for the tramway network that linked all the major Dublin suburbs to the city centre. In 1896, for instance, the tram line to Kingstown and Dalkey was opened. Besides passengers, the trams were ideal for carrying advertising messages and well-known national brand names such as Bovril and Typhoo tea, as well as local brand names like Heiton's coal and Downes' bread, were advertised to the public by means of enamel posters fixed to the front and sides of the tramcars. But alongside the development of public transport came a revolutionary breakthrough in personal transport. Until the motor car was invented in Germany in 1886, people could only travel long distances by train or on occasion by horse-drawn hansom cab. At the turn of the century in Ireland, the effective distance people could travel from their homes was about 17 miles, particularly in the country, where horse and trap was the only means of transport. The coming of the car changed all that; by 1900, there were about 40 cars on the roads of Ireland. That same year saw the opening of what was claimed as Ireland's first garage, Peare's Motor Works of Waterford. It also claimed to be the first firm in Ireland to assemble motor vehicles. In an *Irish Field* photograph of 1901, Dr. J. F. Colohan was depicted motoring in the Dublin area; he was described as "the first Irishman to take up motoring". Over the next 30 years, car ownership became much more widespread, giving people much more freedom to travel and shop, an effect that had great influence on shopping patterns and hence advertising.

Looking on at these advances was a young man called Charles McConnell. His father had founded the Ormond Printing Company at Lower Ormond Quay, Dublin in 1898. Printing techniques and advertising were inextricably linked in those days, so young Charlie's apprenticeship in his father's printing works was a most useful education. In his fifth and final year, he often recalled later, his wages were 12/6d a week. Strangely enough for a printing apprentice who had successfully served his time, in later life, Charlie McConnell showed only slight mechanical aptitude. Friends had to summon up great courage to travel in his car. Charlie in his young days also worked in the newsagency side of Eason's, the first of many great names in advertising to have started off in this venerable company. Young McConnell also worked with a paper stockist called A. Armstrong & Co, during which period, he got to know every printer in town. In later years, he had vivid memories of dealing out reams of paper to Arthur Griffith for *The Nation*.

Many of the classified advertisements in the early years of the new century were for motors and accessories. Motoring quickly caught the public's fancy and soon specialist magazines appeared, carrying advertisements not only for motor cars, but for petrol, garages and accessories. Motoring clubs such as the RAC came into being to look after car drivers' interests. In those days, when motoring just started, there were so few car owners compared with today that the practice in handbooks for the industry was to list each car, together with the owner's name and address. Yet in 1906, *The Irish Times* reported that Dublin was very slow in adopting motor power for commercial purposes. The number of such vehicles in the city could be counted on the fingers of one hand. Cycling, became a popular sport. One turn of the century classified advertisement in *The Irish Times* was inserted on behalf of Rudge-Whitworth, the cycle firm, based at 1, St Stephen's Green, Dublin. It was offering ladies' and gentlemens' safety bicycles priced from eleven to 20 guineas — very expensive for the time. People who bought cycles from the firm were told, in its advertising, that they could be taught to cycle free of charge in the finest riding school in Ireland.

There were charlatans about, too, not only in Ireland, as the *Australian Typographical Journal* pointed out in 1910. "Anyone with porpoise-like effrontery who can possess himself of an old typewriter, a few bottles of red and black ink, and rent a 12 x 8 office, can trumpet forth as an expert in the designing of advertisements. There are a few competent advertising designers, but in their train comes an army of wasters who have picked up a few ideas from the advertising magazines."

One of today's most important brands had its origins in turn-of-the-

in 1922. In March, 1923, the new Irish Government brought in severe restrictions on manufactured tobacco imports, so Clarke's moved to Dublin. Albert Price came here in January, 1925.
The restrictions helped the local tobacco firms win back lost ground and Clarke's never recovered. Belatedly, in 1927, the firm started serious advertising campaigns and early the following year, Albert Price was made head of the advertising department. In 1931, Clarke's and Wills amalgamated and he was made deputy head of the stores and advertising departments, becoming head in 1941. The two departments were not separated until 1958. For many years, he was advertising, marketing and public relations manager of W D & H O Wills. In later years, he was on the board of Aubrey Fogarty Associates.

An 1897 press advertisement for Bushmills whiskey.

This 1917 calendar was produced by the Cork Distilleries Company, distillers of what was then known as "Paddy Flaherty's whiskey". Today, the brand, distilled by Irish Distillers at Midleton, Co Cork, is known simply as "Paddy".
Photograph: Irish Distillers.

28

century Ireland — Carroll's cigarettes. In 1905, the Dundalk family firm of Carroll's bought its first cigarette making machine. The first cigarettes launched by Carroll's were called "Anti Combine", a reference to the monopoly held in the Irish market until then by the big English companies such as Players and Wills. Then in April, 1906, Carroll's launched its next brand, "Emerald Gem", which were sold in packets of ten for 3d. The main type of advertising was in the form of showcards for shops, which featured the cigarette cards carried inside the packs. Similar showcards were used to advertise Carroll's tobacco, including a picture of the real Mick McQuaid, a footballer, which has been used on the firm's plug and cut plug tobaccos from 1889 right up to the present day.

In Cork, the Cork Distillery Company used the name of its most popular salesman, Paddy Flaherty, said to have known every publican in Munster, to "christen" a new whiskey blend. Today, the brand is known as "Paddy". The old distillery salesman has been immortalised. Just as Mick McQuaid became an increasingly well-known trademark in Ireland as the century wore on, so too did the famous "Hero" trademark used by Players, a very popular brand in Ireland. Player's registered the design featuring the sailor's head in 1883 for its "Navy Cut" pipe tobacco. In 1888, the sailor was put inside the lifebelt and his hat lettered. Legend has it that the sailor was Thomas Huntley Wood, who served in the 1880s on HMS Edinburgh. In exchange for the use of his face, Wood was given a pouchful of tobacco and a handful of guineas. Player's "Navy Cut" cigarettes were launched in 1890 at 3d. for ten. Within seven years, the Player's brand, complete with the by now famous sailor on the packs, was the biggest selling cigarette brand in Ireland — with little or no advertising apart from showcards. Carroll's had an uphill struggle to establish its cigarette brands against such competition.

1910 proved a decisive year for advertising — the Bisto launch took place. It was one of the very first big brand convenience foods and within a few years, "Bisto" had become established in the popular mind, in Ireland as well as in Britain, as a virtually generic term for gravy. That very same year, Halley's Comet proved a Godsend to advertisers; Bird's custard, Pears' soap and Philips' light bulbs were among the brands to use the comet in their advertising.

In the early years of this century, advertising was carried in a very limited selection of media, newspapers and magazines, outdoor posters (enamel and litho printed), showcards and little else. As Leo Blennerhassett, in later years the publicity manager of Independent Newspapers, recalled, many businessmen in Ireland saw advertising as merely a vulgar intrusion during the early part of the century. In 1911, Tom Grehan, the then newly appointed advertisement manager of the *Irish Independent,* had the honour of addressing a meeting of the Dublin Chamber of Commerce on the subject of advertising — an advanced topic for the time. Some of the

Kenny's Advertising agency was located in Middle Abbey Street, then the "Madison Avenue" of Irish advertising, from the early 20th century until 1963, when it moved to Lower Baggot Street. The agency is now in Adelaide Road.

The noted Dublin grocery firm Findlater's had its head office in O'Connell Street (then Sackville Street), Dublin.
Photograph: Alex Findlater.

Opposite above:
An advertisement used in certain Irish newspapers around 1905 for the White Star shipping line compared the length of its liners (nearly 900 feet) with the height of St Peter's in Rome (448 feet).

Opposite page:
Interior of a Findlater's grocery shop, Dublin, about 90 years ago. The only instore advertising was for brandy, on the chairback.
Photograph: Alex Findlater.

ALEXANDER FINDLATER & CO., 29, 30, 31 & 32, UPPER SACKVILLE STREET, DUBLIN. 31

ALEX. FINDLATER & CO.

DUBLIN:
- 29 to 32, UPPER SACKVILLE STREET
- 28 and 30, UPPER BAGGOT STREET
- 67, SOUTH GREAT GEORGE'S STREET
- 9, LEINSTER STREET
- 72, THOMAS STREET

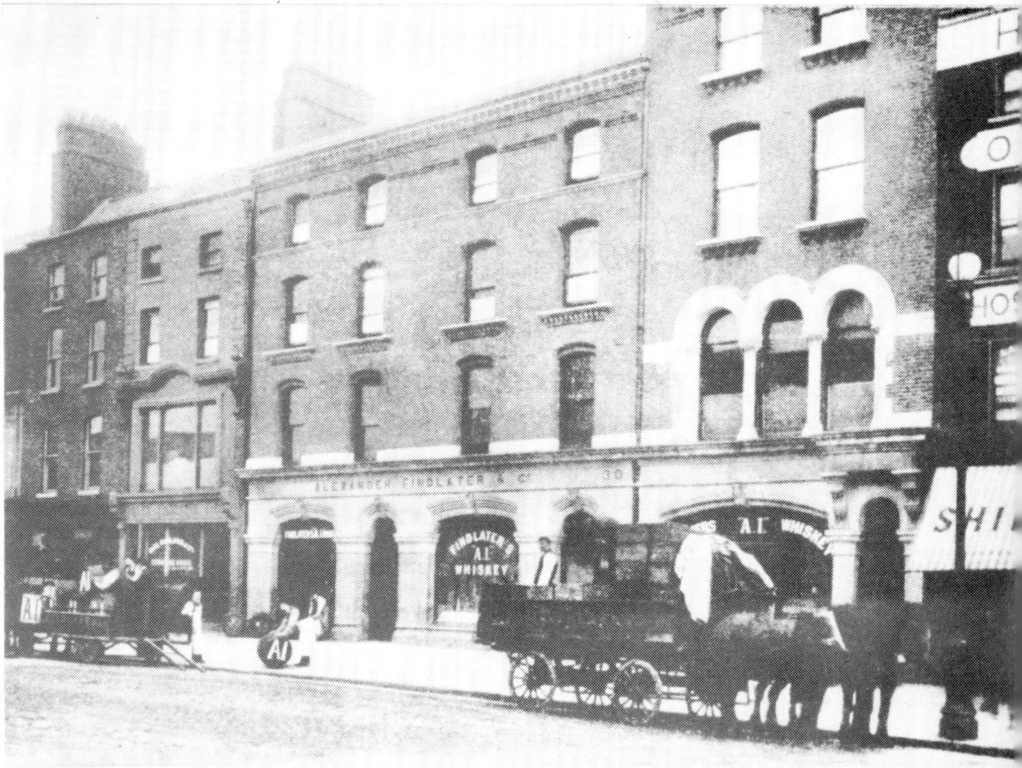

HEAD OFFICE UPPER SACKVILLE STREET, DUBLIN.
Established 1832.

SANDYMOUNT,	The Green
RATHMINES,	Rathmines Road
BLACKROCK,	28 & 30, Main Street
KINGSTOWN,	85, Lower George's Street
HOWTH. Facing the Harbour	(Premises now in course of Erection)

older members of the Chamber still regarded advertising as a less than respectable means of earning one's living and walked out halfway through his talk. One well-known Dublin brand, Varian Brushes, had given its account to John H. Parker in 1906: happily, the brand is still going strong today, with the same agency.

The same year that Halley's Comet arched through the heavens, to the delight of advertisers and the general public, Kevin J. Kenny decided it was time for a move. After 18 years in Amiens Street, he moved his agency to the more fashionable business centre of Middle Abbey Street, No. 65, just opposite Independent Newspapers, thus starting the trend that made the street, during the 1930s and 1940s, the "Madison Avenue" of Irish advertising, in close proximity to what was then the main power centre of the Dublin media. Kenny had a double-fronted shop similar in style to the old one in Amiens Street; in addition to placing advertisements, his magazine publishing business had grown. As early as around 1910, his client list showed such prestige accounts as the Royal Irish Constabulary (recruitment advertising), Boland's Bakery in Capel Street, Dublin Corporation, the

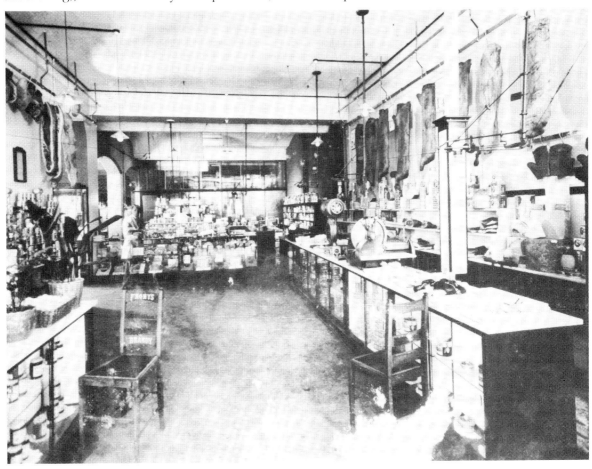

Department of Agriculture and Blackrock and Pembroke urban district councils, long since absorbed into Dun Laoghaire borough and the city of Dublin respectively. Other Kenny accounts were of a more modest nature, like the Dublin Cowkeepers' Association and the puffing and snorting Blessington Steam Tramway.

Shortly after Kenny moved his advertising agency to Middle Abbey Street, Independent Newspapers made the most of a major breakthrough in print technology to boost its advertisement revenue. In 1911, half tone process engraving came into general use in newspaper printing; for the first time, newspapers could use photographic illustrations easily and simply for both editorial and advertisement columns. The *Irish Independent,* under its progressive advertisement manager, Tom Grehan, encouraged the full use of the facility, which also meant more business for advertising agencies. For some years previously, the *Irish Independent* had given its display advertisements a more daring look, with fancy borders and new typefaces. This new layout look was enhanced by the use of photographs; the arrival of photographic illustration coincided with the move by the few Dublin agencies away from the concept of merely placing advertisements, with any attempts at layout and design being done by the primitive art studios of one or two main newspapers, like *The Irish Times* and the *Irish Independent,* with a vital part played by their compositors, towards the idea of the full service agency.

Before World War 1, many large and small firms in Ireland still had a dismissive attitude towards advertising, believing it to be neither necessary nor seemly. English firms, like Bovril and Pears' soaps, were running substantial campaigns, which included Ireland, then part of the United Kingdom, but there were few similar campaign moves on the local front. With the advent of war, severe rationing of newsprint forced big cutbacks in newspaper pagination and availability of

One hundred years ago, D'Arcy's of Usher Street, Dublin, brewers of O'Connell's Dublin ale, was advertising its product purity.

Early this century, James H. North took advertisement panels on the No 10 tram in Dublin. A painting of the tram passing along St Stephen's Green was used on the company's calendars.

advertising space. This scarcity of space heightened the interest of some organisations in doing what was now more difficult. Certain newspapers took advantage of the situation by putting up their rates. Several Irish advertisers kept a "black book" of newspapers that put up their rates during the war and exacted retribution after the war was over: the *Irish Independent* escaped this opprobrium.

MAP OF IRELAND.
WHO OWNS IT?

In this famous lawsuit Plaintiffs stated they did not object to the Map of Ireland being used in the advertisement of

IREL COFFEE.

This delicious beverage is made in Irel-and, and the Map of Ireland is on every bottle.

Note the play on the word Irel-and in this advertisement.

A Rinso advertisement, World War I.

A simultaneous showing of new millinery in this Lees' advertisement.

RINSO is made by Hudson's, a name famous in every household.

That's GOOD ENGLISH *and* GOOD STUFF TOO!

THERE is no difficulty with RINSO, it is all so simple. You soak the clothes in RINSO and cold water overnight—rinse and hang out to dry in the morning, that's all. RINSO does in cold water all that more costly but less scientific preparations do in hot water. It is the easy washer—easy for the housewife—easy for the clothes.

Sold in 2D. & 1D. Packets everywhere.

R. S. HUDSON LIMITED, LIVERPOOL, WEST BROMWICH AND LONDON.

Dublin 48 Mary St. **LEES'** Rathmines

A Simultaneous Showing of

NEW MILLINERY

In Four Noted Shopping Centres

Twenty-Window Display.

The "LEE" Shopping Centres will be especially attractive to Ladies during this week.

The Newest Models and Latest Styles

ECONOMY will be shown in delightful profusion. Fine Materials, Effective Colourings, and Artistic Designs will be in evidence. VALUE.

Quality and Style Abounding

Moreover, "LEE" Value, as set forth in this dainty medley, offers an irresistible inducement to keen shoppers and an education in purchasing possibilities.
Is it not, therefore, worth while to visit one or other of our centres to see, to enquire, to learn?

No Expenditure Necessary.

IMPORTANT.

High-Class Millinery, by expert designers, produced in our workrooms. Customers' individual tastes carefully studied with a view to pleasing and becoming personal styles.

EDWARD LEE & CO., LTD.

N.B.—ALL OUR ROOMS WILL REMAIN OPEN LATE ON TO-MORROW (WEDNESDAY) EVENING

Kingstown **LEES'** Bray

DAWSON'S "LINCONA" BALATA BELTING

THOMPSON'S MOTOR
STAND N
DUBLIN, BELFAS

Telegrams :—
Traction { Dublin / Belfast / Cork }
ROYAL DUBLIN SOCIETY

ALBION
COMMERCIAL MOTORS
Lorries, Charabancs, Omnibuses
World-wide reputation for reliability, long service and *low maintenance charges*

Sole Concessionaires for Ireland, excluding Ulster :
**Thompson's Motor Car Co., Ld.,
DUBLIN.**

ALLDAYS
General Purpose Tractor
FOR PLOUGHING, HARROWING, REAPING, DRIVING STATIONARY MACHINERY, AND ROAD HAULAGE
Driving & Hauling
Threshing Machines
Fitted with Springs to both Axles.   Winding Drum and Wire Rope.

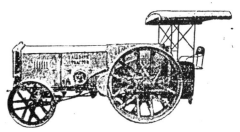

Concessionaires for Ireland—**Thompson's Motor Car Co., Ld.**

CLAYTON
and SHUTTLEWORTH
THRESHING MACHINERY

Sole Representatives in Ireland :—
Thompson's Motor Car Co., Ld.

"COMMER CARS"
Concessionaires for Ireland—
Thompson's Motor Car Co., Ld., DUBLIN.

FOR
GOODS & PASSENGERS
OVER SIXTY
SOLD IN IRELAND
THIS YEAR

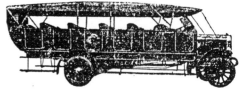

Makers—Commercial Cars, Ltd., Luton, Beds.

34

…AR CO., LTD.

58 AGRICULTURAL SHOW. BALLSBRIDGE

Telephones :
Dublin   5001
Belfast   2961
Cork   936

…CORK

…KINSON
…am Waggons

ON RUBBER TYRES
FOUR AND SIX TON LOADS

…e Finest Under-type Waggon made.

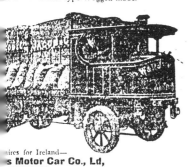

…ires for Ireland—
…s Motor Car Co., Ld,
…DUBLIN.

WYLES
MOTOR PLOUGHS

CALEDON
Industrial Motor Vehicles

THE MOTOR VEHICLE YOU WANT

IS A CAR you can trust
—a car you know some-
thing about, and which has
proved its dependability in
the case of other users who
have tested out its profit-
earning capacity by actual
results.

THE STRONG, simple
design of the Caledon has
proved eminently satisfactory
in the service of hundreds of
important users.

CALEDON MOTORS, Ltd.
DUKE STREET, GLASGOW.

Irish Agents :—Thompson's Motor
Car Co., Ltd. Dublin, Belfast,
Cork, and Waterford.

EVIDENCE.
" I have much pleasure in
stating that the ' Caledon '
Chassis I purchased from you
nearly two years ago has been
running daily up to now and
has not given a moment's
trouble yet. This speaks for
itself. . . . The car has
never let us down."

…DEN STEAM
WAGONS

…ELOQUENT TESTIMONIAL :

Repeat Order from

…. A. GUINNESS, SON & CO.

5-TON WAGONS
4-TON TRAILERS.

…Ireland : Thompson's Motor Car Co., Ltd.

WORTHINGTON
SIMPSON, LTD.

PUMPING MACHINERY
FOR ALL PURPOSES.
OIL AND GAS ENGINES
COMPLETE ELECTRIC LIGHTING PLANTS

WORTHINGTON-CANE
MILKING PLANTS

Demonstrations Daily in the Show Yard.

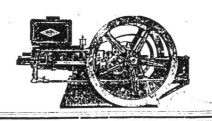

NENAGH
County Tipperary
Fairs and Markets, 1928.

CATTLE AND SHEEP FAIRS.

Monday, 2nd January
Monday, 6th February
Monday, 8th March
Thursday, 29th March
Tuesday, 24th April
Tuesday, 29th May
Wednesday, 4th July

Wednesday, 1st August
Tuesday, 4th September
Wednesday, 10th October
Thursday, 1st November
Monday, 3rd December
Thursday, 13th December

PIG FAIRS.
PIG FAIRS are held on the SECOND and FOURTH
TUESDAY of each Month.

HORSE FAIRS.

Monday, 6th February
Tuesday, 29th May

Tuesday, 4th September
Monday, 3rd December

Special Fowl Markets.
Saturday, 10th November, and Thursday, 13th December.

BUTTER, EGG AND FOWL MARKETS every Monday.
CORN MARKET   GENERAL MARKET
Thursdays.   Saturdays.

By Order, Nenagh Urban District Council.
SEAN T. O'NEILL, Town Clerk.

Fairs and markets
advertisement in
Nenagh, 1928.

Half page
advertisement for cars
and trucks, The Irish
Times, **June 10, 1919.**

35

THANKS TO OUR NAVY WE CAN STILL TOSS A PANCAKE IN THE FRYING PAN CLEANED WITH VIM.

YES, our food comes to us silently—thanks to our splendid Navy—and cleanly—thanks to VIM, which is in every way a splendid Cleanser and Polisher. Both the Navy and Vimmy are exceptionally busy this Shrove Tuesday.

When Jack comes ashore for a well-earned rest he will find Vimmy still busy, for there can be no rest for Vim while there is a speck of rust to remove.

FOR POTS AND PANS, PLATES AND DISHES, DRESSERS AND TABLE-TOPS, AND FOR CLEANING GAS COOKERS.

IN SPRINKLER-TOP TINS OF THREE SIZES.

LEVER BROTHERS LIMITED, PORT SUNLIGHT.

Lever Brothers used a character in their advertising called Vimmy to highlight the cleaning powers of their product Vim.

Opposite page:
Late 19th century advertisements for Cork's two main breweries. Beamish & Crawford dates back to 1792, while Murphy's Lady's Well brewery was founded in 1854.

One of the biggest advertising campaigns during World War 1 was for recruiting for the British Army, which began in late 1914. Kevin J. Kenny was most annoyed to find that the campaign for Ireland, which used newspapers and outdoor posters, was being handled by an English agency. He went to London and met with the people responsible for publicity in the War Office and persuaded them to make Kenny's the placing agent for the campaign in Ireland. For two years, until the Easter Rising of 1916, this British Army recruiting advertising was lucrative business for Kenny's, although no record remains of the total spent. This new business was complementary to existing accounts like that for the Royal Irish Constabulary.

Life in Ireland remained comparatively tranquil from the time World War 1 was declared in August, 1914, until April, 1916, when the Easter Rising took place. During that period of just under two years, commercial and social life in Dublin and the rest of the country carried on as usual, the only outward sign of war being the constant procession of recruits, men, as well as a few women on the catering and nursing side, who had joined the British Army voluntarily and sailed off from Kingstown harbour, with hope in their hearts, to fight for what they thought was the freedom of small nations. 50,000 Irish soldiers never returned home. So calm was the atmosphere in Dublin in early 1916, that young Charlie McConnell, thoroughly addicted to the business of advertising since he started space broking (buying advertisement space in the newspapers for 4d a line and selling it for 6d), that he was determined to start an agency of his own.

Masons was a long-established firm of opticians, founded at Arran Quay, Dublin, just down from the Four Courts, in 1780. For many years subsequently, the firm was at 5 and 6 Dame Street and it was into those premises, according to popular legend, that Charlie McConnell walked one day in the first month or two of 1916. He had an idea that reflected the current feeling that the war must soon be over.

McConnell's advertising slogan for Mason's was "Peace in Sight". He hoped, on the basis of this clever copyline, to win Mason's modest advertising account, confined to small display advertisements in the *Dublin Evening Mail, Irish Independent* and *The Irish Times,* as well as some country newspapers. Mason's did not accept Charlie McConnell's offer, but they did pay him the goodly sum of half a guinea (10/6d) for the use of the slogan. Ireland's greatest advertising man was on his way. He decided to leave his job in the Ormond to set up in the agency business and did so in two small rooms in St Andrew Street in the centre of Dublin, opening for the first time in Easter week, 1916. In later years, Charlie McConnell would trot out the same anecdote at every successive staff party in McConnell's, until the entire agency staff knew the words by heart: "Three important things happened in 1916. McConnell's was founded, my son John was born and there was a little trouble down in Sackville Street (now O'Connell Street)."

His very first account was for a modern invention — Dublin's first mechanically propelled taxis. The idea of such taxis was novel indeed and faced stiff competition from the horse-drawn hansom cabs, a form of public transport that had been used for nearly 200 years and which still had another 30 years of life left. A & B Taxis introduced the motorised taxis to Dublin and Charlie McConnell organised publicity for them in the Dublin newspapers. Before long, other accounts came to the agency, such as Barnardo's Furs, the Dublin Gas Company, and Paterson's matches. But until 1920, Charlie McConnell had to sell paper to the printing trade, an area in which he had much expertise and many useful contacts, in order to keep the new agency solvent. His first right-hand-man was Leo Blennerhassett, later to become publicity manager and then London manager at Independent Newspapers. Blennerhassett did most of the detailed work in the tiny office, everything from writing copy through to collecting accounts, while Charlie McConnell began to hone his "front office" skills so evident in his later advertising career. Another young man who joined the agency not long after was Jack Tate. Serving in an infantry regiment of the British Army during World War 1, he had studied advertising by post while in the trenches.

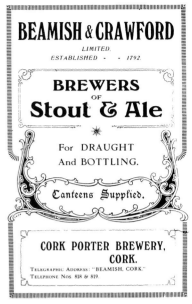

McConnell was lucky with his choice of office location, well away from the destruction of the immediate city centre. Henry Crawford Hartnell, in Commercial Buildings in Dame Street, was equally fortunate, but Kenny's premises in Middle Abbey Street were destroyed and subsequently rebuilt. The back garden also provided a useful means of escape for some of the insurgents at the GPO when they were fleeing at the end of the week. Eason's block, including the advertisement section, at the corner of Sackville Street and Middle Abbey Street, was also destroyed. Some of the newspapers were hit, particularly the *Freeman's Journal* and its associated titles, the *Evening Telegraph* and *Sport.* The *Journal's* offices in Princes Street, by the side of the GPO, were completely destroyed in the shellfire by British forces that ended the Easter Rising. Only the sign was left intact. It was the beginning of the end for the *Freeman's Journal,* although it quickly opened an advertisement office in Westmoreland Street and editorial and printing departments in Townsend Street. *The Irish Times'* paper store in Lower Abbey Street was burned down, but the main offices in Westmoreland Street escaped damage. There was one strangely coincidental casualty of Easter Week: Constable Brosnan, who was on duty at the gates of Dublin Castle on Easter Monday, 1916, was the first person to be killed during the Rising. He was the father of Meredith Brosnan-Warner, "Warner" the cartoonist, who drew the famous cartoons for the O'Dearest mattress advertisements which ran from 1941 until 1967. During the course of the war, the Department of Agriculture bought large volumes of space in Irish newspapers for its tillage campaign. Yet by 1917, the British Government was appealing to newspapers, including the Dublin

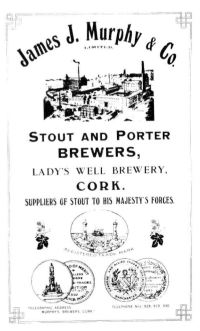

The Bunratty folk park in Co Clare recreates old style village life. Shops have been decorated as they were late last century, complete with enamel signs advertising Player's "Navy Cut" and St Bruno "Flake".

Pawnbroker advertisement.

dailies, for free advertising space to promote the sale of War Bonds.

Once World War 1 was over, in November 1918, the world settled back into a fragile peace marked by recurring economic depression. In Ireland, the uneasy lull that followed the Easter Rising was broken in 1919 by the start of the War of Independence. Apart from cordite, there was a whiff of something else in the air — Bisto. The product had been launched in 1910 and nine years later, one of Ireland's longest-running advertising campaigns began, featuring the Bisto Kids, designed by Will Owen. With their cast-off, cut-down clothes and air of mischievousness, they caught the popular spirit, "smiling through adversity". The advertisements featured on tram sides and posters and used a phrase that soon passed into popular use, "Aah Bisto". Will Owen's designs achieved lasting fame. The Bisto campaign, although widely used in Ireland, was devised in London.

In 1919, Carroll's, the Dundalk cigarette, snuff and tobacco manufacturers, launched their Sweet Afton brand, initially on the Scottish market, where the firm had been well entrenched since the 1850s. At the urging of James Chandler, manager of Carroll's Glasgow depot, the new cigarette was launched, with a specifically Scottish image. Buried in St Nicholas's churchyard, just across the street from the original Carroll's factory in Dundalk, is Agnes, eldest sister of the great Scottish poet, Robert Burns. She lived at Stephenstown, near Dundalk, and died in 1834, aged 72. So Carroll's directors decided to choose a brand name from Burns' poetry and settled upon the poem "Afton Water". The head and breast of the poet were used on the pack design, which has remained unchanged to the present day, with only minor modifications. The cigarette was not introduced to the Irish market until 1927.

Grafton Street

FIRST OF ALL
an Irishman is a sportsman, and sportsmen like straight dealing, such as is experienced by the devotees of all sports at Crotty's, the Sports House, Grafton Street

TENNIS.   GOLF.   CRICKET.   Waterproof Capes

...at **CROTTY'S**
THE SPORTS HOUSE, 62 GRAFTON ST.

SPRING SHOPPING WEEK
May 14th to 19th

HORTONS
at the corner of Grafton St. & Suffolk St. are now showing a new supply of
Jaeger Summer Underwear & Shirtings
Also an attractive range of the inimitable
Burberry Coats in Many Styles
"Clad with a Burberry you are ready for all occasions."
HORTONS.   Also at College Gn., Trinity St.

Barnardos
21 Grafton Street
invite you to call and see the wonderful value they are offering in
all FUR GARMENTS
Beautiful Wolf Ties from £1 9s. 6d.

Switzers
FOR Spring Show week this Distinctive House of Fashion will exhibit some lovely examples of Fashion Art. Three-piece Costumes in beautiful new shades. Exquisite Wrap Coats for all occasions, and Choice Collection of Furs. Latest productions in Millinery, Blouses, Jumpers, and all "ready to wear" Sporting Garments.

LOWER GROUND FLOOR ATTRACTIONS.
Library—Reading and writing room.
Up-to-date Tea Rooms and Ice Soda Fountain.
Public Telephone Exchange.

Brown Thomas
THE HOUSE FOR VALUE
EVERYTHING for Ladies and Children's wear
READY-TO-WEAR Suits for Men and Boys
SPORT REQUISITES
IN THE RESTAURANT DAILY
Popular 4 Course Lunch. Inclusive Charge 2/-
BROWN THOMAS & Co., Ltd., Grafton St., DUBLIN.

PIANOS
Finest Selection of all the World's Best Makes.
Moderate Prices.
Full Guarantee.
Catalogues Post Free.
PIGOTT
AND CO. LTD.
GRAFTON ST.,
CORK   DUBLIN   LIMERICK.

FOR TENNIS
White Blanket Coats, Superior Quality, from **42/-**
Tennis Skirts in Gaberdine or Pique, Perfectly cut, and Special Value at **10/6**
WHITE WOOL SUITS, Bound Silk Braid. Specially Priced at 3½ and 4 Guineas.
FORREST
& SONS, LTD., GRAFTON ST.

Tempting Offer of Charming CHALTON And other English PIANOS AT OLD PRICES.
While our limited Stock of English Pianos lasts we have decided to Sell them at the old prices. You are therefore specially invited to visit our Salons and test these and other instruments, including Behstein and Schiedmayer Pianos.
McCULLOUGH
SOLE BECKSTEIN AGENTS.
39 Grafton Street.

WEST AND SON
DIAMOND RINGS
WRIST WATCHES
IN GOLD AND SILVER.
SILVER CUPS AND BOWLS.
GRAFTON HOUSE

Lunch with your Friends at Kidds

46 NASSAU ST.		ADAM COURT (Off Grafton St.)	
3-Course Lunch	3/-	3-Course Lunch	2/6
5-Course Dinner	5/-	5-Course Dinner	4/6
Afternoon Tea	1/-	Afternoon Tea	1/-

17 HENRY STREET, 3-Course Lunch, 2/6; Afternoon Tea, 1/-.
CHOICE SELECTION OF WINES AND CIGARS.
Our Buffet at Adam Court is select and secluded. An ideal, restful rendezvous for business men and visitors.—Kidds, Limited.

Robert and Co., Limited
THE FASHION CENTRE, GRAFTON STREET.

Summer Gowns
EFFECTIVE Washing Silk Dresses, broad stripe pattern, white collar, full three-quarter sleeves, belted at waist; stocked in rose-white, pink-white, sky-white, and grey-white.
Special Price, **£3/19/11**

DAINTY Flowered Voile Dresses, in light subdued tones, round neck, long white sleeves, finished with frilling; gathered skirt, draped sides. In sky, pink, green, etc.
19/11

Useful Tennis Skirt, in Cream Serge, full length.
LADIES' SUNSHADES
Japanese Sunshades, pretty designs. From 1/11½ to 4/11½.

Robert and Co., Limited
THE FASHION CENTRE, GRAFTON STREET

Robert & Co., Ltd.,
THE FASHION CENTRE   GRAFTON STREET
SMART Striped Sponge Cloth Frock, collar, short sleeves, turnback cuff, one belt. Colours Rose-Grey, Lemon-Blue, Brown-Blue, Green-White, Sky-Black, Navy. Sizes 34, 36, 38, 40. From **15/11**
LARGE Selection of Sponge Cloth Frocks, square and round necks, plain and assorted stripes. From £1/12, 10/11, 12/11 up. **14/11**
GOOD Selection of Cotton Frocks and Knickers, 2/11, 3/11, Stripes and Checks. From 6/11 to £1/3.
EMBROIDERED Voile Frocks, sizes 22 to 26. From 12/11 up to 29/11.

CHILPRUFE
Sweet Lavender
Pexar Underwear.
BOOTS, SHOES
Seaside Wear

HOUSEHOLD DEPT.	ROBERTS	HOUSEHOLD DEPT.
BEDSTEADS BEDDING PILLOWS BOLSTERS BLANKETS SHEETS BEDSPREADS PILLOW CASES ETC. ALL at Lowest Prices	Department for CHILDREN to meet the great and regular satisfaction to many hundreds of parents who discriminating.	TEA SETS DINNER SETS GLASS WARE EARTHENWARE ENAMEL WARE CARPETS RUGS CURTAINS CASEMENTS at Lowest Prices

Prescotts
are the pioneers of
Dyeing and Cleaning in Ireland
Some examples of their work can be seen this week at their
BRANCH OFFICE
6 Grafton St.
where full information may be had. Your visit will be appreciated.

Smyth's for Sunshades
Prices 6/6 to 45/-
Ask to see Pattern Book at their only
—Address—
75 Grafton St
Francis Smyth AND Son
Umbrella and Parasol Manufacturers.
Repairs and Recoverings a Speciality.
All work done on the Premises.

Velka Violet
TOILET SOAP
Made from the special "VELKA" base, perfumed with deliciously natural Triple Violet Essence. Sold in handsome box of Three Tablets each. Neatly wrapped.
MADE ONLY BY
J. BARRINGTON & Sons, Ltd.,
KING'S INNS STREET SOAPWORKS, DUBLIN.

Autocrat
SHAVING STICK
Encased in handsome Aluminium tin, a Pure Emollient Soap, giving a fragrant lather, which will not dry on the face or irritate the most tender skin.
MADE ONLY BY
J. BARRINGTON & Sons, Ltd.,
KING'S INNS STREET SOAPWORKS, DUBLIN.

DAVIS & CO.
(LATE OGILVYS)
COSTUMES
GOWNS
FURS
WRAP COATS
MILLINERY
Prices Strictly Moderate.
45 Grafton St.
Mourning Goods a Speciality.

PETER E. MAGILL, ADVERTISEMENT CONSULTANT, BEACON HOUSE, 85-86 GRAFTON STREET, DUBLIN.

The Dublin Evening Mail **published a page of Grafton Street shopping advertisements in May, 1923.**

1919 saw a new advertising account launch a new agency. The first issue of Dail bonds was authorised by the Dail in April, 1919, to the value of £250,000. Handling the publicity, both covertly in Ireland, (since their issue was considered illegal by the British authorities based in Dublin Castle) and openly in America, was Sean Lynch, who had a strong Republican background. That year saw him start Lynch Advertising in small offices in Suffolk Street, not far from the commercial offices of Independent Newspapers in Carlisle Buildings, where a young lad called Billy King started work in 1917. Lynch Advertising lasted until 1985, when the agency collapsed under the weight of its debts.

Kenny's Advertising agency at 65, Amiens Street, Dublin, pictured in the late 1890s. Right, in the doorway, is Kevin J. Kenny, founder of the agency.

OGLAIGH NA hEIREANN

Ta Adhbhair-Saidiuiri ag teastail i g-coir Airm na hEireann

Ta sli i gcoir a thuille saidiuiri ins na Cathaibh ata ainmnithe ar an dtaobh chle.

Glacfar le h-adhbhair-saidiuiri ag Oifigibh na gCath.

Iad so gur mhaith leo bheith, i gCathaibh a 60, a 61, a 62, a 63, a 64, is a 65, is leor doibh teacht go dti ean-Staisiun Airm, agus cuirfear as son go dti Corrach Cill Dara iad

Ni mor teistimeireacht o dhuine de'n chleir no o'n bhfear go bhfuiltear ag obair do fe lathair no go rabhthas ag obair do.

Leightear na Coingheallacha Seirbhise ar an dtaobh dheas

NA COINGHEALLACHA SEIRBHISE

Fanfar san Arm go ceann bliana no nios giorra do reir mar is toil le Comhairle an Airm.

Pagh Oglaigh :
3/6 sa lo, agus cothu.

Pagh an dreama ata ag brath ar Oglach :
Bean-cheile : 4/- sa lo.
Bean-cheile is leanbh : 5/6 sa lo.
Bean-cheile is 2 leanbh : 6/6 sa lo ; agus 9d. sa bhreis i n-aghaidh gach leanbh eile ata fe bhun 14 bliana d' aois.

Wilson Hartnell was putting more energy into its publishing activities, in contrast to other agencies in town. Henry Crawford Hartnell decided, in 1920, to relaunch the *Lady of the House* as the *Irish Tatler and Sketch*. It was the forerunner of the present *IT* magazine, run by Noelle Campbell-Sharp. Perhaps Hartnell was right in his decision — after all, advertising was such small business in Dublin then that the combined staff of all the city's advertising agencies in 1920 totalled just 18.

Feelings were running high in Ireland: the Black and Tan war was at its height. Anti-Irish sentiment was strong in England, but Charlie McConnell, with his ineffable charm and bonhomie, managed to pull off a remarkable coup in London. The big advertising exhibition at White City, London, opened in 1920 shortly after the Croke Park massacre: hardly an auspicious moment for Irish advertising men. McConnell's had a small stand, which marked its very first involvement with the London advertising world, and Charlie McConnell put up a poster which read: "Talk business not politics". The innate good sense of that slogan, coupled with McConnell's diplomatic and soothing manner, won him and Irish advertising many friends in London that year. Also there were Kevin J. Kenny, founder and managing director of Kenny's Advertising agency and Kenny's general manager, Brian D. O'Kennedy. The two men were to split up seven years later.

Advertisement placed in January, 1923, by Kenny's Advertising agency, for volunteer recruits to the Army.

A press advertisement
for a Bunclody, Co
Wexford, garage in
September, 1924.
*Photograph: Wheels and
Deals/Gill & Macmillan.*

Opposite page:
McBirney's Christmas
advertising, 1924. Its
famous advertising
slogan "40 paces from
O'Connell Bridge" was
devised 20 years later.

Treaty or No Treaty
— April, 1923
advertisement for a
Dublin tailoring firm.

MORRIS CARS
NEW PRICES & NEW PROGRAMME

Our 1923 Programme being now completed, we have pleasure in announcing the Morris Programme for 1924— the prices for which come into force to-day, Sept. 3rd.

The new striking reduction in the prices of Morris Cars has been rendered possible only by increased efficiency in our works at Oxford and Coventry. The world-famous MORRIS QUALITY in material, construction and finish has been enhanced, while the design, improved in detail after exhaustive experiment, remains, as always, that of the ideal owner-driver's car.

THE NEW PRICES.

The Morris-Cowley Cars, 11.9 h.p.,

fitted with Lucas 12-volt dynamotor-starter lighting set (5 lamps) All-Weather hood and side-curtains opening with doors, Smith speed-indicator and 8-day clock, Boyce Motor-meter (radiator thermometer), petrol and oil gauges, Knots pump chassis lubrication, 5 Dunlop cord tyres on 5 detachable steel wheels, spring gaiters, tool kit with jack and pump, spare petrol can and carrier on running board, half-gallon tin of Shell oil sent out with every car, coachwork painted Morris Grey, cost—

The Two-Seater	-	-	£235
The Occasional Four	-	-	£255
The Four-Seater	-	-	£267

The Morris-Oxford Cars, 13.9 h.p.,

fitted with Lucas 12-volt dynamotor-starter lighting set, with 5 lamps and dashboard light, Smith speed-indicator and 8-day clock, driving mirror, electric and bulb horns, Gabriel shock-absorbers to both axles, 5 Dunlop cord tyres (28 x 3½) on 5 detachable steel wheels, Knots pump chassis lubrication, Boyce motor-meter, petrol and oil gauges, All-Weather One-man hood, 3-panel front windscreen, complete kit of tools including jack and pump, spare petrol can and carrier on running board, half-gallon tin of Shell oil. Coachwork painted Blue, Claret, Bronze Green or Morris Grey, upholstered in finest Mottled Grey leather, cost—

The Two-Seater	with folding dickey seat for two built into the body, and fully upholstered, with folding windscreen. The All-Weather hood has windshields, which open with the doors	£356
The Four-Seater	with detachable side-doors, opening with doors, and four-panel folding glass screen with apron for rear passengers	£380
The Coupe	upholstered in Grey Bedford cord, with dickey seat for two built into the body and fully upholstered	£421

ALL PRICES PLUS CARRIAGE.

Coachwork: Note, while the familiar racing lines of our 1923 coachwork have been carefully preserved, the new bodies, in all models, have been built to give considerably more room.

MORRIS MOTORS Ltd.,
Cowley, OXFORD

M. CARTON
BUNCLODY

Agent for the Counties Wexford, Carlow and a large portion of Wicklow.

42

Rowntrees starts manufacturing chocolates at its new Inchicore works, Dublin, 1927. In May of that year, the firm announced a big promotional price cutting campaign.

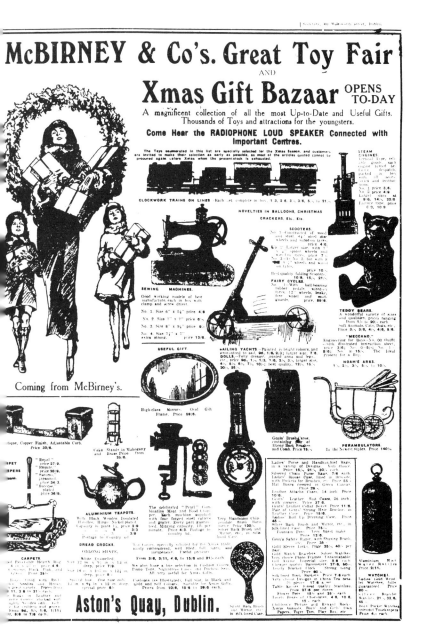

McBIRNEY & Co's. Great Toy Fair
AND
Xmas Gift Bazaar OPENS TO-DAY

A magnificent collection of all the most Up-to-Date and Useful Gifts. Thousands of Toys and attractions for the youngsters.

Come Hear the RADIOPHONE LOUD SPEAKER Connected with Important Centres.

Coming from McBirney's.

Aston's Quay, Dublin.

PHIL 30, 1927.

Mr. York
Comes to Dublin With Great News

Plain Mr. York, of York, Yorks, has arrived in Dublin with a welcome message. His good news will create the furore that it deserves, and plain Mr. York will now be more popular than ever in the Irish Free State. He says quite plainly and emphatically that the price of High-class Chocolates must be reduced now that Rowntrees are making their famous products in Dublin, and that these reductions will be put into force from May 2nd.

Price Reductions from May 2nd

He says further, that still more reductions will be made later on when the full plant is installed at the Inchicore Works. Plain Mr. York, of York, Yorks, is determined that the Rowntree Plant in Dublin shall maintain the great traditions of the York Plant and that in both quality and price, in Ireland as elsewhere, Rowntree's name shall stand supreme. The following are some of the lines that are now to be reduced:

Our York Seal Assorted Chocolates price 4/- per lb. has already been reduced from 4/6

ROWNTREE
& CO., (IRELAND), Ltd., The Cocoa Works, DUBLIN

TREATY OR NO TREATY.

One point we are all agreed on—that THE PEOPLE'S OWN TAILORS, 8 EUSTACE STREET, is the Best House in Dublin for Ladies' and Gentlemen's Tailoring. Cash or Credit. Perfect Fit guaranteed.

Kellett's **advertisements,** Dublin Evening Mail, **May 31, 1923.**

CITY FINAL

Dublin Evening Mail.

No 22,469   DUBLIN, THURSDAY, MAY 31, 1923   ONE P...

RECEIVING OFFICE
FOR
Prescott's Dye Works
AT
THE HOSIERY SHOP,
11A Rathmines Terrace,
DUBLIN.

Information for the Public about THE STRIKE AT KELLETT'S

The Merchant Drapers' Association of Dublin, Ltd., desire to inform the Public that the Strike of a small section of the Assistants employed by Messrs. D. Kellett, Ltd., is due to the following demands of the Irish Union of Distributive Workers, which the Firm cannot comply with—

The Union demands that Messrs. Kellett retain in their employment a full Staff of Assistants, notwithstanding the fact that, owing to the great depression in trade (which the Union admits), there is not sufficient work for them. In January the Firm—in order to deal with this depression and to avoid dismissals—arranged to adopt a system of holidays, which was agreed to by the Union.

This arrangement expired in March; and, owing to the continued depression, the Firm found they were still over-staffed, and wished to continue the holiday arrangement, still being anxious to avoid dismissals.

This proposal was agreed to by the Assistants, but they wished to vary the arrangement by including all the married Staff and others having dependents. To this the Firm could not agree, as they considered it a hardship on those with dependents; but before any settlement was arrived at the Executive Committee of the Union intervened, and turned down the proposals completely, leaving Messrs. Kellett, Ltd., in the position that they had no alternative but to reduce the Staff to a number suitable to the requirements of the business.

The Merchant Drapers' Association feel that this action of the Union is a direct Challenge of the right of Employers to Engage and Dismiss Assistants according to their requirements, and it must, and will be, resisted by the Trade. The claim of victimisation made by the Assistants' Union is wholly unwarranted and without foundation.

The great majority of Messrs. Kellett's Staff, although they are Members of the Irish Union of Distributive Workers, refused to go out on Strike, and no new appointments have been yet made.

Issued by the Merchant Drapers' Association of Dublin, Ltd.
Dublin, 30th May, 1923.

KELLETTS
Stylish Millinery

D. KELLETT, Ltd., George's St. & Exchequer St., DUBLIN.

Kennedy & McSharry advertise coats for the well-dressed man.

COATS

Habitually well-dressed men know the "Kenneth Durward" and "Peltinvain" Coats—and value them highly.

"Peltinvain" Rainproof Coats from 75/-

"The New Peltinvain" Weatherproof Coat, close fitting style, seam back and centre vent — 75/-

The "Wolverton" Slip-on. Full loose fitting style, 75/-, 115/-, and £7/15/0. An ideal Weatherproof Coat for any occasion.

Our Special Rubber Waterproof Riding Coat, extra wide cut; belt all round, with riding flap — 70/-

The New Double-Breasted Light Tarred Coats, very stylish and smart in appearance. Best tailor made, £6/15/0

Our Famous "Peltinvain" Coats, with belt all round, in Blue Grey and Fawn Mixtures — 115/-. Made from the famous "Plume Triune" Cloth.

Our New "Heatherdale Peltinvain" Coats in new shades of Brown and Fawn, semi-fitting — £5/10/0

Agents for "Dexter" Waterproof and Aero Wool Web Golf Jackets.

KENNEDY & McSHARRY,
Westmoreland Street and D'Olier Street, Dublin.

44

Within three years of that White City exhibition, the harmony engendered in London had its effects in Dublin. Leading personalities of the advertising business in the city, such as Charlie McConnell, Kevin J. Kenny and Tom Grehan set about forming the Publicity Club in 1923. A surviving photograph of the Publicity Club's first outing shows that jaunty optimism that characterises the advertising profession. An open-topped omnibus is about to depart from outside Independent Newspapers' offices at Carlisle Buildings for a tour of the Boyne valley. Despite the enticing summer weather, the club members were dressed in the formal business style of the day, dark suits and bowler hats. The Publicity Club was off to an auspicious start.

On June 8, 1923, a memorable letter went out from the controller of the Stationery Office to Wilson Hartnell. Henry Crawford Hartnell must have been as overjoyed as his austere personality allowed, for it read: "Gentlemen, I am directed by the Minister for Finance to inform you that you have been declared Contractor for Government Advertising in accordance with the terms of the Contract Form signed by you on the 16th May last." It was a big breakthrough for the agency and for the next 30 years, until Tim O'Neill of Sun Advertising, who

By the late 1890s, T. B. Browne's was one of London's biggest advertising agencies. This illustration shows the store room for blocks.

STORE ROOMS FOR BLOCKS, &c.

45

Frank Padbury, depicted here by Pyke, was one of the first two teachers of advertising subjects at the Rathmines Municipal Technical Institute in 1929/30.

The first ever Publicity Club outing departs in the summer of 1923. The charabanc is parked outside Independent Newspapers' Carlisle Buildings office near O'Connell Bridge.

O'Kennedy Brindley ran this campaign for Irish-made blankets the year the agency was founded, 1927.

Follow a good lead

THE leading new Dublin Hotels—
The Gresham Hotel and Wynn's
Hotel—are both furnished throughout with new Irish Fleecy Blankets. Such
keen buyers are good judges—they know
that new Irish Blankets are exquisitely
soft and warm, and being made from pure
new Irish wool will wash and wear
splendidly. You will be wise to follow
their good lead and

Buy **Irish**
Blankets

**Leading Irish
Blanket Mills**
" DRIPSEY "
Dripsey Mills, Ltd.,
Cork.
LUCAN:
Hill & Sons, Ltd.,
Lucan, Co. Dublin
PROVIDENCE
Woollen Mills,
Foxford.
THOMOND
Woollen Mills,
Sixmilebridge.
ATHLONE
Woollen Mills Co.,
Ltd.
J. COGAN and
SON,
Ballincurrig
Mills,
Midleton.
CONVOY
Woollen Co., Ltd.

had superb political contacts, snatched away the contract in 1954, Wilson Hartnell was kept busy and reasonably rewarded placing Government advertising in daily and weekly newspapers. McConnell's also did some government advertising work. The media scene was largely limited to newspapers, posters and to a lesser extent, magazines. Not for nothing did Charlie McConnell pay daily visits to his friends in Independent House, but in 1923 came the first chink in the all-print media, when the Marconi Company organised experimental radio broadcasts from the Royal Marine Hotel in Dun Laoghaire to the Dublin Horse Show in the RDS.

As radio was coming to the RDS, so did hundreds of advertising personnel arrive in town. They had travelled to Dublin from the world advertising convention in London, curious to see the centre of Dublin being rebuilt after the Easter Rising damage. Ireland had never before hosted an advertising convention of this size and Charlie McConnell (naturally) and Paddy Montford, advertisement manager of the *Freeman's Journal,* played a sterling role in the organisation of the Dublin event. Sadly for Montford, what should have been his year of glory was marred by the final closure of the 161 year old *Freeman's Journal,* the last issue of which was published on Friday, December 19, 1924.

Charlie McConnell had well settled his agency into much larger premises at 10 Great Brunswick Street (now Pearse Street). He had been in Publicity House since 1918 and although the building was far

Eleven o'clockishness

Bobby turns up his nose at ordinary milk and says it's skinny. Milk makes sturdy legs and bright eyes and rosy cheeks. Bobby must have it and, if he won't take it one way, he must be persuaded to take it another.

And so, when Bobby brings his chin to the kitchen table in the middle of the morning, what does mother do? She gives him a piece of bread or a biscuit spread nice and thick with Nestlé's Milk. And that does it —for Nestlé's Milk is rich, pure, full-cream farm milk, so prepared that the most delicate digestion can take it and absorb all the good that is in it.

NESTLÉ'S MILK

HERE IS AUTUMN!

AND winter is just round the corner. Why not brighten your long winter evenings with clean, new coloured furnishings in the home? Prescott's can dye your heavy curtains, chair covers and carpets to a cheery warm colour, clean them of all their imbedded dust and grime, for a few shillings in a few days. Roll up your furnishings and send them to Prescott's to-day.

Prescott's
DYERS AND CLEANERS
82-84 TALBOT STREET, DUBLIN
AND BRANCHES

Prescott's used an autumn theme in its advertising in late 1927.

Nestlé advertisement, late 1920s.

Remarkable hair care advertisement published in the golden jubilee issue of the Eagle, Skibbereen, 1907.

A REMARKABLE INVENTION FOR THE CULTURE OF HAIR

THE EVANS VACUUM CAP is a practical invention constructed on scientific and hygienic principles by the simple means of which a free and normal circulation is restored throughout the scalp. The minute blood vessels are gently stimulated to activity, thus allowing the food supply which can only be derived from the blood, to be carried to the hair roots, the effects of which are quickly seen in a healthy, vigorous growth of hair. There is no rubbing, and as no drugs or chemicals of whatsoever kind are employed there is nothing to cause irritation. It is only necessary to wear the Cap three or four minutes daily.

60 DAYS' FREE TRIAL!
The Company's Guarantee.

An EVANS VACUUM CAP will be sent you for sixty days' free trial. If you do not see a gradual development of a new growth of hair, and are not convinced that the Cap will completely restore your hair, you are at liberty to return the Cap with no expense whatever to yourself. It is requested, as an evidence of good faith, that the price of the Cap be deposited with the Chancery Lane Safe Deposit Company of London, the largest financial and business institution of the kind in the world, who will issue a receipt guaranteeing that the money will be returned in full, on demand without questions or comment, at any time during the trial period.

The eminent Dr. I. N. LOVE, in his address to the Medical Board on the subject of Alopecia (loss of hair) stated that if a means could be devised to bring nutrition to the hair follicles (hair roots), without resorting to any irritating process, the problem of hair growth would be solved. Later on, when the EVANS VACUUM CAP was submitted to him for inspection, he remarked that the Cap would fulfil and confirm in practice the observations he had previously made before the Medical Board.

Dr. W. MOORE, referring to the invention, says that the principle upon which the Evans Vacuum Cap is founded is absolutely correct and indispensable.

An illustrated descriptive book of the Evans Vacuum Cap will be sent, post free, on application.

THE SECRETARY, EVANS VACUUM CAP CO., LTD., REGENT HOUSE, REGENT STREET, LONDON, W. (437)

An early coffee essence, made in Cork about 1900.

too big for initial needs, he sub-let part of the premises. By the 1940s, Publicity House was packed to capacity by McConnell's. Charlie McConnell was very interested in aviation, an interest shared by J. J. O'Leary of Cahills the printers (uncle of Michael O'Leary of the City Office origination firm) and quickly brought a flying ace into the company. Colonel Charles Russell served in the Royal Flying Corps in World War 1 and lost an eye while serving as an officer in the RFC. For the rest of his life, the injury pained him. In 1922, Colonel Russell was appointed director of civil aviation, being made commander of the Air Corps in 1925. Subsequently, Col. Russell became a director of McConnell's and pioneered many civil aviation "firsts" in the late 1920s and 1930s, aided by Charlie McConnell.

McConnell was busy exploring other new directions in the early 1920s. In 1922, he set up a subsidiary company called McConnell-Hartley with an advertising man from London called Hartley to promote outdoor posters. The new company also became the first in Ireland to produce advertising films, a mantle that later passed to another McConnell company called Irish Photoplays. The first major film production handled by Charlie McConnell was one featuring the new ESB development on the Shannon and the tourist delights of Gougane Barra in Co Cork. In 1926, McConnell's won the account for the Savoy Cinema in O'Connell Street, Ireland's first luxury cinema, offering cinemagoers an unheard of degree of comfort. The cinema was declared open by W. T. Cosgrave, president of the Executive Council, who also happened to be a great friend of Charlie McConnell. Working for McConnell's at the time were Jack Tate, soon to become the leading light of Arks when it was set up in Dublin in 1931 and Harry O'Brien, who set up Arrow Advertising in the early 1930s.

McConnell was involved in so many other schemes it was hard for rivals to keep up with him: no wonder that he was hardly ever home at

Cork Park race course was closed down in 1917 to make way for the Ford car plant. The Ford manufacturing facility was closed down three years ago. This photograph shows advertising umbrellas used by the bookmakers at the course early this century.
Photograph: Cork Examiner.

48

56 Lansdowne Road, Ballsbridge. At least he didn't have far to go for the first of the national military tattoos and historical pageants that took place in 1925 at Lansdowne Road rugby grounds. McConnell's handled the publicity. Ancient sporting practice was revived in 1924 and 1928 with the Tailteann Games: Charlie McConnell was vice-chairman of the publicity committee. He relished being in advertising. One story he loved to tell and retell was about the time he was having a drink in the old Princess Bar at the side of the GPO. A shabbily dressed old man came over to him and engaged him in conversation. Charlie, when asked his line of business, replied: "Advertising." "So am I," replied the old man, scurrying to a dark recess of the bar and fishing out his sandwich board.

Advertisements in the Dublin newspapers of September, 1925, offered the prospect of a new housing development in south Dublin: the 300 acres of the Mount Merrion estate. Sites and houses were being offered at extremely attractive terms. Purchasers were given a two years' free bus ticket into town.

Two years later, the newly formed Electricity Supply Board started building the giant hydro-electric scheme on the Shannon. It took the German contractors, Siemens-Schuckert five years to complete the project at a cost of £5 million. The board's managing director, Dr Thomas McLoughlin, decided to appoint Ned Lawler, political correspondent of the *Irish Independent,* as the ESB's public relations officer, the first such appointment in a public utility in Europe. Lawler's function at the ESB included advertising and to publicise the Shannon

Cork steamship advertisements, early 20th century.

A Bovril can, about 1900.

The Oxo logo has hardly changed since 1900.
Photographs: Nenagh Heritage Centre.

49

scheme, inclusive train and bus tickets allowing people to see it for themselves were advertised extensively. Package deals were advertised in England by the board for this purpose; Ned Lawler prepared copy and concepts for the advertisements, which were designed and laid out by freelance artists. The advertising scheme for Shannon was the first big campaign by a semi-State board in the new Irish Free State.

The Irish Times of January 30, 1926, recorded that the second annual ball of the Publicity Club of Ireland was held in Clery's Imperial ballroom. It was described as a "brilliant success", attended by 600 people, including many well-known Dublin businessmen. Reported

Linen
Handkerchiefs

No. 179. Ladies' fine sheer Linen hemstitched handkerchiefs, hand embroidered initial, about 12 inches.
Per doz. 11/-.

We also have a splendid Selection of Gentleman's Linen Handkerchiefs.

No. 58. Men's Hemstitched Linen Handkerchiefs, hand embroidered initial, about 18 inches, with ¼ inch hem.
Per doz. 21/9.

Handkerchief List G.B. sent post free. Delivery of parcels guaranteed. Carriage paid on orders 30/- upwards to the U.S.

ROBINSON & CLEAVER
MANUFACTURERS OF IRISH LINEN
BELFAST N. IRELAND
Also at Regent St., London and Church St., Liverpool.

An advertisement for linen handkerchiefs from Robinson & Cleaver, the Belfast department store, used about 1900, when the firm was spending the enormous sum of £500 a month on its classified advertising.

Ford advertising trucks to farmers.

Laundry advertisement, 1923.

Every Article We Wash

gets exactly the treatment that best suits it. We take a great deal of trouble to give you a highly dependable service.

Dublin Laundry Co., Ltd.,
MILLTOWN
Phone—Rathmines 57.

Van calls on receipt of a postcard
Ask for particulars of our Flat-finish Service.

To Farmers !

It has been said that no farm is complete without a car, a telephone, and a truck. We believe that on Irish Farms, trucks at any rate are essential. Have you ever considered the time spent on going to and from markets with the horse and cart? A whole day is wasted, and little done. With a truck now, you can carry more and the time is reduced by half at least. The lowest priced and the lowest taxed tonner you can buy to-day is the

1 TON *Ford* TRUCK
£135
AT WORKS, CORK

SEE THEM IN THE AUTHORISED FORD DEALERS SHOWROOMS

SMITHFIELD MOTOR CO. LTD.,
SMITHFIELD (OFF ARRAN QUAY), DUBLIN
Deferred Payments Arranged. 'Phone 4441.

SAVE 50 PER CENT. BY WRITING FOR SAMPLES TO
ROBINSON AND CLEAVER, BELFAST,
IRISH CAMBRIC POCKET HANDKERCHIEFS
ROBINSON AND CLEAVER, LTD. BELFAST.

THE
A I SAUCE.
A FINE TONIC and DIGESTIVE
AN EXCELLENT RELISH FOR FISH, FLESH, OR FOWL.
BRAND & CO., Ltd.

By Royal Warrant
Horticultural
His Majesty

Manufacturers of
Machinery to
the King.

RANSOMES'
LAWN MOWERS.
THE BEST IN THE WORLD.

Royal Botanic Society, 1904, 1905
& 1906, GOLD MEDALS.
R.A.S.E., London, 1904,
SILVER MEDAL.
Royal Horticultural Society, 1906
& 1907, SILVER MEDALS.

Possess
Improvements
contained in no other
machines.

HAND POWER MACHINES | HORSE & PONY MACHINES
in all Kinds and Sizes. | for Large Lawns, Parks,
Thousands in Use | Cricket Grounds, etc

MOTOR LAWN MOWERS.
THE FIRST AND FOREMOST PETROL MOTOR MOWERS
Nearly 200 of these Machines have now been made and
supplied, including two to H.M. THE KING

ILLUSTRATED CATALOGUES FREE
Ransomes, Sims & Jefferies, Ltd., Ipswich
SUPPLIED BY ALL IRONMONGERS.

ROBIN
The New
Starch
Makes
LINEN GLOSSY, STIFF & FLEXIBLE.
Does not Stick to the Iron
Made by the Manufacturers of the celebrated Reckitts Paris Blue

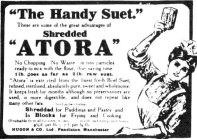

"The Handy Suet."
These are some of the great advantages of
Shredded
"ATORA"
No Chopping   No Waste   in tiny particles
ready to mix with the flour, thus saving time
1 lb. goes as far as 2 lb. raw suet.
"Atora" is extracted from the finest fresh Beef Suet,
refined, sterilised, absolutely pure, sweet and wholesome.
It keeps fresh for months although no preservatives are
used, is more digestible, and does not repeat like
many other fats.
Shredded for Puddings and Pastry and
In Blocks for Frying and Cooking
HUGON & CO. Ltd., Pendleton, Manchester

ALL EXPERIENCED HOUSEKEEPERS USE
KANDEE SAUCE
FOR SOUPS, FISH, CHOPS, STEAKS, &c.
THE BEST SAUCE FOR GENERAL USE.
DON'T TAKE SUBSTITUTES.
In Bottles, 2d. and 4½d. each.

DELICIOUS
MAZAWATTEE TEA
A LUXURY
WITHIN THE REACH OF ALL.
SOLD BY LEADING GROCERS EVERYWHERE.

Kandee sauce, launched at the beginning of the century and still produced by Goodalls.

A Donnelly's sausage poster, about 1910. *Photograph: Nenagh Heritage Centre.*

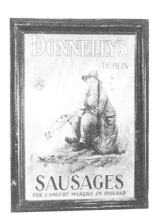

the newspaper: "There was a great display of fancy costumes, which excited favourable comments. The decorated ballroom presented a brilliant scene with the multi-coloured representations of well-known characters in the cinema world, period dresses and proprietary articles. The function was a splendid tribute to the organising genius of this young club in Irish commerce." Two years later, a second advertising industry association was founded, largely inspired by James O'Shaughnessy, the Irish-American Secretary of the American Association of Advertising Agencies, the Irish Association of Advertising Agencies, forerunner of the Institute of Advertising

Magazine advertisement for baby's feeding bottle, about 1910.

Photograph: Nenagh Heritage Centre.

Practitioners. Its first meeting was on June 28, 1928. Chairman of the organisation was William E. O'Keeffe, the advertising agent, and the inevitable Charlie McConnell was the honorary secretary. Other committee members included J. P. Kealy of the Swift Advertising service, Frank Douglas, W. H. Guilfoyle and Brian D. O'Kennedy. The entrance fee was ten guineas and the annual subscription was two guineas. By 1929, the association faced for the first time a member going into liquidation, Guilfoyle Advertising.

In London, two developments in the advertising business foreshadowed similar moves in Dublin by two decades and more. in 1923, the Women's Advertising Society was founded; its first president was Marion Jean Lyon, then advertisement manager of *Punch*. Women were working as account executives, space buyers, production managers, company secretaries and extensively in accounts departments. As Viscountess Rhondda said in 1924: "It is just about the one profession in which women have equal chances with men."

Research too was coming into vogue in London. Statistical studies based on population censuses were published; in 1924, J. Walter Thompson, London, compiled the *Population Handbook of Great Britain and Ireland*. At the same time, an English advertising manager, addressing a

---

ADVERTISEMENTS.

THESE ADVERTISERS are convinced that it pays to issue their advertisements through this Agency. May we have an opportunity of proving that it will pay you also?

Department of Agriculture.	Maxwell Lemon.
Royal Irish Constabulary.	George Mitchell, Ltd.
National Health Insur. Comrs.	Nugent's "Timberoid."
registrar-General for Ireland.	Doyle's Patents Agency.
Dublin Corporation.	P. O'Reilly, Ltd., Boxes.
South Dublin Union.	Bolands, Ltd.
North Dublin Union.	J. J. M'Quillan, Tools.
Rathdown Union.	Battersby, Auctions.
Portumna Union.	Crotty's Waterproofs, etc.
Rathmines U.D.C.	Flower & McDonald.
Pembroke U.D.C.	Women's N. Health Assoc.
Blackrock U.D.C.	Housing & T. P. Assoc.
South Dublin R.D.C.	Royal Inst. Public Health.
Rathdown No. 1 R.D.C.	Kingstown (Holiday Resort).
Rathdown No. 2 R.D.C.	Newcastle (Holiday Resort).
North Dublin R.D.C.	Bundoran (Holiday Resort).
Blessington Tramway.	Bray Amusements Com.
National University.	Industrial Devel. Assoc.
University College, Dublin.	Peamount Sanatorium.
University College, Cork.	Civics Institute.
Rathmines & Pem. Jt. Hosp. Bd.	Blind Flag Day.
City of Dublin Technical Schs.	Slainte Insurance Society.
City Woollen Mills	Century Insurance Co.
Francis Smyth's Umbrellas.	Cooper & Kenny.
Ganter Bros., Jewellers	Dublin Cowkeepers' Assoc.
Eustace Bros., Dry-cleaning.	De Selby Quarries.
Max Boot Polish.	Solicitors' Apprentices Soc.
Dublin Distillers' Co. Ltd.	Dublin Branch Red Cross.
Locke's Whiskey.	Merchant Drapers' Assoc.
Rya-nite Flooring	Blackrock College.
Adamson's Cattle Remedies.	Castleknock College.
"Mutesco" Hair Restorer.	Mungret College.
Pierce Cycles.	Rockwell College.
Elliott's Irish Poplin.	Belvedere College.
Comerford and Brady.	And many other Prominent
Coleman's Seeds.	Advertisers

Our service covers every detail of advertising. We have a specially trained, expert staff for writing, designing, and displaying advertisements, and advice based on years of experience is at the disposal of our clients.

No matter what class of advertising you are issuing, we can help you, at no additional cost whatever. Write to us **now**.

Client list published by Kenny's Advertising Agency about 1910.

Kenny's Advertising Agency,
65 MIDDLE ABBEY STREET, DUBLIN.

Telephone—Dublin, 1797.　　　　　*Telegrams—'Advertise, Dublin."*

2 oz of plug

Ireland's
Best
Value

CLARKE'S PERFECT PLUG

Clarke's tobacco advertising, Dublin, mid-1920s. In the early 1930s, the firm merged with Wills.

McConnell's prepared this advertisement for the new Gresham hotel, Dublin, in April, 1927.

Illustration from the *Principles of Practical Publicity,* **published in Philadelphia in 1906.**

THE NEW GRESHAM

Phœnix-like on the ashes of its old self rises the New Gresham, with old facilities expanded, and old services renewed and re-vitalised. Everything that was worthy in the old associations is here, wedded to all the improvements that experience has indicated as desirable in a modern Hotel.

The New Gresham will be the popular rendezvous for all who value the good things of life, and appreciate a refined interpretation of its social amenities.

No effort or expense has been spared to raise an edifice fit to grace its prominent position in one of Europe's finest thoroughfares.

Interior decorations and fittings in the New Gresham have been designed to combine beauty with the dignity befitting its importance.

The Front, in Portland Stone, is reminiscent of Dublin's best Architectural period—the late 18th century, with details modified to suit a modern Hotel building. There is a handsome metal valance, made by a leading French firm of metal workers, to shelter the entrance.

The building is a steel-framed structure, constructed on the most modern lines. All steel-work is cased in concrete, and carried on massive reinforced concrete foundations. The floors throughout are solid reinforced concrete. Partitions have been built of material notable

for its sound and fire-resisting qualities, which was specially imported from Denmark.

The Hotel is centrally-heated throughout by the latest invisible system, which eliminates all unsightly radiators and pipes, and gives a pleasant, radiant warmth, like that from diffused sunlight. A control from each bedroom permits the heat to be turned off or on at will.

The latest type pedestal wash basins with hot and cold water are in every bedroom. Instant hot water is assured by a circulating pump. In addition a number of bedrooms are provided with private bathrooms, which have been fitted with specially designed fittings in accordance with the latest American ideas.

A telephone is provided in every bedroom, enabling guests not only to ring up the various service departments of the Hotel for their requirements, but also to be connected direct to outside subscribers.

The lighting fittings are a feature of the new hotel; the majority have been specially made in Paris by one of the most famous French firms, who created a sensation with their exhibits at the recent Paris Exhibition.

A high speed Passenger Lift is installed, fitted with a special micro-drive self-levelling apparatus—the first of its kind to be used in Ireland. There is also a complete Vacuum-cleaning installation.

Open in wide welcome to the Nation and its Visitors

The Gresham Hotel Co., Ltd., Upper O'Connell Street, Dublin.

McC.

ARTISTIC USE OF FEMALE FIGURE TO ATTRACT ATTENTION TO A PRODUCT
By permission of The Ethridge Company, New York

53

conference on product marketing, told his audience: "Marketing should take into account investigation into the consumers' habits and tastes, and the kind of product needed, as well as the name, price, packaging, promotion and selling."

"Splits" were developing in the advertising business, another sign that the profession was coming along nicely. Brian D. O'Kennedy had started in the advertising business as a representative peddling round the city on an ancient bicycle selling space for the *St Anthony Annuals*. He had been inspired by an American magazine advertisement which claimed readers could learn advertising by post and earn the then enormous sum of $5 a month from the profession. He went on to Eason's, gravitating to Kenny's. Over a period of some ten years, he rose by degrees to become general manager. He was Kevin J. Kenny's right-hand-man, but since he was of a more go-ahead frame of mind than his boss, a "split" was inevitable.

O'Kennedy wanted to turn the agency into a full service agency, providing a complete copywriting and art service for clients. In later years, he often claimed that Kenny's was first to start becoming a service rather than a placing agency. His other ambition at Kenny's, to be appointed to the board, was frustrated, so he took the plunge and set up his own agency. Most of the capital was drawn from Thomas Brindley, who ran a long established printing works at Eustace Street in Dublin city centre. It is now part of the Dublin printing firm of Brindley Dollard. Brindley the printer put up virtually all the capital for setting up the new agency in 1927, provided half its trading name, but took no active part in running the place. Brian D.

At the end of the 19th century, butter and cheese in bulk was usually packed in wooden boxes, as with this Galtee cheese box.
Photograph: Nenagh Heritage Centre.

Irel coffee was launched in 1913; it is still going strong, made by Johnson Brothers, Dublin. It retailed at 1/- and 6d a bottle. One promotion during World War I gave two full bottles free in return for 12 empties, an offer "not to be despised in war time", was the copyline in one campaign. In 1921, Kenny's Advertising agency won the Irel account.

A new Irish industry has been established in this country for the manufacture of a high-class coffee essence.

Up-to-date plant has been installed by which the real coffee aroma is preserved.

This article is being placed upon the market in a business-like fashion, packed in handsomely labelled cartons, containing

½ doz. 1/- bottles,
1 „ 6d. „

A sample bottle will be sent gratis and post free to any grocer on receipt of a postcard to the Irel Company, Ship Street, Dublin.

"SPREADING OUR WINGS"
We'll meet you at Publicity House

Telegrams
ADCRAFT
DUBLIN

PUBLICITY HOUSE
10 GREAT BRUNSWICK ST.

IREL CO., LIMITED.,
Chancery Lane, DUBLIN.

February 1918.

CALLED TO THE COLOURS.

A dominating advertisement just now is to be seen on the windows of grocers' shops and also the trams of Dublin, Belfast, Cork, and Londonderry. This beautiful transparency is a riot of colour, advertising Irel Coffee.

The "Advertising World" (London) says in the past months "Irel" has been widely and strikingly advertised. It refers to this transparency as a cleverly conceived design, most arresting and unconventional.

By separate post we send you two in a tube (please withdraw carefully). If you do not want to put them up on the windows please post back to us.

Irel Coffee advertising card, 1918.
Illustration: Johnson Brothers.

O'Kennedy bought him out in 1937. O'Kennedy, the managing director, described as a persuasive talker and great ideas man, started with a staff of three on February 27, 1927, heralded by 12" x 4 column newspaper advertisements, in offices over the Rainbow Café in Lower O'Connell Street — the arch can still be seen, but the premises is now a Chinese restaurant. O'Kennedy-Brindley's first account was for Sandeman's port and sherry. O'KB was the first agency to use the brand new advertising medium of radio. When potential new clients came to the office, O'Kennedy moved staff from office to office and brought in friends to make the agency seem bigger than it really was. Before long, O'Kennedy recruited a friend and colleague from Kenny's, Frank Padbury, a most meticulous man who got angry over inaccuracies. 20 years later, Padbury broke away from O'Kennedy-Brindley to form his own agency. The year after Brian D. O'Kennedy landed into fierce political controversy. His agency's election advertisements for Cumann na nGaedheal were strong and hard-hitting against Fianna Fáil, ironical in view of the agency's later work for Fianna Fáil. O'Kennedy-Brindley was also the first Irish advertising agency to announce a foreign connection — in the late 1920s, it had an association with the English firm of W. S. Crawford for advertising outside Ireland.

In the North, too, progress was reported on the advertising front. Thomas G. Wells, an Englishman, had come over to Belfast to work as advertisement manager on the *Irish News*. In 1927, Wells left the newspaper and set up his own advertising agency, which survived until 1980.

When McConnell's moved from St Andrew's Street to Publicity House, 10 Great Brunswick Street (now Pearse Street) about 1918, artist Frank Lean devised this change of address postcard. Depicted in the 'plane are C. E. McConnell, Arthur Thornton, Leo Blennerhassett, George O'Callaghan and Peter Byrne.

Advertisement in the Nenagh Guardian, Saturday, October 28, 1916 — a predecessor of "Head and Shoulders" hair shampoo.

IMPORTANT TO MOTHERS. Every Mother who values the Health and Cleanliness of her Child should use **Harrison's** "RELIABLE" NURSERY POMADE. One application kills all Nits and Vermin, Beautifies and Strengthens the Hair. In Tins, 4½d and 9d. Postage 1d. GEO W. HARRISON, Chemist, Reading. Agent of Nenagh: J. HOLTON, 71, Castle Street, Nenagh.

Charlie McConnell pictured at his desk in Publicity House in Great Brunswick Street, Dublin (now Pearse Street) in 1923.

In 1926, Will Rogers, writer and wit of the American West, visited Ireland. He helped raise funds for the victims of the Drumcollogher cinema fire that year. He is pictured here outside the Shelbourne Hotel, Dublin, with Tony Reddin (left), manager of the Capitol theatre and Charlie McConnell (right). Rogers signed the photograph: "If we had a tenor we would sing." He was killed in a 'plane crash in Alaska in 1935.

Van Houten cocoa was a popular brand in Ireland in the first three decades of this century.

They Simply Love It

What "The Lancet" says about van Houten's Cocoa

The flavour is delicious, while the extreme fineness of the grinding prevents any trace of grittiness in the mouth. There is no evidence of the addition of either starch or finely comminuted cocoa shell. This cocoa is an excellent specimen of its class and maintains the high character we found it to possess when examined in our laboratories over twenty years ago.

A beautiful casket of delicious chocolates GIVEN AWAY Save your coupons.

Van Houten's COCOA
Best and goes farthest

Advertising Ball News

AN EXTRAORDINARY   MORNING NEWSPAPER

4 AM EDITION

No. 1 Vol. 1   Dublin, Saturday, January 31, 1925   SIXPENCE

Great Ball Scores Record Success

GAY THRONG IN THE METROPOLE

Story of Wonderful Night

Coca-Cola was among the first American soft drink brands to develop carry-home packs, in 1923. The illustration shows one of the initial Coca-Cola six pack carriers, dating from about 1925. Carry-home packs took a further 50 years to catch on in Ireland.

The great Publicity Ball held in the Metropole Ballroom, Dublin, at the end of January, 1925 was the first such advertising industry function organised in Ireland.

Drink
Coca-Cola
Delicious and Refreshing

A Coca-Cola poster used in America during the 1920s.

Tommy Wells, who founded Wells Advertising in Belfast in 1927, seen indulging a favourite hobby — car rallying. On this occasion in England, Tommy took a back seat.
Photo: Patrick Wells.

Alfie V. Browne, who had his own printing business in Belfast, approached a London agency called Travers Cleaver. Cleaver was one of the family that owned the now defunct department store of Robinson and Cleaver. The agency had the account and was looking for someone to service it in Belfast: Browne set up his agency in Arthur Street, Belfast, managing to survive the London agency's bankruptcy in 1930. Alfie Browne's "trademark" was a long cigarette holder. Unusually for an agency in those far-off times, Browne had a female director, who shared the running of the business, Hilda McBride.

While the Irish advertising agency scene was developing slowly, but with increasing confidence, a major change in policy startled the

Ford truck advertisement, The Irish Times, **September 17, 1923.**

O'Kennedy Brindley ran an extensive publicity campaign for the Cumann na nGaedheal party in the 1927 general election. A sample of its hard-hitting copy is shown right.

1927 advertisement.

As You Like It
DRY
MEDIUM OR
SWEET
Gaymer's Cyder
AGENTS: ROBERT SMYTH & SONS, LTD.
ST. STEPHEN'S GREEN, DUBLIN

ECONOMY—
By Torch and Petrol Can

IRELAND'S BILL FOR FIANNA FAIL

THE men who boasted during their Civil War of 1922-3 that "the Bill of Costs was mounting to the skies," and who since 1923 have contributed nothing to pay that bill but obstruction and the repetition of foolish pledges which they have now broken, have the effrontery to accuse the Government of extravagance.

They print a long list of Civil Service Salaries in an attempt to bring our National institutions into disrepute and to make their dupes believe that if they were allowed to smash the Treaty they would govern the country for nothing and with no Civil Service at all.

Here is the grim record of the economies **THEY** effected:—

DAMAGE TO PUBLIC PROPERTY

For the reconstruction of Buildings alone which were the property of the Nation, the people have paid in taxation for Fianna Fail · · · £2,000,000

For Bridges blown up and Roads destroyed, the people have paid in Local Rates a1one for Fianna Fail · · · £1,436,845

DAMAGE TO PRIVATE PROPERTY

1. Settled directly by the State:—

For Railways destroyed in the attack on the economic life of the country, the people have paid for Fianna Fail · · · £633,201

For Other Private Property, compensated for outside the Courts, the people have paid for Fianna Fail · · · £1,312,000

2. Claims for Compensation lodged with the Courts in each county.—

IN addition to the damage of which a portion is set out above, and on each side, there was an incalculable amount lost owing to looting, dislocation of transport and trade, depressed credit and so on. In May, 1922, it was estimated by the Bishop of

Ross, an authority on national economics, that Ireland was losing at the rate of A MILLION A WEEK. There is to be added on to all this loss the cost of the army which was required for putting down the Civil War and preventing further destruction. In five years, according to the calculation of the Department of Finance, Mr. De Valera and his friends cost the Nation the enormous sum of

Thirty-Five
Million Pounds

A sum which, invested at five per cent., would produce yearly, £1,750,000, enough to pay the salaries complained of by Fianna Fail twice over each year till the Day of Judgment.

Irishmen! in whose hands is the Country safe?

Distrust the Destroyers

Put your trust in the Builders

GIVE YOUR VOTE TO

Cumann na nGaedheal

Read the "Freeman"—the Organ of Cumann na nGaedheal. Every Friday. One Penny.

An early 200 pack for Carroll's Sweet Afton cigarettes, made in the late 1920s.
Photograph: Nenagh Heritage Centre.

advertising world in London. Guinness started to advertise. In 1926, Guinness sales in Britain started to level off, something that had never happened before. One of the solutions to the problem was advertising, never previously tried. After discussions with a number of agencies, including J. Walter Thompson, which later inherited the account, the Guinness board of directors decided to appoint S. H. Benson, a London agency founded in 1893 to handle the Bovril account. For that brand, they had devised the slogan "Prevents that sinking feeling." Dorothy L Sayers based her fictional agency, Pym's, in her novel *Murder Must Advertise* on Benson's. Copywriter Oswald Greene and junior copywriter Robert Bevan, who in 1944 became chairman and managing director of the agency, set out for Ireland to do some rudimentary market research on Guinness. Again and again, the pair were told by pub customers that they drank Guinness because it was good for them. Greene soon had his copyline: "Guinness is good for you." The first ever posters for Guinness appeared in a test campaign in Scotland in January, 1928. The first national campaign began in Britain in the spring of 1929. John Gilroy, who died in 1985, was the brilliant artist who joined the staff of S. H. Benson in 1925. His most famous Guinness poster showed a man carrying a girder, with the copyline "Guinness for strength." He did his very first Guinness poster in 1930 and carried on the tradition for the next 30 years. He also designed the Johnnie Walker logo. In 1986, when Guinness was staging its successful bid for the Distillers' Group, elements from Gilroy's designs for Guinness and Johnnie Walker were combined in the ad war that ensued.

In America in 1928, a big consumer brand changed advertising agencies: Maxwell House coffee went to J. Walter Thompson. The man who started the brand in 1882, a coffee salesman called Joel Cheek, named it after the Maxwell House hotel in Nashville, Tennessee, where he had test marketed it. When J. Walter Thompson

Wilson Hartnell receives its recognition from the Joint Advertising Committee in 1927.

A really complete Advertising Service

This organisation is equipped to render the most complete, most efficient, and most helpful advertising service in the country.

Each department is staffed by specialists, every one of whom has a long record of successful work in advertising and selling in Ireland. Here is a very brief outline of our method of working:

Investigation

To produce results an advertising campaign should be built on a basis of facts—not guesswork. Therefore the first step is an investigation covering the product to be advertised, the market, the prospective customer, the extent of competition, and the sales resistance which must be overcome.

Planning

With the results of our preliminary investigation before us, we prepare detailed plans for an advertising campaign, together with an estimate of its cost.

Production

Advertisements are originated, designed and written, and submitted for approval. Being based on full knowledge of every factor governing sales these are always attractive, forceful and convincing.

Execution

Advertisement spaces are secured at keenest rates, suitable positions booked, dates of appearances arranged, proofs passed, insertions checked, vouchers forwarded, and a detailed account submitted monthly.

Postal Advertising

A special section is devoted to the carrying out of postal advertising campaigns. The equipment includes addressing machines of the latest type, and selected lists of suitable names and addresses for many purposes.

Outdoor Advertising

This department is equipped to handle every type of outdoor publicity. It attends to the designing, printing, posting and checking of posters, and also undertakes the organisation of house-to-house distribution and sampling.

Printing for Business

We write, design, and produce every kind of printed matter for advertising purposes, from a simple letter to an elaborate catalogue, showcard, or poster. We have our own printing works—one of the best equipped in the country—which is staffed by specially trained craftsmen.

Special Campaigns

The resources of the organisation are such that we can undertake, at short notice, campaigns of the most unusual type, and always carry them through efficiently and successfully. This booklet describes one such campaign.

─[If your goods or service can be sold in Ireland, you can probably avail of our services. A preliminary consultation commits you to]─
nothing.   Write or telephone Dublin 3914 and make an appointment.

O'Kennedy-Brindley
LIMITED
ADVERTISING
53-54 LR. O'CONNELL ST.
DUBLIN
~

O'Kennedy Brindley ran this advertisement on its own behalf in 1928.

started preparing the first campaign for the brand, its creative personnel drew heavily on the atmosphere of the hotel, plenty of moonlight and magnolias.

Although Guinness advertising in Britain was immediately profitable — and controversial — the brewery in Dublin remained immune from the need to publicise its stout for another 30 years, when the first large scale campaign in Ireland in 1959 marked the firm's bicentenary. Here, packaging and advertising changes were far more gradual than the enormously bold step taken by Guinness in Britain. Carroll's decided to market Sweet Afton cigarettes in tens, selling at 6d. The pack design was basically the same as had been used for the Scottish launch nearly ten years previously, except that for the first time, a cream colour was used on the pack. It remains in use to this day. Two years later, in 1929, the 20s pack was slightly redesigned, given a cream coloured hinged lid box. In 1929, the packet of 20 Sweet Afton cost 1/4d.

The decade ended with an appropriate visit by James O'Shaughnessy, the former secretary of the American Association of Advertising Agencies. He was guest of honour at an Irish Association of Advertising Agencies' lunch in Jury's hotel, Dame Street.

The Irish Times.

SPECIAL EXTRA

DUBLIN, WEDNESDAY, SEPTEMBER 16, 1925.　　VOL. LXVII

Faith in the Future

Makers of

All kinds of Household Furniture, including Bedroom, Dining, and Drawing Room Suites, Chesterfield Suites, Cabinets, Sideboards, Bookcases, Chests of Drawers, Hallstands, Tables, Chairs, Wood Beds, Household and Kitchen Deal Furniture. Immense range of Bedding, including Mattresses, Bolsters, Pillows, Cushions, Mattress Cases, Wire Mattresses & Wire Meshes, Stretchers. Most things that go to Furnish the Home.

Factors of

Iron Beds and Cots, Huge Selection of Carpets, Rugs, Mats, Brush Mats, Linoleums, Linoleum Squares, Floorcloths, Blankets, Felt, Mattress Felts, Prams Go-Cars, Overmantels, Toilet Mirrors, Base Rocking Chairs, Deck Chairs, Bentwood Chairs and Armchairs, Pure Hair, Fibre, Wool, Flock, Kapoc, Feathers and Down, Upholsterers' Requisites and Coverings in great variety and at keen Prices.

These magnificent premises, commenced over two years ago when the outlook could not be described as encouraging, are now completed. Designed by Mr. C. J. Dunlop, M.R.I.A.I., and built by Messrs. J. & P. Good, Ltd., Dublin, the structure is entirely of reinforced concrete, and is a revelation of the artistry and finish which can be achieved in this up-to-date form of construction. The fine Offices, with their splendid fittings, the spacious showrooms, and the unique workshops are continually being admired by our customers. They

specially like the arrangement of the workshops and remark that such conditions enable our workers to give of their best—which they do.

This business has been built on the solid basis of Integrity, Quality Goods, Sound Value, Careful Attention to Customers' Requirements—and *in outlook keeping ahead of the times*. To-day we are the Leading Wholesale Firm in our Trade in Ireland, and owing to the superiority of our products the demand for our goods is ever expanding.

FURNITURE

TO meet the situation brought about by the Tariff imposed on Furniture we have greatly increased our staff of workers.

Bigger demand has resulted in our being able to offer customers greater variety without increasing prices.

Our main trade is the production of sound goods for those who have not a lot to spend. Our Bedroom Suites and Upholstered Suites are particularly good value and stand favourable comparison with imported articles.

The Furniture Trade is capable of giving big employment here to skilled men. Hitherto competition of imported goods produced on the mass production principle drove them out of the country. A new era of prosperity is before the trade. By buying our Furniture you get goods you will be proud to show to your friends, and besides you keep the money at home, which is, after all, a very practical form of patriotism, in view of the present excess of imports over exports in the Free State.

Senator Michael O'Dea,

Founder and Head of the Firm, who is SEEKING RE-ELECTION TO THE SENATE. PLEASE THINK OF HIM **To-morrow.**

Our Trade Mark appears on all our Mattresses. None genuine without it

BEDDING

IF people gave more attention to their bedding they would sleep better. The connection between health and sleep is greater than may appear, and for this reason we think the question of suitable bedding may well be termed a national one. We are equipped to supply the country with all the bedding it needs.

As pioneers in the Free State of modern health-bringing mattresses you are safe when you buy one with our well-known Trade Mark (shown on this page) attached to it.

Our bedding is not expensive—you can have a mattress made of Fibre (Four Qualities), Flock, Wool, Kapoc, Hair mixed with Fibre, Pure Hair, Hair mixed with Irish Fleece Wool, or a Luxurious Box Spring of a new type.

Are you satisfied with the Mattress you have at present? Does it give you that restful feeling you seek? If not, get one of ours and then, in the words of the Poet, "Sleep, that great consoler, will set your spirit free."

Wholesale Only

We sell only to the Trade, but our Goods can be obtained all over Ireland, and if you write us we will be pleased to send you the names and addresses of the Merchants in your District who stock our products. Traders who require catalogues and Price Lists are invited to write for them.

Enterprise

and Enthusiasm are what is wanted in Industry today. There is no other way of solving the problem of unemployment. The Merchants who have pluck enough to decide on a policy of expansion are those who will reap the reward in the not distant future when the country definitely strides on the road to progress.

Telephone :
Dublin 1071.
Private Branch Exchange.

Telegrams :
"Bedsteads, Dublin."

O'DEA & CO.

FURNITURE and BEDDING MANUFACTURERS, 41-45 STAFFORD ST., DUBLIN

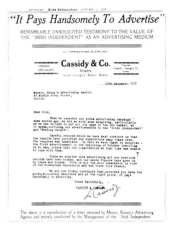

"It Pays Handsomely To Advertise"

REMARKABLE UNSOLICITED TESTIMONY TO THE VALUE OF THE "IRISH INDEPENDENT" AS AN ADVERTISING MEDIUM

Cassidy & Co.

Cassidy's, drapers, found that it paid to advertise in 1929.

Opposite page:
A busy shopping scene — Patrick Street, Cork, complete with Lipton's grocery store, in 1928.
Photograph: Cork Examiner.

Full page advertisement for O'Dea & Co., The Irish Times, **September 16, 1925.**

WELCOME BACK!

SHELL joins the Irish Public in extending a cead mile failte to the gallant airmen who, in the face of appalling odds, accomplished the first East to West Atlantic Flight. Shell is proud of the part it played in the great adventure proud that it was chosen when life and fame were at stake—proud that lubrication was perfectly satisfactory throughout the whole terrific test, and that the great engine of the Bremen was enabled to give of its best.

LUBRICATION BY SHELL

SHELL-MEX (IRELAND) LTD. GRAFTON STREET, DUBLIN DEPOT, VICTORIA ROAD, CORK

This advertisement first appeared in the Irish Times on July 4th, 1928. Irish Shell Limited

Early aviation advertisement for Irish Shell appeared in The Irish Times, **July 4, 1928.**

The Electricity Supply Board advertised the forthcoming power from Shannon in 1928.

Opposite page:

While the huge Shannon hydro-electric project was being built in the late 1920s, the Electricity Supply Board advertised conducted tours of the scheme.

An advertisement for the Shannon scheme under construction, published in 1928.

62

Afterwards, an IAAA delegation saw Mr O'Shaughnessy to the train at Kingsbridge station (now Heuston) for Cork; he was bound for Cove (*sic*), where he would embark on the liner, home to the USA. Later that year, the Wall Street crash sent reverberations round the world's economies.

For the 1929/30 session of the Rathmines Municipal Technical Institute, the principal, G. J. T. Clampett, introduced the first course in advertising held in Ireland. The aim of the course, said a press release, was to "increase the efficiency of the younger generation in advertising". The first two lecturers were Frank Padbury, then production manager at O'Kennedy-Brindley and Brendan Kehoe, a civil servant whose speciality was psychology. The syllabus used was that of the Advertising Association, London. Not long afterwards, the *Evening Herald* reported: "Previously, the advertising man's work consisted entirely of the preparation of advertising. Nowadays, he needs to be a specialist in marketing, with a wide knowledge of every factor that can possibly affect sales policy."The Rathmines course was immediately successful. In 1937, a brand new course was started, with the co-operation of the Irish Association of Advertising Agencies and the Dublin newspaper managers.

Energy!

90,000 HORSE POWER

Of energy will be available from the Shannon Electrical Power Station next year for Irish Industry and Irish homes.

The American workman is the most prosperous on earth, because he has, on an average, three horse-power, the equivalent of thirty human slaves, helping him to produce.

No wonder he can toil less and be paid more than the workman of other lands. He is not a toiler, he is a director of machinery.

Wages and prosperity are determined by output, and the use of electric driven machinery is the key to the maximum of production with the minimum of effort. It is the secret of successful industrial organisation.

The Shannon is being harnessed to enable the Irish industrialist and the Irish worker to use that key.

Shannon electricity will lift the heavy work of industry from human shoulders to the iron shoulders of machines.

The Great Southern Railways are issuing return tickets at single fares (available for 3 days) from all stations to Limerick. Conducted tours daily by I.O.C. buses. Permits for private parties issued on application to The Guide Bureau, Strand Barracks, Limerick.

THE ELECTRICITY SUPPLY BOARD

THIS MODEL OF THE SHANNON WORKS

You'll see at the Show in Ballsbridge.

Have you seen our show of Electrical Fittings and Appliances at 25, St. Stephen's Green?

The model is a perfect reproduction of a wonderful engineering feat.

Our collection of Fittings and Appliances— selected from the most up-to-date American, British, French and German models—has been assembled with the aim of selling you the most perfect means of making use of the wonders of the Shannon Power.

Our Showrooms are only two minutes' walk from Grafton Street—just beside the Shelbourne Hotel. The No. 10 or 11 tram will leave you at the door.

ELECTRICITY SALES SHOWROOMS

Electricity Supply Board

25 ST. STEPHEN'S GREEN ... DUBLIN

Visit the Shannon Works!

See this Mighty Project in the making

Arrangements have been made with the Great Southern Railway to issue Return Tickets at Single Fares from all stations on its system to Limerick on week-days, available for return within three days including day of issue, from now on until the 29th of September inclusive.

Conducted Tours daily from the I.O.C. premises
Sarsfield Street, Limerick :—
1st Tour leaves at 10.30 a.m., returning 1.30 p.m.
2nd ,, ,, 2.30 p.m., ,, 6.30 p.m.
BUS FARE 4/- (Children Half-price)
Guide's services free.

Those not wishing to avail of these Conducted Tours should apply direct for a permit, giving date of proposed visit.
Conducted Tours on SUNDAYS for large excursion parties ONLY—

Apply to The ELECTRICITY SUPPLY BOARD

GUIDE BUREAU, STRAND BARRACKS, LIMERICK

Citroën, in this advertisement in 1924 in The Irish Times, claimed that 250,000 of their cars were then in use.

Lisdoonvarna was good for the health in the late 1920s.

63

CHAPTER THREE

ADVERTISERS AND AGENCIES

Coming of Modern Times, 1930-1949

"I say, why don't we have a few G & T's and get to know each other better?"

— SHORT-LIVED RECRUIT TO McCONNELL'S, 1938

In the early 1930s, children could enter handwriting competitions run by Henry Bell Ltd., a Waterford animal health products firm.

108 PRIZES
FOR BOYS & GIRLS IN A SIMPLE
HANDWRITING COMPETITION

No Entry Fee
Every child
has a chance
of a prize.
Send your
entry NOW.

Every child attending a school in this district should enter for this simple competition. Cash prizes and genuine Swiss watches will be awarded in four classes, ranging from under 10 years of age to 16. Free Entry Forms have been sent to all schools—if your teacher has none you can get one on application to Henry Bell, Ltd., Waterford. There is no entry fee, but simply send one empty carton of Poultrine Fowl Powder and one empty carton of Porkatine Pig Powder. Get an entry form and enter now—don't wait until the closing date.

A S NEW YEAR DAWNED in 1930, prospects were bleak; Ireland, with the rest of the western world, was in financial turmoil after the Wall Street crash shook stock market confidence the previous October. Here in Ireland, as elsewhere, consumer spending plummeted and dole queues grew longer. Soon, one in every third breadwinner was out of work and at virtually every street corner in every Irish town and city, groups of dispirited men gathered to pass the time. In Belfast, these men wore the duncher caps so familiar in that city and later to become a hallmark of noted political artist and cartoonist, Rowel Friers. Dark days, but not all the tidings were gloomy. Advertisers had it cheap; a half page in the *Irish Radio News* cost £5. The Irish Free State's first Fianna Fáil government lay just two years in the future, while ahead of that again was the economic war with Britain. Yet as the country started to plunge to the economic depths, there were hopeful signs that indicated a growing maturity in advertising in Ireland. This very same year saw another major Irish advertising agency, Arks, start its slow take-off towards the creative "hot shop" image it enjoyed in the 1960s and early 1970s.

In Britain, where economic depression was equally endemic, big brand advertising used an increasing variety of advertising media. Between the mid-1920s and 1932, Britain had nearly a thousand extra cinemas and the development of cartoon techniques made cinema advertising there more acceptable to audiences. However, some cinema owners were hostile to the idea and in 1938, the Associated British Picture Corporation banned advertising films from its 500 cinemas. Commercial radio from French stations became a very important medium for southern Britain, when miscellaneous media included airships and the projection of advertising slogans onto clouds by powerful searchlights. New-style motor vans looked like the early 19th century advertising carts; the Mazawattee tea vans carried enormous models of teapots on their roofs. Special offers by popular daily newspapers ran riot with cut prices on books, holidays and insurance. Advertising in Britain was approached on a far more scientific basis, with more research and fewer outlandish copy claims. *John Bull* magazine even analysed all food advertised in its pages — for purity, while the *Radio Times* had a panel of doctors to examine its medical advertisements.

American advertising reflected the country's grave economic crisis which followed the 1929 Wall Street crash. Advertisements were dowdy, blatant and vulgar, according to an advertising specialist, James Rorty. Mass research techniques were used for the first time. At Young and Rubicam, extensive use was made of Gallup poll techniques; its sharp research, plus smart copy, ensured that its billings climbed from $6 million in 1927 to $22 million in 1937. Radio became a major medium in the USA in the 1930s; Young and Rubicam had its first big radio hit, with the *Jell-O* variety show compered by Jack Benny. When a certain coffee brand started its *Maxwell House Showboat* radio variety show, its sales went up by 85 per cent in a year. By the time of World War II, J. Walter Thompson was the biggest American agency, with total international billings of over $70 million. Young and Rubicam was next, with $43 million.

Here in Ireland, a certain humour and lightness relieved the general gloom. C. O. Stanley, the man behind the Pye radio company, set up Arks Publicity in London in the late 1920s. A young trainee was taken on, by the name of Alec Guinness. He was said to have incorrectly marked up for blockmaking artwork for an advertisement for the BBC's *Radio Times*. He was alleged to have used feet instead of inches and the blockmakers, seizing on the challenge to their technical skills, made up the block to measure six feet by four feet. It had to be delivered by lorry. The story caused much amusement in London advertising circles at the time. As the block came in, so was Guinness on his way out. Never cut out for advertising, he decided to follow, with enormous success, his true *métier*, the theatre.

In a way, it was hardly surprising that Alec Guinness found himself working in bemusing circumstances in Arks' office in Lincoln's Inn Field. The magazine *USSR Today* passed from hand to hand among the office inmates, an advertising *samizdat*. Also passing from grubby hand to grubby hand was an illicit copy of *Lady Chatterley's Lover*, in which the sexual passages were as well marked as any preparatory school Bible.

One of the earliest Irish Hospitals' Sweepstake advertisements, in 1931. It was a joint promotion between the Sweep and Carroll's cigarettes.

Sir Henry Lytton of the D'Oyly Carte opera company, London (right) seen on Scott's fruit farm in north Co Dublin in the early 1930s. Scott's was a client of McConnell's.

Arks, London, held a sports social and benevolent dinner in the Connaught Rooms, London, in October, 1930. The menu cover, reproduced here, shows Cecil Dick (right), now of CP & A Advertising, Dublin, complete with broken nose, suffered while he was playing in a rugby match between the London Times and the BBC. The tiny figure to the immediate left of Dick is C. O. Stanley, Arks' chairman, while on the ground, far left, is Philip Zec, famous cartoonist and later managing director of the old Sunday Pictorial newspaper.

ARKS
SPORTS
SOCIAL
AND
BENEVOLENT
DINNER

CONNAUGHT ROOMS
THIRD OCTOBER, 1930

CHAIRMAN: C. O. STANLEY, F.I.P.A.

As Guinness wondered later, in his autobiography, *Blessings in Disguise,* "how many of Arks' office typists retained the image of violets twined in pubic hair". Arks in London employed other people who went on to achieve fame, like William O'Connor, "Cassandra" of the *Daily Mirror,* noted for his World War II columns. Other inmates of Arks in London in those early days of the 1930s were Tim O'Neill, later to found Sun Advertising in Dublin and Cecil Dick, who worked with O'Neill for five years until he went off to found his own agency, City Publicity, in 1951.

The opening of Arks in Dublin was an altogether more sedate affair: no copies of *USSR Today* and *Lady Chatterley's Lover.* When the Dublin branch of the London agency opened its doors for the first time, in September, 1930, it was in a couple of small rooms in St Andrew Street, over what was then the Hibernian Bank, just yards from where Charlie McConnell had started in the advertising business 14 years previously.

Stanley sent over from London a beautiful young man called Clifford Knott to run the new Dublin agency, which opened with a staff of just three — Knott, Jean Keegan, who later became company secretary of Arks and a director, and an office boy. Mrs Keegan, who stayed with the agency until her retirement in 1971, recalls that Knott must have been the epitome of the original "golden boy", tall and slim, with fair hair and skin, elegantly dressed in Savile Row suits and wearing a modern style gold watch chain. As well as his good looks, he had a most charming personality, which allied to his English public school education, gave him an immediate and effortless entrée into Irish society, quite an achievement, given the anti-English hostility then. In London at this time, advertising was peppered with people with names like C. Maxwell Tregurtha, Amos Stote, Dillon Damen and Aesop Glim.

Mrs Keegan says that, to this day, she can never understand why C. O. Stanley sent over Knott, a very English type, to open Arks in Dublin in those turbulent times, but adds that perhaps he realised, innately, that his natural charm would overcome prejudice. Knott was brilliant, but his incandescence, even though ephemeral, did produce one long-lasting benefit to the agency. Knott was said to have been largely instrumental in persuading World War I veteran Jack Tate to leave McConnell's, where he had made a good name for himself in the space of a few years, for the more uncertain waters of Arks. Tate had originally started in the advertising business with Kenny's, just after the war. Tate came to Arks a year after it started. A letter from Arthur E. Snow, the publicity manager at Jacob's the biscuit makers in Bishop Street, addressed to Jack Tate and dated August 29, 1931, says: "I have heard that you have made the big decision and the purpose of this is to offer my sincere good wishes for the health, wealth and business prosperity which your good name in the advertising world entitles you to." Tate had made a previous gamble that didn't work out; in the 1920s, he left McConnell's for a period of nearly three years to partner Sean Lynch in Lynch Advertising. He then returned to McConnell's. The move to Arks was far more successful; he spent the rest of his career with the agency.

Arks' very first account was that of Mineral Water Distributors, makers of Thwaites soda water and Cantrell and Cochrane mineral waters. The firm was based then in Nassau Street in the centre of Dublin, where it drew water from its own artesian well. In those days, the mineral water business was fragmented between many small producers, with only a handful of larger firms, such as Mineral Water Distributors in Dublin and the Ross firm in Belfast. Advertising on a national scale was rare indeed; indeed, some mineral water firms were still using the 19th century style bottles with glass "marble" stoppers. The can and the plastic bottle, now so familiar, were unimagined as were the large scale advertising campaigns by multinational brands like Coca-Cola and Pepsi Cola. In the early 1930s, Coca-Cola was still confined to the USA, where its slogan for the Age of Depression was "The Pause that Refreshes". In Dublin, traditional attitudes to business in Mineral Water Distributors had changed little since the turn of the

Opposite page: Colonel Charles F. Russell, the aviator and a founding director of McConnell's Advertising agency, samples Carroll's "Sweet Afton" cigarettes in June, 1931.

Publicity Club advertisement, Irish Independent, **January 3, 1930.**

67

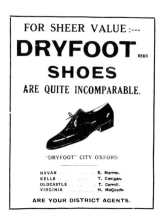

FOR SHEER VALUE:---
DRYFOOT REGD
SHOES
ARE QUITE INCOMPARABLE.

"DRYFOOT" CITY OXFORD

NAVAN	B. Marron.
KELLS	T. Cavigan.
OLDCASTLE	T. Carroll.
VIRGINIA	H. McQuade.

ARE YOUR DISTRICT AGENTS.

This shoe advertisement appeared in 1931 issues of the Meath Chronicle.

Insurance advertisement used in Northern Ireland weekly newspapers, 1935.

Opposite page: Columbia records advertising, 1930.

Advertising to a female target audience, 1938.

Who am I?

I cannot be a husband and father, but I can carry on the work of providing for the family if the breadwinner should die. He will feel happy in the assurance that I shall look after his wife and children. Oddly enough, although a servant I am paid only when I am waiting to begin work; when my work actually commences my wages cease. *Who am I?*

I AM

A PRUDENTIAL
"Heritage" POLICY

I provide for dependants, should death occur within 20 years,

£100 IN CASH, PAYABLE IMMEDIATELY,

£3 A WEEK FOR THE REMAINDER OF THE 20 YEARS,

£900 IN CASH WHEN THE INCOME CEASES.

If death occurs after 20 years, £1,000 is payable immediately.

I cost so little compared with the security I bring your family. Am I not worth considering?

To THE PRUDENTIAL ASSURANCE CO., LTD.
HOLBORN BARS · LONDON · E C1
(Incorporated in England)
Please supply me with particulars of your
"Heritage" Policy. *Age next birthday*_____

Name_____

Address_____

N.T.C.
23/3/35. _____

century, when James Joyce confessed an addiction to Thwaites' lithia water. Club Orange came later. Arks held the firm's account from 1930 for over 30 years. After mineral waters came the Dublin Gas Company, which gave the handling of its advertising to the new agency just a week after Arks opened for business. Meanwhile, as from November 1, 1932, Wilson Hartnell was appointed advertising contractors to the Royal Dublin Society, responsible for all catalogue advertising. Wilson Hartnell was also closely involved at this time in the erection of the famous RDS clock, built in the early 1930s, that still tells the time at the centre of the RDS grounds in Ballsbridge.

As the 1930s began, there were signs of modern marketing and advertising techniques arriving in Ireland. By the early decade, motoring had developed into a popular pastime; Ford cars made in Cork since 1919 were largely responsible for the rapidly growing popularity of motoring in Ireland. The very first big campaign for a petrol company was handled by Kenny's.

Pratt's petrol had been sold in Ireland since the first decade of the century. Its long-used advertising slogan, "Never say petrol, say Pratt's" became very familiar with two generations of Irish motorists. In the early 1930s, however, Pratt's was taken over by the Esso company, big even then. Kenny's handled the overnight change of brand name, from Pratt's to Esso, using mainly newspapers. The name change campaign, a "first" in Irish advertising, cost an estimated £10,000, an enormous advertising expenditure then.

In the mid-1930s, Lyons Tea was a big advertiser with a novel gimmick. Every summer, the firm sent horse drawn drays round the country. These featured hobby horses; children got tickets from their local Lyons' Tea agents and followed the progress of the hobby horses avidly. Gregory J. Dunne of the *Leitrim Observer*, Carrick-on-Shannon, was a small child at the time and remembers well the Lyons Tea dray coming up the Dublin road in the town.

For the cigarette firms, the main means of advertising was with playing cards. There was also extensive free distribution of cigarettes at functions. In the early 1930s, the playing card scheme at Wills became so big that a separate department had to be set up to handle the exchanges. C. K. Smith ran the twin stores and advertising departments at Wills; his deputy was Albert Price, later appointed to run the departments on Smith's retirement.

More new consumer brands came on the market: Punch and Co. of Cork had a major brand with its Science polishes, a forerunner of today's many household cleaners. That account went to Arks, as did the Sunbeam Wolsey account, the Jacob's chocolates account and Fruitfield Jams, for which the agency prepared full colour advertising. Arks' first artist, as visualisers were called then, was Ian Gray, who left after some years to become the advertising manager of Pims, the Quaker-owned department store in South Great George's Street. Pims, in common with the other big stores like Switzers, employed its

Authorised Agents for COLUMBIA GRAFONOLA and the New-Process COLUMBIA RECORDS
Full Range of Instruments & Records always in stock.

PIGOTT
AND CO., LTD.
11 SUFFOLK ST.
DUBLIN.

CLERYS
are authorised Agents for
Columbia Gramophones & Records
Newest Models & Records in Stock.
Come in and hear any Instrument or Record Played. Latest Lists Sent Free on Request
CLERY & CO. LTD. O'CONNELL ST. DUBLIN

A **Resolution !** to get those
NEW COLUMBIA RECORDS
from M°HUGH'S
39 TALBOT STREET

Best Bread
FOR
Women

Ultra-Violet Rays impart feminine fitness without fat. Sunshine Bread is saturated with ultra-violet rays by the Vioroid Process. That is why Sunshine Bread is the best bread for women. And besides increasing the health properties of Sunshine Bread the Vioroid Ultra-Violet Ray Irradiation Process makes the texture of Sunshine Bread smoother and less crumbly while keeping it beautifully light and spongy and gives a subtle richness to the flavour. Sunshine Bread is the same price as ordinary white bread

SUNSHINE
Bread   MADE LOCALLY UNDER LICENCE in our BAKERY

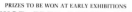

Swollen udders were
the subject of this
"Cataline" cow drench
advertisement in 1931
provincial newspapers.

Opposite page:
Hoover advertisement,
1930.

Motor car
advertisement run in
Northern Ireland
newspapers, 1936.

own advertising manager, who was responsible not only for booking space in the newspapers but for preparing copy and layout, too.

Media developments helped. On September 5, 1931, the *Irish Press* was launched as a new daily, closely associated with Eamon de Valera's Fianna Fáil party. The new title, eventually successful in advertising and circulation terms, caused enormous dissension within the ranks of the newspaper world, because of its political views. The Independent group took a particularly strong line against the new paper, refusing permission for it to use the same newspaper trains as itself. The arrival of the *Irish Press* also encouraged Independent Newspapers to mount a considerable outdoor poster advertising campaign extolling the virtues of its three papers.

Many big advertisers were British and pro-Unionist; they were willing to advertise in newspapers like the *Irish Independent* and *The Irish Times,* but not the *Irish Press.* Jack Dempsey had joined the new paper even before it started publication, to work in the advertisement department, having crossed over from Kenny's Advertising agency. Soon after the inception of the *Irish Press,* a young Erskine Childers joined the paper and for a time was its advertisement manager. He was a great "miracle" worker, putting his numerous business contacts to good use. An early example of his work on the *Irish Press* was the series of "open air" supplements, the first of which was published in April, 1933.

Shortly after the launch of the newspaper, a general election was held in 1932. As in the 1927 election, the Cumann na nGaedheal campaign was handled by O'Kennedy Brindley. The theme of the Duffy's circus poster was adopted to a campaign attacking "Dev's Circus". Copy for this campaign was written by that brilliant copywriter, Frank Padbury, a staunch supporter of Cosgrave's party. A whole series of these posters was produced for the 1932 election; in later years, the agency used miniatures for mailshots to potential new clients. By one of those strange coincidences, Jim Furlong, who later became a bastion of the *Irish Press* group advertisement department, was with O'KB in the early 1930s. The agency held the advertising rights for the Irish Omnibus Company and Jim Furlong was responsible for the bus side advertising. After one particularly good year, he is remembered as going to Brian D. O'Kennedy, looking for a suitable rise. He came out to tell two female colleagues, Maymay Dignam and Elizabeth Somers (later with Padburys and Sun, respectively), that he had won a rise. It turned out to be 2/6d a week and Furlong is said to have marched in to O'Kennedy and to have told him to keep it for the messenger's rise. While O'Kennedy Brindley was selling bus advertising, horse drawn cabs were still going strong. The fare within the city limits was just two shillings.

Mistakes caused changes of job; a particular example was that of the much-liked Tommy O'Sullivan, father of Niall O'Sullivan of the O'Connor, O'Sullivan Advertising agency. At this time, he worked in

Kenny's and handled the Findlater's grocery shop account, among others. A morning newspaper carried an advertisement in which the price of butter was incorrectly listed as "1/8d a lb". It should have been 2/8d, so naturally, large queues began to form outside all the Findlater shops. A correction went into the *Dublin Evening Mail,* whose first edition came out at 3 p.m. The correction read: "The price of butter at Findlater's was incorrectly listed in this morning's newspapers. It should have read 1/8d a lb."

Tommy O'Sullivan made a swift transition from Kenny's Advertising to the new *Irish Press.* The paper itself was not above the odd mistake: a death notice appeared in eleven consecutive issues. A man called Tom Connolly worked on the front counter; when the mistake was noticed, he was told to change his name so that his initials no longer read "T. C.", an invitation to run advertisements 'till countermanded.

In the year of the general election, another big media development suffered a spontaneous abortion: the *Evening Telegraph* was launched as the new Dublin evening paper by the *Irish Press.* A strike of delivery boys put it off the streets and the group had to wait another 22 years before successfully launching the *Evening Press.*

By chance, a man who had an immense influence on the development of many aspects of Irish advertising and display work, set foot in Ireland for the first time within days of the *Irish Press* being launched. Heine Petrie, founder of Modern Display Artists, arrived in Dublin in September, 1931, spending the months of that following winter renovating a small cottage in Glencree, Co. Wicklow, for An Oige, the newly founded Irish Youth Hostel Association. When his six months' visa came close to expiring, he was so keen to stay in Ireland that he enrolled at the Metropolitan School of Art, since there was no difficulty in getting a student visa. In May of the following year, 1932, Mrs Eileen Petrie, now his widow, arrived in Ireland to represent Canada at the international guide camp held at Powerscourt as part of the Eucharistic Congress. She met Heine at the art school in October, 1932. Some time in 1933, Heine worked for Gaelite Signs. There, Heine helped design and fabricate Ireland's early neon signs, such as the one on McDowell's the O'Connell Street jewellers, who claimed to have the country's first animated neon sign.

Eventually, there were meetings with Frank Brandt, the designer and head of the publicity office that the ESB set up in the early 1930s to produce all its own advertisements, including those for the first electrical appliances it had started selling. Brandt explained that while he could not take part in any outside business venture, he thought that his assistant, Sammy Suttle, could do so, provided that it did not conflict with his work in the ESB. A partnership was decided upon, with Heine as chief designer and artist and Sammy as an additional designer and contact man, since he was well connected in the Dublin advertising world.

"WAIT! TRY THE HOOVER FIRST!"

Don't be rushed into buying just any electric cleaner. You can buy a *Hoover* now for less than many ordinary suction machines! And, as you know, the Hoover is an electric beater, an electric sweeper and an electric suction machine—all in one!

This is important. It means that the Hoover cleans through and through—gets out even the embedded grit which is the cause of threadbare patches,

whereas ordinary vacuum cleaners clean only the surface.

With the Dusting Tools attached, the Hoover also does upholstery, curtains, skirtings, stair-carpets and all inaccessible corners. Think what a Hoover will save you this coming Spring cleaning.

FOR SMALLER HOMES There is now the Hoover Minor, an ordinary vacuum cleaner, priced at only £10.10.0 yet fully as efficient as the other vacuum cleaners relying on suction alone.

For further particulars of the Hoover models, write to Hoover Limited, Dept. Q. 1, Hanover Street, Regent Street, London, W.1.

A British Empire Product

HOOVER LIMITED, 1, Hanover Street, Regent Street, London, W.1.

The HOOVER

It BEATS ... as it Sweeps as it Cleans

By Appointment Manufacturers of Electric Suction Sweepers to His Majesty the King

Overleaf:
Gift offers, 1930.

Full page advertisement for Donnelly's, Irish Independent, **January 10, 1930.**

FREE GIFTS
FOR YOU

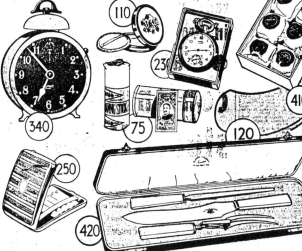

Be sure to read this list

Such simple rules

LIST NO.	GIFT	COUPONS	LIST NO.	GIFT	COUPONS	LIST NO.	GIFT	COUPONS
1	"Ensign" Camera (2¼ × 3¼ photo)	200	17	Ingersoll "Pilgrim" Alarm Clock	340	30	Military Brushes, in Leather Case, ebonised hollow back	200
2	Portable Gramophone, by Decca Co.	1500	18	Atkinson's "White Rose" Perfume	200	31	"Valet" Safety Razor, No. 99	80
3	"Embassy" Case of Cutlery (45 pieces), E.P.N.S. and stainless	2100	19	Atkinson's "Lily of the Valley" Perfume	160	32	"Valet" Safety Razor, No. 55 (Nickel Case)	200
4	Three Table Knives, stainless	100	20	Atkinson's "Violet" Perfume	160	33	"Valet" Razor Blades (5 blades)	70
5	Three Dessert Knives, stainless	80	21	Grossmith's "Lily" Perfume	280	34	Elvery "Swift" Tennis Racket	540
6	Three Table Forks, E.P.N.S.	110	22	Dubarry's "Posy" Powdrette	110	35	Tennis Racket Press	90
7	Three Dessert Forks, E.P.N.S.	90	23	Dubarry's "Wafer" Powdrette	70	36	Dunlop Tennis Balls (6 in a box)	310
8	Three Dessert Spoons, E.P.N.S.	90	24	6 Genuine Gillette Blades and Shaving Soap (Aluminium Holder)	75	37	Badminton Racquet	400
9	Three Tea Spoons, E.P.N.S.	50				38	Badminton Shuttlecocks (3)	100
10	Three Soup Spoons, E.P.N.S.	90	25	Ladies' Silk Hose, well known brand, standard shades. Please mention shade.		39	"Dunlop" Golf Balls (6 in a box)	410
11	Two Table Spoons, E.P.N.S.	40		Grade A	120	40	"Warwick" Golf Balls (6 in a box)	300
12	One Jam Spoon, E.P.N.S.	30		B	160	41	Football	360
13	Set of Carvers (3 pieces, stainless)	420		C	200	42	Football (Youth's)	170
14	Set of Fish Carvers	420	26	Ingersoll "Regina" Wrist Watch (Lady's)	750	43	Hurling Stick	210
15	Bread Knife (serrated edge, stainless)	120	27	Ingersoll "Roi" Wrist Watch (Gent's)	750	44	Hurling Stick (Youth's)	120
16	Genuine "Thermos" Flask (pint)	90	28	Ingersoll "Leader" Watch	230	45	Camogie Stick	120
			29	"Embassy" Gold Cigarette Case	230	46	Hurling Ball	70
						47	Hand Ball	90

1 Free Coupons will be found in every packet and tin of Sweet Afton Cigarettes.
2 All Sweet Afton Coupons, past, present and future are eligible.
3 A Free Voucher, equal to 5 Coupons, is given in this advertisement. Cut it out and use it.
4 Select Gifts from list — send requisite number of coupons, addressed: Afton Gifts, P. J. Carroll & Co., Ltd., Dundalk, enclosing sheet of paper, giving your name and address in capital letters and total number of coupons enclosed. On receipt the gift selected will be sent you at once delivery free.

These gifts are the standard products of well-known manufacturers.
They are given out of profits —NOT out of quality.
The fine standard of Sweet Afton Cigarettes remains unchanged.

Use this Voucher

SMOKE
Sweet Afton CIGARETTES

Manufactured by P. J. CARROLL & CO., LTD., DUNDALK,

BANKS SIZE 10 for 6. 20 for 11½

CUT OUT & SAVE THIS VOUCHER IT IS EQUAL TO **FIVE FREE COUPONS** **5**
ONLY ONE OF THESE VOUCHERS CAN BE USED FOR ANY ONE GIFT

For Announcements of Births, Deaths, Etc., see Page Two.

Irish Independent

CITY SPECIAL

VOL. 39. No. 9.　　　　DUBLIN, FRIDAY, JANUARY 10, 1930.　　　　PRICE, ONE PENNY.

THE IRISH PIG
THE WORST IN THE WORLD!

OUR KILLINGS 1928		OUR KILLINGS 1929		AFFECTED WITH DISEASE AND CONDEMNED in 12 Months ending Dec. 27th, 1929	
Before Inspection		*Inspection Period*			
Pigs	81,449	Pigs	56,107	Pig Carcases	58
Sows	2,793	Sows	2,761	Pig Heads	2,892
Lambs	16,795	Lambs	19,396	Sow Heads	323
	101,037		**78,264**	Livers -	2,599
				Lungs -	2,156
				Tripe -	3,239

The Killings in 1928 were 29·10% more than the 1929 Killings. Inspection was slowly strangling the business last year.

CAN THE IRISH FARMER PAY?

Donnelly's is the first and only factory in Ireland in which modern "scientific" inspection is enforced and Donnelly's necessarily carries the full loss until the passage of the new Bill—when all the Irish curers will be inspected, and the loss will be passed back on the pig producer.

INSPECTION IN DENMARK

Pigs are inspected and classified as follows:—

(1) Certified for Export.

(2) Slightly Affected Certified for Home Consumption

(3) Definitely Dangerous, Sterilized and Sold Cooked.

(4) Condemned.

INSPECTION IN UNITED STATES

A factory may be inspected under three alternative systems:—

(1) Federal Inspection for export.

(2) State Inspection for Home Consumption.
(This Inspection often of the most cursory description.)

(3) No Inspection at all.
(Local butchers' and farm killings.)

WHAT FOREIGN EXPERIENCE HAS THE NEW INSPECTION DEPARTMENT ACQUIRED—ON THE WORKING UNDER ENGLISH REGULATIONS?

ISSUED BY MESSRS. DONNELLY, LTD., BACON CURERS, CORK STREET, DUBLIN.

A rough of a poster for recruiting to the Army, allegedly drawn by Sean Keating RHA, in the 1930s.

In the 1930s, the Electricity Supply Board advertised the many uses to which electricity could be put in the home. All the advertisements were devised and executed by Frank Brandt and his publicity team at the ESB.

A MAID FOR EVERY ROOM!

A DREAM from the Arabian Nights—a dream for the holder of a Magic Ring.

A dream come true when Electricity is the servant in your home.

With perfect service in your home you would have leisure to live—time to think—energy to enjoy the good things that come your way.

Electricity will give you this perfect service if you are willing to have it.

Would you refuse a Wishing Ring if it were offered to you?

Why not give Electricity the chance to drive drudgery away from you—the chance to be a Maid for Every Room in your house?

DO IT NOW!

ELECTRICITY SUPPLY BOARD
Showrooms: 25 St. Stephen's Green, Dublin

Modern Display Artists was set up with the partial help of a £200 loan from its legal adviser, Ronnie Brown. The very first order was from a company called Irish Pharmaceuticals, run by a man called Sam McAuley. Among his brands were Dawn beauty products.

MDA's first ever order was for building 100 trial window displays for the firm. Even though MDA was two weeks late with the order, Irish Pharmaceuticals was so pleased with the outcome that it ordered a further 200. These displays were used for Bayrol products and those two orders were followed by stands for Dawn products. MDA was well under way. Some 15 years later, the famous Dawn beauty contests were lucrative business for Tim O'Neill's Sun Advertising. They also launched Maureen O'Hara on her Hollywood film career.

"Now Mikey, hould tight an' I'll let on to be that quick-startin' Shell!"

Early 1930s advertisement for the Irish Sweep.

Shell advertisement, Irish Independent, February 13, 1930.

Opposite page: Charlie McConnell (far right) beside the KLM 'plane that made the Galway-Dublin-Berlin flight in 1932 in anticipation of a regular service — which never materialised. Also in the photograph are Col. Charles F. Russell, a director of McConnell's (second right) and John Dulanty, High Commissioner, Irish Free State (second left). On the steps of the 'plane is Hugh St. G. Harper, then managing director, Irish Shell.

FOR ALL YOUR WASHING

Rinso

CREAMIER lather **EASIER** washdays
CLEANER clothes

Plainy a packet of
  Rinso,
Over a packet of
  Rinso,
Downy a packet of
  Rinso,
Dashy a packet of
  Rinso,
Right leg a packet of
  Rinso,
Left leg a packet of
  Rinso,
Belly a packet of
  Rinso,
Backy a packet of
  Rinso.
—Dublin street rhyme
used early this century
before the advent of
modern detergents.

A Kenny's
advertisement for its
newspaper
advertisement placing
services in the early
1930s.

Send your ads.
to KENNYS

No matter how small or how large
we will insert your ad. in any
papers you name, anywhere, anytime. And the price will be the
same as you would pay direct to
the newspapers.

KENNY'S ADVERTISING AGENCY
65 and 66 Middle Abbey Street, Dublin

One amusing episode involving Modern Display Artists took place not long after the firm was founded. It designed stands for Smyth's, the Balbriggan, Co. Dublin, hosiery firm, for an RDS Spring Show. Heine designed a freize of naked dancing nymphs for the back of the stand, but the RDS insisted they had to be clothed! Alan Whyte of Smyth's and Heine Petrie worked feverishly, stretching pieces of knitted silk underwear material over the figures. They were made to look twice as titillating, but the RDS passed them!

Locke's Distillery, for long a landmark at Kilbeggan, Co. Westmeath (it closed in 1953), provided another early job. Locke's (an employee of which claimed to have invented Irish coffee about 1920, some 25 years earlier than Shannon) marketed some of its whiskey in stone jars. MDA made a huge mock-up of one of these jars for display purposes. The art of exhibiting goods was starting to develop in Ireland.

Kenny's had a copywriter who later gained much political notoriety: Frank Ryan, the republican and socialist. He went on to fight on the Republican side in the Spanish civil war; eventually, he died on a German submarine during World War II and was buried at Dresden in Germany in 1944. While he was a copywriter with Kenny's, the Special Branch was said to have been assiduous in keeping him company.

Arks gained more recruits and more accounts. In 1934, Dick Young, the man who was to found R. Wilson Young nine years later, joined Arks. He had started as an analytical chemist, training in the old Royal College of Science in Dublin. In 1917, he became a radio officer in the Merchant Navy. One day in New York, undecided as to his next course of action, he tossed a coin, whether to stay in America or come home to Ireland. As he said himself later, Ireland lost. Young was described as a strange man, gifted with a great sense of humour and a dangerous capacity for fun of every kind. He was a cousin of Jack Tate, who had come into Arks to take over from the "golden wonder", Clifford Knott. Young teamed up with his cousin, although he later left to set up his own agency after a blazing row that took much healing. Young's scientific prowess stood him in good stead at Arks, where he devised an extensive piece of market research, carried out all over Ireland in 1938, one of the very first occasions that research for advertising was done here, although the practice was well established in London and America by this time. Other big accounts came into Arks: the Irish Hospitals' Sweepstakes, a major advertiser in the 1930s, with frequent newspaper spaces and constant sponsored radio programmes, changed from Lynch's. No doubt that decision had been helped by Jack Tate's arrival at Arks he took charge of the account. The Turf Development Board, forerunner of Bord na Mona, also came to Arks for its advertising. In 1935, the Educational Building Society was founded; Kenny's immediately won the account.

One of the great old timers passed away. In August, 1935, Henry Crawford Hartnell, who had founded the agency of Wilson Hartnell back in 1879, died at his home in Idrone Terrace, Blackrock, Co.

THIS PRETTY GIRL HAS A LOVELY COMPLEXION
(As you can see)

SHE USES ICILMA CREAMS

···· always keeps these two jars on her Dressing Table, (She's finished trying others)

AND *NOW* ···

In her handbag she always carries these 6ᵈ tubes

SPECIAL OFFER. *Prove to your own satisfaction that no other preparations can equal those made by Icilma. We will send a complete Beauty Treatment, including generous samples of Icilma Vanishing Cream, Icilma Cold Cream, Icilma Face Powder, four shades, Naturelle, Rosée, Crème and Prunette, and FULL SIZE Icilma Wet Shampoo and Icilma Hair Powder. Simply forward your name and address, with 6d. (in stamps) to ICILMA (Dept. 79A) 37/45 King's Rd., St. Pancras, London, N.W.1*

Icilma
VANISHING and COLD CREAMS
Vanishing Cream, 6d. tubes, 9d., 1/3, 2/- jars.
Cold Cream, 6d. tubes, 1/3 jars.

Made to prevent the growth of superfluous hair

Outstanding Superiority

Player's Please

PLAYER'S NAVY CUT

MADE IN DUBLIN

Player's advertising, 1930.

Beauty products' advertising, 1930.

YOURS FOR 10/-

Per Month, delivered on receipt of first payment.
GREAT RESERVE SALE OFFER

Solid Oak GATELEG TABLE

Packed free and carriage paid. Solid Oak throughout, beautifully figured grain, rich Jacobean finish Satisfaction fully guaranteed. Size, 4ft. x 3ft. 90/-, at, per month.

Other Sizes:
3' 6" x 2' 6",
83/-, at 10/- per Month; or 76/6 Cash. 4' 6" x 3' 6". 105/-, at 10/- per Month; or 93/6 Cash.

10/-

Or, Cash Price, 83/6.

BABY'S PRAM.

Roomy and comfortable. Latest design and finish. Storm-apron. Laced hood with corner shields. Safety belt. heavy ribbe. cushion tyres. Size 30" long, 17" wide, 18" deep. Packing free. Carriage paid. Cash price. 83/6; or 10/-, at per month

10/-

BARRON'S

COMPLETE HOUSE FURNISHERS,
1 North Earl St., Dublin
(Facing the Pillar).

**Household utilities
advertisement, 1930.**

Dublin. The running of the business was taken over by his son Noel, who finally emerged from the wings after 20 years as understudy. Noel, who remained a bachelor, also stayed on in the family house and continued his lifelong habit of travelling into town by train from Blackrock station. Joan Tighe, the *Evening Herald* columnist, worked for Noel Hartnell over 20 years later; she recalls him as a man very fixed in his ways. People set their watches by the time he arrived in town each morning. If new passengers intruded on the "club" on the train to town, he got very annoyed.

In 1934, William Nesbitt of Arnotts, the Dublin department store, decided almost on the spur of the moment to set up an advertising agency to handle the department store's advertising. The firm was spending one per cent of turnover on advertising a high level for pre-war. As 1934 turned into 1935, Janus came into being in three rooms in the Arnott's building in Henry Street: in addition to William Nesbitt, the other partners involved were a man from Belfast called T. H. Wallins, who produced showcards for the firm and Harry Jauncey, the printer who owned the Temple Press and who had been advising Nesbitt on advertising. The first major appointment to the agency, as manager, was an Englishman called Reg Wilks, recalled by Ronnie Nesbitt as being very thorough. He had started in advertising in London in 1927, with Curry's, the electrical retailers. Three years later, Wilks went to work in Nigeria, before coming to the Dublin job.

Besides running the new agency, Wilks also worked for Arnott's, where he made himself very unpopular by imposing new stock control systems on the buyers, then virtually independent. The new agency had much difficulty in gaining recognition, for the Dublin newspapers considered, wrongly, that Janus was merely a department of Arnott's. It may have been housed in Arnott's, but the store had no financial involvement in the new agency. Naturally, though, Arnott's was the new agency's first account, a progressive move for the time, since nearly all stores did their own advertising.

Hard on the heels of Wilks joining Janus came Ken Murphy, who had started his advertising career with Kennys in October, 1931. He joined Janus in 1936. He stayed for about six years, before joining Domas. He concluded his career with O'Kennedy Brindley. A young Denis Garvey joined Janus in 1938.

A recruit into Arnotts itself, in January 1937, was young Ronnie Nesbitt, son of William Nesbitt. Ronnie trained in Benson's agency in London and after returning to Dublin, maintained his keen interest in publicity. As Arnott's advertising manager, he was responsible for the frequent and well-illustrated catalogues for customers which Arnott's started before the war and which lasted until well into the 1950s, designed needless to remark by Janus. Ronnie Nesbitt, for many years Arnott's managing director (a post now held by his son Michael) is now chairman.

An interested new participant in the business was young Terry

Spillane, son of M. J. Spillane, once an *Irish Independent* journalist, later assistant editor of debates in Dail Eireann. Terry joined Arrow Advertising in Middle Abbey Street in 1935 (the agency had been founded four years previously by Harry O'Brien, a former employee of McConnell's), as the firm's only junior trainee. His salary was £1 a week. After a year, O'Brien sacked Terry because he could no longer afford to pay him. Terry's brother, Eimar, who spent the rest of his career in agencies, first McConnell's and then O'Keeffes, from which he retired in 1986, also started in Arrow. The agency, at 97 Middle Abbey Street, beside the Adelphi Cinema, had such accounts as McCairns Motors, Imco the dry cleaners and Todd Burns, the department store. Another account was Prescott's the opticians in O'Connell Street; its advertisements contained a visual produced by trick photography. The impression given to people was that they really did need glasses! Such advertising would not be allowed today. O'Brien was also said to have placed job advertisements in the Dublin press from time to time; these gave the impression that the agency was indeed expanding, but the job vacancies were often figments of his imagination. Similarly, another agency in town at this period had impressively labelled doors off its main reception area. A daring young newcomer to the advertising business had the temerity to open the door marked "Marketing Department", only to find the broom cupboard.

SHIPPING.

WHITE STAR

COBH & GALWAY to U.S.A. and CANADA.

Largest Steamers from Ireland.

COBH to BOSTON and NEW YORK
Cedric......Sun., Mar. 30 †Baltic ... Sun., Apl. 20
Arabic......Sun., Apl. 13 Cedric .... Sun., Apl. 27
†Omits Boston.

GALWAY to BOSTON and NEW YORK
Cedric......Sun., Mar. 30 Cedric ... Sun., May 25
Cedric......Sun., Apl. 27 Cedric ... Sun., June 22

GALWAY to QUEBEC and MONTREAL
*Megantic .... Tues., April 1
Megantic .... Mon., May 5
* To Halifax, N.S., only.

For further particulars, apply WHITE STAR LINE, 31/37 Victoria Street, Belfast, Liverpool, 1 and 2 Eden Quay, Dublin;
SCOTT and CO., Cobh (Queenstown);
Or, LOCAL AGENTS.

Shipping advertisement, 1930.

In 1937, Charlie McConnell challenged the London Publicity Club's golfing members to a match in Dublin. The London team arrived on an Aer Lingus flight; pictured here at Baldonnel, second from left, is W. Buchanan-Taylor, publicity director of J. Lyons. The team left their desks in London at 1.30 p.m. on the Saturday, enjoyed a banquet in Dublin that night, played the match on Sunday and were back at work by 12 noon on the Monday.

In 1933, the staff of Kenny's Advertising agency presented a silver salver and tray to Kevin J. Kenny (seated at desk) in commemoration of his silver wedding anniversary. Pictured from left to right are Ken Murphy (later with Janus, Domas and O'Kennedy Brindley), Leo Blennerhassett (later to become publicity manager, then London manager of Independent Newspapers), Ned O'Neill (later to become general manager of CIE's outdoor advertising department), Tommy O'Sullivan (who later joined the Irish Press. He was father of Niall O'Sullivan of O'Connor O'Sullivan Advertising agency), Colum E. Kenny (son of Kevin J. Kenny), Mrs Cecilia Wallace (on Kenny's staff from 1927 until 1977), Miss Conroy, Con Kenny (nephew of Kevin J. Kenny), Molly Miller and Miss Derham.

Early 1930s motor spirit advertisement.

This advertisement for Robertson, Ledlie, Ferguson & Co was published in the Munster Express, Waterford, in 1934.

Despite the "chancers", the advertising business was slowly becoming professional and disciplined. Terry Spillane was recorded as having passed the advertising and publicity examination of the Rathmines Technical Institute in 1937. It was sponsored by the Dublin Newspaper Managers' Association and the Irish Association of Advertising Agencies. Topics covered such matters as copywriting and advertisement construction, media and space buying, advertising routine, layout, illustration, printing and reproduction methods and marketing policy, the last-named a real innovation for the pre-war business.

McConnell's had become a limited liability company in 1932, with Charlie McConnell and Colonel Russell the aviator on the board. Many of the newly set-up Irish subsidiaries of British firms floated share issues; the advertising of these issues meant good business for McConnell's, which handled issues for such firms as Ranks, Irish Shell, Ever Ready, May Roberts, Dunlop and the Industrial Credit Company. In the years between 1933 and 1935, McConnell's claimed to have handled the advertising for industrial capital issues amounting to over £6,600,000. In January 1935, Charlie McConnell became a director and vice-chairman of the Ormond Printing Company, where he had served his apprenticeship years before. Simultaneously with Charlie's appointment, Waddingtons, the Leeds-based printers, bought into the Ormond.

Parliamentary legislation that came into force after the election of the Fianna Fáil government meant a great boom for the advertising business in Ireland. After the economic war started with Britain in 1933, many sources of cross-channel advertising dried up for the local media, still mainly newspapers. The Control of Manufacturers Act gave great incentives to British firms to set up subsidiary firms in the Irish Free State, so that they were manufacturing within the tariff barriers of the State. Chivers was the first British firm to take advantage of the Act and start manufacturing in Ireland, at Henrietta Street, Dublin. These new Irish operations, such as Bovril (meat extract) and Ever Ready (batteries), in serving the local market also had to organise their advertising locally, an excellent fillip for the eight or nine advertising agencies then active in Dublin.

1935 saw another milestone for McConnell's: the rebuilt Theatre Royal in Hawkins Street was opened on September 23. Charlie McConnell was not far away from the publicity. The new theatre was enormous, with 4,000 seats to fill. The souvenir programme prepared by McConnell's was considered by expert sources in the trade to have been one of the finest examples of printing, layout and design of the period. Almost just across the street from the Theatre Royal was a trade house that did so much business with McConnell's that it was considered practically a branch office: the Dublin Illustration Company, run by the McManus family and popularly referred to as the "DICO". At one stage, there was even a direct telephone link between the two firms. However, there was a drawback from Charlie McConnell's point of view, if not that of his dedicated staff. Going across to the DICO was a handy excuse for a quick "snifter" or even better, a prolonged lunch at the Red Bank in D'Olier Street, a restaurant popular with McConnell personnel.

In 1938, Charlie thought he would put an end to this carry-on by bringing in a tough, no-nonsense English advertising man to run the day-to-day business of the agency and reveal the true nature of all those visits to the DICO. On his first morning at McConnell's, the new appointee was being introduced by Charlie McConnell to all the staff. "I say," said the new arrival, in his best Belgravia tones, "why don't we all have a few G & Ts and get to know each other better. "He was on the boat back to Britain that same night.

In the 1930s, Kenny's Advertising agency (it always "signed" its work KAA), spent £10,000 on the first overnight brand name change ever carried out in Ireland, when Pratt's petrol became Esso.

PRATT'S
PERFECTION
Motor Spirit

Means fullest engine efficiency with every type of car. Because of its matchless purity there is no waste. PRATT'S is pure spirit to the last drop. That's why there is a constantly increasing call for this Brand.

THE "NEXT BEST" IS "TAXIBUS" SPIRIT.
Specially Packed for commercial vehicles, and for cars adjusted to take a somewhat heavier spirit than PRATT'S PERFECTION. Packed in aluminium cans.

ANGLO-AMERICAN OIL COMPANY, Ltd.

Wrigley's chewing gum advertisement, 1930s.

Lux soap advertisement, 1933.

Why do men like to dance with her?

NOT merely because she is a good dancer. She dances as if she *enjoys* it. She radiates vitality. Nothing seems to tire her.

Her simple rule is—Wrigley's after every meal. The great secret of feeling fresh is to keep the *mouth* fresh. And the pure, cool flavour of Wrigley's Chewing Gum refreshes the mouth as nothing else can. Removes all trace of eating, drinking and

smoking. And sweetens the breath.

Wrigley's also aids digestion. And cleanses the teeth. It is recommended by doctors and dentists—for reasons of health, of mouth hygiene and of efficiency.

In two flavours—P.K., a pure peppermint flavour—and Spearmint, a pure mint leaf flavour. Only 1d. a packet — but the finest quality money can buy.

WRIGLEY'S 1D PER PACKET

IF YOU WANT A COMPLEXION AS LOVELY AS THIS

USE HOLLYWOOD'S WAY OF GUARDING SKIN BEAUTY

As the close-up brings her near Loretta Young's smooth skin is irresistible—thrills you—fills you with envy. And it's true of all the lovely stars you see on the screen. Wouldn't you like to know how they keep their skin so marvellous—so youthfully clear and smooth?

They use Lux Toilet Soap—actually 705 of the leading 713 stars in Hollywood and England use this lovely white soap.

Millions of women everywhere use Lux Toilet Soap, for they have discovered how marvellous it is for keeping skin smooth. Surely you wish to give your skin the same care as the film stars — order Lux Toilet Soap tomorrow. Your grocer or dealer sells it.

4 REASONS WHY YOU SHOULD TRY THIS BEAUTY SOAP OF THE STARS
1 Quick, luxurious lather.
2 No harmful alkali—made from purest materials.
3 Delicious perfume — a pure white lovely tablet.
4 Wrapped — safe from handling and dust.

4d a tablet MADE IN IRELAND

LUX TOILET SOAP

a LEVER PRODUCT

Arnotts

Irish Goods of the finest quality, and at most moderate prices, are available in all our Departments. We cordially invite you to inspect our stocks.

Almost every requirement for personal or household use can be obtained of Irish Manufacture in style and finish unsurpassed.

♣

DRAPERS • OUTFITTERS • AND • HOUSE • FURNISHERS
HENRY STREET DUBLIN

Plain advertisement used by Arnotts in 1933, before the setting up of Janus Advertising.

Window
splay that
a study!

xtent that K & S Products have ...ed ahead within the past few months shown in the window display this week at J. SHEIL'S, 50 THOMAS ST.

K & S
PRODUCTS

This display is in itself a study of the wonderful range of Pure Food Products now being produced in our Irish Factory. They embrace K & S Jellies, Custard, Jams, Marmalade, Lemon Curd, Mince Meat, Egg Substitute, Candied Peel, Glace Cherries, Cornflour, Peas, Sausages, and Puddings.

See the exhibit of
J. SHEILS
50 THOMAS STREET, DUBLIN

MANSION POLISH AT JUNGLETOWN.

" I was just scrubbing the lino, Mrs. Fox, when this young rascal upset my pail of water."

" I wonder you scrub lino, Mrs. Bear. I always use Mansion Polish for it. It's such an easy way to keep it clean and bright, and makes it last so much longer!"

MANSION POLISH

GIVES A QUICK, BRILLIANT FINISH
TO FLOORS AND FURNITURE

In tins 6d., 10½d., and 1/9.

Also large household tin containing 2-lbs. net 3/-

MADE IN IRELAND. THE INCHICORE MANUFACTURING CO., LTD., 83 GT. SHIP ST., DUBLIN

Advertisement used in 1933 for K & S Pure Food Products.

Mansion Polish advertisement, early 1930s.

1936 saw Aer Lingus take to the air for the first time, with a flight from Dublin to Bristol. In view of Charlie McConnell's close aviation links, it was hardly surprising that the account for the brand new airline went to McConnell's. A small scale newspaper advertising campaign announced the launch.

In 1937, Charlie McConnell was able to celebrate two important events, the coming of age of both the agency and his son John. That little bit of bother down in Sackville Street, as it was in pre-independence days, even came into the picture, for McConnell's produced a lavishly illustrated, spiral bound book that told not only the story of Ireland's emancipation, beginning on Easter Monday, 1916, but also the development of the country's premier agency. The book contained many historic photographs of the 1916 to 1923 period, many more showing the progress of McConnell's and a number showing Charlie McConnell with personalities such as W. T. Cosgrave, first president of the Executive Council, who happened to be a good personal friend of the advertising man. The booklet, which later inspired a young lad called Brian Cronin to take up the career of advertising, gave rise to the often-told story about Charlie McConnell that he always took the extreme left-hand place in photographs, so that the caption read: "From left, Charles E. McConnell ... "This legend isn't entirely true; a number of photographs exist in which he is in the *middle* of groups. Another story began to circulate after the publication of this booklet, that Charlie McConnell had won the War of Independence, signed the treaty and quelled the civil war single-handedly, in brief moments of time snatched from running Ireland's top advertising agency.

Young John McConnell got the "works" as well, arriving on the scene with a "pop" of champagne. In 1937, he graduated from Trinity College, Dublin, with an honours degree. He also reached his majority and joined his father's firm. To mark these momentous occasions, Charlie threw a lavish coming of age party on May 21, 1937, in the Gresham Hotel, for 400 guests, members of the Dail, of the diplomatic corps, university professors and leaders of industry. Young John was promptly sent to London to learn the advertising business, working for a period with the London Press Exchange. The following year, 1938, McConnell's opened a London office, again with lavish celebrations. It was the firm's first branch office and the first time an Irish agency made such a move.

Arks was also on the move: in 1937, it left its cramped quarters in St Andrew Street for the elegant Clonmell House at 17 Harcourt Street. This fashionable townhouse had been built in the 18th century for the Earl of Clonmel. Around the turn of the century, Sir Hugh Lane, the art collector, who drowned on the *Lusitania* in 1915, lived in the house. Until 1932, it housed the Municipal Gallery of Modern Art. After World War II, Arks expanded by acquiring the two adjoining houses, as well as a couple of small houses just at the rear, in Montague Street.

McConnell's, in this house advertisement, advertise the fact that they were responsible for handling the advertising of industrial capital issues amounting to over £6,600,000.

McCONNELL'S
ADVERTISING
SERVICE
LIMITED

Ireland's Leading Advertising & Marketing Service

FINANCIAL ADVERTISING
NEW CAPITAL ISSUES

McConnell's were responsible for conducting the advertising of Industrial Capital issues amounting to over

£6,600,000

made in the Irish Free State since January 1st, 1933

PUBLICITY HOUSE, DUBLIN
Phones 43141 2, 3 and 43227

Every minute counts!

Many a busy housewife has been heard to say: "I never have a minute to spare."

This is not strictly true. She has many minutes during the day, but they come at odd times and they are wasted.

An Electric Kitchen will organise these minutes—and add to them many other minutes.

An Electric Range and an Electric Water-Heater offer the housewife a kitchen organisation that saves time, labour, space and money.

ELECTRIC COOKING DEMONSTRATIONS will be given daily in the following places next week:

LIMERICK Technical Schools, 3 p.m. and 7 p.m.

WATERFORD Town Hall, 3 p.m. and 7 p.m.

MALLOW Parochial Hall, 3 p.m.

A WHITE ENAMELLED WATER-HEATER with constant hot water. Really hot water at any hour of the day or night, at a negligible cost because of the specially low rate charged for water-heating.

A WHITE ENAMELLED RANGE easily cleaned, equipped with a perfect heat-control, designed to give not only the best cooking results but the utmost ease and speed in attaining them.

These economical luxuries are now within the reach of every woman who has Electricity in her home, and they may be had from us on Hire Purchase Terms.

ELECTRICITY
SALES SHOWROOMS
(Operated by the Electricity Supply Board)

25 ST. STEPHEN'S GREEN, DUBLIN

Call and talk to our Home Service Experts in the Demonstration Kitchen at 25 St Stephen's Green. They will give you every assistance and information and you can arrange to attend a free demonstration at our Grafton St Showrooms.

OH, WHERE IS THAT SUN

Fog, rain, cold. Brr! Oh, where's that sun? No wonder you shy at journeying abroad in this not-so-Californian winter. But, say, did you ever realise that the sun's still in business, all the time, even in those drear days when you think it's quenched for keeps? Right above those clouds the sun is blazing eternally, just a few minutes flying time up from Baldonnel — sunshine all the way, every day, to Bristol and Croydon. That's the way we fly you.

IRISH SEA AIRWAYS
39 UPPER O'CONNELL ST.
Phone: 72372-3
Our Night Booking Agent is L.S.E. Motor Co., Ltd.
Phone: 76511

Travel The Sunny Way Next Time

ESB advertisement for an electric range and water-heater, 1930s.

An early Aer Lingus advertisement.

In the mid-1930s, the imposition of tariff barriers forced many British companies to set up subsidiary manufacturing operations in the Irish Free State, providing a healthy increase in billings for Dublin advertising agencies. This photograph shows the first tyre to be made at Dunlop's new Cork factory in 1935 being taken from the mould. Dunlop closed its Cork factory four years ago.

Aerial view of General Textiles factory under construction at Athlone in 1935.

In the late 1930s, ice cream carts sold the product at outdoor venues. This photograph was taken at a Cork agricultural show in 1937.
Photograph: Cork Examiner.

ESB advertisement for electric fires, 1930s.

CARRY THE COMFORT WITH YOU

when you leave one room for another. Take the Electric Fire upstairs, downstairs, anywhere. Plug it into a convenience outlet—and there, on the instant, is its genial warmth. No delay—not even for a match. No cleaning up afterwards.

Up-to-date Fires at pre-tariff prices may be seen at our Showrooms.

ELECTRICITY
SALES SHOWROOMS
(Operated by the Electricity Supply Board)
25 ST. STEPHEN'S GREEN, DUBLIN and Branches

Arks occupied this very elegant Harcourt Street location, where the main hall was tiled in marble, for nearly 50 years, until it moved to the more functional but less architecturally interesting development at the other end of Harcourt Street, the Harcourt Centre.

War was fast approaching, although everyone in the advertising business kept hoping that all the scares of war in 1938 were unreal, that somehow the nasty German business would go away. This year, a young man by the name of Denis Garvey joined Janus, by now moved to Middle Abbey Street, by then the Madison Avenue of Irish advertising, from Arnott's building. Garvey had been working on a newspaper called *East Coast* owned by that remarkable newspaper and trade publisher, John Flynn, who apart from being blind and mean, had a perfect ability to make up a page layout in his head. The young Garvey had been a reporter with the newspaper, covering numerous events along the coast, from Booterstown southwards. A fellow reporter on the paper was J. J. McCann, who went on to found the *Radio Review* immediately after the war and later still became joint managing director of *The Irish Times*. With the advent of war, the English personnel at Janus, including Reg Wilks, went away for war service. Denis Garvey, who had joined the agency as general dogsbody but with the fortunate ability of being able to type, suddenly found that he was the right person in the right place at the right time and began his long years of running one of Dublin's top agencies. In 1942, he became general manager and in 1946, managing director.

Brilliant exhibitions were held in Dublin just before the war, such as the great radio show, held in the Mansion House in 1938. That same year, Fords, the motor manufacturers, staged the first ever major Irish motor show, also at the Mansion House. But the storm clouds were gathering.

The Spring Show of 1939 was a financial catastrophe for the RDS and in June of that year, the minutes of Modern Display Artists record that because of the show's poor results, the entire MDA staff, with the exception of the van driver, agreed to a 15 per cent cut in salaries. After the declaration of World War II in September, 1939, much worse was to come. At the ESB, where Frank Brandt had recruited very talented commercial designers and artists, Norman Penney, Anne O'Donovan and Patricia Lynes, the advertising campaigns in national and provincial newspapers to boost the consumption of electricity and the sale of the domestic appliances, were now put into reverse. Consumers were soon being urged to use less electricity. For the duration of the war, the RDS shows were cancelled and newsprint supplies went on ration, with newspapers being cut back, first to eight, then four pages an issue. Modern Display Artists found itself using the oval shaped wooden offcuts from toilet seat manufacturers to make air raid warning rattles, with the curved sections being used to provide "rockers" for small toys. The *Northern Whig* in Belfast carried advertisements from the Registrar-General, Northern Ireland, stating that "Persons over 14 should always carry their identity cards." That same year, Janus placed an advertisement for Arnott's in *The Irish Times:* "Figured crepe suede slip and pantie set, 12/11d. Postage 6d extra."

Yet, as often happens in times of great adversity, people's ability to "make do and mend" in the most creative way, comes to the fore. The dark days of the Emergency, as World War II was called in the Irish Free State, encouraged people in the advertising business to create much of worth from very slight resources, such as the Advertising Press Club. Melville Miller, better known as "Sandy", who had been working with McConnell's before the war, went off to fight with the Royal Artillery, returning unscathed after the war to work in Aer Lingus. Denis Guiney, closely involved with McEvoy's Advertising, bought Clery's in 1940. He held one of Dublin's biggest ever sales, much advertised, which realised £54,000 in its first week.

Perhaps the best-known advertising campaigns ever mounted in Ireland, that for O'Dearest mattresses, began in 1941 and ran without a break until 1967. Peter McCarthy, the man who owned the mattress firm, was very go-ahead on the question of advertising and when Arks came up with the idea for a campaign using cartoons and topical limericks, he gave an immediate start. Frank Durley was the man who started the campaign in 1941, using advertisements in the Saturday editions of *The Irish Times.* The drawing in the very first advertisement showed a seaside hotel; the word "bed" in the "bed and breakfast" sign was crossed out and replaced with "O'Dearest". The limerick read:

> Business was bad until Cassidy,
> The new manager, showed his sagacity,
> Crossed out the word "bed",
> Put "O'Dearest" instead.
> Now the hotel is filled to capacity.

For the next 26 years, the 8" double column advertisements in *The Irish Times* on Saturdays and later in the *Irish Independent* as well helped mark off the weekend for countless readers.

In the midst of war, what was to become one of Dublin's best-known agencies, Domas, was set up in 1942. Dick and Kevin Duggan, two of the three sons of R. J. Duggan, who had played a major part in setting up the Irish Hospitals' Sweepstake twelve years previously, together with Joe Delaney, were in at the start of the agency. Joe Delaney, the man who ran Domas for many years, was born and reared in Cork city and never forgot his childhood roots. He also had a particular addiction to drink and at one stage was rumoured to have kept a half barrel of beer on his desk in Domas. Delaney had qualified as an architect, but never practised; before the war, he had worked for an agency in town called Artwey, in which one of the partners was Tommy Thomas, later advertisement manager on *Radio Review, Sunday Review* and *The Irish Times.*

Delaney's move from Artwey, into Domas was propitious, for while Thomas was away during the war fighting with the Crown forces, his

Charlie McConnell (left) playing golf with Hector Legge, editor, Sunday Independent, **at Bundoran, June 3, 1939.**

In 1940, this air raid shelter at the top of O'Connell Street, Dublin, was painted with advertisements for the wartime Red Cross sweepstakes organised by the Hospitals Trust. *Photograph: Hospitals Trust, Dublin.*

announce
a Specially Designed

HEAVY WEAR
wooden-soled EMERGENCY BOOT

The Emergency has affected leather but after considerable research and experiment Hallidays have pleasure in presenting their newest line in Men's Heavy Duty Footwear. Properly cared for, they will give reasonable service and are available at a price within everyones reach. They will endure rough work on the land and provide dry and comfortable support for the feet. You have Hallidays assurance that these boots will provide suitable foot protection for outdoor workers and you can buy them with confidence.

The leather thread or other protection on the sole and heel should be replaced when worn. Above all remember the wood will burn — **Don't roast the boots in front of the fire.**

Dundalk has a long shoe making tradition. One firm, Hallidays, advertised these special Emergency Boots during the period of World War II.

Below and overleaf: Letterheadings used by local firms in the 1930s. Full colour printing was often used on these letterheadings, as a form of advertising.

Illustration: Nenagh Heritage Centre.

partner Andy Knox Galwey, formerly of McConnell's and *The Irish Times* advertisement department, drank not only the profits but the turnover. The agency collapsed in a heap of debts, the worst agency collapse to date. Hereafter, it was referred to as "Arseways". To cover the liabilities and retain the good name of the advertising business, the other agencies combined to offer their skills to the tune of £3,000 each in continuing to produce advertising for Artwey's clients until such time as the debt was cleared. In Domas, Delaney quickly became respected; he was also well-known for his rugby refereeing and also for his interminable car trips down the country to see clients, journeys that became notorious for the number of pubs visited. Delaney also set part of his house in Templeogue to the even more famous advertising "character", G. J. C. Tynan O'Mahony, otherwise known as "Pussy", who had joined *The Irish Times* as art editor in 1928 and who was appointed general manager of the newspaper in 1943, after the death of J. J. Simington. Very soon after the start of Domas, Ken Murphy joined from Janus as general manager.

Bill Bergin came out of his time as a printing apprentice in 1942, having served the then customary seven years. Printers were kings of the industry then, but with 500 of them out of work, the 20 year old Bergin decided to go into advertising. Janus, with such accounts as Arnotts, Twilfit corsets and Rolex watches, was considered the best agency. The young printer applied to a box number advertisement: it turned out to be Janus. He stayed 12 years.

High jinks took place on the Great Northern Railways' outings to Bundoran, where newspaper men and advertising people let their hair down. Terry Spillane remembers one Bundoran incident with clarity. It was in 1942 and an American bomber was running out of fuel on its approach to an airfield in Northern Ireland, just a few miles away. The 'plane circled the bay before making an emergency landing on the beach. Terry Spillane and Victor Penney, a self-employed commercial artist who was on a retainer from Hely's and who freelanced for a number of agencies, were the first to reach the 'plane and greet the crew.

1942 also saw the start of the Advertising Press Club. The Publicity Club had been going for nearly 20 years; the new "rival" was given a friendly reception. Many of the leading young men of the Dublin advertising business were involved in its inception, particularly Denis Garvey and Pat Conlon.

Its first chairman was David Fogarty, a printing ink representative, while on its first council were Desmond O'Kennedy (O'Kennedy Brindley, still over the Rainbow Café in O'Connell Street), Denis Garvey (Janus), Ken Murphy (Domas), Terry Spillane (*The Irish Times*), Frank Padbury (also O'Kennedy Brindley) and Pat Conlon (advertisement manager of *Model Housekeeping* magazine, who died tragically young in 1946 and after whom the Conlon Gold Medal is named). The new club went well; by the December of that year, it was

INTERVAL IN THE IRONING

In this series we may seem to have represented advertising agents as master minds. Actually, advertising people do not include any known supermen. They have wives and families and income tax and twinges of rheumatism and other troubles, just like the rest of you.

So when they are deciding how advertisements should read and look and so on, they are not thinking, in terms of remote beings, like the planetary people of the comic-strips. Although perhaps addressing hundreds of thousands simultaneously, through the Press, the experienced advertising agent adopts the orator's idea of settling on one likeable person and really talking to him. Or it may be her — and about four-fifths of consumer goods purchases are made by women.

Who's our lady friend in the picture?

Oh, she's just a neighbour, having her elevenses (note the labour-saving device of not having a saucer, when you're alone) and a glance at the paper. You'll be glad to note, after all we've gone through in this series, showing the toil that goes into good advertising, that Mrs. M. has paused a moment at the page on which that "Déanta" advertisement appears.

Her married son noticed the "Déanta" advertisement in a different paper, going in on the bus. Her husband's eye was caught by the "Déanta" poster on the hoarding near his office. Her daughter-in-law stopped to look at the window-display at her grocer's. Frankly, if someone doesn't buy "Déanta" sometime, we shall be surprised. Shall we be surprised?

FOR THE ANSWER

Watch for No. 6 of this series issued by the Association of Irish Advertising Agencies in the interests of Better Advertising and of the practitioners who comprise their membership.

List of Members on application to the Secretary
IRISH ASSOCIATION OF ADVERTISING AGENCIES, 36 Dawson Street, Dublin

In the late 1940s, McConnell's prepared a campaign extolling the benefits and virtues of advertising for the Irish Association of Advertising Agencies. These examples are taken from the campaign.

COMPOSITOR AT WORK ....

The client who is manufacturing "Déanta" was delighted with the picture and text for the advertisement, as submitted by his agent — and after consultation with some members of his staff, passed them unaltered. (We need not tell advertising men that we have created an utterly imaginary client.)

Away went the "artwork" then to the engravers, to be reproduced as a printing block by many intricate processes, involving photography by mercury lamps, sensitised plates, acid baths. The agent had dictated the exact process, the metal, the relative texture of the engraving.

And away went the copywriter's words to the printer, to be typeset in styles, sizes, widths and spacings precisely specified.

Technical knowledge and professional experience in the advertising agency ensured that mechanical processes were used to maximum advantage at minimum cost in advertising "Déanta". Who's the chap pictured in the overall?

He's the compositor who is assembling machine-set lines of text type, handset headings and rules, and the printing block, to conform with the agency layout-plan. A proof printing will be sent to the agency. If all seems well (but printers say agency people are per-nickity), then the "Déanta" advertisement in this metal shape will go to the stereotypers. They in turn will produce facsimiles, in the form of matrices or stereotypes. From the agency offices, the matrices or stereotypes will issue forth, accompanied by orders specifying where and when the advertisement is to be published.

Soon, the public will learn for the first time about that excellent product, "Déanta". But what then? Aha!

Watch for No. 5 of this series issued by the Irish Association of Advertising Agencies, in the interests of Better Advertising and of the reputable practitioners who comprise their membership.

List of Members on application to the Secretary
IRISH ASSOCIATION OF ADVERTISING AGENCIES, 36 Dawson Street, Dublin

HUNTING THE DÉANTA PHRASE:

A committee never wrote a good letter. This is a one-man job and the rule applies also to advertising. Writing the message about that fine product "Déanta" is entrusted by the Advertising Agent to one man in his organisation—a trained "copywriter".

Before he writes a word, the copywriter is briefed on the campaign — its reasons and objectives. He is supplied with technical data, research statistics, market analysis, policy notes and rough suggestions. He can have more and often does, for the asking. The basis of good advertising is sound and sufficient information. Only when this has been obtained, does a properly organised Agency look to the copy writer for the words which will go into the advertisement.

What's the fellow in the picture doing?

He's seeking ways to cut his "copy" without losing any of its effectiveness. This is one of the arts of copywriting ... writing a selling message to "fit" a selected size of newspaper space. When finished, the copy will undergo the ordeal of criticism from a "committee" of the agency's executives, to be followed, perhaps, by more rewriting. Only then, does the "Déanta" copy go to the studio to be illustrated. A cameraman has already taken photographs. The Director in charge of the creative department has the responsibility of seeing that the artwork and the copy are welded together into a true advertising weapon — accurate, economical and distinctive.

But what will be the client's reaction?

FOR THE ANSWER

Watch for No. 4 of this new series of advertisements issued by the Irish Association of Advertising Agencies in the interests of Better Advertising and of the reputable practitioners who comprise the Association's membership.

List of Member on application to the Secretary.
IRISH ASSOCIATION OF ADVERTISING AGENCIES, 36 Dawson Street, Dublin.

Genuine Saffron BUNS.

OWING TO THE PREVALENCE OF MEASLES IN THE TOWN

PETER LYONS

BEGS TO INFORM HIS CUSTOMERS THAT HE IS MAKING FRESH DAILY

GENUINE SAFFRON BUNS

RECOMMENDED BY MEDICAL MEN AS THE MOST EFFICACIOUS AND NOURISHING FOOD DURING THIS ILLNESS.

ON SALE AT HIS SHOP—

112 West St., Drogheda

Or delivered by Vans if required.

In the 1930s, health "scares" provided copy platforms for much consumer advertising. An outbreak of measles in Drogheda in 1935 prompted this advertisement for Peter Lyons' bakery in the town.

holding its third presentation, the story of the *Times Pictorial* (not long launched, the transformation of the *Weekly Irish Times* in 1941) told by editor George Burrows and art editor, E. F. MacSweeney. The comparative lack of advertising activity during the war years meant that people in the business had plenty of time for the new Advertising Press Club and trips to Bundoran. One advertising man who worked in Dublin during the war years remembers that mornings were often filled by coffee in Bewleys (even if it was the ersatz variety), while afternoon boredom could be relieved by a drink in the old Jury's in Dame Street. Still, the Dublin advertising men were fortunate. In the great Belfast blitz of April, 1941, which did so much damage to the *Belfast Telegraph* offices, also wrecked the office and studio of A. V. Browne Advertising in Royal Avenue, one of only two advertising agencies in Belfast then.

In 1943, co-operation was in the air. The committee of the Publicity Club recommended that a dinner and informal concert should be organised for the combined membership of that club and of the newly-formed Advertising Press Club. "Members who have been to Bundoran will know what a good time usually results when admen get together, and others will have heard secondhand reports. "In making the recommendation, it was stated: "The cost per man (no mention of the women!) will be moderate, depending on individual thirsts". After all, that was the year that brick-built houses at Ailesbury Park, Dublin, were being advertised for £1,800 and the *Mayo News* of Westport advertised everything to build a new house with four large rooms and hall for £125. An £80 grant was available. Seven O Clock slotted razor blades were on sale, 9d for five. There were even a brand of blades from Argentina, Okey, made in Buenos Aires, for which the Irish advertising was handled by Janus.

The war years threw up many strange brands. With tea rationed to half an ounce per person per week, raw carrots were grated, then

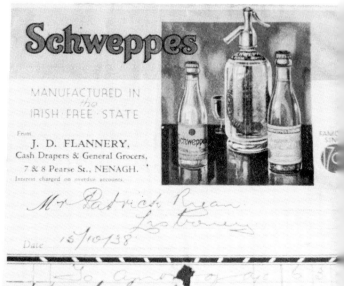

roasted, as a substitute. Cured mutton was passed off as bacon, while the only soap powders were Rinso, Persil and Lux. One of the few brands of soap on the wartime market was Dirt Shifter.

Despite the Emergency, the Advertising Press Club got off to a flying start, with its programme showing a zest and enthusiasm rarely repeated in later years. After the lecture given in the Central Hotel, Exchequer Street, by George Burrows and Eddie MacSweeney, the second session of the club began on September 20, again in the Central Hotel. For the winter of 1943, an impressive list of speakers was lined up. First of all, Daniel S. Terrell, who before the war had been advertising director for Metro-Goldwyn-Mayer eastern division theatres in Washington and also film and theatre critic of the *Washington Herald*, who was press attaché at the American Legation in Dublin during the war, gave a talk on "Advertising with Nothing to Sell". He was followed, the month after, by G. J. C. Tynan O'Mahony of *The Irish Times*, on "A Journey through the Press: My Life and Times." There must have been a hefty volume to narrate! Then club members were invited to the dress rehearsal of the revue, *Hello Wonderful* at the Capitol

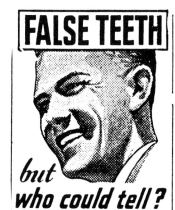

You can laugh, talk and enjoy your meals free from embarrassment if you sprinkle your plate in the morning with Dr. Wernet's Powder. It forms a soft antacid cushion which holds your plate firm and secure, gives "all day" confidence and prevents sore gums and all discomforts.

Advertisement for Dr. Wernet's Powder, Clare Champion, **1947.**

COMES TO BROWN THOMAS
MONDAY NEXT, NOV. 6th

Pat Rooney, the Great Fleet Street Cartoonist, will be with us next Monday, November 6th. If you want either a really clever cartoon of yourself or a "speaking likeness" portrait you can depend on Mr. Rooney. Many dog lovers will, of course, wish to have their pets sketched, and if affection for your tail-wagger runs to 5/- then Mr. Rooney will give you a delightful picture of which you'll be proud

In 1933, Brown Thomas advertised the arrival of Pat Rooney, the Fleet Street cartoonist.

TEST

ULSTER'S BEST
GLEN
LAUNDRY SERVICES

NEWTOWNARDS.
Phone 21.

Northern Ireland
laundry advertisement,
1935.

FASHION
Sensation at
Brown
Thomas

Special offer of
Fashionable
TEDDY BEAR
COATS at
Half Usual Prices !

52/6
SPECIAL PRICE

PERSONAL SHOPPERS

Theatre. Also in October, 1943, the Advertising Press Club and the Publicity Club got together to hold a joint dinner and smoker in Jury's Hotel, Dame Street. In November, Victor Salter, advertisement director of the *Belfast Telegraph*, which was still recovering from the damage inflicted in the German blitz 2½ years previously, gave an address on the advertising business in Northern Ireland, still in a very rudimentary state with just two agencies, Wells and A. V. Browne. For January, 1944, the AP Club billed Dan Nolan, then general manager of *The Kerryman*, speaking on the importance of the provincial press.

Government advertising provided a major fillip for the industry, when the Post Office Savings Bank section of the Department of Posts and Telegraphs decided to mount a £6,000 campaign. The campaign ran for six weeks and covered daily and provincial newspapers, weekly and monthly magazines, posters (in Irish and English), strips on buses, trams and trains and 800,000 leaflets — all for £6,000!

A special meeting of the Irish Association of Advertising Agencies was called and a delegation consisting of Brian D. O'Kennedy, Charlie McConnell, Jack Tate and Denis Garvey met representatives of the Department. Then a committee was formed to prepare the campaign; it consisted of Frank Padbury (O'Kennedy Brindley), Denis Swords (McConnells), Pat O'Daly (McEvoys), Denis Garvey (Janus) and Ken Murphy (Domas). All 16 Dublin agencies took part in the campaign, with all copy preparation done on a co-operative basis. The following agencies were involved: Arks, Arrow, Artwey, Caps, Domas, Eason's, Janus, Kelly's, Kenny's, Lynch's, O'Keeffes, O'Kennedy Brindley, McConnell's, McEvoy's, R. Wilson Young and Wilson Hartnell.

The newest agency on the list, R. Wilson Young, had literally just opened its doors. Young set up his own agency in 1943 at 115 Grafton Street, soon moving to 111, over Dixon & Hempenstall. Seven years later, he moved to premises in Fleet Street owned by Colm O'Lochlainn, the man behind the Three Candles' printing firm and father of Dara O'Lochlainn, artist and jazz expert. Young used to claim in later years that he had not "pinched" any accounts from anyone else to start the agency, that all his accounts came from firms new to business in Ireland.

During 1943, the general election provided fair work for some agencies: Lynch's handled Fianna Fáil, Kellys, Fine Gael, R. Wilson Young, Labour and Domas, Sean McEntee. Despite the privations of war, there was still consumer advertising being done. Bread was a topic of perennial interest, since it was on ration. The flour being used ensured that the bread was a dark grey colour: people yearned for the pure white bread that was produced until the war. O'Kennedy Brindley managed to mount a small campaign for Kennedy's bread — Kennedy's/DBC was one of Dublin's best known bakeries. It closed down ten years ago. Bermaline, a speciality bread rather similar to Hovis, was also being advertised very modestly. Domas won the Procea bread account.

Arthur Snow, for many
years advertising
manager of Jacob's the
biscuit makers. He
served with Jacob's for a
total of 50 years,
retiring at the end of
the 1950s.

A Congress brand
range, made by the old
Drogheda Foundry and
Ironworks, once a major
employer in the
Boyneside town.

Other mid-war advertising gives a strong flavour of the times. Locally-made washing powders proliferated; Hurley's soap powder was one popular brand, while Domas was using big newspaper spaces to get across the message for Foamex. Arks handled the appropriately named Blitz powder. Nylons had been invented and put on sale in the USA in 1940; they were not on sale in Britain until after the war and became available in Ireland in the late 1940s. Nylons helped ease the path of many a wartime romance for American servicemen in Europe. Here in Ireland, women had to put up with ersatz leg coverings: paint. One brand on the Irish market was called Abbey Tan, produced by Irish Pharmaceuticals; Miners made Liquid Stockings. McEvoy's held the Miner's account, which went to O'Kennedy Brindley when McEvoy's took aboard Abbey Tan. For the latter account, McEvoy's prepared copy which read: "The success and popularity of 'Abbey Tan' is not due to its originality, but to its superiority".

Plans were afoot for an advertising campaign to combat the fast growth of venereal disease. At Dr Steevens' Hospital, Dublin, attendances in the VD clinic jumped from 15, 184 in 1941 to 25,790 in 1943. The Advertising Press Club newsletter said: "Surely no responsible newspaper or magazine proprietor in Eire could refuse to co-operate in a drive to stamp out this horrible disease." Nothing came of the advertising notion. Charlie McConnell was on much safer and

Opposite page:
Teddy Bear coats were
very fashionable in the
1930s. This Brown
Thomas advertisement
shows them at the
special half price of 52/6.

93

Introducing the New Policy at
BROWN THOMAS's

EVERY Buyer in Brown Thomas's is making an outstanding effort during this event to introduce the New Policy, and quality articles in all departments are down to very low prices, in some cases as low as half usual. Come in yourself to-day or any day during the week and see all the new things that are continually arriving.

Post Orders for any of these quality articles receive immediate attention. Satisfaction guaranteed or money refunded. Orders of 10/- or over sent post free.

MR. MARTIN
Buyer of Silks and Dress Materials, says —

MR. COFFEY
Buyer of Sheets, Table Linens, Fancy Linens, Towels, Blankets, Quilts, etc., says —

"I have secured some beautiful Silks and Dress Materials for the Spring and am selling them at wonderful prices to make this week a real introduction to the New Policy. There are just a few examples of my prices this week.

"This week I am making outstanding offers in my Department and everything is down in price, same as in all others. A few are shown below. There is nothing in my Department but is an exceptional value.

After the McGuire family bought out Brown Thomas from Selfridges in December, 1933, John F. McGuire, chairman and managing director, instituted a new selling policy, which included featuring the store buyers in advertisements.

Biro pens were a new fad in the late 1940s, when they cost the equivalent of a working man's weekly wage (about £2 10s/£2.50). The first advertising campaigns for Biro in Ireland were prepared by Domas.

These advertisements for Kingston's ties, run in the late 1940s, sold a total of 13,000 dozen ties. The ties retailed at 12/6d each, post free.

(handwritten note) 2 ...been promised a Biro for Christmas. Dorothy got one for her Birthday — says its terrific — makes writing a pleasure. Bill got one the day he saw the first ad. Says its just the thing for an office, writes on anything and makes six perfect carbon copies. I'm sure you'd love one too; why not drop John a few hints

Biro
THE PEN WITH A POINT

NEW REDUCED PRICE 49/6. At Stationers, Jewellers and Stores.
Refill units (inserted by Dealer while you wait) 1/-.
Patents granted or pending.
Sole Distributors in Eire: Kevin McDonnell, Ltd., 2 Anne's Place, Dublin.

Gay as a fiesta!

Gay as a fiesta ... colourful as California these Continental ties are to-day's smartest neckwear choice. They have that wonderful supple feel that only silk has. They have that deep rich sheen that only silk has. They have that rhythmic design and colour harmony that make them exclusive to Kingstons. And wrinkles evaporate overnight! The design shown is called plumage. Background colours include blue, wine, brown, green, grey.
Price 12/6. Post free.

Kingstons

Kingstons Ltd., O'Connell Street and George's Street, Dublin.

THE MIGHTY ATOM

A GOOD many years ago a quiet, unassuming man, living in a small town in England, came into possession of a very good recipe for a hair tonic. He saw its possibilities, but unfortunately he had no means to develop them. Nevertheless he decided to try what advertising on a small scale would do.

The first advertising cost a few pounds. It brought returns. The next advertising cost a little more. Results were better. And, as the sales grew, the advertising grew. To-day this tonic is one of the largest sellers in the country.

How do we know? Well, the writer of this advertisement handled the advertising right from the start. It is but one of many striking examples from our records of what can be achieved by that mighty atom of commerce, advertising, when skilfully handled.

O'KENNEDY BRINDLEY
ADVERTISIN

O'Kennedy-Brindley Limited, 53-54 Lo...
O'Connell Street, Dublin. Telephone 7351...

---

less contentious ground when he won the advertising account for the Monument Creameries, run by the Ryan family. Janus won the Irish Permanent Building Society account. It was worth £4,000 a year and was the first time for this small building society to advertise. Now it is the largest building society in the country and spends an estimated £2 million a year on advertising, through O'Keeffes.

Personalities dominated the local advertising scene. In 1943, Ed Carrigan joined O'Kennedy Brindley as a youngster and remembers finding a whole portfolio of posters in the agency, done for the 1932 general election. Michael Carr, who was to spend much of his career with Arks, until his recent retirement, was reported as being a staffer at O'Keeffes and a winning tennis player.

Tony Lokko, the artist and father of Greg Lokko of Colour Repro, the Dublin trade house, spent much of the war years working for Kelly's advertising agency in D'Olier Street. He was also reported as designing the covers for a womens' magazine called *Maeve*. In July 1943, Ken Murphy, then with Domas, announced his engagement to a young lady called Molly Smyth. It was one of the worst-kept social secrets of that summer, as was the announcement in early 1945 that Terry Spillane was getting married to Eileen Clarke, also of *The Irish Times*.

Gerry Keenan-Hall, manager of the McEvoy Publishing Company, was doing well with his play writing. In March, 1944, his third drama,

My Friend, the Senator, was staged at the Peacock Theatre. It was stated to be a satire on the political life of Ireland. McEvoy's was an agency with similar origins to Janus: an offshoot of a department store in its early days. Denis Guiney, who bought over Clery's store in Dublin's O'Connell Street in 1940, was said to have largely funded McEvoy's agency, set up by P. L. McEvoy, in order to benefit from the commission from Clery's advertising that would otherwise have gone to an outside agency.

GET YOUR
STORM LAMP
FOR
3/6
FINEST QUALITY.
FROM
GEORGE WHITE & Sons
O'CONNELL STREET, LTD
WATERFORD.

Storm lamp
advertisement, 1934.

Paddy Montford (right) on
the roof of Independent
House, Dublin. Left is
Leo Blennerhassett,
honorary secretary
Publicity Club while
centre is Sam
McCauley, managing
director, Irish
Pharmaceuticals.

Opposite page
(near right):
An O'Kennedy
Brindley advertisement
on the Saturday leader
page of The Irish Times,
August 11, 1945.

Iron tonic
advertisement, early
1940s.

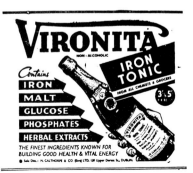

VIRONITA
NON-ALCOHOLIC
IRON TONIC
FROM ALL CHEMISTS & GROCERS
3/5
Contains
IRON
MALT
GLUCOSE
PHOSPHATES
HERBAL EXTRACTS
THE FINEST INGREDIENTS KNOWN FOR
BUILDING GOOD HEALTH & VITAL ENERGY

ANOTHER HUGE OFFER

£40

FILL IN A SQUARE NOW—it takes only a few minutes

Closing FIRST POST JAN. 11—Result JAN. 18

2d. PER SQUARE 4 SQUARES 6d.

Adjudicating Committee:— Senator Michael Hayes, M.A., B.L., Lecturer in Modern Irish, University College, Dublin; Tadhg O Neill, B.A., Associate Editor, "The Irish Digest"; V. M. McMahon.

MUST BE WON

PENNYPOTS CROSSWORDS No. 48

Unlimited Consolation Awards

CLUES ACROSS.

8. Man walking may sometimes have to take ——.

8. Nurse will like to —— worried patient at ease.

9. Man will sometimes —— book to friend fond of reading.

10. Exclamation.

13. Sometimes very pretty.

16. Lights at sea often appear to ——.

17. A lot is sometimes learned from a ——.

CLUES DOWN.

1. Man at meeting asked to assent to proposal may ——.

2. Good —— is often applauded.

3. The time of slave traffic might be described as "days of ——."

4. It is often next to impossible to reason with man while they ——.

5. Often seen on farm.

7. Schoolboys are often anxious to —— their class.

8. There is often a lot in some waters.

11. Trainer will probably —— racehorse before big race.

12. Sportsman out shooting often has good ——.

14. Is often very deep.

15. Housewife is sometimes on the look-out for bread ——.

RULES:—This contest is a test of skill and knowledge. The Prize will be awarded for what the Adjudicators consider the best set of answers in one square. Aptness and accuracy form the sole standard of their judgment. The competition is governed by the full rules and conditions which have already appeared in the "Irish Times" on June 1—or may be had free on application to Pennypots, Ltd.

I accept the rules of the Competition as final and legally binding.

NAME ....
BLOCK LETTERS. State Mr., Mrs. or Miss.

ADDRESS ....
....

Cross P.O.'s and make payable to Pennypots, Ltd. In lieu of P.O. Stamps may be pinned or affixed by corner. I.T. 48.
P.O. No.................................

Send all Entries to:

PENNYPOTS CROSSWORD
2 Lr. O'Connell St., Dublin
Additional Entry Forms Free on Request.

As No. 47 was a two-week competition result will appear next week.

96

3 Doctors
out of every 4
use gas fires

They have selected them as the healthiest method of heating their homes, and the most convenient. You will find them so, too—ideal for bedrooms, dining rooms, and other rooms where a fire is not required all day long.

Instal gas fires and smile at sudden changes of temperature.

Ask about the Cooker and Coke Boiler Installation for Kitchens.

GAS SERVICE DEPARTMENT, DUBLIN, DUN LAOGHAIRE, BRAY

Dublin Gas advertising in 1934 had a distinctly medical tone — "3 doctors out of every 4 use gas fires".

Opposite page: Crosswords were important features of newspaper promotions through to the 1950s; this one, which appeared in The Irish Times in January, 1941, offered an enormous prize fund of £40.

Electric washing machines came on the market in Ireland in the 1930s: this early Miele model was manufactured in Germany and marketed in Ireland just before World War II.

Another agency, O'Kennedy Brindley, was doing a little advertising on its own account. Newsprint was so scarce that by 1940, restrictions had been imposed on newspapers' pagination. The only newspaper launched in Ireland in the Emergency Years after 1941 was that of the *Drogheda Argus,* brought to life in 1943 after having been out of circulation since the mid-1930s. Joe Stanley, a Dublin printer and publisher, was said to have been active in 1916 and to have put his close friendship with de Valera to good use in obtaining newsprint supplies. So with the national papers bringing out A and B editions (display advertisers could go into either), O'Kennedy Brindley's neat little coup with *The Irish Times* caused a certain amount of envious admiration.

Since 1941, the agency had been advertising itself on the front page of the private circulation gazette published weekly by the Dublin Mercantile Association. In late 1943/early 1944, O'Kennedy Brindley extended its self-advertising to *The Irish Times*, where it occupied a 5" single column on Bertie Smyllie's leader page every Saturday. O'KB also created another minor wartime sensation when the agency produced a six colour folder for a client; the print run was just 1,000.

In March, 1944, it was reported that Michael Carr was moving from O'Keeffes to Arks, while Alan Tate, son of Jack Tate joined the same agency. Soon afterwards, Bill O'Donoghue was named Arks' general manager; from 1935 until 1937, he freelanced for a couple of Dublin space dealers, then he went to Kelly's, where he became production manager. From Kelly's, he went to the new agency of Domas. After a year there, he joined Arks as its production manager. As O'Donoghue was moving up at Arks, Jimmy Cranwell was moving out, into R. Wilson Young, which had just acquired the Bird's Custard account, a mainstay of that agency for many subsequent years. Cranwell was one of four advertising people who played "stiffs" in "Arsenic and Old Lace" at the Gaiety Theatre, Dublin. The others were Dick Young, Ben McConnell and Denis Garvey.

Into this easy-going advertising life came a youngster with a fine aptitude for drawing: Jarlath Hayes. His mother went into Kenny's in Middle Abbey Street, climbing past the turf banked on the stairs; she asked Kevin J. Kenny for a job for her son. Master Jarlath was taken on; his wages were 10/- a week and his immediate boss was studio manager Patrick Joseph Dempsey, brother of Jack Dempsey of the *Irish Press*. Just after the war, P. J. Dempsey bought out the Parker agency. Dempsey's assistant in Kenny's, Eamonn Geraghty, remembers an advertisement being placed by the agency for a Thomas Street store during the war for a newly arrived consignment of clogs. The gardai had to be called to control the crowds that suddenly materialised. A young advertising student called Bill Bergin remembers being given lifts home on the handlebar of his tutor's bicycle: by 1944, public transport, especially in the evenings, had become very spasmodic.

Paper restrictions meant that poster advertising had to be cut back, but the Government commissioned some fine posters for the Army, done by Jack McManus of Arks, the Post Office Savings campaign and

In the 1930s, laundries were an important feature of the economic landscape, for cleaning, dyeing and dry cleaning. In Dublin, big names included Imco, Prescotts and the White Heather. All advertised extensively; this advertisement for the long-defunct Dunlop Laundry and Dye Works, Dublin, appeared in the Irish Local Government Officials' union magazine in April, 1936.

Dunlop Laundry and Dye Works, Limited.
MOUNT BROWN AND KILMAINHAM
——Try Our Three Services——
" UTILITY " LAUNDRY, FULLY FINISHED LAUNDRY, CLEANING AND DYEING.
City Receiving Offices:—13 STEPHEN'S GREEN, N.; 18 TALBOT STREET; 3 UPPER CAMDEN STREET, AND 5 MOUNT BROWN, DUBLIN.
Telephones :—22318-9.

the Grow more Wheat drive. Young Eimar Spillane, brother of Terry, won a prize for his poster design for the latter campaign. Cosmetics advertisements for brands such as Miners, Dawn and Outdoor Girl occupied many bus sides (an increasingly popular medium). Kelly's did an advertising campaign with the headline "Give Him Wolsey Socks" featuring the head of Wolsey, portrayed as a very ill-humoured prelate. A new vegetable extract called Vegex came on the market, but didn't survive. Neither did the many brands of "artificial" coffee that came on the wartime market. As soon as consumers could buy real coffee after the war, there was no longer any place for brands like Pasha Coffee.

With McConnell's advertising in 1944 for Rawson's shoes, the change in advertising techniques was noticed. Just before the war, shoe advertising in Dublin was characterised by polished, photographic and air-brushed layouts, but this style had given way by the end of the war to freer drawing techniques, using wash and line drawing, sometimes charcoal. In advertisements for Donaghy's shoes prepared by Janus, artwork appeared to be white chalk on grey paper with highlights in black.

Charlie McConnell out riding with the South County Dublin Harriers, Inchicore, Dublin, December, 1938.

The late William
P. Cavanagh of Chivers,
a former chairman and
administrator of the
Association of
Advertisers in Ireland.
Bill Cavanagh began his
career with the firm of
O. R. Fry in Hawkins
Street, Dublin, before
joining Boileau and
Boyd. In 1919, he joined
Armour's Dublin office.
At the time, there was a
huge trade here in
American bacon, but
Armour's canned meats
were popular. Its canned
jam did not, however,
sell well. From 1927
until 1933, Bill
Cavanagh worked for
Armour's London office,
returning home that
year to join Chivers,
which had just started
manufacturing in
Dublin.
Chivers had been
represented in Ireland
since 1899. In the early
years of the 20th
century, its crystal
jellies were popular
here, in a seasonal
market that lasted from
April to September. By
the 1930s, tablet table
jellies gained popularity
in Ireland, helped by the
advent of both Birds and
Chivers into production
in Ireland in 1933. For
many years, Bill
Cavanagh was Chivers'
sales manager.
Deeply involved with
the Association of
Advertisers in Ireland
from its formation in
1951, he became a
chairman of the
organisation. When he
retired from Chivers in
1967, he became full-
time administrator of
the AAI. Bill Cavanagh
died in 1986.
*Photograph: The Green
Studio.*

For Christmas, 1944, with clear signs that the war would last only a few months longer, an increasing use of colour in magazine advertisements was noted within the advertising industry, although few of these pages were described as being noteworthy in design, production or printing. Clark's shoes ran full pages in four colours, while McConnell's featured Santa (no appearance fees!) in a pre-Christmas campaign for Keiller's Little Chip marmalade and showed diners in an appetising two pages in full colour for Chef sauce. It was suggested

100

that production managers in the Dublin agencies should rotate their artists, layout men and copywriters in order to replenish the creative flow.

By the middle of 1944, the Advertising Press Club had an impressive array of members, who included Bill Bergin, Frank Chambers, Basil Clancy, Jimmy Cranwell, Horace Denham, Dickie Duggan, Jim Furlong, Denis Garvey, Gerry Keenan-Hall, Colm Kenny, Tony Lokko, J. J. McCann, Fred Mullen, Ken Murphy, Dan Nolan, Alpho O'Reilly, Peter Owens, Albert Price, Pat Ryan, Terry Spillane, Alan Tate and Jack Webb. Brian D. O'Kennedy, Frank Padbury and Dick Young were associate members. For the 1944/45 session of the club, the following officers were appointed: chairman, Desmond B.

Optician's advertisement, mid-1940s.

A corset and underclothing advertisement for Brown Thomas, the Dublin department store, published in Dublin newspapers in November, 1934.

Furnishings advertisement, 1941.

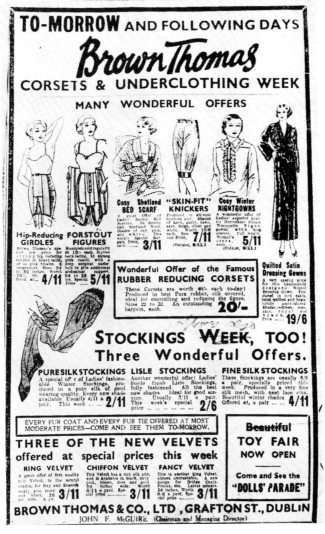

CUMANN LUITH-CHLEAS GAEDHEAL

12th Annual

CONVENTION CEILIDHE

At QUEEN'S HOTEL, ENNIS

On Sunday Night, 19th January

Rinnce—9 go 3.

Presentation of County Championship Medals and League
and Tournament Trophies won by the Clare Senior Hurling
Team during 1946.

Admission 3/6

CEAD MILE FAILTE

Advertisement for a
political ceilidhe, 1947.

O'Kennedy; vice-chairman, J. C. McConnell; hon. secretary, Denis Garvey; hon. treasurer, P. J. Conlon; public relations officers, Terry Spillane and Tommy Mangan. In July, 1944, appointments were made for the 1944/45 session of the Publicity Club. Chairman was Jack O'Sheehan; vice-chairmen, Desmond B. O'Kennedy and G. J. C. Tynan O'Mahony; honorary treasurers, G. S. Childs and C. B. McConnell; honorary secretary, Gordon Sutton Kelly. Leo Blenner-hassett of Independent Newspapers was elected an honorary officer. In that same month, at the Tramore, Co. Waterford, golf club, J. J. Walsh of the *Munster Express* was reported as being congratulated on winning the Publicity Challenge Cup at Bundoran.

People were constantly on the move. A young, up-and-coming advertising man called Peter Owens joined Kelly's agency in 1944; it had just acquired such accounts as Villa boot polish and Paramount Pictures. Philip Callan also joined Kelly's from Easons. Pyke, the noted cartoonist, who became appreciated in later years in the advertising industry for depicting its "heads", joined the *Irish Independent* as art editor. Another famous cartoonist, Bob Fannin, whose work has graced Independent Newspapers and *Business and Finance* magazine for many years, joined the production department of R. Wilson Young Advertising from the commercial department of the *Irish Press*. Philip Callan moved on quickly from Kelly's to O'Keeffes; when he wasn't writing copy, he was writing plays for Radio Eireann and the BBC. Jack Lyons, who had been publicity manager of the Theatre Royal and who went to work for MGM in Belfast and then Dublin, was succeeded at the Theatre Royal by a young man called Jack Cruise, later to be a great comedian and entertainer.

The 1938 motor show at the Mansion House, Dublin. On show was the 25,000th car made at the now closed Ford factory in Cork.

Newest of the New Spring Modes at Brown Thomas's

HERE are some of the very latest Spring Modes now showing in our Windows and on the Fashion Gallery. Come and visit us to-morrow Every day will see some new Arrivals.

BROWN
THOMAS & CO.
Grafton St., Dublin

John F. McGuire

Brown Thomas Spring Modes were advertised in the *Dublin Evening Mail* in February, 1934. Shortly afterwards, the firm had 10,000 copies of a three colour fashion brochure printed by Hely's. The total cost was £70, including artist's fees of £5.

The advertising and publicity examinations at Rathmines Technical Institute in the early summer of 1944 showed some promising newcomers. The Irish Association of Advertising Agencies' prize went to Bill Bergin, who also won a full course certificate. This latter achievement was shared with Peter M. Owens. Not long afterwards, when Bergin was working for Janus in Middle Abbey Street, it was reported, humorously of course, that he could be seen with his foot "plastered", the offending member projecting from the window. The unfortunate young adman had had an accident which necessitated his foot being encased in plaster for some time.

In December, 1944, Benny Greene of *The Irish Times*, one of the best-known personalities on the advertisement side of that paper, was referred to in the Advertising Press Club newsletter as "the year's most conscientious, hard-working and generally run-ragged pressman".

On a more serious note, as 1944 came to a close, restrictions on consumer items began to be eased a little, a fact reflected in the advertising of the period. McConnell's was advertising Willwood's jams and marmalades, made in the old Willwood factory in Parnell Street, Dublin, as well as Toblerone chocolate, also made by the same firm. Chef sauce, another Willwood speciality, was also advertised extensively by McConnells, but it was noted that the emergency rations' newsprint did not show up the half tones to good effect. Janus was busy advertising the carpet department at Arnotts, while for the ladies, Zenobia talcum powder was advertising with refinement. Bradmola Mills took advertising space to announce that the return of silk stockings was imminent, while Flexee foundations advertised their

A Wilson Hartnell space order dating from the 1930s.

A 383

Telephone: DUBLIN 2161
Telegrams: "HARTNELL" DUBLIN
Contract No. ....

WILSON HARTNELL & CO., LTD., *Advertising Contractors*

CONTRACTORS TO
THE GOVERNMENT OF EIRE
W.H.
CONTRACTORS TO THE
ROYAL IRISH AUTOMOBILE CLUB
ETC., ETC.

COMMERCIAL BUILDINGS, DUBLIN, 1.

To ....

Please insert undermentioned Advertisement and charge to our Account

No. of Insertions ....

Size of Space ....

Position ....

Date of Insertion ....

Rate per Insertion ....
Less our Commission

Memorandum ....

For *WILSON HARTNELL & CO., LTD.*

COMMERCIAL A.C

Date of Order ....19....

INVOICES must be furnished not later than the last day of each month. Each invoice must have a cutting of the advertisement to which it refers pasted on the back.
TWO VOUCHER COPIES for each insertion must be sent to this Office on day of publication certain.

This photograph was taken in Jury's hotel, Dame Street, Dublin, in 1942 just after the start of the Advertising Press Club. The grouping was the same as that for the Bundoran poker school. From left: Desmond O'Kennedy, Ken Murphy, Denis Garvey, Pat Conlon, Terry Spillane, David Fogarty (the printing ink representative who was first club chairman) and Frank Padbury. All were on the first council of the AP club.

ladies' corsets — in silhouette. Advertising for ladies' underwear was a subject of consternation in the media; Denis Garvey remembers well how reluctant the advertisement department of Independent Newspapers was in accepting layouts that showed models wearing brassieres. On at least one occasion, the late John Charles McQuaid, long before he was elevated to become Archbishop of Dublin, was said to have complained privately to members of the newspaper's advertisement staff about ladies' underwear advertising in the *Irish Independent*. Recalls Ronnie Nesbitt of Arnotts, "the *Irish Independent* would not accept corset advertisements showing legs. *The Irish Times* had no such qualms. However, it meant making two sets of blocks.

More serious matters were afoot, however. October 13, 1944, saw what was described as the biggest night out in advertising since the mid-1920s. 500 advertising people and their friends and relations packed into the Metropole Ballroom for the gala event organised with military precision and efficiency by the Advertising Press Club. Thoughts of the war were far from people's minds as they were

determined to enjoy themselves; Sean Mooney, the Theatre Royal's top singer, brought the crowds to their feet with his singing of "Lil' Marlene" and "Don't be Cross". Noel Purcell's performance added to the merriment. With dancing and spot prizes, the event went on until 3 a.m. By 2 a.m., the *Times Pictorial* had produced a special two page souvenir of the event, complete with photographs. Everyone at the "do" said it was the best since the great advertising ball held in the same ballroom on Saturday, January 31, 1925.

The Irish Association of Advertising Agencies announced a new constitution; it provided the same ethical standards as those of the older professions, such as accountancy, with severe penalties for breaches of the code. The new constitution was the first attempt by the Irish advertising industry at self-regulation and precursor of many post-war regulatory curbs on the industry, culminating in the establishment of the Advertising Standards Authority and the powerful Government moves against cigarette publicity. The Advertising Press Club started planning for the new year of 1945, with the big event being the launch of the technical group committee to ensure better technical liaison between members. On April 5, 1945, the Publicity Club held its 21st anniversary dinner, slightly belatedly, since it was set up in 1923, 22 years previously, in the Gresham Hotel, Dublin. Honorary secretary Gordon Sutton Kelly said that letters and telegrams of congratulations had poured in from Britain and America.

Chairman Jack O'Sheehan (Hospitals' Trust) said that Ireland would have to protect her hard-won economic freedom, while vice-chairman Brian D. O'Kennedy referred to Denis Guiney's "arsenal of distribution" across the street — Clery's. P. L. McEvoy urged protection of Irish industries against foreign propaganda. Charlie McConnell, who had been chairman of the club six times, was presented with a replica of the gold medallion on the chain of office. He told the assembled crowd that he foresaw a brilliant future for advertising in the post-war world.

When Peace Day came on May 8, 1945, marking the end of $5\frac{1}{2}$ years of conflict, the advertisers were ready. *The Irish Times* carried a number of advertisements with a peace theme. Martin Mahony and Bros (hosiery) had an 8" double column (Janus), Mineral Water Distributors (Arks) had a similar sized space and McConnells booked an 8" double column for Sweet Afton cigarettes. The same agency took a 4" double column for the B + I shipping line. Later, other newspapers in Dublin and the provinces carried some of the peace advertisements. At 11.30 p.m. on the night before the special *Irish Times'* issue, at least five advertising agency men were at the newspaper to make last minute checks. Janus had had the blocks for the Mahony advertisement with the newspapers since the previous July, so that as soon as the censor gave the go-ahead at 6.50 p.m. on May 7, the advertisement was ready to be used. One agency in town put up a notice: "We have a special welcome for publishers' representatives at any time".

Winter Can't hurt HIM..

Winter's rigours lose their sting when you give up their strength and resistance to infection. That's why children who take Carragol nearly always get through winter free from colds and other winter ills. This palatable emulsion of Cod Liver Oil, hypophosphites, and Carrageen Moss is the ideal winter tonic. Put your children on it and keep them safe. Bottles 1/3, 2/-, 3/6 from chemists.

...he's taking CARRAGOL

Essence of Sun and Sea

Health advertisement, 1941.

Overleaf:
Henry Ford & Son of Cork took this full page advertisement in the Irish Press on January 1, 1938.

An advertisement prepared in the 1930s by Arks on behalf of Macardle, Moore & Co., Dundalk.

New Year's Greeting

Ford

and an invitation to all Irish Motorists to make 1938 a prosperous year for Irish Industry

WESTPORT — IRISH SEWING COTTON CO. LTD. SEWING THREAD

DROGHEDA — AUTOMOTIVE INDUSTRIES LTD. SPARK PLUGS

GALWAY

DUBLIN — EXIDE BATTERIES (IRELAND) LTD. AUTOMOBILE BATTERIES
THE LEINSTER ENGINEERING CO. LTD. SPARK PLUGS

BRAY — SOLUS TEORANTA AUTOMOBILE BULBS

ENNIS — L. JORDAN LTD. ELASTIC TAPE

WEXFORD — JOHN BROCKHOUSE & CO. (IRELAND) LTD. CHASSIS SPRINGS

CORK — THE IRISH DUNLOP CO. LTD. TYRES AND TUBES
HARRINGTON & GOODLASS WALL LTD. ENAMELS AND PAINTS
O'BRIEN BROS. LTD. UPHOLSTERY CLOTH

Ford Products incorporate the greatest percentage of Irish Labour and Irish-made Materials.

This diagram illustrates the movements of local purchases to Cork for use in the manufacture of Ford Products.

A large number of miscellaneous items bought in Ireland for non-production purposes are not Included.

MAKE up your mind to join the great band of Ford users in 1938 . . . the greatest motoring community in Ireland. Enjoy with them all the benefits of Ford ownership, including value far above the price, the unique Ford Service organization, low, fixed charges for repairs, and the Ford Engine and Parts Exchange Plan. This is a New Year Resolution it will <u>pay</u> you to make.

The Ford "Eight" - £165
The Ford "Ten" - from £190
The Ford V-8 - from £230
Ford Commercial Vehicles
for every type of load
Fordson Tractors from £150

★ **Here's wishing you a very Happy New Year** ★

HENRY FORD & SON LIMITED CORK

Don't mope in misery there is a
MACARDLE'S NO·1 STRONG ALE
round the corner

Brewed in the good old-fashioned way by
MACARDLE, MOORE & CO., LTD., DUNDALK.

Brown Thomas

VALUE

Downright VALUE to the last nut—
that's the secret of the amazing popularity of these famous cycles. You'll
find them in every town in Ireland.
First-class components assembled by
skilled labour. Each machine is
thoroughly tested, and equipment includes Dunlop Tyres, Pump, Tools,
and Reflector. And, to crown its
other attractions, it is priced at a price
which makes it a thoroughly sound
investment.

CASH PRICE
£3 : 17 : 6   6/- A MONTH
is all you need pay for this
superb machine. There is also a Ladies'
model. Cash Price, £3 5 0, or 6 6 a
month.

WRITE FOR CATALOGUE
Which gives you full particulars of all the models in our range
of first-class cycles.

Grafton & Duke Streets.   Phone 4206.   Dublin.

Before World War II, a bicycle could be bought at Brown Thomas for 6/- (30p) a month.

In September, 1946, Edward F. MacSweeney was appointed publicity manager of Metropole and Allied Cinemas, Dublin. He had been art editor of the Times Pictorial since 1941.

Jack O'Sheehan of the Irish Hospitals' Sweepstakes, was chairman of the Publicity Club in 1945.

Opposite left: Frank Durley, well-known advertising copywriter, who said in 1944 that "the creative man's brain is his office and it knows no hours". He also pointed out that the copywriter is rarely allowed the "temperament" of the artist.

In late May and early June, the Publicity Club organised the first-ever exhibition and competition of current advertising work in the old Engineers' Hall in Dawson Street. Entries were judged by a panel that included the advertisement managers of the three Dublin morning newspapers and Frank Brandt, the publicity manager of the ESB. At this time, Billy King organised a fascinating night-time visit to Independent Newspapers by members of the Advertising Press Club's technical group. He said: "There is a high degree of co-operation between the advertisement and editorial departments, a co-operation all the more necessary during the peak period of the space famine, now happily showing signs of moderation."

With the coming of peace, John Flynn, the well-known publisher, told the Advertising Press Club that individual brand names should be banished in export markets. He urged the setting up of trade bureaux in all parts of the world, as well as the sale of goods under generic titles, such as "Irish Jam", "Irish Shoes" or "Irish Clothing". He well anticipated both the establishment of Coras Trachtala, the Irish Export Board, and brands like Kerrygold. Sean Lynch was elected I.A.A.A. Chairman.

The first post-war international move by an Irish agency was made by Janus, which opened a London office at St. Mary's Chambers, 161A-166 Strand, in 1945. It was managed by Reg Wilks who had been the first manager of Janus before the war.

A great veteran of the business barely survived the peace; John H. Parker, who had set up his placement agency back in 1888, died at his home in Howth. The agency was taken over by Patrick Dempsey, who had been studio manager in Kenny's. Within four years, Dempsey's own agency was to handle the launch publicity for the *Sunday Press*. As

Gordon Clark, for many years actively involved in the publicity business. He had close connections also with Mount Salus Press. He was pictured (right) in 1945 when he won the Gold Medal of the Advertising Press Club, organised in conjunction with the Rathmines School of Commerce. He was 22 at the time and managing editor of the Leinster Express. He was elected chairman of the Advertising Press Club in 1952/53.

soon as the war was over, the newspaper business began to blossom once more. With the easing of restrictions, the *Irish Independent,* which had carried very few display advertisements in the last months of 1944 and the first months of 1945, was able to expand. Its issues went up to six pages and within each of those early expanded issues, it was able to carry up to 90 display advertisements.

Two new agencies came into being, Padbury's and Sun. Both had a major impact on post-war advertising. Frank Padbury left O'Kennedy Brindley at the end of April, 1945, to start on his own. He started his career as a compositor in his native Waterford and in 1922, joined Kenny's before moving to England, where he worked with Heritage Peters Advertising agency in Coventry, in the English Midlands. When O'Kennedy Brindley was set up in 1927, he returned to Dublin to join the new firm. For many years, he was production manager at the agency; he was made a director in 1938. He also lectured on advertising at the Rathmines Technical Institute for some years. Padbury was a skilled photographer with a keen interest in both still and movie photography. On one publicity outing to Killarney, remembers David Luke, Padbury went missing. Eventually, he was found in the lavatory of the hotel, changing film in his camera in the semi-light. A stickler for production accuracy, Frank Padbury was often known to ring up newspapers when he spotted errors in advertisements he was responsible for and complain vociferously. On one occasion, remembers Bob Nealon, he gave out hell because a newspaper

The Empire, Belfast, advertised this pantomime featuring Jimmy O'Dea in 1936. Adam Findlater of the Dublin grocery family was the first chairman of the Empire and responsible for its rebuilding in 1894. This Belfast landmark closed in 1961. At one time, the Findlaters also owned what is now the Olympia Theatre, Dublin.

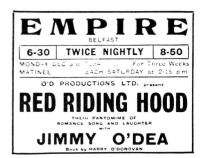

EMPIRE
BELFAST
6-30 | TWICE NIGHTLY | 8-50
MONDAY DEC 3rd ... For Three Weeks
MATINEE EACH SATURDAY at 2-15 p.m.
O'D PRODUCTIONS LTD. present
RED RIDING HOOD
THEIR PANTOMIME OF
ROMANCE SONG AND LAUGHTER
WITH
JIMMY O'DEA
Book by HARRY O'DONOVAN

Charlie McConnell (left) seen playing golf at Bundoran in 1940 with Bertie Smyllie, editor of The Irish Times.

reproduction of a Kennedy's Bakery advertisement made the slice of bread appear like a sod of turf.

Frank Padbury was joined in his new venture by Maymay Dignam, who also worked in O'Kennedy Brindley, where she was secretary to Brian D. O'Kennedy. Maymay, who later bought out the holding left by Frank Padbury to his wife, remembers him as a man of great energy, a fast worker. "He could write copy very quickly. He was a brilliant man, who also read a lot. Frank was always keen to help other people." Just the year after the agency started, a youngster called Robert Nealon joined the staff. He is still there, the present managing director.

Padbury Advertising opened for business at 97-99 Grafton Street and within a month of starting, was granted recognition by the Dublin Newspaper Managers' Committee. The agency's first accounts included Galligans, for whom Padbury devised the slogan, "Every Pillar Box is a Branch of Galligans", Leinster Engineering and Brownlee

Brothers. Smith & Pearson, the structural steel firm, came in soon afterwards, as did Kennedy's/DBC, the Dublin bakery firm. Within two months, Padbury won a store account, Kellett's of South Great George's Street; previously, this retail drapery outlet had followed the practice of the time and advertised direct. In the July, 1945, issue of the *Irish Tatler and Sketch,* the agency placed its very first colour advertisement for Dolcis shoes. Victor Penney, an accomplished finished artist, did much work for the new agency.

If Your
TIME
Is NOT worth Anything—

Otherwise—

IRISH SEA AIRWAYS
" The Shortest Distance Between Two Points "
39 UPPER O'CONNELL STREET
PHONE—72872-73
Twice Daily Services to Bristol, Croydon, and Isle of Man.

An early Aer Lingus advertisement, published not long after the airline had been established in 1936.

111

To tell the story of one of the great romances of the world we go back nearly two thousand years to the days when Mark Antony loved Cleopatra. Following the death of Cæsar, Antony summoned the lovely Queen to appear before him to answer charges that she had helped his enemies. She sailed up the river Cydnus to meet him:

The barge she sat in, like a burnished throne,
Burn'd on the water; the poop was beaten gold;
Purple the sails and so perfumed that
The winds were love-sick with them; the oars were silver;
Which to the tune of flutes kept stroke.

Like Cæsar, Antony lost his heart and head and in doing so sacrificed domination of half the world on the altar of infatuation. He had become ruler of the eastern division of the Roman dominions; but soon the Senate declared war on Cleopatra. In the battle at Actium (31 B.C.) she was defeated and fled—Antony followed her, deserted by his troops. A year later he stabbed himself and died at her feet. History has called her "the serpent of the Nile," Octavian has described her as "this accursed woman." Yet the secret of her strange fascination for men has never been explained—this fascination that made men like Cæsar and Mark Antony willing slaves to her loveliness. She passed out of life by letting a poisonous asp, the deadly viper of the Egyptian sands, bite her, having first witnessed the death of one of her slave girls from the same cause.

MARTIN MAHONY  & BROS., LIMITED
BLARNEY, CO. CORK   ESTABLISHED 1750

Manufacturers of Blarney Tweeds, Hosiery and Knitting Wools

Advertisement for Mahony's of Blarney, Co Cork, The Irish Times, **May 19, 1945.**

John McConnell received his BA degree at Trinity College, Dublin, in 1937. He is seen here being congratulated by his father, Charlie, founder of the advertising agency of the same name.

The second major agency to open its doors for the first time in 1945 was Sun Advertising, set up by Tim O'Neill. He had graduated in economics from UCD in 1932, then had gone to work in Arks in London, where a close colleague was Cecil Dick. At the end of the 1930s, he started his own publishing business in Dublin, doing *O'Neill's Who's Who* and the *Irish Medical Directory,* later selling out to J. J. O'Leary's Parkside Press, part of Cahills, the printing firm. O'Neill was made secretary of Cahill & Co. in 1939, as well as a director of Parkside. Later, he became a director of O'Kennedy Brindley, before severing his connection there to join Kelly Advertising. In 1945, he decided to start his own agency, operating from Grafton Street. His right-hand woman was Elizabeth Somers, who had worked with him in O'Kennedy Brindley.

O'Neill had excellent political connections, which enabled him to get the agency off to a good start with some important accounts, including Aer Lingus (then just resuming its post-war services) and CIE. He gave a start to many well-known people in the business, such as Cecil Bell (later with Arks, now managing director of W & C McDonnell), Iain MacCarthaigh the copywriter and Brian Cronin. He was a generous man, always ready to help people. He was sociable and affable, too. One story told during his Parkside Press days related how he entertained two clients at the Windmill Theatre in London, then the only theatrical establishment in the British capital to have naked women on stage. O'Neill and one of his clients enjoyed the show; the other client was quite disgusted and O'Neill had a major pacification job to do. In retrospect, however, his greatest achievement was bringing in the

Dutch artists. Until then, Ireland had no tradition of graphic design in advertising, but from the arrival of the first Dutchman, Gus Melai, the situation began to improve.

Throughout 1945, there was news of up-and-coming young people making their mark in the industry. Gilbert Pollard, a staunch member of the Advertising Press Club, was promoted assistant manager (Denis Swords was his boss) and production manager at McConnell's. 22 years old Gordon Clark, who had been a traffic officer with Aer Lingus and who now worked in the editorial department of the *Leinster Express* in Portlaoise, was awarded the Advertising Press Club's gold medal in a competition organised in conjunction with the High School of Commerce in Rathmines. O'Kennedy Brindley announced a number of appointments. Jack McManus, who had started his advertising career with McEvoy's in 1932 and subsequently worked in Amsterdam, before coming home at the start of the war to work in Arks and then going on to become display manager of the Swastika Laundry, became a member of the visualising team at O'KB. Bill Lindsay, who had been an artist with the agency for nine years at this stage, was promoted to art director. The third major appointment was of copywriter Jack O'Donoghue, who had worked with Artwey and Arks before the war. A young Pat O'Rorke joined the agency and is still with it, Dublin's longest serving copywriter. With the arrival of Padbury and Sun, Dublin now had 19 agencies, turning over in total £3/4 million. Bolton Street Technical Institute looked for part-time teachers of window and shop display, for ten shillings an hour.

Maclean's toothpaste advertisement, 1938.

Photograph taken by Frank Padbury on the last Great Northern Railways' "junket" to its hotel in Bundoran, May, 1946. Front row, from left: Jarlath Hayes, Sam Suttle (ESB), Charlie McConnell and J. J. Walsh. Back row, from left: Brian D. O'Kennedy, unknown, Jim Furlong, Jack Tate, Billy King, Gerry Power, Fred Hamly and Basil Sheppard.

113

This photograph was taken at the dinner held to mark the opening of McConnell's London office in 1938. Included are W. Buchanan-Taylor, publicity director, J. Lyons (front row, second from left), Tom Kenny, Connacht Tribune, Galway (back row, eighth from left), Charlie McConnell (front row, second from right), John McConnell (back row, tenth from left) and Alfie Byrne, Lord Mayor of Dublin (front row, far right).

To Shareholders

and Customers !

WE ARE NOW OPEN TO BUY

SEED AND MILLING WHEAT.

BLACK & WHITE OATS.

AN UNLIMITED QUANTITY

YMER BARLEY.

WE HAVE NOW OBTAINED A COMMISSION LICENCE FOR
WHEATEN MEAL.

WE WILL STORE, DRY AND MILL AT VERY REASONABLE COST

LOC GARMAIN CO-OP. AGRL. SOCIETY LTD.,

The Castle & 87 North Main St., WEXFORD.

'PHONE: WEXFORD 35.

(12711-9)

TRIALS OF AN ADVERTISING AGENT

CREATIVE TALENT IN IRELAND

INDICATED BY HOME FIRMS' EXPENDITURE

IN a paper on "The Trials of an Advertising Agent," read before a meeting of the Publicity Club of Ireland in Jury's Hotel, Dublin, last night, Mr. John W. Tate, Managing Director of Messrs. Arks, Ltd., said that there was a popular idea that the advertising copywriter sat with copies of the London evening papers before him, from which he was supposed to get his bright ideas.

IRISH TALENT

It was a mistake to believe that all the brains in the advertising business were across the water; there was quite an amount of talent in advertising in this country, and while large London salaries and prospects allured their best young men away, they still, to a great extent, had people who preferred to work and live here, and were brilliant in their own sphere as writers of advertisements.

Referring to territorial or national distributive advertising, Mr. Tate said that distributive advertising could be handled very easily and efficiently in County Dublin and district. Whether territorial or national advertising was taken depended on individual tastes and on the times.

VALUE OF AGENT'S ADVICE

The advice of the advertising agent was, said Mr. Tate, really worth having, and he thought that people did not realise that, or the advertising agent would be used more.

The standard of production of creative ability in this country was extremely high, and compared favourably with the best work of the most highly commercialised countries. There were small advertising agents who sometimes were very good indeed. Nobody should despise the small man.

Mr. Brian D O'Kennedy said that, in comparing advertising in this country and advertising across the water, they must bear in mind that the advertiser on the other side was spending very big money, and had a great advantage over the agent here in productive work.

Advertising here was up to a very high standard, and was quite as good as advertising on the other side.

ADVERTISING CONSCIENCE

One of their difficulties was that most of their advertisers were not really advertising-minded. They had not the advertising conscience here that they had on the other side, and he thought that until they got it, they would be very much behind in advertising. Last year Messrs. Guinness spent £94,000 on advertising; Players, £120,000; Craven A, £70,000; Ovaltine, £223,000; Horlicks, £152,000; and Rountrees, £108,000.

Mr. S. McCauley said that the advertising agent was looked on as an expert, and was given as much latitude as possible.

Mr. P. L. McEvoy said that he thought that one of the greatest trials of the advertising agent in this country was that virtually everybody knew everything about advertising. He thought that one of the things wrong in this country was that people got too good value for the money they spent on advertising.

Mr. L. C. Blennerhassett sympathised with advertising agents and consultants on the limitations put on them.

Mr. J. O'Dockery said that he knew of copy which had been passed by executives, sent in to a newspaper by agents, set up, and cancelled at the last moment. It was a compliment to agents that so few alterations were made in their copy.

Mr. T. Merry was of opinion that manufacturers should be informed of the advantages to be obtained from the services of advertising agents.

Mr. E. C. Maguire supported the view that there were in this country men capable of giving manufacturers service as good as, if not better than, that given on the other side.

Mr. T. O'Neill said that there should be an advertising manager or chief clerk deputed by firms to look after advertising, and interpret the wishes of the Board.

Mr. J. O'Sheehan said that while advertising agents here could turn out as good work as was done in England, one could see as bad advertising in Ireland as anywhere else.

Mr. C. E. McConnell, Chairman of the Club, said that as one who had conducted an advertising agency for a quarter of a century, he could state that he never had had anything but the greatest courtesy and help from the Press in this country in the preparation and issuing of his advertisements.

At the opening of the meeting, the Chairman said that they were glad to see Sir Lauriston Arnott, Bart., managing director

Opposite page:
Getting ready for the Advertising Press Club dance in the Metropole, 1944, from left: Rita Newell (later Mrs Denis Garvey), Pearl Garvey, Alva Hughes (later Mrs Gordon Clark) and Betty Whelan.

Co-operative advertisement published after the end of the Emergency.

This report on the advertising industry appeared in The Irish Times, January 3, 1941.

Reg Wilks, first general manager, Janus Advertising.

115

★

A fitted carpet almost furnishes the room!

The problem of furnishing a room is half solved when the right carpet is fitted. Choose at Arnotts where choice is wide and where quality is your guarantee of satisfaction later on.

Seamless Axminsters

Axminster Hearthrugs

Beautiful Linoleums

MATS and MATTING

We also have in stock a fine choice of all kinds of mats and mattings. Carpets, etc., fitted by expert fitters. Patterns and quotations free on request.

GRADUAL PAYMENTS

You can obtain any of Arnotts carpet, furniture, mattresses, etc. on the gradual payment system. Your further enquiries are invited.

Arnotts Autumn Catalogue   ★   October 1941

From the late 1930s until the mid-1950s, Arnott's, the Dublin department store, produced a regular Trend catalogue, mailed out to customers. The catalogues were produced by Janus Advertising and printed by the Temple Press, Dublin, which also had close connections with the store.

Vitriol was poured on the advertising industry by the late Dr Cornelius Lucey then of Maynooth, later Bishop of Cork: "Time was when newspapers really were newspapers. Now they are truly adspapers, drawing half their revenue and allocating half their space to advertisements. Ads must attract the attention of the reader and so they flaunt themselves overmuch."

Jack McManus also produced some award-winning anti-TB posters; tuberculosis was the scourge of the era and with the active assistance of Dr Noel Browne, the Minister for Health, consideration was given in 1948 to setting up an advisory body from the advertising and publishing industries to plan anti-TB publicity. Dr Browne told the Advertising Press Club: "There are a number of simple methods by which it would be possible to reduce in Ireland the simply staggering incidence of diseases like TB, gastro-enteritis and infantile paralysis". There was even a suggestion that "Health Queens" should be elected at local carnivals. Speakers at that meeting included Frank Padbury, Jack Tate, Fred Mullen, Walter Mahon-Smith, Sam Suttle and David Luke.

There was great sadness at the passing of Pat Conlon on December 4, 1945. A very popular man in the business, he had worked on the advertising side of such publications as the *Irish Grocer, Woman's Life* and finally, *Model Housekeeping*. Ken Murphy of Domas said in an appreciation that Pat Conlon had a great heart and a man for whom hard work assumed the pleasures of a hobby. Less than three years later, another great personality of the Dublin scene passed away, G. J. C. Tynan O'Mahony, manager of *The Irish Times*.

On a happier note, in 1945, Ernie Keogh, a young man working in Arrow Advertising announced his engagement to Florrie Heather, while on September 3 that year, Terry Spillane, vice-chairman of the Advertising Press Club, got married in University Church, Dublin, to Eileen Clarke. No wonder that by the time Christmas, 1945, came round, the Advertising Press Club and the Publicity Club combined

This photograph was taken during an Advertising Press Club outing to Howth in 1944. From left: Jack Webb, unknown, Desmond O'Kennedy, Mrs Breda Gilmartin (sister of Denis Garvey), Denis Garvey, Tommy O'Sullivan and on his back, Tommy Mangan.

The Quick and easy BREAKFAST DISH Rich in Whole Wheat Energy

There is no quicker or easier way to serve cereal than Brown & Polson's light and digestible Wheat Flakes. Equally tempting for child or adult, it's the ideal breakfast Cereal. Why? Because the way Brown & Polson make them.

"So delicious—So thrifty So light and digestible for all the family".

BROWN & POLSON WHEAT FLAKES

BROWN & POLSON (IRELAND) LTD TERENURE DUBLIN

forces to throw a party for 500. It was held in Clery's ballroom and featured a turkey dinner for six shillings. Artistes providing entertainment included The Antlers and Sean Mooney.

With the coming of peace, one of the big brands came to Ireland. Aspro had been well-known in Ireland since before the war. A pharmaceutical chemist in Lower Mount Street, Dublin, called V. E. Hanna, started packing them for local distribution in 1930, but it wasn't until 1945 that Aspro (Ireland) was set up to manufacture in Dublin. Quickly, it became one of the country's biggest advertisers, taking half pages at frequent intervals in practically every daily and weekly newspaper. Most of the copy, remembers Norman McConnell, later managing director of Aspro-Nicholas, came from England. The creative work in Dublin, done by O'Kennedy Brindley, consisted largely of cutting out the Union Jack from the British advertising copy.

When making gravy, thicken with cornflour

The result is better and more nourishing

BROWN & POLSON
PATENT CORNFLOUR

SUPPLIES STILL LIMITED

BROWN & POLSON (IRELAND) LTD., TERENURE, DUBLIN

Opposite and above: Just after the end of the Emergency, Brown & Polson of Terenure, Dublin, was advertising its wheat flakes and cornflour. Later, as part of CPC (Ireland), it made cornflakes under licence in Dublin for Kellogg's, a practice that lasted until the late 1970s. Kellogg's now imports all its breakfast cereals directly into Ireland from the UK, a trade worth an estimated £20 million a year.

'It's her complexion that puts men off!'

I'm afraid Phyllis's friends rather take it for granted that she's billed for a single life. Not that she's hopelessly unattractive. In fact, she's got such a pretty figure that many a man catching sight of her says to himself: 'By Jove, that looks like a charming girl!' But when she moves nearer, he changes his mind.

What a wretched complexion the girl's got! Muddy, blotchy—with tell-tale lines under her eyes.

'And when I try to patch things up by putting on a lot of make-up, it only seems to look worse,' says poor Phyllis sometimes.

If only she wouldn't 'try to patch things up!' If only she'd realise that a skin like hers is a sure sign that she is neglecting her system!

What a different girl she'd be if she took Eno's 'Fruit Salt' every morning!

How gently and thoroughly Eno would disperse those poisons which are spoiling her looks. How swiftly Eno would purify her blood and set it coursing healthily through her veins.

Why, after only a few weeks, that unhappy complexion of hers would be as clear and clean as flowers after rain. She'd see a new person smiling at her in the mirror. A bright-eyed, rosy-cheeked Miss Can.

But how many of us are like Phyllis — putting up with shabby complexions and trying to treat them outwardly with creams — when we ought to be treating ourselves to inner cleansing with Eno! Take yourself in hand. Get a bottle of Eno. You couldn't take a step that could do more for your looks, your health and your happiness. Eno every morning is the basis of all true beauty.

Now if only she took Eno's 'Fruit Salt' ... how different her skin would be

Have you any of these symptoms?

BAD COMPLEXION
IRRITABILITY
OBESITY
HEADACHES
DEPRESSION
INDIGESTION
SLEEPLESSNESS
CONSTIPATION

ENO'S 'FRUIT SALT'

Eno's 'Fruit Salt' is pure, harmless and perfectly natural in its action. It contains no harsh aperients—no sugar to encourage fat. Its work is simply to clear poisons and impurities from your blood—to keep your system in first-class order and your skin clear and fresh. For very many years doctors have approved it. Get a bottle to-day. Ensure 1/9 or (double quantity) 3/-. The words Eno and 'Fruit Salt' are registered trademarks.

Eno's Fruit Salts used extensive newspaper advertising in the 1930s, aimed at a female audience and promising a cure for obesity, depression and constipation.

117

BLACK & WHITE
It's the Scotch!

Established 1720
WEST & SON
Jewellers, Silversmiths, and Watchmakers. Order for Weddings, Anniversaries and all occasions.
Grafton House,
102-103 Grafton Street · Dublin

Boys' Shirts 8/11
GALLIGAN'S
HENRY STREET, DUBLIN

BM!
BRADMOLA MILLS, LTD.,
BLACK ROCK, CO. DUBLIN.

The Irish Times

CITY

PRICE 3d.   DUBLIN, SATURDAY, MAY 12, 1945   No. 27,395

CENSORSHIP AND MANY EMERGENCY RESTRICTIONS ABOLISHED

British-U.S. Attitude On Polish Crux

Allied Move To Stamp Out Nazi System

Mines Off Wexford

SEVEN V.C.s WON BY IRISHMEN

Hitler's Bomb-proof Cellar

Where He Was Wounded

RUMOURED JAPANESE PEACE FEELERS

Cabinet's Loss Country's Gain

SUPPLIES ORDERS

SALE OF LORRIES

THEY CAN BE PUBLISHED NOW—I.

Pictures That Were Stopped by the Censor During the War

Air raid damage in London. Masonry falling during bombing. St. Paul's Cathedral is in the background.

PRAGUE FIGHTING

HENLEIN'S SUICIDE

Appeal to Trade Unions

Fourteen U-Boats In British Harbours

Mayo Farmer's Will Contested

Irish News in Brief

Woman Found Guilty Of Murder, But Insane

T.D.'s Story in Appeal Against £100 Fine

G.N.R. Defence in Train Meals Case

German Prisoners To See Atrocity Films

Goering Says Hitler Refused His Advice

Camp "Break" Disclosed Invasion Plot

Bredavan Drivers' Dispute In Cork

PEACE

CAVENDISH FURNITURE CO., LTD.

Todd Burns

THE IRISH ASSURANCE COMPANY LTD.
and
THE INDUSTRIAL AND LIFE ASSURANCE AMALGAMATION Co., Ltd.

Principal Figures from the combined Accounts for 1944

NEW LIFE POLICIES IN 1944
Ordinary Branch - - - 7,107
Industrial Branch - - - 162,887

NEW SUMS ASSURED IN 1944
Ordinary Branch - - £3,151,505
Industrial Branch - - £4,495,513

Total Income - - - £2,305,886
Life Funds - - - £7,264,037
Investments in Government of Eire Securities - £4,135,717
Investments in and Loans to Municipal, County and Public Boards in Eire - £1,220,118
Total Assets - - - £7,742,939
Claims paid since 1939 - £4,920,281
Total Assurances in force - £35,219,106

THE IRISH ASSURANCE COMPANY LIMITED

O'Dearest "Peace" advertisement published in *The Irish Times*, **Saturday, May 12, 1945.**

118

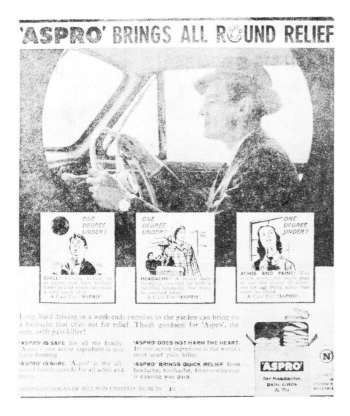

Perhaps the most talked-about party of the immediate post-war years was that thrown by O'Kennedy Brindley to celebrate its 21st anniversary. At the party in the Gresham Hotel in 1948, Brian D. O'Kennedy was presented with an inscribed walnut table by Bill Lindsay, while other tributes were paid by Michael Carr (account executive), Jack McManus (production executive) and Vera Hill (chief accountant). Edmundo Ross and his orchestra were brought over from London; no expense was spared to make a memorable night out. An excellent souvenir booklet was produced, a lavish piece of work at a time when many consumer goods were still on ration. A few copies of this book are still in circulation, giving a tantalising glimpse into advertising nearly 40 years ago. The night at the Gresham Hotel went well, except for two account losses. One major advertiser, Alec Buckley of Buckley Motors was said to have expressed disgust at his money being used to help fund such entertainment, while another advertiser objected even more vociferously to the scantily-clad dancers whom Brian D. O'Kennedy had "imported" from London. "So this is what the service fee is for," the client said.

The *Capuchin Annual* for 1946/7 carried a full page advertisement for Biros. They were recommended for needing no nibs and no blotting paper; the slight snag was that they cost 49/6d each, the equivalent of a week's wages for a working man. On the household front, Villa polish

Health care advertising was important for many provincial newspapers through the late 1940s and 1950s. "Aspro" was a regular quarter page advertiser in weekly newspapers.

Insurance advertisement, late 1940s.

Pat Conlon, who died on December 4, 1946 and after whom the Conlon Gold Medal is named.

THE DUBLIN EVENING MAIL 10th Nov.

While reading the smalls in the Press
One advertisement did me impress,
For ten shillings more
I'd have comfort galore,
For **ODEAREST** *is worth the excess.*

TRADE ENQUIRIES TO —
O'DEA & CO., LTD. WOLFE TONE HOUSE, DUBLIN

was being promoted throughout the country; a total of over 4,000 window pelmets were put up in shops in every city, town and village in the 26 counties.

In September, 1947, it was reported that luxury items were gradually coming back onto the market. Advertisements started appearing in the Dublin newspapers for Lentheric "Tweed" perfume. Domas Advertising ran 35 insertions, mainly in Dublin evening newspapers, for Kingston's ties. 13,000 dozen were sold, mostly in Dublin, but orders came in from all over the country and a number from England. Hughes Bros., the dairy firm, advertised extensively to announce its new pasteurising and refrigeration equipment, while Miwadi, in anticipation of the "Big O" campaign in the mid-1980s for Club Orange, ran advertisements in which copy read: "A for Horses, B for Mutton, C for ships, but O for Miwadi". A critic said the children might be amused working it out, but that the campaign would leave the average adult cold.

Two grocers, Eamon Quinn, father of Feargal Quinn of

SEASON'S SAVOURY SOCIAL

Clare Creamery Managers'
THIRD

ANNUAL DANCE

At Thomond Hotel,
Lisdoonvarna

SUNDAY NIGHT, 5th JANUARY, 1947

Dancing from 8.30 sharp.　☛ DRESS OPTIONAL

★ Music by Stephen Garvey's Radio Orchestra ★

CATERING BY ATLANTIC HOTEL

★ ★ ★

Where are you going, my pretty maid ?
Where are you going, my hearty ?
Right over the hills to the CREAMERY DANCE,
'Tis there I'll meet my fancy.

Tickets (including Sit-down Supper) 12/6

CEOL SIDHE, BIADH RIOGH, RINNCE AERACH

The Clare creamery
managers danced to the
music of Garvey's radio
orchestra in 1947.

Opposite page:
The Publicity Club was
revived in 1940 after
being dormant for a
number of years. This
photograph was taken at
the inaugural meeting,
in Jury's hotel, Dame
Street, Dublin, on
February 20, 1940.
*Photograph: Dublin Evening
Mail.*

A selection of early
O'Dearest mattress
advertisements. The
campaign started in The
Irish Times in 1941,
using Saturday editions.
Later, the campaign was
extended to Saturday
editions of the Irish
Independent.

Brown & Polson Corn Flakes will now cost **you** only **7½**d. per packet—a more than welcome price reduction in these days of higher prices and increased costs.

Why not join the thousands of housewives who are already serving this delicious and nourishing breakfast food? Corn Flakes are pre-cooked to an appetising golden brown, can be served straight from the packet and are most easily digested. With children they are a prime favourite.

BROWN&POLSON
Corn Flakes

FREE COOKERY BOOK—Send a postcard giving your name and address (block capitals) to Brown & Polson (Ireland) Ltd., Dept. (C) Terenure, Dublin, for Free Cookery Book—One Hundred and One Easy Recipes.

MANUFACTURED IN DUBLIN BY BROWN & POLSON (IRELAND) LIMITED

Brown & Polson cornflake advertisement, 1941.

Dick Young, who founded R. Wilson Young Advertising in 1943.

Superquinn, and Malachy Quinn, father of QMP's Conor Quinn, had an idea that helped revolutionise the pattern of post-war shopping and hence, advertising. They launched a series of shops in Dublin called "Payantake", in which shoppers enjoyed keen prices because they picked their own groceries. The traditional form of grocery selling, across the marble topped counter, was put under notice for the first time in Ireland. McEvoy's handled the modest advertising for this new idea.

Agencies were also on the move; in the summer of 1947, Domas moved from 63 Dawson Street to 76/77 Grafton Street, where it had three floors of offices. Joe Delaney and Ken Murphy hosted a cocktail party for friends of the firm from the advertising agency and newspaper worlds. At the gathering, Charlie McConnell, chairman of the Irish Association of Advertising Agencies, made a plea for more co-operation among the Dublin agencies. At McConnell's, Denis Swords fell very ill and was out of action for some time. His deputy, Gilbert Pollard, filled in for the absent manager. Denis Swords, who worked with all his papers laid out on the office floor, and who walked round Publicity House in Pearse Street with his hands behind his back, was later to collapse and die in his office. Colleagues felt that his spirit hung in the air for many months afterwards; for years, he had been the linchpin of the agency. Pearl Garvey of Janus was reported engaged, while Tony Lokko (by now with Janus) was newly married. Eoghan Plunkett joined Domas in 1948 and is still there.

1948 saw a big change in the fortunes of O'Keeffes Advertising. In existence for about 60 years, it had long been a placement agency alone, operating from offices in Dawson Street. Then it moved to cramped offices in Upper O'Connell Street, near the Carlton Cinema.

Eimar Spillane, who retired as a director of O'Keeffes in 1986, remembers that when Ray O'Keeffe, present chairman and managing director, took over the agency, it was practically on the point of collapse. He financed the take-over with the help of money from Matthews, Mulcahy and Sutherland, the insurance brokers and also a couple of relatives, one of whom was in the Dublin fish trade. O'Keeffe managed to turn the agency into a full service firm. He also managed to drag the firm into the black within a short space of time. On one occasion soon after the take-over, Ray O'Keeffe was trying to win the Sunbeam account: that firm had started as a small knitwear factory in Cork just 20 years before, in 1928. Offices were borrowed from the insurance brokers and filled with "dummy" staff. The right atmosphere must have been created, since O'Keeffes won the account and went on to create many distinguished advertisements for the garment brand.

Staff who were in the agency in the late 1940s remember vividly the day that Ray O'Keeffe walked in and told everyone that the agency had won the Irish Permanent Building Society account, then billing £6,000 a year. It was enough to warrant a week-long celebration in the agency. In the early O'Keeffes advertisements, the then managing director of the building society, the late Edmund Farrell, appeared, until a member of the agency staff hinted to him that his photograph made him seem a little too much like a member of the Mafia. Today, it is the main account at O'Keeffes, worth £2 million a year and responsible for generating about one-third of the agency's turnover. O'Keeffes is hardly likely to lose the account, since Ray O'Keeffe also happens to be chairman of the Irish Permanent Building Society.

Bill O'Donoghue was made manager of Arks Advertising in 1944. Ten years later, he started up O'Donnell Earl.

Coca-Cola promoted itself extensively to American forces at home and abroad during World War II; this was the start of the brand's international marketing. The copy line, "the pause that refreshes", had been introduced in 1929.

Buckfast tonic wine advertisement, The Irish Times, January 30, 1941.

123

Two fashion advertisements from *The Irish Times*, February 24, 1941.

In the late 1940s, well-known personalities were paid modest fees to endorse Pond's Creams, in a long running campaign prepared by Arks.

PRACTICAL AND INEXPENSIVE

Coats

FOR

Spring

DAYS AT

Todd's

A very smart and useful double-breasted Tailored Coat with half belt and high fastening. Cut on youthful lines in fine wool material. In shades of new Cherry, Grey, Saxe, Navy and Black. As sketched above. Only ... 4½ GNS

Popular Swagger Coat in soft Mohair cloth, featuring the new unpressed pleated effect at back and stitched pockets. Available in becoming shades of new Fawn, Dusty Pink, Pastel Blue, Off White, New Grey, Sea Green, etc. As sketched on right. Only ... 75/-

TODD, BURNS & CO., LTD. MARY ST. DUBLIN

fabric

begins to-day

Week

Dressy woollens . . . lovely silks and crepes . . . delightful prints! To make the most of the season's new pastel shades and vivid colours use ARNOTTS PATTERN SERVICE—the short cut to chic. Write or call to-day. Patterns free.

ALL WOOL ARGALAINE	ALL WOOL CARDELLE
54" wide. Rich all wool argalaine in many smart shades including blue, green, wine, etc. Will make up beautifully. Per yd. - - - **5/11**	This delightful all wool Cardelle is available in shades of cherry, grey, dusty, pink, tan, red, brown, blue. 54" wide. Per yd. - - **7/11** and **6/11**
LIGHT WEIGHT BOUCLE	★ SPECIAL OFFER
Here is the new light weight for two-pieces and frocks. All new seasons shades available. Excellent value. Per yd. - - **10/11** and **7/11**	English light weight boucle for coats and two-pieces. Grey, dusty, pink, dahlia, green, fawn, blue. Outstanding value. Per yd. - - - **9/11**
OFF WHITE COATINGS	ALL WOOL COATINGS
These off white coatings are smart too, and we are offering a good selection. 54" wide. Prices are 16/11, 12/11 and **9/11**	Glorious all wool coatings. 54" wide in beautiful shades of green, blue, tan. Price per yd. - - **14/6**
FANCY CHECK COATINGS	
A big range of all the smart new fancy check coatings. 54" wide. At various prices. Per yd. - - **13/11**	16/11, 15/11,

Also SILKS & PRINTS

Flowered Lingerie Crepe	Bemberg Crepe
Flowered lingerie crepe. Guaranteed washable. Pink, sky, peach, ivory. Per yd. **2/3**	Bemberg lingerie crepe. Pink, peach, sky, nil, mauve, ivory. Per yd. - - - **2/11**
Flowered Lingerie Crepe	Rimbalaine
Flowered lingerie crepe. Shades: Peach, turquoise, pink, ivory. Per yd. **2/11**	Some lovely colourings in check designs. Ideal for out-of-doors suits. Crease resisting. Per yd. - - - **2/9**
Rich Quality Crepe	Fergusons Lingerie Cloth
Rich quality lingerie crepe. Pink, champagne, turquoise, nil. Per yd. - - - **1/11**	Ask for Fergusons lingerie cloth in a choice of several colours. Per yd. **2/6**

Prints ranging from 1/- Fast colours 1/3, 1/6, 1/11, 2/3.

ARNOTTS

HENRY STREET, DUBLIN

Terry Spillane and Eileen Clarke got married in University Church, Dublin, on September 3, 1945. At the time, Terry was vice-chairman of the Advertising Press Club.

Charm in Irish life

Mrs. Cyril McCormack

There is no shortage of Pond's Powder, Pond's Creams and Lipsticks are becoming easier to secure. Soon all Pond's trusted products should be at beauty's service once again.

THE daughter-in-law of the world-famous Irish tenor, John Count McCormack, is slim and of medium height. Her clear blue eyes and perfect skin are the chief characteristics of a beautiful face, framed in lovely auburn hair. Her poised bearing gives her a quiet distinction which is most alluring.

Mrs. McCormack says, " I have always relied on Pond's to safeguard my complexion."

Pond's Creams

Still your Passport to Beauty

WHEN
IN
DUBLIN

Meet at the

PILLAR
ICE-CREAM
PARLOUR

---

*For the Best
Cream Ices*

Sundaes, Melbas,
Parfaits, Ice-Cream
Sodas and other
Ice-Cream and
Soda Fountain
Specialities

◦◦◦ ◦◦◦

Also Kinema Cups

**62 UP. O'CONNELL
STREET · DUBLIN**

HIS FIRST . . .

A KINGSTON SHIRT
MAKES ALL THE DIFFERENCE

KINGSTONS LTD. O'CONNELL ST. AND GEORGE'S ST., DUBLIN

The Pillar ice cream parlour, a popular O'Connell Street, Dublin, rendezvous, placed this advertisement in various publications in 1946.

A Kingston shirt made all the difference in 1946.

The Advertising Press Club held a gala dinner dance in the Metropole Ballroom, Dublin, in October 1944. It had an attendance of 500.

Jack McManus, the noted artist, joined O'Kennedy Brindley in 1945 after 2½ years as display and advertising manager for the Bells - Swastika laundry and dry cleaning chain. Before the laundry appointment, he worked in Arks where he produced some notable recruitment posters for the Defence Forces.

THIS IS SATURDAY!

Aw nuts! this is Saturday

how about some —

Lemon's PURE SWEETS

The Quantity is rationed but THE QUALITY IS MAINTAINED

Through the 1940s and 1950s, Lemon's pure sweets advertisements were as much a feature of The Irish Times on Saturdays as those for O'Dearest mattresses. "This is Saturday, how about some Lemon's".

Beer advertisement, 1948, when the pint was 8d (3p).

Patent medicines and remedies, similar to Angiers' Supavite, Beecham's Pills, Milk of Magnesia and Clarke's Blood Mixture, seen here, were widely advertised in the provincial and national press in the late 1940s.

In other advertising, in late 1947, early 1948, the artist responsible was told he could make the sod a little less symmetrical. The sod in question was winter turf, featured in the Bord na Mona campaign. "Nylon" was still a thrill-packed word for women, an advertising man noted in referring to a campaign for Miner's Liquid Stockings. Pepsodent announced that "it really does make teeth white", while Gibbs' SR toothpaste played on the fear of gum rot.

A quaint side-light on attitudes to women was given by Betty Whelan in 1948. She was then a director of the Betty Whelan Model School and Agency in Grafton Street and was also well-known as Pyke's Betty in the *Evening Herald*. She quoted a Dublin businessman as saying: "It is the woman in the home, the shop, the factory, and office who really matters. She is the person you have to reach with your advertising, because the spending of two-thirds of the nation's income is left to her." Added Betty: "So straight away we come to realise how valuable is the pretty girl appeal in advertising. The things which interest the majority of women are those little things which American advertisers stress so much — to be lovely, to be loved, to be young, exciting, charming, clever or dangerous. All of which lead to capturing and sustaining male interest."

you can't beat it — 8d. a pint

BREWED IN WATERFORD *Since* 1792

STRANGMANS STRONG BEER

Recommended in the treatment of
BLOOD AND SKIN DISORDERS
The Name speaks for itself!
CLARKES BLOOD MIXTURE
In Liquid & Tablets form   Of all Chemists and Stores

For COMFORT after EATING
chew a couple of
'MILK of MAGNESIA' TABLETS
By correcting acidity they give prompt relief from indigestion. 'Milk of Magnesia' Tablets are handy to carry in handbag or pocket. 6d.1/-, 2/-, & 3/6d.
'Milk of Magnesia' is the trade mark of Phillips' preparation of magnesia.

FITNESS
FOR THESE DAYS
You can help your system to adjust itself to the most strenuous conditions with 'Supavite' Capsules. They tone and fortify nerves and brain, providing the body-building vitamins and minerals needed. 'Supavite' contains vitamins A, B₁, B₂(G), C, D, E and Nicotinamide with Iron Calcium and Phosphorus ... FITNESS for these days! Just take two 'Supavite' Capsules once daily in a little water.
Angiers
SUPAVITE
CAPSULES
Price 5/- per box (15 days' supply), at all chemists.

More personnel moves were announced. At the end of 1946, the youthful Peter Owens had moved from Kelly's Advertising to head the advertisement section of Abbey Publications, just as Billy McFeely returned to the *Standard* newspaper from Abbey. Young Brian Doyle joined Domas Advertising. J. J. Dunne was appointed manager of Independent Newspapers in succession to the recently retired James Donohoe. Jack Webb of *The Irish Times* was named chairman of the Advertising Press Club in the summer of 1945. Jim Kane, later remembered as a tough, no-nonsense production manager at McConnells, joined the copy and layout department at Kennys. His earlier agency experience included McEvoys and he had worked in the *Irish Press* in its founding days. Jimmy Gooch came to the creative side of O'Kennedy Brindley; described by former colleagues as an "out-and-out English loyalist", he came to Dublin from the Charles F. Higham agency in London. At the Metropole and Allied Cinemas, Edward F. MacSweeney was appointed publicity manager, 15 years after joining *The Irish Times* reporting staff. L. J. Lewis, who had been publicity manager of the Santry Speedway, a popular sporting venue just after the war, went to work for an office equipment firm called J. A. Miller and Son selling the new-fangled adding machines. John Player & Sons promoted their Dublin advertising manager, John McNeill, to a similar post in Nottingham; he was succeeded by R. B. Cobbe. David Hayes, a brother of Jarlath's, joined CIE as assistant to public relations manager Leslie Luke.

Easy payment terms for furniture, late 1940s.

George Bernard Shaw turned advertising copywriter in 1948 for this Pan American World Airways' advertisement. Two years previously, he had drawn a suggested layout for an O'Dearest mattress cartoon. Since he didn't know what the product was, he recommended placing a "bottle of O'Dearest on the floor" in the drawing!

127

The big news of the early summer of 1948 was the decision by the Irish Association of Advertising Agencies to impose a minimum five per cent service fee. The fee was calculated on the gross cost of press advertising inserted as from May 1 that year. J. C. Oakes, the association's secretary, pointed out that some agencies had been charging ten per cent and more for some years past and that agencies were far more than bookers of space.

Tragic news during the autumn of 1948 was that Colm O'Sheehan, second son of Jack O'Sheehan, publicity director of the Hospitals' Trust, died at the age of 28. Young Colm had worked in the FOS Display Centre and before his death, had joined the staff of the newly formed Radio Eireann Repertory.

The standards of advertising continued to advance. Stuart H. Blofeld, director and general manager of Creative Art, Dublin's first large scale commercial art studio, noted that advertising in Ireland had made many advances, particularly since the easing of trade restrictions, which enabled businesses to spend more on advertising. He said that the processes and equipment used by engravers and printers were far superior and that the artist was now able to play a far more important rôle in advertising. Previously, before the war, most advertisements were purely typeset and quite unimposing. Colour and technique had also improved in the preparation of showcards,

A house advertisement for Domas published in a 1949 issue of Print magazine, edited by David Luke.

Even by the late 1940s, the O'Dearest mattress advertisements had built up quite a reputation for accurate horse racing tips. In May, 1948, Walter Mahon-Smith, then of Arks, had some good luck with an O'Dearest tip.

When W. Mahon Smith of Arks ordered his weekly 8" d/c for the Irish Times of Derby Day he optimistically tipped one for the ladies. To their delight (and his own) it came off, and one grateful punter wired The Times to record a win. Pictured at right in his Malahide studio is artist Warner, unknown by appearance to most of his wide readership.

GIVE HER FURS THIS CHRISTMAS

HERE ARE A FEW
SUGGESTIONS FOR GIFTS
OF LASTING VALUE

SILVER FOX
JACKETS from
69 GNS.

NAT. BLUE FOX
CAPES from
21 GNS.

NAT. CANADIAN
SILVER FOX
TIES from
9½ GNS.

& hundreds of
others to choose
from . . . . .

EXAMPLE
ILLUSTRATED IS A
TWO-SKIN NAT.
SILVER FOX
CAPE ONLY 21 GNS.

OTHER STYLES IN
SILVER FOX
From 10½ GNS.

HERE IN OUR SHOWROOMS YOU
WILL ALWAYS FIND A TRULY
WONDERFUL SELECTION OF EVENING
CAPES, BOLEROS & JACKETS

swears
AND
wells LTD.

70 GRAFTON STREET, AND 33/34 WESTMORELAND STREET,
DUBLIN
ALSO AT 84 GRAND PARADE (Facing Patrick St.) CORK
OPEN ALL DAY SATURDAY AT 33/34 WESTMORELAND STREET, DUBLIN & 84 GRAND PARADE, CORK

Swears and Wells, the furriers, ran 6″ double column advertisements such as the one illustrated, in the late 1940s. The advertisements, which were placed by McConnell's London office, featured a single coat in screen and line.

A POWDER LIKE STARDUST

FROM *Hollywood*

"Stardust" powder featured in campaigns prepared in the late 1940s by O'Kennedy Brindley. The model was Jean Power.

catalogues and sales material; the advent of the airbrush, allied to recent advances in letterpress and litho printing, had been a great boon. Granted, the advance of art in Irish advertising had been tardy compared with Britain and America, commented Blofeld, adding that money was the big problem. A page in a high class Dublin magazine cost just £30, hardly an incentive for lavish production expenditure. A black and white page in the American *Saturday Evening Post,* in contrast, cost £2,660.

At Janus Advertising in Middle Abbey Street, a young girl called Rena Dardis was starting to make her mark, having decided she wasn't going to stay in Guinness to collect her pension. She was to spend 15 years with Janus, then regarded as one of the "hot" shops in town. Her

129

GOOD SHERRY
is the best appetiser
—is the best natural tonic. There is no
wine showing such a delightful variety—
always insist on the best.

The Best

PALOMINO and
VERGARA of JEREZ

HEALTH
KEEPS YOU LAUGHING
health depends
on a clean system

Beecham's PILLS

Worth A
Guinea A Box

keep you "In
the pink."

A Kenny's
advertisement for
sherry, late 1940s.

Gerry Keenan-Hall,
McEvoy's manager, who
was also a noted
dramatist in the 1940s.

Beecham's Pills
advertisement, 1940s.

sister Margaret had an equally close and fruitful relationship with the agency. She was widely regarded at the time as one of the best artists working in Dublin and her work on Janus' fashion accounts, including of course Arnotts, was considered superb.

A young artist from Belfast helped to pioneer the revolution in Irish advertising art. Paddy Considine, the founder of Adsell, started off running his own studio in Belfast. There were only two major Belfast agencies, A. V. Browne and Wells, both living largely on printing and poster work, since the *Belfast Telegraph,* by a curious anomaly, gave recognition at this stage to the Dublin agencies, but not to those in Belfast. After a while working in his tiny studio at the back of the Belfast City Hall, doing illustration work, he went to Arks in Dublin for a short while and from there to Domas, where he was the agency's first full-time layout man. Previously, Domas had relied on freelance layouts, done by the Chapman husband and wife team. Paddy Considine was considered the artist to have introduced the scraper-board concept to the Dublin agency scene.

Addressing the Irish Association of Advertising Agencies, Charlie McConnell said that in 1948, the annual wages bill of the Dublin advertising agencies was between £20,000 and £30,000. The industry was reaching respectability; the Publicity Club celebrated its 25th anniversary. Speakers included the Taoiseach, John A. Costello, S.C., and the chairman of the club, George Childs.

At a monthly luncheon of the club held in 1949, Brian D. O'Kennedy, managing director of O'Kennedy Brindley, complained about Irish Government departments seeking competitive tenders for their advertising. He gave the example of an advertising agency recommending the slogan "The Country Needs More Wheat" during a wheat growing campaign. A civil servant had altered this to "The Requirements of the Country Call for the Production of More Wheat".

Still, the 1940s ended on a humorous note.

The O'Dearest mattress campaign had already been running for nearly ten years, becoming the best-known advertisement series in the country. Permission was sought to feature George Bernard Shaw in one advertisement; when he was asked, he replied, unsure of the exact nature of the product: "I've no objection, as long as you put a bottle of O'Dearest by my bedside." When the Republic was declared in 1949, O'Dearest naturally came up with a suitable limerick and cartoon. The latter showed a Colonel Blimp, dressed in plus fours and accompanied by his butler. The limerick went:

By Gad, sir, the thing is absurd,
To give the old Empire the bird.
But there's one consolation,
For in this new nation,
On an O'Dearest, I'll rest undisturbed.

The declaration of the Republic meant a new beginning for the country; that new-found confidence was also reflected in the growing maturity of Irish advertising. The media side of the business was expanding, too, with the return of sponsored programmes to Radio Eireann after the war and the launch of the *Sunday Press* in September, 1949, which broke the *Sunday Independent's* monopoly of the Sunday newspaper market among Dublin-produced publications. It was the first big newspaper launch since the *Irish Press* 18 years previously. New opportunities were fast opening for advertisers.

1949 was a memorable year too for Denis Garvey of Janus. For a few glorious weeks, he chaired both the Advertising Press Club and the Irish Association of Advertising Agencies.

Read this wonderful testimonial from a grateful mother :—

"After writing you for a sample of your food, we put baby on it, and he has never looked back. We tried nearly every food on the market, and nothing agreed with him. He used to vomit it all up as soon as he had taken it, but the first feed of Neave's put him on the road to recovery, and he is a beautiful boy now : weighing 21 lbs., and nine months old. I recommend it whenever I can, as I am certain that Neave's Food saved his life "

This testimonial is one of many from grateful mothers all over the Country, whose babies enjoy robust health and strength, thanks to the body-building qualities of Neave's Food.

ON SALE EVERYWHERE.   CARTONS 7½d.   TINS 1/10d.

In the late 1940s, Neave's Food for babies was still going strong, heavily advertised in the press, just as once it had been a main user of tram advertising. It also had a long term contract, early in the 20th century, for poster space on Dublin's Ha'penny bridge.

CHAPTER FOUR

ADVERTISERS AND AGENCIES

Preparing for Television, 1950-1960

"Advertising was fun, sometimes uproarious".

— GEORGE GAMLIN, McCONNELL'S, 1951-1957

WITH THE START of the 1950s, the stranglehold of wartime austerity started to lift. The past ten years had been a dull time for the advertising business in Ireland; economic growth was sluggish and few firms were inclined to advertise substantially. Firms like Jacobs, the biscuit makers, were actually forbidden to export, by Government decree, in an effort to build up the slack local economy. So Jacobs had no great need to advertise its biscuits in the immediate post-war period. Yet within a very few years, more changes in the media heralded great growth in advertising; new agencies and new brands came along to take advantage of the improving economic climate as the decade developed.

1954 was an apocalyptic year for the media. *The Irish Times,* so long regarded as a Protestant, Unionist newspaper, had been changing, slowly, to accommodate the realities of life in the new State. Its great, but totally eccentric, editor, R. M. Smyllie, had nudged the newspaper in this new direction, but it was still half planted in the past. In 1954, he died after a two years illness which began around the time of the great fire at the newspaper and which had effectively prevented him from taking an active rôle in its running. With his death, the old order in Westmoreland Street was well and truly over. The time was fast approaching when priests and nuns would buy the newspaper without fear of moral censure. On the evening newspaper front, the *Evening*

Herald and the *Dublin Evening Mail* battled it out, discreetly. Jack Dempsey and his colleagues at Burgh Quay, put in good heart by the success of the new *Sunday Press,* launched in September, 1949, decided to go for the hat trick of titles by launching the *Evening Press,* in September, 1954. The brash new broadsheet, edited by Douglas Gageby, later to be equally successful with *The Irish Times,* soon made its impact on a countrywide readership. On the advertising front, it was the first Irish newspaper to take the business of selling classified advertising seriously. Under Jim Furlong, scores of teenagers canvassed small ads from households all over the Dublin area. Some of these teenagers, like Dick Birchall, went on to develop their own advertising agencies. Gerry O'Boyce, later with the *Farmer's Journal* and Don O'Connell, the talented head of Doherty Advertising, were also in on the start of the newspaper.

For years, Denis "Dinny" Swords was general manager of McConnell's.

Advertisers in the other Dublin evening newspapers were canvassed, with promises that they wouldn't have to pay if their ads in the *Evening Press* didn't work. Usually they did, for the new paper quickly built an impressive readership. The *Evening Press* soon had a reputation for being the small ad medium, just as well, since agencies were much slower in accepting its worth. As it turned out, the *Evening Press* was one of the last successful newspaper launches in Ireland. Flickering television screens had been seen in American films shown in Ireland since the late 1940s; the images were so much redolent of science fiction that few took much notice. In England, the BBC had started its television service after World War II; in 1953, a transmitter was opened in Belfast, for a handful of sets. The BBC was very staid in those days and its programming dull and worthy. The Coronation of Queen Elizabeth II in 1953 was the turning point for British television; crowds gathered round every television set to watch the marathon broadcast. The public imagination was fired; pressure also began for a commercial television channel with more popular appeal. In 1955, Rediffusion was appointed the first contractor as ITV went on the air in the London area. Within three years of ITV starting transmissions, its Belfast station, where the contractor was Ulster Television, came on the air. Inexorable pressures in the Republic ensured that by the end of 1961, Telefis Eireann would be on the air, changing for ever the whole world of advertising in Ireland.

Around 1950, official figures showed that the total annual turnover of the combined Dublin advertising agencies came to £½ million. The wages bill for the Dublin agencies came to £30,000 a year.

In 1950, Youngs left Grafton Street, where the agency had been started in 1943, for Kevin Barry House in Fleet Street. Dick Young was a tenant there of Colm O Lochlainn of the Three Candles Press. In 1956, the agency had grown so much that it was on the move again, this time to South Leinster Street.

At the very start of the decade, pressure came from another quarter: the advertisers. The agencies had had their own organisation, the Irish

Early studio conference, O'Kennedy Brindley.

Opposite page: Photographs of the O'Kennedy Brindley agency in Lower O'Connell Street, Dublin, about 35 years ago.

Association of Advertising Agencies, since the late 1920s. Two newspaper bodies, one for the Dublin papers, the other for the provincials, had long been in existence. So the advertisers were the last to organise themselves; they were prompted by the refusal of the newspapers to give detailed readership figures.

Newspapers had been producing audited circulation figures since before World War I; the *Irish Independent* had led not only the Irish newspaper industry, but also that of London too, by giving advertisers totally authenticated figures for cover sales. But the advertising world, now grown more sophisticated, wanted more data, like the age groups of readers, their socio-economic rating and their distribution throughout the country. The newspapers were unwilling to supply this type of information, so Albert Price (advertising manager of WD&HO Wills), Bill Cavanagh, sales manager of Chivers' jams and Phil Ryan of Cerebos Salt came together, the prime movers in the campaign to set up the new advertisers' association. Many of the meetings took place in Albert Price's house at Butterfield Crescent, Rathfarnham, fuelled by endless cups of tea made by Albert's charming wife Eileen.

Pictures above and below show senior
account executives and their assistants

Above: account executive and layout specialist
Below: part of the studio and some staff artists

Above: the production director, D. B. O'Kennedy
Below: an artist who specialises in fashion artwork

Above: another account executive and assistant
Below: a section of the general office

Above: the space ordering and media section
Below: part of the accounting staff

Above: mechanical production executive
Below: some of the insertion-checking staff

135

McCONNELL'S ADVERTISING SERVICE LTD.
Publicity House, Pearse Street, Dublin
St Stephen's House Westminster, London, W 1

34 YEARS
IN BUSINESS
Now Finally Getting Time to Hold the
1st STAFF DINNER
PORTMARNOCK COUNTRY CLUB
Portmarnock, Co Dublin

Thursday, March 16th, 1950 B.M.
hereinafter to be known as
Thursday March 16A for Advertising 1950
(Punctuation at Diners' disposal)

Before MCDAY, old calendar—explanation
consideration and penetration overtime!

**Menu cover from
McConnell's first staff
dinner at Portmarnock
Country Club in 1950.**

**Opposite page:
In 1950 an important
international
advertising conference
was held during
London's Festival of
Britain. Afterwards
many delegates of the
conference visited
Ireland, some of whom
are photographed here
together with members
of the Publicity Club of
Ireland. Delegates
represented Denmark,
Germany, Holland,
India, Sweden and the
U.S.A. Irish hosts
include Maura Fox
(Domas), Albert Price
(W. D. & H. O. Wills),
C. E. McConnell
(McConnells), David P.
Luke (Fleet Printing
Co) and Eddie
MacSweeney (Odeon).**

There was good backing for the move: the tobacco manufacturers, Jacobs, Aspro, Chivers, Cadburys and Rowntrees were all keenly interested. So too were firms like Lever Brothers, then headed in Dublin by Tom Milner, who were sufficiently concerned about the money they were spending on advertising to want to be part of an advertisers' grouping. The first formal meeting to set up the association was held in the Metropole in 1952. A list of the subscribers, dated July 4, 1952 showed the following: Arthur E. Snow (Jacobs), Charles W. Chesson (Aspro), George Stuart Childs (Irish Assurance Company), G. Patrick L. Cook (general advertising manager, Lever Brothers), Cornelius P. Kelleher (Bovril), Richard Barton Cobbe (Players), Eric S. Williams (Birds), Victor M. Woods (Cadburys) and Albert Price (Wills). Albert Price was the first honorary secretary, while Bill Chesson was first honorary treasurer. Jack O'Sheehan of the Hospitals' Trust was founding president. The first offices were in Kildare Street and for the first five years of its existence, George Childs administered the association on a voluntary basis.

In those far-off days of the early 1950s, remembers Norman McConnell, former managing director of Aspro-Nicholas (Ireland) in Dublin and a past president of the association, the concept of marketing was so little understood that when you talked about the subject, people thought you were referring to the cattle markets! Many advertising techniques were similarly primitive. Pat Ryan, who now runs his own advertising agency in Dublin and who spent many years working for Janus, had served his time at the old Wood Printing Works — the full seven years. Then in the early 1950s, the Yendoles had just bought the print supply firm of Millers, founded in 1831. Millers was in Upper Abbey Street, not far from a clatter of advertising agencies and within striking distance of the main newspapers. Pat Ryan became manager of the advertising typesetting department. Type, he remembers, was sold by the pound weight. Besides being manager and salesman for the department, Ryan also did typesetting himself, for nearby agencies based in Middle Abbey Street, such as Arrow, Janus, Kennys and McEvoys. Three other advertising typesetters were going strong, Cosmon, Koningsveld and Zoon and the Dublin Illustrating Company, popularly known as "DICO".

Willie O'Toole, now production manager with Brian Cronin & Associates, started as an office boy in O'Kennedy Brindley in 1956: on Friday evenings, in his recollection, up to 40 printing blocks would be sent out to the provincial newspapers.

Technology may have been primitive, but advertising was still fun. Bernard Share, after a short time in publishing with the Fleet Publishing Company, run by Donal O Morain and Hugh McLaughlin, joined O'Kennedy Brindley, still based over the Rainbow Café in Lower O'Connell Street, in 1952. Brian D. O'Kennedy, the man who started the agency back in 1927, offered the young Share £5 a week, a sizable salary. "Make it five guineas a week and worthwhile," replied

the young recruit to the advertising business, with a certain
insouciance. He was paid in guineas. He remembers how in those days,
advertising executives did not have big, flashy cars; you went to see
clients by courtesy of CIE. One day, he was waiting for a bus outside
Clery's in O'Connell Street when it started to rain. He hoisted his
umbrella and a whole collection of cigarette butts and other office junk
fell out, placed in the umbrella by mischievous colleagues. He took the
"jape" in good part and went on to participate in many more
mirthmaking escapades to relieve the occasional boredom of the
advertising profession.

Bernard Share went to Australia in 1954, spent three years there
teaching and returned to Dublin and O'Kennedy Brindley. On his
second time with the agency, he remembers some of the great
personalities with whom he worked, Tony Lokko, the photographer,
who died tragically young, Val Kiely, on the public relations side and
Jarlath Hayes, the designer. One of Share's career highlights at
O'Kennedy Brindley was to invent the immortal characters of "Don"
and "Nelly" for Donnelly's sausages. For years, they bounced a neon

Winter Clothing
from Wm. JENKINS

Keep dry and warm this winter by getting value with quality at JENKINS

SHIRTS
Working Shirts; Khaki, Navy, Flannelette, etc., from **9/11**

Horrockses' O.P. Flannelette from **16/11**

SUNDAY SHIRTS
Special Value in Stripe and Dice Pattern Collar-attached Shirts with Trubenised Collar, at **13/9**

Tunic, with Two Collars, from **14/11**. Usual Price, 21/-.

BLANKETS
Lucan, Killarney, etc., FROM **54/9** PAIR.

SHEETS
TWILL **37/5** PAIR.
FOLK-WEAVE BEDSPREADS 70 x 90, **25/6**

LADIES SHOES
Our Selection is now wider than ever. Courts, Flat Heel, Slip-on and Laced Styles of every well-known brand.

SPECIAL—Ladies' Flat Heel Laced Leather Shoe, in Black or Brown, **24/6** pair.

UNDERWEAR
Gents' Cotton Pants and Vests from **7/11**

Gents' Wool Garments, Rock, Wolsey, etc., from **12/11**

Ladies' Vests, from **3/6**
Knickers, from **3/9**

OVERCOATS
A most Outstanding Selection of all types.
Men's **78/3—£16/16.**
Boys' and Girls from **32/-**

GENTS' WATERPROOFS
Double Texture, **45/8—£6/10**
Gaberdine Coats, **84/-—£14**

LADIES' WATERPROOFS
Single and Double Texture, from **39/11**

CHILDREN'S WATERPROOFS
Boys' and Girls, from **19/6**

MEN'S HEAVY BOOTS
Our reputation for the very best in Men's Heavy Boots is well maintained this year.
Splits & Whole Kip from **36/9**
Bison and Box, from **52/-**
Boot-Dry, Lee, Farmer's Friend and Guernsey Brands in stock.

WELLINGTONS
Dunlop and English Brands at Lowest Prices.

LADIES' DRAPERY
Our New Ladies' Drapery Shop is now fully stocked and the selection is unbeatable. Come once and you will come again.

THESE ARE ONLY A FEW ITEMS FROM THE BEST STOCKED STORE IN TOWN.

VALUE WITH QUALITY. **WM. JENKINS, WEXFORD** COMPLETE OUTFITTERS

Clothing advertisement by a Wexford outfitters, Wexford People, October, 1952.

An Advertising Press Club outing to the Old Conna hotel in Bray in the early 1950s. The "can can girls" were, from left: Jack McCann (Radio Review), **Tom Spelman (Philips), Gerry Quinn (managing director, Brown Thomas), Horace Denham** (Irish Press) **and Ken Murphy (O'Kennedy Brindley).**

sausage backwards and forwards high over the junction of D'Olier Street and Westmoreland Street, overlooking O'Connell Bridge. In print advertisements, grey plasticine made up some lifelike Donnelly's sausages.

Aubrey Fogarty, who founded Fogarty Advertising in 1961, had started on *The Irish Times* in the late 1940s. He started to do "roughs" of advertisements and take them to the clients, selling them the idea of the advertisement, rather than the space. Ed Carrigan, then in O'Kennedy Brindley and teaching in Rathmines, used his influence with Desmond O'Kennedy to get young Fogarty into the agency. He worked as a trainee visualiser, serving his apprenticeship under Jimmy Gooch, whom Fogarty remembers as a "diehard English loyalist". Fogarty says that during one studio argument, Gooch picked up a scalpel. "If it hadn't been for Noel Byrne, I probably wouldn't be here today", says Fogarty.

Later, Bernard Share went to Janus, where he and Bill Bolger (now with the National College of Art) formed a creative team of rare intensity. At Janus, settling into its new residence at Parnell Square, management was puzzled at the prompt arrival of studio personnel. They kept turning up for work at 9 a.m. sharp, every morning, thereby destroying a long-held and otherwise accurate belief about creative

A TRUE LUXURY CAR

IT'S THE
VAUXHALL CRESTA

From the inside, looking out; from the outside, looking in: the impression is of grace & luxury. This Vauxhall is a GENUINE six-seater with generous hip and shoulder room. And performance and economy are outstanding in a car of its class.

CURTLEIGH
MOTOR ENGINEERING CO.
32, O'Connell St., Waterford.
'Phone 4411.

FINEST TRUCK VALUE EVER!

£1120 FROM EX WORKS

FORD 'F' SERIES PETROL TRUCKS!

COMPARE THESE PRICES !

154" F500 Chassis and Cab £1120
Truck £1195
with Hoist £1275
with Tipper £1275

154" F600 Chassis and Cab £1285
Truck £1360
with Hoist £1440
with Tipper £1620

172" F500 Chassis and Cab £1245
Truck £1330
with Hoist £1400

All Prices Ex Works Cork

Only Ford manufacturing methods and Ford resources could have made this possible ! Here are the toughest heavy duty petrol trucks built today—with a range of chassis lengths—and prices starting at only £1120 ex works. Every Ford heavy duty truck in this famous ' F ' Series is specifically designed to last longer, and earn more'! There's reliability too; over the roughest country with the heaviest load you can be certain that a Ford Heavy Duty Truck will deliver the goods, and give the fastest turn round for bigger profits ! Comfort, ease of handling, manoeuvrability . . . it pays in every way to go FORD, with heavy duty trucks !

FORD HEAVY DUTY TRUCKS
save you money all the time

HENRY FORD & SON LIMITED · CORK

REVOLUTIONARY
PETROL ECONOMY !
New Minor '1000' gives
NEARLY SIXTY MPG !

PERFORMANCE TOO ! Just as impressive were the tests made with the standard carburettor needle, driving at average speeds. Though these tests were made to prove the car's performance, petrol economy was little short of miraculous.

Fitted with an economy needle in the carburettor the new Minor '1000' has been tested exhaustively and has given the following remarkable performances. Driving at 40 m.p.h.—53 m.p.g. Driving at 35 m.p.h.—54 m.p.g. Driving at 30 m.p.h.—59 m.p.g. These figures were obtained without coasting, using measured amounts of petrol filled into a dry tank and carburettor. The car, other than the economy needle, was standard in every detail. The economy needle is available to all Minor '1000' owners.

DUBLIN/LIMERICK
Distance 120 miles. Time 129 mins. Average speed 55.8 m.p.h. Petrol consumption—48 m.p.g.

DUBLIN/CORK
Distance 158 miles. Time 183 mins. Average speed 51.8 m.p.h. Petrol consumption—46 m.p.g.

INDEPENDENT PROOF UNDER THE WORST CONDITIONS

The Editor of a leading Irish motoring paper on hearing of the remarkable petrol economy of the Minor '1000' asked to be allowed to 'see for myself' ! . Starting in the Phoenix Park, Dublin, he drove across the city and back and got 48 miles to the gallon ! This was without the economy needle !

And, THIS IS LUXURY MOTORING

There's nothing missing from the equipment of the Minor '1000' — from heater (standard in all Minors !) to deep, fitted carpets, from windtone horn to Dunlopillo upholstery, there's everything driver and passengers need for comfort : plenty of room for everyone and their luggage too ! This is economy motoring you enjoy !

the NEW MINOR '1000'

SERIES II MINOR
2-door £489-10
4-door £529-10
(Ex Dublin)

(Ex Dublin)
2-DOOR MODEL £515-0-0
4-DOOR MODEL £549-10-0

JOHN KELLY (Waterford) LTD.
CATHERINE STREET, WATERFORD.

Morris Main Dealer :: 'Phone 4988

people. Management never found out the real reason for the prompt and excellent timekeeping. The top floor studio windows looked straight into the nurses' home of the Rotunda nursing home in the centre of the square. 9 a.m. happened to be shift change time and the night nurses would rush into their rooms and strip off.

If Denis Garvey, the Janus managing director, ever heard sheep bleating on the stairs, he never let on. Bernard Share and Bill Bolger were doing splendid sheep imitations. Similarly, Garvey pretended never to notice when sticky buns or even on occasion, brassieres, were dangled on lengths of string outside his second floor window, particularly during important meetings with clients.

Copywriter Frank Sheerin started his career in Kenny's in Middle Abbey Street. He had funny incidents to recall in later years, like the time Dermot Larkin appeared in the office wearing a wet suit, complete with a large fish caught off Killiney the day before: Michael Kenny was said to have found man and fish stretched out in the studio that Monday lunchtime, drying out, literally. While he was at Kenny's, Sheerin was studying at Rathmines. A lecturer there, Rex McDonnell, had just moved from Janus to O'Kennedy Brindley; he was a big help to the young Sheerin. One day, McDonnell was lecturing at Rathmines on the subject of "Print and Reproduction". He was in an awful state, confiding later that his wife was expecting a baby that day.

Contrasts in car and truck advertising from the early 1950s.

For over 50 years . . .

One of the first Austins, a 40 h.p. Phaeton designed in 1905.

Austin has meant dependability and for over thirty years the name Austin in Ireland has been associated with Lincoln & Nolan. From the famous " Seven " to the sensational new Farina-designed A 40 and A 55 Austin have produced, and Lincoln & Nolan have assembled, a range of fine cars always a little better than the rest ! As has been so truly said : " You buy a car, but you *invest* in an Austin ! "

LINCOLN & NOLAN LTD., DUBLIN

Main Dealers for Cars and Light Commercials
Cork City & County:

CROSS'S GARAGE
SOUTH MALL CORK

WHAT BLADE
MAKES YOU SMARTER
STARTER?

7 O'CLOCK,
COCK!

Get off to a good start in the morning with a 7 O'CLOCK
shave! These triple-ground blades simply glide over
your face, leaving a smoothness that lasts all day. And
7 O'CLOCK are so well-matched that you never find one
that's less of a stayer than any other. If getting dressed
is a race against time, 7 O'CLOCK are the blades for you!

7 o'clock Blades
4 D. EACH

Available in packets
of 5 and 10

Trade enquiries to Desmond Murray, National Bank Chambers, Westland Row, Dublin.

Dublin
Mont Clare Hotel

MERRION STREET,
CORNER OF MERRION SQUARE.

Comfortable! Convenient! Quiet!
Two minutes' from Westland Row.
HOT AND COLD WATER IN
EVERY BEDROOM.
FULLY LICENSED.

'Phone: Wires:
Dublin 62896.   Montclare, Dublin.
                                  (a3083-2)

The rooftop lavatory at Kenny's caused Sheerin momentary embarrassment. Only the women of the agency could use the inside washroom, while the men had to go to the roof. Sheerin was engrossed in the *Irish Independent* when a gust of wind blew open the door and he found himself facing the typists in the Indo across the street. As he says himself, shock, horror, for them and for himself.

Upstairs in Janus, colleagues played worse tricks on each other. Leaving the office at five in the evening could be quite hazardous, because an open wardrobe had been placed outside the door. On one occasion, an account executive is said to have forgotten to take off his Mickey Mouse ears when seeing a client. "It was all good fun, but it seemed to have faded away with the start of television," reflects Bernard Share now. The atmosphere in Janus, on a creative "high", was far more relaxed than at O'Kennedy Brindley. Janus had tremendous staff parties; O'Kennedy Brindley held rather more formal annual staff dinners, where the placing of people was of the utmost importance. If you were seated near the door, you were quite literally on the way out. One senior executive found himself at one of these dinners perilously close to the restaurant entrance, with the top table far removed, hazy in the distance. Soon afterwards, this top man parted company with O'Kennedy Brindley.

Stephen O'Flaherty created a minor sensation in the motoring world of 1950: he launched the Volkswagen on an unsuspecting Irish market. He had been working for McCairn's Motors, but in 1949, despite many doubts in his mind, signed the Volkswagen franchise for Britain and Ireland. Initially, the first of the ugly German cars were assembled at premises at Shelbourne Road, Ballsbridge. The marque

Friendly, open-fire appearance
with real 'central-heating'
comfort!

Whether you leave the
doors of the Rayburn
Room Heater open, to
enjoy the cheer and glow
of an open fire, or closed,
it gives on warming your
room by convection.

The Rayburn Room Heater takes in air at
the bottom, heats it, sends it out again as a
warm air stream which penetrates to every
corner of the room until you are surrounded by warmth. The fire need never go
out . . . you can let it burn all winter long
if you like and still save fuel! Turf gives
excellent results, and compared with an ordinary fire, the Rayburn gets at least twice as much heat out of every shovelful
of fuel. Dimensions: only 23¼" high; 18" wide; 12½" deep. See
it at your nearest Waterford Foundry dealer.

RAYBURN
ROOM HEATER

Burns beautifully on turf!

Irish made throughout by the
Waterford Foundry—a subsidiary company
of Mosser-Waterford Ironfounders Ltd.

To: Waterford Foundry Information Centre, 71 Nassau St., Dublin.
Please send me all details of the Rayburn Room Heater.

NAME
ADDRESS
ME

GLOW
on your way with
BOVRIL

The concentrated goodness of Beef

It's cold and wet out . . . you've
promised to visit friends—but
your hot Bovril keeps you glowing
cheerfully. Bovril is concentrated
beefy goodness . . . it takes 2¼ lbs.
of prime lean beef to make one
4-oz. bottle of Bovril.

The beef in Bovril livens up your appetite
and aids your digestion. Bovril builds up
your resistance to ills and chills and helps
you to come well through the winter.

IN BOTTLES: 1 oz : 2 oz : 4 oz : 8 oz : 16 oz   (a18-1)

Who runs most risk?

"The soldier, of course," you'd say. But
you'd be wrong. The baby has far more
enemies. Millions of them, in fact. And he
has less protection.

Wherever there is a trace of dirt—on face
or hands, on clothes, on floors or toys—
there disease germs breed in millions,
waiting to pounce on your baby. And only
you can protect him.

Where there is dirt there is danger of disease.

Cleanliness is the surest protection. Therefore, for your baby's sake, make
"cleanliness" your watchword.

Hands and faces must be washed regularly,
and *always* before meals. Make it a rule
to wash your own hands *always* before
touching food. Keep clothes clean. And
see that floors where children creep and
play, are washed regularly and
thoroughly.

THERE'S DANGER IN DIRT

but *CLEANLINESS means safety*

There's
Danger
in Dirt

Issued by the Women's National Health Association of Ireland (Inc.)

was launched at the Shelbourne Hotel, Dublin, in October, 1950. The 22 horse power car cost £365 for the cloth upholstered version, while leatherette covered seats cost an extra £20. Some advertising by O'Kennedy Brindley helped the launch — the reliability of the car did the rest. There were some 60,000 cars on the road, less than ten per cent of today's car population in the Republic and petrol cost 2/9¾d (14p) a gallon.

In 1951, W & C McDonnell opened its new factory in Drogheda, first making margarine and then a wide range of convenience foods. Not long after, Mitchelstown Creameries, an early user of radio, launched new products. Calvita was a mild cheese: the campaign's copyline was "Slim, trim and brimful of energy". Galtee was a stronger cheese, using a boxer in some of its designs.

Opposite page:

Razor blade advertisement, 1952.

Hotel advertisement, 1952.

Solid fuel stoves are now back in fashion: in the 1950s, Rayburn, made by Waterford Foundry, was the brand leader.

Bovril advertisement, 1952.

Forerunner of Health Education Bureau advertising: the Women's National Health Association of Ireland published this advertisement in the early 1950s.

At the Advertising Press Club Christmas party, 1952, Maura Fox (honorary secretary, AP Club) with Gordon Clark.

Irish Advertising Conference

CORK 1952.

REGISTERED DELEGATES

The number before each Delegate's name is the registration number.
This is also the mail box number.

37	Allen, W. E. D.	41	McGuire, Senator E. A.
38	Allen, Mrs. W. E. D.	36	McKay, W. F.
54	Boll, C.	15	MacSweeney, E. F.
22	Bergin, W. J.	16	MacSweeney, Mrs. E. F.
80	Bergin, Mrs. W. J.	2	Maguire, K. C.
39	Busteed, Professor J.	23	Mahon-Smith, W.
21	Byrne, B.	55	Malone, D.
5	Clancy, J. B.	60	Mangan, T. J.
44	Clarke, M.	45	Miller, M.
74	Clarke, Mrs. M.	50	Mullen, F. J.
30	Cook, G. P. L.	8	Murphy, K. A.
79	Colley, M.	72	Murphy, Mrs. K. A.
42	Crosbie, Condr. G.	56	Murray, Mrs. L.
67	Crosbie, George F.	70	Milner, T. E.
43	Crosbie, T.	68	Nolan, D.
14	Dardin, Miss R.	69	Nolan, Mrs. D.
7	Denham, H.	50	O'Donoghue, W. D.
78	Devlin, L.	51	O'Donoghue, Mrs. W. D.
65	Dignam, Miss M.	28	O'Farrell, L. A.
18	Dowling, P. J.	82	O'Neill, T.
84	Fitzpatrick, P.	10	O'Regan, P.
9	Fox, Miss M.	83	O'Rorke, P.
59	Furlong, C. J.	75	O'Kennedy, B. D.
66	Furlong, Alderman W. J.	76	O'Kennedy, Mrs. B. D.
34	Geirn, A. J.	63	Padbury, F. W.
35	Geirn, Mrs. A. J.	64	Padbury, Mrs. F. W.
48	Gemlin, G.	26	Rackow, J.
19	Garvey, D. J.	27	Rackow, Mrs. J.
20	Garvey, Mrs. D. J.	25	Rackow, P. M.
81	Gray, W. J.	31	Rooney, E.
6	Gubbins, Miss R.	53	Somers, Miss E.
17	Hartnell, N. C.	49	Spillane, E.
1	King, W. G.	13	Spillane, T. D.
57	Kitchen, W.	71	Stacey, Miss W.
61	Luke, D. P.	47	Stokes, M. H.
62	Luke, Mrs. D. P.	29	Sutton Kelly, G.
46	McConnell, C. E.	52	Tate, A.
32	McConnell, W. J.	33	Thomas, A. R.
40	McCourt, K.C.	11	Walsh, J. J.
73	McCourt, Mrs. K.C.	12	Walsh, Mrs. J. J.
24	McFeely, W.	86	Hyde, John
77	McGovern, C.	87	Delaney, W. J.
85	Isach, Miss G. M.		

List of registered
delegates at the
advertising conference
of 1952 in Cork.

Major concerns, too, were becoming much more conscious of the value of advertising in the early 1950s, often led by semi-State organisations. Aer Lingus was a pioneer in the advertising business. After the war, the first publicity manager was a New York Jew called Hermann Harris, who had been a copywriter on the TWA account in New York. He stayed with Aer Lingus for six months, being succeeded by Major Eamon Rooney, brother of Michael Rooney, editor of the

Page Five

ENJOY YOUR OWN SPORT

— in the FORCES

● In the Army a soldier must keep himself physically fit. That is one reason why he is encouraged to play games. Each barracks has its own sports field where a soldier can play the game of his choice - and the Army caters for all games. If a man be keen on athletics or any form of indoor sport he will be given every facility to practice and improve his standard. The Army has its own coaches, well equiped gymnasiums and expert advice is always available for the novice.

● Life in the Army is in the main an open air life. It's a manly, disciplined life. Work in the open air, good food, meals at regular intervals, physical training as part of the day's routine, plenty of exercise - these are the things which develop a man's physique, give him a zest for living, and, in the case of the soldier, enable him to acquire that bearing and carriage which single him out from his colleagues in civilian life.

JOIN THE FORCES

Issued by the Department of Defence.

(#2590-3)

Defence Forces'
recruiting advertising,
1952.

Irish Independent during the 1960s. Major Rooney was rather a martinet, bringing military discipline to the running of the publicity department, at this time based over the "Flowing Tide" public house in Lower Abbey Street. Wags in the department said this put the "pub" into publicity as far as Aer Lingus was concerned. Major Rooney was succeeded in turn by Gerry Draper, who later moved high up the management ladder at British Airways.

Some of the very earliest holiday advertising in Ireland was created by Aer Lingus, for companies selling package holidays did not start up until the early 1960s, notably Joe Walsh Tours, begun in 1961. In 1951, a very early holiday advertising campaign mounted by Aer Lingus ran into mild censorship problems. Frank Fitzpatrick, then a youngster at the airline, remembers that Gerry Draper insisted that all models had to wear one piece swimsuits. The bikini had been invented in 1946, but took a further 20 years to gain acceptance in Ireland. While advertising was starting to come of age in Ireland, young talent was flowing out of the country. Wave after wave of emigration bled the country of young people in the late 1940s and through the dreary days of the 1950s. The biggest queues in the Dublin area were to be found each night at the Dun Laoghaire mailboat departures. Jack Cronin, now director of European operations for J. Walter Thompson, a native of Charleville, Co. Cork, worked on the *Limerick Chronicle* between 1951 and 1953, for the grand sum of £1 a week. While there, he came to the realisation that he could make far more money writing the copy for advertisements than writing up court reports. So he set sail for Canada, where he eventually became head of JWT's operations. He is now based in London. Jack Cronin has a cousin in Irish advertising, Bill Walshe, of the Innovation Group.

The very first large scale conference ever held in Irish advertising took place in Cork in May, 1952, organised jointly by the Advertising Press Club, the Irish Association of Advertising Agencies and the Publicity Club of Ireland. The publicity for the conference said: "This is the first occasion in which the various advertising clubs and associations have joined forces to speak with authority on the problems already facing advertising in 1952." The adverse trade balance, changes in supply and demand and in purchasing power were all challenges for those engaged in the advertising business, so "Publicity Promotes Prosperity" was chosen as the conference theme.

The official conference train left Kingsbridge Station, Dublin, at 10.30 a.m. on Friday, May 16, 1952. The return fare was 48/- (£2.40) and included reserved first class coaches, lunch on both journeys and transport to and from the station in Cork. Honorary secretary of the conference, which was held at the Imperial Hotel, was Gordon Clark of Montford Publications, O'Connell Street, Dublin. The conference was opened on the Friday at 4 p.m. by the Lord Mayor of Cork, Alderman Patrick McGrath. The first business session then followed, "Advertising and the Cost of Living". It was chaired by Noel Hartnell of

National brand underwear and slumberwear advertising, 1950s.

143

At the advertising conference of 1952 in Cork, the Lord Mayor of Cork, Patrick McGrath, Brian D. O'Kennedy (O'Kennedy Brindley), W. G. King (Independent Newspapers) and Denis J. Garvey (Janus).

Scribbans Kemp was a popular Dublin-made cake brand in the early 1950s. This Christmas advertisement appeared in the *Wexford People*, December 13, 1952.

Wilson Hartnell, chairman, Irish Association of Advertising Agencies. Speakers were John Busteed, professor of Economics and Commerce at University College, Cork, Brian D. O'Kennedy, managing director, O'Kennedy Brindley and Walter Mahon Smith, editorial secretary, *The Standard*. A reception was given that night in City Hall, Cork, with a film premiere at 11.15 p.m. in aid of charity.

On the Saturday morning, the first session started bright and early, chaired by Frank Padbury, chairman of the Advertising Press Club, on "The High Cost of Not Advertising". Speakers were Kevin C. McCourt, director, P. J. Carroll & Co., T. J. Hickey, editor, *The Statist* and C. E. McConnell, managing director, McConnell's Advertising Service. The second session on the Saturday, "Aesthetics and Advertising" was chaired by Gordon Sutton Kelly, chairman of the Publicity Club. Speakers were Senator E. A. McGuire, president of the Federated Union of Employers and a member of the Arts Council, Sean McManus, managing director, Dublin Illustrating Company and Denis Garvey, managing director, Janus. The concluding open forum was chaired by Billy King of Independent Newspapers, the conference president. The formal dinner that night was hosted by the *Cork Examiner*. The Sunday programme included church services (nearly all the advertising people attended) and afternoon coach tours to neighbouring beauty spots. On the Monday morning, various Cork factories were visited. All in all, a most successful first advertising conference, prelude to the much bigger event held in Galway two

Here are some of the famous and delicious biscuits baked by

Jacob's IRELAND

Made from the finest ingredients, they are firm family favourites

KEY TO ABOVE
1. Thin Arrowroot
2. Custard Cream
3. Marietta
4. Marie
5. Lincoln Cream
6. Cream Cracker
7. Goldgrain
8. Butter Cream
9. Kimberley

W & R JACOB & CO. LTD. DUBLIN IRELAND

"Particular People Prefer"

PERRY'S
Quality ALES

IN BOTTLE
and
On Draught.

which are the talk of the country.

Brewed by: Robert Perry & Son Limited, Rathdowney.
'Phone: Rathdowney 8.

(a5399-5)

Shooting a Janus advertisement in O'Connell St., Dublin. The time 06.00 hrs., the traffic nil — 1960.

A Jacob's biscuit advertisement of 1953; the firm did not start serious brand advertising until the late 1950s.

Perry's ales, Rathdowney, Co Laois, 1952.

years later. 1952 also saw the foundation of the McConnell Award, for meritorious service to advertising, by the Advertising Press Club; Charlie McConnell had just celebrated 35 years in advertising.

That year also saw much interest in a label for a new brand of tinned steak designed by Louis Le Brocquy. Michael Scott said that he had recommended Le Brocquy "because he is one of our greatest living artists" and added that the Le Brocquy tin was selected from a shelf of other tinned products by no less than 14 out of 14 "typical men in the street". There was no mention of housewives in this piece of research!

In between the Cork conference in 1952 and the one in Galway two years later, a major graphics trend was developing in Irish advertising, one that had repercussions for the betterment of the industry that are still felt today. The Dutch artists started arriving. The man behind the graphics revolution was Tadgh (Tim) O'Neill of Sun Advertising. O'Neill, who had worked in publishing and advertising, notably Kellys and O'Kennedy Brindley, started his own agency, Sun Advertising, in 1946. His political connections were impeccable and within a few years, he had won such major accounts as Aer Lingus, CIE and Bord Failte. O'Neill came from Abbeyfeale, Co. Limerick and like other personalities from that region, such as Vincent Browne, editor and publisher of the *Sunday Tribune* and Bill Walshe of the Innovation Group, he was not only forward-looking but possessed of immense energy, although some sources say he was not good at organisation. He was good at giving women advancement, in an industry that was well disposed towards sex equality years before most other sectors of Irish business. Many now well-known people worked in Sun, Cecil Bell (who also worked in Arks and Aer Lingus and is now managing director of W & C McDonnell) and Michael Lunt, the designer. Patsy Dyke, one-time *Sunday Press* columnist and now public relations person, wife of Cathal O'Shannon, was also a Sun staff member.

145

George Gracie, responsible for the start of Guinness advertising in Ireland. The brewery's first campaign was devised in 1959 to mark the bicentenary of the firm; it was placed in The Irish Times **and cost £900.**
Photograph: Guinness group.

Arks produced this press advertisement in 1959 to mark the 200th anniversary of the foundation of the brewery.
Photograph: Guinness Museum.

Included at the 1959 Publicity Club annual ball are: Douglas Gageby (The Irish Times), Winnie Stacey (Cerebos), Mrs W. Convery, David P Luke, Mrs E. Keogh, Mrs Albert Price, Mrs Eileen Luke, Ernie Keogh (Arrow), Hilda Carron (Woman's Way), Peadar Pierce (Evening Press), Joe Bigger (Hammond Lane), Terry Flanagan (Irish Press) and Laurence Maloney.

GUINNESS IS GOOD FOR YOU

The copy department of McConnell's about 1960: from left: Niall O'Sullivan, Joan Walker and C. J. (Mac) McCormick.

A famous copyline, "You're never alone with a Strand". Advertisement in Derry Journal, 1960.

When Arks lost the O'Dearest account in 1960 it placed this advertisement on the front page of a Saturday issue of The Irish Times. The account went to Sun Advertising and later reverted to Arks.

YOU'RE NEVER ALONE WITH A STRAND

The moment you handle the packet you know. This is a different cigarette. Flip top pack. Sleek. Smart. Modern. No loose bits in the pocket. New Strand.

The moment you touch the cigarette you know. This is a different cigarette. Rounder. Firmer. Perfectly made — perfectly packed. New Strand.

The moment you draw you know. Taste all there. So smooth. So cool. Rich Virginia tobacco and millefil tipped. New Strand.

The moment you offer them you know. They're wanted. They're expected. They're absolutely *right*. New Strand.

The cigarette of the moment

STRAND
TIPPED CIGARETTES
W. D. & H. O. WILLS

MILLEFIL TIPPED 3'2 for twenty (1/7 for ten)

MADE BY W. D. & H. O. WILLS

*palmam
qui
meruit
ferat*

Nineteen years ago Arks Ltd. took over the advertising of a first-class Irish product and began their contribution to making its name as familiar as Sunlight, Bovril or Kodak. That product was a spring-interior mattress and its name was . . . . *Odearest*. In these advertisements that brilliant Irish cartoonist "Warner" first made his bow to the Irish public. It has been a story of success and Arks are proud of the part they have played in it. To-day Messrs O'Dea & Co. Ltd. have decided to hand over the conduct of this advertising to another advertising agency and we at Arks Ltd. desire to inform the business community of this fact, and to wish continued good fortune and success to a fine Irish product and a first-class Dublin firm to whom our thanks are due for their friendship, confidence and patronage over so many years.

ARKS LIMITED
ADVERTISING AND MARKETING
harcourt street DUBLIN

P.S. The same service which has also been responsible for many other outstanding schemes, is available to firms selling goods which do not compete with existing clients. It seems odd but, for instance, we advertise no motor car, no nylons, no department store.

Advertisement for Philips' radio sets, 1953.

Morris Minor advertisement prepared by Young Advertising in the early 1950s, when car tax for these models was £12 a year.

In the early 1950s, an O'Dearest advertisement was the subject of an unsuccessful libel action, brought by the English artist Bob Gibbings, who featured in the cartoon and limerick. It was the only occasion that O'Dearest advertising was the subject of such an action.

O'Neill's Christmas parties were legendary; the hospitality flowed freely. On occasions when O'Neill felt that members of staff needed a break, he was only too willing to help. One senior artist with the agency found that not only had O'Neill organised a hire car for a fortnight, but also a succession of hotel bookings round the country (all at his own expense) so that his senior executive could go off on a relaxing tour. Kitty O'Neill, his widow (he died at the age of 56 in 1967), remembers that the young accountant who looked after the agency's books was a very efficient and personable man called Charles Haughey. O'Neill was a man in pursuit of excellence, particularly in the design field. Apart from his agency, he also ran the Dolphin Studios, named after his favourite hotel, where he often entertained in splendid style. Dermot Malone, who also enjoyed this level of hospitality, was studio manager.

O'Neill, since his agency was handling the Aer Lingus account, looked to a continental airline for possible design recruits. At the start of the 1950s, there was little or no design training in local art schools in Ireland that was oriented specifically towards the world of advertising. KLM in Amsterdam was very design conscious, even at this early stage in aviation and had a large design studio. O'Neill persuaded Gus Melai to leave KLM and join Sun in 1951; he worked more or less full-time on the Aer Lingus account. Melai, who later married a German countess, and spent his time painting on the island of Ibiza. He is now a semi-invalid in Holland. While he was at Sun, he wrote to a friend, Bert van

"When I am tired of sitting at the wheel
I go inside into my boudoir on wheels,
and take a rest on my 'O'DEAREST'."

Bob Gibbings in Kerr, Van Hoek —
'The Way of the World' — West Texas

"In a caravan, writing," said Bob,
Can at times be a wearisome job,
Then it's nice to enjoy
One's ODEAREST nearby,
So completely cut off from the mob."

TRADE INQUIRIES TO—
O'DEA & CO. LTD. WOLFE TONE ST. & CAPEL ST., DUBLIN

BUY YOUR ODEAREST from
Todd Burns
MARY STREET DUBLIN

Select your ODEAREST Mattresses at LEE'S
DUBLIN (48 Mary St.)
RATHMINES
DUN LAOGHAIRE & BRAY   Edward Lee and Co. Ltd.

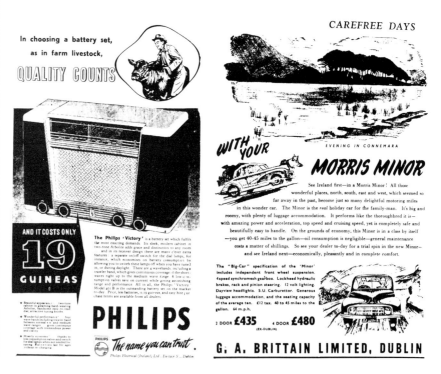

In choosing a battery set, as in farm livestock,
QUALITY COUNTS

AND IT COSTS ONLY
19 GUINEAS

The Philips 'Victory' is a battery set which fulfils the most exacting demands. Its sleek, modern cabinet in two-tone Arbolite adds grace and distinction to any room and in its receiver design there are many clever extra features — a separate on/off switch for the dial lamps, for instance, which economises on battery consumption by allowing you to switch these lamps off when you have tuned in, or during daylight. There are a wave-band, including a trawler band, which gives continuous coverage of the short-waves right up to the medium wave range. 6 low-consumption valves save on current while giving astonishing range and performance. All in all, the Philips 'Victory' Model 470 B is the outstanding battery set on the market to-day. Price, less batteries, is 19 guineas, and easy hire purchase terms are available from all dealers.

● Beautiful appearance — two tone cabinet in gleaming hard-wearing Arbolite, handsome easy-to-read dial, attractive tuning knobs.

● Wonderful performance — four wave bands including trawler band between normal s-w and medium wave ranges, gives continuous coverage with tremendous power and clarity.

● Miserly economy — thanks to low consumption valves and switch for dial lamps when not needed for tuning. Batteries last for ages without re-charging.

PHILIPS
The name you can trust.

Philips Electrical (Ireland) Ltd., Portage S., Dublin

CAREFREE DAYS

EVENING IN CONNEMARA

WITH YOUR MORRIS MINOR

See Ireland first—in a Morris Minor! All those wonderful places, north, south, east and west, which seemed so far away in the past, become just so many delightful motoring miles in this wonder car. The Minor is the real holiday car for the family-man. It's big and roomy, with plenty of luggage accommodation. It performs like the thoroughbred it is — with amazing power and acceleration, top speed and cruising speed, yet is completely safe and beautifully easy to handle. On the grounds of economy, this Minor is in a class by itself — you get 40-45 miles to the gallon—oil consumption is negligible—general maintenance costs a matter of shillings. So see your dealer to-day for a trial spin in the new Minor—and see Ireland next—economically, pleasantly and in complete comfort.

The "Big-Car" specification of the 'Minor' includes independent front wheel suspension. 4-speed synchromesh gearbox. Lockheed hydraulic brakes, rack and pinion steering. 12 volt lighting. Dayview headlights. S. U. Carburettor. Generous luggage accommodation, and the seating capacity of the average tan. 64 m.p.h. £12 tax. 40 to 45 miles to the gallon.

2 DOOR £435   4 DOOR £480
(EX-DUBLIN)

G. A. BRITTAIN LIMITED, DUBLIN

Bill Cavanagh (front row, left) with his team of sales representatives at Chivers, Dublin, in 1953.
Photograph: The Green Studio.

Emden, asking if he was interested in his job as art director in Sun. About 14 days before van Emden arrived in Dublin, Gerrit van Gelderen came over to work in Sun. Jan de Fouw, who knew Melai well, had come to Dublin to renew the acquaintance and decided to stay, building up a freelance practice. He remembers that his first major agency job was doing a 2″ double column drawing of a steaming kettle for Arks; the fee was £5. Some of the Dutch artists arrived by the freelance route, like de Fouw, while others followed Melai into Sun Advertising, like Karl Uhlemann, father of Rai Uhlemann, the Aer Lingus designer. Bert van Emden brought over Piet Sluis, still around and is well-known today for blowing a mean jazz trumpet, and Ries Hoek, now with RTE. Willie van Velzen was another immigrant artist into Sun. Of that clannish Dutch school, most stayed in Ireland and proved themselves to have a decisive influence on the future standing of Irish advertising art. Apart from Gus Melai, one of the few to leave was Piet Stroethof. He left O'Kennedy Brindley to start a photographic company and then left Ireland, for Australia, about 1974. Win de Boer only stayed a short while in Ireland, with Sun.

Iain MacCarthaigh, who worked in Sun Advertising when a copywriter or layout man could expect to be paid £13 a week, says that the Dutch designers brought a whole new concept to design. One said to him: "I have done a fantastically lettered layout; I want 34 words of copy and 74 character spaces for the headline. We have beautiful descenders on the lower case "g", so could you put plenty of lower case "g's" in the headline?"

Why a *self-winding* wat

In 1953, Edmund Hillary and Sherpa Tensing reached the peak of Everest. On June 24 that year, the Irish Independent carried a special advertisement feature on the achievement, with this advertisement for Rolex watches, devised by Janus.

OVER 25,000 FEET the effects of altitude become marked. The tissues of the muscles waste away and the mind becomes progressively more numb and dazed. A climber tends to forget details such as winding his watch; he doesn't want to be bothered with this when all his energy is needed for the climb.

There was no need for the members of the British team★ who climbed Everest to remember this detail. For they were equipped with Rolex Oyster Perpetual watches. The Perpetual self-winding "rotor," a Rolex invention, kept their watches fully wound all the time. No need, either, for them to slip off their warm gloves, which would have been necessary with a hand-wound watch.

Nor did they have to worry about accuracy. Their Rolex Oyster Perpetuals had all passed the severe tests of accuracy carried out at the Rolex factory at Bienne and again in Geneva. These include being tested in various positions and at widely differing temperatures.

On an Everest expedition, a watch must stand up to the worst conditions — extreme heat, tropical humidity, and drenching rain on the Indian plain and in the foothills leading to the mountain; driving blizzards, immersion in snow, extreme cold, and the continual jarring of step-cutting on the mountain itself. The Oyster case, another Rolex invention, is guaranteed to be waterproof and to give complete protection against the hazards of humidity, snow, and dust.

SEVEN TIMES ON EVEREST — FINALLY TO THE TOP

The story of Everest is not one of sudden achievement. Ten previous expeditions, during 30 years, had gathered experience, giving help to those following. On seven of these, climbers wore Rolex Oyster watches. And on almost every Himalayan expedition, including Eric Shipton's many Himalayan climbs,

Rolex Oyster watches have accompanied the pioneers. Rolex has become an acknowledged part of high climbing equipment.

In everyday life the advantages of the Rolex Oyster Perpetual, though less dramatic, are equally as great. The Perpetual self-winding mechanism will save you trouble, but its normal purpose is to maintain a constantly even tension on the mainspring. This makes for greater accuracy than is possible with a hand-wound watch. The movement is of such remarkable precision that thousands of Rolex watches are certified each year as wrist-chronometers by Official Swiss Government Testing Stations and Observatories. And the famous Oyster case keeps the movement permanently

The Rolex Oyster Perpetual that accompanied the victorious British Everest Expedition. Waterproof, self-winding, and a miracle of accuracy, this watch is the highest achievement of the watchmaking industry.

THE   ROLEX   WATCH   COMPANY   OF   EIR

150

was necessary on Everest

daily hazards of dust,
ater. Everest experience
hat was already certain
watches will remain
very possible condition.

*team, including Mr. E. P. Hillary,
itish Himalayan Expedition, were
erformance of their Rolex Oyster
hen, that they insisted on taking
o Everest this year.*

HIMALAYAN ROLL OF HONOUR
Rolex Oyster watches were worn on these historic Himalayan Expeditions

1933 British Everest Expedition that reached 28,150 feet.

1933 Houston Expedition that flew over Everest for the first time.

1934 Expedition to Nanda-Devi. Eric Shipton and H. W. Tilman.

1935 British Everest Reconnaissance Expedition led by Eric Shipton.

1936 British Everest Expedition led by Hugh Rutt-ledge.

1937 British Reconnaissance Expedition to Snakagam led by Eric Shipton.

1938 British Everest Expedition led by H. W. Tilman.

1939 Expedition to Karakoram led by Eric Shipton.

1947 Swiss Alpine Club Expedition to Gangotri.

1949 Swiss Himalayan Expedition to Garhwal.

1952 Swiss Alpine Everest Expedition led by Dr. Wyss-Dunant.

1952 Swiss Alpine Everest Expedition led by Dr. Chevalley.

1952 British Himalayan Expedition led by Eric Shipton.

1953 BRITISH EVEREST EXPEDITION LED BY COL. HUNT.

ROLEX

A landmark in the history of Time measurement

IMITED,   9b   LOWER   ABBEY   STREET,   DUBLIN

Gerrit van Gelderen, one of the design recruits into Sun Advertising in the early 1950s.

Another Dutchman created a big stir on the agency front, Johnny van Belle. He had served with the Free Dutch Air Force in the Far East during World War II, and after the war, when he returned to civilian life, he found himself appointed managing director of Philips (Ireland), the Dublin subsidiary of the giant Dutch electrical goods firm. This type of consumer product started to become available again, so it was an exciting time for van Belle, building up the Irish market for the firm.

A small, cherry-faced man, Johnny van Belle has always had a dashing approach to business. In 1953, he decided to leave Philips and start his own advertising agency. He says he was always very interested in modern ideas in advertising and marketing, but before he could put this particular idea into practice, he had to run the gauntlet of opposition from some of his peers in the industry. They were none too happy at seeing a go-ahead Dutchman starting up an Irish advertising agency. Pressure was exerted on the Department of Justice to try to get his work permit revoked, but happily for Irish advertising, van Belle rode out the storm. He set up shop in Parliament Street, taking the name of "Grosvenor Advertising" at random from a quick look through the *Advertisers' Annual*. Jan de Fouw remembers that van Belle's first employee was a young lad in short trousers, complete with bicycle for deliveries. He was called Jim Nolan, until recently vice-chairman of Arks, now director of the Institute of Advertising Practitioners.

The new agency started with some small accounts and lots of help from people in the media like Horace Denham, Jack Dempsey and Jim Furlong. An early account was Ryans' car hire; later came the big accounts like Hoover, Burtons, Andrews Liver Salts and Smiths Crisps. The agency pitched for and won the Condor tobacco account. And soon it handled the entire Gallaher account in Ireland. People who later became well-known in the advertising business worked in Grosvenor Advertising, Don Lemass, George Gaffney, Aubrey Fogarty, Brian Davitt, Hugh O'Donnell and Alf Humphries, who joined from McConnells and who later went to Australia. Grosvenor's

Bridie Gallagher, the singer, at the opening of the Chivers' factory in Clonskeagh, Dublin, in 1953.
Photograph: Tony O'Malley.

Jan de Fouw, who arrived on the Irish design scene in the early 1950s.

Inspecting a production line at the new Chivers' jam factory in Clonskeagh, Dublin, during the 1953 official opening ceremony.
Photograph: Lensmen.

art director was Gerry Doherty, who later set up the G & S Doherty agency.

Some sources in the industry reckon that Johnny van Belle had a slightly "anarchic" approach to business, that he was too ready to try to "poach" clients off other agencies. Whatever the truth, for a number of years, Grosvenor helped inject a new vitality into Irish advertising. After two years, it moved from Parliament Street to Leinster Street and then to premises in Fitzwilliam Square, which proved too costly to maintain. The agency was set on the path that led to its eventual takeover by Collett, Dickenson Pearce, London.

Also in 1953, Chivers, the jam manufacturers, opened its new factory at Clonskeagh, Dublin. Bill Cavanagh, sales manager, assembled his team of sales representatives for the official opening. Dressed in double breasted suits, complete with neatly folded handkerchiefs in breast pockets.

Desmond O'Kennedy probably brought in more than he anticipated when he recruited Cor Klaasen in 1956. Klaasen saw an advertisement in Holland for artists/designers for O'Kennedy Brindley; he applied and was interviewed at The Hague by Jack McManus. He was successful; Desmond O'Kennedy picked him up at Dublin airport one winter's night in 1956. Klaasen's wages were £15 a week, very good money for those times. He remembers that O'Kennedy Brindley was run very strictly — if you were consistently late, you got a note with your wages warning you of your shortcoming. When Klaasen arrived, towards the end of the wave of Dutch artistic immigration, he took a while to settle into the local ways. He remembers: "When I was first in

A Young advertisement for Irel coffee, early 1950s, when a bottle cost 1/3 (6p).

A Cadbury's press advertisement prepared by Arks in 1953. Visuals were drawn by Rowel Friers.

George Childs of the Irish Assurance Company, Dublin, was chairman of the Publicity Club in 1948/49 and one of the founders, in 1951, of the Association of Advertisers in Ireland.

Dublin, I thought all the girls by the cinema queues were whores, until I realised they were selling tickets." An apocryphal story about his digs, arranged for him by the agency bears out this sense of newness in Dublin for the young Dutch artist. His command of the English language was not too hot in those days; language in the studio at O'Kennedy Brindley tended to be rather free and easy, in the best artistic tradition. His landlady was an upright Catholic soul, who kept a strict house. When Cor arrived after his first day in the agency, she asked him how it went. He is reported to have replied: "It was fucking marvellous."

He did not get on well with Desmond O'Kennedy, whom he later referred to as "the man with the blue Gillette Porsche". Neither did he get on too well with Jack McManus, the man who had interviewed him in Holland. After three months in the agency, Klaasen was fired by McManus. After a short spell freelancing, Klaasen went to Youngs where he built up the studio over a seven year period. Then he switched to McConnell's for a similar length of time.

Cor Klaasen quickly imbibed the sense of fun that often permeated Irish advertising in the 1950s. Early in the decade, one incident provoked much mirth. It is still told with gusto by Brendan Byrne, who worked first with Janus, then with O'Kennedy Brindley for many years. It concerns a Bloomsday promotion carried out by Janus for Hely's the stationers one June 16 in the early 1950s.

Hely's shop was in Dame Street and the idea was for a "snake" of men, each bearing a letter of the firm's name, painted on their hats, to make its way down to the city centre. There was even a hat for the apostrophe. Out-of-work men were hired for this Joycean parade; the only snag was that they enjoyed themselves far too much, even at that early hour of the morning. The parade ambled down Dame Street in distinctly ragged order. Hely's name was spelled with consistent inaccuracy that Bloomsday.

Over at McConnell's, much of the hard work was done by the legendary "Dinnie" Swords, who sometimes stamped round the office, because of his lame leg, clapping his hands as he went. At other times poring over his paperwork spread over the linoleum in his office at Publicity House, Pearse Street. Charlie McConnell was brilliant on the publicity side and at glad handing people — on one occasion, remembers John O'Neill of Design and Art Facilities, who was once production manager in the agency, McConnell said to his staff: "We are now affiliated with this American agency and what's more, they are affiliated to us." On another occasion, McConnell went into the studio and chastised two of the layout artists, as they were called in those days. He said that he had seen a tremendous advertisement, very creative, a good "selling" production. Why couldn't McConnell's studio produce work of equal brilliance? Two small layout voices piped up: "But Mr McConnell, we did that advertisement." Another time in the 1950s, McConnell's devised a new campaign for Carroll's Sweet Afton

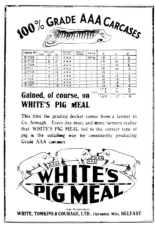

Pigmeal advertisement, Coleraine Chronicle, **April, 1955.**

155

ALEX THOM
& CO. - LTD.

PRINTERS
LITHOGRAPHERS
and BOOKBINDERS

:: This Magazine is a ::
specimen of our work

2 CROW STREET, DUBLIN
IONA WORKS BOTANIC RD.

Advertisement for Alex Thom the Dublin printers in the Dublin Magazine, **autumn, 1953.**

The 30th anniversary dinner of the Publicity Club of Ireland was held in the Metropole, Dublin, on April 14, 1953. From left: George Childs (past chairman, Publicity Club), Maura Fox (honorary secretary, Advertising Press Club), Victor Woods (chairman, Publicity Club), Gordon Clark (chairman, Advertising Press Club), Liam Boyd (TWA) and Audrey Boyd.

cigarettes. Naturally unknown to them, another agency in Dublin was working on a new campaign for Wills' cigarettes. Both campaigns used an identical slogan. McConnell's had all the blocks made and dispatched by train to the provincial papers, for in those days, weekly newspapers were an important medium for national brand advertising, before the days of television. All the blocks had to be recalled and the McConnell's campaign rejigged.

John McConnell says that the most interesting campaign he ever worked on at the agency was done about 35 years ago, for Carton Brothers, the egg firm. The campaign was handled jointly by McConnell's and O'Kennedy Brindley. Ireland was exporting so many eggs that the trade could not keep up with the demand. Egg production had to be stimulated, so a weekly news sheet called PEP — Profitable Egg Production — was produced and a campaign mounted with the slogan: "Yesterday's egg on the table tomorrow". The campaign aimed to persuade farmers to increase the amount of grain for feeding hens and old ladies in the country to sell eggs instead of eating them.

Meanwhile, David Luke, that well-known publicity personality, had occasion to ask Charlie McConnell did he really believe in advertising. Luke, then chairman of the Publicity Club, was discussing details of a forthcoming meeting with McConnell — the two men were on first name terms with each other, in McConnell's usual affable style. All went well; Luke left the room at the conclusion of the meeting, knocked on the door, returned and asked Charlie McConnell: "Do you believe in advertising? "McConnell was astounded. His agency had

Dog fanciers Jack and Alan Tate photographed in the early 1950s.

been promising copy for many days for Luke's magazine, *Print*, but nothing had arrived. It came later that day.

George Gamlin, who worked in McConnell's from 1951 until 1957, when he went to the USA, has fond memories of that time 30 years ago. He now runs his own agency in Honolulu. He was a copywriter, hired by McConnell's from Bristol because he came up with a variety of ideas for Paddy whiskey which had exhausted all McConnell's people. His fledgling idea was "At least ten years old the day you drink it". They must have thought that was pretty good. At least they hired him, for which he was grateful. Dublin was the beating heart of advertising in Ireland and Charlie McConnell was a towering figure.

Charlie was of the old school, a fine looking man, tall, handsome with beautiful hands, recalls Gamlin. He went out and entertained the clients and brought back the business. The rest of the work, other people did. The office was a collection of rooms, basements, stairs and a back alley for parking if you were lucky enough to own a car. Advertising made money and for that it was paid attention, whether anyone ever really believed it sold anything. The client was king. "Write him an idea. If he likes it, fine. If he doesn't, write him another one. Advertising was fun, sometimes uproarious," recollects Gamlin.

Copywriters came and went, mostly types from England. One man had a farm in England and wrote copy on the side. He was put on the Sweet Afton account which was driving everyone crazy.

After 12 rejections of ideas, he wrote: "The perfect smoke for the stony broke, for Christ's sake smoke Sweet Afton". He put it on John's

At the 1954 Publicity Club Ball of the Year under the chairmanship of David P. Luke (Irish Press group), from left, front row: Horace Denham (Irish Press group), Mrs H. Denham, Jack O'Sheehan (Hospitals Trust), David P. Luke, Mrs D. Luke, Brian D. O'Kennedy (O'Kennedy Brindley) and Mrs F. Padbury. Back row: Albert Price (W. D. & H. O. Wills), Mrs A. Price, Charles E. McConnell (McConnells), Mrs D. Garvey, Frank Padbury (Padburys) and Denis J. Garvey (Janus).

157

From left: Gordon
Sutton Kelly, Noel
Hartnell (Irish Tatler &
Sketch), Peter Rackow
(Cinema & General
Publicity), J. J. O'Leary
(Cahills), W. G. King
(Independent
Newspapers) and Brian
D. O'Kennedy
(O'Kennedy Brindley)
during one of the
breaks between
sessions at the Galway
advertising conference
in 1954.

desk and quit. Days started at about 9.30, working until a break for lunch about 1 p.m. Lunches were heavy, with lots of booze followed by working long into the night.

O'Connell Street was filled with people at 3 a.m. At 8 a.m. you could shoot a cannon down the street and not hit anyone. Hilarious conversations ensued with American clients, arranging early morning meetings. Charlie McConnell would say with his brogue which he loved to put on, "Ah sure, anytime at all is fine with us. 9 o'clock! Certainly, let's say *to be exact* nine ten, that's ten minutes after nine in the morning; we'll all be there." Everyone would show up about ten.

At lunch one day a new copywriter — George Gamlin was copy chief by then — told a joke to which John McConnell didn't listen. It was at the Red Bank restaurant at the bar. The new writer, a large red faced Englishman called O'Brien said to John: "well the least you can do is listen; after all I have to listen to *your* fucking jokes!" Brendan Behan was at the end of the bar and he laughed his head off. John laughed with everyone, then it was back to the grind.

In Galway during the 1954 advertising conference — J. E. McEllin (Irish Press group), D. J. Garvey, President of the conference , and Albert Price, secretary.

May Kneafsey (The Standard), **L. V. Whitehead (Incorporated Sales Managers Association) and C. E. McConnell (McConnells) at one of the receptions in Galway.**
Photograph: G. A. Duncan.

James Mansfield (RGDATA) dancing the light fantastic with one of the delegates in Galway.

Checking the delegates' papers in Galway — D. J. Garvey (Janus) and Melville (Sandy) Miller (Irish Times).

Charlie McConnell didn't believe much in research. One day a whole group from Kayser Bondor came over from England. The agency team was in the boardroom and one KB executive said: "Mr McConnell, do you have research facilities?" Without pause, Charlie said "Research facilities? Certainly." He then poked Gamlin in the ribs with his elbow and said, "George, tell them all about it." He then launched into a description of the agency's mythical research department praying that they wouldn't ask to see it. Mercifully they didn't. At the pub that night, John McConnell clapped George Gamlin on the back and said "You have become Irish by absorption."

They were good days. John McConnell drove a Jag. One December, George Gamlin and he went to Dundalk to attend the annual sales dinner of Carroll's. They got back at 8 a.m. the next day and went immediately to a Colgate Palmolive presentation which they improvised walking down Bachelors Walk. CP was tremendously impressed, they said. After that, McConnell and Gamlin went to their big lunch and then to the office to catch up.

Gamlin was one of the few Englishmen working in McConnells; he spent some years, as the creative director. He loved all the people he worked with. They were amongst the happiest days of his life. History was made. One day Shell asked for new ideas for its petrol. McConnell's presented a new theme in the early 1950s, "Super Shell". It was turned down by Shell as being too flashy and not conservative enough. In the following years, somehow it became a worldwide theme for Shell. McConnell's never got any credit to Gamlin's knowledge. Not that they cared. Gamlin says now: "I always think that the Irish had a secret cynical smile in their minds about advertising in those days. What lay behind that smile I'll never know and really don't care either. Maybe that was why Brendan Behan was laughing"!

In those dear, dead days of over 30 years ago, one of the best advertising "japes" of all time took place in McConnell's. The agency sought a top class copywriter for its Dublin headquarters — not the far-flung outposts of empire like Colwyn Bay or Derby — and advertised accordingly in London. The advertisement was seen by a lowly employee of an agency there, who borrowed a couple of sheets of his firm's notepaper, some work samples and with the help of one or two friends, concocted a job application. He was called to Dublin for an interview, managed to sail through it quite brilliantly and won the job. A condition of his contract was that he would spend a month in Dublin settling into the place, which he didn't know, getting the feel of the city, so that he could write suitable copy. A month went by; the London man really enjoyed himself at McConnell's expense. From time to time, Charlie was told, yes, the young man was settling in very nicely and what fine restaurants Dublin had, the Red Bank and Jammets to name but two. Indeed he had met so many of McConnell's staff in the Red Bank that it was almost like the agency's canteen. Towards the end of the month, senior staff at McConnell's grew a little restless and wanted the young man to start earning his living. Two and three days went by and still no sign of copy on a very straightforward job. The imposter fled Dublin, having enjoyed a month's "holiday" in town at the agency's expense.

At the Irish Press dinner during the 1954 advertising conference in Galway, Brian D. O'Kennedy (O'Kennedy Brindley), Jim Furlong (Irish Press group), Mrs B. D. O'Kennedy, Major Vivion de Valera (Irish Press group) and Mrs J. Furlong.
Photograph: G. A. Duncan.

After the big catch on the River Corrib in Galway in 1954 — Joe Clancy (Easons), Tommy Mangan (Irish Press), Hugh Walker (J. Walter Thompson, London) and Kay O'Neill (Agricultural Ireland).

In Galway during the advertising conference, Mrs J. J. Walsh, J. J. Walsh (Munster Express) and Nell O'Reilly (Connacht Tribune).

John Hickey (Connacht Tribune), **Nell O'Reilly** (Connacht Tribune) with **Mrs Hickey and Leo O'Farrell (Rumble Crowther & Nicholas, London).**

At the Galway 1954 advertising conference opening session: From left: **Thomas Milner (Esso), David P. Luke,** (chairman, **Publicity Club of Ireland and** Irish Press **group), Albert Price, (hon. secretary, Publicity Club of Ireland and W. D. & H. O. Wills), Alderman J. Owens, Mayor of Galway, Denis J. Garvey,** conference president (**Janus**), **William G. King (Independent Newspapers), Frank W. Padbury (Padburys), Horace C. Denham** (chairman, **Advertising Press Club and** Irish Press **group), and Arthur R. Thomas** (The Irish Times**).** Included in the background: **W. H. Orr (Lever Bros.), Nell O'Reilly** (Connacht Tribune**), Gordon Clark (Montford Publications), Terry Spillane** (Irish Hardware & Allied Trader) **and Walter Mahon-Smith** (The Standard).

163

In Galway during the advertising conference — Maymay Dignam (Padburys), D. J. Garvey, President of the conference (Janus) and Albert Price (W. D. & H. O. Wills).

The support of women in advertising at the 1954 conference in Galway was evident with this attendance: Rena Dardis (Janus), Maymay Dignam (Padburys), Elizabeth Somers (Sun), Maura Fox (Domas), Winnie Stacey (then IPA, London), Mrs L. Murray (Woman's Life), May Kneafsey (The Standard), Ita Hynes (Sunday Independent), Eithne McBrien (O'Kennedy Brindley), and Nell O'Reilly (Connacht Tribune). *Photograph: The Irish Times.*

At O'Kennedy Brindley, an artist called Willie Curran had an amazing ability to hand draw the most intricate lettering — any typeface, any point size could be drawn freehand by Willie with great dexterity. By about 1956, the first Letraset began to trickle in to the Dublin agencies; the skills of hand lettering started to become redundant. Jack Tate in Arks often used to reminisce about the days of hand-drawn lettering to younger members of staff in the agency; even 25 years ago, not all knew exactly what he was on about. Rena Dardis, who worked in Janus until 1959, when she went to O'Kennedy Brindley, remembers how the Arnotts' advertisements used to be 8" double columns; she says that when she increased the space to 11" x three columns, it was quite traumatic for Arnotts.

Her sister Margaret was the most prominent fashion designer in the late 1940s and through the 1950s. Also outstanding as freelance fashion designers were Jack and Eileen Chapman. Rena Dardis remembers well the time she persuaded Sloweys to have a full page for just one dress in both *The Irish Times* and the *Irish Independent,* in the early 1950s. The impact of such an advertisement created a colossal sensation at the time and Sloweys reported a big increase in sales as a direct result.

At the same time, a more down to earth advertising campaign was being run by the Department of Health. In the early 1950s, tuberculosis was still a major scourge. To try and prevent the spread of the disease, the department ran an advertising campaign urging people not to spit in public. Advertisements were placed in buses to this effect. Not long after, Erskine Childers, who was a director of Arks advertising in the 1950s, was heard to complain that of all the

Mr and Mrs Jack Tate of Arks with Mrs Erskine Childers (right) at the 1954 Galway advertising conference.

Leo O'Farrell (Rumble Crowther & Nicholas of London) decides to purchase a hen during a break in the Galway conference. Jack McCann (Radio Review) **lends support.** *Photograph: G. A. Duncan.*

Government departments, only health had an effective public relations department. In the 1950s, the notion of public relations and advertising campaigns by Government departments was regarded as almost too fanciful to be true, although there were some pioneering government health films, promoted by Dr Noel Browne when Minister for Health.

1953 saw the first An Tostal, a national festival designed to lift the spirits of a gloomy nation. Terry Balfe, later publicity manager with Irish Shell, was appointed secretary and he worked diligently to organise publicity for the event. Sun's resident Dutch artist, Gus Melai, designed the symbol. Newspapers made great play of the ugly looking bowl erected on O'Connell Bridge by Dublin Corporation that disappeared speedily during the course of the festivities. It was dubbed "The Tomb of the Unknown Gurrier" and dumped in the River Liffey. Sadly, An Tostal faded out after a couple of years; today, it is only celebrated in Drumshanbo, Co. Leitrim.

Forward progress was made on another front — women in advertising. Since the 1930s, a handful of women had been working in Dublin advertising, mostly on the administrative side, although some agencies did employ women on the creative side. In the early 1950s, Janus had an excellent female artist called Kay Nolan, who died tragically young. At this time, too, Maura Fox, now with McConnell's, was with Janus as well. She was elected to the committee of the Advertising Press Club when she was just 19 years old.

It was the first time that a woman had been elected to the committee of an advertising body in Dublin. The night that she was elected, Denis Garvey got up and said: "We'll all be making history tonight." Garvey was also instrumental, in 1953, together with Gordon Clark, in setting up TABS, the advertising benevolent society that helps less well-off members of the profession. Until then, advertising people or their dependants who had fallen on tragedy and hard times had no

Menu produced for the dinner sponsored by the Irish Press **group at the 1954 Galway advertising conference.**

organisation to turn to for financial help. The death of an advertising man inspired Denis Garvey and a small group of similarly minded samaritans to get TABS off the ground. In the early days, it was designed to cover both the advertising and journalistic professions, but the journalists soon dropped out. Their own union organisation, the NUJ, was reasonably able to help such cases. The completely voluntary TABS became a legal entity in November, 1954. Over the last 30 years, TABS has been of immense benefit to less fortunate members of the advertising profession.

1954 was a momentous year for advertising. Wilson Hartnell lost the Government advertising account to Sun and the second big advertising conference took place, this time in Galway. There were also signs of encouraging developments in the publicity industry in Northern Ireland. 1954 was amazing for another reason; Irish Shell ran a campaign in Latin and no-one blinked so much as an eyelid. The

If you study dietetics . . .

Students of dietetics discovered years ago that, for genuine health-giving nourishment, cheese stands in a class of its own. People more concerned with flavour have discovered that there is no cheese made that can compare with any of the now famous three—Galtee, the cream cheese, Whitethorn, the delicious gruyere, and Three Counties, the new spreadable cheese. Remember *for health and flavour they are unbeatable.*

GALTEE. WHITETHORN
and
THREE COUNTIES
Mitchelstown Creameries, Mitchelstown, Co. Cork.

Early 1950s advertisement for cheese produced by Mitchelstown Creameries, Co. Cork.

In the 1950s, when emigration was at its height, Bord na Mona advertised extensively to persuade potential recruits not to emigrate, but to work for it at an hourly rate of 2/1. Currently, the Board is seeking to lay off about 2,000 workers.

Religious advertisements, Coleraine Chronicle, March, 1955.

REVIVAL & HEALING CAMPAIGN
HANOVER PLACE HALL, COLERAINE
Commencing
27th MARCH over 8th APRIL
Weeknights 8 p.m.; Sundays 6 p.m.

Speaker: Pastor A. D. Strathdee

Jesus still Saves and Heals—THE BLIND SEE, THE DEAF HEAR, CANCERS, TUMOURS, ARTHRITIS GO IN HIS NAME.

ALL WELCOME.

SOCIETY STREET MISSION (Interdenominational)
IMPORTANT NOTICE REGARDING QUEEN STREET MEETING
Sunday Night's Service at 8 p.m. will be held in the METHODIST CHURCH, COLERAINE (kindly granted)
LONDONDERRY GOSPEL MALE VOICE CHOIR (Leader: Mr. W. W. Leech) and COLERAINE GOSPEL MALE VOICE CHOIR (Leader: Mr. E. F. M'Dermott) will be united in leading the Praise and will also render several Choir Pieces.
The Special Speaker will be Mr. FRED J. PURCHAS, Representative in Ireland of the China Inland Mission.
Everyone heartily invited to this special meeting. Do keep Sunday night free.

BORD NA MONA
WORKERS! WANTED.

☆ **NEW INCREASED RATES**
1/8 PER HOUR FOR 48-HOUR WEEK ENABLE AVERAGE WORKERS ON PIECE RATES TO EARN AT LEAST
per **2/1** hour

THERE IS A CAREER HERE *for* **YOU**

VILLAGES ARE BEING BUILT TO PROVIDE FAMILY LIFE FOR WORKERS

ENJOY: High earnings. Opportunities for promotion. Free travel. Credit facilities. Abundant meals. Varied recreation; Football, Dances, Cinemas. High-class living accommodation. Spring beds. Bed linen.

All-in charge **20/-** *weekly*

For Details of Employment and conditions. applications should be made to: Your Employment Exchange Office or Bord na Mona, 26 Lr. Hatch St., Dublin, or, In Person, to any of the following works:

Timahoe South near Robertstown, Co. Kildare   Boora   near Kilcormac, Offaly
Ballydermot   „   Rathangan. Co. Kildare   Timahoe North   „   Enfield, Co. Meath
Clonsast   „   Portarlington, Leix   Glashabaun   „   Edenderry, Offaly
Littleton   „   Thurles, Co. Tipperary   Shean   „   Edenderry, Offaly
Attymon   „   Athenry, Co. Galway   Mountdillon   „   Lanesboro', Co. Longford

DON'T EMIGRATE—WORK AND EARN GOOD WAGES IN IRELAND

company had been selling on the Irish market since 1908, but for the following 50 years, its publicity was directed towards the motoring market and towards the market for agricultural and industrial lubricants and fuel oil. It did not start advertising for oil fired domestic central heating until 1960. In the mid-1950s, when central heating oil sold at just 1/- a gallon, Shell decided to run a campaign aimed at encouraging boarding schools, convents and other institutions to install oil-fired central heating. Since the campaign was aimed mostly at the religious, the campaign featured a figure from Greek mythology, Prometheus, inventor of fire and saviour of mankind, and ran in such publications as the *Capuchin Annual.*

A NEW STANDARD
OF WHISKEY
DRINKING

CROCK O' GOLD
The lightest, the mildest, the smoothest of them all, Crock o' Gold was produced only after 2½ years' experimental research with 87 different blends. A number of fine, rare old pot still and grain whiskeys were finally selected from the separate distilleries, each contributing in some unique way to the blend — one for body, one for flavour, yet another for bouquet and aroma — and all for great age. Gilbey's consummate skill makes every golden drop of this superb whiskey a rich experience you'll enjoy. Yes, it's true to say that Crock o' Gold introduces new standards of whiskey drinking to Ireland.

LONDON DRY GIN   GILBEY'S SPEY ROYAL

Liven up cocktail parties with London Dry Gin. Internationally known, this smooth gin has a flavour every appreciative drinker enjoys.

There's a great deal to be said for tradition, as you'll discover when you've had your first mellow sip of Spey Royal. It's a fine old Scotch Whisky.

GILBEY'S

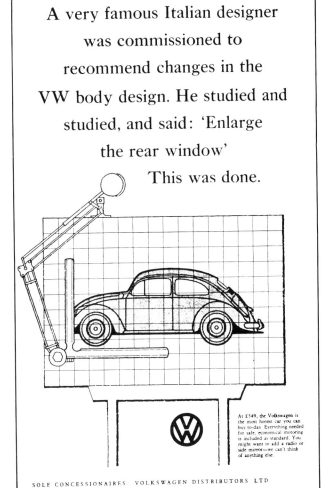

A very famous Italian designer
was commissioned to
recommend changes in the
VW body design. He studied and
studied, and said: 'Enlarge
the rear window'
This was done.

At £549, the Volkswagen is the most honest car you can buy to-day. Everything needed for safe, economical motoring is included as standard. You might want to add a radio or side mirror—we can't think of anything else.

SOLE CONCESSIONAIRES: VOLKSWAGEN DISTRIBUTORS LTD

Gilbey's whiskey and gin advertisement, 1958.

A Volkswagen advertisement by O'Kennedy Brindley for the ICA (Institute of Creative Advertising) publication Campaign, late 1950s.

GILES TALBOT KELLY P.I.C.A.

is inaugurating his own
Design Consultancy Group
and hopes to be in a position
to accept commissions before the
first of June.

Preliminary enquiries should be addressed to
FIR LODGE, *Sheilmartin Road,*
Sutton, Co. Dublin.

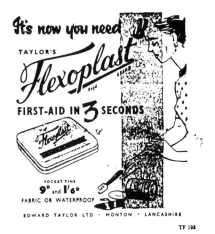

It's now you need
TAYLOR'S
Flexoplast
Regd.
FIRST-AID IN 3 SECONDS

POCKET TINS
9ᴰ and 1/6ᴰ
FABRIC OR WATERPROOF

EDWARD TAYLOR LTD · MONTON · LANCASHIRE
TF 193

Giles Talbot Kelly, then president of the Institute of Creative Advertising, took this advertisement in 1960 to announce the start of his own design consultancy group. The advertisement was published in Campaign, the institute's journal, which was launched in 1959. Stalwarts in its production included Bill Bolger, Jimmy Gooch, Jarlath Hayes, Cor Klaasen and Bernard Share.

First-aid advertisement 1950s.

Early beer advertising — Bass ran this advertisement in the Dublin newspapers in 1954.

Youngs ran this campaign for the new Austin A30 in 1954. The 4 door model cost just £449.

For Noel Hartnell of Wilson Hartnell, 1954 got off to an inauspicious start. Back in 1923, his father had won the Government advertising account; it was not especially lucrative and involved placing hundreds of classified advertisements a year, for tenders and the like, on behalf of Government departments. The contract had been placed with Wilson Hartnell through the Stationery Office. One day in early 1954, Wilson Hartnell was given 3½ days' notice of the termination of the contract. Sean MacEntee was Minister for Finance in the Inter-Party Government of the time; he was also a close personal friend of Tim O'Neill of Sun Advertising. The account moved to Sun, which at the time had such accounts as Caltex (Ireland), Sunbeam Wolsey, Harringtons and Goodlass Wall, the paint manufacturers, and O'Dea and Co, makers of O'Dearest mattresses. However, some government advertising was handled by McConnell's, where P. X. Bradley was in charge of the account. Shortly afterwards, Sun moved from Grafton Street to Earlsfort Terrace. The sudden switch of account after so long a period gave rise to angry questions in the Dail. Robert Briscoe (Fianna Fail) asked if the transfer had been made on the basis of a lower tender and if the difference was such as to justify changing from the former contractor, who had built up and maintained a highly specialised organisation specifically to service the account. Minister MacEntee replied that from the assurances given by Sun, its tender would be substantially more advantageous. Noel Hartnell was 62 years old when the bombshell dropped; he had spent 44 years working in the agency, started by his father in 1879. His two fellow directors were D. M. McCracken, a Dublin solicitor and P. J. Dowling, who had been with the firm since 1940 and who was described as a Dublin man with long experience of advertising in Ireland and England. Noel Hartnell, a life-long bachelor, who lived at Idrone Terrace, Blackrock, never really recovered from the shock and the agency remained in a doldrum until Michael Maughan was instrumental in buying it out ten years later.

The second Irish advertising conference was held in Galway in May, 1954. It was staged at the Great Southern Hotel in Eyre Square and was welcomed by Alderman Joseph Owens, Mayor of Galway. Over a hundred delegates came, from almost every agency and major advertiser in Ireland. For some delegates, the journey began when they took off from Northolt Airport, London, predecessor of Heathrow. At Galway, the president of the organising committee was Denis Garvey, managing director of Janus, described as a founder, with the late Patrick Conlon, of the Advertising Press Club in 1942, a past chairman of the Irish Association of Advertising Agencies, a council member of the Publicity Club and acting honorary secretary of the recently founded Advertising Benevolent Society. He had been joint honorary secretary of the Cork advertising conference held in 1952.

David Luke, chairman of the Publicity Club, chaired the first business session, on the topic of "Advertising Lowers the Cost of Living." Speakers were W. H. Orr, director, Lever Brothers (Ireland) and F. W. Brownlee, managing director. Orr pointed out that in 1952, total expenditure on advertising in the USA was three per cent of the total spent by private individuals on consumer goods. In Britain, the figure was between 1½ and two per cent, while here in Ireland, the figure was just 0.6 per cent, or 1½d's worth of advertising for every £1 spent by the consumer. The reception and dance that first night were sponsored by the *Irish Press*.

Clarks shoe advertisement, 1958.

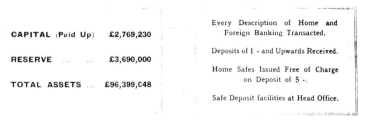

Until the late 1960s, most bank advertising was of the "tombstone" variety, ready to be slotted into advertisement features, annuals and the like. This example by the Bank of Ireland was used about 1954.

171

Jack Tate was a mainstay of Arks in the 1930s, 1940s and 1950s. He joined McConnell's in its infancy and did the same with Arks, not long after the latter agency started in Dublin in 1931. He had started as a weaver in Atkinson's Irish Poplin Mill, later moving to Dockrell's. He was a president of the Publicity Club and a chairman of the Irish Association of Advertising Agencies. He was a McConnell award winner. His hobbies were painting and golf. After he died in March, 1973 at the age of 79, an Irish Times appreciation said that "the computerised advertising game would have offered little joy to a man who was essentially an artist, an individualist, a humorist and above all a man who was deeply and warmly concerned about human relationships."
Photograph: The Irish Times.

Andrews liver salt advertisement.

Inner cleanliness comes first!

BEFORE YOU WASH your face and hands remember the kind of cleanliness that matters much, much more. Remember *inner* cleanliness. Remember Andrews.

Drink a lovely sparkling glass of Andrews and see how much better you'll feel. It tastes nice, freshens your mouth and banishes 'parching head'.

Andrews is very good for bilious headaches and indigestion. It tones up your liver. Settles any ' acid stomach ' bothers. Tactfully reminds your system to be regular.

Always keep the Andrews handy. Be sure of your *inner* cleanliness.

Andrews

Standard size 1/6d.   Family size 2/7d.

Ireland's Greatest Band Attraction

ROYAL SHOWBAND

(WATERFORD)

CORINTHIAN   Ballroom,   DERRY

WEDNESDAY, 9th MARCH

DANCING 9 - 2   ADMISSION 6/-   (Including Tax)

Derry Journal advertisement, March, 1960.

If it's worth doing at all—

—it's worth doing well!
Take the tip and go to
MOUNTJOY
MOTOR CYCLES LIMITED
18 BERKELEY ST., DUBLIN
Brindley

If it's worth doing at all —

—it's worth doing well!
Take the tip and go to
MOUNTJOY
MOTOR CYCLES LIMITED
18 BERKELEY ST., DUBLIN
Brindley

If it's worth doing at all —

—it's worth doing well!
Take the tip and go to
MOUNTJOY
MOTOR CYCLES LIMITED
18 BERKELEY ST., DUBLIN
Brindley

TO COMMEMORATE 50 YEARS OF

HILLMAN

AND 25 YEARS OF

MINX

NEW *Jubilee* MINX

EVEN MORE REFINEMENTS

EVEN GREATER PERFORMANCE

Price £635   Optional Extras: Smiths Heater (fitted), £13.

Over-riders, £4.   Rootes Rimfinishers (5), £8.

●

BUCKLEYS MOTORS LTD., SHANOWEN RD., DUBLIN.

TELEPHONE 79641.

The very first campaign produced by Brindley Advertising when it started business in 1956 was a series of cartoon drawings by the renowned artist Rowel Friers. The client was Mountjoy Motor Cycles, which is still going strong at its Berkeley Street, Dublin, premises although the founder Ted Barrett died some years ago.

A commemoration advertisement for Hillman cars.

Jack Lynch, then Minister for Industry and Commerce (left) pictured with Bill Cavanagh, outgoing chairman of the Association of Advertisers in Ireland, at the association's dinner in the Shelbourne Hotel, Dublin, in January, 1960.
Photograph: Irish Press.

173

You save Pounds on shoe repair bills with

'Dinkies'

THE ORIGINAL NICKEL-RIMMED HEELS

Rimmed heels
advertisement, 1950s.

Photographed in the
early 1950s from left:
Ernie Keogh, Maura
Fox, Dermod Cafferky,
unknown journalist,
Ray O'Keeffe,
unknown, late Jim
Kane, manager
McConnells, who had
also worked on the
Evening Press and as
manager of Kennys and
Brendan Byrne.

Opposite page:
Pictured at an
Advertising Press Club
annual dance in the
early 1950s were
1. Eithne McBrien (later
media manager, O'KB,
the first person in an
Irish agency to hold
such a title), 2. Ken
Murphy (Domas),
3. Winnie Stacey (then
IAP, London), 4. Maura
O'Neill (Janus), 5. Joan
Tighe (then Wilson
Hartnell, now Evening
Herald), 6. Brendan
Byrne, 7. & 8. Rita and
Denis Garvey,
9. Desmond
O'Kennedy, 10. Brian
D. O'Kennedy, 11. Jack
McManus (O'KB) and
12. Charlie McConnell.

On the Saturday, the first business session was chaired by Horace Denham, chairman of the Advertising Press Club on the subject of "Advertising Protects the Consumer". Speakers were James Mansfield, general secretary of RGDATA, the grocery trade organisation and L. V. Whitehead, chairman of the Irish branch of the Incorporated Sales Managers' Association. Mansfield said that the standardisation and branding of commodities guaranteed uniformity of quality. Some advertisers did however indulge in spectacular and expensive schemes which might be classified as stunt advertising. Demand created by them was transitory and sales fell rapidly as soon as the stunt was discontinued.

The lunch that Saturday was hosted by J. J. McCann's *Radio Review*. The business session that afternoon was chaired by Frank Padbury, chairman of the Irish Association of Advertising Agencies, on the theme of "Advertising Serves the Community". Speakers were Erskine Childers, T.D. Minister for Posts and Telegraphs and Jack Tate, managing director of Arks. Frank Padbury was able to indulge his life-long hobby of photography: he filmed most of the proceedings of the conference and delegates were later able to see the edited final version. Independent Newspapers hosted the Saturday night conference dinner.

On the Sunday morning, the *Connacht Tribune* hosted a coach tour of Connemara, while Wilson Hartnell, publishers of the *Irish Tatler & Sketch,* organised the lunch at the Renvyle House Hotel. Afternoon tea at Ashford Castle Hotel was organised by May Kneafsey, secretary and manager of the *Standard.* On the Monday, the closing day of the

conference, the open forum was chaired by Denis Garvey, while lunch was hosted by *The Irish Times*. It was a memorable conference, ably organised by the committee, made up of D. J. Garvey (Janus), Billy King (Independent Newspapers), Albert Price (W D & H O Wills), David Luke *(Irish Press* group), Tom Milner (Esso), Frank Padbury (Padbury Advertising), Horace Denham *(Irish Press* group), Jack Briggs *(Irish Times)*, Gordon Clark (Montford Publications), A. J. Gairn (David Allen & Sons), George Gamlin (McConnell's), John Hickey *(Connacht Tribune)*, Walter Mahon-Smith *(Catholic Standard)*, Brian D. O'Kennedy (O'Kennedy Brindley) and Mrs Nell O'Reilly *(Connacht Tribune)*. The fashion parade committee did a good job too: Rena Dardis (Janus), Horace Denham, Maymay Dignam (Padburys), Mrs John Hickey and Mrs Nell O'Reilly. Brendan Byrne has fond memories of the conference: he met his wife there.

Remarkably few of the delegates or the organisations they repre-

Neil Renton (right) of McConnell's London office, who died in tragic circumstances, with Charlie McConnell in the 1950s.

Caricature of Basil Brindley by Billy Lindsay.

sented are no longer with us. Gone to greater rewards from the Galway conference are Dr Oliver Chance (Independent Newspapers), Erskine Childers, George Childs (Irish Assurance Co.), Gordon Clark (Montford Publications), Horace Denham, Jack Fitzgerald *(Connacht Tribune)*, Noel Hartnell, C. E. McConnell, Tommy Mangan *(Irish Press)*, "Sandy" Miller (then *Irish Times*), Frank Padbury, Albert Price.

Among the organisations no longer in existence, but well represented at the conference in Galway, were Montford Publications, *Radio Review, Woman's Life* magazine, *Times Pictorial, Agricultural Ireland* magazine, *Galway Observer* newspaper, Sun Advertising. The Galway conference still evokes fond memories — it was the last such all-embracing advertising conference held, although there is talk from time to time of reviving a similar venture.

While the Irish advertising conference was deliberating in Galway, movement was discernible in Northern Ireland, where the publicity business had long lagged behind its counterpart in Dublin. 1954 saw McConnell's open its Belfast branch office, as a subsidiary of McConnell's (London). The new Belfast agency started life in Whitehall Buildings in Ann Street, in central Belfast, with just Ron Chapman and a secretary. The only other competition on the Belfast agency front then was from Wells Advertising, over 25 years in existence, and A. V. Browne Advertising, almost as long established. It had been set up by Alfred Browne, father of Val Browne, who took over his father's business in the 1950s. A chartered accountant, Val Browne worked as a travelling auditor for American Express before joining his father's agency. Then, suddenly, to everyone's surprise, Belfast got a fourth agency. Osborne Peacock of London opened a small branch office. Until 1954, that other offshoot of the publicity business, public relations, was a totally unknown quantity in Northern Ireland. Even in Britain, public relations was in its infancy; the Institute of Public Relations had only been set up in 1948. By 1954, when the annual price review was in operation and the Ulster Farmers' Union realised that it had to do public relations work on behalf of its members for both newspapers and radio. John Caughey, who had been editor of the *Ulster Farmer's Journal* since 1952, suggested the setting up of a public relations department in the union. Caughey found himself organising its work — arranging radio interviews, organising farmers' protest meetings and letting the public know all about the union. The Northern Ireland Government press office did exist, but this was the first time that Northern Ireland had an official public relations organisation. Caughey also became the first person in Northern Ireland to become a full member of the Institute of Public Relations, in 1954.

In 1956, remembers Willie O'Toole, O'Kennedy Brindley was one of the top three agencies then, the others being Arks and McConnell's. Just prior to O'Toole joining the agency, another aspiring recruit to advertising came into O'Kennedy Brindley, almost by accident. John

Hunter, founder of Hunter Advertising, had been working as a teacher in Bray, earning £3 a week. He heard that a job was vacant in O'Kennedy Brindley for £8 a week, an enormous sum of money in those days. He dropped into the agency and asked to see Brian D. O'Kennedy. He was very surprised, that day in 1954, when the receptionist actually showed him into O'Kennedy's office — "she must have been expecting someone else with a similar name for an appointment with him". Hunter was put to work helping to write radio scripts. Within a few weeks of his arrival, the firm moved to Lower Gardiner Street. In 1955, it was the first Dublin agency to open an office in Cork, run by Dick O'Hanrahan. Hunter also remembers that Joe O'Byrne ran the studio upstairs and Jack McManus the production department downstairs, with the non-specialists in between. The idea of agency specialisation was only just starting to come in. Pat O'Rourke was there, having joined the agency just after the war and who has gone on to spend his whole career with the one agency, a rare event indeed in the world of advertising. O'Rourke, recalls Hunter, was about the last of the old-style advertising men who could do everything, write the copy, get the photographs taken, do the layout and book the space. A more specialised approach came in during the 1950s and interestingly, O'Kennedy Brindley was the first Dublin agency to appoint a media manager, Eithne McBrien.

Just as John Hunter was excited by the allegedly big salary levels in advertising, even more excitement was engendered by the salary Michael Carr was said to be getting after his arrival at Arks in 1954 — all of £1,000 a year, or £20 a week. Carr had worked in O'Kennedy Brindley for the previous eleven years; he joined Arks as a copywriter

Solus lamps introduced the self-service concept in the 1950s.

Bird's instant whip was the new convenience food of the 1950s, joining the same brand of custard powder, which dates back to 1837. Now, the instant whip has been joined by such new products as mousse, while the custard is also available in ready-to-eat form. Bird's jellies were also a popular product then, as now. Maxwell House instant coffee was launched about 1957. In the 1950s, sponsored radio, backed by newspaper advertising, were the main media used to promote the products.

Bernard Share, now editor of Cara **magazine and** Books Ireland, **worked first in O'Kennedy Brindley and then Janus in the 1950s. In those days, he recalls, account executives (itself a new title) often had to take a bus to see clients.**

An unusual advertisement mock-up produced in 1956. The photograph was taken by Tony Lokko for O'Kennedy Brindley.

and then became an account director. When he came to Arks, Erskine Childers was on the board. He remembers the first Fiat cars being marketed in Ireland in 1955 — they cost less than £400. Arks had the Fiat account for nearly 30 years and Carr started off the early campaigns for the car using just newspapers and magazines.

Hunter considered himself lucky to have been able to change jobs so easily. Unemployment was high: by the end of 1956, the national level stood at 80,000 and on several occasions groups of unemployed protesters blocked O'Connell Bridge in Dublin.

Jacob's Nut Plain, wholesome, satisfying, the most delectable of flavours, 1/4 lb. 4 1/2 d.; 1/2 lb. 9d.

Jacob's Plaza Plain, packed with goodness, tempting, delicious. 1/4 lb. 4 1/2 d.; 1/2 lb. 9d.

Jacob's Nutana Plain, delicious chocolate with nuts and sultanas. 1/4 lb. 4 1/2 d.; 1/2 lb. 9d.

And she says she's strong-minded

It was all our fault. We packed a pound of temptation in a box and called it Jacob's *Patricia* Chocolates. Someone gave it to her yesterday. Till then she was strong-minded — she could even eat one chocolate and stop. Now we're rather worried. We wonder whether we should have made them quite so good, whether we should have taken six whole days to make each melting bite. Because, you see, she reached the second layer during the evening — and thinned it out considerably. And *she* calls herself strong-minded. Just think then of all the people who are *fond* of chocolates. It's just as well we have a big factory and machines that work day and night.

JACOB'S CHOCOLATES

Jacob's Patricia Chocolates, a superfine assortment, deliciously flavoured, hard and soft centres. 1 lb. Box 4/-.

Arks

Jacob's the biscuit makers used to market a selection of chocolate, in bar and box form. This advertisement was designed by Arks in the 1950s for Jacob's "Patricia" chocolates.

179

The bar of the Dolphin Hotel, Essex Street East, much frequented by Tim O'Neill and the staff of Sun Advertising and its associate company, Dolphin Studios.
Photograph: G. A. Duncan.

A 1950s advertisement, prepared by Arks for the now-defunct Bolands' bakery in Dublin.

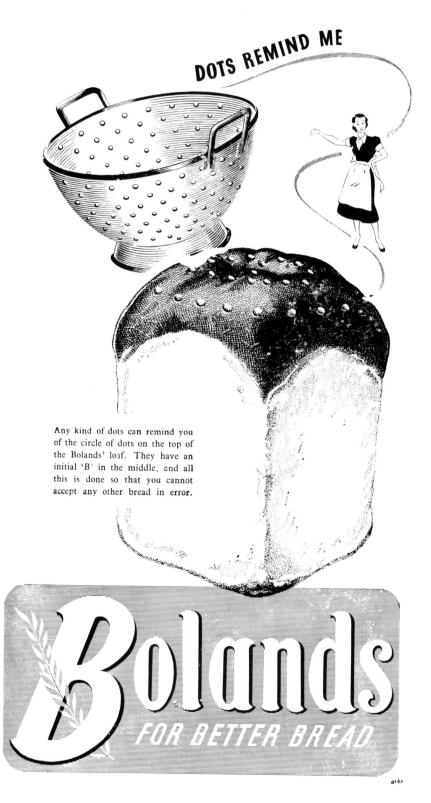

DOTS REMIND ME

Any kind of dots can remind you of the circle of dots on the top of the Bolands' loaf. They have an initial 'B' in the middle, and all this is done so that you cannot accept any other bread in error.

Bolands
FOR BETTER BREAD

arks

The big influence on Arks of course, as well as having a seminal effect on much other advertising in Ireland, was Luke Dillon-Mahon. He had worked with Mather & Crowther in London, which gave him a good grounding in the tasks of an account executive. He wanted to come home to Ireland and the departure of Bill O'Donoghue in 1954 to set up his own agency, O'Donnell Earl, gave Luke Mahon, as he was known then, the chance to work in Dublin. Jack Tate was chairman, his son Alan was also in the agency and Bill Molloy was production manager. The total staff of Arks in 1954 was just 20; there were only two copywriters, Jack Tate, often compared in style to Alastair Sim, the actor, and the newly arrived Michael Carr. O'Donoghue had taken such big accounts with him to O'Donnell Earl, such as Mitchelstown, a major spender on sponsored radio programmes. Gradually, Luke Mahon built up the business, introducing an urbane style into Irish advertising that had never previously existed. As John Hunter says: "There was no comparison at all between the Arks of 1954 and the agency ten years later — thanks to Luke's influence."

Michael Hayes, now teaching advertising at the College of Commerce in Rathmines, joined Arks in 1956 as a space buyer. He had started his advertising career with the *Southern Star* in Skibbereen, Co Cork; in his time there, not so long ago, wooden poster type was still being used, set by hand, and dance posters were big business. After four years in Clery's, Hayes went into Arks. Luke Mahon had just set up an advanced in-house administration system. The media department in those days had a staff of three; dispatch, accounts and media all worked in the same room. A bright young lad called Dick Birchall was the voucher clerk.

The year after Michael Hayes arrived in Arks, the agency did the launch campaign for Boland's Biscuits. It was one of the first large scale consumer product launches; Boland's bakery had been established as a bread bakery for nearly a century and built a brand new biscuit factory in Deansgrange, Co Dublin, offering a major home-grown challenge to Jacobs, for the first time ever.

There was no television of course, so Bolands depended heavily on newspaper advertising. "Change over to Bolands" became a well-quoted slogan. L-shaped spaces were booked in the nationals and Dublin evening newspapers, outdoor advertising, using planes towing banners, were major components in the campaign. Another big print campaign in those days, remembers Michael Hayes, was for Cadbury's chocolates, using the "Bridge that Gap" theme. Drawings of various people filling the gap with a bar of Cadbury's were done by noted Northern artist and cartoonist, Rowel Friers. The campaign ran from 1956 until 1958 and ran to a total of 137 insertions in the national press. Friers also drew cartoons for a major campaign for Churchman's cigarettes.

Another young arrival at Arks at this time was John Allen, now administrator of *Cara* magazine, the Aer Lingus inflight publication.

George Gamlin, now of Honolulu, who was McConnell's copywriting "ace" for much of the 1950s.
Photograph: Elson-Alexandre, Los Angeles.

Ron Chapman (above) and Dave Dark (opposite page) of McConnell's, Belfast. The agency opened there in the mid-1950s as a subsidiary of McConnell's, London. Later, Chapman and Dark bought out the Belfast agency from McConnell's.

Tim O'Neill of Sun Advertising with his daughters Catherine and Suniva.

He spent three years with Arks, working first as a voucher clerk, then as a production assistant, before joining Aer Lingus in the same capacity. Arks was terribly gentlemanly and John Allen recalls being summoned to see Luke Mahon, the general manager, who said: "We already have one Mr John in the firm. Could we possibly call you John?"

Frank Sheerin, widely regarded as a brilliant copywriter, responsible in recent years for writing the Sally O'Brien campaigns for Harp lager and the Guinness "island" series of commercials in 1977, has good recollections of his time at Arks. He joined the agency in the late 1950s; he says that Jack Tate was a very good-humoured person to work with and bit of a "ham" actor. Jim Nolan says that Tate never got on well with machinery; he would often drive cars with no oil. When the O'Dearest account left Arks after many years, Tate had an advertisement drawn up for the *Irish Times,* saying that Arks was now in a position to take another mattress account. Very courteous; only Arks under Jack Tate and old Etonian Luke Mahon could have made such a dignified farewell gesture.

April 16, 1956, saw the ebullient Basil Brindley open his agency in two rooms over the Lincoln Inn. The premises had been owned by Charlie Houlihan, a colourful solicitor accustomed to driving round town in a violet coloured Rolls-Royce. Brindley got the keys to the offices for £100; the contents included a typewriter, two desks and a few chairs.

Basil Brindley made his name as a sporting journalist — Jim McGuinness, then with the *Irish Press,* gave him his first "break". He went on to write five books, all on sporting themes. Eventually,

Brindley decided to go into advertising rather than follow his father into the Stock Exchange. His first agency job was with McConnell's, where he remembers vividly Denis Swords, Gilbert Pollard, Eimar Spillane, Basil Sheppard and Frankie Byrne. On one occasion, going to an advertising conference in Harrogate with Charlie McConnell, Charlie told a story for the fifth time. Brindley retorted, with the cheek of youth: "You've told me that already." Charlie replied: "If I tell a story for the 44th time, you will listen and laugh with reverence." Brindley also studied at Rathmines; he was 26 years old when he started his advertising studies there. His teachers included Ed Carrigan and Bill Bergin.

Directly after leaving McConnell's, the youthful Basil Brindley started his own agency. Recognition took two years. His first account was that of Reg Armstrong, then based in Halpin Street. For Armstrong, Brindley's launched the NSU Quickly, followed by the NSU Prinz series. Advertisements for the latter car had a humorous twist, helped by puns on the car's number plate in the advertisements: "For Reg". Reg went on to get the concessions for General Motors and Opel, which meant good advertising business for the agency. Brindley also acquired the Downes' bakery account: he had been at school with Desmond Downes, the firm's managing director. For the bakery, Brindley invented the "Butterkrust" slogan. The first two years were tough for the agency, with recognition slow to arrive, but Basil, later helped by his brother Donald, progressed well. Eileen Byrne has been with the agency since it started; she was first paid 30/- a week.

Pictured holding a gallon glass at McConnell's Christmas party in 1955 were Terry Balfe and Charlie McConnell. Seen in the mirror is the then managing director of McConnell's, John McConnell.

...957, a presentation was made to David P. Luke, vice-chairman of the Advertising Press Club, on the occasion of his visit to the United States of America to study communications after leaving the Irish Press group following the successful launching of the Evening Press. Included in the photograph are: (seated) Fergus O'Sheehan, chairman, Publicity Club of Ireland, David Luke, Mrs Eileen Luke, Michael Kenny (Kennys), Matt Kavanagh (Ireland's Own), George Childs (Irish Assurance Co), Walter Douglas (Lamb Bros.), Winnie Stacey (then IPA, London), Tom Milner (Esso), Tom Spelman (Philips), Pat Carrigan (Irish Press), A. McCabe (McCabe Auctioneers), Peadar Pierce (Irish Press), Albert Price (W. D. & H. O. Wills), Hilda Carron (Woman's Way), Eithne McBrien (O'Kennedy Brindley), W. G. King (Irish Independent), Mrs W. G. King, Terry Spillane (Irish Hardware & Allied Trader), Terry O'Sullivan (Evening Press), Walter Mahon-Smith (The Standard), Jack O'Sheehan (Hospitals Trust), Denis J. Garvey (Janus), Mrs D. J. Garvey, George O'Toole (Ormond Printing) and W. G. Spencer.

NOW I feel better, Mummy!

What a blessing to know you can now relieve children's pains with the new aspirin specially made for children by Angiers. 'Junior' contains 1¼ grains pure aspirin—the correct dose for a small child—in pink orange-flavoured tablets. Di-calcium phosphate ensures that there is no digestive upset. 'Junior' quickly and safely relieves pain and discomfort of children's ailments.

Angier's
JUNIOR
Aspirin
Specially made for Children

Angiers Junior Aspirin may be given as directed for rapid relief of teething troubles, feverishness, headache and all childish discomforts for which aspirin in this new form, is indicated. Consult your doctor if a child is in pain. FOR ADULTS. 4 tablets equal the normal 5 grain dose.

The Angier Chemical Company Ltd., 86, Clerkenwell Road, London, E.C.1. Laboratories: South Ruislip, Middlesex.

(a1111-11)

Pluvex roofed
is weather proofed

Pluvex is the roof felt that all can rely upon to make a lasting roof for sheds, summer houses, poultry houses and all small buildings. Full instructions inside every roll. Rolls contain 12 sq. yds., 36 ins. wide. When you buy roof felt from your Ironmonger or Builders' Merchant insist on getting Pluvex.

PLUVEX ROOF FELT

It's a RUBEROID Product, so it must be good.
THE RUBEROID COMPANY LIMITED

Make sure of...

WHITE TEETH

and HEALTHY GUMS

Your teeth are only as safe as the gums they grow in. Gibbs S.R. keeps teeth white and because it contains Sodium Ricinoleate guards gums against infection. So remember — use Gibbs S.R. night and morning.

Family tube 2/1

Standard tube 1/6

use Gibbs
S.R.
TOOTHPASTE

(a6085-1)

Just Arrived

CHOICE PRUNES
IN SYRUP

only 3/6 Tin.

ALSO

ORIED PRUNES

Ac 1/4 Lb.

AT THE

L. & N.
Tea Co.

We are now adding to our Stock
of FREE GIFTS.

Many useful Household Articles,
Including:

Aluminium Teapots, Aluminium
Saucepans (from 1 Book).

Hot Water Jars and Bottles, Mats,
Hearth Rugs and Shopping Bags,
Tea Sets (In beautiful patterns).

WATCH OUR WINDOW
DISPLAY.

If you don't see what you want,
please ask us. Get a Collecting
Book To-day, and

Save As You Spend

AT THE

L. & N.
Tea Co.

Cash Supply Stores,

Wexford, New Ross

and Enniscorthy.

(ijk940-1)

**IN OUR CHINA DEPARTMENT
ALL THIS WEEK.**

We have just received large deliveries of Beautiful China Tea
Services from all the leading Pot-
teries, including Wedgwood, Doul-
tons, Tuscan, Royal Albert, and
New Chelsea.

Also our 12-month Quota of Col-
lough China 21 Piece Tea Sets
approximately forty designs,
ranging from 59/6 per Set.

Long overdue deliveries of all
kinds of Glass Ware, from the
Continent have also come to hand.

TRADE ENQUIRIES FOR THE
ABOVE INVITED.

OPEN ALL DAY.

HEARNE & Co., Ltd.,

1/66 The Quay, WATERFORD

(ijk101-1)

CHEST
COLDS

Rub chest, throat and back with
Vick Vapour-Rub. Its combined
poultice-and-vapours action eases
congestion, loosens phlegm, calms
coughing.

Just
rub on **VICK**
VAPOUR-RUB

(a1114-10)

FLY

VISCOUNT

TO

GERMANY

Now you can fly by Aer Lingus Viscount from Dublin to
Germany. Take advantage of this new service for business
or holiday travel. Flights to and from Dusseldorf every
Sunday, Tuesday and Friday, and flights to and from
Frankfurt every Monday and Thursday.

DUSSELDORF

£29 - 18s.
RETURN

FRANKFURT

£35 - 15s.
RETURN

AER LINGUS

For reservations consult your travel agent or Aer Lingus,
40 Upper O'Connell Street, Dublin, 'phone 42921: 38 Patrick
Street, Cork, 'phone 24331; or at Cruises Hotel, Limerick,
'phone 556.

Opposite page:
Selection of
advertisements from
the Wexford People,
1952.

Aer Lingus to Germany
advertisement.

185

In 1957, Ron Chapman, then managing director of McConnell's in Belfast, was instrumental in setting up the Publicity Association of Northern Ireland. At the time, there was no forum in the North for advertising people to meet up socially, so Chapman and two artists, Gary Gilmore and Bob Beattie, invited everyone they knew in the publicity business to attend a dinner at the Orchid Room in the Midland Hotel, Belfast. About 50 people turned up and an *ad hoc* committee was formed, of which Ron Chapman was first secretary. He is now an honorary life member.

Another agency in town occupied a lowly ranking in the 1950s but was clearly destined for greater prominence: Arrow. It had been started just over 30 years previously by Harry O'Brien, who had learned his craft in McConnell's in the 1920s. He was the uncle of Ernie Keogh, who bought out the agency in the mid-1950s, along with his great friend, Dermod Cafferky. It was said at the time that the purchase was completed with a threat hanging in the background that the two young men would leave with many of the accounts.

At Domas, similar "splits" were developing. The agency was well-regarded in the 1950s; it trained more of the big names in present day Irish advertising than any other single agency. Peter Owens was there as managing director; he says that in 1956, he got an offer to head up the reorganised creative area of Domas. "I brought Domas from being a very small agency to fourth or fifth in Ireland", he claims. He went to the USA in 1958 and 1959 and when Domas was reluctant to have him back, he started his own agency. Ken Murphy, previously with Janus, later with O'Kennedy Brindley, was in Domas from the start as general manager. Paddy Considine, who started Adsell in 1963, spent

Brooklax was a regular advertiser during the 1950s.

A Christmas party organised by Sun Advertising in the 1950s. From left: Patsy Dyke, Jan de Fouw, Gerrit van Gelderen and Michael Gorman.

FRYS
CHOCOLATE CREAM

Here it is again, the same delicious flavour, the same high quality . . . . living up to Fry's tradition—but wrapped for protection in silver foil.

A Fry's chocolate advertisement, 1950s.

A 1950s party held by Sun Advertising. From left: Sir Raymond Grace (The Irish Times), Cathal O'Shannon, Gerrit van Gelderen, Tony Kelly, Helen Redmond and Mike Butt.

the previous ten years with Domas, ending up as joint managing director with Joe Delaney after the departure of Peter Owens. Brendan White, later to start his own agency, was also a "graduate" of Domas. Frank Loughrey, from Belfast, worked in Domas 25 years ago. He recalls clearly the personalities of the agency, including Paddy Schofield, there as an account executive and Bill Kampf, the production manager, who died young.

Later, Michael Maughan and Sean O Bradaigh, both of whom worked in Domas, bought out Wilson Hartnell from Noel Hartnell. Accounts worth some £70,000 moved from Domas to Wilson Hartnell. Domas, now a much smaller agency than its heyday in the late 1950s, early 1960s, when it employed about 40 people, served as a real forcing ground for Irish advertising talent. Joe Tiernan, who joined the agency in 1962 and took over after the death of Joe Delaney in the early 1970s recalls "Domas was at its height when it moved from Grafton Street to Granite House in Pembroke Road, Ballsbridge, in 1958." Michael Maughan was to spend a total of seven years in Domas around this time; he began in the voucher department working with Agnes Russell, who joined him in Wilson Hartnell and who has been a familiar figure at the latter agency for many years as its receptionist. One pre-Christmas sighting at Domas is still remembered by many: the directors were to be seen on the floor playing with a train set loaded with "balls of malt".

Domas had such major accounts as Bachelors, DuPont, Proctor and Gamble, Smithwicks, TWA and Vauxhall. Growing consumer pressure in the late 1950s in the biscuit market led to the start of a veritable revolution in marketing and to the arrival on the Dublin

Just a minute

is all

you need

to make

delicious

coffee

with

IREL

*and it
costs only
1/6 a bottle*

An Irel coffee
advertisement,
published in 1961.

Jack Farrer, a
McConnell's designer
(right) with John
O'Neill in the 1950s.

advertising scene of a London advertising agency, Royds, which had far reaching consequences for local advertising. John Hunter, who was very familiar with the London advertising scene in the late 1950s, remembers that marketing was very much in vogue there, the new motivating factor. In Dublin, by contrast, little was heard about the need for professional marketing. The launch of Bolands' biscuits in 1957 created an air of unease in Jacobs; for the first time, the latter company was under serious local competitive pressure. Gordon Lambert, who joined Jacobs as assistant accountant in 1944, becoming chief accountant in 1953, had long had a keen interest in sales and marketing. He got his big chance in 1958 when he was appointed commercial manager, being made marketing director the following year. It was the first time an Irish company had taken the marketing function seriously.

He recalls: "In the late 1950s, only a handful of companies, such as Guinness and Jacobs, were exporting in a worthwhile way. Jacobs was one of the first firms to appoint young men to senior management positions."

Before the arrival of Bolands on the biscuit scene, there was no need for Jacobs to advertise; it was simply a question of selling what products you could get the ingredients for. In addition, the existing management at Jacobs had the traditional hostility towards advertising, seeing it as something intrusive, vulgar and altogether unnecessary. The advertising manager, Mr Snow, had little to do when it came to publicity, a little bit of advertising for the Jacob's cream crackers, a venerable product launched by the firm in 1885. A small amount of "public relations" advertising was done as well. The tiny advertising expenditure was handled by McConnell's.

NOW <u>YOU</u> CAN ENJOY AMERICA'S FAVOURITE COFFEE

Maxwell House
Rich, mellow coffee <u>made instantly in the cup!</u>

Americans know good coffee when they meet it—and the one they love best is Maxwell House. Now you can meet it too! And make it in a moment—right in the cup! Maxwell House Instant Coffee is here, and all good grocers have it!

So quick and easy to make! Just put a spoonful of Maxwell House Instant Coffee into your cup. Pour on hot water, or hot milk if you prefer—and there's your cup of coffee! Take a sip and—"Ah!" you'll say,

"This is coffee." It is. Coffee as it's meant to be. Coffee at its rich, mellow, most satisfying.

Maxwell House Instant Coffee is made from nothing but 100%, pure, fresh-ground coffee.

The very next time you're shopping ask for Maxwell House Instant Coffee—and when you get home relax and enjoy the best cup of coffee you've ever tasted! Look for the bright red tins.

5/- and 2/9 at your grocer's

Maxwell House
≡INSTANT COFFEE≡

"GOOD TO THE LAST DROP"

One of the very first Irish advertisements for Maxwell House instant coffee, Cork Examiner, April, 1957. The brand was named after the hotel in Nashville, Tennessee, where Joel Cheek test marketed his ground coffee in 1882.

Bile Beans were an important press advertiser throughout the 1950s.

Feel, and look, a new woman

HELPED BY THIS 'BALANCED-ACTION' FORMULA

Like this school-teacher—who is also a housewife and mother—you too can feel young and radiantly healthy, however busy you are. The secret? *Good health and regularity.* So, at the first sign of constipation, take today's Bile Beans.

EXTRA THOROUGH . . . EXTRA GENTLE

The 'balanced-action' formula in today's Bile Beans includes 12 selected ingredients, balanced to bring extra *thorough* relief, blended to bring extra *gentle* relief from constipation. And today's Bile Beans not only restore regularity—ridding you of the headaches, heaviness, biliousness and other troublesome ailments caused by incomplete elimination: *they also break up and clear away undigested fats.*

NORMAL REGULARITY RESTORED

So restore your normal regularity with today's 'balanced-action' Bile Beans—the safe, non-habit-forming remedy that is extra *thorough*, extra *gentle*. Overnight you'll feel better . . . look better . . . be your own radiant self again.

TODAY'S 'BALANCED-ACTION'
BILE BEANS
FOR RADIANT HEALTH AND VITALITY

Here's food for thought

appeal to you. They're not very complicated, in fact they're rather easy but you'll be delighted with the difference they make. None of them takes more than a few extra minutes to prepare: just chop, sprinkle or add and you'll have big mealtime enjoyment at a small cost. When you've tried some of them you'll probably think up a few of your own. That's a great thing about Batchelors foods. The range is so wide and so very versatile that you'll never be at a loss for good ideas.

Peas are fine when they're straight from the can.

You can also liven them up ~

Add ring of bacon or heat them in ham or bacon stock.
Or sprinkle on a little cleverly chopped mint.

Or go way out and add some chopped, fried or grilled rashers to a plate of peas,

mmmh!!

Batchelors means freshness — FRESH FOODS - FRESH WAYS OF USING THEM!

Sausage, pork or bacon, of course, cooked & chopped, blend in beautifully with beans.
And/or some chopped, fried onion.

You can also liven up beans by ~ An added spoonful of curry powder can make exciting eating!

And the adventurous should try covering beans with brown sugar, adding some rashers & baking. Irresistible!

Batchelors means freshness — FRESH FOODS - FRESH WAYS OF USING THEM!

Spaghetti goes with almost everything. And grated cheese goes marvellously with spaghetti!

Carrots & white parsley sauce are old friends.

How about French carrots (ours) Slice them lengthwise, watching your fingers! and fry in a little butter.

Batchelors means freshness — FRESH FOODS - FRESH WAYS OF USING THEM!

Batchelors prunes and strawberries are summer on a plate. TRY

Strawberries with jelly, custard or cream ~

Or, even better, a drained can of strawberries fills a flan perfectly. Especially when you top it up with cream. What to do with the syrup? Give it to the kids, they love to drink it!

N HALL THEATRE

GALWAY

th JULY, at 8.30.   MATINEE 3.30
gerald, June Dupree and Louis Hayward in
TEN LITTLE NIGGERS
A thrilling detective story

A LUCOSE and DUKE MITCHELL in
MONSTER MEETS THE GORILLA
Baldwin Agent

ed TUESDAY Only   At 8.30
ST RE-ISSUE THE BEST OF THE ROAD SHOWS
BY, DOROTHY LAMOUR and BOB HOPE in
THE ROAD TO BALI
FILMED IN TECHNICOLOR
laughter, song, music and exciting adventure.
AD TO BALI" is a film you must not miss!
MATINEE TUESDAY AT 4 P.M.

Y and THURSDAY (1st and 2nd Race Days)
Midnight Matinee 1st Race Day at 11.30.
SIGMUND ROMBERG'S
THE STUDENT PRINCE
at 8.30
ED IN CINEMASCOPE AND COLOUR
the golden voice of MARIO LANZA.
AL MATINEE THURSDAY AT 4 P.M.

SATURDAY Only   At 8.30
Brothers, Tony Martin and Virginia Grey in
THE BIG STORE
a masterpiece packed with music and song.
AT G. ROBINSON and VERA ELLEN in
BIG LEAGUER
MATINEE SATURDAY AT 4 P.M.
(TB)

HALL • LOUGHREA

Wednesday, July 31st, for 3 Days at
8.30 Show starts at 8.10
hot hits.

THE SEARCHERS
Also John Ford's Masterpiece
JOHN WAYNE and VERA MILES

Sunday and Mon, July 28 and 30
CinemaScope and Technicolor
MR. ROBERTS
Warner Bros great laugh hit starring
JAMES CAGNEY, HENRY FONDA
and JACK LEMMON

CENTRAL CINEMA, BALLINASLOE

(various listings)

CHAEL'S HALL, CRAUGHWELL

CEILIDHE

Sunday Night, July 28

BALLINAKILL CELI BAND

TAIRE BALLROOM

Sunday, July 28th

CEILIDHE and Old-Time Waltz

THE ASSAROE CEILIDHE BAND
(BALLYSHANNON)
CING 9—2   ADMISSION 3/9

IRST RACE NIGHT
(WEDNESDAY, JULY 31st)
the and Old-Time Waltz

E ASSAROE CEILIDHE BAND
Dancing 9—2

ADMISSION   5/-

COND RACE NIGHT
(THURSDAY, AUGUST 1st)
the and Old-Time Waltz

E INNISFREE CEILIDHE BAND
(CAVAN)
Dancing 9—2

ADMISSION   5/-

AND OPENING OF NEW SPORTS FIELD
AT TULLYCROSS, RENVYLE
SUNDAY, AUGUST 4th, at 3 p.m.
UP CONTEST: TULLYCROSS v. ROUNDSTONE
GAME: TUAM STARS v. CONNEMARA SELECTED
J. Kivane, J. Mahon, B. O'Neill and J. Young.
Ceilidhe that night. Clifden Juvenile Pioneers
d. All-Ireland and National League Cups on display
ADMISSION 5/-
AND DANCE in C.B.S. HALL, LETTERFRACK
ASSAROE CEILIDHE BAND, Bally-shannon.
ADMISSION 5/-

GALWAY RACE COMMITTEE
1 Eyre Street, Galway.

RACE CARDS

Will be available to sellers
at wholesale price of

9 - per dozen

on both mornings of Races

SECRETARY.
3924/TB-30757

KILKERRIN

CARNIVAL

SEPTEMBER 8th—22nd
1957

Full particulars later

CENTRAL CINEMA, GORT

(listings)
CRANIUM MOB
ATHENA
THE ROARING TWENTIES
CRASH DIVE
HONDO
With John Wayne, Geraldine Page and Ward Bond

LOUGHNANE MEMORIAL HALL
LABANE, ARDRAHAN

DANCE

Sunday Night Next, July 28th
Hours 9 - 1 (s.t.)
JOHNNY GUITAR

Dec Kelly and his Quick Silver Band
ADMISSION, 4 -

Athenry Town Hall

Sunday, 28th July, at 8.15 p.m.
Pier Angeli, Ricardo Montalban
and Yvonne De Carlo in
SOMBRERO

Tuesday, 30th July, at 8.15 p.m.
James Cagney, Humphrey
Bogart, Priscilla Lane in
THE ROARING TWENTIES
Hollywood's toughest men in
their toughest gangster film.

Friday, 2nd August, at 8.15 p.m.
Greatest of all Western's
HONDO
With John Wayne, Geraldine
Page and Ward Bond.

Woodford Cinema

Friday, 26th July:
JOHNNY GUITAR

Sunday Special Attraction:
DOUBLE EXPOSURE
A thrilling murder and detective drama.

New Inn Cinema

Sunday, July 28th:
Starring CARY GRANT and
BETSY DRAKE in
Room For One More

The story of a young couple just married. The wife is so fond of children that, before her husband realises, she has adopted dozens of them with all sorts of complications ensuing. From here on the film becomes a riot of mirth.
Programme commences at 8.15 p.m. sharp.

TYNAGH CINEMA

Sunday, July 28th:
CHARLES LAUGHTON and John Mills in
HOBSON'S CHOICE
This happy laughter-raising film is one of the great screen comedies of recent years.

ESTORIA

SPECIAL NOTICE
ADMISSION PRICES from August 1st, 1957: Balcony, 2/7; Back Parterre, 1/9; Front Parterre, 1/-. Children 1s. Matinees 7d. (including Tax).

SUNDAY, July 28th   Matinee 4.30
BRETT KING, BARBARA LAURENCE, JAS. GRIFFITH
JESSE JAMES Vs. THE DALTONS
Powerful Outdoor Filmed in TECHNICOLOUR. Also
MARIE WINDSOR, RICHARD ROBER, ALLEN NIXON
OUTLAW WOMEN

MONDAY, July 29th   Two Days   Matinee Tuesday, 3 p.m.
Anthony Steel, Anna Maria Sandra, Donald Sinden
THE BLACK TENT
(IN VISTA VISION AND TECHNICOLOUR)
Stirring and Spectacular Desert Adventure set in North Africa—1942

WEDNESDAY, July 31st   Two Days
Matinee Thursday, 4 p.m.
Return visit of the Classic Drama. The Picture that requires no introduction.
JANE WYMAN, ROCK HUDSON, BARBARA RUSH
MAGNIFICENT OBSESSION
(COLOUR BY TECHNICOLOR)
Unforgettable in its Dramatic Force, its Intimacy, its Feeling.
★ WE UNRESERVEDLY RECOMMEND ★

FRIDAY, August 2nd   Two Days   Matinee Saturday, 4 p.m.
Thomas Mitchell   Rose Stradner   Vincent Price
THE KEYS OF THE KINGDOM
A. J. Cronin's Best Loved Book Relief. A Film to see again and again.

E.P.P.O. WATCHES
LADIES' 15 JEWEL LEVERS, 20 micron Rolled Gold Case, £6-18-6.
GENTS 15 JEWEL LEVERS, Chromium and Steel Waterproof Case, £6-18-6. Same in 20 micron H.G., £7-10-0.

A. HARTMANN & SON
MAINGUARD ST.   Phone 473   GALWAY

COMMERCIAL BALLROOM
★ Race Week 1957 ★

Presenting Ireland's Greatest Band Attractions
at Prices to meet your Pocket!

★ **CARNIVAL DANCE TIME** ★

TO-NIGHT (FRIDAY, July 26th)   9—1   3/9 (inc. Tax)
The Sensational
Pete Browne and his All-Stars
with Four Vocalists

SUNDAY, July 28th   9—1   3/9 (inc. Tax)
Galway's Greatest Band Show
The Arabian Dance Band
with MAXIE on the Univox, and Vocalists

TUESDAY, July 30th   9—1   3/9 (inc. Tax)
VISITORS' RACE EVE DANCE
Pete Browne and his All-Stars

FIRST RACE NIGHT
9—2   5/- (inc. Tax)
J. J. FLYNN AND HIS ACES
WITH FOUR TOP-HIT VOCALISTS

SECOND RACE NIGHT
9—2   5/- (inc. Tax)
CIARAN McNAMARA
("THE MODERNAIRES")
WITH VOCAL GROUP

FRIDAY and SUNDAY, August 2nd and 4th
The Arabian Band Show
9—2   3/9 (inc. Tax)
RIGHT OF ADMISSION STRICTLY RESERVED

GREAT HOLIDAY ATTRACTION
"SHOW-TIME"
ALL-STAR DRAMA AND VARIETY SHOW
WITH
FRANK O'DONOVAN
MARTIN CROSBIE
AND FULL COMPANY

In the Big Tent at the
Fair Green
(OPPOSITE RAILWAY STATION)
EVERY NIGHT AT 8.30
3/-, 2/-, and 1/6

WEST OF IRELAND'S GREATEST CENTRE
OF ENTERTAINMENT

Show Band Singer
LILY FITZPATRICK

Show Band Singer
DON GERAGHTY

Seapoint

... Now, here's the Gen on Galway's Race Week Dancing—
and here are the Bands...

The Melody Aces   and   **Johnny Butler**

The Seapoint 13-Piece Show Band
Directed by JACK BARRETT

JIMMY KEENAN
Alto-Sax

JOHNNY MURRAY
Drums

JACK BARRETT
Musical Director

IAN HENRY
Pianist

PADDY MILLANE
Bass

FRANK HOGAN
Tenor-Sax

CHARLIE WYMS
Trumpet

Programme

SUNDAY, July 28—Afternoon 3—6   Adm. 2/6 (inc. Tax)
    Night   8—2   Adm. 6/- (inc. Tax)
MONDAY, July 29   8—2   Adm. 5/- (inc. Tax)
TUESDAY, July 30   8—2   Adm. 5/- (inc. Tax)
Two Bands—Johnny Butler and his T.V. Orchestra
and the Seapoint Show Band
WEDNESDAY, July 31   8—2   Adm. 10/- (inc. Tax)
(FIRST RACE NIGHT)
Two Bands—The Melody Aces
and the Seapoint Show Band
THURSDAY, August 1   8—2   Adm. 10/- (inc. Tax)
(SECOND RACE NIGHT)
Two Bands—The Melody Aces
and the Seapoint Show Band
FRIDAY, August 2   8—2   Adm. 5/- (inc. Tax)
SUNDAY, Aug. 4—Afternoon 3—6   Adm. 3/9 (inc. Tax)
    Night   8—2   Adm. 7/6 (inc. Tax)
MONDAY, August 5   9—2   Adm. 5/- (inc. Tax)
(GALA BANK HOLIDAY HOP)

SPACIOUS RESTAURANT GROUND FLOOR
Seating Capacity 350

OPEN 11 A.M.—11.30 P.M.   RACE NIGHTS UNTIL MIDNIGHT

Table d'Hote Luncheons Two Race Days
11.30 A.M.—3 P.M.

DENIS LOUGHLIN
Alto-Sax

PADDY O'LOUGHLIN
Tenor-Sax

BILLY McDONALD
Trumpet

PHIL DALY
Trombone

Galway Bay

The former premises of Domas, Granite House in Pembroke Road, Dublin, next to the present day US Embassy.

Opposite page: An advertisement for Batchelors designed by Domas, 1966.

Page of entertainment advertisements from the *Connacht Tribune*, July 27, 1957.

Biro advertisement, 1957.

Above:
Don Finan, O'Keeffes, in a spoof advertisement for the ICA (Institute of Creative Advertising) publication Campaign, late 1950s.

Gordon Lambert came to his new job with the blessing of having no previous experience in the publicity field; he saw what needed to be done with a totally fresh eye. He constructed his "marketing diamond"; at the centre was the marketing director, with responsibilities extending to advertising, sales, product development, packaging design, distribution and merchandising. The outer setting for all these facets was public relations. This thinking was revolutionary in the Irish marketplace.

With his keen interest in contemporary art, Lambert was able to make a substantial input into the packaging redesign. Before he took over responsibility for Jacob's advertising, it had been of a general nature, designed to increase biscuit sales generally. Lambert started individual brand advertising, giving each brand a separate identity, starting with cream crackers and moving on to fig rolls. Although McConnell's had the account — soon after the firm also "provided" Frankie Byrne, who was appointed by Lambert to look after the firm's public relations, there was little scope for it to expand the Jacob's advertising. Out of the blue, in 1958, Royds wrote to Jacob's, without prior introduction and asked if the agency could make a presentation. Eventually, they won the Jacob's account, having opened a Dublin office in 1959 at 7 Dawson Street. Gordon Lambert remembers that John McConnell was "very annoyed" at the account switching to Royds, so for a time, the two agencies worked in tandem on the account. Eventually, Royds in Dublin was to merge with Sun in 1966 to form Irish International.

In the old-style Jacobs, run like a homely family firm, on paternalistic lines, the Quaker Bewley tradition was strong. Quaker tradition is strongly against advertising and self-promotion — only within the last two years has the Bewley's cafe firm done any serious consumer advertising. In Jacob's, too, the feeling was that producing the very best in biscuits was enough to sell them. Advertising expenditure ran to about 0.05 per cent of turnover. Under Gordon Lambert's influence, that figure soon crept up to five per cent. The antipathy to advertising in the old-style Jacobs was widely accepted throughout Irish industry as late as the 1950s. One shining exception was O'Dea's, the firm that makes "O'Dearest" mattresses.

Frank Chambers, the man who wrote so many of the limericks for the "O'Dearest" advertisements, which ran for many years first in *The Irish Times* on Saturdays and then in the *Irish Independent,* as well, maintaining the Saturday tradition, worked on the mattress account in Sun from 1955 until 1957, when he returned to Arks. He had been with the agency since the Emergency, until 1947, when he joined the *Standard.* For years and years, the formula of the Saturday advertisements never varied. First of all, the limerick was written and approved by the client; then Warner drew his cartoon and finally, the whole combination of copy and layout would be approved on the

Friday. Cecil Bell, who worked as an account executive on the O'Dearest campaigns, first at Arks then at Sun, wrote some limericks himself. Very often, the advertisements contained winning tips: the ad that appeared the day of the 1958 Grand National provided a good monetary return for careful readers of the "O'Dearest" publicity that day. Peter McCarthy, the managing director of O'Dea's, was surprisingly liberal as a client; in the 1950s as today, clients really called the shots in advertising campaigns and it was a rare agency that dared to contradict a client. On one occasion in the 1950s, Warner and Chambers concocted an advertisement that made them slightly nervous: how would Mr McCarthy react?

Eileen Byrne, director and secretary, Brindley Advertising.

The drawing showed a horse drawn caravan. The limerick read as follows:

> I find caravanning great gas,
> On O'Dearest I travel first class.
> I go at my ease and stop where I please,
> As I'm towed on the road by my ass.

Peter McCarthy loved the limerick and it went into print the next day, when it caused a minor sensation.

A death and a birth in 1957 caused sadness and joy. Frank Padbury, the man who started Padburys, died on December 8, 1957. He left his holding in the agency to his wife, who sold it in 1962 to Maymay Dignam, who had been involved in the agency since its start in 1945 and who had worked in O'Kennedy Brindley (where Padbury was in charge of production for many years) as secretary to Brian D. O'Kennedy. Maymay thus became the only woman ever to own an Irish advertising agency, over 20 years before the feminist issue started to become "live" in advertising. She has fond memories of Frank Padbury: "He was full of energy, a very fast thinker and worker. He could write copy very quickly. He was a brilliant man and used to read a lot to learn as much as he could. He was always keen to help people find jobs and also taught in Rathmines from the time advertising courses were started there, in 1929. Shortly after Padbury died, Seamus Dignam, Maymay Dignam's nephew, joined from *The Irish Times,* where he was head librarian. He started as a copywriter and eventually became chairman.

Basil Brindley, who founded Brindley Advertising in 1956. *Photograph: The Irish Times.*

The "birth" in 1957 was of the *Sunday Review,* the tabloid Sunday newspaper run by *The Irish Times.* In many ways, it was ahead of its time. If full colour printing facilities had been available, it might still be in circulation, some agency sources believe. Yet the Dublin advertising agencies were very reluctant to support the publication; Clodagh O'Kennedy, the dress designer and wife of Desmond O'Kennedy, was roped in to write a weekly fashion column, but not even this swayed O'Kennedy Brindley into buying more space in the newspaper. It lasted until late 1963, the year after the *Dublin Evening Mail* published its last edition.

'Don 'n' Nelly', Donnelly's sausages campaign 1959, by O'Kennedy Brindley. The caricatures in plasticine were created by Bill Bolger.

When Boland's Biscuits started production in 1957, Arks placed a series of L-shaped advertisements in the daily newspapers. This page was from the Evening Press of September 12, 1957. Top right hand corner is an advertisement for Neave's Foods, a baby food marketed in Ireland since the early 19th century.

EVENING PRESS, THURSDAY, SEPTEMBER 12, 1957

U.S. schools move
'Peace talk' with President

PRESIDENT EISENHOWER and the defiant Governor of Arkansas, Mr. Orval Faubus, will meet to-morrow on Saturday to talk over the school integration conflict at Little Rock between Arkansas and the Federal Government.

'Worse than Hungary'

'Rabble rouser'

Planned robbery, but not guilty of murder

Dublin Fever Hospital

GRAND CHARITY DANCE
In aid of
Cappagh Hospital Building Fund
CRYSTAL BALLROOM TO-NIGHT

To dance on TV

Hungarian exile vanishes

Secret file

Won't be taken back to Italy

Daughter for Mr. Lloyd-George

Honoured by Pope

OVER 300 DROWNED

WELCOMED

Car crashed into house, woman died

SHE IS ANNIE OAKLEY OF DRUMCONDRA

Football final broadcast

Minister opens Show

Back to School
In a Waterproof Duffle Coat
25/-

Young man with a long way to grow

All the more need for giving

Neave's FO

Be kind to your nose!

Pink Paraffin scores again
—now the first paraffin to smell pleasant

Aladdin
PINK PARAFFIN

Where have those Bolands Biscuits gone?

BOLANDS BISCUITS
the Quality You've been waiting for

A judicious juxtaposition of advertisements in a Saturday issue of the Irish Independent, January, 1958.

Frank Padbury, who founded Padbury Advertising in 1945 and who died in 1957.

Candles advertisement.

C A N D L E M A S
2nd February, 1952.

FOR BEST BEES WAX CANDLES 65% AND 25% ORDER FROM

W. & S. Armstrong Ltd.,

WHOLESALE IMPORTERS AND DISTRIBUTORS,

Enniscorthy.

'Phone (2 Lines) 15 and 38.

(a573-1)

21 VITAL YEARS.

In the year 1937 McConnell's celebrated its 21st Anniversary, and at the time published a booklet with the above title.

It is now out of print, and there is only one copy in the possession of the company.

Would anyone, therefore, having a copy which he would be prepared to sell, kindly get in touch with

The Chairman,

McCONNELL'S

ADVERTISING SERVICE, LTD.,

Publicity House,

Dublin.

Y-Front advertisement, The Irish Times, **March 29, 1958.**

Roscrea bacon and sausages — a Parker account in 1957.

McConnell's advertisement in The Irish Times, **in 1955.**

195

1958 saw another publication cease — the *Times Pictorial*. It was the old *Weekly Irish Times* transformed into a picture newspaper in 1941. By the end of the late 1950s, with TV on the horizon, it had outlived its usefulness. It was a traumatic time for the national print media, yet in 1959, *The Irish Times* was able to celebrate its centenary with considerable style. Bernard Share and Jarlath Hayes, working in O'Kennedy Brindley, were responsible for producing the agency's advertisements for the supplement. They were created in the authentic style of 1859, using wooden type, still to be found quite often in 1959 in Dublin printing houses, even if down in the basement. Bernard Share ransacked century old file copies of the *Illustrated London News* for authentic Victorian commercial phrases. Not realised at the time, design for newspaper advertisements was on a peak that was soon to pass, irretrievably, with the advent of television. Iain MacCarthaigh, just coming into Sun after a nine year spell with Bord Failte, says that at the end of the 1950s, most advertising was placed in newspapers. With the help of the Dutch designers in Sun, the standard of design was often brilliant, yet as he says now, somewhat ruefully, the art of newspaper advertisement design has gone.

1958 also saw a major milestone in the progress of Irish advertising. The Institute of Creative Advertising was set up, forerunner of the more recent Institute of Creative Advertising and Design, that has done so much to foster and improve good standards of creativity in the industry. First president of the Institute was Bill Bergin; Jarlath Hayes was first vice-president, while Francis Ryan was treasurer and Giles Talbot Kelly, a flamboyant Englishman who worked for Janus, was both secretary and public relations officer.

The names of the subscribers were listed as Jarlath Hayes (designer), Bill Lindsay (designer), W. O'Rourke (designer), R. G. T. Kelly (advertising executive), Gerry Doherty (designer, the man who set up the G & S Doherty agency with his wife Sybil and three Dublin businessmen), T. E. O'Sullivan (designer) and Marcella Kerin (spinster).

The articles of the new Institute stated, among other things, that the office of a member of the council shall be vacated if "he become bankrupt or make any arrangement of composition with his creditors or if be found lunatic or become of unsound mind."

O'Keeffes moved from cramped and poky offices at Upper O'Connell Street, by the Carlton cinema, to a fine Georgian house in Fitzwilliam Square, where it remains to this day, although the premises have been much enlarged. It was a shrewd move on the part of managing director Ray O'Keeffe, reckoned to be among the least publicity conscious of all Dublin agency heads. Well-placed sources believe that when O'Keeffes made the move into Fitzwilliam Square in the late 1950s, the house cost around £8,000. The appreciation of the value of the property in the intervening years has been truly colossal. One of the reasons for the move was the acquisition of the Sunbeam

Wolsey account: to make a good impression on the Cork firm, O'Keeffe's was said to have hired offices in the area just for the day. Even the offices of Matthews, Mulcahy and Sutherland, the insurance firm which had backed Ray O'Keeffe in his takeover of the agency ten years previously, were said to have been called into use for the day. The ploy was successful: O'Keeffes won the account. Celebrations were intense, but not quite as intense as when the agency won the Irish Permanent Building Society account from Janus in the late 1940s. It billed £6,000 a year. The people in the agency toasted Ray O'Keeffe's health for a week following that news. The ploy used by O'Keeffes in winning the Sunbeam Wolsey account, of making the agency seem more grandiose than it really was, is common in the advertising industry.

When O'Kennedy Brindley was still above the Rainbow Café in Lower O'Connell Street, the agency was said to have brought in people for the day to staff up the offices while a presentation was being made to a potential client from overseas. Later that day, the personnel from the client firm went to a city centre travel agents and were puzzled to find some of the people they had met in O'Kennedy Brindley earlier in the day now writing travel tickets and answering timetable queries.

Some forms of advertising lacked subtlety but were money spinners for both the agencies and the newspapers. In the late 1950s, when education was still paid for by parents, schools and colleges competed in the marketplace for custom. For a couple of months every summer, there was an advertising bonanza, when all these educational establishments took space (Kenny's had a useful near monopoly in this

On location for Powers' gin launch campaign 'There's a new power in the land' by O'Kennedy Brindley in 1959, were Niel O'Kennedy (centre wearing sunglasses) and Bernard Share (hand on head).

197

sector) to advertise the starting dates of the new school term in the autumn. Daily newspapers would run two or three pages of these advertisements at a time, remembers Michael B. Kenny, who says, with a degree of wistfulness, that the practice went out with the arrival of free secondary education in 1966.

Just as Jacob's started to advertise seriously for the first time at the end of the 1950s, 1959 saw Ireland's biggest commercial concern, Guinness, do likewise. In Britain, Guinness began advertising for the first time in the late 1920s, using the S. H. Benson agency. Bobby Bevan began his advertising career as the copywriter on the account, which Benson's held until 1969; he later became managing director and chairman. Bevan talked to Guinness drinkers in Dublin pubs and from that elementary market research came the memorable copy line, "Guinness is good for you." In the 1930s, Guinness was advertised in Britain with some of the most striking posters ever designed, the work of John Gilroy, who drew all the cartoons for the product which have passed into advertising mythology. Guinness improved its market share in Britain in the 1930s, at a time of deep economic depression, with the help of the Gilroy-designed advertising. The firm did not follow suit in Ireland.

Lucozade advertisement, Irish Independent, **January 30, 1958. The same issue reported that Dermot C. Jordan, a 31 years old Dubliner and a trial motor cycle rider, had been appointed manager of the advertising and public relations department of Esso Petroleum Co (Ireland). He succeeded W. J. Delaney, who retired after 44 years' service.**

Better value, 1957. A Dunne's stores' advertisement, Cork Examiner.

Here, the management of the firm never considered serious advertising: during the 1930s and 1940s, right through into the late 1950s, Guinness in Dublin spent about £10,000 a year on advertising, taking small spaces in programmes for community events, producing Guinness playing cards and sometimes bringing over the odd showcard from England. In 1951, there was brief Guinness advertising on Dublin buses. One Dubliner told *Time* magazine "It was like advertising potatoes." So low a priority did advertising have in the Guinness scheme of management up to 1958 that it was looked after by the company secretary and two girls in his department. Just as the new threat from Boland's biscuits helped push Jacob's into advertising for the first time, so did the challenge of competition from UK beers such as Double Diamond arriving in the Irish market persuade Guinness that it should start the dreadful business of advertising.

Two men played a crucial role in the start-up of Guinness advertising in Ireland, Ken Tyrrell and George Gracie. Tyrrell had spent 20 years in the advertising department of Guinness at the Park Royal brewery in London; he had been "exported" to London in 1939. He returned home to Dublin in 1958 to set up the advertising department at the St James' Gate brewery. Initially, Arks in Dublin

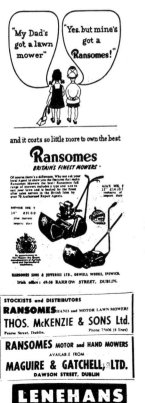

Lawnmower advertising, 1958.

The Dublin-London tourist return air fare in 1958 was £12.18s, while that from Dublin to Manchester was just £6.19s.

Phoenix beer advertisement, 1957.

was chosen to be the media buying agency, while the creative input came from Benson's in London. Gracie, who died at the end of 1985, joined Guinness in Dublin in 1938 after graduating from Trinity College, Dublin. In 1940, he followed in Ken Tyrrell's footsteps and went to work for Guinness in London. During the war years, he spent much of his time persuading publicans to sell less Guinness because of the rationing, but at the same time, ensuring that the brewery lost no goodwill. By accident, he ended up back in Dublin. He met the late Guy Jackson, like "Sandy" Miller, killed in the 1972 air crash at Staines near Heathrow airport, in the North of England. Jackson had got lost and when he met up with Gracie, the two men spent ages chatting in a lay-by, in the recollection of Gracie when interviewed in 1985. The upshot was that Gracie came back to Dublin to head up the new marketing function in Guinness.

The first advertising campaign for Guinness in Ireland, to commemorate its bicentenary in 1959, cost the grand sum of £900 and was confined almost entirely to *The Irish Times.* Stanley Penn of Benson's came up with the copy line: "200 years of Guinness — what a lovely long drink". Once Guinness had taken the plunge with advertising, it soared onwards and upwards, becoming one of the first major advertisers on Telefis Eireann, becoming a big user of outdoor posters and starting large scale campaigns in the print media. The conversion of the house of Guinness to the cause of advertising was swift and thorough; within two years, the firm was closely involved in the launch of Harp lager. Other beers were promoted by Guinness as well, such as Smithwicks. As George Gracie, later to become president of the European Brewers' Association, remarked: "It was great fun playing our left hand against our right."

Ford truck advertisement from a campaign that ran in major provincial newspapers, 1957.

"Aertex" ladies shirts advertisement, 1950s.

Sandeman's port, as advertised in the Irish Independent **in the mid-1950s.**

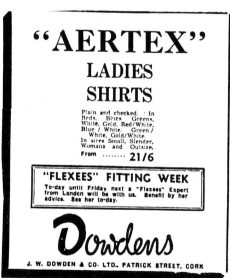

21ST BIRTHDAY

To-day we are proud to announce the addition of the new

1936-1957

VISCOUNT 800

BUILT BY VICKERS — POWERED BY ROLLS-ROYCE

to our fleet

Exactly 21 years ago to-day the first Aer Lingus aircraft, a twin engine De Havilland Dragon — carried a full complement of 5 passengers from Dublin to Bristol at 114 miles per hour. What a far cry that is from the powerful 65-seater Vickers Viscount 800 — the latest addition to the Aer Lingus fleet. The Viscount 800, with its four Rolls-Royce turbo-prop engines, cruises smoothly at 320 miles per hour high above the weather. The cabin is pressurized and the air conditioning system keeps the atmosphere as fresh as a spring morning. The new airliner will be in service on the Dublin-London route from 1st July. Aer Lingus, with the Viscount 800, brings to its 1957 passengers all the comforts and advantages of the most up-to-date airliner in Europe.

The D.H.84 — AN t-IOLAR — the first Aer Lingus airliner. In 1936 Aer Lingus carried 773 passengers and a few parcels of freight —last year the airline carried 457,974 passengers and 6,331 tons of freight.

1936

1957

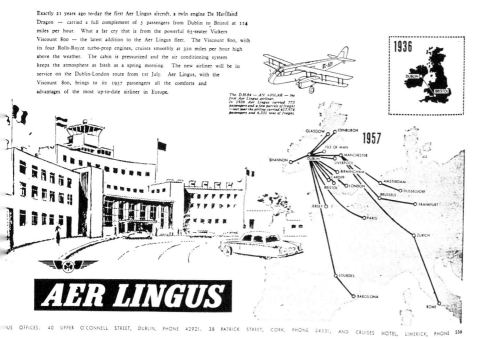

AER LINGUS

US OFFICES: 40 UPPER O'CONNELL STREET, DUBLIN, PHONE 42921; 38 PATRICK STREET, CORK, PHONE 24331, AND CRUISES HOTEL, LIMERICK, PHONE 556

Full page advertisement in the Cork Examiner, May 27, 1957, for the new Viscount aircraft for the Aer Lingus fleet. Five years later, with the start of the Sunday Times colour magazine in London, Aer Lingus started a memorable series of advertisements aimed at the British market.

201

Woodbines cigarette
advertisement, 1957.

Post Office Savings
Bank Account
advertisement, 1957.

Best of all-
smoke
WOODBINES

1'2 FOR TEN

2/4 FOR 20

Firmly packed and of unvarying quality
WOODBINES are wonderful value at 1/2 for ten.
Give yourself the pleasure of a cooler,
smoother smoke with all the satisfying flavour
of PURE VIRGINIA tobacco.

The GREAT little cigarette
Made ENTIRELY of PURE VIRGINIA Tobacco
MANUFACTURED IN DUBLIN

PERSONAL

SHANAHAN'S STAMP

AUCTIONS, LTD.

present

A

" Calm Before the Storm "

Sale

(SALE NO. 76)

which will be held on

SATURDAY,

1st NOVEMBER, 1958,

At 2.45 p.m.

A U.S.A. Section valued at $50,000 superb G E R M A N STATES, particularly strong in SAXONY; British Colonies; Europeans, etc. Many Collections, Wholesale, etc.

Nearly 1,000 lots valued at over £40,000 ($110,000) incl. comm.

Ask for our 94 page Catalogue incl. 35 pages of illustrations and inserts.

SHANAHAN'S STAMP

AUCTIONS, LTD.,

39 Upper Great George's Street,

Dun Laoghaire,   Dublin.

Bridge that gap with Cadbury's

dairy milk chocolate

How your vitality ebbs when you wait too long between meals.	How Cadbury's Dairy Milk chocolate restores your energy.
THERE'S REAL NOURISHMENT IN CADBURY'S	

Don't nurse a grievance when there's too big a gap between meals — too big a gap between you and your vitality. Take positive steps. Treat yourself to Cadbury's Dairy Milk Chocolate. It's a positive treat. More than that, Cadbury's is *nourishing*. It sustains and fortifies you — as indicated in the diagram above. Yes, Cadbury's restores your energy and keeps you going — which is only natural for a $\frac{1}{4}$-lb. is worth a glass of milk and two poached eggs in food value. So bridge that gap with Cadbury's.

ARKS

Back page advertisement for Shanahan's stamp auctions, The Irish Times, October, 1958. Later, Dr Paul Singer, who ran the auctions, faced criminal proceedings over the major financial swindle involving countless old age pensioners who had invested in the firm. The Irish Independent claimed to be the only newspaper not to have accepted advertising from Singer.

From 1956 until 1958, Arks ran a "Bridge that Gap" campaign for Cadbury's chocolates, using the Irish Independent, Irish Press, Evening Press, Sunday Independent and Sunday Press. Drawings were by Rowel Friers.

Stanley Wilson, now with Bord Fáilte, as a space buyer in Janus 1960.

Paraffin advertising in The Irish Times, October, 1958.

Rex McDonnell visualiser (below), Janus and later O'Kennedy Brindley, 1960.

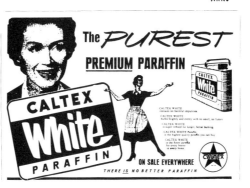

The *PUREST* PREMIUM PARAFFIN

CALTEX White PARAFFIN

CALTEX WHITE contains no harmful impurities.
CALTEX WHITE burns brightly and evenly with no smell, no fumes
CALTEX WHITE is super-refined for longer, better burning.
CALTEX WHITE is the highest quality paraffin you can buy
CALTEX WHITE is the finest paraffin for every home

ON SALE EVERYWHERE
THERE IS NO BETTER PARAFFIN

203

*After a long morning in the ring,
all good judges are of the same mind,
for all good judges know that . . .*

only the best pigs are in

Clover SKINLESS PORK SAUSAGES

EXTRA NICE WHEN PARTNERED BY CLOVER BACON OR HAM
CLOVER MEATS LTD., WATERFORD, LIMERICK, WEXFORD, AND DUBLIN DISTRIBUTING CENTRE

**A Clover skinless
sausages
advertisement,
published in 1957.**

Bringing Guinness into the world of advertising was great fun and the participants enjoyed themselves. Tyrrell, Gracie and the third person in the Guinness sales and marketing triumvirate, Bobby Howick, made a formidable team. The tubby but genial Howick was in charge of the sales department and colleagues in Guinness used to refer to himself and Gracie as the "brawn and the brains." Gracie quickly established a formidable reputation with agency people in Dublin for making them feel that his ideas were in fact theirs; agencies had a worthy client with whom to work.

No wonder that with signs of advertising in Ireland starting to move onto a more elevated plane, the Advertising Press Club was able to celebrate. It had a record-breaking 15th gala dance on December 6, 1958. Club chairman Horace Denham ensured that the throng really enjoyed themselves. The attendance included Mr and Mrs Jack Dempsey, Mr and Mrs Bill Cavanagh, Mr and Mrs Gordon Clark, Mr and Mrs Brendan Byrne, Noel Montaine and party from Cosmon, Mrs and Mrs Liam Yendole (Millers), Mr and Mrs Peter Rackow (Cinema and General Publicity), Mr and Mrs Joe O'Byrne. The following year, 1959, the Advertising Press Club held an even bigger and better gala dance, under the auspices of club chairman Billy King.

The serious business continued; Peter Owens set up his own agency. When he returned from the USA in 1960, he was unable to return to Domas, which he had joined in 1948 and decided to set up shop for himself. He put a small advertisement in *The Irish Times* one day in 1960, announcing that he was in business. Peter Greville of Albright and Wilson in Dun Laoghaire gave the brand new agency its

**McConnells' football
team, 1958. Front row,
fourth from left, Niall
O'Sullivan; second
from left: John O'Neill.
Back row far right,
Peter Jay, designer;
Fourth from left, late
Eric Kerr, director,
McConnells; First left:
Pat O'Kelly, production
manager, McConnells.**

first business. Owens claims that he brought to Irish advertising the concept of marketing planning done in tandem with the communications element. "You cannot have an advertising campaign unrelated to strategic marketing planning. When you get the marketing strategy right, you put down enormous roots for the advertising." When Owens, inspired by his studies in the USA in 1958/1959 of the coming age of television, preached his new found revelations to Irish advertisers, they fell on deaf ears. He started business with a small staff — Phyllis O'Kane was the very first employee and is now agency deputy chairman — and for the first five years, life was tough. Brian Ebbs, his copywriter, was killed in a car crash in 1969. Peter Owens hung in and his agency survived well.

McConnell's started a Cork branch in 1960; later it merged with the Communicators' agency, which folded in 1972. A young man called Manus O'Callaghan began his advertising career with O'Kennedy Brindley in Cork. Today, he heads Southern Advertising, which in a neat piece of rôle reversal, opened a branch office in Dublin in the summer of 1986.

As Peter Owens was starting his agency, Bernard Share was creating a revolution with the help of Bill Bolger: they started doing advertisements on location: few other Dublin agencies ventured out of their studios then. Share and Bolger did one series of advertisements featuring Nelson's Pillar and other Dublin landmarks. Then there was a series of advertisements for Janus itself, published in *Management*

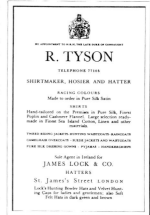

Tyson's was a high quality mens' outfitters in Grafton Street. Through the 1950s and into the 1960s, its "Savile Row" style advertising was familiar in newspapers and magazines.

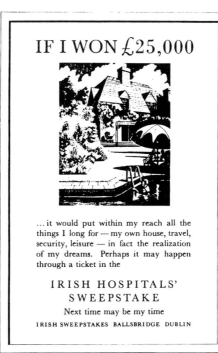

Yodel, a long vanished chocolate spread, advertised in the Derry Journal, **February, 1960.**

An up-market advertisement for the Irish Hospitals Sweepstake, used in the 1950s.

Harry Byers, then with Janus, as a model in a Janus advertisement 1960.

magazine. For one of the advertisements, it was decided to photograph all the Janus staff at five in the morning in a totally deserted O'Connell Street. In those days, the street was quiet enough at midday, but the creative heads wanted it totally deserted. Few of the Janus staff had their own cars, but everyone was rounded up. The camera packed up, so the following morning, again at 5 a.m., the sequence had to be reshot. At O'Kennedy Brindley, an advertisement for Power's gin was shot on location in a field — great excitement.

Within months of those advertisements being prepared, Denis Garvey sent Share and Bolger on a training course in London, to learn about television advertisement production. It was, says Share now, a far-sighted move. Other agencies began to hire people from London to head up their new television departments; the biggest single impetus ever given to the Irish advertising business was about to get under way. Eamonn Andrews, who little more than ten years previously, had been introducing Kavanagh's pure foods on sponsored radio, was now appointed chairman of the committee appointed by the Government to set up the Irish television service.

Heine Petrie, founder of
Modern Display Artists
in 1935, and his wife,
Eileen.

CHAPTER FIVE

The Start of Market Research 1961-1973

"How do Jacob's get the figs into Fig Rolls?"
'MR FIGGERTY' CAMPAIGN BY IRISH INTERNATIONAL, MID-1960s

Flurries of snow greeted the guests arriving for the gala dinner in the Gresham Hotel, Dublin, on December 31, 1961, to mark the opening of the Telefis Eireann service. For months beforehand, the main agencies had been gearing up for television production, importing TV producers from London, where commercial television had been in operation since 1955. The first-ever advertisement to appear on Telefis Eireann was not included in the draw for the first advertiser: a CIE bus lumbered into view, complete with advertisements. The next day, New Year's Day, 1962, the television service started its scheduled programming. Advertising in Ireland would never be the same again.

Moves started in 1961 to abolish the old Irish Association of Advertising Agencies and replace it with the Institute of Advertising Practitioners in Ireland. Captain Oliver Walsh was appointed to the association in 1961 and a committee was appointed to oversee the change, comprised of Capt Walsh, Desmond O'Kennedy, Dermod Cafferky and Luke Dillon-Mahon. The new institute was formally inaugurated in November, 1964. After the founding of IAPI, John Young became first president; he went on to do a second term. When he joined IAAA in 1961, Walsh had just retired after a long and successful career in the Army; he was also a secretary of the Show Jumping Association of Ireland, another of his keen interests. Walsh, who died at the end of 1985, used to admit that his entry into the advertising business presented a big hurdle, since he knew little or nothing about the industry. However, he was a keen "student" and in 25 years with the advertising industry, he gave sterling service. He was also closely involved in the Advertising Standards Committee and later the authority and a prime mover of the Joint Advertising Education Committee.

1960 saw a brand new alcoholic product launched — Harp lager. The concept of lager was unusual then and Bensons in London created a TV campaign, which Arks placed. It wasn't a particularly warm summer in 1961, so weather conditions weren't ideal for the copyline — "Have a Harp, a cool, refreshing Harp", but the TV campaign had an enormous impact. Arks did interesting work on beer accounts, handling the campaigns in the early 1960s for New Ross-brewed Cherry's Ale, one of the Guinness group's first ventures outside the stout market. Later, the beer was brewed in Waterford and renamed Phoenix. Another venture by Guinness, some 25 years ago, fizzled out. It produced a yeast-based product rather similar to Marmite and called Gye, a by-product of the brewing process. Despite Arks' press campaign for Gye, it failed to win customer acceptance. Later, the Phoenix account moved to McConnell's, where Jack Farrer ("a wonderful draughtsman") and Iain MacCarthaigh devised the copy line: "Phoenix, the bright pint." George Gracie and Bobby Howick were enthusiastic, but Guy Jackson, the managing director, said that

In September, 1960, Maurice Dockrell, Lord Mayor of Dublin, presented young Niall O'Sullivan with the Conlon gold medal. Also pictured are Michael Kenny (second from left) and Tom Milner. Overleaf in a photograph taken in 1985, Maurice Dockrell, chairman of the ICS Building Society congratulates Niall O'Sullivan, managing director of O'Connor O'Sullivan on winning the ICS account.

"pint" was a Guinness word, so the slogan had to be changed to "Phoenix, the bright beer". A series of TV commercials was devised, built around conversations with Malachy the barman and an unknown customer.

New appointments, new agencies characterised the start of the 1960s; not alone was the new television service injecting some much needed excitement into the advertising scene, but within a couple of years of the start of Telefis Eireann, the economic development of the country was set in train by Sean Lemass, the Taoiseach. A new confidence, a willingness to experiment and try new ideas, came into play. No-one picked up vibrations more quickly than Gordon Lambert at Jacobs; by 1961, he was marketing director at the company and putting all his new ideas on packaging design, advertising and sales promotion into practice. In October, 1961, he announced that Frankie Byrne had been appointed public relations officer to the company. Frankie, who had previously worked for McConnell's, joined Jacob's, which became one of the first commercial organisations in Ireland to put public relations on a sound footing. An interesting footnote shows how much Gordon Lambert was ahead of his time. The original press release announcing Frankie's appointment described her as "Ms Frankie Byrne". The term 'Ms' did not come into general use for a further 15 years. In 1961, Jacob's enjoyed much public relations coverage from its association with the first Aer Lingus flight from Dublin to the brand new Cork airport.

Lambert met his advertising match with another great personality: Corwin Mack Kile, managing director of Irish International. Often remembered for his jokes and japes, Kile brought a serious professionalism to the business of advertising that is often overlooked in the flood of reminiscence. He put a "zip", a brashness into Irish advertising that never previously existed. Born and brought up in Wisconsin in the American mid-West, Kile served his time with a local radio station. During World War II he served with the American forces in Europe; he was said to have taken part in the D Day landings in Normandy, France, in June, 1944 and to have gone ashore at Cherbourg. Later in the war, he was said to have taken part in the Allied landings in southern Italy.

One of the stories told and retold about him had him watching an American-made film on RTE; it covered World War II and included actual footage shot during the landings in Italy. Kile is said to have recognised himself and to have rung up RTE demanding his appearance fee! He returned to the publicity business after the war, having done a stint on the American forces' newspaper in Europe, *Stars and Stripes*. About 1960, he was working on a big public relations contract for Turkish tourism, a contract said to have been cancelled

In 1961, a gathering was held of previous chairmen of the Publicity Club of Ireland. They are seen with host, Edward Murphy, and chairman of the year, Oonagh McWhirter — front row: Albert Price (W. D & H. O. Wills - 1946, 1971); Jack O'Sheehan (Hospitals Trust - 1944); Brian D. O'Kennedy (O'Kennedy Brindley - 1945); Edward Murphy (Independent Newspapers), Oonagh McWhirter (Variety Club of Ireland - 1961); Charles E. McConnell (McConnell's - 1929, 1939-44, 1970); Fred Summerfield (F M Summerfield, Chrysler Cars - 1927); George Childs (Irish Assurance Co - 1947). Back row: David P. Luke (Irish Press group - 1954); Liam Boyd (TWA - 1955); Victor Woods (Fry Cadbury - 1952); Edward F. MacSweeney (Odeon - 1950); Melville Miller (The Irish Times - 1949); J. M. McNeill (Players - 1959); Andrew Gairn (David Allen - 1960); Walter Douglas (Lamb Bros - 1957); Fergus O'Sheehan (F.O.S. - 1956).

when the generals took over in Ankara. Royds had opened a branch office in Dawson Street, Dublin — its very first account was Jacob's biscuits — and Mack Kile was "headhunted" to run the office. This he did so well that by 1963, Royds had moved into more palatial premises at 9 Fitzwilliam Square. Meanwhile, Tim O'Neill's health began to deteriorate — he died in 1967 at the age of 56 — and he decided to sell out. The three directors of Sun Advertising, by now well ensconced in Earlsfort Mansions, Earlsfort Terrace, were O'Neill, his wife Catherine ("Kitty") and Elizabeth Somers. After the sale, Royds'

An advertisement for O'Kennedy Brindley, Cork, placed about 1960.

our game is your business...

Planning, designing and placing advertisements is very much a team effort. So too is Public Relations and Marketing. At O'K-B we have brought together just such a team—talented people all expert in their own fields. Working together as one force on over one hundred accounts. Smashing profit targets for our clients. Always scoring heavily. Winning a place on this side means a lot of hard work and even more expertise. Toothy grins make for nothing, flashy ties make for less. Knowing the score in the Advertising, Marketing and P.R. field means dropping down for a team talk—we're playing at home most days.

Directors: D. B. O'Kennedy, R. M. O'Hanrahan, N. A. O'Kennedy, E. W. Mooney, R. O'Kelly.
Team Members: Sean Power, Pat Barry, Anne Stenson, Jack Sweeney, Manus O'Callaghan, Jo. O'Sullivan, Sylvia Hennessy, Margaret Baker, Rita Barry, Seamus O'Farrell, E. W. Mooney, R. O'Kelly.
Insert: Linda Lavery—on transfer from English First Division Side.

okb O'KENNEDY-BRINDLEY (CORK) LTD., 26 MacCURTAIN ST., CORK, TEL. 51203, TELEX 6013.

DESTINATION DUBLIN

Sportiest of town cars, liveliest of country cars, the handsome Anglia takes anything and everything in its cheerful stride. On trips to the city you'll find the Anglia nips merrily in and out of the busiest traffic, parks with neat precision. On country outings the roomy Anglia carries four passengers more if they're children quickly and comfortably to the sea or the hills.

- Wonderful 997cc oversquare engine gives speeds over 75 mph yet remarkable economy up to 50 mpg'
- Rake-back rear window gives extra passenger room, big boot gives generous luggage space.
- 4-speed gearbox helps sporty acceleration, safe sure overtaking.
- Insurable in 9 hp class, taxed at the lowest rate.
- Backed by Ford Service in Ireland and overseas.

ANGLIA THE WORLD'S MOST EXCITING LIGHT CAR FROM **FORD** OF CORK DE LUXE £535

Dublin office and Sun Advertising merged to form Irish International in 1966.

Kile had an amazing ability for writing "jingles" and commercials: none showed his talents to better effect than the "Mr Figgerty" campaigns for Jacob's fig rolls. The copy theme of the "Mr Figgerty" campaign was "How do Jacob's get the figs into fig rolls?" Kile was one of the few advertising people then to understand the totality of the marketplace, according to a former colleague. In an unsuccessful pitch to the ESB for its account, he told the advertising "heads" at the board about the psychology of colour in advertising, the use of "hot" and "cold" colours, but his ideas were ahead of their time. A generous, extrovert man who loved dining at Jammets, the Royal Hibernian or the Russell Hotel — now all sadly gone — he insisted on entertaining in style. He was also the first person in Ireland to use a video recorder, ten years in advance of their general acceptance here.

He brought in a clatter of new accounts to Irish International including Allied Irish Banks (during the pitch for the AIB account, legend has it that the safe opened and out stepped Mack Kile and his team), Ryans Hotels, Cantrell and Cochrane. For Bord Bainne, he launched Kerrygold butter on the home market in 1972 with the copy theme: "Welcome Home Kerrygold". His presentations for clients often bordered on the flamboyant: at one Dunlop presentation, he was said to have arrived in the room curled up inside an enormous tyre. Sadly, several people who were also present at that presentation deny the authenticity of the story. His parties were good too: at one fancy dress affair, both Kile and senior executives from Jacob's were seen dressed in grass skirts, in keeping with the Hawaiian theme of the

Advertisement for Ford Anglia cars, Irish Press, November 2, 1961, when the Cork-based firm was market leader. By 1986, Ford's share of the Irish car market had slumped to a mere 14 per cent.

CHURCH OF THE MIRACULOUS MEDAL

C L O N S K E A G H

Blessed and Dedicated on Our Lady's Birthday

Clients of Our Lady have already given us over 100,000 bricks. We still need the gift of 900,000 bricks to clear the debt on our church.

How many will you donate in honour of Our Blessed Lady?
Offering for each brick: Two Shilling and Sixpence.

VERY REV. T. R. CONDON, P.P.
Church of the Sacred Heart, Donnybrook, Dublin

Church building fund advertisement, Irish Press, **November, 1961.**

party. On the serious side, he persuaded the International Advertising Association to hold its world conference in Dublin: 2,000 delegates came to town.

One thing is for sure, remembers John Conway of Irish International: "He taught me how to live beyond my means". Yet despite all his flamboyance, he was regarded as a very honest man, said by friends and enemies alike of being incapable of stabbing anyone in the back. Another of his moves was to set up a subsidiary agency in London, Image International: only later, it was said, did Royds find out about it. One of the Saatchi brothers was a freelance copywriter for the Image agency. Although Mack Kile left Ireland in 1975 to live in southern Spain and California — for some years he has been touring the world with Wayne McMahon's show of TV commercials — his influence, both serious and flippant, on Irish advertising, remains potent.

Despite the enormous interest created by the new advertising medium, TV, the print media determined to fight back. In February, 1962, *The Irish Times* had its first ever full colour advertisement, for Jacob's biscuits. The advertisement was pre-printed by Hely's on East Wall Road, closely connected with *The Irish Times* through Frank Lowe and George Hetherington.

The *Irish Press* was also experimenting with colour and that same year, Independent Newspapers installed its gravure printing plant at Middle Abbey Street for full colour printing. In October, 1962, the *Irish Independent* ran its first ever full colour advertisement, from Janus for Carlsberg. Also in 1962, Bob Milne came home to Ireland, rather reluctantly. He had spent a long time working in the London advertising agencies and his urge to come back was fading. One day, he received a letter from Tim O'Neill of Sun Advertising, who wrote: "You're probably a West Cork Protestant (he wasn't), but will you come for an interview?" He came over to Dublin for a rugby match, stayed in the Dolphin and decided to accept O'Neill's offer. He started by looking after Carroll's international brands and remembers well those first advertisements in full colour in the *Irish Independent*.

Ralph Leonard (right), publicity manager, Aer Lingus, pictured with Brian Lenihan about 1960.

214

At the annual meeting of the Irish Association of Advertising Agencies, held in Athlone in 1962, Desmond O'Kennedy, outgoing chairman (third from left) makes a point. Also from left: Luke Mahon (Arks), Dermod Cafferky (Arrow), Tom Linehan and J. B. Clancy.
Photo: Lensmen.

Group taken at the Irish Association of Advertising Agencies' conference in the Shamrock Lodge hotel, Athlone, in February, 1962, at which plans were discussed for a phasing out of the association and its replacement by the proposed Institute of Advertising Practitioners in Ireland. From left: Ernie Keogh (Arrow), Luke Mahon (Arks), Michael B. Kenny (Kenny's), Oliver Walsh (IAAA), Desmond O'Kennedy (O'Kennedy Brindley) and John Young (R. Wilson Young).

215

Monday's child—a brilliant sales idea

by a
special correspondent

SMALL cars, big cars, medium cars . . . long cars, wide cars, utility cars and status symbol cars . . . English cars and Continental cars—Ireland has them all!

Into this highly competitive, complex, buyer's market Brindley Advertising successfully sought and found a slot for the NSU Prinz on behalf of their client Reg Armstrong Motors Ltd, who were the first firm outside Germany to be entrusted with the assembly of NSU Prinz.

In the NSU Prinz, Brindley Advertising had an excellent product with numerous advantages over its competitors. The problem was to communicate these advantages to potential buyers in an unusual, quick and easily digestible way and to avoid cramming all the sales points into an advertisement reminiscent of a store "Bargain Week".

Brindley Advertising started by asking the basic questions "Who is the market for a car of this type?" and "What features has the NSU Prinz got that this market looks for in a car?" Potential buyers obviously lay in all income groups amongst bachelor men and women as well as families. It is extremely well designed, good to look at, astonishingly roomy for its size, and is very economical to run.

A nippy car, it is capable of speed, amazing acceleration and yet is easy to drive with fantastic manoeuvrability. The NSU Prinz, then, was highly suited as both a family pleasure car and for every day business use in city traffic with its attendant parking problems.

These pluses gave Brindley's a platform for their campaign—"The car for every day of the week" and a copy platform, parodying the nursery rhyme "Monday's child" was evolved.

It was decided to run a series of 11 in by four-column advertisements every week in selected papers, each advertisement to feature a different selling point. Visual impact was attained by the bold use of white space and unusual angle photographs of the car. Reversed type on a black panel reiterated in rhyme all these selling points appearing on different days.

The result was a striking hard hitting series of advertisements which hammered home all the major selling features of the car in an interesting and easily assimilated manner with excellent continuity.

Every advertisement carried a keyed coupon inviting application for a full-colour brochure on the NSU Prinz. Coupon returns exceeded all expectations and provided a valuable mailing list for future sales contacts. A whimsical touch was added in the "FOR REG" number plates on the illustrations of the car giving extra emphasis to Reg Armstrong Motors as distributors.

The press campaign was backed with extensive television and cinema advertising which echoed the main theme.

Sales were highly satisfactory and pushed the NSU Prinz up into the top selling bracket of 800 cc cars on the Irish market—confirmation of the old adage "Find out what they want and tell 'em you've got it quickly and concisely!"

Brindley Advertising successfully sought and found a slot for the NSU Prinz on behalf of their client Reg Armstrong Motors Ltd

THURSDAY'S PRINZ

Sunday's Prinz is fair of face.
Monday's Prinz has lots of space.
Tuesday's Prinz is noted for thrift.
Wednesday's Prinz can really shift.
Thursday's Prinz can turn on a button.
Friday's Prinz is an "extras" glutton.
Saturday's Prinz with these extras galore.
Ex works costs five two-nine, and no more!

REG ARMSTRONG MOTORS LTD
Ringsend Road, Dublin 4 Telephone 683533

PLEASE SEND ME FULL COLOUR PRINZ 4 BROCHURE

NAME
ADDRESS

Thursday's Prinz . . . .
"Manoeuverability" seems a frighteningly big word when it comes to describing the Prinz 4's small-space handiness. There are more parking places for the apparently double-jointed Prinz—parking spaces passed in despair by drivers of other cars. With such intelligent shortness of body and an amazing turning circle of 28 feet, the compact Prinz runs rings inside them all! But there's no sacrifice of interior roominess—there's more passenger space in the Prinz than most 1200 c.c. cars! Perhaps "nimble" is the suitable word for the COMPACT Prinz 4.
* Up to 50 m.p.g. * 75 m.p.h. * Luxury fittings * Stove enamel finish * 36 b.h.p. * 4,500 mile service interval * 11.9 cu. ft. luggage space * Silent heater/demister * £13 tax

Reference—Association of Advertisers in Ireland

THE Association of Advertisers in Ireland. Council and officers for 1963: Chairman, J. C. Bigger (Hammond Lane Foundry Co Ltd): vice-chairman, J. M. McNeill (John Player & Sons): hon treasurer, F. C. Palmer (Reckitts (Ireland) Ltd): hon secretary, D. C. Jordan (Esso Petroleum Co (Ireland) Ltd).

Council: W. P. Cavanagh (Chivers & Sons (Ireland) Ltd); J. A. Chapman (Switzer & Co Ltd):

G. P. L. Cook (Lever Brothers (Ireland) Ltd); J. F. Kearney (Williams & Woods Ltd); C. P. Kelleher (Bovril (Ireland) Ltd); C. G. Lambert (W. & R. Jacob & Co Ltd).

N. McConnell (Aspro-Nicholas of Ireland Ltd); J. O'Sheenan (Hospitals Trust (1940) Ltd); K. Rowe (Sunbeam Wolsey Ltd); K. E. J. Tyrrell (Arthur Guinness Son & Co (Dublin) Ltd); and V. M. Woods (Fry-Cadbury (Ireland) Ltd).

★ **DONEGAL DEMOCRAT**

CERTIFIED NET SALE 8,970 COPIES WEEKLY   BALLYSHANNON, CO. DONEGAL—115 HIGH HOLBORN, W.C.I.

In 1963, Brian Doyle was named advertising manager of W. D. & H. O. Wills, in succession to Albert Price, who had retired. Before Wills, Doyle had worked for Domas and Masser-Waterford Ironfounders. Price became a director of Fogarty's. City Publicity, started by Cecil Dick in 1951, moved to Upper Leeson Street in 1963; it had been in Suffolk Street. Interesting people worked for the agency, like Derek Morris, who went to live in Florida, Fred MacDonald, who had been with Lynch's and who had worked as a reporter in the Spanish civil war and ex-Luftwaffe pilot, Freddie Heinzl, who later worked for Bailey Son & Gibson and who died some years ago. In 1973, City merged with Admar, whose leading lights (still with the merged agency) were Phil Fitzpatrick and Gerry Dunne, son of John Dunne, once manager of Independent Newspapers. Carmel Bruce, who was with Cecil Dick, in Sun, also shines in City. Elizabeth Somers, for so long Tim O'Neill's right hand woman, spent only a short time in Irish International after the Royds/Sun merger and joined City in 1965.

At Janus, still regarded as a top creative agency in the early 1960s, Mia Ffrench-Mullen joined as secretary to Pat Ryan, the general manager. Later, she became an account executive, before moving, some years later to a similar position in Fogarty's. She is now retired. During Pat Ryan's time in Janus, many now familiar names in the business were with the agency. On the media side, Harry Byers was there, with Padraic Guilfoyle as a junior. Ciaran Havelin was there as a junior, so too was Ken Grace, also Michael Bowles. Janus was almost as much a training ground as was Domas. One very talented copywriter, Bert Weiner, went from Janus to McConnell's in 1970. He died of a heart attack less than a year later. He was a Cockney Jew, a delightful man, remembers Ryan. One young man who worked in the Janus studio committed suicide by putting his head in a gas oven. Giles Talbot Kelly, a rather flamboyant English designer, was at Janus too. Later, he was involved in the setting up of ICAD as well as Group Three design, an early design consultancy in Dublin, before going to the National College of Art.

At Arrow, then an up-and-coming agency, young Brian Murphy was making headway. He had trained as an illustrator in New York, but returning home, found there was no demand for those skills in the magazine field, so he joined Arrow, which had just been bought out by Ernie Keogh and Dermod Cafferky from Harry O'Brien, Keogh's uncle. Brian Murphy was made creative director in the early 1960s; the agency staff numbers had crept up to about 14. In 1964, he was made a director, buying a ten per cent stake in the company; Joe Dillon, who had started the agency's public relations department three years previously, making Arrow one of the very first agencies to take public relations seriously, did the same. Such accounts came the way of Arrow as the First National Building Society and Renault cars. O'Kennedy Brindley was on a creative upswing too, with the arrival of

Try it when you are tired

GUINNESS Yeast EXTRACT
A glass of Hot Gye rapidly
restores energy whenever
you feel tired

A Guinness brand failure from the early 1960s: Gye, a yeast based, by-product of the brewing process, similar to Marmite.

Opposite page:
In 1962, Brindley's mounted a major campaign using press, television and cinema for the NSU Prinz car. The copy platform parodied the nursery rhyme, Monday's Child. 11" x 4 cols newspaper advertisements included a keyed coupon inviting applications for a full colour brochure. The huge number of replies gave a valuable mailing list. The campaign soon pushed the car into the top selling bracket of 800 cc cars.

In the early 1960s, O'Kennedy Brindley prepared many campaigns for Volkswagen cars that had a distinctly humorous touch, as in this example from national newspapers in November and December, 1963. The campaigns also made extensive use of outdoor posters.

Musgrave tea competition, 1963.

people like Rena Dardis, the copywriter and Rex McDonnell, a highly regarded illustrator. In 1962 also, McConnell's in Belfast became a subsidiary of the Dublin firm, rather than of McConnell's, London.

One of the top agencies of the 1950s, Domas, was starting to "split". By 1962, it had been going for 20 years; Joe Tiernan joined the agency that year. He had been with its accountants. When Tiernan came in, Domas was in Granite House in Pembroke Road, Ballsbridge (since demolished) and had a staff of 42, making it one of the largest agencies in town. It came to be regarded as the prime "nursery" in the agency business, since so many of its employees broke away to set up their own shops. Peter Owens, Adsell, the modern Wilson Hartnell, Brendan White, all these agencies had their origins in Domas. Peter Owens had worked in Domas from 1956 until 1958, when he went to the US. On his return, in 1960, he started up his own agency. Paddy Considine was joint managing director of Domas, with Joe Delaney, after Owens left. Considine remembers that he did not find it a satisfactory situation, so he decided to leave and set up his own agency, Adsell. Considine, strong on the visual side of advertising — he was reckoned to have been the first artist in Dublin to use scraperboard

Heard any good VW jokes lately?

 VOLKSWAGEN 1200

techniques — says that his was one of the very first agencies to have been set up by a creative rather than a management person. He brought with him Noel Foley, who became production manager, account executive and company secretary. From Domas, Considine acquired the Smithwicks beer account, which remained with the agency until 1982. Between Domas and Adsell, Paddy Considine worked on the Smithwicks account for the best part of 40 years. Betty Griffin was a colleague from Domas; she teamed up with Considine to run the public relations side of Adsell as a separate company.

The departure of Michael Maughan and Sean O Bradaigh from Domas to take over Wilson Hartnell was perhaps the biggest blow suffered by Joe Delaney's agency.

When Joe Tiernan joined Domas in 1962, Michael Maughan was with the agency. So too was Sean O Bradaigh; Dickie Duggan, the insurance man, had long been involved with Domas. Michael Maughan remembers that at the time of the takeover, Wilson Hartnell, then based in Commercial Buildings in Dame Street, was like something out of Dickens' Pickwick Papers. At the time, the firm was more concerned with its publishing side, the *Irish Tatler & Sketch*. Advertising played a secondary rôle. Some sources say that at the time of the takeover, Wilson Hartnell was turning over £10,000 a year on its advertising accounts: Michael Maughan says the figure was as low as £5,000. Maughan had had a Jesuit education — useful in advertising — shared with Finbar Costello, managing director of Irish International. Maughan, who gained experience on handling client accounts at Domas, but who was never made a director there, did not want to have a fashionable "hot shop" that was named after him. He wanted a solid, traditional name that was well respected in the advertising business. Wilson Hartnell provided the perfect takeover opportunity. Henry Crawford Hartnell had set up the firm in 1879 and eventually handed it on to his bachelor son, Noel, who often used to say: "O'Keeffes claims it was the first service agency. They haven't a leg to stand on. We were. "When Maughan took over Wilson Hartnell, he kept on the aged Noel Hartnell — signing cheques. Sean O Bradaigh looked after internal administration including personnel, while Maughan looked after account procurement and the agency image. Richard G. Duggan, who had been a founder of Domas and chairman of that agency until two years previously, came in as chairman of Wilson Hartnell. The vice-chairman was R. F. Browne, who had been chairman of the Electricity Supply Board for 30 years and who had just retired from that position. At the time of his appointment at Wilson Hartnell, he was still a director of Lyons Irish Holdings and Unidare. Browne was a major influence on Maughan's early career.

At the time, Michael Maughan was described as having been responsible for the successful campaign for DuPont's "Orlon" brand on the Irish market. He had also handled advertising for such brands as Dorothy Gray, Manhattan shirts, Cooper's Jockey underwear, Viyella

A 1962 advertisement for the now-demolished Grand Central hotel in Royal Avenue, Belfast. It was described as "Ulster's premier hotel" and boasted that its bedrooms were fitted with universal type electric razor plugs.

Noel C. Hartnell, who inherited the Wilson Hartnell publishing house and advertising agency from his father, H. C. Hartnell. In turn, Noel Hartnell sold out to Michael Maughan and Sean O Bradaigh.

Members of the Irish Institute of Marketing and Sales Management pictured leaving Dublin in 1964 for the sixth international congress of marketing and distribution in Barcelona. Included in the group are H. V. Woods (secretary), Mr and Mrs Bill Cavanagh, Mr and Mrs A. F. Corduff, Mr and Mrs R. L. Bates, Mr and Mrs M. J. O'Reilly and Messrs S. Doyle, D. B. Fennessy, T. H. Quinn and T. C. Manweiler. *Photograph: Independent Newspapers.*

Smith's potato crisps cost just three old pennies a packet back in 1963. Main competition came from the Tayto brand, launched by Joe Murphy in 1954. Later, Murphy sold out his firm to Beatrice Foods of Chicago.

-all you need for a package of

SMITHS

NEW POTATO CRISPS

and Alpine knitwear. Sean O Bradaigh, a winner of the Conlon gold medal in 1948, had worked in O'Keeffes and Kenny's before joining Domas, where he was account director on such accounts as TWA, Canada Dry and Proctor and Gamble, the washing powder manufacturers. Soon, Wilson Hartnell began bringing in new accounts, such as the Irish Sugar Company, the Gresham Hotel, Manhattan shirts, Hardy's frozen foods (which were just starting to come into the Irish market) and British Paints (Ireland). 24 Lansdowne Road was rented from Nan Morgan, founder of the model agency, and the new shop started with a staff of 14. In 1965, the year after the agency began under its new ownership, Frank Young, now managing director, joined from the Pigs and Bacon Commission. In June of that year, Nick van Vliet joined; he had been with McCann Erickson in Holland for the previous eight years. Another talented Dutchman had come into Irish advertising.

Not long before the takeover of Wilson Hartnell, two major newspaper close-downs took place. The much loved *Dublin Evening Mail* closed down: affection was not enough to sustain it in a much changed marketplace. In the following year, November, 1963, the *Sunday Review* was closed down by *The Irish Times.* Despite a circulation of 160,000, it failed to attract agency support. It had a brilliant editorial team which included John Healy and Ted Nealon, but despite its sound editorial content, it was not a viable commercial operation. On one occasion, such was its desperation for advertising, that it ran a feature on caravanning, with two pages made up of suppliers' advertisements,

Pictured at the Association of Advertisers in Ireland annual dinner in the Shelbourne Hotel, Dublin, in January, 1964, from left: Hugh McLaughlin (Creation), Mrs Noel Cautley, Ray O'Keeffe (O'Keeffes), Mrs Nuala McLaughlin, Ken Rowe (Sunbeam Wolsey), Mrs Ray O'Keeffe, Noel Cautley (O'Keeffes) and Mrs Ken Rowe.

nearly all 1" single column affairs. Perhaps its greatest drawback was that it could not carry adequate colour advertising: very often, colour advertisements had to be withdrawn late on a Saturday night because the quality would not pass muster. Sources said, in retrospect, that if the *Sunday Review* had been allowed to survive for another couple of years, with better facilities for colour advertisers, it would never have closed and the *Sunday World* would never have started.

A full colour advertisement for Fit Kilkenny Remoulds won a major European prize for J. H. Parker in 1964. This small Dublin agency, with a present staff of nine, including Kingsley Dempsey and his father, P. J., geared up in the 1960s, adding a complement of services, like public relations. It has about 60 clients, including Ritchie's Mints and the Irish Linen Guild. Tony Lokko did Ritchie's familiar design, still used today.

Michael Colley of the Electricity Supply Board was talking about advertising. He said, in a feature for an early issue of *Business and Finance* magazine: "It is the exception rather than the rule for an advertising agency to get a really full briefing from the client on the overall market position when initial campaigns are being discussed. It is seldom that such discussions are held far enough in advance for the agency to produce its best in publicity material. Forward planning is not a characteristic of most Irish advertising and frequently, the blame for indifferent campaigns is laid at the agency door, when in fact it is lying fairly and squarely on the client's mat."

Colley went on to complain about a reluctance by clients to use consumer and market research. "Good marketing and advertising is based on knowledge; knowledge of the scope of the market, competitors' activities, consumer attitudes. Whilst I am convinced that some organisations carry their research to absurd lengths — US-based companies particularly — I am equally well convinced that well-planned and reasonably priced research can point to the proper approach in a marketing and advertising programme."

Michael Maughan, chairman, Wilson Hartnell. Up to the early 1960s, he worked for Domas, then in 1965, he was instrumental, with Sean O Bradaigh, in buying out Wilson Hartnell, then known primarily as publisher of *Irish Tatler and Sketch* magazine. Its billings as an advertising agency were reckoned to have been as low as £5,000 at the time of the takeover.

221

Norman McConnell, left, (Aspro) and Ken Tyrrell (Guinness) pictured at the 1963 dinner of the Association of Advertisers in Ireland.

Rena Dardis, the copywriter, who worked first in Janus, before transferring to O'Kennedy Brindley in 1959. She played a key rôle in the latter agency's creative "fizz" of the 1960s.

While Colley was lamenting short-sighted attitudes to market research, the man who did more than anyone else to change the situation was arriving in Ireland, John Lepere. Born in Belgium of English parents, his life got off to an exciting start when as a young boy at the beginning of World War II, he had been evacuated through France to escape the German advance. He spent the early years of his career in market research in London and had been on the point of going to Zurich as managing director of J. Walter Thompson's Swiss office when a call came through from Don Carroll of Carroll's, the cigarette firm. He persuaded Lepere to come to Dublin to discuss a job offer, even though Lepere was not particularly interested. Out of courtesy, he came over and ended up by taking the job at Carroll's, in charge of marketing. Although "marketing" had been a vogue word in London for the previous ten years, it was scarcely used in Ireland in the early 1960s. Lepere brought to his new job and to Irish industry generally an enthusiasm for marketing and the sciences it engendered, particularly scientifically-based market research. He was one of the early directors of Irish Marketing Surveys, set up by John Meagher at about the same time, in which Carrolls became a major stakeholder, along with Guinness.

The new science of market research had a profound effect on the advertising business in Ireland. Already, media managers were being appointed to the larger agencies and with the rapid growth of

PUT
A
TIGER
IN
YOUR
TANK

ESSO
EXTRA

CALL AT THE ESSO SIGN

FAST!

Don't suffer pain—nerve pains, neuralgia, headache, backache. Take two or three 'Aspro' and stop pain *fast*. **Medical science** has now proved that the 'Aspro' formula is the world's most effective pain reliever. So for quick, safe, relief take 'Aspro'. There's no better medicine.

YOU ARE RIGHT TO TRUST 'ASPRO'

A NICHOLAS N PRODUCT

'ASPRO' IS PROVED

One of the most famous advertising campaigns of the 1960s, Esso's "Tiger in your tank". The campaign was devised in Britain and adapted for use in Ireland by Kenny's. This example appeared in the Sunday Review, July 28, 1963.

Until the mid-1960s, Aspro used frequent large spaces in national and provincial newspapers, before switching irrevocably to television. This advertisement appeared in the Sunday Review of November 17, 1963, the second last issue of the newspaper.

television, the need for accurate research into listening, reading and viewing patterns became paramount. John Meagher had returned from Canada to Dublin in 1963; a good salary in the latter city that year was £2,000. Having worked in market research in Canada, he was determined to set up his own market research firm. A. C. Nielsen was already in Dublin and Jack Jones had set up his Market Research Bureau of Ireland in 1962. Twice in the first year, Meagher thought of packing up and going back to Canada, then in 1965, he persuaded Guinness and Carrolls to become shareholders in Irish Marketing Surveys. Their arrival allowed for the eventual departure of all but one of the UK shareholders. NOP, a subsidiary of Associated Newspapers, is the only remaining UK shareholder. Today, the IMS group has four companies employing about 70 people. It also employs, on a casual basis, about 450 researchers. Lansdowne Market Research is complementary to IMS, while in the North, there is Ulster Marketing Surveys. IMS also has 51 per cent of IMS Condon, Sean Condon's marketing consultancy. Infoscan is run by Eamonn Williams. Meagher is also a director of CIE and of TAM; he is also deputy chairman of Independent Newspapers.

Dick O'Hanrahan of O'Kennedy Brindley, poses for a backache advertisement in the early 1960s.

Joan Walker, now retired, once a stalwart of McConnell's copywriting department.

John Lepere became one of the prime movers in the shift towards a more scientific approach to the advertising business and the evaluation of its audiences, so from that point of view, his place in the development of Irish advertising has indeed been seminal. He believes that the agency is vital in protecting the integrity of the brand. He had opportunities to put his beliefs into practice with some of the last big cigarette launches before the big Government clamp-downs on tobacco products' advertising. In 1966, three years after Lepere's arrival, Carroll's launched its Major brand. Until then, male smokers had an overwhelming preference for plain cigarettes. Tipped cigarettes were perceived as being feminine, so the advertising campaign devised by Peter Owens had a major rôle reversal job to do. The copyline was: "Major breakthrough in big smoking enjoyment." The new brand of cigarettes cost 3/11 for 20; upwards of £200,000 was spent on both television and full colour advertisements in the printed media, including Independent Newspapers' publications. It was one of the last times that a major cigarette launch could take place, free of the restrictions that later shackled the market. Soon, Major captured 25 per cent of the market, an extraordinary achievement and a brand domination it has retained to this day. John Lepere, unfashionably, believes that concerns about the health aspects of smoking as well as the resulting restrictions, are overdone. The launch was also a big success for the Peter Owens' agency, then only six years old. However, other cigarette launches at the time flopped: Arks ran big campaigns for Player's Shannon cigarettes, which failed to take off, partly because

A McConnell's golf outing to Delgany, 1965. From left: Des Bradley, Mike Tobin, John O'Neill, John Brown and Niall O'Sullivan.

In the early 1960s, the "16 Group", members of staff at Arks, held an exhibition of their art work.
As at early 1986, members of that group had scattered to a wide variety of other occupations; just one person from the group remained with Arks. Exhibitors, with recent location, were as

the brand name had the wrong connotations. Another cigarette launch that failed at this time was Wills' Woodbine Export.

Three years after the Carroll's Major launch, Gallaher's made one of its first big launches in Dublin. In 1969, it brought out Silk Cut, the first low tar cigarette, a prescient forewarning of the health concerns to come. Just two years later, the UK Royal College of Surgeons' report on the alleged links between cigarette smoking and poor health, was published, starting the debate that has culminated in more and more restrictions on tobacco products' advertising.

exhibition

16 group exhibition

follows: Eric Bannister (Arks), Michael Bolger (Irish International), Peter Bolt (retired), Joseph Byrne (Peter Owens), Noel Byrne (retired), Francis Cray (Youngs), Edmond De Reymonth (own photographic business), Jim Harkin (own business), Ronan Henry (Swan Design), Clare Hurley (married), Marcella Kerin (retired), James Leahy (Dun Laoghaire VEC), Victor McBrien (Kenny's), Raymond McCaffrey (emigrated), Desmond McCarthy (own business, DMA), Jack McGouran (Quest public relations), Francis MacMahon (O'Kennedy Brindley), Luke Mahon (retired), Terence Murphy (emigrated), Gilda Mason (married), Kenneth Mosley (emigrated), James Nolan (IAPI), Brendan O Broin (CDP), Joseph O'Mara (retired), Kay Owens (Mrs John Fanning), Terry Pattison (QMP), Sean Redmond (own business), Annette Smyth (Hunters), John Tate (deceased), John Thompson (Irish Farmers' Journal), Shamus Wade (re-emigrated), Edward Weinmann (O'Kennedy Brindley) and Frank Sheerin (own business).

Very shortly after Carroll's had brought Major cigarettes on the market, Peter Owens handled another big consumer launch. Galtee launched a vacuum packed bacon joint, the first product of its type on the Irish market. The bag had to be boiled by the housewife; the media campaign had to do a two-fold educational job, with this new kind of product and in the way it was cooked. Owens did an admirable job. Owens' creative marketing strategy was proving effective, appreciated by Galtee's go-ahead marketing expert, Ed Cussen.

In 1965, Dublin had 27 major advertising agencies. Admar was still in Upper Fitzwilliam Street (before its merger with City Publicity). Adsell was then as now in Upper Leeson Street, Arks was at Clonmell House in Harcourt Street. Pat Ferguson was already a director: on the

An elephant livens up the opening of an early Quinn supermarket in 1965. Now, the group is far better known as Superquinn and is celebrating its 25th anniversary.
Photograph: Superquinn.

retirement of Luke Dillon-Mahon, he became chairman and managing director. Arrow listed four directors: Ernest Keogh, Dermod Cafferky, Brian Murphy and Joe Dillon. Brindleys had no fewer than six members of the Brindley family listed as directors, while Caps Publicity, majoring on just two accounts, the Hospitals' Sweepstakes and Bord na Mona, had three directors, Niall O'Rahilly, Mrs. Bridie O'Rahilly and John Sweetman, G. & S. Doherty had been set up two years previously by Gerry Doherty, who had worked in the *Irish Press,* Janus and then as creative director of Grosvenor, and his wife Sybil, hence the G. & S. Three other Dublin business people were involved in the agency, Walter Maguire, John V. Rafferty and David McIlvenna. Domas directors were listed as Joseph A. Delaney, Brendan T. White, Joseph A. Tiernan O. Delaney and Eoin Plunkett, who had joined the agency in 1948 and who is still there. Edward J. Kelleher and William H. Clarke were listed as directors of Easons Advertising. About this time, Noelle Campbell-Sharp was starting her business career, as a rather junior employee of Easons. Fogarty's was already at Haddington Road, while Janus was in Parnell Square. Kenny's was in Lower Baggot Street; the great "splits" were about to happen. John Doyle, who now runs a seafood restaurant in Dingle, Co Kerry, remembers that with the divided board in Kenny's, rival groups of directors were meeting in different houses. Eamonn Geraghty, the general manager, was ousted after 25 years' service: John Doyle recalls Eamonn Geraghty well: "he wasn't one of the shiny suit brigade. He cared about the agency and helped young people, including myself, to get on. He is one of the most

When Wilson Hartnell designed this advertisement for Phoenix beer in the mid-1960s, agency staff turned to beer drinking. Included in the photograph from left are: Nick van Vliet, Brian Martin, Alan Cooke (now Bell Advertising) and Pat McIntyre, who now runs his own design and origination studios. The second person from the right is unidentified.

A Morrissey's advertisement for the letting of Liberty Hall, Dublin's first 'Skyscraper', 1965.

Noel, Ken, Vinnie and the boys like what's happened to

PHOENIX

There's a new generation of beer drinkers; different attitudes, different tastes. Takes a good beer to keep pace — and stay on top. Phoenix does. Clear-cut, cool-headed Phoenix. A taste for the times. Gaudeamus igitur.

WILSON HARTNELL

MORRISSEY'S

LIBERTY HALL
(NOW NEARING COMPLETION)

PRESTIGE OFFICE ACCOMMODATION TO LET

CLOSE TO O'CONNELL STREET, CUSTOMS HOUSE AND PORT OF DUBLIN

AVAILABLE LETTING SPACE: 12,000 SQ. FT. NETT FROM SEVENTH TO TWELFTH FLOORS INCLUSIVE

ALL MODERN AMENITIES

TWO HIGH-SPEED LIFTS
CENTRAL HEATING

Each floor contains approximately 2,000 sq. ft. nett and lettings of one or more floors will be considered

THERE ARE ALSO FOUR LOCK-UP SHOPS FACING ON TO EDEN QUAY AVAILABLE FOR LETTING ON LEASE TO APPROVED TENANTS

FULL DETAILS OF RENTS AND ACCOMMODATION AVAILABLE FROM SOLE LETTING AGENTS
DANIEL MORRISSEY & SONS LTD.
MERRION BUILDINGS, LR. MERRION ST., DUBLIN

227

Frank Young,
managing director,
Wilson Hartnell. He
joined the agency from
the Pigs and Bacon
Commission in 1965.

human men in advertising, yet after 25 years' service in Kenny's, got just hours' notice."

Jarlath Hayes, who had graduated from Kenny's to work in other agencies, such as O'Keeffes and McConnell's, found his most exciting agency niche at O'Kennedy Brindley in the 1960s. He says then, that the place was "pulsating". Eventually, he was invited back to O'Keeffes, where he became tired of the agency scene. He found Ray O'Keeffe too fond of minute detail; in the end, Hayes quit advertising agency work in 1972 to found his own design practice.

Lynch's was still going strong in Amiens Street, while directors of McConnell's, apart from the McConnell family, included John Brown, financial controller and Eric Kerr. Mike Tobin, McConnell's media director, remembers well arriving in the agency after leaving school; there was no such thing as a "media department". The order department was the correct terminology and the only data required was the cost per column inch in individual newspapers and the cost per 1,000. There was no science to it at all and account executives and clients worked out the campaign schedules together. TV's arrival focussed attention on the need for readership and audience data; about 1969, Tobin was appointed to the board of McConnell's. He headed the new media department; only one other agency in town could claim such a title — O'Kennedy Brindley.

McConnell's sometimes had home movies for its Christmas party. One such film, a ten minute affair, was shot on location at Howth

Mr and Mrs Luke
Dillon-Mahon (Arks) at
a water colours'
exhibition in Dublin,
1968.
Photograph: The Irish Times.

228

Head and featured Owen O'Connor as the "baddie" and Niall O'Sullivan and John O'Neill (who now has his own production company, Design & Art Facilities, as well as a close involvement in Datapage, the new Dublin typesetting firm), as the two "crooks". An old horse was hired for the production, which went under the working title of "Jest passing through". In those days, remembers O'Neill, there was a great family atmosphere in McConnell's and Charlie, the benevolent father figure, had a habit of calling everyone "boys and girls".

John Lepere, who joined Carroll's, the cigarette manufacturers, in the early 1960s, bringing new skills in marketing and market research to the Irish market.

Belfast Telegraph advertisement, 1965.

229

McEvoy's was still in Middle Abbey Street, coming to the end of its life as an advertising agency and trade publisher. In 1965, directors were listed as Niall F. McEvoy and Robert L. McDowell. O'Donnell Earl was at 15, Leeson Park, part of the present location of Wilson Hartnell. O'Keeffes, then as now, was in Fitzwilliam Square. Its directors included Raymond J. O'Keeffe, Brendan J. Matthews and William G. Sutherland, the latter two names showing the insurance broker connection that had existed since Ray O'Keeffe's takeover of the agency in the late 1940s. Directors of O'Kennedy Brindley included Desmond and Niel O'Kennedy, William L. Lindsay, R. M. O'Hanrahan, Rena Dardis, Bill Bergin and Kenneth Murphy. A separate company was listed for O'Kennedy Brindley in Cork. Directors of Padburys were listed as Marie J. Dignam, Robert Nealon and James F. Dignam. Other agencies included Parkers, then at Grafton Street — the last agency to locate in this street — Royds, Sun, Wilson Hartnell and R. Wilson Young. It was an impressive tally. Sadly, in 1965, one long-time employee of Young's died — Tommy O'Sullivan, father of Niall, who had worked in the *Irish Press* before joining Dick Young in his agency. A gregarious and popular man, always ready to mimic, O'Sullivan was a great favourite in the advertising business and his death at the age of 53 came as a great shock to many friends.

One of the newest agencies was Fogarty's, started in 1961 by Aubrey Fogarty. He had started in O'Kennedy Brindley, then worked with Kenny's as a copywriter, then spent five years in Grosvenor. At one stage in his career he had been general manager of Kelly's agency

Cyril Lord recruitment advertisement, Belfast Telegraph, **November, 1965.**

Mrs. Basil Brindley (left) with Mrs. Hugh McLaughlin whose husband played such a major rôle on the Irish printing and publishing scene for over three decades.

230

and publishing house in D'Olier Street. One day, Kelly offered Fogarty 60 per cent of the agency; when the young man saw how deeply in debt the agency was, he agreed, but did a deal with the newspapers to pay them off within a year. Kelly went off to pursue another line of business unsuccessfully, then he returned to the agency and according to Fogarty, "tore up the agreement", so the young man left. He had had a good insight into the Machiavellian politics of the agency business. Also at Kelly's, Aubrey Fogarty met Anne Gill, who later became his wife. She died tragically, of leukaemia, in 1972.

Fogarty's started up in Grafton Street; Frawleys of Thomas Street was its first account. Three months after beginning, a heavy fall of snow blocked all the drains up and the embryonic agency was flooded with sewage. He had only been three or four days in temporary premises in Parnell Street when these went on fire. Then he was back in Grafton Street, moving about a year later to Leeson Street. Fogarty's claimed to have got recognition faster than any other agency at the time. In Leeson Street, where he employed 12 people in three rooms, a potential client arrived from the UK. "Extras" were dotted around the offices and in Fogarty's words, a show was put on. After a suitably impressive lunch, the UK advertiser turned to Fogarty and said: "Now you can let all those people go." It wasn't the first time an advertising agency had put on a big show to win an account and it won't be the last. In Fogarty's case, the client did come in and stayed for 20 years. After a year in Leeson Street, he bought the present Haddington Road premises for £4,500.

At a Publicity Club lunch in 1969, the "chain gang" comprised, from left: B. A. Boyd, chairman, Publicity Club of Northern Ireland, Dermod Cafferky, Publicity Club of Ireland and Michael Hayes, Advertising Press Club.

A testimonial written in 1967 by Don O'Connell, then general manager of G. & S. Doherty.

231

Tommy Johnston (left), director of McConnell's and secretary of TABS Golfing Society in 1965, presenting John O'Neill with his "trophy" following one golf outing.

Citibank Ireland was the first foreign bank to open in Ireland, in 1965. The 20th anniversary of its opening was well advertised in Dublin daily newspapers.

Opposite page:
In May, 1965, Brindley's prepared this prize winning advertisement in French on behalf of the Department of Agriculture. It was used in a supplement on Ireland in Le Monde, the Paris daily newspaper.

Milo O'Shea appeared in this 1965 campaign for Harp lager.

CITIBANK◆

20 Years Ago on this day . . .

We became the first foreign bank to open in Ireland

"*We're here for keeps*"
said Jack Arnold, Senior Vice-President, Citibank New York, at the official opening in Dublin, 1965. (The Irish Times)

CITIBANK◆IRELAND
20th Anniversary

71 St. Stephen's Green, Dublin 2. Tel: (01) 780488
12 South Mall, Cork. Tel: (021) 21953

232

Le Chef, seul, est Français

Everywhere they're drinking

HARP

The Gold Medal lager beer

Oui!

Photographie prise à l'Hôtel Intercontinental de Dublin

The lager you enjoy so much—
Ireland's own favourite

is now drunk in 73 countries
right round the world.

It takes a fine lager to go that far.

tout le menu est IRLANDAIS

La France peut aujourd'hui savourer en toute fraîcheur les délices gastronomiques de la verte Irlande!

La délicatesse de l'agneau de printemps irlandais séduit Gourmets et Chefs de cuisine dans tout Paris. Le bifstek irlandais, savoureux et saignant, ainsi que le porc de première qualité font l'enchantement des plus difficiles.

L'île d'Emeraude est renommée pour son goût de la bonne cuisine.

Les poissons frais de ses mers, de ses lacs, de ses rivières sont transportés par avion en France, à quelques heures des lieux de pêche. (Vous pouvez, bien entendu, venir en Irlande les pêcher vous-même dans un cadre idyllique.)

Tous les produits alimentaires irlandais sont conservés avec toute leur fraîcheur naturelle, leur goût et leur qualité intactes. Demandez à votre hôtel, à votre restaurant favori de mettre à leur menu des spécialités irlandaises.

Boeuf Agneau Porc	Saumon Truites Homards Langoustes Ecrevisses Bigorneaux Scampis	Beurre Fromages Crème

L'Irlande fait aussi l'exportation d'une gamme de plus en plus étendue de fromages, de beurres, (salé et non-salé), de crème, de lait en poudre et condensé, de flocons de chocolat.

Pour tous renseignements sur les produits ci-dessus et sur toute autre denrée irlandaise susceptible de vous intéresser, veuillez vous adresser à:

Department of Agriculture,
Foreign Trade Division,
Upper Merrion Street,
DUBLIN 2.

Brindley Adv./Dublin

Have an Irish brewed
Harp lager — and enjoy yourself.

233

Quinn's supermarket (now Superquinn) opened in a converted cinema at Sutton Cross, Co Dublin, on February 22, 1968. It burned down in September, 1986. The photograph shows crowds on the opening day — the retail grocery revolution was well under way.
Eamonn Quinn, father of Feargal, wrote at the time: "We are an all-Irish firm and while we at Quinn's are a little old-fashioned, the housewives of Sutton and surrounding area are entitled to modern, up-to-date shopping methods. The new premises are bright, airy and hygienic with plenty of room to display all the goods so that a free choice is available. There is easy access to the car park". In June, 1965, the extension to the firm's Dundalk store had been completed, while the same month, Ireland's largest supermarket, Quinn's in Finglas, Dublin, had also been opened.

Eamonn Quinn pointed out in 1968 that his late father, John, himself and his son Feargal, between them had nearly 100 years in the grocery business.
Photograph: Superquinn.

While Fogarty was making progress with his new agency and Maughan and O Bradaigh were building up Wilson Hartnell at a pace that stunned the rest of the advertising industry, young Bill Walshe was turning O'Donnell Earl into an agency with a good spread of medium-sized accounts, including Mitchelstown. Walshe had begun his advertising career in Grosvenor, then went into O'Donnell Earl as managing director: big accounts there at the time included Gateaux, Bovril and Imco. Three years after he arrived, and at about the same time that Maughan and O Bradaigh were buying over Wilson Hartnell, Walshe decided to do the same with O'Donnell Earl. Bill O'Donoghue, the agency's founder, retired from the business. The chairman of the company during O'Donoghue's tenure, Lord Killanin, no longer had any connection with the agency either. Walshe says that O'DE was not called such because of the Lord Killanin connection — the name was simply a convoluted effort dreamed up by Bill O'Donoghue to reflect the then current Madison Avenue trend for big names.

Philip Stobo, chairman of S. H. Benson, the London advertising agency, told a 1965 conference of the Advertising Press Club that "Ireland is one of the most exciting countries in western Europe to live and work in at present. You know where you want to get to by 1970 and the means of achieving it have been blueprinted in the Second Programme for Economic Expansion. But there is one thing missing from the programme: a deep enough understanding of the part that advertising can play in achieving those aims." Harry Byers was director of the conference. Almost simultaneously, RGDATA was holding a conference on self-service in the grocery trade, which was coming into vogue. Three years later, Quinn's supermarkets, later Superquinn,

Bandwagen.

The official name for this Volkswagen is the Micro-Bus. Which, if you think about it, is pretty apt.

Admittedly there's a little less headroom in our 'Bus than in the traditional type.

But what you lose in headroom you gain in doors. Our model has four on the sides and one at the back.

And if you have more things than people to carry, two of the three bench seats can be removed.

A bulky drive-shaft and a radiator are things you don't waste fuel hauling around.

In the VW 'Bus, the engine is at the back and it's air-cooled.

You can expect to get roughly 24 m.p.g.

Oil? Only 4 pints—and never a drop added between changes.

Tyres? 35,000 to a set is about average.

No, you certainly don't have to be Millionaires to jump on this Bandwagen.

Ⓥ VOLKSWAGEN

Noted socialites of the 1960s: Clodagh O'Kennedy, the designer and her husband, Desmond O'Kennedy of O'Kennedy Brindley. *Photograph: The Irish Times.*

The 1960s saw the emergence of the showband era; it provided the copy theme for this Volkswagen advertisement prepared by O'Kennedy Brindley for the 1966 and 1967 editions of the *Golden Irish Show Band* annual.

Mr and Mrs George Kealy (Glen Abbey), pictured at the 1966 dinner of the Association of Advertisers in Ireland.

started on its big supermarket expansion. In late 1986, Superquinn celebrates its 25th anniversary.

At Brindley's, Basil Brindley and his brother Donald, were about to have some of the best fun of their advertising careers. Pat Quinn, a long-standing friend and client, was running his supermarkets — later sold to Westons and now known as "Quinnsworth". Quinn's stores, not to be confused with those run by the other Quinn families in the supermarket trade, were advertised heavily. Pat Quinn fronted much of the advertising for his stores, with the help of comedian Hal Roach. Some rare times were had during recording sessions and Basil Brindley considers this time with this client unparalleled in its enjoyment.

Opposite page:
Until the late 1960s,
provincial newspapers
carried much national
brand advertising.
O'Kennedy Brindley
ran this campaign for
Volkswagen cars in
eight major provincial
newspapers in August,
1966.

"Sound man, Brendan"
— an outdoor poster
used as part of the
Beamish stout
campaign prepared by
Arrow Advertising in
the mid-1960s.

At Rowntree-Mackintosh, managing director Melville ("Sandy") Miller was predicting in 1965 that soon Ireland would catch up with the UK in confectionery consumption. In 1961, per capita consumption of confectionery in Ireland was 4½ ounces a year; by 1965, that figure had gone up to seven ounces. When he was announcing the good news, Melville Miller also stated that the Mackintosh toffee factory in Rathmines, acquired when the two companies merged, would soon be closed down. Within ten years, another big name in the confectionery trade, Urneys in Tallaght, went out of production. Later still, Lemon's, famed for its "crinoline lady" also closed. "Sandy" Miller's predictions had been over-optimistic, just as the general optimism of the 1960s faded away with the arrival of the 1970s.

Louis O'Sullivan, then information officer at Erin Foods, later to found *Checkout* magazine, was masterminding the editorial publicity for the new brands emanating from the Irish Sugar Company's subsidiary, busy launching a plethora of new products, such as instant soup and freeze dried vegetables. Even product launches had sparkle in the 1960s; Rena Dardis, then with O'Kennedy Brindley, remembers one flamboyant occasion when the agency launched a champagne perry drink called White Velvet to combat Babycham. The reception was held at the Mansion House; Clodagh, Desmond O'Kennedy's wife, designed the models' dresses. A large label was hand-painted for a champagne bottle; a waiter put the bottle in an ice bucket to cool and the colours ran off. It was a miniature disaster, but everyone laughed it off, in the spirit of the 1960s.

1966 saw the formation of the United Distillers of Ireland, a merger

This may shake you a little, but—

all over the country
Volkswagens are being taken off the road.

Is this a good thing?

Well, it certainly doesn't do them any harm.

The Volkswagen is built to take the rough with the smooth.

8" boulders are no obstacle to a car with independent torsion bar suspension on all wheels.

Of course, if you try to tackle something bigger you'll notice a difference.

But there will be no hard feelings on your part.

And your VW? It isn't easily rattled. Its body is welded in one piece.

And its works are protected by a solid steel plate.

The VW always makes good ground in bad conditions because its air-cooled engine is at the rear, where the extra weight gives the drive-wheels real go-ahead grip in sand, snow, mud—even in freshly cut wheat.

And used VWs always fetch good prices because everyone knows that even an old VW still has a long way to go.

If a spare part is ever necessary, any VW dealer can do the necessary: quickly and cheaply.

In future, used VWs are going to fetch even better prices.

For the simple reason that new VWs will never cost less than now.

Ⓥ VOLKSWAGEN

Charlie McConnell, who was made life president of the Publicity Club of Ireland in 1969. He founded his agency in 1916 and ended up running a total of 16 companies. A pioneer of many aspects of publicity, in 1918, he was instrumental in organising meetings to try to get the planned all-Ireland Irish Institute of Publicity off the ground, but it was one of the rare McConnell ideas that failed to materialise. His dictum was: "If you stand still, you don't stand a chance." His son John became managing director of the Dublin agency in 1954; he carried on as chairman for nearly 20 years more. He died in 1977 at the age of 89.
Photograph: The Irish Times.

of Jameson's and Power's distilleries and the Cork Distillery Company. The move was spearheaded by managing director Kevin McCourt, who had been TE director general. For the first time, the distilleries were working together, rather than against each other, on the home as well as the export markets. Advertising and marketing showed distinct improvements too; by 1969, there had been a big change of agencies, to

Peter Owens at the Association of Advertisers in Ireland dinner, Shelbourne Hotel, Dublin, 1964.

Jammet's restaurant, Nassau Street, which closed in 1967; it was a popular rendezvous for Dublin advertising people.
Photograph: Patrick Jammet/Lost Dublin, Gill & Macmillan.

include Arks, Peter Owens and Easons. Gilbeys went from Arks to Hunters, where Michael Bowles had just joined from Peter Owens. In 1970, Wilson Hartnell won the Jameson Crested Ten account. Then a new brand was brought in, Midleton Reserve, aimed at the segment of the whiskey market which did not drink the traditional Irish whiskey. To reach this market, Wilson Hartnell devised a £30,000 national newspaper campaign over three months. It was the first time that full colour had been used extensively in Ireland to promote whiskey. The Kiskadee white rum launch was in 1971.

In 1966, Young Advertising moved from South Leinster Street, where Chubb, the safe firm, is now located. About ten years earlier, John Young had started to run the agency founded by his father. Young's was one of the first agencies in town to take in graduates. Donald Helme spent some 16 years with the agency, before working for an unsatisfactory year as managing director of Arks; Robin Robb was also with Young's before emigrating to Canada to work for the R. J. Reynolds tobacco company. Peter O'Keeffe trained at the agency before moving on to CDP. Also in 1966, Arrow, then enjoying a top creative reputation, created a major campaign for the Cork-brewed Beamish stout, brewed by one of that city's two breweries, Beamish and Crawford. The campaign featured conversations between a Dublin drinker and a Cork drinker; the copy theme was "Sound man, Brendan." In one Cork hurling match, someone shouted out the catchphrase to Christy Ring. Thereafter, there was no stopping the public appeal of the campaign, which involved TV, press and point of sale. The fact that the brand failed had nothing to do with Arrow's advertising work, maintains Brian Murphy, then the agency's creative director. Apart from Beamish & Crawford and the First National Building Society, which had just started big advertising, Arrow also began campaigns for RTV Rentals. TV set hire was just beginning in the mid-1960s and Arrow helped popularise the idea.

238

In the mid-1960s, the Publicity Club made several visits to its opposite number in Northern Ireland; one such Dublin party is seen on arrival at the old Great Victoria Street railway station in Belfast. This particular party was greeted by R. B. "Brum" Henderson, the managing director of Ulster Television and chairman of the N. Ireland publicity association. The Dublin party was entertained at City Hall, Belfast, by the then Lord Mayor, Sir Robin Kinahan.

O'Donnell Earl grew quickly under Walshe's leadership. Staff numbers grew considerably but there were incipient problems that were to prove the agency's undoing in the next decade. "I knew nothing about management and cash flow and we over-traded like hell," Walshe now admits, candidly.

In 1967, Bill Cavanagh became administrator of the Association of Advertisers in Ireland, having been one of the organising committee back in 1951 and then an early chairman (the position was later restyled "president"). Cavanagh was sales director of Chivers for many years; wearing his sales managerial hat, he worked for long on the council of the Irish branch of the Incorporated Sales Managers' Association, later to become the Marketing Institute of Ireland. He was administrator of the Association of Advertisers in Ireland until he retired in 1979; he was also very involved in the International Union of Advertisers' Associations. Apart from his family, his other great love was Spain. At the age of 60, he learned Spanish. During the many meetings of the IUAA in Brussels, he had his favourite Spanish café, where he could enjoy a few glasses of Sangre de Toro, listen to the guitar group and contentedly puff his pipe, which was almost his trademark.

Frank Sheerin, who joined the Arks board in 1967, at the same time as Eamonn O'Flaherty, recalls that much of that decade was a period of intensive creativity in the agency. Bill Felton was there, so too were Phil Walsh, Brendan O Broin, Catherine Donnelly, Barry Devlin, Pat Ingoldsby (doing some not-so-zany copywriting), Jimmy Strathern, now McConnell's creative director, Terry Pattison, Michael McAuley, Sean O'Connell, Shamus Wade, Marcella Kerin and an account executive called Pat Ferguson, later chairman and managing director and the man who played a large part in engineering the sale of the agency to Lopex.

Arthur Garrett was advertising manager for Dockrell's, the Dublin hardware firm, from 1956 until 1983. Not only did he have to book press advertisements, but he had to write the copy as well. He did the same with radio commercials; his duties even included window displays.

1967 saw another "character" emerge onto the agency scene, Don O'Connell, one of the *Irish Press* group stalwarts. O'Connell had been in at the start of the *Evening Press;* he became general manager of the G. & S. Doherty agency, set up in 1963 by Gerry Doherty. At one stage, O'Connell claimed to have worked in the Merchant Navy. For years, Doherty's has remained a middle grade agency; in the early 1970s, O'Connell, Ray Kennedy (another *Irish Press* stalwart, who now runs his own public relations business and reckoned one of the most gregarious PR people in town) and Cyril Boden engineered a buy-out of Doherty's. While O'Connell and Kennedy both had newspaper advertising experience, Boden was a banker, an alternate director with the Chase and Bank of Ireland in Dublin. This purchase resulted in a bitter legal action.

As Don O'Connell was coming into advertising, two other personalities were departing this life, Tim O'Neill, founder of Sun Advertising and Peter McCarthy, the managing director of O'Dea's, makers of "O'Dearest" mattresses. From the start of Sun in 1946, O'Neill made the agency into one of the shining creative shops in Dublin for a ten year period. In retrospect, his greatest achievement was to have brought in the Dutch artists, a move that improved immeasurably the standards of design in advertising in Ireland, as well as commercial design education. He died young, having been in poor health for some years previously. Sensibly, he took steps to ensure the continuation of the agency, even if in merged form. The present day Irish International agency owes a strong legacy to O'Neill. Towards the end of his life, O'Neill had to be absent so often from the office,

Old-style grocery shop, with counter service, Clonakilty, Co. Cork, 1968.
Photograph: Bord Failte.

Ann Quinn of O'Keeffes, Miss Advertising 1968. She was crowned at the Advertising Press Club Christmas party in Clery's.
Photograph: Irish Press.

The late Guy Jackson, then managing director, Guinness Group Sales, addressed the Advertising Press Club in 1968 at the Royal Hibernian Hotel on the rôle of the State in the marketplace.
Photograph: The Irish Times.

because of his illness, that he was called, cruelly, the "absentee landlord".

Peter McCarthy had a keen eye for good advertising; he had sanctioned the start of the O'Dearest cartoon campaign in 1941 and remained its greatest advocate, until his death in 1967. The "O'Dearest" cartoon by Warner, with accompanying limerick, usually written by Frank Chambers, became firm favourites with readers of the Saturday editions of *The Irish Times* and later with the *Irish Independent* as well. A well-organised routine of copy clearance between the agencies involved in the campaign (Arks and for a time, Sun), meant that there were rarely any delays to the production schedule. McCarthy was a good client, perceptive and encouraging. He even let slightly risqué limericks through, at a time when any material of that nature was severely frowned upon. Through the 1940s, 1950s and well into the 1960s, the O'Dearest advertisements continued, backed up, after the war, by a sponsored radio programme. On the death of Peter McCarthy in 1967, cartoonist Warner was confident that the series would be continued. After all, the campaign had been running for the past 26 years, an unheard of length of time in Irish advertising. How many mattresses were sold directly as a result of the campaign was never calculated, but the advertising made O'Dearest a generic term for mattresses. Frank Chambers thought differently to Warner about the survival prospects of the campaign: he remembers saying at the time, "new kings, new rules". He was proved right; within a few weeks, the campaign was dropped for good, joining that other immortal Saturday advertisement series, for Lemon's sweets, featuring the crinoline lady and the output of the famous factory at Drumcondra, now very regrettably closed down.

John Hunter set up his own agency, Hunter's, in 1968: he later sold out, but the agency is still highly regarded within the industry. Hunter began his advertising career in O'Kennedy Brindley, where he spent his first few weeks sorting out the guard books. The idea of specialisation was starting to come in; upstairs, Joe O'Byrne ran the studio. Downstairs, Jack McManus ran the production department. Georgina was the typist, so fast that she was said to have had ten fingers — four on each hand, plus two extra, her generous bosom!

By the late 1960s, the advertising scene in Cork was starting to burgeon: O'Kennedy had opened a Cork office, run by Dick O'Hanrahan, in 1955. By 1968, the office was turning over about £130,000. Manus O'Callaghan was to become managing director. 1968 saw Eddie Mooney leave Brindleys after a long stay to go to O'Kennedy Brindley in Cork. Mooney was to spend nearly 20 years in Cork, where he set up O'Kelly Mooney with Dick O'Kelly; he died there, tragically, in 1986.

The 1968 McConnell Award went to Fred C. Palmer, managing director of Reckitts (Ireland). He is seen here (left) receiving the award from Michael Hayes, chairman, Advertising Press Club (right). Looking on is Norman McConnell, president of the Association of Advertisers in Ireland.

Michael O'Hehir interviewing Sir Billy Butlin at the Ward Union Hunt's point-to-point race meeting at Fairyhouse in 1970. Basil Brindley (centre) was secretary of this fixture for 15 years. His firm also handled the Butlin account for the same length of time.

MEET THE DALEKS
IN ANN STREET

They arrived at Aldergrove by Emerald Airways.   To-night at 8 p.m. they will invade Ann Street when they will accompany the Right Honourable The Lord Mayor of Belfast, Councillor William Jenkins, J.P., up to Dr. Who's spaceship the "Tardis," which has arrived for its Christmas visit.   The Lord Mayor will then perform the official switch-on ceremony, setting the street and its Christmas tree ablaze with light.   The shops are open, too, in Ann Street where one-stop shopping is possible in Belfast's most compact shopping centre

Bring the children to see the procession. They'll thrill to a visit to the "Tardis" and receive a parcel from a real talking Dalek.   Vouchers are available at shops displaying the Dalek sign.

Clip 'n Save
This coupon entitles the holder to 6d off one Dalek voucher. Offer ends on SAT. 4th December

WORTH **6d** When you buy your DALEK VOUCHER before 4th DEC. ANN STREET ASSOCIATION

SHOP EARLY

PRESENTED BY THE ANN STREET ASSOCIATION

Advertisement for Ann Street traders, Belfast, published in the Belfast Telegraph, **November 22, 1965.**

Hunter spent the late 1950s and early 1960s working as an account executive in London, waiting for the right opening to present itself in Dublin. Luke Mahon, as he was then known, offered him a job in Arks. Remembers Hunter: "There was no comparison between the Arks of 1955 and the Arks of 1965, thanks to Luke's influence." There was a sense of innovation about the place, equal to that in any London agency, a feeling that Arks really knew what it was about. He describes his two years in Arks as his most enjoyable time in advertising, but Hunter was determined to set up on his own. He left Arks in the autumn of 1967; Roger Wornell took over from him. Hunter's first effort was a failure, the first sales promotion company to be set up in Ireland, yet within a year of setting up his agency, Hunter's had three big consumer accounts. The first was Club Orange from Cantrell and Cochrane. The soft drinks firm had just been restructured and was starting to create brand strategies. This account had been with City Publicity, whose managing director, Cecil Dick had a close connection

At a meeting in 1969 of the Advertising Press Club on campaign planning are the speakers, with club chairman Michael Hayes. Included (from left): Luke Dillon-Mahon, president, Institute of Advertising Practitioners, John Meagher, chairman, Market Research Society, Norman McConnell, chairman, Association of Advertisers, Michael Hayes, G. F. Maher, chairman, Marketing Institute and Aidan O'Hanlon, president, Public Relations Institute of Ireland. This was the first time in Ireland that the heads of these various bodies had come together to address the same meeting.

The second ADMAP world advertising workshop was held in Dublin in October, 1969. Pictured from left were: Michael Hayes (Arks), Simon Tilley (Belfast Telegraph), the late Brian Dawson (The Irish Times) and Dr. A. Kitchener (Wilkinson Sword), who read a paper at the workshop.

with Cantrell and Cochrane — his brother, Rex, was managing director there. From City, the account went to Irish International, after a superb presentation by Mack Kile. It stayed at the agency for just six months, before shifting to Hunter's. John Hunter's business strategy was to win accounts that were big enough in themselves to keep an agency running; he didn't want a string of fiddling little accounts. By the time he finished his ten years running the agency, he had won a total of ten such accounts. He now runs a biscuit factory in Bray, making the "Braycot" pure food brand.

Brian Cronin returned to Ireland in 1968 after eleven years in the USA. Before he left, he had been running O'Kennedy Brindley in Cork. Originally, he had been a copywriter in McConnell's. When he started in Dublin in 1968, he took an advertisement in *The Irish Times* which read: "Today, a little bit of Madison Avenue moves back home." He took offices in Earlsfort Mansions, where Sun Advertising had been. The new agency started with no clients and one secretary. The first account was the Canada Dry brand for Batchelor's, with a copy line: "Ireland's going on the dry". On the strength of that, the new agency won the Carlsberg lager account and then the main Batchelor's account, for which the agency devised the famous Barney and Beaney campaign in 1970. The cartoon characters have been used mainly on TV during the intervening 16 years and feature also on product packs. The cartoon characters took off so quickly in the public esteem that they soon rivalled the Lyons' Tea minstrels. So well did the new agency do that by 1973, it was moved into the former Canadian Embassy

Pictured on an Advertising Press Club visit to Belfast in 1969, Jean Jaffray (David Allen) and Ted Mullen (then Irish International, now marketing services executive with The Irish Times).

245

At a beer and ballads session organised by the Advertising Press Club at the old Grosvenor Hotel, Westland Row, in 1968, from left: Pat Flood (Arrow), Paddy Neilan (Independent Newspapers), Leo Blennerhassett (Independent Newspapers), Harry Byers (Janus), Padraic Guilfoyle (Janus), Alan Pascoe (Sunday Times, London), Frank Loughrey, Michael Brotherton (The Times, London) and Dympna Monaghan (Arks).

Tony Lokko did the original designs for the Ritchie's mints wrappers in the late 1960s; the same basic design is still being used today.

premises in Clyde Road, Ballsbridge. Its first year's turnover had been £40,000; by 1972, that figure was £345,000. Shortly after the move to Clyde Road, Brian Cronin's senior staff included Harry Byers, account director, who had joined from the Ryans' tourism and traders' group, where he had been marketing manager, Frank Loughrey, media manager, who had spent eight years in Domas and Dermot Quinn, art director, who had previously worked at Adsell, Padburys and Peter Owens. Flemming Christofferson from Copenhagen joined from O'Kennedy Brindley as assistant art director, while Brendan Byrne, another Domas man, was production manager and Ashling Foster, copywriter, joined from Irish International. Gerry Lawlor ran Communique, Cronin's public relations firm.

Brendan White Advertising was just starting up in the late 1960s, with former Domas director Brendan White as managing director and senior staff including Frank Loughrey (from Cronin's) and Paddy Schofield. Accounts included the Green Isle brand for Batchelors.

Meanwhile, while John Hunter, Brendan White and Brian Cronin were starting up their agencies, Noelle Campbell-Sharp was starting her media career, in Eason's Advertising. She remembers devising a campaign for men's hair shampoo; her plan was 20 years ahead of its time. She also remembers that Harold Clarke was strongly against her wearing trousers to work and tried unsuccessfully to get her to replace them with a skirt, then normal working garb for women in advertising.

On a day trip to Belfast in 1969, from left: Leo Mooney (then Independent Newspapers, now Esso), Michael Hayes, John Harwood (Belfast Telegraph) and John Conway (Irish International).
Photograph: Belfast Telegraph.

In 1969, the Advertising Press Club organised a design competition to devise a symbol for the club. Judges of the contest were Jarlath Hayes, Brian Murphy and Michael Hayes. The winning design, still in use today, was the work of Marie Mooney (right) then with Young Advertising. Also in the photograph, Ken Grace (left) and Michael Hayes.

247

**Time beer
advertisement, 1960s.**

When the game is rough,
and the opposition tough—
stop! you need . . .

E. SMITHWICK & SONS LTD.   ADSELL

In 1968, just as the Northern troubles were starting to dominate the TV and radio news bulletins for the first time, trouble flared on the cigarette front. Players and Wills, the two tobacco products' firms, had merged their interests, despite the intense rivalry between the two firms. In Dublin, Player Wills (Ireland) was formed; Wills vacated its factory at Botanic Road, Glasnevin, which later became the headquarters of Hugh McLaughlin's Creation group. By the time it launched the *Sunday World* from there in 1973, strands of tobacco fibre were still turning up. Player Wills operated from the existing Players' factory on the South Circular Road. The new company decided on a major brand launch: Corsair. Much preparation went into its launch, over a 42 week period. The packs were designed by Walter Bernardini and printing was done as far away as Finland in order to ensure total secrecy. The hull of the pack was printed in Holland. As the launch, with the code name of "Operation Victor", drew near, Frank O'Reilly, the company chairman, appeared on the factory floor and urged the entire workforce to absolute secrecy.

The man behind the marketing of the new product was Peter Prendergast, now Government press secretary. The key, novel element in the advertising campaign devised by O'Kennedy Brindley, where John Watchorn was in charge of the account, were coupons for a poker style competition. Within days of the launch, using TV commercials made in New York, print advertisements and 48 sheet posters, in August, 1968, the directors of Player Wills were summoned to a meeting with the then Finance Minister, Charles Haughey, and told, to their great astonishment, that the competition contravened lottery regulations and would have to be scrapped, otherwise extra tax would have to be levied. The Player Wills directors wondered whether other cigarette manufacturers had had anything to do with pressurising the Government. Before December of that year, the brand was dead. After Corsair, came the launch of Shannon, in 1970, for which advertising was handled by Arks. This brand was aimed at

Cardinal O Fiaich (then Monsignor Tomás of Maynooth College) addressed a monthly lunch of An Ciorcal Fógraíochta agus Caidreamh Poiblí in 1970. He was pictured with Pat Ferguson, then of Arks.

Pictured at the first lunch, in 1969, of the then newly formed Ciorcal Fógraíochta, from left: Michael Hayes, Mary Finan, Brian Murphy and Captain Oliver Walsh. The Irish language has not had a major impact in the advertising arena, with a few exceptions. The Guinness "Tá said ag teacht" commercial in 1977 won accolades for the brewery, its agency, Arks and Frank Sheerin. In the early 1980s, there were some clever Toyota press advertisements in Irish. However, in July, 1969, through the efforts of Brian Murphy (then of Arrow, now of Diners Club) and Sean O Loingsigh (then of Lynch Advertising), An Ciorcal Fógraíochta was formed. The group met for an informal lunch through the medium once a month. Formal functions were also organised. Starting with people working in advertising, the group later expanded to include the whole field of communications. Its present name is An Ciorcal Cumarsáide. The chairmanship rotates on a six monthly basis; among the cathaoirligh of ciorcal have been Brian Murphy, Sean O Loingsigh, Liam O Lonargain, Pat Ferguson and Michael Hayes. In recent years, a more or less permanent venue has been the Arts Club.

the king sized market, then starting to develop, but Shannon failed to make the grade, partly because the brand name had the wrong connotations.

In 1968, F. C. Palmer was awarded the McConnell Award; he had been sent to Ireland to set up Colman's manufacturing unit in 1934. By 1968, he had responsibility for the whole Reckitts and Colman group in Ireland, which included factories in Dublin and the Zip firelighter factory at Castlebellingham, Co Louth. For two years chairman of the Advertisers' Association, he was one of the chief architects in getting advertisers' co-operation with representatives of agencies and media in the establishment and functioning of the Irish code of advertising standards.

1968 and 1969 saw the biggest collective voluntary effort made by the Irish advertising and media industry. The Biafran civil war was at its height in Nigeria and Irish advertising personnel pooled their talents to create a huge advertising campaign. All newspapers and magazines

Guest speakers have included Micheál Mac Liammóir, Niall Toibin, Cardinal O Fiaich, the late President Cearbhall O Dalaigh and Michael Mills, the Ombudsman.

Cork agency people pictured back in 1970, looking suitably determined before the big match. Back row, from left: Pat Barry, now corporate affairs manager, Guinness Ireland, Dick O'Hanrahan, O'KB, Margaret Baker, now Southern Advertising, Sean Power, pr consultant. Middle row: Dick O'Kelly, O'KM, Sylvia Hennessy, the late Eddie Mooney, O'KM, Jo O'Sullivan. Front row: Rita Barry, Manus O'Callaghan, now Southern Advertising, Anne Stenson, Seamus O'Farrell.

throughout Ireland were asked to donate space (90 per cent did) and printers, blockmakers and poster firms all gave freely. The end of the summer of 1969 saw the total cash raised from the public for Biafran relief, as a result of the advertising campaigns, climb to nearly £½ million. Hubert Popplewell ("Pop"), copy chief at Fogarty's, died in 1968. In a tribute, Jim Caulfield said: "He helped everyone, from office junior to managing director. Despite his 50 years, he seemed a Peter Pan, involved in the ballad revival and co-editing *A/Progress,* the Advertising Press Club's newsletter.

Despite the burgeoning troubles in the North, members of the Advertising Press Club had memorable outings to Belfast, with the active encouragement of AP chairman Michael Hayes, then in the much expanded media department of Arks. Boozy day trips took place from Dublin to Belfast, visiting such establishments as Mooney's in Belfast and the *Belfast Telegraph*. On the return part of one such trip, a healthy sex equality crept into the proceedings: the bus had to make a watering stop near Balbriggan. While the advertising men lined up at the back of the bus, the advertising women ran into the bushes. In late 1969, Gerry O'Boyce of the *Irish Farmers' Journal* started a weekly get-together at a heated, indoor swimming pool. *A/Progress* said that

Lux is a nice soft feeling.

Daughters soon learn that there's more to Lux than just meets the eye. It's a nice soft feeling too.

You see, Lux is quite different from your usual detergent. For one thing, it's made with delicate flakes of pure white soap and doesn't contain any harsh additives.

Lux Flakes are specially made for the handwash. Feel the luxury of that soft rich lather. See how beautifully Lux works, cleaning as only pure soap can. (Lux is a highly effective cleaning agent.)

Washed the Lux way, your special things keep their colours bright, stay soft and are left whiter, too.

Dresses, trousers, jumpers, blouses, sweaters, babies' clothes, all these are safe with Lux. You stay safe and confident, too.

You can actually feel the difference.

Lux cares for your special things like no detergent can.

Lux advertisement placed for Lever Brothers, 1970.

252

"Georgina O'Sullivan of Arks is one of the few who breaks the all-stag profile." The days of heavy socialising on the advertising scene were drawing to a close. From the early 1970s onwards, in an increasingly computerised environment, more work by less people in the face of an on-going recession, helped cut down the amount of social activities in advertising.

Maura Fox, by now moved from Janus to McConnell's, reckoned however that by the late 1960s, she and Rena Dardis of O'Kennedy Brindley were among the very few women working at senior level in Irish advertising. One of Fox's favourite campaigns at McConnell's was for Cantrice, a DuPont material used in the manufacture of tights. Public relations for the brand included *Late, Late Show* coverage and a small TV campaign, using slides. Yet this modest campaign gave the brand a higher market share in Ireland than in most other markets. "Per capita, we became the biggest sellers of the brand and the campaign became an object lesson for DuPont elsewhere in Europe," remembers Maura Fox. In McConnell's public relations department, Marilyn Bright (now the well-known *Irish Independent* cookery writer) and Mary Timmons joined the staff.

1969, when the North erupted into serious violence, a big conflict emerged in Janus. With the arrival of television, Janus, found that

Brian Cronin &
Associates' most
famous creation, the
Barney and Beany
characters for
Batchelors. They have
been widely used in
media advertising,
including TV and on
pack designs for the
past 15 years.

Opposite page:
Pat Ferguson, who
succeeded Luke Dillon-
Mahon as managing
director of Arks in
1973.

This photograph was
taken in 1973 when Des
O'Meara & Partners was
set up at South Anne
Street, Dublin. From
left: Adrian O'Brien,
Des O'Meara and Colm
Cronin.
*Photograph: Robert Dawson
Studio.*

many of its clients were not particularly suited to the new medium. To preserve its standing in the agency league, it needed more clients. All of a sudden, Janus found itself a little less than fashionable. Some employees, like George Gaffney, now of Gaffney McHugh, had not got on well with Denis Garvey, the managing director. When Dick Birchall joined the agency in 1969 for two years that he found frustrating and unhappy, the discontent seemed to crystallise. A committee was set up, with the blessing of Denis Garvey, to find ways in which the agency could improve its position. Members of this committee included Pat Ryan, the agency's general manager, Dick Birchall and Eddie Edmonds, who came from Hely Thom as production manager and who kept a low profile during the dispute. He was later made a director of Janus. After leaving advertising, he became managing director of Cahills the printing firm. The Janus committee had a weekend meeting at the La Touche hotel in Greystones; it returned to Dublin with a rather unwise resolution, that Denis Garvey should be promoted to chairman and a new managing director appointed, with the aim of bringing in new business. Garvey was, needless to remark, extremely annoyed, believing that this could have been the nucleus of an agency breakaway. Firings followed; Pat Ryan, who says he played an honest rôle throughout the proceedings, resigned. Some sources believe he may have been too naive, although honest. Garvey remained managing director, although he was eventually succeeded by Jack Downey, when Garvey *did* become chairman.

At the first meeting of the new council of the Institute of Advertising Practitioners in Ireland, held in the Shelbourne hotel in May, 1970, were from left: Denis J. Garvey (Janus), Oliver P. Walsh (director, IAPI), Noel B. Cautley (new president), Luke Dillon-Mahon (Arks), Dermod J. Cafferky (Arrow, outgoing president) Stafford C. McConnell (McConnell's), John F. Young (Young's) and Sean O Bradaigh (Wilson Hartnell).

254

In early 1973, Stephen
O'Flaherty watched the
first Irish-assembled
Toyota car, a 1200 cc
Corolla, being
completed at the
Bluebell, Dublin, plant
of Toyota (Ireland).
O'Flaherty had been
responsible, nearly 25
years previously, for
bringing the
Volkswagen marque to
Ireland. Now, Toyota is
brand leader in the Irish
car market.
*Photograph: Eddie Kelly, The
Irish Times.*

At a TABS "race night"
in the Irish Farm
Centre in the early
1970s, from left: Eileen
Ball (Johnson Bros),
Michael Hayes (Arks),
Gerry O'Boyce (Irish
Farmers' Journal) and
Carmel Bruce (City
Publicity, now
CP & A).

Between 1970 and 1971, there was a slight fall in employment in the advertising business, from 1,000 to 990. Advertising through agencies was worth around £12 million in 1971, according to the Central Statistics Office. Dick Birchall set up his agency in 1970; his other work experience had included being brand manager at W & C McDonnell, where he claimed he took Royco packet soups from near zero market share to brand leadership in 18 months. He also claimed another first, in 1967, with the introduction of price tickets on products.

In 1969, Wilson Hartnell acquired three big accounts, which brought total billings to £½ million. Agency people in Dublin were awaiting with great interest the first shop to pass the magic £1 million mark. Wilson Hartnell's new accounts were Phoenix beer, United Dominions Trust and Youghal Carpets. Earlier in the 1960s, when the Youghal Carpets' account was with Padbury's, Seamus Dignam claimed an input into the famous copyline: "The soft, deep pile of a Youghal carpet". The great consumer goods boom was just beginning.

Ian Fox, who had been an associate director of McConnell's and manager of its marketing and promotions division, joined Wilson Hartnell in 1972 as an account director. He joined the agency not long after Barry Healy, later to set up his own agency, which eventually collapsed, joined the Wilson Hartnell team. Healy had worked in London with Campbells Soups and Young and Rubicam. After returning home to Ireland, he was with Mahony's of Blarney and had been marketing manager of Lentheric, the toiletries' firm. Also joining

Opposite page: Pictured at an RDS Spring Show reception in the early 1970s, hosted by Independent Newspapers, from left: Vincent Fanning (Independent Newspapers), Eamon Carolan (O'Donnell Earl), John Thompson (O'Keeffes), Fred Hayden (Temana Ireland) and Michael Hayes (Arks).

In 1973, Brian Murphy, then creative director, Arrow, receives the first Clio won by that agency (for Hennessy) at the New York advertising festival. Presenting the award is Bill Evans.

257

Wilson Hartnell at this time were Norman McIlroy, as account executive, Eamonn Moore, its new financial controller, who had been with Rank Xerox and Cahill Holdings, Sally Anne Egan, who joined as personal assistant to Michael Maughan and Ian Lush, who joined the agency's media department as space and time buyer; he had been with Arks and Kennys. In 1970, Sean O Bradaigh, then joint managing director of Wilson Hartnell, predicted that by 1980, the advertising industry could be employing 2,000 people.

1971 saw the passing of Noel Hartnell, the grand old man of Irish advertising; he was 81 years old. He is buried at Mount Jerome. In 1965, he sold out the agency to Michael Maughan and Sean O Bradaigh. Not long before his death, the Institute of Advertising Practitioners named him as one of three honorary members.

Peter Owens became one of the first Irish agencies to announce a link with a foreign agency, in 1971. It became the associate in the Republic of the British office of the US agency, McCann Erickson. It was a trading relationship, without any overtones of ownership. Peter Owens said that the link could mean £100,000's worth of extra billings; in 1970, the Dublin agency, which employed 48, had billings of just over £900,000. Also in 1971, Pat Ferguson took over as chairman at Arks. Ferguson eventually reorganised the agency and brought in the Allied Irish Banks' account, worth £150,000 a year, to replace the departing Aer Lingus account. Meanwhile, O'Keeffes claimed it had reached billings of £1 million. In 1971, McConnell's became the biggest buyer of time on radio and TV. 90 new radio commercials were produced and 40 new ones for TV; time on television bought by the agency amounted to £335,000. 27,000 print space orders were written by the agency in that year.

1971 saw O'Donnell Earl move from Leeson Park into Hume House, Ballsbridge, while at about the same time, Wilson Hartnell moved into Leeson Park from Lansdowne Road. Michael Maughan bought 12 Leeson Park, which had been the first headquarters of the Irish Management Institute. Then he bought Number 13, where Lady Grace, widow of Sir Raymond Grace of *Irish Times'* space selling fame, ran a company called Irish Media Research. Lady Grace still lives in Number 13. Number 14, where Donagh McDonagh ran a public relations company, was also acquired, along with Number 15. Also in 1971, O'Kennedy Brindley's billings topped the £1 million mark for the first time; added to that were billings of £200,000 for the firm's Cork office. The Dublin agency was the second largest buyer of television time, after McConnell's.

Joe O'Byrne says that in O'Kennedy Brindley, the first wave of highly creative talent, such as Rex McDonnell, Bernard Share and Jarlath Hayes, was followed by such people as Phil Walsh (later to go to Kenny's), and Sean O'Connell, who went to England. A miniature immigration of Scottish talent included Drew McDonnell, a good all-rounder, and Jimmy Strathern, now with McConnell's. Then, says

O'Byrne, "O'Kennedy Brindley changed from being a highly creative agency to a service agency." The change virtually coincided with the agency topping the £1 million turnover mark. That was the year that the agency also employed 100 people for the first time. At one board meeting, O'Byrne, who was the youngest director, said to Desmond O'Kennedy: "Why don't you employ half that number of people and double the salaries."

The first of the big UK take-overs of a Dublin advertising agency happened: Collett, Dickenson & Pearce bought out Grosvenor in 1970. The agency had been ailing for some time, a problem attributed by some well-informed sources in the industry to over-drinking by one or two top executives. Gallaher's, the cigarette manufacturers, was making aggressive moves into the Republic's cigarette market, with the opening of its Tallaght factory. Grosvenor handled the brand advertising. There were close dealings between Grosvenor and CDP, which handled the Gallaher brands in the UK; they culminated in CDP buying out Johnny van Belle and his co-directors. A two man team was picked to run the agency: Hugh O'Donnell, who had been creative head of Grosvenor and Bob Milne, who had been with Adsell. Milne had returned to Dublin in the early 1960s to work in Sun; after three years, Tim O'Neill fired him. "We were great friends and he was a great character, but very difficult to work with", recalls Milne. Then he joined Peter Owens. From there, he went to Adsell, busy gaining such accounts as the Roscrea Bacon Company. "Very quickly, we built up a healthy business. Within two years, the situation had become very

St. Patrick's night dinner, Hilton Hotel, London, 1972. From left: Charlie McConnell, Peter Finnegan, Grainne and Eamonn Andrews.

relaxing. I learned a lot from Paddy Considine and Noel Foley." Milne was reluctant to leave Adsell when he was headhunted by CDP. However, one factor that persuaded him was the fact that O'Donnell and himself had been great friends since their time together in Sun. Milne joined CDP. Many small accounts were disposed of, so too were some of the staff, for as Milne says now, "the place was staffed with a lot of the wrong people." The agency had bad debts, but within a year of Milne and O'Donnell taking over, CDP was back in the black.

Fortunately for CDP, there was a major merger being digested at the Bank of Ireland, which was in the process of absorbing three smaller banks, including the Hibernian and the National. Similarly, the Allied Irish Banks group was being formed from three smaller banks, the Munster & Leinster, the Provincial Bank and the Royal Bank, a merger that was finalised in 1972 shortly after that of the Bank of Ireland. With the two new groups, advertising became a serious consideration for the first time.

CDP (Ireland) landed the Bank of Ireland account and persuaded the client that a campaign should be run, primarily on TV, for cheque book accounts. Once banking management had got over the shock of mass media advertising for the first time, the campaign was seen to be working. Little further persuasion was needed for further advertising. After the Bank of Ireland came the Ford Motor Company, which was probably the turning point in the agency's fortunes.

Pictured at the Institute of Advertising Practitioners' dinner in the Burlington hotel, Dublin, in 1973, were Rena Dardis (chairman, ICAD), Michael Kenny (president, IAPI) and Dan Nolan (president, Provincial Newspapers' Association of Ireland).

Wilson Hartnell suffered its first major breakaway. Conor Quinn, brother of Minister for Labour in the present Government, (Ruairi Quinn), Charlie McDonnell and Barry Healy decided to set up their own agency. Rather than starting from scratch, they followed the example of Michael Maughan by buying over an existing agency. McEvoy's in Middle Abbey Street was rather run-down, based in drab offices run by Niall McEvoy, son of the founder, and Niall's sister, Miriam, but it still turned over £50,000 a year. Its main account had been Clery's department store, for which much space was bought in the evening papers, and which had just left the agency after more than 30 years. In order to get instant recognition, Quinn, McDonnell and Healy bought McEvoys. They thought that two or three accounts might follow them from Wilson Hartnell, but none did. Quinn has a vivid recollection of sitting in a car parked off Moore Street one night with his other partners. They were all gloomy after realising they were committed to the big move and reflecting that they were opening for business without a single account. Happily, that situation did not last long. Neither did the original partnership, since Barry Healy left in 1976 with the Murphy beer account to form his own agency, which eventually crashed with sizeable debts. Terry Pattison, who had been creative group head in McConnell's, joined Quinn and McDonnell, making QMP.

At Kenny's, Des O'Meara, who had come back to Dublin in 1966 to become creative director of the agency, suddenly found that his job

At the IAPI 1973 dinner, from left: Eric Cooke (chairman, Association of Advertisers in Ireland), Mrs Eric Cooke, James O'Connor (director, Institute of Practitioners in Advertising, London), Mrs Michael Kenny and Michael Kenny.

261

was being done by two other people. He says he never had an adequate explanation for the move by Kenny's management, but decided, wisely, that he should get out and start his own agency. He teamed up with Colm Cronin, head of public relations at the Pigs and Bacon Commission and then, as now, a noted theatre critic. Colm Cronin had worked in Arrow and Kenny's before the Commission so he was well used to the wiles of the agency world. The two men set up Des O'Meara and Partners; very recently, Cronin has left the agency to pursue his own public relations' interests. There were hopes that since O'Meara's father was managing director of Lyons Tea, that the new agency would win the prestigious Lyons' Tea account, for which Gunther Wulff, the film production man, had recently created the cartoon characters of the Lyons' Minstrels in conjunction with McConnell's. Des O'Meara was not satisfied in his ambition with Lyons, but he did win from that company the smaller one for Lyons' "Readibrek", an instant breakfast cereal. Within a short time, however, the agency, which had begun life in South Anne Street, by dint of knocking on many doors came up with the Quinnsworth supermarket account. By now, it has blossomed into a major advertising spender, of about £1 million a year, making it the agency's biggest account. A young man called Maurice Pratt joined the media department of the young agency from Hunter's, where he had been a junior media executive; after two years with the firm, he went to the client, Quinnsworth, where he is now marketing manager and one of the

Peter Finnegan (left) and John Meagher, IMS, signing the agreement for one of the first JNMR surveys. They were started in 1972.

best-known performers on television through his constant appearances in the Quinnsworth commercials.

At McConnell's, Charlie McConnell finally stepped down in 1970 as chairman of the agency. The general consensus of opinion was that he had held on far too long — when he officially retired from the agency, he was 83 years old. The mantle of chairman finally shifted to his son John, who was born in 1916, the year that the agency opened for business. John had been managing director since 1954. Charlie had spent a record-breaking 54 years at the head of the firm; only Noel Hartnell, with 60 years in Wilson Hartnell then mostly a publishing house, was able to claim greater length of service. Within two years of Charlie McConnell retiring, the agency was on the move, from Pearse Street to its new, present building at Charlemont Place. A photograph taken by *The Irish Times* at the 1972 opening of the new building shows Charlie McConnell at repose on a chair, a rather plump, elderly man slightly bewildered at the new surroundings. Charlemont Place may be functional and efficient: the old Publicity House in Pearse Street (an anonymous office block now stands on the site) may have had more character, but it was a maze of corridors and poky little rooms. Just opposite the new building is another modern structure, the head office of Carroll's, the cigarette manufacturers, for so long a major client of the agency. After the move to the new base, McConnell's continued to expand; it remains the biggest Irish agency in terms of billings and is still Irish-owned, unlike many of the other large agencies in town. In the North, too, McConnell's was on the move. In 1970, it shifted offices from the drab Cromac Square, on the edge of the Markets area, to the more refined Malone Road. In 1972, the year that McConnell's moved in Dublin, three executives of the agency in Belfast, headed by the then managing director, Ron Chapman, bought out the equity of the Belfast firm from McConnell's. Even though the company became a locally owned and independent entity, it continued to trade as "McConnell's". Chapman, who comes from Chepstow in Monmouthshire, had come to Northern Ireland on war service during World War II. He met his wife Lily in Portrush and then decided to stay in the province.

After the war, he started work with the Old Beach Linen Company, eventually becoming its advertising and publicity manager and then sales manager. He never particularly liked the latter job, so when McConnell's opened in Belfast in 1955, he accepted the post of managing the new office. It was mainly a contact office for servicing McConnell's existing clients in Northern Ireland. Chapman began to acquire new accounts, a slow process; the first big acquisition was of the White, Thompson and Courage account. The product promoted was Speedicook porridge oats. In 1955, the McConnell's office in Belfast was turning over less than £10,000 a year. By 1983, that figure had risen to £1 million. Also in 1972, the Cork agency in which McConnell's had an interest, Communicators, was wound up. The

When Michael Hayes
left Arks in 1973, he
was given an unusual
going-away present for
achievements in space
by Fred Mullen of
David Allen, the poster
firm. Fred was then
acting Lord Mayor of
Dublin.

managing director was James Orr; the other director was John McConnell. Communicators had only been set up at the end of 1971.

When John Fanning joined McConnell's in 1972 after a brief spell selling advertisement space for the Institute of Public Administration and with the research firm, A. C. Nielsen, he worked with account executives on strategic planning, a forerunner of account planning which came into vogue in the late 1970s, formulating the strategic development of brands in relation to advertising. Market research was starting to come into its own in the early 1970s.

The 1972 air crash at Staines just outside Heathrow airport, of a BEA Trident en route to Brussels, was a devastating blow to Irish industry and indirectly, advertising. When the 'plane came down, killing all on board, among those who died were Con Smith of the Smith car group, distributors of Renault, Guy Jackson, managing director of Guinness and Melville Miller, once advertisement manager of *The Irish Times* and managing director of Rowntree Mackintosh. The loss of their talents left an enormous gap, never satisfactorily filled since.

While McConnell's in Belfast was being bought out amicably by its senior management, Aubrey Fogarty was involved in litigation over three executives of his Belfast agency who left to start their own agency. Fogarty opened in Belfast in 1967 and Audrey Ralston was employed as local manager. Business improved and by 1970, further staff had been taken on, including Michael Mitchell. A separate company was then established; Des Bingham joined the Belfast firm in 1973. Business went well and so capable was the local management that Aubrey Fogarty's trips to Belfast grew more infrequent. But management personnel were dissatisfied with their remuneration; Audrey Ralston offered to buy out Fogarty for £20,000. He refused the offer, Ralston, Mitchell and Bingham resigned from the company and soon afterwards, when Fogarty went to Belfast, he found that his entire staff there had walked out, to work for the new agency, RMB Advertising. Almost all the accounts of the Fogarty agency changed sides as well; only two small accounts were left with Fogarty's firm. Aubrey Fogarty took legal proceedings: he says, in recollection, that the incident happened just after his wife Anne had died tragically young. "It was good therapy for me preparing for the case," he says. In an important decision for the advertising industry. Aubrey Fogarty won his case. He was awarded damages of £21,700 plus costs against the three defendants, Audrey Ralston, Mike Mitchell and Des Bingham. Fogarty's Belfast office was closed down; RMB still flourishes in Belfast.

A cheeky takeover was foiled in Dublin. In June, 1971, O'Donnell Earl made a £78,000 cash bid for Wilson Hartnell, a much larger agency. Bill Walshe, then joint managing director of O'Donnell Earl, said that many Irish agencies were not as conscious of profitability as they should be; they tended to think in terms of turnover and not

Opposite page: Sean O Bradaigh, who was first managing director of WH Associates, later renamed Bell Advertising. Illness forced his retirement two years ago, but he continues on the board of both the Wilson Hartnell group and of Bell Advertising. He worked in Domas with Michael Maughan and together they bought over the old Wilson Hartnell agency from Noel C. Hartnell; Maughan and O Bradaigh became joint managing directors. In 1973/74, nearly ten years after the Wilson Hartnell takeover, the agency began developing the idea of a second agency to handle smaller accounts. O Bradaigh recollects now: "It was a new concept, which we were first to develop in Dublin. In the event, it turned out much better than we had anticipated and it really turned into a competing agency." Bell is totally separate from Wilson Hartnell, except for financial services and a limited number of employees it shares with the rest of the group. Words and Pictures, run by Nick van Vliet, developed as a studio service out of Wilson Hartnell.

profitability. He said that there was an urgent need for agencies to rationalise, pointing out that in 1971, Dublin had 31 agencies with a combined billing of £9 million. Michael Maughan, managing director of Wilson Hartnell, described the bid as "utterly ludicrous". Wilson Hartnell claimed billings for the previous year, 1970, of £850,000, with a five per cent profit level. O'Donnell Earl had a 1970 turnover of £460,000. It acquired new accounts and new staff. Bovril and Berney Mastervision joined, while the Gateaux account went to McConnell's. David Rudd, previously managing director of Imco, became a partner in the agency. Deirdre McQuillan joined as librarian and research assistant.

Niall O'Sullivan and Owen O'Connor started their agency at cramped premises in Belvedere Place, Dublin, in 1971. O'Connor had been in McConnells, Janus and Peter Owens, while O'Sullivan had been account director at McConnell's. No accounts came over from McConnell's and while O'Connor O'Sullivan started with a blank sheet, the new agency grew quickly, winning the Carling Black Label lager account, the handling of the Carroll's GAA All Stars award, Warner Lambert brands, Premier ice cream, HB chocolate bars and Carroll's system buildings. Then came work for Mitchelstown Creameries, Datsun cars (now Nissan), Bass ale and Beamish stout. With O'Connor O'Sullivan was a good creative team, including Ian Calder, Brian Wallace (both shareholders in the agency) and Charles O'Connor.

Cor Klaasen spent seven years with McConnell's, a much happier period than his time with O'Kennedy Brindley. He left McConnell's in 1972 to set up his own agency, together with Michael McHugh (who had been production manager in Knights, as McConnell-Hartley had been rechristened after Des Knight's takeover) and Ray Wasserman. KMW changed into the Key Communications group, which foundered in January, 1985.

Danny Moroney, now retired from *The Irish Press* recalls the time he attended a media conference in Galway. An agency man asked him what he wanted to drink. Moroney replied: "A Scotch, anything except Haig. I can't stand the stuff." Replied the agency man: "You can cancel the order for four ½ pages for Haig I've just sent in to the *Irish Press* group." Moroney has a pet hate: media managers who can never be found in their agencies, but in various hostelries, then get up and say they haven't seen a newspaper representative for the past 12 months.

In the summer of 1973, Joe O'Byrne, former creative director of O'Kennedy Brindley, joined Des Knight, managing director of Knights Advertising, the former McConnell-Hartley company. By the end of its then current financial year, Knights expected to have billings of £1¼ million. Arrow was flying high. In July, 1973, it won a Clio award in the international beverages section of the 14th Clio Advertising Awards Festival, for a full colour advertisement for Hennessy brandy. Producing that advertisement on location in France had been an

Today, a little bit of Madison Avenue moves back home.

In late 1968 a large advertisement appeared in The Irish Times showing an eye-catching photo of the New York skyline over the ocean.

Its headline: "Today a little bit of Madison Avenue moves back home". Its purpose: to herald the arrival of a new advertising agency. Its name: Brian Cronin & Associates.

That advertisement was the new Agency's first, for it had no clients other than itself. Not the recommended way to open an advertising agency perhaps, but the founder was willing to gamble on two things: 1) Having made it in America, he could make it at home; 2) In any event, there's always room for another good one.

So much for the blarney . . . .

The advertisement worked (it had to!) and, from a standing start as number 28 in the Irish agency race, Brian Cronin & Associates now rank in the top 10 out of a total of some 50.

Opening in Earlsfort Terrace with six offices (five too many at the time), the Agency ran out of space after a few years, as happens to the best organised companies. So, in early 1973, it moved to more commodious and prestigious quarters at 10 Clyde Road, Ballsbridge. The former Canadian Embassy building, no less.

From an attitude of "don't see us . . . we'll see you" which the Agency had in its original offices, we now operate out of one of the nicer offices in Dublin.

An advertisement placed by Brian Cronin & Associates in the 1980s, reflecting the agency's growth.

267

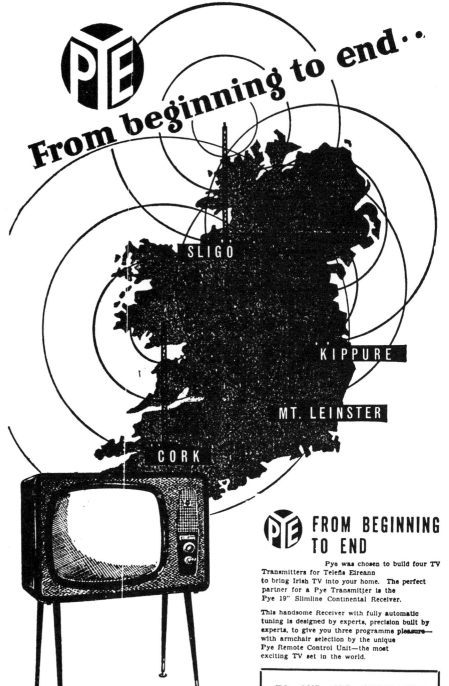

From beginning to end··

PYE FROM BEGINNING TO END

Pye was chosen to build four TV Transmitters for Telefís Eireann to bring Irish TV into your home. The perfect partner for a Pye Transmitter is the Pye 19" Slimline Continental Receiver.

This handsome Receiver with fully automatic tuning is designed by experts, precision built by experts, to give you three programme pleasure—with armchair selection by the unique Pye Remote Control Unit—the most exciting TV set in the world.

TO OUR OLD CUSTOMERS

If your SLIM LINE 19" CONTINENTAL AUTOMATIC Television Receiver is not adjusted for TELEFIS EIREANN — CHANNEL 7 — please contact your dealer before December 31.

If for any reason he cannot facilitate you, let us know and we will do our best to help so that you can participate in the first programme in the IRISH TELEVISION SERVICE on New Year's Eve.

All PYE Television Receivers manufactured since 1954 are suitable for Channel 7. Send your name and address on a POST CARD (no letters please) to:

SALES DEPARTMENT
PYE (IRELAND) LIMITED
DUBLIN 14

LIST PRICE:	70 guineas
REMOTE CONTROL:	3 guineas extra
LEGS:	1½ guineas extra

Pan Collins wrote the Irish Press supplement on the new Telefis Eireann service, published at the end of December, 1961. Pye (Ireland) was an advertiser.

268

PYE (IRELAND) LIMITED, DUNDRUM, DUBLIN 14

enlivening experience, in the recollection of Brian Murphy, the then creative director of Arrow. 1973 saw Mary Finan joining Wilson Hartnell's newly established public relations subsidiary; she is now its managing director. Well-known as a TV quiz show hostess, her first job after leaving college had been as Joe McAnthony's assistant on the public relations side of Kenny's. Then came a stint at Peter Owens. Wilson Hartnell's newly separate public relations company, highly marketing oriented, grew fast after Finan's arrival. The agency's first pr person, in the late 1960s, had been Emer O'Kelly, now the RTE newscaster. Other pr talent to have worked in the firm included Michael O'Reilly, Brian Keogh, Patrick Crane, Sean O'Riordáin, Dave Holden, Jack Mooney and Liam Ó Lonargáin.

1973 proved to be a decisive year for Irish advertising and media. Not alone did Ireland join the EEC, with enormous implications for the economy and hence the advertising business, but there was a flourish of international tie-ups.

Immediately after Ireland joined the EEC, O'Kennedy Brindley announced that the UK group, KMPH/Pemberton, was taking a 26 per cent stake in the Irish agency. By this link, O'Kennedy Brindley joined the International Needham Univas world network of agencies, which included Needham, Harper and Steers in the USA and Havas Conseil in France. Commented Desmond O'Kennedy, the Dublin agency's chairman and managing director: "Today, I believe there is no room for an agency confined in its thinking and its operation to a purely domestic market." Prophetic words indeed as Ireland closed the door on years of inward-looking economic policies, with home industry supported by tariff barriers and joined the outward-looking European Economic Community. At the same time, McConnell's joined the new ten nation agency network called Publimondial, with its headquarters in Brussels. Janus also joined an international grouping. In some advertising circles, these groupings were criticised for being little more than "paper chains". However, the then managing director of McConnell's, Brendan Redmond (now chairman) said: "Joining the EEC is the most exciting prospect. In every EEC country to date, prices have gone up, but wages and salaries have gone up even faster, so people have more purchasing power. A big increase in the Irish public's purchasing power means a big increase in advertising to win their extra custom. In addition, free trade will bring in many new products from abroad to compete on the Irish market — new advertisers with still more advertising money."

Also in 1973, with the collapse of Creation not far away, a major development startled the media world and attracted widespread public interest. Hugh McLaughlin and Gerry McGuinness risked all on the new *Sunday World*. The print run of 200,000 for the first issue sold out — if it hadn't, the paper would have folded shortly afterwards. For advertisers and advertising agencies, a new, largely downmarket, mass circulation newspaper was born, with good country coverage and full colour advertising facilities.

Luke Dillon-Mahon stepped down from Arks in 1973; he recalls that when he joined the agency in 1954, clients were always the boss. By the time he left advertising, agencies had gained much more prestige, while on the client side, the marketing function was starting to develop. Dillon-Mahon's retirement was a major loss to Irish advertising; he had done much, through the 1950s and 1960s, to drag it, elegantly, into the modern era. The year following, 1974, the great recession started, just as Pat Ferguson started to gain control at Arks.

CHAPTER SIX

To the present, 1974-1986

"Women are often better copywriters"

BARRY DEVLIN

Since the mid-1970's, the face of advertising has changed more dramatically than during any other period in its existence, while the cult of personality and "characters" has become subservient to computerised statistics. Agencies have become slimmer, more productive and less prepared to take creative risks. Advertisers have become far more marketing oriented in the face of a recession that seemingly continues for ever. Media has expanded too, with new newspapers like the *Sunday Tribune* and the *Sunday World,* a big expansion of television advertising sales to take nearly half the entire advertising "cake" in the Republic and more radio stations, with the opening of RTE Radio 2 and a proliferation of "pirates". On television, colour has become the accepted norm, of vast benefit to advertisers, particularly in the food categories. Symptomatic of these big changes over the last dozen or so years has been the restructuring of the agency business. Two spectacular collapses and several more minor ones have shaken out the advertising world, but the most far-reaching change of all in the advertising business since 1974 has been the drastic shift in ownership among larger agencies, part of an on-going trend towards greater internationalisation, pan European, if not global advertising. McConnell's is the largest Irish agency in terms of billings; it remains the only big agency in Dublin to remain in Irish ownership. Other well established agencies like Arks, Hunter's, O'Kennedy Brindley and

Cecil A. Bell, managing director, W & C McDonnell. Before joining the Unilever group, he worked in Aer Lingus, Arks and Sun Advertising.

Monday, fry-up (yawn) Tuesday, fry-up (not again)
Wednesday, fry-up (ho-hum) Thursday, fry-up (xx!!•*)
Friday, fry-up (say no more)

Have a change for a change.

With a new recipe from Vesta: Beef Strogonoff. Tasty beef in a sauce, with pasta shells and mushrooms, herbs & spices-a real change. Simple and quick to prepare too.

VESTA
READY MEALS

Beef Strogonoff

Vesta ready meals advertisement for W & C McDonnell, 1974.

Youngs have all sold out; Wilson Hartnell, an agency that has brought a new style of management professionalism to the business over the last 20 years, is now 80 per cent owned by Ogilvy and Mather. While control of the larger agencies has been slipping out of the country, there is now a growing trend for some major accounts to do likewise, as with Harp Lager, which went in 1986 to Dorland's, a London agency, which in its copy themes is now busy extolling the Irishness of the brand.

1974 was the year that the recession, induced by the ten-fold increases in world oil prices, started to bite. In the intervening 13 years, the Irish economy has spasmodically threatened to shown signs of slight improvement, but overall, the economy has stayed static. Consumer demand has flattened out, with year-by-year growth in spending staying in single figures. Only unemployment has showed spectacular growth: ten years ago, the figure of 100,000 unemployed was considered horrific. Today, the unemployment figure is verging on $\frac{1}{4}$ million, draining much consumer spending from the economy and imposing tremendous financial burdens on the State finances. Against this gloomy scenario, the advertising industry (media, advertisers and agencies) have been forced to run much tighter operations, economical on personnel and overall costings. It is only ten years since Sean O Bradaigh, now in semi-retirement from Bell Advertising, was forecasting that employment in Irish agencies would

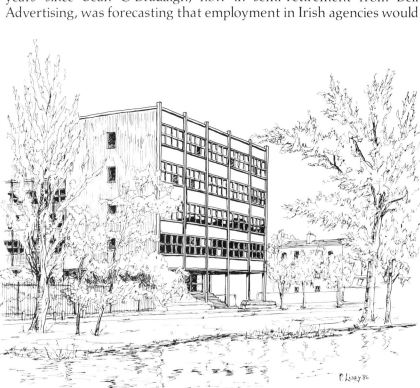

McConnell House, on the banks of the Grand Canal, Dublin, home of McConnell's Advertising agency since 1972.
Drawing: Pat Liddy.

top the 2,000 mark. Instead, over the last five years, agencies have cut personnel numbers by a quarter. Now, Dublin's 50 plus agencies are employing in total just 800 people: fewer people are doing far more work.

With the slimmer times that arrived in 1974, permanently, not only did the "Slimline" theme become a useful copy theme for food and drink advertisers, as they capitalised on a new calorie controlled consciousness, but it became management practice too among advertisers and agencies. Changes in the structure of the media have been dramatic in the last ten years. In print media, there have been a few new developments. First of all, the *Sunday World,* launched back in 1973 as a colourful "pop" tabloid, took off rapidly. It is now the largest selling newspaper in Ireland, selling over 360,000 copies a week. Its most recent development has been in Northern Ireland, where its weekly sales are well over the 80,000 mark, putting it well ahead of the Belfast owned and published *Sunday News.* On the Sunday newspaper front, the *Sunday Journal,* originally started with a farming bias, later

Still from the Kinsale section of the Bank of Ireland commercial produced in 1974 by CDP. The "Ireland's bank" TV commercial was for 75 seconds long and was shot in Dublin, Kinsale, London and New York. Production costs were £40,000. Director was Brian de Salvo; Gay and Terry Woods, a well-known vocal duo, did the backing.

Similar advertising moves were made at the same period by Allied Irish Banks, similarly formed from a number of banks. The two big bank mergers of the early 1970s reduced the number of banking companies in Ireland from ten to four.

Arks' former offices, Clonmell House, Harcourt Street, Dublin.
Drawing: Pat Liddy.

273

The right choice for the housewife
and your store!

SPECIAL RELAUNCH PRICES

**Vim was relaunched by
Lever Brothers in 1975.**

came into the orbit of Joe Moore's PMPA motor insurance group. In the process, it changed its editorial bias to urban and attempted to be a no-nudity version of the *Sunday World*. After just three years in existence, it foundered.

Another Sunday newspaper launch turned out to be more successful: the *Sunday Tribune*, which began as a joint effort between Hugh McLaughlin and John Mulcahy. The transformation of the well-respected *Hibernia* magazine into a Sunday newspaper was an uncertain business. McLaughlin bought out Mulcahy and brought in the Jefferson Smurfit group. The *Sunday Tribune* Mark 1 foundered after three years. In early 1983, Vincent Browne resuscitated the title and changed its fortunes. Now the paper sells just under 100,000 copies a week, has a strong ABC1 profile and presents what many agencies and advertisers consider a very well produced colour supplement in Irish newspaper publishing. It is the first newspaper in Ireland to be bar coded. Elsewhere on the national newspaper front, the most dramatic development has been *The Irish Times'* commissioning of its own coldset web offset press, enabling it to print full colour at competitive rates. The newspaper is now running full colour advertisements every day of publication. Negotiations continue at Independent Newspapers for its eventual change-over to photocomposition and web offset printing, the modern processes by which *The Irish Times* and the *Sunday Tribune* are produced. Independent Newspapers has had considerable success with its *Evening Herald*, changed to tabloid four years ago, partly in response to the short-lived threat posed by Hugh McLaughlin's last newspaper venture, the *Daily News*. The *Evening Herald* has dramatically improved its share of the Dublin evening newspapers' classified advertising. However, at the present rate of progress, it could be at least two years before Independent Newspapers typesets and prints its three Dublin titles by modern methods. The *Irish Press* group, still suffering the effects of closure during the course of its transition to modern origination systems, still has to make the final transition to web offset printing. Some newspaper sources speculate that Michael Smurfit is still interested in coming back into newspaper publishing and that if he did so by acquiring the *Irish Press* group, he could print its three titles, plus the Southside series of controlled circulation newspapers, at one of his existing printing plants.

The development of controlled circulation newspapers, which once promised so much, now seems less assured. Hugh McLaughlin, with the *Dublin Post*, launched 18 years ago, started this revolution in newspaper publishing. The *Galway Advertiser*, now 16 years in existence, is generally acknowledged as the first "free" country newspaper. At the same time, Century Newspapers in Belfast, publishers of the *News Letter* and the *Sunday News*, went into the "free" newspaper business in the Belfast area. The biggest development came in 1979 with the launch of the *Southside* series in Dublin. This series is now owned by the *Irish Press* group and covers much of the greater Dublin area, but with the cutdown on print advertising, such newspapers are now less profitable. Smaller circulation country "freesheets" often have a better chance of survival, since their print runs are shorter and less costly. Some provincial newspapers, like the *Meath Chronicle,* have entered the controlled distribution market successfully. Also on the newspaper front, the National Newspapers of Ireland organisation, representing eleven titles, is starting to make a cogent case for the use of the national newspapers as an important and worthwhile advertising medium. Over the last ten years, the volume of display advertising in the national newspapers has remained static, while the advertising revenues of RTE radio and television have soared. Now, the national newspapers, through their collective promotional work, are starting to bring back a little of the glamour that is now enjoyed almost exclusively by television advertising. Even the paid provincial press, long in the advertising doldrums, has started to fight back, modestly, with the establishment of a centralised advertisement sales bureau in Dublin. Over the past 25 years, national brand advertising, once so important in the provincial newspapers, has gone almost entirely to TV and radio. Whether the provincial press can start winning back some of this national display advertising remains to be seen. Food advertisers now use TV, radio and to some extent magazines: food advertising in full colour is rare in newspapers and remains an area to be developed.

On the media side, the biggest development by far has been the advent of colour television. RTE screened its first colour advertisement back in 1972: six years later, in 1978, the station opened its second channel, which is now securing a more equitable share of the audience.

Nowadays, colour advertising is taken for granted. It is particularly useful for food advertisers, who can show their products in natural colours. The growing importance of TV as the main advertising

Kevin McCourt, a former director general of RTE, who was appointed managing director of United Distillers of Ireland in 1968. This merger brought together the Republic's distillers; in 1971, it was renamed Irish Distillers' Group. Later, Bushmills joined the group. Under McCourt's guidance, the new distillery grouping began new marketing and branding strategies at home and abroad.

Donald Helme, new president, IAPI, takes over from Dermod Cafferky (right) of Arrow, in 1975.

medium is reflected in the revenue figures. 1986 will have seen RTE bringing in television advertising revenue worth £38 million, while in Northern Ireland, advertising revenue on Ulster Television and on Channel 4, is likely to be worth around £20 million. Ironically, there are now more homes in the Republic capable of receiving Ulster Television (about 500,000) than there are in Northern Ireland itself. The coming of satellite television is likely to have major repercussions on television in Ireland. For an experimental period, the main cable television company in the Dublin area, Cablelink, which is owned by RTE, is going to transmit a selection of satellite channels to test viewers' reaction. At present, about 18 English-language satellite channels can be received in Ireland: their main disadvantage is poor quality programming. In theory, satellite television, whether distributed by cable television or picked up directly through receiving dishes on viewers' houses, will make the whole country multi-channel. How quickly this fragmentation of the television audience takes place remains to be seen.

In the meantime, 60 per cent of the commercials used on RTE television come from the UK, with the benefit of Irish voice-overs. The UK advertising industry is regarded as the world's most sophisticated, ahead even of the USA in areas like production quality and sophistication of research. In the UK, advertisers and agencies have the advantage that not alone are budgets much bigger, but that media costs and production costs are more equitably balanced. A UK

The first ever winner of the JAEC diploma, Ireland-Canada scholarship was Claire Cronin. The scholarship is sponsored by O'Keeffes and Jemma Publications. From left: Noel Cautley (O'Keeffes, chairman, JAEC), Claire Cronin, Marion O'Reilly (director, O'Keeffes) and Michael Hayes (director of advertising studies, College of Commerce, Rathmines, Dublin).

1977-78 presentation in TCD library. From left: **Danny Moroney,** Irish Press, **Peter Finnegan,** Independent Newspapers, **Rory Yates-Hale, Irish Printing Federation and Jack Restan, Jack Restan Displays.**

campaign, with fine production standards, can cost £½ million: the media costs can be five or ten times that figure. In Ireland, production costs can sometimes equal time costs. An expensive Irish-made commercial can cost up to £100,000, yet it has to compete in production values against much more expensively-made UK commercials. One discrepancy thrown up is the lack of "dialogue" commercials made in Ireland. Dialogue costs much more to produce, so an Irish advertiser is more likely to go for an endorsement type commercial.

As John Fanning, managing director of McConnell's, makes the point that advertising agencies need sympathetic clients willing to pay the extra costs involved in making dialogue commercials. If the Irish advertiser is part of a multi-national group, his agency can "cannibalise" videos made elsewhere in the world, merely adding Irish voice-overs. Multi-national advertisers, like the Unilever group, can call up commercials used in other markets and adapt them for use in Ireland. The Irish advertiser with no international connections cannot do so and must rely on locally-made material. Recently, when McConnell's did commercials for Golden Vale Easi Singles cheese portions, they used a full scale production, creating effective advertising. Local productions of this type are increasingly rare with the pressures on budgets: the desire to "cannibalise" is always present. Seven years ago, when McConnell's was producing the Guinness Light commercials (the advertising was acclaimed, the product sales were not), footage from American space rocket launches was incorporated into the commercials. Present production practices in the Irish commercials' production industry are likely to continue. John Fanning

Ian Fox of Brian Cronin & Associates. **He has worked in the advertising industry since the early 1960s. He also writes on music for the** Sunday Tribune **and is presenter of the** Top Score **programme on RTE Radio 1.**
Photograph: RTE.

277

Maura Fox of McConnell's; in her time as head of radio at Janus, she started the careers of Larry Gogan, the RTE Radio 2 disc jockey and Hugh Leonard, the writer.

cannot see an increase in dialogue commercials here. Another factor mitigating against their development is that the UK television channels have many comedy and other series' programmes that develop actors and actresses into well-known personalities. Says Fanning: "Characters have already been developed in ½ hour programmes and are then used in commercials. Viewers' understanding of those characters is dependent on them having seen the actors and actresses in these full-scale programmes. You cannot develop that understanding just in 30 second commercials." Another major drawback is that RTE has produced few series like *Glenroe* that have built up acting personalities who could perform in dialogue commercials. "Not nearly as many actors have become well-known here through their television work as is the case in the UK," concludes Fanning.

Concurrent with the development of TV channels has been the fragmentation of the radio audience. RTE radio has developed into two main channels, Radio 1 and Radio 2, the latter started partially in response to the threat posed by "pirate" stations. RTE radio is now bringing in advertisement revenue of about £14 million a year, or four times what is accruing to the pirate stations. Since the disappearance of Radio Nova earlier this year, the pirate radio scene seems to have settled down into something approaching respectability. In the Dublin area, older established stations like Sunshine and newer ones like Q102 slog

In 1977, W & C McDonnell advertised Flora margarine — with a strong health angle — in Image and other consumer magazines. Health considerations were starting to permeate food and soft drink advertising.

Part of the elaborate recruitment campaign devised for the Defence Forces by Arrow Advertising in the late 1970s.

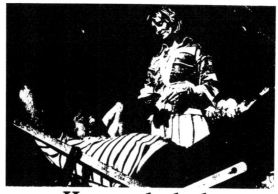

Have you looked at your husband lately?

Really looked at him? Does his waistband betray that he's desk-bound too often? Do his fingertips tell you he's smoking too much? Do his eyes give a clue to his business lunches?

Get back the husband you had. Plenty of exercise. Fewer cigarettes. And evenings and weekends, something light to eat—with Flora. Why Flora?

Flora is higher in polyunsaturates than any other spread because it's made with pure

sunflower oil and contains no animal fats at all. Flora has the kind of light, delicate taste that men often prefer.

So when he's home, look after him. Because he'll never look after himself.

Flora. Good taste that makes good sense.

JOIN THE DEFENCE FORCES

and go places

it out in the ratings, while in many country areas, pirate stations come and go. Much of the glamour and excitement that was attached to pirate radio up to 12 months ago, seems to have waned. Talks go on, endlessly, about legalising local radio, yet the problem seems no nearer a solution now than was the case five years ago. Community broadcasting, seen as a "respectable" form of pirate transmission, is currently considered to be one option for local radio development, so that stations are not entirely dependent on the commercial whims of private owners.

Just as the radio audience has broken up into many component parts, so too has another section of the advertising industry — outdoor. Together with newspapers, outdoor advertising is the longest established medium in Ireland. For many years, it doddled along without great glamour or excitement. The "scare" six years ago, when cigarette advertising was banned from outdoor, jolted the contractors into a more marketing conscious attitude. Long established poster contractors like Allen's and More O'Ferrall are now using the highly

IT'S TIME
HE GAVE YOU ONE
MRS DUKES

Two years ago we offered Alan the chance to open a Switzer Group Budget Account ... he didn't.
Perhaps he was too busy trying to balance the country's budget.
But maybe Mrs. Dukes would like some help to enjoy a smooth ride over the ups and downs of the forthcoming economic policies.
Our budget strategy is simple ... credit related to your spending power. A Switzer Goup Budget Account gives you 24 times your monthly payment in credit. For example, £20 a month gives you credit of £480.
Its a sound economic package that's politically popular, so call into your local Switzer Group Store and give it your vote.
How about it Alan ... for the wife!

SWITZER GROUP

Switzers Dublin · Cashs Cork · Todds Limerick · Moons Galway · Accent Plus Henry Street

Switzers, the Dublin department store, ran this advertisement in January, 1986, just before the budget. It was placed by the firm's advertising agency, The Innovation Group. Alan Dukes, then Minister for Finance, said that the advertisement had been published without the consent of his wife and himself. He called on Switzers to apologise publicly to Irish women for the contempt shown them by this advertisement.

Manus O'Callaghan,
chairman and managing
director, Southern
Advertising, Cork. In
1986, the agency opened
a branch office in
Dublin.

Joe O'Byrne, founder
and managing director
of O'Byrne
Associates, the Dublin
advertising agency.

Brian Cronin,
managing director,
Brian Cronin &
Associates, Dublin. He
started his agency in
1968 and created
"Barney and Beany" for
Batchelors, one of the
best-known
advertisement cartoon
creations since the start
of Irish television.

professional skills of Outdoor Advertising Services, Poster Management and Walter Hill.

The various advertisement media have fragmented over the last decade; so too has the agency world. 20 years ago, Dublin had fewer than 30 agencies. Today, despite the recession, it has just over 50. In addition to the "veterans" of the business like Arks, McConnell's and Wilson Hartnell, many small operations have come to the fore, employing just two or three people. Symptomatic of the agency shake-out have been several collapses, two spectacular, the rest less so.

The sound of breaking glass was heard loudly in 1974, with the collapse of O'Donnell Earl. The agency had been started in the early 1950s by Bill O'Donoghue, a former general manager of Arks and a talented copywriter. At the same time that Michael Maughan and Sean O Bradaigh were buying out Wilson Hartnell in 1965, Bill Walshe was busy buying out O'Donnell Earl from O'Donoghue when the latter decided to retire.

O'Donnell Earl had some good accounts, like Gateaux, Mitchelstown Creameries and Sterling Winthrop. In 1969, it had moved from Leeson Park to Hume House; at its peak, the agency was employing about thirty people and with a turnover in 1973 of £517,000 equivalent in today's money terms to about £5 million. It was ranked about 7th among the Dublin agencies. Walshe admits now that he knew "damn all" about cash flow and management; those were the heady days in Dublin advertising when clients poured out advertising money like wine. Suddenly, with the big recession of 1973/'74, caused by the huge hike in oil prices by Middle Eastern producers, the Irish

economy, along with all others in the Western economy, was in big trouble. The first item to be cut was advertising expenditure. Particularly troubling to O'Donnell Earl were the cutbacks at Sterling Winthrop, a major client, which was spending around £¼ million a year with the agency on brands such as Andrews Liver Salts and Milk of Magnesia. When those allocations were chopped, O'Donnell Earl was in trouble and in 1974 went into receivership with accumulated liabilities of around £180,000. Eventually, every penny of those liabilities was paid off, says Walshe. After the appointment of Alex Spain as receiver, Walshe and a few of the staff continued working so that client service could be maintained. After a time, the agency simply ceased trading. "The day we went into receivership was like Christmas for the other agencies," remembers Walshe. He claims that he had lots of offers, but didn't want to be absorbed into another agency. Dermod Cafferky came up with the solution: Phoenix Associates was set up as a totally separate company from Arrow Advertising. Bill Walshe says that only one big client, Bovril, left him at this stage. Phoenix Associates ran for seven years. Says Bill Walshe: "It never had recognition; that meant Arrow could keep it under control. I was locked in there for life and not terribly happy. I had given Dermod Cafferky my word that I wouldn't leave." The setting up of Phoenix Associates was the start of the Marcom group; not long after Janus came into the fold. The later collapse of Arrow itself, in April, 1983, was the most spectacular financial catastrophe ever seen in Irish advertising.

The next failure was of Barry Healy & Associates in early 1982. Healy had worked for Wilson Hartnell and was a founding partner in the Healy, Quinn, McDonnell agency, which took over McEvoy's Advertising in 1973. Three years later, he left to form his own agency. Healy's agency collapsed in early 1982, with debts estimated at around £100,000. Its biggest client had been Brennan's Bakeries, then

Owen O'Connor founder, with Niall O'Sullivan, of O'Connor O'Sullivan Advertising.

Ten years ago, Michael Bowles left Hunter's to set up The Media Bureau, the first independent media buying firm in Ireland.

Award winning Black & White whisky advertisement produced by Irish International.

281

Bob Milne, joint
managing director,
CDP.

Peter O'Keeffe, joint
managing director, CDP
started his advertising
career with the Irish
Press in 1966. He then
joined the then Wilson
Young agency, before
joining Cadbury Ireland
in 1970 as advertising
manager with
responsibility for the
modernisation of
Cadbury's packaging.
He joined CDP Ireland
in 1973 to handle the
Bank of Ireland account,
becoming a director in
1977 and jt managing
director in 1981.

spending around £100,000 a year. Brennan's moved to Cronin's, where its spend is now five times that figure. Prominent on the creative side at Healy's was Ian MacCarthaigh, now with O'Kennedy Brindley. Healy himself is working in American advertising. The biggest ever advertising agency crash was yet to come — just 12 months later.

The collapse of the Arrow agency in April, 1983, was the largest ever recorded in the Irish advertising industry. It had liabilities of £1.2 million. RTE alone lost £300,000 and as a result introduced new credit

A De Lorean
advertisement produced
by A. V. Browne, the
Belfast agency, in 1982
for use in Northern
Ireland. The De Lorean
car project later
collapsed, having
absorbed £70 million of
Government funding.

282

DE LOREAN

why every reader of this magazine can feel proud

Just over 2 years ago work began on a green field site near Dunmurry. It now boasts one of the world's most sophisticated car plants, housing ultra modern, high technology, manufacturing processes.

What we have all shared in is the creation of something unique in the car world — the De Lorean Sports Car.

The De Lorean presents performance with economy and safety with comfort, all in an image uniquely De Lorean.

This massive undertaking was made possible with the help, co-operation and endeavour of the people, business concerns and government agencies of Northern Ireland.

The effort that has gone into this project has been thoroughly worthwhile.

control procedures, to prevent a repetition. The start of Arrow's troubles dated back to the end of the 1960s, when it had its first big loss. The liquidation of Palgrave Murphy, the shipping company, cost the agency around £25,000. Through the 1970s, the expansion of Arrow continued unabated. In 1976, for instance, it started an award winning recruitment campaign for the Department of Defence. Three years later, the Department's advertising budget was slashed, causing big problems at Arrow. A dispute involving Gallaher's, the cigarette manufacturers, cost Arrow £70,000. It had been running a campaign for the Health Education Bureau, in the early stages of that organisation's existence. However, the "Conquest" dummy cigarette pack devised by Arrow resulted in Gallaher's taking successful legal

Bill Walshe of The Innovation Group. Previous agency encounters included O'Donnell Earl and Phoenix.
Illustration: Jim Cogan.

Field research being carried out for MRBI.

283

Michael Maughan, chairman of the Wilson Hartnell group, who was principally responsible for the agency's revival in the '70s and '80s. The growth of Wilson Hartnell was one of the most significant features in Irish advertising during that period.

A caricature of Brian Davitt, of Davitt and Partners, by Martyn Turner.

action against the agency, because the anti-smoking pack was similar to one of its own brands.

The board of Arrow had decided on expansion in the late 1970s and the group name, Marcom, was used for the first time in 1978 when it was registered by Arrow directors Dermod Cafferky, Brian Murphy, Joe Dillon and Ernie Keogh. The original idea of the group was never implemented, that of each company retaining autonomy in its services and having at least one director on the group board. This plan was never fully implemented.

Janus Advertising was approached by Arrow Advertising in 1975 for a merger; this was declined, but in the late 1970s, Janus sold its premises in Parnell Square and moved to Merrion Square, next to

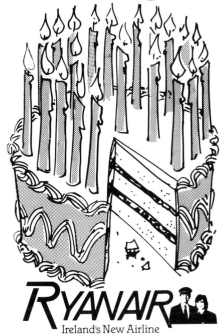

Happy birthday Aer Lingus!

RYANAIR
Ireland's New Airline

Joe Burke, marketing director, Batchelors.

RyanAir advertisement, in The Irish Times, on the morning of the 50th anniversary of Aer Lingus, 27 May, 1986.

Rex McKane is chairman of Belfast Progressive Advertising, now BPA McCann. He has been chairman of the Northern Ireland Association of Advertising Agents since 1984, is a past chairman of the Institute of Marketing in Northern Ireland and a past chairman of the Publicity Association of Northern Ireland.

Arrow Advertising. Janus continued to operate independently, but did share certain creative and financial facilities with Arrow and Marcom. However, Denis Garvey was far seeing in insisting on the retention of his agency's autonomy; no director of Janus was a director of either Arrow or Marcom and neither was a director of these two companies a director of Janus, a vital factor that saved Garvey's agency when Marcom crashed.

Arrow Advertising's first expansion had been with the setting up of Public Relations Practitioners as a subsidiary company, with Joe Dillon as managing director. In 1981, shares in PRP were sold to Hill & Knowlton, a J. Walter Thompson subsidiary and one of the world's largest public relations practices, for a sum believed to be around £50,000. At the beginning of 1983, PRP separated from the Marcom group when Hill & Knowlton bought a majority shareholding in the Dublin public relations firm.

The "rumblings" started at the Marcom group in early 1983, when

Opposite page:
Andrew McMeekan,
who spent two years
recently as marketing
director of Guinness
Ireland. During his
brief stay in Ireland, he
organised a major
restructuring of the
marketing department
in Guinness.

Dermod Cafferky,
lately of Arrow.

Karen Flynn,
advertising and sales
promotions manager of
Coca-Cola Ireland.
Before joining the firm a
year ago, she worked
with Bell Advertising;
her previous work
experience included a
TV video production
company. At Coca-Cola,
she is responsible for an
advertising budget of
over £1 million a year,
mostly TV, but also using
some magazines. She
has responsibility for
three Coca-Cola brands,
including Diet Coke,
Fanta, Fresca and Lilt. In
the West of Ireland,
Sprite, a lemon/lime
carbonated soft drink, is
marketed in competition
to 7-Up. Karen is one of
the few female
advertising managers in
Ireland.

Mary Finan, managing
director of Wilson
Hartnell Public
Relations.

four top executives left to start their own agency. Ken Flynn, creative director, Padraig Doyle, copywriter, Gerry Hanlon, visualiser and Jim Donnelly, account director started what is now DDFH & B. They were joined almost immediately by Jerry Brannelly, general manager/ director of Brian Cronin & Associates. He spent most of his career with Lintas in London, before returning home to Cronin's in 1979. The new agency's first account was Scholl (Ireland), the health shoe makers, closely followed by Laird's jams.

Cost cutting went on at Marcom; Brian Murphy, who was vice-chairman at the end, says that the high salaries had little effect. He was on £30,000 a year, while chairman Dermod Cafferky was on £33,000 and Ken Flynn was on £25,000. "If we had each been paid £5,000 less, it would not have made much difference. Our salaries were not out of line with the rest of the industry." Lopex, ironically, had made an offer to buy out Marcom in the late 1970s, but Dermod Cafferky turned down the bid. Later, Lopex bought Arks and Young's.

As part of the fall-out from the Arrow collapse, three of that agency's creative people, Frank O'Hare, Kieran Hayden and Alan Smyth set up a new consultancy in late 1983, called The Creative Department, offering services for TV, radio, press, design and finished

The Lynch Advertising sign still stands outside its former offices in Lower Leeson Street, Dublin; the agency closed down in April, 1985. It was founded in 1919 by Sean Lynch, who had previously been in the publicity business with Jack McDonagh. Lynch's first big advertising campaign was for the 1919 Dail Bonds. In 1926, Lynch founded the Irish Travel Agency, which was later sold and which is still trading successfully. The advertising agency had started in Suffolk Street, but for many years, it was located above the travel firm in D'Olier Street, where the Irish Travel Agency is still based.

Sean Lynch died in 1961; he was father-in-law of Sean O Loinsigh, who took over the running of the agency and moved it to Amiens Street. In 1979, the agency moved to Leeson Street. When Dara O Loinsigh, son of the 1960s Sean O Loinsigh joined the agency ten years ago, it had a staff of about 28. He now works with Doherty Advertising.

art. At the same time, Brian Murphy, who had been vice-chairman of the Marcom group, was named managing director of Diners Club International in Dublin.

Colin Anderson, who had started Anderson Advertising in Belfast with an Arrow involvement, had bought out the Dublin firm's interest before the crash. Phoenix Associates, run by Bill Walshe, formerly of O'Donnell Earl, and now of The Innovation Group, shut shop.

After the crash of Arrow Advertising, Bill Walshe had another extrication job to do; the day after Arrow stopped trading, he started The Innovation Group. All his clients from Phoenix Associates came with him: "they appreciated good service". Walshe also says that any debts incurred through Phoenix Associates were all cleared. "I have a very clean record". Many of his clients, like Whelehan's of Finglas, have been with him since his O'Donnell Earl days. The Innovation Group has a staff of 12; it buys in all its creative work. "We get tremendous creative variety that way. We're the planning end and have no obligation to use any one creative group. By going where we want for our creative work, we save about £200,000 a year on overheads," says Walshe. He says that last year, the agency turned over £4.8 million; in 1986, he is aiming for 16 per cent net profit, very high for the agency business. He seems to have learned his lesson from the O'Donnell Earl days: "We have very full management information. Four days after the end of the month, we have the full financial data for that month, including profit levels. I use cash to buy forward in the media," he claims. In one recent deal with a newspaper group, he says he did a deal for six months' space and got 30 per cent commission. His next aim is

to do a private placing. His ambition after that is to buy an agency abroad. "I want a big stage to play on. I'm 50 this year and sure as hell, I'm beginning a new career". Only one person remains with him from his O'Donnell Earl days — Eamon Carolan, his media manager. Daragh Cafferky works with him (he was also in Phoenix Associates). "He's very loyal and very bright". Walshe always plans forward nowadays. 20 years ago, after a rather drunken rugby dance in his native Limerick, he bought his own tombstone. Today, it sits in his garage, so he says, complete with inscription: "At least he tried." He also remarks: "My grave has long been bought in Kilkee, Co. Clare, where I spent many of my formative years."

Dermod Cafferky, former chief executive with Arrow Advertising, which collapsed in 1983, made an unsuccessful attempt to return to the advertising/media business in 1985. He set up a company in Blackrock, Co. Dublin, called Irish Media Representation Service to sell advertising space on behalf of provincial newspapers, organise copy from advertising agencies and handle invoicing and voucher copies. In the Arrow crash, provincial newspapers lost almost £67,000.

In early 1985, Key Communications ceased trading. All trade creditors were paid in full. Cor Klaasen set up KMW in 1973 with Michael McHugh (now with Gaffney McHugh) and Ray

Opposite page: Modern style bank advertising, devised by AFA for its client, the Ulster Bank.

In May, 1986, Dr Eamon de Valera, controlling and managing director of the Irish Press group, presented medals to some past chairmen of the Publicity Club.
Pictured here from left are Paddy McKenna (Guinness Ireland), Dr de Valera, back row: Bill McHugh, Bill Tyndall, John Culliton, Joe O'Grady, Billy King, Donal O Maolalaí and Frank Fitzpatrick (present chairman). Seated, front: Tim Dennehy (left) and Niall O'Flynn.
Photograph: Matt Kavanagh, The Irish Times.

When the budget lapses occasionally

So you break out of
conformity once-in-a-while.
That's human. It's then you'll
be glad of a friend in the Ulster
Bank. Have a chat with the branch
manager at your local Ulster Bank.
You'll find him more than willing to
advise and help on family budgeting for;
school fees, mortgage repayments . . . car
repayments, holidays (yes, and even a built-in-
reserve for the occasional flutter). Get to know each other

better by the year. And if at some
future time you need financial help for the
children's further education or some home
improvements, who better to approach
than your friend in the Ulster. Because
he understands, more than you know,
of the various demands on a family budget.
Call into the Ulster Bank — the friendly one.

You'll be glad of a friend in the Ulster ⟳ Ulster Bank Limited

Wasserman. Later, it became Key Communications, in which Paul
Kelly had a majority controlling shareholding. The creative side
of KMW was handled by Cor Klassen, while Tom Rafferty looked
after production. Then he joined Golley Slater Beckett, the sales
promotion and marketing firm, as did Paul Kelly. Michael Mackey,
account director at Key Communications, who left the agency before
its collapse, became general manager of Aubrey Fogarty and brought
a number of clients with him, including Windsor Motors. He had
joined Key in 1983 when his own company, Mackey & Partners, ceased
trading.

Fred Hayden, director,
Association of
Advertisers in Ireland.

Mike Tobin, media
director, McConnell's,
Dublin. He joined the
agency, from college, in
the early 1950s; in
1960, he was made
media manager, one of
the first such
appointments in
Dublin. Ten years later,
he became media
director. His
department has a staff
of 12, probably the
largest media department
in a Dublin agency.
Besides planning and
buying space and time
in Ireland, it does much
work abroad; previous
international buying
has been for such
clients as Aer Lingus
and CIE. It now
handles the IDA
account worldwide.

289

The Arrow creative team in 1973, left to right: Tom Connolly, Brian Murphy (forefront), Bill Bolger, late Brian Fry, Joe Dillon, Valerie Kemple, Pat Loughran, Alan Smyth, Bob Oakley (rear), Brendan Kelly and David Best (forefront).

In 1972, Padraic Guilfoyle and Georgina O'Sullivan got married; both were working in Arks at the time and colleagues at the agency organised this large poster in the agency. Included in this photograph are Tony O'Leary (1), Sandra Lyons (2), Bill Molloy (3), John Cruise (4), Michael Vaughan (5), Pearl Manning (6), Tom Doherty (7), Brian Carolan (8), Alan Tate (9), Ray Carrigan (10), Eamonn O'Flaherty (12), Tony O'Grady (14), Jim Murray (15), Sally Kerins (16) and Jim Nolan (17).

CONGRATULATIONS GEORGINA AND PADRAIC

You've seen the poster, now read the card.

A caricature of John
Fanning of McConnell's
Advertising by Martyn
Turner.

291

Also in early 1985, the Brangan Luhmann Knight agency was wound up, terminating a link that went back to 1921. In that year, Charlie McConnell founded McConnell-Hartley (the Hartley was a London advertising man), to promote both outdoor advertising and film advertising. Colm Brangan, who worked in Britain before coming home to work with Cahills, joined Peter Owens on the account executive side in 1969. He stayed there seven years, setting up Brangan Luhmann Knight in 1976 with David Luhmann, who was a former creative director with J. Walter Thompson in New York and Des Knight, who had been the main partner in Knight O'Byrne, which grew out of McConnell-Hartley. Joe O'Byrne had split with Knight to go off and form O'Byrne Associates. BLK went well until 1983, when there was an accumulation of bad debts from clients. Des Knight left in 1983 to set up his own company, somewhat after David Luhmann had gone back to the USA. At its peak, the agency had a staff of around 20 and a total of 60 clients. With the collapse of firms like Tara Travel and the loss of accounts like Allied Irish Finance (which went to McConnell's when that agency acquired the whole Allied Irish Group account), the collapse of BLK itself in early 1985 was inevitable. At the time of its closure, its most notable client was Memory Computer.

A 1986 collapse was that of the WS group, run by Bill Watson, noted for his bow ties. He started his advertising career with Dolphin Studios, an offshoot of Sun Advertising. From there he went to Peter Owens, which he recalled recently was an experience everyone should

Still from the "Oil City" campaign devised by KMMD for Irish Shell in 1984. The TV commercial was produced in England and was said to have been the most expensive ever produced for use on RTE, with production costs estimated at well over £100,000.

A mixer campaign prepared for Savage Smyth, the Dublin soft drinks firm, in 1985 by what was then known as KMMD Advertising.

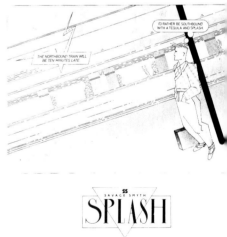

 OIL FOR EVERYTHING. CHILLED DRAUGHT MIXERS FROM SAVAGE SM' ·RED·WHITE·ORANGE·COLA·SODA·TOI

292

Martin Larkin,
managing director
of O'Kennedy
Brindley. He started his
advertising career with
McConnell's and when
that agency fired him
in 1974, he joined
O'Kennedy Brindley,
being made managing
director at the time of
the Saatchi & Saatchi
takeover in 1981. Since
the agency moved to
Clonskeagh Square in
1984, it claims to have
put on substantial extra
billings. At the end of
1985, it acquired the
Coal Information
Services, Fruit
Importers of Ireland
and Crown Paints
accounts — "£1 million
extra business in four
weeks," he said at the
time. O'Kennedy
Brindley now employs
about 50, compared
to its early 1960s'
peak of 120. "There is
no-one at O'KB doing
nothing," he says,
adding that the days of
the long lunch in the
advertising business are
gone.

go through. Working with him at Peter Owens were Niall 'Harry' Bracken, Doug Ross and Michael McGarry, whom Watson says was one of the most talented people in the business, because he could turn ideas round so quickly. Then came five years in White & Partners. Eventually, Watson set up Wordsmiths, which went through a tricky patch when Paul Lynch, Philip Nutley and David Kelly set up Hibernia Advertising; Wordsmith's major account loss was Atlantic Homecare and Carpets. Watson, who thinks that local design work is weak and plagiaristic, keeps a low profile: "My best lesson is to lie low. You come across all the big shots. You see how brightly the stars burn and then disappear."

While these local agencies were collapsing, the internationalism of advertising was highlighted by big international agencies buying into the Irish agency scene. Saatchi & Saatchi, which had its origins in London, is now the world's biggest advertising agency, billing $1.5 billion. Irish advertising agencies in total turn over just around £100 million. 60 out of the world's top 100 advertisers are now Saatchi & Saatchi clients; the group operates in 57 countries, offering multi-national clients a totally global service. Here in Ireland, it bought out Hunter's, started by John Hunter in the late 1960s and O'Kennedy Brindley.

In 1979, Saatchi & Saatchi took a controlling interest in O'Kennedy Brindley; the two agencies had a number of clients in common, such as Procter & Gamble and Rowntree-Mackintosh. Saatchi & Saatchi took

Nurse Jean Burke from Douglas, Cork, working in St Vincent's Hospital, Dublin, draws the £250,000 ticket in an Irish Hospitals' Trust sweepstake in 1978.

Product endorsement: Barry McGuigan, then world champion, and his wife, Sandra, were signed up by CBF, the Irish Livestock and Meat Board in 1986 to advertise and endorse Irish beef and lamb on the home market.

The photograph shows from left: Nicholas Ryan of Clerihan, Co Tipperary (chairman, CBF's home market advisory committee), Barry McGuigan and Paddy Moore, CBF's chief executive.

an 80 per cent stake in the Dublin agency for £106,975, a further payment of an identical amount after the financial year ended in March, 1979 and a further £100,000 in respect of the 1979/80 year. A fourth and final payment was made after the financial year ended in March, 1981. In 1978/79, O'Kennedy Brindley billed £2½ million and made a pre-tax profit of £100,000; its main shareholders were brothers Desmond and Niel O'Kennedy. The takeover came six years after KMPA/Pemberton took a 26 per cent minority shareholding in O'Kennedy Brindley. In October, 1984, O'Kennedy Brindley moved out from the offices it had occupied in downtown Lower Gardiner Street since the mid-1950s, to Clonskeagh Square in South Dublin. Now only one agency, Easons, is still north of the River Liffey. All others have followed the move southwards, towards RTE. Here it has some of the most stylish modern offices to be found in Irish advertising, a world away from the inner city problems now found in the Lower Gardiner Street area. Between the sell-out of O'KB in 1981 and its move to Clonskeagh in 1984, the agency's present managing director, Martin Larkin, claimed to have increased billings by 74 per cent. The agency now has a staff of about 50 and is dropping its time honoured

Anti-smoking logo, created by Doherty Advertising for the Health Education Bureau.

295

George Gaffney,
Gaffney McHugh
Advertising.

Pip Kirby, managing
director, Young
Advertising.

Paddy Considine,
managing director,
Adsell Advertising.

Stuart A. Kenny,
chairman, Kenny's
Advertising.

Dick Birchall,
managing director, The
Birchall Co.

Martin Wright, creative
director, Momentum.

Mal Stevenson, art
director, McConnell's.

Declan Hogan, creative
director, Peter Owens.

**Kevin Casey,
copywriter at Peter
Owens.**

Jack Gillen, creative
director, O'KB.

Jimmy Strathern,
creative director,
McConnell's.

297

name soon in favour of Saatchi & Saatchi Compton Ireland. In the early 1960s, in its creative heyday, the agency employed 120.

Rowe Advertising, which had been set up by John Rowe in 1979 as an offshoot of Young Advertising, announced rationalisation plans in early 1983, following Rowe's departure. It moved from offices in Clyde Road to Leeson Close, next door to Youngs, and Pip Kirby of Young's took over as managing director. At the same time, bright young talent at the agency was made redundant, including copy chief Cathy Gilfinnan, creative director Mal Stevenson, production director Jack Hayden and media manager Geraldine O'Loughlin. Rowe Advertising,

DE OSCAR-WINNENDE DRANK

We knew Ballygowan was performing well.
But we were thrilled when Ireland's leading figures
in the grocery trade agreed with us.

SON SUCCÈS LUI A VALU UN OSCAR

They judged Ballygowan to be the best
non-alcoholic drink product of the last two years at the recent
Today's Grocer/AIDA-SIAL New Product Awards.

ΕΒΡΑΒΕΥΘΗ ΤΟ ΚΑΛΥΤΕΡΟΝ ΑΝΑΨΥΚΤΙΚΟΝ ΤΗΣ ΧΡΟΝΙΑΣ

Which is the equivalent of an Oscar nomination.
It means representing Ireland at the
International Oscar Awards Competition in France.
And . . . we won!

EN OSCARSVINDENDE DRIKKE

Ballygowan Spring Water, in competition with
soft drinks and non-alcoholic products from nine different
countries, won the coveted international Oscar.

UNA ACTUACIÓN GALARDONADA CON OSCAR

Like most Oscar nominees we had a speech prepared —
just in case. It was like all acceptance speeches,
a little modest, a little tearful and a little long.

LA PRESTAZIONE VINCENTE

However, here's an excerpt: "Thank you all for
enjoying our Ballygowan Spring Water and helping
us win the SIAL Oscar (with a capital Eau!)."

AN T-UISCE A GNÓTHAIGH OSCAR

AN OSCAR WINNING PERFORMANCE

BALLYGOWAN
SPRING WATER
THE REFRESHING CHANGE

In the 1986 new product awards scheme, organised in Ireland by Today's Grocer, **Ballygowan spring water was judged the best non-alcoholic drink product of the previous two years. A print advertisement produced by McConnell's celebrated the win.**

298

75 per cent owned by Milne Estates, controlled by the Young family, finally closed down a year later. Lopex then bought Young Advertising.

Five years ago, in the spring of 1981, Arks was sold to Lopex, the holding company of a number of agencies operating in London, New York, Amsterdam, Brussels and Paris. Lopex acquired the entire share capital of Arks; Pat Ferguson stayed on as chairman and chief executive, but Alan Tate, son of Jack Tate, associated with Arks since 1931 and who died in 1973, retired to live in London. Others on the board after the take-over who have subsequently left include Michael Carr (retired), Jim Nolan (now with IAPI), and Frank Sheerin (own company).

With Wilson Hartnell now 80 per cent owned by Ogilvy & Mather, the take-over of top Dublin agencies is almost complete. The only large agency still Irish owned is McConnell's, which remains resolutely in local control. Still, the buy-out process has not been all one way.

In July, 1984, Brian Cronin bought an agency in New York, Walsh Rinehart & Puccio, handling mainly travel accounts. Cronin's intention was that his son Jim would run it, but Jim had to travel west for health reasons, so the running of the agency was handed over to Cronin's daughter Claire.

The very first buy-out of an Irish advertising agency had been of Grosvenor back in 1970, when Collett Dickenson Pearce of London bought out Johnny van Belle's interest. CDP placed the running of its newly acquired Dublin agency in the hands of Hugh O'Donnell and Bob Milne. Five years ago, they were instrumental in buying back the agency from its London owners. CDP retained a share of just five per cent. Now, the agency, through that shareholding, has been able to retain the CDP name, but is 95 per cent locally owned. Turnover is now claimed to be well over £8 million. Hugh O'Donnell, well regarded as a copywriter, retired in 1985, while Milne became joint managing director with Peter O'Keeffe. CDP's executive creative director is Brendan O Broin, while general manager Michael Fennell worked with Bob Milne in Sun.

1981 saw Doherty Advertising acquiring a majority shareholding in Padbury Advertising from that doyenne of advertising people, Maymay Dignam, the only woman to have run an advertising agency in Dublin. In Belfast, for a number of years after its inception, Audrey Ralston was managing director of RMB Advertising. Padbury's was founded in 1945 by Frank Padbury and after his death in 1957, Maymay took over the running of the agency. When Doherty's acquired its majority stake, in 1981, her nephew, Seamus Dignam, with the agency since 1958 and Bob Nealon, with Padbury's since a few months after its inception, became chairman and managing director respectively, as well as being shareholders. Doherty's had been acquired in the 1970s from the founding group by Don O'Connell, Ray

Phyllis O'Kane, first employee of Peter Owens Advertising when the agency started in 1960; she is now its deputy chairman.

299

Kennedy and Cyril Boden. In the late 1970s, the agency changed its name from G & S Doherty to Doherty Advertising. Ray Kennedy left to form his own public relations practice. Doherty's managing director is Don O'Connell and assistant managing director Brendan P. Hickey; in 1986, it was employing 24. Also in 1986, O'Connell was claiming that the Doherty/Padbury alliance made it fourth largest among the wholly Irish-owned agencies.

Finbar Costello, managing director of Irish International, reversed the trend of big Dublin agencies selling out to international groups by buying out his agency. Sun Advertising and the Dublin branch of Royd's merged in 1966 to form Irish International; Mack Kile was managing director of the new agency for nearly ten years, until he left Ireland in 1975. Costello was recruited from Irish Glass Bottle, where he had been marketing manager. When he arrived, Irish International's billings were down to £800,000, with the departure of such accounts as Allied Irish Banks. The agency had a good reputation for creative work, a poor one for account handling. After Costello's arrival, John Conway was brought back as media director. In 1979, Royd's sold its 60 per cent holding in Irish International to Extel, the London advertising agency. A year ago, Finbar Costello bought back this holding, together with the 20 per cent held by the O'Neill family (Tim O'Neill was the founder of Sun Advertising). Now the division of the shareholding is Finbar Costello (40 per cent), Bill Felton, creative

These advertisements for Fiat Croma cars appeared within days of each other in Dublin and Paris newspapers, September, 1986. Copy themes and illustrations were almost identical.

FIAT CROMA. A WHOLE NEW WORLD.

Now, from Fiat...

A new generation car, for a new era.

No ordinary executive class saloon, but a unique combination of power, refinement, space and comfort. A combination made possible only by a massive investment in car technology by a renowned world leader.

And this is technology that shows, in the power and efficiency of the transversely-mounted, twin overhead camshaft 2-litre engines.

Whether you choose the classic 120 bhp Croma 2000 ie with integrated electronic ignition and fuel injection, or the stunningly swift 2000 Turbo ie with a top speed of 130 mph, you'll find power and smooth delivery, coupled with a measure of economy that sets the Croma in a class of its own.

With that power comes the security of front wheel drive, all-round independent suspension and disc brakes making for truly superb roadholding and safer driving–no matter what the conditions.

The high performance Turbo ie is enhanced by the even greater reassurance of ABS anti-lock brakes fitted as standard.

Whichever Croma you choose, you'll find that comfort now takes on a whole new meaning. Th Croma's luxuriously appointed interior, comprehensive instrumentation, practical large tailgate and spacious boot combine to give you n only comfort, but relaxed, easy driving on even th longest journey.

The New Fiat Croma.

New elegance, new power, new luxury.

And a whole new world from Fiat.

O TEST DRIVE THE FIAT CROMA CONTACT YOUR FIAT DEALER OR PHONE 01-266581

FIAT
ALTOGETHER BETTER.

FIAT CROMA. CROMA 2000 ie £15,700. CROMA 2000 TURBO ie £19,990. (PRICES SHOWN ARE
SPECIAL LEASING AND FINANCE RATES ARE AVAILABLE THROUGH FIAT AU

FIAT CROMA

Un nouveau monde de technologie

SOMMATIONS (NORMES CEE A 90/120/EN VILLE) : CROMA CHT (9 CV) : 5.5/7.2/8.8. CROMA I.E. (9 CV) : 6.0/7.6/9.2. CROMA TURBO I.E. (9 CV) : 6.3/8.3/9.9. CROMA TURBO D (7 CV) : 5.2/6.9/8.5. FIAT EN FRANCE 1350 CONCESSIONNAIRES ET AGENTS. FIAT CRÉDIT FRANCE FINANCE VOTRE FIAT

Près de 30 milliards investis en 5 ans : c'est la mesure de l'énorme effort entrepris par Fiat pour se mettre à la pointe de l'industrie mondiale. Avec quel succès !

Reconquête du marché à l'aide d'une gamme de modèles dont l'âge moyen est le plus bas d'Europe. Réussite éclatante de la Uno, élue voiture de l'année et déjà produite à 2 millions d'exemplaires. Naissance du FIRE, le premier d'une nouvelle génération de moteurs, des moteurs simples à entretenir, plus compacts, plus performants.

Et voici qu'apparaît la Croma, la grande berline de Fiat.

Traction avant et moteur transversal, carrosserie "2 volumes 1/2", des dimensions intérieures record rapportées à l'encombrement : la meilleure synthèse entre l'aérodynamique et l'espace habitable.

Fiat Croma. Un concept unique servi, dans chacune de ses déclinaisons, par des motorisations d'exception.

Croma Turbo i.e. Turbocompresseur Garret T 3 refroidi par eau avec intercooler, injection électronique. 155 ch et plus de 210 km/h sur circuit. Avec elle, vous atteignez les sommets de la souplesse et du confort de marche.

Croma i.e. Gestion électronique intégrée des fonctions injection et allumage. Une motorisation de pointe qui vous assure des performances brillantes pour une consommation mesurée.

Croma CHT. Son double circuit d'admission "Hautes Turbulences", une première mondiale en matière d'automobile, vous permet d'économiser jusqu'à 20 % d'essence à régime modéré.

Croma Turbo Diesel. Turbocompresseur KKK avec intercooler. Stupéfiante de vivacité et d'aisance, elle donne la pleine mesure de ses 100 ch et dépasse les 185 km/h. Un record !

L'aménagement de l'habitacle obéit à des règles strictes d'ergonomie et tout concourt à faire de la Croma une voiture supérieurement efficace. Le freinage antiblocage est de série sur les versions ABS des Croma i.e., Turbo i.e. et Turbo Diesel.

Fiat Croma. Entrez avec elle dans un nouveau monde de technologie.

FIAT

Finbar Costello,
managing director of
Irish International.

director, recently returned from O'Kennedy Brindley, John Conway and Willie Nolan, the agency accountant, 20 per cent each. Today, the agency employs about 30 and its billings for 1986 about £5 million. Of all the campaigns produced by the agency, Costello's favourites are those done for Black and White whisky, an award winner nearly every year. Costello, a son of the late Lt Gen Michael Joe Costello, who as general manager of the Irish Sugar Company for over 20 years, did so much to change the Irish food processing industry, hopes that he can start a trend with agency ownership. Indeed, he went one step further, by setting up a UK agency with an existing London agency to form Kilmartin Baker Costello, to service Irish International's UK clients as well as its Irish clients with UK interests.

When Guinness was staging its successful takeover of Distillers in 1986, part of the Guinness advertising strategy used illustrations based on work done in the 1930s by John Gilroy for the Guinness and Johnnie Walker brands.

FOR A STRONGER SCOTCH JUST ADD GUINNESS.

Scotch whisky is one of our leading exports. Over 16,000 jobs depend on it.

Johnnie Walker & Co. must be made stronger if they are to win the fight for overseas sales.

There is opposition from the Far East, America and Canada. Each has its own thriving whisky brands. And powerful international corporations to market them.

Scotch whisky needs a similar champion. And our merger with Distillers would create one.

Time and time again Britain has failed to wake early enough to the challenge from overseas.

The alarm bells are now ringing on the world whisky market. Help us respond. Support the Guinness Distillers bid.

GUINNESS PLC

Guinness and Distillers. A stroke of genius.

This advertisement is published by Morgan Grenfell & Co Limited and The British Linen Bank Limited on behalf of Guinness PLC. The Directors of Guinness PLC are the persons responsible for the information contained in this advertisement. To the best of their knowledge and belief (having taken all reasonable care to ensure that such is the case) the information contained in this advertisement is in accordance with the facts. The Directors of Guinness PLC accept responsibility accordingly. SOURCE: Scotch Whisky Association.

302

Local agencies continue to proliferate. Small agencies have been started in recent years, like PFA, set up in Dun Laoghaire by Peter Finnegan, when he retired four years ago as advertisement director of Independent Newspapers. Over the last four years, PFA has kept going on electrical appliance advertising. Campaign Advertising was started by Brendan Bonass and Malcolm Mitchell, both formerly with Adsell. They have now been joined by Ciaran Stacey, formerly of PFA. Pat Ryan, long with Janus, now runs his own small shop. Yet another breakaway has been O'Sullivan Ryan, run by Ted O'Sullivan, formerly with O'Kennedy Brindley. Another O'Kennedy Brindley man running his own agency is Joe O'Byrne. After leaving O'Kennedy Brindley, where he had been creative director, he was involved with Des Knight in buying out McConnell-Hartley to form Knight O'Byrne. He went on, from Knight O'Byrne, to work for Barry Healy's agency. He left well before the collapse, setting up his own agency in 1979. Since then, he says he has never looked back. The agency remains a smaller agency on the Dublin scale, employing about ten people. Major accounts include Mitsubishi cars, featuring the jingle "Have a Mitsubishi day" and the Trabolgan holiday centre in east Co. Cork. By coincidence, O'Byrne's agency is based in Portobello House, built in the early 19th century as a canal hotel. In a previous existence, the building was a nursing home, where Desmond O'Kennedy was born. An early 70's agency which has continued to do well is Des O'Meara's although founding partner Colm Cronin left in 1986. 1976 saw Des O'Meara move his advertising agency from South Anne Street to Fitzwilliam Place. The agency's biggest account is Quinnsworth, spending about £1½ million a year, or almost half the agency's turnover. O'Meara claims that with the Quinnsworth account, his was the first agency to break the rigidity of the national newspapers' rate cards. "We went to Peter Finnegan in the 'Indo' and he agreed to do three pages for the price of two." Maurice Pratt worked in the agency for about 18 months, before going to Quinnsworth, where he is now marketing manager. Thanks to the personalised TV, radio and to a lesser extent, press campaigns for Quinnsworth, using Pratt, he has become one of the best-known media personalities in the country. At about the time that Pratt worked in the agency, Ian Fox came in as an account executive. He spent three years with O'Meara's. Other notable campaigns to have emanated from the agency included that for Mona yogurt. "That was a greenfield project; we won the account with our grocery know-how. The first campaign for Mona was a teaser type, using bus shelters and TV slides. It lasted a fortnight and cost £5,000. After three months, the product had a 36 per cent unprompted awareness," says Des O'Meara. His agency played a crucial role in the Fianna Fail landslide in the 1977 general election, the first in which publicity razzmatazz had been so heavily used. Among the items used was a special record, called *Your Kind of Country* with vocals by Colm Wilkinson, aimed at youthful voters.

Padraic Guilfoyle, now running his own media firm.

Conor Quinn, joint managing director of Quinn McDonnell Pattison.

Kevin and Joyce
McSharry, who started
Advertising Statistics
Ireland in October,
1981 to quantify
advertising expenditure
in Ireland across all
major media groups.

The late Colman Leigh-
Doyle, chairman of the
Pork and Bacon
Commission until his
untimely death in 1985.

One old established agency that has seen a lot of changes is Kenny's. When Stuart Kenny joined the firm in 1967, his father Michael and Michael's brother, Anthony, were joint managing directors. After the various "splits" in the agency, it has put on a modern face in Astral House, in Adelaide Road. Bertie Simmonds, who was once caseroom overseer in Millers, the typesetting firm, has been with the agency 25 years and is long time managing director. Several subsidiary firms were set up, like the public relations company, which has had a chequered career, but which now appears to have stabilised. Astral Films is run by Phil Walsh, who is Kenny's creative director, while Research Surveys of Ireland has remained dormant following the departures of Michael Fitzpatrick and Helen Kirby. An Englishman, Simon Howard, was brought over from the UK in 1978 to be its first chief executive; two years later, he died after catching scarlet fever and taking aspirins on doctor's orders. He was 33.

Domas remains, a pale imitation of its 1950s self: based at Ranelagh Road, Dublin, its chairman, managing director and principal shareholder is Joe Tiernan, the accountant who joined the agency in 1962. He took over from Joe Delaney, who retired from Domas in the early 1970s and who subsequently died. Eoghan Plunkett, who joined the firm in November, 1948, is still there; Tiernan, Plunkett and two others make up the staff complement of the present day agency, whose biggest account is Chadwicks, the do-it-yourself firm. Of the changes in the industry between the 1950s, when Domas was at its peak, and now, Plunkett says pithily: "Then, the agency business was more dependent on creativity. Now, there is much more dependence on research." Domas, from which four other agencies sprang, still survives.

One or two of the larger agencies adapted the second agency principle, long tried in the USA and UK, to cope with conflicting accounts. Ten years ago, Wilson Hartnell set up Bell Advertising. Today, Bell runs as a virtually autonomous agency, with Richard Strahan as managing director. The agency has grown with some large sized accounts as well as the smaller accounts that would not be of interest to a larger agency, but which in total, add up to profitable turnover. Bell runs all its own departments, independently of Wilson Hartnell, except for shared financial services. Young's tried the same idea with Rowe Advertising, but McConnell's attempt at a second agency has been rather more successful.

King Myers Moy Dobbin was set up in 1981 to handle new business that would conflict with the main agency. Joe Dobbin, Paul Myers and Paul Moy were all in McConnell's at the time; Jim King was chief executive of Kilkenny Design. A year after the start, Jim King went to Guinness Peat Aviation, while the year following, Paul Moy went to Maiden Posters. In 1986, Paul Myers left to set up his own agency, Javelin. With the clear-out of the original personnel, the initials are no longer appropriate: the agency is now renamed Momentum. It claims a turnover of about £3 million.

In Cork, there has been a certain development of advertising agencies. Cork has always been a difficult area for agencies, since so many accounts are based in Dublin and the national media is based in Dublin. O'Kennedy Brindley set up a separate Cork company as far back as 1955, run by Dick O'Hanrahan. When Saatchi & Saatchi bought out O'Kennedy Brindley in 1981, it did not want to buy the Dublin agency's Cork branch. This was bought out by the then managing director Manus O'Callaghan, who together with other senior staff from the office, including Kay McGuinness, Margaret Baker and Frank Dowling, art director, rechristened the agency Southern Advertising. For the last five years, the firm, with a Cork staff of 12, has done well, with many local accounts, as well as a certain amount of national accounts, such as the parts and service division of Ford's and Cooper's Animal Health. Southern Advertising has a branch office in Limerick with a staff of five and in 1986, has opened an office in Dublin. Southern Advertising's 1986 turnover is £2 million. Also in Cork, Concept Marketing was set up recently by Seamus Martin, formerly of the *Cork Examiner,* while O'Kelly Mooney and Associates was set up by Dick O'Kelly and Eddie Mooney, who both used to work for O'KB. Tragically, Eddie Mooney collapsed and died in Cork earlier this year. Southern Advertising is the sole member of the Institute of Advertising Practitioners in Ireland, based in Cork.

Michael O'Reilly, managing director of his eponymous public relations firm, which he formed in 1971 and merged into Wilson Hartnell five years later. In 1981, he left Wilson Hartnell to once again run his own firm. It is now part of the Daniel J. Edelman group, the world's largest independent pr company.

In Belfast, the agency scene has blossomed in recent years, although many accounts, such as Bank of Ireland, are handled on an all-Ireland basis from Dublin. Wells Advertising ceased trading six years ago and Ted Jerram, who had been managing director, went to Australia. A. V. Browne, which had been set up at the same time as Wells, in the mid-1920s, continues in existence. Val Browne, son of the agency's founder, sold it in 1983 to current owners, Patrick Wells and George Lavery. A. V. Browne is now the second largest agency in the North, with a turnover of about £2½ million. It has a staff of 20. Patrick Wells, related to Tommy Wells, founder of Wells Advertising, has built up Browne's with international clients based in the North, like Courtaulds, Berkshire, ICI and Du Pont. Queen's University and the education and library boards have also provided additional account spending. For a five year period, the agency handled the De Lorean car account, until the latter firm folded.

A. V. Browne has survived various other vicissitudes: In 1977, its offices on the Antrim Road in Belfast were bombed — twice. Two days after the offices had been repaired following a bomb attack, they were totally destroyed by fire.

Armstrong Long was a breakaway from A. V. Browne: John Armstrong and Roland Long left the latter agency in 1973 to set up their own shop. Roland Long later decided to pursue his advertising career in England.

In 1983, R. D. Beattie, creative director of Armstrong Long in

Bovril then and now. This current print advertisement for the brand uses a health platform and is a visual reversal of the theme used by artist Will Owen in 1925.

BOVRIL IS WORTH LOOKING INTO. RICH IN VITAMIN B,
BUT VERY THIN ON CALORIES (20 TO THE AVERAGE CUP) BOVRIL'S THE NATURAL CHOICE.

Jim Nolan, director of the Institute of Advertising Practitioners in Ireland.

Louis Hughes, marketing director, P.J. Carroll & Co.

Belfast was appointed to the board; before joining the agency in 1975, he had been a director of McConnell's in Belfast and also ran his own studio, which he subsequently merged with Armstrong Long. Also in 1983, David Lyle joined the agency board. He came to the firm at the same time as Beattie; his account executive responsibilities included the Northern Ireland Electricity Service, Valley Gold, Cantrell & Cochrane and Smiths Chemists. In 1984, several senior appointments were made at Armstrong Long Advertising. Terry Graham, who had been marketing manager at Hollywood and Donnelly, the wine and spirits firm, was made director of marketing services. Ian Erwin was promoted to account director the same year, after rejoining the agency. He had spent nine months with George Hynes and Partners. Peter Montgomery was promoted to the board of the company, while Anita Wilson was made an account executive.

Another of the leading agencies founded in the early 1970s is RMB Advertising. Its three founders were Audrey Ralston, Mike Mitchell and Des Bingham; of those three, only Des Bingham remains, as managing director. Belfast Progressive Advertising, now BPA McCann whose chairman is Rex McKane and managing director is David Lyle, has been established many years. It used to be located in Donegall Square West; about ten years ago, it moved to College Gardens, in the Queen's University area. Also near Queen's is McConnell's, begun as a subsidiary of McConnell's, London, in the mid-1950s and later a subsidiary of McConnell's, Dublin. Ron Chapman, who has since retired, and Dave Dark bought it out in the early 1980s, but retained the title.

Ron Chapman's son, Mike, became chief sub-editor at the *Belfast News Letter*. His wife, Sandra, is the well-known *Belfast Telegraph* columnist. Over the last five or six years, other agencies have been set up, including George Hynes & Partners, a branch of the Hynes agency in London. The Northern Ireland agency, based at Bangor, is headed up by Bill Trimble, who used to work for the Bushmills company. George Hynes, the founder of the agency, comes from Bangor.

Hynes started in 1980, soon acquiring such clients as Audi cars and the Northern Ireland Tourist Board. In 1984 and 1985, the Bangor-based company claimed to have shown the most dramatic growth in its existence, winning eight consecutive presentations, including British Midland airline, Unipork, the Department of the Environment and the Milk Marketing Board's Spelga dairy products brand. It has also opened an office in New York. Gilmour Carter Adamson Symington Advertising (GCAS) has thrived since its inception in 1981.

Anderson Advertising was formed in 1981 by Colin Anderson, who used to work for Armstrong Long. A year after Colin Anderson set up his agency in 1982, it had such accounts as Tyrone Crystal and Hamilton Holidays, as well as handling the worldwide campaigns for the Industrial Development Board. Colin Anderson, the agency's managing director, came from Armstrong Long, as did its art director,

Graham Wilkinson
(left) and Des Byrne set
up the Behaviour and
Attitudes market
research firm in 1985.
Previously, both had
worked with Irish
Marketing Surveys,
where Byrne was
managing director.

Raymond Douglas, who had been studio manager with the latter agency. Not long after launching the agency Anderson extricated himself from the Arrow fall-out. Also in Belfast is Septembers Advertising and Betty Carter Advertising, run by Betty Carter.

Various appointments have been made at Belfast Progressive Advertising over the last 12 years; it has been established in Belfast for about 30 years. In 1974, Hugh Harrison was made a director; he joined the agency in 1968 to work on personnel recruitment advertising. Before joining BPA, he had worked for four years with Morton Publications as an advertisement manager. He started his advertising career with the *Belfast Telegraph*, where he worked for 15 years. His directorship followed on the appointment of Peter Thompson as general manager; he had been marketing services manager at Barbour Threads, responsible for advertising and sales promotion. Shortly after Harrison's promotion, John A. H. Kelly joined the agency as an account executive; he had worked first with McConnell's and then with Armstrong Long. In 1978, Brian Watson, who had been advertisement manager of the *Ulster Grocer*, joined BPA as a senior account executive. Finally, in 1984, Rex McKane also took the title of chairman in addition to retaining his existing post. At the time, he was chairman of the Northern Ireland Association of Advertising Agents.

Martin Swords,
marketing controller,
Gallaher (Dublin).

Father and son: Aubrey
Fogarty, managing
director, Aubrey
Fogarty Associates and
son Stuart, now a
director of the agency.

Bill McBride, the international rugby player, was appointed marketing and public relations manager at the Northern Bank in Belfast. He joined the bank in 1959; in his rugby career, he captained Ireland from 1971 to 1975.

In September, 1984, Harland and Wolff helped break the nearly all-male bastion of public relations in Northern Ireland by appointing Dr Maria Moloney as head of its public relations function. She had been senior information officer with the Northern Ireland Housing Executive. She described the Belfast shipyard as a "throbbing place" and said it was amazing how many visitors it got from all over the world, keen to see where the Titanic was built. Also in 1984, Billy McEvoy was appointed head of marketing at Belfast airport. He succeeded Gerry Willis, appointed chief executive. Billy McEvoy's first responsibility was for developing new business, particularly in international traffic.

Various unsuccessful attempts have been made over the years to unionise the advertising industry, the most recent in 1977. The Irish Advertising and Design Association was formed to serve the interests of creative workers in advertising, communication and design. In 1976, threats were made to IAPI that work emanating from people not recognised by three printing trade unions would be blacked. This news was said to have taken six months to have reached the majority of people directly affected, in the creative departments of agencies and freelancers. A meeting of creative workers in the Burlington Hotel on August 16, 1977, decided overwhelmingly to join No. 16 branch of the Irish Transport and General Workers' Union. The committee of the association comprised Victor McBrien (chairman), Catherine Donnelly (secretary), Walter Bernardini, Ian Calder, Jim Cogan, Colin Gardiner, Ronan Henry, Cor Klaasen, Michael Lunt, Anton Mazer, Noel Mooney, Rex McDonnell, Gerry Murphy, Frank O'Hare, Dermot Quinn, Paul Richards and George Wood.

The association covered the following job areas: artists, photographers, writers, typographers, visualisers, creative directors, retouchers, paste-up and flat artists, illustrators, cartoonists, photographic technicians, photosetters, sign writers and display artists. The attempt at organising the creative section of the industry, although well-intentioned, faded away. Creative people are notoriously difficult to organise in trade union activities and the blacking threat from print unions, once so strong, also faded away too.

Eamonn Moore, financial director of Wilson Hartnell, points out the fiscal disabilities under which Irish advertising labours. During the 1980s, employment in the advertising industry has dropped by 25 per cent; about 800 people now work in the agencies. Disposable income has been squeezed: over the last ten years, the tax take on average income has doubled. The company tax rate of 50 per cent, plus disallowances on cars and entertainment are major disincentives to the advertising industry. Entertaining now costs twice as much in cash flow terms because of the tax system. In the UK, by contrast, the advertising industry has had explosive growth in the last few years, showing a 24 per cent increase in 1984.

Symptomatic of the pressures under which the advertising industry is labouring is the fragmentation of awards. When the Advertising Awards Festival started in the mid-1960s, closely followed by the setting up of the Institute of Creative Advertising and Design, no other awards system existed in the industry. Now, there are so many awards that some sources consider, flippantly, that the industry should start awarding awards to the awards. Media awards for advertising have proliferated. In outdoor advertising, the poster contractors' association now runs its own annual awards' scheme for posters, while the recently constituted National Newspapers of Ireland ran its first scheme of awards for advertisements appearing in national newspapers, earlier this year. This award scheme is likely to be made a bi-annual event. The *Sunday Tribune* runs its own scheme for advertisement of the month, chosen by an independent panel of critics drawn from the industry.

Audiences' appreciation of advertising has become far more sophisticated over the last ten years. As Brian Martin of Wilson Hartnell says: "Children are very perceptive about corner cutting on production costs. With the development of global brands, huge amounts can be spent on campaigns. Multi-national advertisers selling in Ireland can use these campaigns here, adding Irish voice-overs if necessary. For example, United Biscuits can use its UK material here, while firms like Jacob's have to fund their advertising out of their own local resources." Changing perceptions of advertising have been well documented by McConnell's Advertising, which notes that every day, the average Irish adult is exposed to over 200 print advertisements, almost 100 television commercials and 100 radio commercials. Market researchers, say McConnell's, now report a very different relationship between advertising and younger consumers. Today's consumers enjoy advertising, are capable of an acute understanding of the marketing objectives behind advertisements and are suspicious rather than resentful, knowing that the ultimate aim of all advertisements is to make a sale. McConnell's suggests a number of reasons for these changes: the younger generations have been brought up with television and have been exposed to a much greater variety and quantity of advertising than previous generations, they are more visually literate and are at ease with non-linear messages and many have been given insights into marketing and the media at school. A recent research study quoted by McConnell's says that there are four categories of people influenced by advertising. Firstly, the sophisticated critic accepts advertising as a legitimate part of his or her environment and wants to have an equal relationship with the advertisers. Secondly, the uninhibited appreciator loves advertising and responds unashamedly to good entertainment. Thirdly, the

Ken Grace (above) media director of Wilson Hartnell. He began his career in Janus, before moving to the media department of Arks for four years. He was appointed media manager of Wilson Hartnell in 1968 and media director in 1981. When he started buying and planning, available information was very sparse; from early 1974, computerisation started, bringing far greater sophistication. On TV time buying, he reckons the Dublin advertising industry is on a par with the UK industry in terms of planning and ahead in terms of time buying skills, since there are six TV channels received here, four of them commercial.

311

THE DAY MUNSTER BEAT THE

Christy Cantillon crosses the line for the only try of the match.

Greg Barrett takes a pass from Seamus Dennison.

Gary Knight, the All Blacks prop, in full cry.

Colm Tucker helps Les White to feed the ball back at a lineout.

Larry Moloney caught in possession but holding on for dear life.

It's not every day we beat the All Blacks!

Gerry McLoughlin moves in to rut off Andy McGregor.

But whoever said this is an every day whiskey?

BLACK BUSH

The special occasion Irish liqueur whiskey. From the world's oldest distillery. Established 1608. Distributed by Seagram Ireland Ltd.

Top picture... Gerry McLoughlin leads a footrush; below... Andy Haden has recovered but Les White is looming on the right.

Advertisement for Bushmills' Black Bush in the Limerick Leader **the day after Munster defeated the All Blacks November 4, 1978.**

312

LL BLACKS AT THOMOND PARK

The All Blacks perform the Haka.

Brendan Foley under pressure in the lineout.

al Canniffe, No. 9, is not quite in such mortal danger as this picture would indicate!

Staff photographers John F. Wright, A. F. Foley and Dermot Lynch were at Thomond Park on Tuesday to capture these dramatic shots of Munster's historic victory over the All Blacks.

Tony Ward, on the burst, supported by Donal Canniffe.

Blacks hooker John Black tries to bring the ball through at his feet, but Pat Whelan, Brendan Foley, Les White and Gerry McLoughlin aren't having any.

Donal Canniffe kicks for touch.

Tony Ward puts everything into a long clearing kick.

Mick Donaldson evades Donal Spring to launch a New Zealand attack.

HISTORY MAKERS! Munster, who made history by becoming the first Irish side to beat a touring All Blacks team at Thomond Park. Standing, left to right; Sean Gavin, president; John Cole, touch judge; Gerry McLoughlin, Les White, Moss Keane, Donal Spring, Colm Tucker, Pat Whelan, Brendan Foley, Corris Dorman (Watson) the referee; Martin Walsh, touch judge; Seated: Tony Ward, Christy Cantillon, Moss Finn, Seamus Dennison, Donal Canniffe (capt.), Greg Barrett, Jim Bowen, Larry Moloney.

313

Aine O'Donoghue,
Market Research
Bureau of Ireland.

Ciaran Havelin, now
sales and marketing
director of JS
Publications, a former
media manager in Arks.
While in Arks, he set
up that agency's
subsidiary, Scope Media
Centre.

careful deliberator enjoys some advertising but is wary of being manipulated. Lastly, the suspicious rejector reacts negatively to all advertising except messages which are completely rational.

John Fanning, managing director of McConnell's since 1981, epitomises the new breed of advertising person: more than half his working life has been in research. Planning and strategy are his particular strong points. "Account planning has become more and more important over the last 13 years. As budgets and production costs go up, you have to know how and why you are saying your brand message. The business is much more systematic now and in our agency, we've hired people with a market research background over the last seven or eight years. "McConnell's now employs about 90 people. It no longer has any links with UK agencies, although McConnell's former branches in Belfast, Colwyn Bay and Derby are still going strong — after local buy-outs. Fanning, whose brother is Dave Fanning, the Radio 2 DJ, says that in certain cases being Irish-owned is an advantage. "Many clients might not fully know the implications of foreign ownership of their agencies."

A concomitant of this emphasis on account planning is the market research industry. As Des Byrne of Behaviour & Attitudes, a company set up two years ago, points out, market research has been available in Ireland since the late 1950s. A. C. Nielsen was first into the field, offering a retail audit. Then, in the early 1960s, major steps forward came with Jack Jones setting up the Market Research Bureau of Ireland and John Meagher doing likewise with Irish Marketing Surveys. Jones is about to celebrate the 25th anniversary of his company. Then with the start of Telefis Eireann came Irish TAM. As Byrne demonstrates, the basic market research facilities and techniques have been available to the Irish advertising industry for a long time. "From 1963 onwards, there was increasing use of group discussions for pre and post campaign testing. Group discussions are still very important and widely used but now there is the question of using qualitative and quantative research to feed into the overall advertising strategy," remarks Byrne. He adds that in the last five years, with the advent of account planning in the agencies, this concept of market research has come on by leaps and bounds. Research is being used to provide long-term strategic objectives for brands. But Des Byrne notes that advertising doesn't always work in literal ways and that as far as the market research industry is concerned, there is a shift away from trying to assess information transference towards assessments of general feelings and moods generated by advertising.

Qualitative techniques are still important on the pre-testing scene today, certainly in this country and Britain. The emphasis of pre-testing research has moved completely away from statistical prediction or even prediction of any kind, since those predictive techniques were undoubtedly grossly overclaimed and have been replaced largely by group discussions, the results of which offer the advertiser and the agency better understanding, or at least a "feel" for the consumer response to the advertising concepts and/or material.

Over the last 20 years, Irish manufacturers have built up a vast pool of market research information, so that brand managers are working with a much greater depth of knowledge. Des Byrne says that with the first wave of marketing men from the 1960s now reaching middle age, they need research to keep in touch with fast-moving consumer markets. At the same time, marketing departments have been pruned during the past decade of recession so that over-worked marketing managers have to buy in much more research data. All areas of advertising have cut back on recruiting new talent over the last ten years, no area more so than marketing. Fortunately, says Byrne, there are signs of new marketing blood coming into the industry.

In 1983, Eamonn Williams, managing director of Irish Tam/Attwood Research of Ireland, moved to London to join the board of Audits of Great Britain, with responsibility for the Broadcasters' Audience Research Board. He was succeeded at Irish Tam/Attwood by Peter Curran, although Williams remained on the board of the Irish company. He later returned to Dublin to set up his own market research company, Infoscan, which is now part of Lansdowne Market Research.

On the research side, John Meagher, when managing director of Irish Marketing Surveys, said that pre-testing can contribute to more effective advertisements and campaigns. Advertisement pre-testing

Brendan Miller, now account director, former media manager, O'Keeffes Advertising.

Present generations of McConnell's in the McConnell Advertising agency, founded in 1916. From left: Stafford McConnell, John Henry McConnell and John C. McConnell.

315

involves investigation of the end consumer responses to the advertisements in concept or artifact form. The term "investigation of the responses" is a broad one which encompasses the assessment or measurement of attention, communication, comprehension, credibility, empathy, involvement and even propensity to purchase or use. Pre-testing is used by advertisers and their agencies to help them make major creative decisions as to the direction of advertising on the one hand and on the other for very limited enquiries — designed, for example, simply to establish understanding of an intended headline or copy phrase.

Although Ireland has a low representation of major market research networks compared with the rest of Europe, largely home grown companies have made research here as sophisticated as that in the UK. Des Byrne again: "Many UK companies operating in Ireland have been suitably impressed by the depth and skills of market research facilities and techniques used here." Total expenditure in Ireland through

Some examples from Cronin's campaigns in Irish for Toyota cars. From a standing start in 1973, Toyota's market share has crept up year by year. Ten years ago, it had 7.5 per cent; today, it has around 18 per cent.

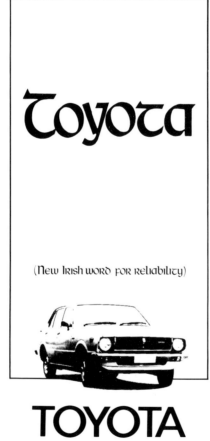

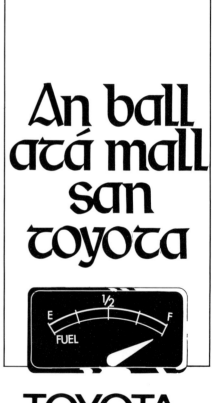

market research companies is running at about £7 million a year. Ad hoc research accounts for about 60 per cent of that total, continuous the rest. Ad hoc is broken down by Des Byrne as follows: qualitative — 19 per cent, omnibus — seven per cent and other quantitative — 36 per cent. In continuous research, Attwood Research of Ireland operates household retail panels while Infoscan does dustbin audits. AC Nielsen continues to do retail audits. With ad hoc research, Behaviour & Attitudes does omnibus, other quantitative and qualitative, while Dale Parry does other quantitative and qualitative and Irish Consumer Research does qualitative. Irish Marketing Surveys does omnibus, other quantitative and qualitative, the same as Lansdowne Market Research. The Market Research Bureau of Ireland does other quantitative and qualitative research, while Wilton Research does qualitative. While basic techniques have changed little, Des Byrne reckons that telephone interviews are more feasible now,

Go raibh mílte maith agaibh

TOYOTA

Bí an gan teip.

(Níl thuigeann toyota teip)

TOYOTA

Desmond O'Kennedy
(left) of O'Kennedy
Brindley and Eamonn
O'Flaherty of Arks at a
Kinsale festival, early
1970s.

Neil McIvor, advertising
manager, Industrial
Development Authority.

**The advertisement on
the opposite page was
published in Japan
recently by the
Industrial Development
Authority, a major
overseas advertiser**

with microcomputer technology useful in tabulating the resulting data.

While market research has flourished, so too have other aspects of service to advertisers and agencies. Dublin now has about a dozen trade houses producing phototypesetting for the advertising industry, while about six colour trade houses provide a wide variety of services, from planning to separations. Among these trade houses are Colour Repro, run by Greg Lokko, son of Tony Lokko, Litho Studios, run by Pat Leamy and Master Photo Engraving. The quality of colour, now that the print industry has changed entirely to litho, has improved enormously, while screen printing is also fast improving as a method of production. The largest screen printing firm in the country is Print & Display, which screen prints many full colour posters for the advertising industry. Photography has blossomed too, with Tony Higgins, Walter Pfeiffer, Dave Campbell and Neil MacDougald being joined by newcomers like Kieran Gallagher and Dave Keegan. Not alone are photography and typesetting farmed out (no Dublin advertising agency now has a resident photographer, as was once the case with larger agencies like O'Kennedy Brindley), but copy and artwork are handled by outside individuals and studios. In early 1984, the Peter Owens agency followed a common trend in Dublin advertising agencies by deciding to farm out its artwork. Production manager Jimmy Quinn was let go, along with four other studio people, including visualiser Martin Collins.

A newish agency buying in creative material is Gaffney McHugh, set up seven years ago by George Gaffney, once with Janus and Sun and 14 years with Grosvenor/CDP, and Michael McHugh, a founder

318

of the now defunct KMW agency. Gaffney McHugh has a total staff of just three, but claims billings of over £1½ million. It has no creative staff at all, buying in all its needs. Says Gaffney: "There are only about five good copywriters in town. We use people like Jon Chandler and Terry Bannon for layout and design. Creative partnerships are much more loosened up now — we pick the most appropriate one for the job." Bill Walshe, founder of The Innovation Group, which has a staff of a dozen and which claims a rare profit level for the agency business of around 16 per cent, says that his agency saves around £200,000 a year by buying in copy and artwork. He claims that he can shop around to pick the best talent, since he is not committed to any one group.

In 1983, Frank Sheerin, responsible for some of Arks' best copywriting for many years and a key participant in the great creative "buzz" that Arks enjoyed in the early 1960s, left the agency to set up his own company. He had joined the board of Arks in 1967 at the same time as Eamonn O'Flaherty, but must have felt that at the time he was leaving the agency, it was a rather dim shadow of its former self.

In early 1986, a media buying company was set up by Padraic Guilfoyle, formerly of the RTE television sales department. He offers a full service in media planning and buying for advertisers and agencies, particularly in the broadcast media. The first such media firm was set up by Michael Bowles back in 1976. He says that with the forthcoming fragmentation of the broadcast media, with the rapid development of satellite broadcasting likely over the next two or three years, the extension of cable television and the likely arrival of legitimate local commercial radio, he is confident that the need for media specialists will grow. A former media manager in Arks, his previous agency experiences, before spending seven years with RTE, included Youngs and Janus.

While the common themes of fragmentation and tightening up are seen right across the advertising spectrum, the industry is also haunted by a growing bureaucratic clamp-down on its activities. Not only is the industry labouring under the burden of financial disincentives, not being able to offset entertainment expenses, but many restrictions and restricting bodies have come into operation. Not only is there a Director of Consumer Affairs (Jim Murray) looking after the public's complaints on failures of products and services, but the Consumers' Association is much more active too. Even the Ombudsman, Michael Mills, former *Irish Press* political editor, can find himself in the thick of the consumerist fray on occasion.

The Advertising Standards Authority is closely modelled on that in the UK, although it covers all media, unlike the UK. The first discussions on the need for a code of standards for the advertising industry took place in the 1960s; the authority was set up in 1981 and funded by a levy of 0.2 per cent on advertising budgets. The chairman of the authority is Joseph C. McGough, SC, formerly with Bord Bainne, while the authority's administrator is Kevin O'Doherty. Its

with a current foreign advertising budget of IR£2.4 million. Until 1983, the IDA's advertising was aimed at selling Ireland as a profitable manufacturing base. In 1984, the IDA started the first of its new direction campaigns, aimed at selling the skills of Ireland's workforce. The campaigns are run in Europe, the USA and Japan and include major international airports. The campaign is designed to last five years and to change foreign perceptions of local work skills. Most of the IDA's advertising is handled through McConnell's. Neil McIvor is manager of the advertising and overseas press department in the IDA; he joined in 1978 from Aer Lingus, where he had been publicity manager.

IDA Ireland

319

Copywriter, Frank
Sheerin.

Tony O'Sullivan,
creative director,
Hunter's.

Graham Stone, an
Australian-born
copywriter, now with
CDP.

Catherine Donnelly,
copywriter at
McConnell's.
Illustration: Jim Cogan.

board members represent consumer interests and the interests of the advertising industry — advertisers, agencies and media. The committee of management represents the Association of Advertisers in Ireland, the Institute of Advertising Practitioners in Ireland and the media. The number of complaints received is low: in the year to June 30, 1985 for instance, just 54 pursued complaints were recorded. 29 were upheld.

One of its early "battles" was in the margarine versus butter controversy. In 1982, the Margarine Manufacturers' Association complained about "misleading" advertisements put out by the National Dairy Council. Both sides to the dispute quoted medical opinions and eventually, the ASA found in favour of the margarine makers. In another case, a bus side advertisement for a plumbing service used a cartoon showing a woman waiting outside an "out of order" lavatory. Four people complained and the authority recommended that the advertisement contravened the standards of taste and decency. CIE withdrew the advertisement, but in the ensuing media controversy, the owner of the plumbing service received so much publicity that he reported an enormous rise in business.

Health advertising has also become much more a feature of the advertising industry; since the advent of the Health Education Bureau in 1979, it has been spending increasing amounts of State funding on health publicity, the bulk on anti-smoking campaigns. In 1985, it spent £375,000, including production costs, on its anti-smoking drive, while in 1986, the anti-smoking figure is £370,000. Half of that budget goes on outdoor, while the remainder is divided between press, cinema and TV. Proponents of the cigarette industry cannot fail to point out that the Bureau is able to use TV, cinema and outdoor, all of which media are banned from carrying tobacco products advertising. Doherty Advertising has been running the anti-smoking campaign for the Bureau; by June, 1986, research showed that 81 per cent recognised the knotted cigarette symbol.

The campaigns must be having some effect, because the number of people in the population still smoking has dropped dramatically. In 1972, 43 per cent of the population smoked, but by 1986, that figure had fallen to 32 per cent. Consumer spending on tobacco products in the Republic is still £500 million a year. By the end of the century, cigarettes may have become a minority pastime, socially unacceptable in polite company. Even more stringent restrictions on the tobacco products industry are now being brought in, such as a ban on instore sampling and further cutbacks on the amount of shop displays and the amount manufacturers can spend on publicity. So severe are the latest set of impositions on the tobacco products industry that there is likely to be a three month moratorium in the near future on cigarette advertising while the three main manufacturers, Carrolls, Gallahers and Player-Wills, define their new advertising strategies. The incoming regulations dictate for instance that 15 per cent of the area of

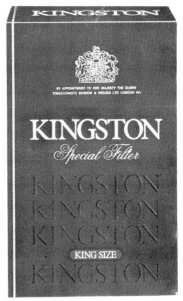

Earlier this year, Gallaher (Dublin) launched a new king-sized cigarette, Kingston, on the Irish market — despite media restrictions on tobacco products' advertising. Radio and TV banned such advertising in 1973, while posters were put out of bounds six years ago.

Says Martin Swords, marketing controller, Gallaher (Dublin), "King size is the only growing sector of the cigarette market. We saw a gap between our own king sized brands, such as Benson & Hedges and Silk Cut, selling at the top price and no frills, no nonsense brands like John Player Blue."

Gallaher's, has 26 per cent of the total Irish cigarette market, which is showing a year-by-year decline of 3 per cent.

321

Bill Davis, media director of O'Kennedy Brindley. He joined the agency from Arks in 1963 and was made media manager two years later. He started his advertising career in Janus. At one stage in the early 1970s, he lectured on the subject at the Rathmines College of Commerce. He is also a past chairman of the media conference. In addition to being media director of O'KB, he is also assistant managing director.

a cigarette pack has to be devoted to even stronger health warnings. A 2 per cent levy on advertising budgets will be used to help fund the Health Education Bureau.

One tobacco products' manufacturing source says that the Irish anti-smoking regulations are among the most stringent in the world, harsher even than those in Britain. With restrictions on publicity (tobacco products' firms can only advertise now in printed media), manufacturers are turning to sponsorship as another means of publicity. The Carroll's Irish Open golf championship, held every summer, is long established, a prestige event that costs the company an estimated £1/4 million a year. Drinks companies too, although not so thwarted in their publicity campaigns, are also turning to sponsorship. Guinness, for example, pours an estimated £1/4 million a year into the Cork Jazz Festival, held each October. Budweiser, the newcomer American beer brand, is also spending large amounts on Irish horse racing. Sponsorship is also returning to radio and television under a new guise: on RTE Radio, for instance, the Bank of Ireland has helped sponsor the quality programming on FM3, while the main Dublin newspapers have been involved with Radio 2 sponsorship. The *Evening Herald* is closely involved in a nightly chart selection show on Radio 2. Calor Kosangas sponsors the "Housewife of the Year" competition, televised by RTE. On television, Fords of Cork is spending an estimated £100,000 a year providing prizes of cars for *Murphy's Micro Quiz-M* show, hosted by Mike Murphy. Ford's advertising agency, CDP, is even said to provide the copy extolling the virtues of Ford cars on the show. The Irish Permanent Building Society spent an estimated £1/4 million earlier this year promoting Barry McGuigan, the boxer. Shortly afterwards, he lost his world title. As one noted advertising man said at the time: "How permanent is permanent?"

The vehemence of the Health Education Bureau is not reserved solely for the anti-smoking campaign. Between this year and last year, it has spent £260,000 on an anti-measles campaign, while back in 1982, it spent around £1/4 million on an anti-drugs campaign. The Bureau's current anti-drugs campaign, using largely TV, is costing around £100,000. Its work benefits a number of agencies, not just Doherty's. Similarly, road safety absorbs up to £100,000 a year in publicity costs. Just as State-funded organisations such as Bord Failte and the IDA now have some of the biggest advertising budgets in the country, so further State publicity spending, like that by the Health Education Bureau is making an important contribution to the advertising industry.

Ireland's first alcohol-free beer was launched in 1981 by Murphy's of Cork. Moussy, brewed in Switzerland, tastes like lager, but in addition to having no alcoholic content, is also low calorie. In the first two years of its sales in Ireland, Moussy did well, but since then, its brand leadership of the alcohol-free beer market has been ousted by the Guinness brewed Kaliber, which now has world-wide sales estimated at £10 million. In Ireland, Kaliber is reckoned to have 90 per cent of the £6 million alcohol-free beer market.

Changing life styles among young consumers has led to many changes in drinks marketing — and plenty of new products. Showerings launched Ritz aimed at the new young female drinker, described as "an experimenter, fashion conscious and independent." From Irish Distillers comes West Coast Cooler, described as a pleasant fruity alcoholic drink, projected at the younger age group. West Coast Cooler is aimed at the 25 to 36 age bracket and claims over 65 per cent of the cooler market. Another new product in this market segment is St Leger, a mixture of white wine, orange juice and spring water, aimed at the female drinker in her mid-20s, who does not want a high alcoholic content. Many of these new drinks are aimed not only at the younger generation of drinkers, particularly female, but also have a strong bias towards the health slant. Low calorie content is essential for the success of many food and drink products nowadays, along with a "purity" theme. No additives and no preservatives form one of the current marketing bandwagons. Even old products are making use of the purity theme; Bovril, for instance, celebrating its centenary this year, is capitalising on the fact that the product is completely pure, with no additives or preservatives.

In the beer market, there have been many changes, particularly in the 1980s. Twenty years ago, the beer market in Ireland was accounted for almost exclusively by Guinness stout; beers like Smithwick's and Cherrys had small brand shares.

Although stout with sales of £416 million a year still accounts for 50 per cent of all beer sales, and ale has fallen to 22 per cent, the big increase has come from lagers, now worth £224 million a year. In 1960, all lagers sold in Ireland were imported and had a two per cent market share; that year, Guinness bought the old Great Northern Brewery in Dundalk. 1960 saw the first production of Harp, just 5,000 bulk barrels in the first year; today, the brewery, much expanded, produces one million hectolitres of several lagers and exports to 70 countries. Even as recently as 1979, lagers had just ten per cent of the beer market; between then and now, lager's market share has crept up to 26 per cent and Stephen Hayes, then marketing manager of Tennents Ireland, reckons that lager may be the most popular type of beer in Ireland. The firm has done its bit in promoting change: in 1982, it introduced a draught lager, weaker and cheaper than existing brands. Tennents has 8.3 per cent of the market. Guinness then launched two low-strength lagers, Steiger and Hoffmans.

In early 1985, the Guinness group launched Hoffmans lager, in the south of Ireland. 48 sheet posters were used in the initial publicity, followed up by a TV commercial produced by Wilson Hartnell, with the theme "What a Night — What a Lager". German Pilsner lagers became increasingly popular, culminating with the importation by Guinness of the Fürstenberg brand. Steiger, Hoffmans and Fürstenberg have over seven per cent of the market between them. Guinness claims that it still has brand leadership in the lager market

The first ever advertisement for the Irish Stock Exchange appeared in The Irish Times **on March 14, 1986. The exchange was set up 200 years ago and had never previously advertised; its first campaign promoted the Smaller Companies Market.**

323

When Aubrey Fogarty was made chairman of the Publicity Club of Ireland in 1971, he was congratulated by Bart Bastable (left) and Dr Conor Cruise O'Brien (right).

Stills from the third phase of the Wilson Hartnell campaign for Paddy whiskey, May 1984.

Philip Cozens, purchasing and marketing director, H. Williams.

with Harp. Meanwhile, one new development has been the extension of own label to the lager market, with Quinnsworth's new own brand lager. The fastest growing branded lager is Heineken, brewed by Murphys in Cork. Carling and Carlsberg, brewed in Cork by Beamish and Crawford, have a combined market share of 30 per cent.

A new arrival on the Irish market at the end of 1985 was Caffrey's ale, a draught brand brewed by the Ulster Brewery in Belfast and marketed in the Republic by Tennents Ireland. Through Brian Cronin & Associates, the brand spent £1/2 million in initial launch advertising, including TV, national press, 48 sheet outdoor posters and bus sides. According to John Simms, managing director of Tennents Ireland, one third of Irish adult male drinkers are regular ale consumers and that over four-fifths of the market is draught.

1986 has seen Tennents spending £1 million on advertising its products in the Republic. These include the new Caffrey's ale and Tennents lager. In early 1986, the Harp lager account moved to Dorland's in London after more than 20 years with Arks. In recent years, Harp has lost brand share to rivals such as Heineken, Carlsberg and Tennents. The introduction of Fürstenberg from Germany by Guinness has also had a big effect on the beer market. Dorland's already handled Harp in the UK; now that it also handles the brand in Ireland, the aim is to reinforce its appeal to younger consumers in Ireland by taking a fresh, more modern creative approach. Harp, first launched in 1960, still claims to have 40 per cent of the lager market in

Ireland, despite the advent of many rival brands that have fragmented the market. In 1982, it had 64 per cent. Rival brand owners claim that Harp's market share figures may be too high. To beat the increased competition, Harp, in addition to its new media campaigns, has introduced a complete new look on its labels, bottles and taps. Promotions for the brand have included the use of rock bands like Queen. In 1986, Harp has also been using the Trivial Pursuits game as a promotional tool; so far this year, in its image revamp, Harp lager has spent well over £1 million.

Four years ago, Irish Distillers ran a major advertising campaign for hot whiskey, through Wilson Hartnell. Brendan Kelly came up with the copyline: "Wrap yourself 'round a hot Irish", while visualiser Brendan Magee and WH director Mike Curley added the hands, warming themselves round a glass of the "magic potion".

In 1984, a major new emphasis on whiskey advertising was developed by Wilson Hartnell. As Murrough MacDevitt, account director, said, research showed that Irish whiskey brands were failing to attract sufficient new drinkers to maintain long term brand well-being. The traditional forms of drinking whiskey reduced the limited appeal of Irish whiskey to many drinkers under 40. Spirit brands cannot be promoted on TV, radio or cinema, so a campaign strategy was devised for Paddy whiskey; the initial campaign, using posters, bus sides and magazines was devised in the spring of 1983, using the Paddy and mixer logo with such words as "Ridiculous", "Scandalous" and "Preposterous". The second phase used such copylines as "Orange goes ape over Paddy" and "White's just wild about Paddy". Post-advertising research indicated an initial trial rate of around 30 per cent in a drinks market beset by an overall depression. The third phase of the campaign, featuring young ladies who represented white, orange and red, moved into magazines. In the past two years, McConnell's has run an effective and evocative campaign for Power's whiskey, another Irish Distillers brand, using copy by Catherine Donnelly and colour wash paintings of traditional Irish pubs.

In one test run by Behaviour & Attitudes on the Powers' campaign, 200 young males formed the target audience. Of all the colour advertisements in the issue of the *Sunday Tribune* that they were shown, in terms of spontaneous recall, the Powers' advertisement was the best remembered. More than a quarter of respondents remembered it without prompting. Half the people who remembered seeing the advertisement claimed to have read all or part of the rather lengthy text. A number of people even pointed out a minor mistake in the artwork!

The soft drinks market has experienced difficult trading conditions in the last few years; not until 1983 was that slide halted. That year, a 5.4 per cent increase was reported. Some of the major soft drinks manufacturers opted heavily for generic or private label production, where generic products were made for specific supermarket chains,

Frank Fitzpatrick, current chairman of the Publicity Club of Ireland. He joined Aer Lingus in 1947 and spent nearly all his career there in the publicity department; he worked for Harmon Harris, Major Eamonn Rooney, Gerry Draper, T. P. Byrne, Ralph Leonard, Neil McIvor, Sean Bradden and the present manager, Bob Fitzsimons. In addition to print buying, he was long responsible for print production of Cara magazine. Recently retired from Aer Lingus, he still acts as a print consultant to it and runs his own company, PF Marketing.

Bord Bainne magazine advertisement in Germany (above) and a shelf sticker in Arabic.

with no advertising. Generic soft drinks sell for appreciably less than branded lines. 7 Up, first bottled in Ireland by Kiely in Tipperary in 1951, claims good support in both the grocery trade sector and in the pub trade; it is unusual for a soft drinks brand to achieve both.

One of the major Irish brand successes over the past two years has been Ballygowan spring water. Geoff Read spent years planning the launch of Irish spring water; critics scoffed. An early attempt at launching the brand was less than successful, but then Read teamed up with Nash's, the Newcastlewest, Co. Limerick, soft drinks firm. Using a source near the factory, the brand swung into full production. The label on the bottle was designed by Noel Hayes, of the Aston and Hayes design partnership. After two years, the brand now claims leadership in the Irish spring water market, a peak once held by Perrier water, distributed by Cantrell & Cochrane. The latest accolade for the Ballygowan brand came in late 1986, when it announced a major link with Anheuser Busch, the giant American brewery and soft drinks firm. The new link, which will give the brand access to the US market, is described as a "partnership agreement", but in fact Anheuser Busch has taken a shade over 50 per cent stake in the Ballygowan brand. Here in Ireland, Ballygowan has been challenged in recent months by some other local brands, most notably Tipperary, bottled by Gleesons in Borrisoleigh, Co. Tipperary.

At the end of 1985, one Cork firm broke with a lifetime's tradition and started advertising. Barry's tea, a popular brand first in the Cork area and more recently, nationwide, spent an initial £55,000 on a 15 second TV commercial produced by Arks. Previously, the brand had relied on word of mouth advertising. At the time of the start of its first major advertising campaign, it claimed a 22 per cent share of the tea market.

Despite the recent run-down of the Rowntree-Mackintosh factory in Dublin, Ireland remains one of the most highly developed confectionery markets in the world. Per capita consumption is around seven ounces a week. In 1978, the chocolate sector was valued at IR£44 million (today, it is valued at around IR£80 million). Almost three-quarters of the market, then and now, was accounted for by a handful of small brands. Cadbury's had a particular problem in 1978: with 55 per cent of the chocolate market in Ireland, it wanted to gain extra tonnage without doing so at the expense of its existing brands. Nunch was launched, using a new production process that allowed caramel to be wrapped all round a product, instead of conventionally layered. In the sweltering heat of July, 1977, the brand was launched onto the Irish market, with the aim of getting breadth of distribution rather than high levels of stock. A 15 second TV commercial by Wilson Hartnell was followed by a 30 second concept. Demand far exceeded production, so the product had to go on allocation. The Nunch 30 second commercial was the first Cadbury's commercial made in Ireland to be used in the UK; as for the product itself, it became the most successful new chocolate confectionery brand launched in Ireland for a decade. Despite the ballyhoo, Nunch did not last the pace: five years ago, Cadbury's replaced it with Star Bars.

One of the few bakeries to spend heavily on media advertising is Brennan's of Walkinstown, Dublin, developed over the last 20 years. Until three years ago, the account was with Barry Healy and Associates, but following the collapse of that agency, the account went to Brian Cronin & Associates. The media spend, mostly TV and radio, but with some outdoor and bus sides, is estimated to be worth around £400,000 a year. Joe Brennan, the founder and chief executive of the bakery, says that the amount the bakery spends on advertising is directly related to sales projections. It has brand leadership in the Irish bread market; with its new £3 million computerised bread plant, which came into operation in 1986, the firm has the capacity to supply an estimated 40 per cent of the Dublin area bread market. Apart from Johnston Mooney & O'Brien, now with QMP, no other bakery firm in Ireland spends so heavily on advertising as Brennan's. There is no collective advertising for bread in Ireland, unlike Britain. The last major campaign run collectively by the Irish Flour Millers' Association was in the late 1950s, through Arks, and failed to have any major impact on the slight year-by-year decline in the overall bread market.

Boland's bakery spent £100,000 on advertising in 1983 in a bid to improve its slice of the bread market. The TV campaign was produced by Cinetel for Doherty Advertising. Packaging on its 30 bread lines was redesigned by The Drawing Room and a new logo created; the bakery claimed to be the first in the Republic to use the new EEC food ingredients' listing, to meet the then new EEC food labelling requirements. It was also an early user of bar coding, which is now in general use in the food industry. Unfortunately, despite its go-ahead approach to advertising and packaging, the bakery closed down the following year, largely due to interminable management-union problems in the firm.

Former agency owner John Hunter has been able to put his advertising talents to use with his biscuit firm, Cobbett's of Bray, set up in 1980. It now trades as Braycot, because the Cobbett's name was already registered in the UK when Hunter decided to try marketing there. The brand of biscuits and wholesnacks spent around £20,000 a year on advertising in the Irish market in 1984 and £80,000 that year on a test launch in the UK.

Dairyland, set up by Waterford Co-op in 1974 to make and market the co-op's range of yogurts and salads, has achieved impressive market penetration. In the early 1970s, Waterford Co-op gained the franchise from Sodima, the French co-op group, to make Yoplait yogurt under licence in Ireland. Although the yogurt market, now worth £14 million a year, has taken a downturn in the past year, Yoplait remains brand leader with a market share of 64 per cent.

Imaginez l'homme qui a bâti sa maison ici.
Irlande
Allez loin sans aller loin.

Bord Failte magazine advertisements used in France (above) and the USA (right).

The board is a major advertiser, both at home and abroad. Its account for the home market recently moved to DDFH & B; next year, it will be worth around £400,000 in the Republic and £200,000 in Northern Ireland. The bulk will be spent on TV.

In the UK, where its 1987 advertising budget is likely to be over £1 million, it used TV for the first time this year, in the London ITV area. In France, its yearly spend is about £$\frac{1}{4}$ million, using magazines and cinema; the latter is an important medium there. Otherwise in Europe, all campaigns are placed in magazines. In Europe, it works closely with Aer Lingus

Dairyland has over 70 lines in all, including many new lines developed in the last couple of years, including low fat yogurts and cottage cheese. A rival brand, Mona, despite good advertising by O'Meara's, failed to make its targetted impact, because the market was over-crowded. Between both parts of Ireland, Dairyland spends about £1 million a year on promoting its products; last year, it launched Yop, a new yogurt drink, backed by an initial £100,000 publicity campaign. The initial consumer reaction was good: within five weeks, the new brand had reached its first year sales target. Its latest product is prepared salads, under the Rhoma brand name, with advertising produced by Doherty Advertising.

In the yogurt market, up to 20 per cent is accounted for by own label products. In recent years, own brand grocery products have come to the fore, their proponents claiming that because they did not need advertising, prices to the consumer could be cut. Two years ago, Jacob's belatedly entered the generic biscuit market, previously supplied from the UK. The generic-versus-branded products controversy continues unabated in the grocery market.

Such is the present day competition in the grocery trade that Paud Horan, then Dairyland's general manager, said in 1985: "Grocery retailers are being bombarded with new products and haven't got the chilled space. This pressure means that in future, products will be spectacular successes or spectacular failures — there will be no room for the medium selling product." Waterford Co-op has also moved into the British market within the last two years, becoming a major dairy products' exporter.

Through 1986, the Peter Owens agency has been promoting a new image for the H. Williams' supermarkets. A new house style and colour scheme were brought in following extensive research into the local supermarket market and retail operations outside Ireland. Owens also personalised the supermarket's advertising, featuring some of the store group's female staff and using the copy theme, "Notice the Change?" Superquinn is a major account for Hunter's, while Quinnsworth spends an estimated £1 million a year through O'Meara's.

Big brand spending in 1985 showed some interesting trends. Out of 20 food brands surveyed, 9 showed more spending for that year than 1984, giving an overall increase of 3 per cent. Pharmaceuticals and proprietaries showed a 15 per cent decrease in advertising spending, while household goods and appliances showed a similar increase. Wines and spirits showed healthy advertising increases, but still only spent £1 million in 1985 among the eight brands surveyed by Wilson Hartnell. Seven car brands analysed spent over £4 million on advertising in 1985.

In the car market, where unit sales have fallen from around 100,000 a year five years ago to just over half that figure, promotional competition is fierce. Fiat, a client of Arks Advertising for 30 years, left that agency at the end of 1984 for Hunter's. The car company currently spends about £300,000 a year on advertising. Fiat, in common with other major car manufacturers, spends its advertising budget on above and below-the-line work; above-the-line is media advertising — TV has been an important medium for car advertising since the mid-1970s and below-the-line on catalogues and displays at shows. Car manufacturers also have budgets covering promotional and discretionary discounts for special actions with dealers; building and maintaining dealer networks is a major preoccupation with all car manufacturers. With unit car sales falling back to around 55,000 in 1986, representing a halving of the new car market in Ireland over the last few years, and an unprecedented number of marques on the market — about 25 in late 1986, competition is unbelievably fierce. Ford, which once had a quarter of a market worth 100,000 new units a year, now has 15 per cent of a much smaller market. Larger car manufacturers — now that local assembly of cars has finished — spent up to £1 million a year each on advertising and promotion. Much money is spent on short-term "fire brigade" promotional discounts, while long term, TV and full colour newspaper advertising is vital in building brand image.

After the closure of the Dunlop factory in Cork in 1983 and the closure of the Goodyear facility here, Semperit found itself the only tyre manufacturer in Ireland. Semperit was set up in Dublin in 1969 by the Austrian tyre manufacturers of the same name. During 1984, it decided to expand its market share and appointed Wilson Hartnell to handle the account. Before this appointment, the firm's publicity had been low key; research showed low awareness and knowledge of the brand name and product. In March, 1984, a TV campaign of 30 second commercials was launched, with the theme "Irish made … and hugging every corner of the world." It was followed up by a national 48 sheet outdoor poster campaign. Follow-up research following the advertising showed a big jump in both spontaneous and prompted awareness of the local manufacture, a key point of the advertising campaign.

The PMPA motor insurance firm, taken over by the Government three years ago, despite the claims of former head Joe Moore that his company was financially sound, has been a strong advertiser in the last two years as it has rebuilt its image. The account went to McConnell's in early 1984; it is worth about £½ million a year and McConnell's has created effective TV and radio advertising in line with the insurance company's determination to have a strong marketing impetus.

In the last few years, some financial services, previously forbidden to advertise, have been allowed to do so, following a relaxation of the rules in the UK. In 1984, for instance, the advertising deregulation of the Institute of Chartered Accountants in Ireland enabled members of that body to advertise to the public for the first time. However, newspaper advertisements could be no larger than a quarter page, fees could not be advertised and comparisons could not be drawn with

and ICL. Says Stanley Wilson, Bord Failte's advertising manager: "All campaigns are closely monitored through coupons or now more importantly, telephone replies." The conversion rate from enquiries to bookings is usually between 15 and 20 per cent. In the USA, the budget for 1987 will be around £1.7 million, all in magazines, since TV is too expensive. Next year, the board's global advertising spend will be about £4½ million; in 1984, it was £4.2 million.

Charles Coyle is managing director of Irish Marketing Surveys, which he joined in 1966, not long after it had been started by John Meagher in what is today the premises of Irish Consumer Research. Over the past 20 years, IMS has grown to become a dominant firm in the market research field. In 1985, for instance, it completed about 300 separate surveys.

The market research market in Ireland is estimated to be worth about £7 million a year, with ad hoc studies accounting for £3.5 million of that figure.

any other practices. In Northern Ireland, accountants and solicitors have been able to advertise since 1984, but there has been no great rush to take advantage of the new advertising freedom. The most recent liberalisation of advertising practice among Irish financial institutions has been with the Irish Stock Exchange, which in 1986 advertised its services for the first time ever in its 200 year existence.

1982 was the year that Irish advertising finally broke through the £100 million barrier; as Frank Young, managing director, Wilson Hartnell, pointed out, for the previous three years, no real increase had been recorded in advertising billings.

Speaking at the 1985 media conference, Brian Davitt, that year's president of the Institute of Advertising Practitioners in Ireland, said that the days when agencies were set up on one major account were gone. He added that client lethargy in paying fees had put an intolerable strain on the industry.

In October, 1985, Noel Cautley of O'Keeffes Advertising, then chairman of the JAEC, the advertising educational body, announced that the number of people employed in advertising had fallen by 30 per cent between 1981 and 1985. Advertising students were finding it much more difficult to get jobs after finishing their courses, he said. During the same period, bad debts suffered by the agencies totalled £2 million.

The end of 1985 saw a new head of the Association of Advertisers in Ireland. Brian Doyle, a former advertising manager of Player Wills, had been part-time director general on a consultancy basis for two years, but when he retired, Fred Hayden was appointed chief executive. He had been managing director of Temana Ireland, insecticide manufacturers and is a past president of the association.

With agencies, too, there are continually new permutations of people. In January, 1985, Dickie Duggan, for 30 years chairman of Domas and a founding director of Wilson Hartnell when that agency was bought from Noel Hartnell in 1965, was made WH president. Michael Maughan is now chairman of the agency, while Sean O Bradaigh, also closely connected with that take-over, is now semi-retired because of ill health. His main achievement at the group was the setting up ten years ago of what became Bell Advertising, the group's second agency. Five years ago, Wilson Hartnell diversified further when Nick van Vliet set up Words and Pictures to handle the group's non-advertising communications.

A tragic death in early 1985 was that of Winnie Bigger, managing director of McConnell's Public Relations; she collapsed and died following a business trip to England. She had been made managing director of the firm in 1983; she originally joined McConnell's from Arks in 1968 and transferred to the former agency's public relations firm in 1975. She was succeeded as managing director by Roger Greene.

In December, 1984, Arks lost its managing director, Donald Helme, who had held that job for just 12 months. His departure coincided with the loss of the Fiat account (held by the agency since the mid 1950s) to Hunter's, which already had the Lancia account. Arks had lost other vital business at this time, including CIE, Irish Distillers and Allied Irish Banks.

The summer of 1985 saw Arks with another chief executive, Brian Grant, who took over after the agency had been left without a managing director for six months, following the departure of Donald Helme. Grant helped set up Public Relations of Ireland in 1964 and joined Arks from IBM, where he had been communications manager.

In August, 1985, Donald Helme, a past president of the Institute of Advertising Practitioners in Ireland, started his own agency, The Helme Partnership. His first account was Bailieboro Co-op, said to have been worth £250,000. The account had been with O'Byrne Associates.

One of the bright lights of advertising, Aidan Cosgrave, went to prison following on a charge of importing cocaine for his own use. Drugs Squad detective Thomas Madden told the court that cocaine was now a popular vice among bright young people in the glamour professions, such as advertising. Cosgrave had had a "brilliant" career in advertising, first in the radio sales department of RTE and then in O'Kennedy Brindley. He left that agency to set up his own firm, Creative Advertising and Marketing. After the case, the agency merged with Donald Helme's agency. Helme was chairman of the 1986 Irish Advertising Awards Festival, winning a top prize himself, for a commercial produced by his agency for RTE Radio 2.

In the early 1980s, a long time stalwart of Easons Advertising retired, Joe Clancy, who had been manager for 30 years. He is a brother of Basil Clancy, long-time publishers. Eason's is run today by Thurlo Butterly; it has about 120 clients, many of whom are institutions, such as county councils. A separate company within the Eason's organisation since 1965, Easons Advertising has given starts to many people in the business, from Noelle Campbell-Sharp to Noel Cautley. Even Charlie McConnell is reputed to have worked with the firm for a while. Of all the advertising agencies, Easons can claim the longest antecedents, since the original firm, from which the present day Easons derives, was started 167 years ago.

A major London agency opened a branch office in Dublin in the early summer of 1986 — D'Arcy Masius Benton and Bowles. The firm's Dublin managing director is George Benson, who spent ten years with Young & Rubicam in London and Brussels as well as working with several Dublin agencies before heading up the new agency; account management is the responsibility of Roger Delves. Media director is Colin Clark and creative director is Tony Bodinetz, whose work as a copywriter has included the "Probably the best lager in the world" theme for Carlsberg. The main account at the agency is Mars confectionery; working on that account as well as on the Uncle Ben's Rice account is Patricia Slevin, formerly with Bell. DMB & B intends to

Jack Jones, chairman, Market Research Bureau of Ireland, one of Ireland's first such companies, founded by him in 1962. He says that measuring the effectiveness of advertising is difficult, but that market research, advertising and public relations are sister professions.

Anton Mazer, a Dutch-born designer who started his career here in Sun Advertising where he spent two years.

331

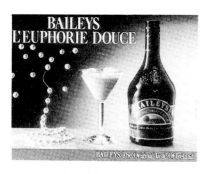

Visual from a recent Bailey's campaign in Brittany, France.

Bailey's Irish Cream was launched, modestly, by Gilbeys in November, 1974. The initial advertising campaign in Ireland, devised by Hunter's, which continues to handle the brand here, cost £10,000. From Ireland, the product was rolled out to Holland, Denmark and the UK.

Now that Bailey's is sold in 146 countries, its global advertising budget is about $30 millions, or about $1 a bottle.

Malachy McCloskey, Boyne Valley Foods.

pitch aggressively for local business, apart from its international accounts.

In the last ten years, women have become much more prominent on the account handling side of advertising, a reflection of the changing rôle of women in society. 20 years ago, only Maura Fox and Maymay Dignam could claim senior positions in the advertising hierarchy; Irish advertising awaits another Maymay Dignam as an agency boss. The *Sunday Tribune* has a female managing director, Barbara Nugent, again a rarity on the media side. However, in the creative echelons of advertising, women now play a much more important function.

Catherine Donnelly is the best-known female copywriter in the business; recently, she was made a director of McConnell's. She came to public notice early in 1986 by winning a sheaf of awards at the ICAD awards. For Ballygowan mineral water, she wrote copy that parodied the "Table for Two" restaurant critique style; a bonus is that client Geoff Read never changes a syllable of what she writes. "The writing has a fluidity that you cannot achieve with countless rewrites," he says. She has been with McConnell's for nearly seven years; the same creative "buzz" that overwhelmed her the first time she took the lift to the third floor in McConnell House on the banks of the Grand Canal still assails her. She finds the agency full of that self-perpetuating enthusiasm that is so necessary for good creative work. Her first agency job was at Arks; then followed the customary trek round the agency scene, O'Kennedy Brindley, CDP and Peter Owens. Much of her recently noticed work has been for press advertisements, not just for Ballygowan, but for other brands, such as the memorable series for Power's whiskey. She has also enjoyed working on the Smithwick's account: "The beer had been an enormous success in the 1960s, but it needed regeneration, with campaigns to change people's attitudes." She is equally at home in television, although it can be a much more tedious and time consuming medium, with up to a year elapsing from the creation of the first concept to the final editing and optics on the commercial. "Hours hanging round the set I don't enjoy so much," she says. After nearly 12 years in copywriting, Catherine Donnelly is still hooked on the process. She does not see it as a poor relation of literary writing: "It's a different discipline". However, she enumerates some past proponents of the copywriting craft who have gone on to become successful writers in other fields: Martin Amis, William Trevor and Fay Weldon. In Dublin, Kevin Casey, a copywriter with Peter Owens, is a noted novelist.

Why do women make such good copywriters? Barry Devlin says that they are more studied in their writing, more careful. They are often better writers, most often responsible for creating memorable words and phrases. Other senior women writers include Barbara Lightfoot, senior copywriter at Wilson Hartnell, whose work has included Hibernian Insurance, the Sandeman's Hot Port campaign and the current Slimline soft drinks' slogan: "If someone you love would like to see less of you." Byna Twomey was responsible, as senior copywriter at Young's, for the Britvic caveman copy and more recently, copy for IBM business media campaigns.

Hilary Curtin is senior copywriter at O'Kennedy Brindley, working on such Saatchi & Saatchi accounts in Dublin as British Airways. Other clients she has written for include JWT holidays and Texaco. Kathy Gilfinnan, senior copywriter at Irish International, is one of the best regarded in the business, creator of the current copy lines for Black and White whisky and its two shaggy terriers: "Dogs don't stray" and "Dogs on the Rocks". Other work at the agency includes Brown Thomas. Paddy O'Doherty at DDFH & B has created such slogans as the one for the National Newspapers of Ireland campaign: "When your advertising is worth a second look." Jan Wynter at Hunter's has written award winning copy for the *Evening Herald* promotional campaigns, while a freelance copywriter, Una Hand, aged 25, has created some memorable puns for Wilson Hartnell's DART advertising. The agency was quick to promote women: in 1981, it had promoted senior copywriter Barbara Lightfoot to creative group head.

In 1983, the Public Relations Institute of Ireland elected its first female president, Barbara Wallace of Wexford. The institute was set up in the early 1950s. She was subsequently re-elected for a second term.

Michael J. Murphy, home trade director, Irish Distillers.

Look who's talking about us.

Freshly ground for extra flavour.

Goodall's of Ireland is the country's largest independent food manufacturer, making table sauces, salad products, baking and cooking aids. The company was incorporated in 1932 by Charlie Hogg and had a franchise to sell products made by Goodall's Backhouse, Leeds, but it has long since been an independent, privately owned Irish firm. Goodall's of Ireland has advertised on Irish television since the service started; its current campaign, devised by Irish International, also uses magazines. The advertisement shown left was used in a recent trade press campaign. Among its brands is Kandee sauce, launched in 1906.

333

Paul Myers, former managing director of KMMD. He left that agency earlier this year, together with Joe Dobbin, to set up a new agency called Javelin Advertising. The new firm's joint creative directors are Dobbin and Conor Kennedy; account director is Marie Claire Sweeney.

KMMD was set up by McConnell's in 1981. Following the departure of Dobbin and Myers, the last of the founders, the agency was renamed Momentum Advertising and Marketing, with a new logo designed by Ralph Steadman, the British political cartoonist.

The predicted break-up of the JNMR survey, financed jointly by the newspapers, magazines and RTE did not after all happen. In late 1986, after threats that the newspapers would disengage from the research, all was sweetness and light and the proponents of the JNMR agreed to stay together, at least for another while. The new contract expires in just under two years' time. Now more equitably financed, the next JNMR report is due in September, 1987. The research costs about £90,000 a year to produce.

Advertising in the last decade has changed substantially, in response to changing market conditions. The period under review had begun with the advertising exhibition of 1974, which was a good year to look back on the previous 50 years; many sections of the advertising industry got together to organise a retrospective exhibition on the industry in the Bank of Ireland exhibition centre in Lower Baggot Street. People like Denis Garvey played a key rôle in its organisation; Frank Grennan, for long a leading light in the Advertising Press Club, was responsible for organising the champagne. The exhibition created much interest; sadly, in retrospect, no-one saw the necessity of preserving the assembled material. 12 years on, only a few panels remain in existence. 1974 also saw Jim Nolan, then with Arks, now with the Institute of Advertising Practitioners, receive the McConnell Award. In the testimony, he was described as quiet and efficient, a consistent supporter of industry organisations and a senior advertising man of depth and experience.

1974 also saw the Advertising Press Club bring Harry Wayne McMahon to Dublin with his 100 best TV commercials. It provided an entertaining and enlightening day for the local advertising industry; the following year, 1975, Mack Kile left Irish International, where he had established such an indelible reputation, to work with the McMahon travelling roadshow. He was perhaps the last of the momentous "characters" to work in Irish advertising.

Now, as the advertising industry takes stock and assesses the retrenchment that has gone on, thanks to the grey recession of the last decade, certain facts remain immutable. TV is the most important medium, for as Brian Martin of Wilson Hartnell says, "In today's communications environment, national noise so often means television advertising". Newspapers have to recapture some of that glamour attached exclusively to television. Advertising remains, however, cautious. Agencies no longer even "sign" their work as in the old days, such is the competition. Gareth Oldham, managing director of Hunter's, comments "that Irish advertisers want their products promoted prestigiously and with care". In promoting their sales messages, humour is fine on occasion. Creativity sells, too, as can be seen in the response to the Power's whiskey advertising. Above all, advertising is the engine of the consumer society, even if demand has flattened out. What Johnston's started all those years ago in 1819 continues today with undreamed of sophistication, despite the hiccups along the way.

Dublin artist Gerald Davis first masqueraded as James Joyce's Leopold Bloom when he created 'Paintings for Bloomsday', an exhibition based on 'Ulysses', in 1977. This etching by him made for the Graphic Studio, Dublin is entitled: "The only authentic photograph of Leopold Bloom, taken on Wellington Quay, June 16th 1904 and discovered by Gerald Davis in December 1979". No doubt James Joyce, something of an ad man himself, would have appreciated the joke.
Reproduced by permission of the artist.

Findlater's calendar, full colour nearly a century ago.

A famous Bovril poster of 1896, with the copyline: "Alas! my poor Brother". The brand was launched in Ireland and Britain in 1886.

Cadbury's Chocolates poster, 1906.

CADBURY'S CHOCOLATES

"IT'S AN ILL WIND THAT
BLOWS NOBODY ANY GOOD."

Ross's of Belfast, the soft drinks firm, advertised its table waters, making the most of the "Royal" connection, in a magazine insert of 1900.

Early 20th century
biscuit tin tops
produced by W & R
Jacob.

A poster created 80 years ago for Welsbach gas mantles.

John Player's hero. The cigarette firm started using this design for its trade mark in 1891. Players began production in Dublin in 1924.

Coca-Cola
advertisement used in
the USA in the early
part of this century.

DRINK
Coca-Cola

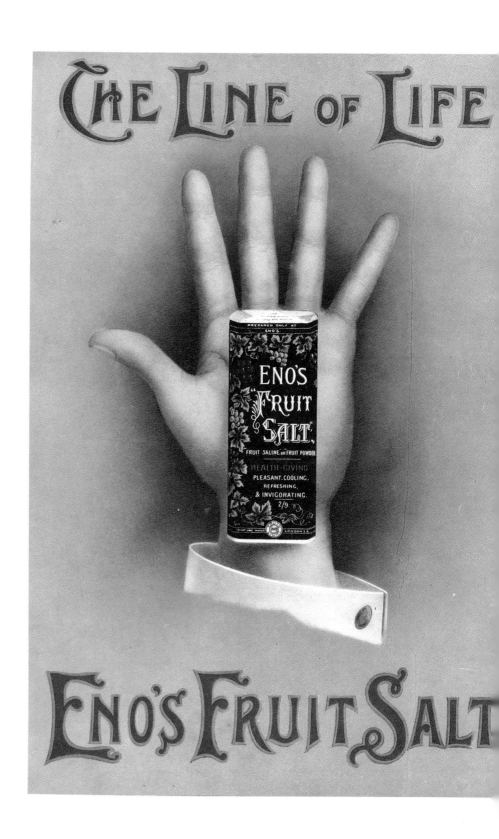

**Advertisement for
Eno's Fruit Salts,** Lady
of the House,
Christmas, 1917.

342

"The Pride of Tipperary."

"For Health and Beauty."

Advertisement for Fry's Cocoa, Lady of the House **Christmas issue, 1917.**

344

The Robert Opie
Collection at his
packaging museum in
Gloucester, England,
highlights brand
development over the
past 100 years. This
illustration shows some
of the countless historic
brand packagings at the
museum; nearly all the
brands featured
were marketed in
Ireland.
*Photograph: Robert Opie
Collection.*

THE BISTO KIDS

The Bisto Kids, first
devised by artist Will
Owen in 1919 and used
almost continuously
ever since.

Mick McQuaid tobacco showcard, 1920s. He was a footballer, whose name has been used on Carroll's tobacco pack designs and advertising since 1889.

An advertisement prepared by Arks for Fruitfield jams in the early 1930s.

346

347

SWEET AFTON

348

A Sweet Afton full colour poster, produced in the 1930s.

Packaging for Cadbury's confectionery, late 1960s.

A CIE Number 19 bus decorated in the colours of Spike, a soft drink from Cantrell & Cochrane, passing through O'Connell Street, Dublin, in 1979. Spike was discontinued three years ago and was replaced by a similar style product, Club 90. It was the first painted bus.

349

"it's here"

-the real thing!

FROM AMERICA   ... TO DUBLIN!

Y ou will thrill to Pepsi-Cola's pure,
delicious, thirst-quenching goodness when you
open up that big cool bottle! Tangy, sparkling
Pepsi-Cola gives you finest value for your money.
A quality drink! A better buy! Tops in flavour,
tops in taste, tops in size. Millions say "Why
take less when Pepsi's best!"

QUALITY

Pepsi-Cola
TRADE MARK

QUANTITY

Look for the signs!

Pepsi-Cola

BOTTLED BY
SLÁINTE MINERAL WATERS
(Cumhlacht Uisate Teo, 45-47 Montpelier Hill, Dublin, Ph
UNDER APPOINTMENT FROM
PEPSI-COLA COMPANY, NEW YORK

Pepsi advertisement on
its introduction to
Ireland in 1951.

Photo of shiny trucks driven by neat,
courteous salesmen will take Pepsi-Cola
to thirsty thousands.

In the spacious bottling store gleaming
rows of robot-like machinery take charge,
scrupulously cleaning each bottle and
filling with Pepsi-Cola on a modern
automatic process!

The Cola nut, one of Pepsi-Cola's
ingredients, grows on trees in Africa and
the West Indies. Natives call it "the
tree of Life! All the zest and energy of
natural cola are captured in the quality
beverage Pepsi-Cola.

St. Patrick's Day

TIME..... for Ireland's finest beer!

he quality beer that outsells all others

ime for a beer that is full of golden goodness, a beer that will lift you
that will satisfy your thirst pleasurably . . . it's time for TIME. TIME
has a rich, full flavour, a sparkling quality —products of 250 years of
ing experience. When you're among friends, TIME enhances your pleasure;
n you're alone, TIME is companionable; only a truly good beer like TIME
s you that glow of satisfaction that tells you you're enjoying yourself. Have
E—have a wonderful time.

EAT SLOGAN COMPETITION FOR TIME BEER

IZE : 7-days in NEW YORK
RIZE : 7-days in ITALY
RIZE : 7-days in PARIS
olidays including pocket money

AER LINGUS
INTERNATIONAL AIRLINES
IROCK JET · VISCOUNT

All you have to do is place 5 TIME slogans in order of
merit—and then write one slogan yourself. It's that easy !
And when you write your name on the entry form, you
also write the name of your favourite barman. If you
win a prize, your barman will get an equal prize ! Get
your entry form now at any bar.

izes totalling £3,000 to be won

shmen have   for a really good beer

Time beer
advertisement, Irish
Press, St. Patrick's Day,
1961.

Lyon's Tea uses the leprechaun theme in its "Pot of Gold" campaign, 1961.

Pot of Gold?

To find the leprechaun's pot of gold—you have to catch your leprechaun first! But to start on the trail of the Lyons pot of gold*—all you have to do is buy Lyons tea. And Lyons tea is not nearly so hard to find as a leprechaun! Your grocer has four different blends at four different prices—a packet for every pocket. So get in on the treasure hunt today—by buying Lyons Tea from now on. Choose the packet that suits you best— Green, Yellow, Mauve or Buff.

You get something EXTRA in Lyons Tea!

LYONS TEA

THE
GREATEST
NAME
IN TEA

PUT
A
TIGER
IN
YOUR
TANK

Esso "Tiger in Your Tank", 1963.

Players and Wills have gone to great lengths to bring you smooth, cool smoking.

Now Players and Wills have come together to bring you the best cigarette yet: Shannon Extra Long. Shannon offer a new dimension in smooth, cool smoking—the result of months of research. Among a great many cigarettes tested, Shannon were clearly a long way ahead. In fact, many smokers expressed surprise that a cigarette so long on quality could be so short on price! Try Shannon for yourself. They're extra long. And they bring you a new dimension in smooth, cool smoking.

Shannon
extra long

A marketing flop — Players' Shannon cigarettes, late 1960s.

MADE BY PLAYER & WILLS (IRELAND) LIMITED   4′3 FOR 20

dull wallpaper, depressing room

It needs the woman's touch and Valspar

A little thought. Some Valspar Emulsion.
Some Valspar Super Gloss. Bright new walls.
Bright new paintwork. A satisfying day's work.
That's the woman's touch with Valspar.
And, well, maybe just a touch of the man.

Valspar
Super Gloss and Emulsion ▪ -for a bright new look all around the house

Home decorating
advertisement by
Valspar, late 1960s.

Rinso advertisement, 1966.

Raelbrook shirt campaign from the 1960s, featuring Boeing 707 planes, then new to Aer Lingus. The airline's last 707 left its service in October, 1986.

Today, in Ireland's soft water, no other washing powder has the real-soap cleaning power of Rinso

Rinso's real-soap cleaning power gives you three great advantages no other washing powder can offer:

1 Real-soap whiteness. Rinso's rich soap lather gives clothes a pure natural whiteness. That's because its rich soap suds work harder and last longer in Ireland's soft water.

2 Real-soap kindness. Rinso's soapy lather is so much kinder to clothes than harsh detergents. Kinder to hands, too. You can even feel the creaminess in the lather. And, of course, the lather rinses easily away.

3 Real-soap value. Being a soap powder, real-soap Rinso gives you more hardworking suds for less powder. So it's more economical. Prove it for yourself: there's no better washing powder for Ireland's soft water.

Look for the bright new pack!

Real-soap Rinso is Ireland's only soap powder

The 707 man gets there on the Bri-Nylon ticket

...and everyone knows he's arrived.

raelbrook 707 BRI NYLON shirts

MADE UNDER LICENCE BY KIERAN & CORCORAN LTD., IN THEIR FACTORIES AT BLACKROCK, SKERRIES AND DONEGAL.

356

Why we killed the Anglia.

Ford Anglia advertisement, 1968; it appeared in the Irish Press.

ou may have noticed we haven't changed Anglia for eight years.

nd that, in all this time, nobody has been to touch it for value.

t recently one or two other cars have n to snap at our heels. So we've been king like beavers to see if we could give a bit more Anglia without whacking up price.

e put curved glass outside to make more lder-room inside.

nd we threw in our Aeroflow system to w out the fug every 40 seconds. (It also s your toes nice and warm).

hen we set to work under the bonnet. e snipped 7 seconds off the 0-60 rating sing our new bowl-in-piston engine. And a load off the big-ends with our five-ing crankshaft.

hen we slipped in a crisp all-syncromesh box. So you could crash into first and no more about it.

We even managed somehow to clip 3ft off the turning circle.

And, as we went along, we simplified one or two working parts.

So servicing is needed half as often.

By the time we'd finished (adjusting body-work to fit and so on) we found a different car on our hands.

And frankly, a better one.

But the price of all this had us worried for a moment. It came out at £49 more than the Anglia De Luxe.

Which isn't chickenfeed.

But it's stacks less than any other manu-facturer charges for a new model with all these features. (For instance, you can't buy a car with a bowl-in-piston engine for less than £100 more than our price).

So we felt you'd feel quite pleased with us.

Finally, after all these changes, we thought we ought to change the name.

To Escort. From today, you can try it at any Ford dealer.

Until you do, console yourself with this thought: if we hadn't made a similar killing in 1929 you'd still be driving round in the Model 'T'.

Ford Escort.

The Successor.

Midland Litho Printers Ltd., Oundle Road, Peterborough.

HENRY FORD & SON LTD., CORK. ESCORT: £653. ESCORT DE LUXE: £687. ESCORT SUPER: £748. ESCORT G.T.: £829. ALL PRICES INCLUDE ALL TAXES.

Colour '70.
The Brown Thomas plan.

We started planning your Spring and Summer wardrobe a year ago.

Studying forecasts by leading designers. Reading reports from colour councils all over the world. Sending our staff overseas to watch for trends. Sifting through thousands of colour swatches.

Finally, we decided which colours would lead the fashion market in 1970.

Then we told our buyers: whatever you buy— whatever style, size, cut, or type—buy it in these colours. Pale Lime. Cream. Peach. Bright Yellow. Bitter Brown. Lilac. Navy.

They're the colours you see in the picture. And they're the ones you'll see this year on anybody who knows what's happening in fashion.

You'll find them looking understated and elegant or jet-set cool in our fashion department. Or looking sort of wild in our new Miss B.T.

shop. And you'll find everything from belts and scarves to shoes and bags co-ordinated to complete the total look.

So you might have a bit of difficulty selecting a style. But you won't have trouble deciding on colour.

We've already done that for you.

Brown Thomas. Dublin, Cork, Tralee.

Brown Thomas advertisement, 1970.

How we've grown.

e De Havilland Dragon by the nose of the Boeing 747 was the entire Aer Lingus fleet when we commenced operations in 1936. :arried one pilot and five passengers. It would take three of them just to transport the crew of one of our new 747s.

The Guinness "Island" cinema and television commercial was directed in 1977 by John Devis. Creative director was Eamonn O'Flaherty and script was by Frank Sheerin. The commercial was filmed off the Aran Islands and at Ardmore Studios; through the 1970s, Guinness, Dublin, had used strong photographic images in its poster campaigns, while in 1982, the brewery started using testimonials from well-known personalities like Elkie Brooks, The Chieftains and Sean Kelly.

Aer Lingus advertisement, 1971, for introduction of Boeing 747s to its fleet.

Time was when the De Havilland Dragon was the newest and finest airliner in service with Aer Lingus. Today it's the Boeing 747. In 35 years nothing much has changed. The airline and the aircraft it flies have grown larger. But the truly important things about Aer Lingus haven't changed at all. Like our interest in the welfare and comfort of our passengers.

Aer Lingus people are helpful people. That's how we filled the Dragon in 1936. It's the secret of how we've grown.

There is an Aer Lingus brand of flying

(Get it from your local Travel Agent, at no extra charge.)

359

Kerrygold butter was launched on the Irish market in 1972. The brand had already been well established in the UK and other markets. The "Welcome Home Kerrygold" campaign was produced by Irish International at a cost of around £90,000. It included this poster used for instore promotional work.

Atmospheric photograph taken at the Five Lamps, Dublin, prior to the opening of Marks and Spencer in the city, late 1979.

360

One of the famous "Friday" series for Smirnoff vodka. The Smirnoff advertising began in 1971 with the copyline "Accountancy was my life until I discovered Smirnoff". The "Friday" campaign ended two years ago. Says Fergus McDermott of Gilbeys: "That was a campaign of the 1970s. The market is much more difficult now, so we are running tighter campaigns using the 'Looks Like Smirnoff' theme". Smirnoff claims a 57 per cent share of the Republic's vodka market.

Fridays and Smirnoff

leave me breathless! SMIRNOFF

The controversial
Huzzar vodka campaign
by McConnell's, early
1980s.

362

Butter is the Cream, from the world's greenest dairyland

National Dairy Council

Advertisement for
Marketing Opinion
magazine photographed
in Hollywood by the
Ron Smith Lookalike
Agency in Los Angeles,
in 1982.

National Dairy Council
advertisement for
butter, 1978.

363

Example from current Power's whiskey campaign, with copy by Catherine Donnelly, McConnell's.

The Educational Building Society account has been with Kenny's Advertising since 1935. The agency set out to achieve a campaign that other agencies could not copy. Kenny's claims to have done this with the "yes, yes, yes" campaign. Kenny's also claims that the EBS was the first financial institution to have treated its advertising like consumer product advertising.

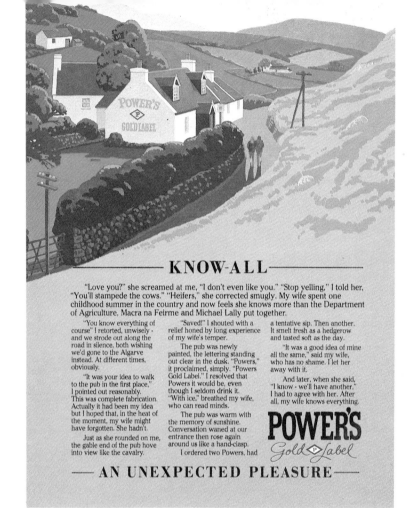

KNOW-ALL

"Love you?" she screamed at me, "I don't even like you." "Stop yelling," I told her, "You'll stampede the cows." "Heifers," she corrected smugly. My wife spent one childhood summer in the country and now feels she knows more than the Department of Agriculture, Macra na Feirme and Michael Lally put together.

"You know everything of course" I retorted, unwisely - and we strode out along the road in silence, both wishing we'd gone to the Algarve instead. At different times, obviously.

"It was your idea to walk to the pub in the first place," I pointed out reasonably. This was complete fabrication. Actually it had been my idea but I hoped that, in the heat of the moment, my wife might have forgotten. She hadn't.

Just as she rounded on me, the gable end of the pub hove into view like the cavalry.

"Saved!" I shouted with a relief honed by long experience of my wife's temper.

The pub was newly painted, the lettering standing out clear in the dusk. "Powers," it proclaimed, simply. "Powers Gold Label." I resolved that Powers it would be, even though I seldom drink it. "With ice," breathed my wife, who can read minds.

The pub was warm with the memory of sunshine. Conversation waned at our entrance then rose again around us like a hand-clasp.

I ordered two Powers, had

a tentative sip. Then another. It smelt fresh as a hedgerow and tasted soft as the day.

"It was a good idea of mine all the same," said my wife, who has no shame. I let her away with it.

And later, when she said, "I know - we'll have another," I had to agree with her. After all, my wife knows everything.

POWER'S
Gold Label

— AN UNEXPECTED PLEASURE —

Is our future sure?

with the **EBS** *YES!*

Educational Building Society Head Office, P.O. Box 76, Westmoreland St., Dublin 2. Tel. (01) 775191/775599. Branches throughout the country. A member of the Irish Building Societies Association. Authorised for Trustee investment.

Sunday Independent

Vol. 85. No. 25.　　SUNDAY, JUNE 23, 1985.　　Price 47p

Don't Miss It.

AN POST **National LOTTERY**

The new National Lottery logo prepared by Wilson Hartnell, which recently won the £1 million a year account. Frank Young, WH managing director says: "Since the campaign for the lottery, which begins operations in February, 1987, will be aimed at every adult in the country, all media will be used." The lottery, which replaces the Hospitals' Sweepstakes, starts with instant games and is likely to move into computerised games in a year's time.

Advertisement for Carroll's Irish Open golf, 1985. Ralph Steadman did the illustration.

365

A classic advertisement for Bailey's Irish Cream liqueur, used on the Irish market in the early 1980s. The campaign was prepared by Hunter Advertising.

This advertisement for Brown Thomas, the Dublin store, was the first full colour advertisement to be printed on the new five unit web offset press at The Irish Times, August 18, 1986. Layout and art direction was by Margaret Healion, art director, and copy was by Casey Evans, copywriter, Irish International Advertising. Fashion co-ordination was by John Redmond, Brown Thomas and photography was by Dave Campbell. Colour separations were by Colour Repro.

Vincent Whelan, chairman Outdoor Advertising Services.

Tom Goddard, who runs his own outdoor company, Metro poster advertising, which operates in Ireland and the UK.

Donal O Maolalaí, former manager of CIE Outdoor Advertising now manager, Public Affairs, CIE.

Dave Richards, joint managing director, Poster Management.

CHAPTER SEVEN

Newspapers and magazines

"Make a great effort this time to have advts up to the mark"
— PATRICK PEARSE TO HIS ADVERTISEMENT MANAGER, 1910

Editions of the Ennis Chronicle **in Co Clare in late 1791 carried advertisements for 1792 almanacks.**
Illustration: Clare Champion.

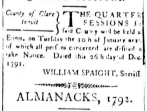

THE PRINTED PAGE has long been the most powerful publicity weapon in the publicist's armoury; for nearly three centuries, advertisements in newspapers, and for the past 80 years, in magazines as well, have been the main means of publicising products and services. Only within the last 20 years in Ireland have the electronic media, notably television, come to occupy the first rank. The idea of using newspapers for advertising purposes was slow to catch on, compared with the development of television as the top advertising medium within the space of 15 years. The first time newspapers anywhere in the world carried an advertisement was in Germany in the year 1591; the very first advertisement was for a book, details of which are now lost in the swamps of history. Just to show the time span of development in newspapers, the Hungarians claimed to have published the world's first news publication, in 1485. It took just over a hundred years for the idea to emerge of using newspapers as advertisement vehicles and a further one hundred years for that idea to catch on in Ireland.

Ireland's very first newspaper is generally acknowledged to have been the *Irish Monthly Mercury*, published by Cromwell's forces in Cork in 1649 and 1650. Being a military publication, it had no need for advertising. In the ensuing 30 or 40 years, there were spasmodic attempts at newspaper publishing in Ireland. Technical drawbacks hampered progress: type had to be handset and the speed of printing depended on the muscle power of the printer. A strong man could turn out 150 sheets an hour. In 1685, Robert Thornton managed to bring out Dublin's first regular newspaper, the *Dublin News-Letter,* which appeared every three or four days, for seven months. Its columns carried all editorial; there was no advertising. Three years later, the first advertisement to appear in an Irish newspaper was published; it offered for sale a copy of a sermon delivered before King James II and his Queen.

The *Flying Post* or the *Post Master* was launched in Dublin in 1699; it lasted for ten years and had the reputation of being the first Irish newspaper to carry regular advertisements, although since all copies have been lost, no record remains of its contents. In 1725, George Faulkner, printer to Dean Swift of St Patrick's Cathedral, started his *Dublin Journal.* The four page newspaper was published twice a week; two years after it started, it published the first illustration ever to accompany an advertisement in an Irish newspaper. A dentist advertised his services; the advertisement included a crude woodcut, which showed him pulling a patient's tooth — without any anaesthetic. Faulkner's was the first Irish newspaper to achieve popular success; he was also the first newspaper proprietor to blend editorial and advertising content in a consistent manner. By the late 1730s, the newspaper carried so many small ads for the sale and renting of lodgings in the city that it had a virtual monopoly on this

Lotteries have been run in Ireland for over 200 years; in 1792, the Ennis Chronicle carried this advertisement for Walker's Irish Lottery.
Illustration: Clare Champion.

The front page of the first issue of The Roscommon Herald, 1859, with (inset) Mrs Lillie Nerney, its present owner.

The Clare Journal,
And Ennis Advertiser.

THURSDAY, APRIL 25, 1811.

FITZGERALD'S SHIRTS.

44, PATRICK STREET, CORK.

Established over a Quarter of a Century.

These high-class and well-fitting Shirts give perfect comfort in Evening Dress. The front retains its proper position, the Collar fits to the band as if sewn to it. A measure and directions will be sent on application, and a pattern Shirt two days after receipt of order enclosing postal note for amount.

Branch House at

69, FENCHURCH STREET, LONDON, E.C.

Where every size is kept in Stock ready for wear, and a Cutter is at work who will take orders.

Prices—6/6, 7/6, 8/6. Leading price, 7/6.

FITZGERALD, Shirt Maker and Hosier.

Front Page of The Clare Journal and Ennis Advertiser, **April 25, 1811, showing a very early use of woodcuts to illustrate advertisements.**
Illustration: Clare Champion.

Parsons bookshop at Baggot Street Bridge Dublin, used to be a receiving depot for classified advertisements for The Irish Times. **The sign was still in place in 1986.**
Photograph: Hugh Oram.

type of advertising. Faulkner was dependent on clients bringing advertisement copy to his offices, off Castle Street. No canvassing was done in the style of today's newspaper advertising.

While Faulkner was getting his *Dublin Journal* under way, the provincial press was starting up. But while Cork had its first newspaper, the *Cork Idler,* in 1715 and Limerick had its initial news publication, the *Limerick Newsletter* set up the following year, the emphasis was on editorial content: any advertisements that came in were a bonus. The first commercially oriented newspaper was *Saunder's Newsletter,* founded in Dublin in 1755. Its owner, Henry Saunders, ensured that within a short while, three out of four of its pages per issue carried advertising. It provided a very comfortable living for Saunders, who lived and had his printing works at Christchurch Place.

In 1769, the *Freeman's Journal* newspaper started carrying advertisements from Thwaites, apothecaries, of Marlborough Street. Not long before, Augustine Thwaites junior, a medical student at Trinity College, had invented soda water. The family firm immediately launched Thwaites' soda water on the market.

An insight into newspaper production of the latter part of the 18th century can be gleaned from the *Limerick Chronicle,* started in 1766 and today, the oldest newspaper in the Republic. Its founder was a poet and historian called John Ferrar, who had a small shop in the centre of Limerick. Customers brought advertisement copy to this shop. Ferrar wrote most of the paper himself, sometimes lifting weeks old material

THE EAGLE
IS THE
LARGEST PENNY PAPER IN THE WORLD.

Offices : { CORK.
BANDON.
SKIBBEREEN. } Offices.

IMPORTANT TO ADVERTISERS.

ATTENTION is requested to the **EAGLE** as an Advertising Medium. It is the only COUNTY PAPER published in the County of Cork, which has a population of over Half a Million. The **EAGLE** circulates generally throughout the Province of Munster, but particularly in the County and City of Cork. The circulation in the West Riding alone of this great "Shire" is guaranteed to be CONSIDERABLY LARGER than ALL the other Papers sold in West Cork combined. This statement is not made as a mere boast, but as a matter of fact that cannot be contradicted. The **EAGLE** is largely supported by the nobility, gentry, and great wealthy middle class. Being thoroughly Independent, and consequently not confined to the limits of any particular party, it decidedly enjoys a LARGE AND INCREASING CIRCULATION AMONG ALL CLASSES. The **EAGLE** is the recognised organ for the County Advertisements, Official Notices, and is used by all Public Institutions, Solicitors, Merchants, Auctioneers, Traders, &c., as a sure means of giving publicity to their announcements.

HEAR WHAT IS SAID OF IT :—

The *Daily Argus*, Rock Island, Illinois, U.S., says :—

"The *Eagle* lies before us, and we have no hesitation in saying that it is not only a credit to its spirited and enterprising publisher, but a sheet that the South of Ireland may boast of. As a typographical production it is simply a marvel, and one wonders how such an amount of solid matter can be so neatly put together and elegantly printed. Surely the 'Art preservative of Arts' has found a congenial home in the *Eagle* Office. The *Eagle* is, we believe, as its Editor claims, the largest page paper in the world, while the news and articles it contains are well written and selected with a care that makes this mammoth broad sheet acceptable to every class of reader. We Yankees boast a good deal of our 'wondrous works,' but this achievement of the *Eagle* puts us completely in the shade as far as the production of large sheet journals. We wish the promoters, whoever they may be, that success they deserve, for producing such a magnificent paper. It is published at the extraordinary low price of two cents."

The *Bulletin*, a prominent daily Paper, published in Freeport, Illinois, says :—

"The *Eagle* is one of the most enterprising journals the Irish provincial Press can boast of. It is well conducted, and always full of able Articles, fresh News, and excellent Reports. It is what Americans term—'a living sheet.'"

The *Dublin Evening Mail* says :—

"The *Eagle* quite surprises us. It now appears in an enlarged, improved form, its pages being of enormous size, and crowded with good news. We wish it success. Its 'eye' will, no doubt, be upon people as steadfastly as in former times, and with even greater effect. The pages, in the matter of size, are quite curiosities in journalism."

United Ireland says :—

"The *Eagle* is one of the ablest Provincial Weeklies in the South of Ireland."

The *Hackney Gazette*, a leading London Paper, says :—

"The *Eagle* has assumed an enlarged form, and is undoubtedly the largest broad-sheet newspaper we have ever seen. With eleven long columns of small type per page, the reader is presented with an immense amount of reading matter, all carefully selected and compiled. The enlarged *clientele* of the *Eagle* will enable it to soar still higher in the literary sphere, and bring all the success that is the proper and deserved reward of a spirited management. We wish our large Irish contemporary every prosperity."

The *Irish Builder* says :—

"The *Eagle* can challenge any print, either metropolitan or provincial, as to its 'get-up' in paper, type, or the purity and independence of its articles."

HEAR WHAT IS SAID OF IT :—

The REV. WM. IRWIN, of the Termoneeny Rectory, Knockloughrim, Belfast, writes :—

"Please let me have a copy of the *Eagle* weekly in future. Whatever other paper I omit subscribing for, I feel I cannot deprive myself of the pleasure of the usual visit, to which I have been so long accustomed, of 'The Great Bird of the South,' who so watchfully 'keeps her eye' on all matters interesting to the public and impartially and independently reports and advises for the best interests of the common weal, without any respect to consequences or private interests, and sometimes, even, at the expense of losing a feather out of her own wing, by exposing the partisan practices of political poachers."

CAPT. P. J. MELLING, J.P., of North Alton, Madison Co., Illinois, writing to one of our Editors, says :—

"I, of course, admire the style and get-up of our American journals ; but I think you produce some wonderful papers in Ireland —the *Eagle*, for instance. Why it is a monster from Munster ! I venture the assertion that it has more square acres of printed matter than any American paper you have ever seen."

The *Madison Co. Sentinel* says :—

"Captain P. J. Melling, of North Alton, favours us with a copy of the *Eagle*. As a newspaper sheet it is somewhat of a curiosity, being an eleven-column folio, measuring 28 inches across the page, and with columns 40 inches in length. The journal is evidently one of the best in Great Britain, and contains an abundance of varied and interesting matter. It is well edited, discusses current events in the Green Isle in a fair, broad, and independent spirit, and is taken all in all, a journal which reflects credit upon the place from whence it hails. Long may its scream be heard."

A literary gentleman of high standing says :—

"Perhaps it is only right that I should say that I always look forward with pleasure to seeing your paper. Not only do I find a large amount of news, local and otherwise, which I would not elsewhere meet with, but articles well calculated to teach valuable lessons, and stories which hold up what is good and noble for imitation, and what is base and bad for just abhorrence."

The *Hull and Lincolnshire Times*, an old and influential paper, published in Hull, says :—

"The *Eagle*, a four-page newspaper, published in the South of Ireland, may well claim to be 'the largest penny paper in the world.' It is a curiosity in journalism, and a marvellous typographical production. Some idea of the enormous size of the 'sheet' may be gathered from the fact that each page contains eleven columns of closely-printed matter, the columns being over a yard in length. The paper possesses some excellent literary features, and is undoubtedly *the* 'family newspaper' of the large district in which it circulates."

The "EAGLE" is the only COUNTY PAPER published in the County of Cork.

Opposite page:
An advertisement for Fitzgerald's of Cork in Punch magazine in 1889.

An 1897 trade advertisement published in London for the Eagle, Skibbereen. The famous newspaper claimed to be the largest selling penny paper in the world!

from London newspapers; he then set the type by hand, locked up the frames and printed off a couple of hundred copies. Shortage of time prevented him doing any canvassing for advertisements. That side of the newspaper business grew up almost by default, with newspaper managers waiting for advertisement copy to come to them, rather than going out after it, in present day fashion. Yet some major steps towards the development of newspaper advertising were taken in the North of Ireland: the *Derry Journal* was set up in 1772. Its owner, a Scots printer called George Douglas, printed and published the newspaper at his stationery office in the Diamond. He advertised in the very first issue for an apprentice for his firm, someone who "must be a Protestant and well recommended." Unusually for the times, advertisement rates were published, 2d a line, with 1d a line for "every

371

continuance". The classified advertisements gave a good insight into the life of Derry over 200 years ago: James Galbraith, a self-professed mathematician, advertised tuition to young gentlemen, while a Dublin dancing master called Morris announced his Dancing School in the Town-Hall of London-Derry. By this time, the *Belfast News Letter*, founded in 1737 and Ireland's oldest newspaper, was carrying a useful quota of classified advertising. Advertisements in the 18th century Irish newspapers have a strange stylistic fascination: a formality and certainty in the copy allowed for no self-doubts. Sugar cakes were not only most excellent, but worm destroying as well, and that was that. They were 1s 1d each. Similar certainty was shown by one of the very few women handling newspaper advertising in those days: Catherine Finn took over the running of *Finn's Leinster Journal* in Kilkenny in 1777, after the death of her husband. Not only did she run the editorial and production sides of the newspaper, but she packed in the advertisements as well.

After the Act of Union in 1800, Irish newspapers became altogether more circumspect. A tax on advertisements dampened down expansion in that direction, but those newspapers that supported the official Government line found themselves in receipt of handsome subsidies by way of Government advertising and proclamations. In 1810, advertisement duty on newspapers was increased, but still the spirit of innovation existed in some newspaper offices.

In the early 1800s, a man called Thomas Bish ran an extensive

Late 19th century advertisement for The Irish Times **and** Weekly Irish Times.

THE
IRISH TIMES,
The leading Journal in Ireland,
And Best Advertising Medium.

CHIEF OFFICES:
3 & 4 LOWER ABBEY ST.,
DUBLIN,
And 153 Fleet Street, LONDON.

THE
WEEKLY IRISH TIMES.
Price **ONE PENNY**.

Is the most popular and best-circulated Weekly Journal in Ireland.

CHIEF OFFICES:
3 & 4 LOWER ABBEY STREET,
DUBLIN,
AND 153 FLEET STREET, LONDON.
1—a-d

Advertisement by the Cork Examiner, about 1900.

THE SOUTH OF IRELAND PUBLICATIONS:

THE CORK EXAMINER
Established 1841   ::   Daily 2d.

THE CORK WEEKLY EXAMINER
AND
WEEKLY HERALD
Every Thursday 2d.

THE CORK EVENING ECHO
Daily 1d.

Head Offices:
95, PATRICK STREET, CORK.

Branch Offices:
DUBLIN	-	-	1 & 2, EDEN QUAY.
LIMERICK	-	-	61, CATHERINE STREET.
LONDON	-	-	180, FLEET STREET, E.C., 4.

sweepstake and lottery broking business in both Ireland and England. He was far ahead of his time: he employed writers and poets to devise his press advertisements. He also had public relations men slipping in advertisements as news a century before public relations became well accepted.

The *Clare Journal* in the early 19th century became the first newspaper in that county to start illustrating advertisements with woodcuts. By 1820, printing technology was changing. The basic design of the newspaper press, little changed since the 17th century, became mechanised. Soon, many Irish papers started to install Columbian presses, which could often turn out 60 or more copies an hour. The press was becoming a mass medium. The *Londonderry Sentinel* soon after its launch in 1829, put in a steam press that could turn out 1,000 copies an hour. Public transport was coming into use for the first time, with Bianconi's mail coaches and the canal system. Both helped to extend the distribution area of newspapers, hence the appeal of them to advertisers was increased.

In 1823, the first of the major Dublin press launches of the 19th century took place: the *Dublin Evening Mail*. Editorial considerations had priority over advertising,although in the 20th century, it became famous for its columns of classifieds. 1823, the year that saw the launch of the *Dublin Evening Mail,* also saw the establishment of two Dublin business houses that were destined to become major advertisers in the press: Alex Findlater's grocery store and Pigott's house of music. In 1830, a forerunner of modern baby foods was launched on the British market, which included Ireland then. Neave's Food was advertised in Irish newspapers as being "admirably adapted to the wants of infants". The brand continued to thrive well into the 20th century.

The growth of advertising in newspapers was, however, a leisurely business: the firm of Johnson's, predecessors of Easons, was set up in 1819. It placed personal advertisements in newspapers on behalf of individual customers; the firm was the first "placing" agency in Ireland. It did not place much advertising for business houses; after all, the concept of the large display advertisement had yet to be developed. All newspapers carried small advertisements on their front pages; when the *Cork Examiner* was published for the first time in August, 1841, it had three columns of advertisements and, unusually, two of editorial copy on the front page. Equally unusually for the time, four of the advertisements were headed by illustrations. The celebrated "Malabar" coffee, sold from 82 Patrick Street, Cork, was advertised in that first issue with the help of a line drawing of a tin of the coffee.

The North of Ireland largely escaped the effects of the famine that devastated much of the south and west of the country in the late 1840s. The North was benefitting, too, from the industrial revolution that brought huge numbers of people into Belfast to man the new factories. When advertisement tax on newspapers — a 1/6d levy on

Ireland's Own **was founded in Wexford in 1902. In 1905, it ran this advertisement in the** Advertiser's ABC, **London.**

"Ireland's Own"

(the Premier Penny Weekly) reaches each of the thirty-two Counties of Ireland in

NUMBERS
UNAPPROACHED

by any other publication of its class.

NO IRISH ADVERTISING PROPOSITION COMPLETE WITHOUT IT.

24 Large Pages and Coloured Cover.
Columns 12½ in. long by 2½ in. wide, 4 columns each page.

Rates and particulars on application to the Advertisement Manager, "IRELAND'S OWN," 2, Creed Lane, London, E.C .

Scale of Advertising Rates in The "Guardian."

Small Advertisements not exceeding twenty words, one insertion, 1s ; three insertions, 2s 6d, prepaid.

Births, Marriages, and Deaths, 2s 6d each.

Legal Advertisements, 6d per line.

Parliamentary and Election Addresses, 1s per line.

Auction Advertisements, 3d per line, with commission off.

All larger advertisements for a are especially quoted for

In future all small advertisements inserted in the "Nenagh Guardian" must be pre-paid (unless advertisers are regular customers). Our rates are :— Notices not exceeding four lines 1/6 per insertion. Every additional line 4d per line (first insertion). Repeats half price per insertion.

Advertisement rates in the Nenagh Guardian, 1916.

Front page of the first issue of the new look Irish Independent, Monday, January 2, 1905. The front page, in keeping with newspaper custom then, was all advertisements.

Opposite page: Letterheading of the Irish Tatler & Sketch magazine when published by Wilson Hartnell & Co.

each advertisement — was finally lifted in 1853, followed two years later by the abolition of stamp duty, the way was clear for an enormous upsurge of new newspaper titles. In Belfast in 1855, the *Belfast News Letter* changed from tri-weekly to daily publication, while the Read brothers launched the *Belfast Morning News,* forerunner of the present day *Irish News.* With the lifting of the impositions on the newspaper industry, new titles blossomed; in 1855, Ireland had 100 newspapers. By 1859, that total was 130.

In the 1850s, there were also several newspapers in Dublin, Cork, Belfast and Limerick, all weeklies, which carried only advertisements. At that time, newspaper advertisements had little illustration, apart from the occasional small block showing a ship, coach or some such ornament. There was little attempt at spacing type. The *Dublin Advertising Gazette,* which distributed nearly 30,000 copies a week, had a higher standard of advertising than competing newspapers and even ran a page devoted to advertising profusely illustrated with line blocks. The other major advertising-only newspaper in Dublin was the *General Advertiser,* which handed out 25,000 copies weekly. In that latter year, the 23 year old Major Laurence E. Knox revived *The Irish Times;* it sold for one penny. A pioneer in newspaper advertising then was the department store of Todd Burns. With the rise of the middle classes in the mid-19th century, department stores had sprung up as purveyors of their material needs; Cannock and White, later to be renamed Arnotts after its purchase by Sir John Arnott, opened in Henry Street in 1843. Todd Burns was one of the first advertisers to make use of the new style of newspaper advertising that came in at the time that Knox launched *The Irish Times:* more white spaces, more illustrations, even though these had to be in the form of line drawings. Todd Burns was heavily into newspaper advertising; in one 1859 issue of the *Dublin Local Advertiser,* it gave away a map of the northern Italian war zone.

14 weeks after its launch, *The Irish Times* went daily. Eleven years on, in 1870, the Baird brothers' *Belfast Telegraph* was equally successful, having been put together at breakneck speed to thwart the proposed *Evening Press* competition. Between a Monday morning and a Thursday afternoon one week in September, 1870, all departments of the *Belfast Telegraph* were put together from scratch, including the advertisement

T. J. (Tommy) O'Sullivan (1912-1965), who was advertisement representative and then advertisement manager of the Irish Press; he joined the newspaper in the mid-1930s. Later, he worked for Wilson Young, now known as Young Advertising. He was the father of Niall O'Sullivan of O'Connor O'Sullivan.

EGRAMS : HARTNELL, DUBLIN.

TELEPHONE : DUBLIN 22551.

The Irish Tatler & Sketch

IRELAND'S PREMIER SOCIAL & SPORTING PICTORIAL

Founded in 1890

Published by

WILSON HARTNELL & CO. LTD.

SOLE ADVERTISING CONTRACTORS TO THE GOVERNMENT OF ÉIRE.

ertisement Manager :

J. DOWLING.

CONTRACTORS TO THE ROYAL IRISH AUTOMOBILE CLUB. ETC.

Editorial and Advertising Offices :

Commercial Buildings,

Dublin, C.1.

"Pussy" O'Mahony of The Irish Times, pictured (second from the right) at the official opening of the Brockhouse factory in Wexford, August, 1935. O'Mahony joined the newspaper in 1928 and eventually became its manager. A son is Dave Allen, the comedian, who is said to have taken his stage name from David Allen, the poster contractors. "Pussy" O'Mahony occupied half a house at Templeogue, Dublin; the occupant of the other half was Joe Delaney of Domas Advertising.

department. In Dublin, meanwhile, *The Irish Times* maintained its quickly won position of superiority in the newspaper field, especially after it was bought by Sir John Arnott in 1873. The paper was described as "the leading advertising medium in Ireland". In 1875, its companion paper, the *Weekly Irish Times*, described as the "best and largest penny paper in Ireland" was launched.

The Irish Times had a well-organised system for collecting copy for small advertisements, through its depot in Rathmines and a second depot in Parsons of Baggot Street Bridge. In the latter location, the newspaper's advertising sign can still be seen above the doorway. If advertisers had their copy into the depots by four in the afternoon, they were guaranteed publication in the next morning's paper. Copy

In 1938, the Irish Association of Advertising Agencies made a special presentation to Tom Grehan, advertisement manager, Independent Newspapers. Jack Tate of Arks (fourth from right) made the presentation of the silver salver. Looking on were Harry O'Brien, founder of Arrow Advertising (extreme left). Brian D. O'Kennedy is second left, while Charlie McConnell is third left.

was put aboard a city bound tram: there was little problem about missing a tram, since they ran every 3½ minutes. Ironically, all the trams carried emblems which denoted their routes, since many passengers could not read. In the *Dublin Evening Mail* in the late 19th century, advertisements took up seven out of the 24 columns in each issue. Advertisements were still hand-set, with no attempt at improving layout and appearance.

Around 1880, many new provincial newspaper publications were launched, such as the *Westmeath Examiner* (1882) and the *Western People* (1883). In few cases was provision made for systematic advertisement canvassing. If anyone had responsibility for overseeing advertisement sales, it was the proprietor and editor, John P. Hayden in the case of the *Westmeath Examiner.* The *Midland Tribune,* for example, was printing eight page issues from 1896 onwards; its advertising rate was 3d a line. Out of those eight pages, just over two were devoted to news. The rest was advertisements, yet of the staff of seven, including journalists and printers, only one, W. J. Bateman, the manager, was involved on the advertisement side of the newspaper. An important source of advertising revenue for the *Midland Tribune,* as for all other provincial newspapers at the time, were the County Grand Juries, replaced by county councils in 1899. A major technical advance helped the development of newspaper advertising: the invention of the Linotype machine, which enabled type to be set mechanically at far higher speeds than the previously used hand-setting system. Although the Linotype system was first used at the *New York Tribune* in 1886, it was not until over ten years later that it started to infiltrate Irish newspapers. The *Longford Leader,* started by J. P. Farrell in 1897, the same year as the *Meath Chronicle,* boasted that it was one of the very first newspapers in Ireland to use a Linotype, the year of its foundation.

Connaught Telegraph, **February 7, 1942. A Government advertisement urged farmers to sow more wheat, since the price had been increased to 50/- a barrel.**

The offices of the Sun newspaper published in Cork from 1903 to 1905.

The front page of the last issue of the *Freeman's Journal*, Friday, December 19, 1924; it was packed solid with advertisements, as were four inside pages.

PROGRESS OF IRELAND'S GREATEST NEWSPAPER

AND NEW JOURNALISM

RIKING CHANGE

INDEPENDENTS" ACHIEVEMENT

ose who were newspaper at the time can appreciate ificance and completeness revolution made in Irish m when, through the and enterprise of the W. M. Murphy, the *dependent* was founded as nny newspaper in 1905

vent of the *Irish Independent* a complete departure in tail from the old, slovenly style of journalism. Un- other journals of the day it or the general reader by pre- n a fair, dispassionate and form news in which all d parties were interested.

STYLE.

who remember how news was and published in pre-*Irish* nt days, or who may care to the newspaper files of the ill readily acknowledge how and valuable to the public change then made by the d staffs of this journal.

y Irish newspapers tended everything in their news well as in their editorial from the narrow party and standpoint.

hus biassed by such pre- d obvious colouring and naturally left the public dary. What were they to What could they believe?

aper which, whatever its own uld present news relating to nd other transactions fairly, and without prejudice was public wanted, and this want is still, supplied by the *Irish nt*.

NEW STYLE.

rom the unreliable and ab- on in which political events t with in the columns of nals prior to 1905, those re in all other respects dull iting to readers.

recording events with fair- mpartiality and in accordance r value as news, the *Irish nt* can claim that it is to-day the brightest, and the most newspaper produced or circu- reland.

STAT DAIRYING INDUSTRY

AT PROGRESS IN 1929

ess was made in the dairying y in the Saorstat during the ust closed, writes an *Irish dent* representative.

reorganisation proceeded apace ondensing industry has been eloped. The re-equipment of at Limerick, the largest of he world, is now complete, and commodation considerably in-

e improvements has been asso- ppreciable development in the e of the higher-priced milk d the outlook for the coming o promising than at any time he history of the industry.

POSITION.

e past season the creamery Kerry was tackled so thoroughly ly all the private creameries a were acquired by the Go- nd the first stage of the re- , involving the closing of ndant creameries, and the others to co-operative societies, he way to completion.

Cork reorganisation work has ced that its end might be said sight.

172 private creameries have ht, and not more than 40 re- taken over.

the industry was definitely

PRICES.

he increased supplies of milk le from the existing cream- quent on the reorganisation, **been a substantial improve- milk prices in relation to the** inable for butter.

o new scheme has been in general feeling of security is ce the creameries have now a velop in the absence of unfair and if the world prices of ove business is certain to the dairying side of the agri- ustry.

KNOW?—ANSWERS

as so called by the inven- es Hargreaves, after his

und Malone, who was born n, 1741. He exposed the oems of Chatterton and forgeries.

ssor Albrecht Penck com- o present human popula- e earth at 1,800,000,000.

stions are on Page Four.)

on for Honey.

annual report to the Co. **keepers'** Association at Ennis- E. Davis, hon. sec., stated hey gathered in July was a t was the best season since caused a great glut on the the price was 50 p.c. less r. Mr. S. Doyle suggested ociation should send a com- to get the Irish Wholesale ade the honey and to vary ording to quality. Irish bee- they could not get good gland as long as the prices at present.

WRITING ASSISTANTS.

Day Class for the next Exam. tion. 9 Successes, April, 1929. LLEGE, 76 Stephen's Green. (Advt.)

MAIN PAGE OF OUR FIRST ISSUE REPRODUCED

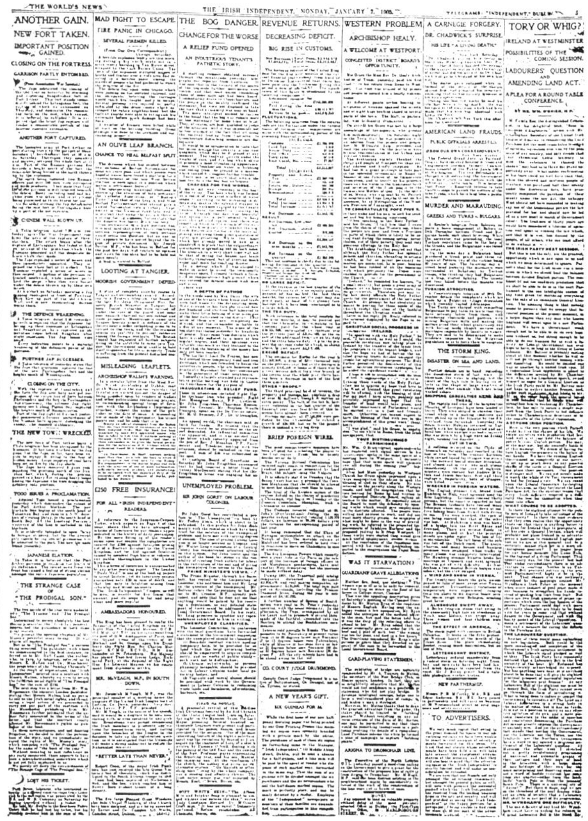

The above is a reduced facsimile of the Main Page of the first issue of the *Irish Independent* on 2nd January, 1905. A cursory glance will show the great progress in the arrangement, treatment and display of news which has taken place in our columns in the last quarter of a century.

ANOTHER SHOP MURDER

BRADFORD WOMAN'S END

The body of Mrs. Edith Warne, aged between 40 and 45, with her head terribly battered, was found under a rug in her little greengrocer's shop in Wakefield Rd., Bradford, on Tuesday night.

Mrs. Marks, a neighbour, states that the deceased had told her that she was married in her 23rd year, but she left her husband, who was 30 years her senior, at Darlington, after a disagreement. After he died she went to Leeds, where she again married and went to live in Sheffield, where she and her husband had a small business. They sold out the business and later went to Shipley, and thence to Bradford.

WOMAN'S HUSBAND.

The woman's husband, Mrs. Marks understood, left about six weeks ago. On Monday her (Mrs. Marks's) little daughter saw a man trying the door and looking through a back window. When Mrs. Warne was told she said it did not matter as the back door was locked. Mrs. Marks stated that Mrs. Warne was a powerfully built woman and would not be easily overcome. It is believed that she was struck down from behind.

The weapon with which the crime was committed and the keys of both back and front doors are missing. Both doors were locked and the front door was barred. A purse which the woman had is also believed to be missing.

AN EVENTFUL YEAR

PRESIDENT'S MESSAGE TO CORK

President Cosgrave in a New Year's message to the people of Cork, conveying his good wishes for 1930, says:—

"The year which has passed has been marked by events of outstanding significance in our national and international life. Ministers of the Irish Free State were appointed to the Holy See, Germany and France, and have taken up their duties.

"Towards the close of the year we received notification of the appointment of his Excellency, Archbishop Robinson, as Papal Nuncio. By selecting an Irishman for this exalted position his Holiness the Pope has given a sign of remarkable interest in, and affection for, his people here.

"For the people of Cork the outstanding event of the past twelve months has been the extension of the great Ford factory, which is of such benefit to the city. I trust that during 1930 it, and the other progressive industries of Cork, will continue to extend and prosper."

Over Four Miles of Advertisements in 1929

The steadily increasing Circulation of the Irish Independent has resulted in a correspondingly increasing demand for Advertising space.

Below we publish the total Advertising space taken for each of the past four years. The figures represent single column inches.

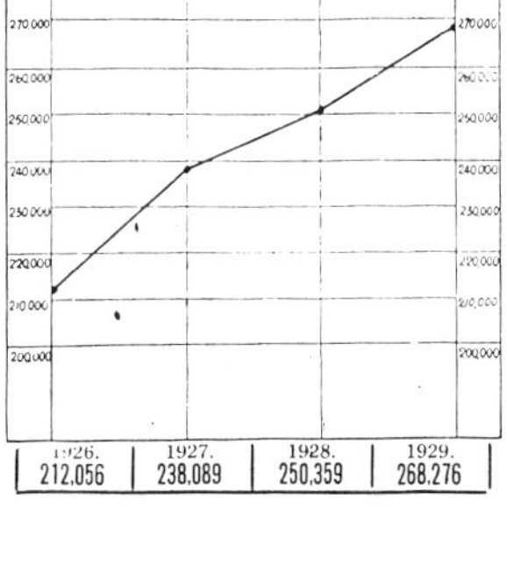

KILL HARRIERS' DANCE

GALA FUNCTION AT TRIM

The Kill Harriers' annual dance, held in the Town Hall, Trim, was a very successful function, and many members of both the Meath and Ward Union Hunts attended, as well as practically all the followers of the Kills.

The pack is very popular in South Meath, and under the mastership of the Duc de Stacpoole the Harriers have had an excellent season.

Some 170 couples attended at the dance. The hall was tastefully decorated, and the green colours of the Harriers predominated. Mr. Malone and Mr. Eivers, hon. secs., were mainly responsible for the success of the night.

THE ATTENDANCE

Amongst those present were:—The Duc de Stacpoole, M.F.H., and the Duchesse de Stacpoole and party; Mr. P. D. Cullinan and Mrs. Cullinan and party; Capt. Collins and Mrs. Collins, Messrs. Cosgrave and Miss Cosgrave, Ballinakill; Dr. O'C. O'Reilly, Trim; Mr. Malone, solr.; Mr. Moorhead, solr.; Mr. D. Reilly, V.S.; Mr. Jiles and party; Mr. H. J. Kirwan, Tullyard House; Mr. V. Eivers, Rorlstown; Mr. and Mrs. Smith, do., and party, Messrs. Gasteen, C. Wylie, J. Ward, I.E.O.

Miss M. Maher and party, Dunboyne; Mr. Rogers, Ratoath; Mr. J. Malone, P.C., Newboggart; Mr. Newman, Athboy; Mr. Higgins, P.C., do.; Mr. and Mrs. J. McGuinness and party, Dangan; Mr. Eadie, Bank of Ireland; Mr. Ryan and party, Hibernian Bank; Mrs. Lee's and party; Miss Gearty and party; Mr. P. Maher and party; Miss Hope and party; Mr. W. Sweeney, P.C.; Miss Miggins, Mr. Constantine, Mr. Mercer, Miss Canty, Mr. P. O'Hara, Miss Duignan, the Misses Anderson.

U.S. PRISON REVOLT

PRIEST WHO PLEADED WITH MEN

Another priest has become a hero in a U.S. prison riot. He is Father Donald McCleary, one of the chaplains at Auburn Prison here, where 25 long-term prisoners started a riot in an effort to gain their freedom, says the New York correspondent of the "Catholic Herald."

The rioting started with hand-to-hand combat between prisoners and guards and ended only when National guardsmen had tear-bombed the jail and surrounded the walls. Eight died in the riot.

Father Cleary was one of those who pleaded with the men to abandon their hopeless attempt to gain freedom and give up the fight. The story of his heroism is told by the Warden in the following words:

"Later they became more threatening, and soon Father Cleary came up bravely under their guns and started to plead with them. He asked them in all decency to drop the effort to escape, which was doomed to failure."

One of the mutineers, however, replied that the riot had gone too far for the men to recede.

THE RESULT OF ENTERPRISE.

This chart shows the Average Daily Nett Sale of the

Irish Independent

for each of the past four years.

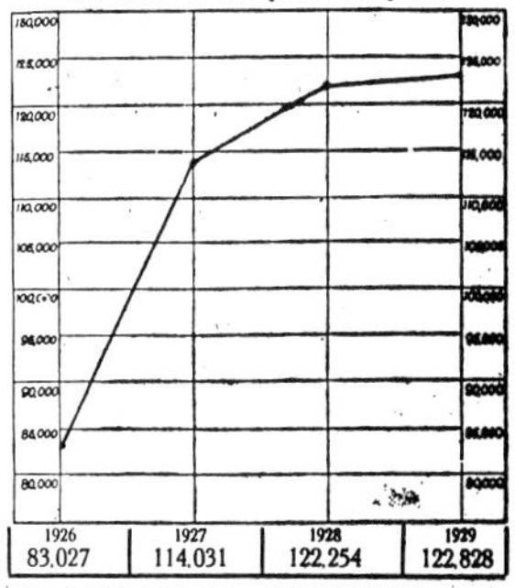

March 14th, 1927, Price of Irish Independent Reduced to 1d.

A FAMILIAR LIST

ADVERTISERS IN OUR FIRST ISSUE

On looking through the first issue of the *Irish Independent*, dated 2nd January, 1905, one is at once struck with the familiar aspect of the advertisement pages. It is like looking at a family photograph taken twenty-five years ago.

Just as the individuals in the photograph would have changed and grown, so have the various firms' announcements.

To-day Advertising has become a very exact science. A new generation has sprung up, ready and eager to use its driving force, and the demand for space in the *Irish Independent* has become greater than ever.

An Interesting List

Below we give a list of firms whose announcements appeared in our first issue, and are still appearing in our columns:—

Booth Bros., Upper Stephen Street.
Brooks, Thomas & Co., Ltd., Sackville Place.
C. Bull & Co., Suffolk Street.
Cantwell & McDonald, Wellington Quay.
Clery & Co., Ltd., Lower O'Connell Street.
Dolphin Hotel and Restaurant, Essex Street.
D.W.D. Whiskey.
Eason & Sons, Ltd., Lower O'Connell Street.
J. W. Elvery & Co., Ltd., Lower O'Connell Street.
M. H. Gill & Sons, Ltd., Upper O'Connell Street.
Great Northern Railway Co.
Great Southern Railway Co.
The Henry Street Warehouse (now Roche's Stores).
W. Holmes, South Great George's Street.
Kane's Hairdressing Saloon, Dame Street.
D. Kellett, South Great George's Street.
Kinahan's L.L. Whiskey (now Baggots, Hutton and Kinahan).
Ed. Lee & Co., Ltd., Mary Street.
McBirney & Co., Ltd., Aston's Quay.
O'Dea & Co., Ltd., Stafford Street.
O'Reilly & Co., Ltd., North Earl Street.
Paul & Vincent, Ltd., Blackhall Place.
Reamsbottom & Co., Geashill.
Rowan & Co., Capel Street.
Robert & Co., Grafton Street.
Skerry's College, Stephen's Green.
Switzer & Co., Ltd., Grafton Street.
Todd, Burns & Co., Ltd., Mary Street.
D. Towell, Upper O'Connell Street.
Wallace Bros., D'Olier Street.
J. H. Webb & Co., Ltd., Cornmarket.

Theatres and Auctions

Our Theatre announcements included the **Abbey Theatre, The Pavilion**, Dun Laoghaire (then Kingstown), **The Queen's**, and the **Empire** (now the Olympia); while in our Auction Columns we had **D. Condren, Arklow; E. A. Coonan**, Rathcoffey; **Gavin Low**, Prussia Street; **A. J. Keogh, Lower** Ormond Quay; and **Messrs. R. and J. Wilkinson**, Prussia Street.

Girl Motorist Killed After Dance.

Miss Lilian McClory (22), The Gables, Hathersage, near Sheffield, was killed when, while motoring home with a party from a dance at Grindleford, the collapsible hood of the car was caught by an overhanging bough of a tree and struck her on the head.

Regulation of British Coal Output.

The Lancashire and Cheshire coal-owners have decided to continue their association for the regulation of output, which has been operating, in conjunction with the Five Counties scheme, for 21 months and which, from Jan. 1, will be a separate organisation, and will be in a position to compete with other districts.

In January, 1930, the Irish Independent reported record progress on the circulation and advertising fronts, as this full page shows.

Rita Gubbins, who was appointed advertisement manager of Dublin Opinion **in 1944.**

The best portrait of a newspaper advertisement canvasser of the time was painted by James Joyce in *Ulysses;* its central character, the seedy and shifty Leopold Bloom, was required to scout out and obtain advertisements for the *Freeman's Journal* on long-term contracts. He was paid a small retainer, but much of what he earned came from commission. Peter Costello, in his book *Leopold Bloom: a biography,* faithfully recreates the shabby world of Bloom. There was a great variety of printed matter in turn of the century Dublin: the *Freeman's Journal, The Irish Times, Daily Express, Evening Herald, Evening Telegraph* and the *Dublin Evening Mail,* as well as sporting publications (like *Sport,* published by the *Freeman's Journal)* and glossy social publications, such as *Lady of the House,* brought out by the house of Wilson Hartnell. In this magazine, Findlater's the grocery firm, took eight or 12 pages an issue for its products and services. It then undertook to distribute 3,000 copies an issue to its customers, at one penny a copy. Other magazine titles of the era included *Hibernia, Irish Figaro* and *Illustrograph,* all full of advertisements.

Into the varied, but incestuous world of Dublin publishing, Joyce set the character of Leopold Bloom. He sought advertisements from establishments like the Royal Marine Hotel in Kingstown, whose copy read as follows:

"The magnificent hotel, unrivalled in situation, opposite the Royal Mail Packet Pier and commanding extensive views of Dublin Bay, is now being made up to date by the addition of Electric Light.

Hot and Cold Salt Water Baths. High-Class Cuisine. Very Moderate Charges. Table d'Hote 3s 6d."

Cantrell and Cochrane advertised its 31 gold and prize medal table waters, bottled under pressure at the well of St Patrick, St Patrick's Well Lane, Nassau Street, Dublin.

In early 1945, the Advertising Press Club newsletter nominated Terry Spillane of The Irish Times **as "the year's most obvious candidate for matrimony". He was pictured with his bride to be, Eileen Clarke, who also worked in** The Irish Times.

Subscribers and Readers of the
WESTERN NEWS.

Send your Papers to your Friends in
ENGLAND or IRELAND.

Every Reader Becomes a Subscriber.

Send them to
MEMBERS of PARLIAMENT.

To Leading
BRITISH and IRISH NEWSPAPERS

Spread the Light.

Do a Little Free State
Propaganda Work.

Buy extra copies of
THE WESTERN NEWS,

Benny Greene of The Irish Times. In a 1944 newsletter published by the Advertising Press Club, he was described as "the year's most conscientious, hard-working and generally run-ragged pressman."

The Western News of Ballinasloe, Co. Galway, ran this promotional advertisement for itself in April, 1924. The newspaper made no secret of its Free State sympathies.

THERE'S
GOOD NEWS *in the*
ADVERTISEMENTS

—Read Them!

You may miss some of the best news in "The Irish Press" if you don't read the Advertisements.

Advertisements ARE news—news about bargains and fashions, news about ideas that save time and work and money.

Before you go out shopping you should get some ideas of comparative prices and styles. This will save going around from shop to shop comparing and weighing up value.

If you live at a distance "The Irish Press" Advertisements are to you the shop windows of the Capital. You can buy from them with confidence. "The Irish Press" only accepts Advertisements from firms of repute.

The Irish Press **advertised itself in 1938.**

McGlade, an advertising contractor of 2 Chapel Lane off Great Britain Street, Dublin, announced that he gave satisfaction to his clients. He offered street advertising vans at the lowest city prices.

"Kandee" was the new Irish sauce. Its advertising described it as appetizing, delicious, digestive, price 2d and $4\frac{1}{2}$d a bottle. Sold everywhere. Annual sales exceed one million bottles. It is one of the few Irish-made grocery products to survive from that date to the present.

James Hill & Son, auctioneers and house furnishers of Dublin, offered to fully furnish bungalows for just £59.10.0. The National Benefit Trust of Dame Street offered mortgage at interest rates from three to $4\frac{1}{2}$ per cent.

From advertisers such as these, Bloom sought business. When he won his contracts, he went to great lengths to ensure that advertisements were properly set and placed in the paper. Costello described Bloom thus during his fictional time on the *Freeman's Journal*: "His thick legs had the appearance of a wading bird's, slightly ludicrous when viewed from the rear. His brown brilliantined hair grew on the long side and came slightly over the collar. Approaching middle age brought minor ailments. Constipation was one, piles another. He was given to flatulence after cider and cabbage. He was attracted by the large claims of patent medicines, then much advertised in the daily and weekly newspapers. "Wonderworker" for rectal complaints, the world's greatest remedy, Coventry House, South Place, London EC. For his breakfast, he gorged on kidneys."

A genuine advertisement canvasser working the city at this time was Tommy Mangan's father, Joe, who started on the *Dublin Evening Mail* in 1890 and who worked on the paper for 53 years. In 1943, he died on the job, collapsing with a stroke while out canvassing. In all his 53 years with the *Mail* he received no salary, selling advertisements on a commission rate of six per cent. A very conscientious man, Joe Mangan would accept no payment for advertisements he didn't bring in personally. Himself and a Mr Davy were the only two representatives on the advertisement side of the *Evening Mail* for many years. Yet despite his commission-only earnings, Joe Mangan managed to bring up his whole family in reasonable comfort.

In January, 1905, William Martin Murphy relaunched the *Irish Independent* in a bright, new format, albeit with advertisements on the front page in the manner of the time. The new-style paper was an immediate success; 50,000 copies were printed of the first issue and as sales climbed, Murphy introduced the concept of audited net daily sales, giving advertisers an assurance for the first time that the paper's sales figures were genuine.

Murphy's concept was a major landmark in the professionalism of the press and it was soon taken up, not just by other Dublin newspapers, but by new, popular titles in London like the *Daily Express* and the *Daily Mail*. The new *Irish Independent* had a substantial advertisement department, itself unusual for a local newspaper of the time. Among the personalities working there was "Alderman" Edward Hollywood, whose book learning was neither wide nor deep, but whose inexhaustible stock of Dublin stage and musical lore stretching back over half a century made him a welcome figure in many business houses. His bonhomie enabled him to fit into any company. Also on the staff was Martin Lacey, who always wore a hard hat on his outsize head. A Wexford man, he was described as "kind hearted and gentle, but as cute as a pet fox". He was a very popular figure, despite the fact that he was often late for appointments — the present chairman of Independent Newspapers, Dr A. J. F. O'Reilly is said to have a similar timekeeping trait. "Tommy" Barden was another canvasser, with an encyclopaedic knowledge of Dublin personalities. Finally among this quartet of advertisement canvassers who presented such an old-fashioned picture, but who kept the paper full of advertisements, was "Joe" Aylward.

In a 1946 booklet, The Story of Michael Davitt, **the** Mayo News **advertised its properties as a tablecloth.**

MERRICK'S,

BOOTS, SHOES and FANCY GOODS,

THE CORNER HOUSE,
CLAREMORRIS.

Telephone : Claremorris, 30.

Micheal Ua Muircheadha
(Michael Murphy)

DRAPER, GROCER, HARDWARE
and SPIRIT MERCHANT,

SHIPPING & INSURANCE AGENT.

The Square : Coillte Maghagh.

ALBERT MADDEN,

General Draper,

4, MAIN STREET, BALLYHAUNIS.

Still maintains the high standard set up fifty years ago by his predecessors, Messrs. Eaton, for the best in

MILLINERY, MANTLES, BOOTS, & SHOES.

Agent for Mocassin & Denaghy's Shoes.

M. Ronayne & Sons, Ltd.
MANUFACTURERS OF ALL KINDS OF BRUSHES.

THE WEST OF IRELAND BRUSH FACTORY,
CLAREMORRIS.

Telephone : Claremorris, 23.

THE NEWS OF THE WORLD

Sounds better when heard on

PYE or EKCO RADIOS

Bought from or Serviced by :

JAMES O'HARA,

Western Egg Depot,

COOLEGRANE, FOXFORD.

'Phone: Foxford, 3.

Gaelic Culture is the Life of the Nation.

THE FLATLEY DANCING TROUPES

Have won renown at Feiseanna all over Connacht, including Sligo Feis Ceoil. All these were trained by :

LIEUT. T. FLATLEY,

T.C.R.G.,

BALLYHAUNIS.

Hollybrook Delicious Cream Ices
ARE THE CHILDREN'S DELIGHT.

Obtainable in all parts of the West.

Ask for Hollybrook and get the Best.

Manufactured by the

Hollybrook Farm Produce Co., Ltd.,

CLAREMORRIS. 'Phone, 21.

JOHN O'HARA,

Victualler,

CAN SUPPLY YOU WITH FIRST-QUALITY **PRIME BEEF** AND **MUTTON.** CHOICEST CUTS— **BEST MEAT.**

Parcels made up and posted to your relatives and friends in England.

SWINFORD.

Telephone : Swinford, 4.

Not only to-day but every day I supply the farmers of South Mayo with the best

IN SEEDS & GRAIN,

as well as

HARDWARE & PROVISIONS.

To please the customer is my ambition.

MARTIN B. GARVEY,

Wine and Spirit Merchant, Grocer and Newsagent,

HOLLYMOUNT.

The Life of a Newspaper is longer than you would think; the Journal of to-day is often the Tablecloth of To-morrow !

Remember this when Planning your next Campaign.

The MAYO NEWS,
(Printers of this pamphlet)
Will Help You.

'Phone: Westport, 70.
'Grams : "News," Westport.

JOHN MURPHY,

WHOLESALE MERCHANT
and IMPORTER.

Church Street, CLAREMORRIS.

Telegrams: "Wholesale, Claremorris."

Telephone : Claremorris, 14.

" NEWS IS WHERE YOU FIND IT. "
— For —

NEWSPAPERS, PERIODICALS AND MAGAZINES,

You cannot get better service than from

JOSEPH FLATLEY,
MAIN STREET, BALLYHAUNIS.

Stationer, Tobacconist and Newsagent, China and Earthenware, Fancy Goods and School Requisites Always in Stock.

383

A page from the first "outdoor" advertisement feature organised by Erskine Childers in the *Irish Press*, **April, 1933.**

...and the wind be always behind you

The *Donegal Democrat* is one of the few provincial newspapers to have a female advertisement manager — Liz Crawford.

Photograph: Donegal Democrat.

GET YOUR OUTFIT NOW

OUR ADVERTISERS CAN SUPPLY ALL YOUR NEEDS

(Continued from Page 6.)

out. It must bear the photograph of the member, not larger than two inches by two.

Sleeping Quarters.

After inspecting the sitting-room and kitchen in Huntpgreystown, with were swept and garnished (although we were not expected), we went up-stairs to the sleeping quarters. The beds had been made by one of the committee, and I have seldom seen pieces of furniture that combined originality, cheapness, and comfort, in the way these beds did.

They were, as far as I remember, bright blue in colour—that is their wooden frameworks were. Two beds are fixed in tiers, something after the manner of ships and trains, and the two beds may be moved as a single entity, so to speak, to the middle of the floor. This has the advantage of rendering them more accessible for "making."

A piece of canvas is stretched across the framework and thus all the essential elements of a bed are present. The members must provide themselves with sheet bags. These are available in certain shops in Dublin and can also be made at home.

It is obvious that an organisation with a nominal subscription like An Oige can only be successfully run if the members are willing to co-operate with one another.

Thus, before leaving people are expected to leave the place tidy for the next set of members, wash up, sweep the floor, arrange the blankets, etc.

During week-ends times of church services are shown in the hostels. In certain countries smoking is forbidden in the hostels, but it is allowed in Ireland, except in the sleeping quarters. "Nur dass ist verboten," says a German Youth Hostel motto, "was sich selbst verbietet." ("Only that is forbidden which forbids itself.")

Travelling Facilities.

Membership of An Oige entitles one to numerous travelling facilities—reductions on certain 'buses, for instance, and special terms in some hotels.

It is wrong to imagine that on a walking tour every inch of the way must be walked. It is quite legitimate to take the train or any other type of conveyance to the west, or south, and start a walking tour in any place one prefers. But it would be definitely against the rules to drive or a hostel in a car and expect to be welcomed there for the night.

During the day, while one's walk is in progress, it is a good plan not to eat too much food, or to make a heavy meal in the middle of the day. Strange though it may seem, one lives on air when one is walking, and if one spends the whole day out, one is less hungry than if one were in town.

Chocolate is, of course, one of the most satisfying things that can be taken for the journey. Cheese is also very satisfying. Many people bring sandwiches with them on a walking tour and tea is available at all sorts of unexpected places in Ireland.

If one goes right off the beaten track one must have one's food in the open air, accompanied by a drink, of water and an orange. But what, after one has scaled a mountain, could be more delightful?

Hiking.

It will be noticed that I have not used the word hiking. A prominent member of An Oige asked me to omit it as it has, through its associations, become distasteful to genuine walkers.

"I found two old ladies in a County Wicklow village," he told me. "They were almost invalids. The hotel was seven minutes walk from the village. 'We hiked to the village this afternoon and back again,' they said."

In the same way, young German walkers no longer speak of "wandern." That word has been done to death.

However, for those that want to "hike" Ireland is there for it. If they like the word, and it brings them a sense of achievement that ordinary "walking" would not bring, let them use it, and let them hike.

The main thing is to hike—whether it is called walking or not—for then you will discover the real Ireland.

Wherever you go

Shoes tell tales

Neglected shoes soon tell a sorry tale. Wherever you go they make it plain that they are not receiving the attention that good shoes deserve.

Keep your shoes bright and fit with "Nugget" and they will serve you well. Every morning after a "Nugget" shine they'll be good for another day's work, for "Nugget" keeps the leather in perfect condition.

NUGGET
BOOT POLISH

Sold Everywhere in Tins at 3d. and 6d.

MADE IN THE SAORSTAT

McC2

HIKERS!
EAT MORE IRISH MILK

The pure whole milk of Irish cows and no other is used in making : :

SAVOY
Good Health
6 OZS. MILK CHOCOLATE 6D

Obtainable in 1d. and 2d. Bars 3d. and 6d. Cartons.

Made by the Savoy Cocoa Co., Ltd., Dublin

HIKERS' & CYCLISTS' SETS FOR THE WHITSUN HOLIDAYS

Comprising Hiking Tent, Ground Sheet, Blanket and Pan—the ideal equipment for the week-end hiking or cycling tour.

No. 1.		No. 2.	
S/W Blanket	2/11	New Blanket	5/9
G. Sheet	3/3	G. Sheet	3/3
Hike Tent	11/6	Hike Tent	11/6
Army Pack	3/4	Army Pack	3/4
Complete Set	19/2	Complete Set	23/9

Weight of outfit, 13 lbs. Carriage extra. Other Sets supplied with larger Tents. Prices on application.

LAWLERS, 2 Fownes Street, Upper (off Dame Street) DUBLIN

MAPS!

In the bookshop at the Sign of the Three Candles in Fleet Street, members of An Oige, ramblers and all lovers of the countryside can obtain Ordnance Survey Maps of any part of Ireland. A complete stock is always on hand, either in paper or linen-backed. The prices are:—

1" Linen-backed, folded   Dublin District 1" Map, for pocket, 3/-.
1" Paper, folded   pocket or flat, 1/6.   3/-.

Here are also many interesting books for walkers and all parts of An Claiceadal for those who like to shorten the road with song.

THE SIGN OF THE THREE CANDLES, LTD.
FLEET STREET   ::   DUBLIN

"She's not afraid to show her legs . . ."

she wears
BALBRIGGAN

Balbriggan Lisle thread stockings—well of course when you wear Balbriggan you never need be afraid to show your legs. Balbriggan stockings look pleasant, they're pleasant to wear, and ladders you say—not unless you wilfully tear them. For hiking —just the thing. We're inclined to say ; you never get tired wearing Lisle thread stockings.

PRICES

1/11	MEDIUM	2/6	HEAVY
2/11	FINE	3/11	EXTRA FINE
4/11	EXTRA FINE EMBROIDERED CLOX		

To be had in all the latest shades

BALBRIGGAN
HOSIERY

Smyth and Co., Ltd., Hosiery Manufacturers, Balbriggan, Ireland.

THE LONG AND THE SHORT

HIKIN

RUCSACS

Bergen Patten—Made from stout quality double texture rubbing-proofed lawn twill, fitted double shoulder straps, leather coat straps. With one large outside pocket. Size 16 in. x 18 in. **8/11** Other Bergen rucsacs at 11/6, 14/7, 19/6, 26/9, 37/-.

The Raby—An outside pocket, made from lawn rubbing-proofed double twill, also with adjustable slides, eyeletted top with drawcord. Size 15 in. x 14 in. Price...

The Caldy—With one outside pocket. Price...

The Arnside—A super rucsac made from proofed double twill. One outside pocket found there, r-cap and buckle fasteners, one with adjustable slides, eyeletted top with drawcord. Size 17 in. x 16 in. Price, each...

PICNIC OUTFITS

Consisting of Vacuum flask, cups, milk container, provision box and spoons, all clipped in position in a small leather cloth attaché case, which can also be used at any time without the contents is required. A 4 persons, 35/-; 3 persons... **15/-**

Aluminium Picnic Sets. Strong, yet lightweight picnic sets made from polished aluminium. Set consists of polished aluminium kettle fitted with wood handle, four cups and spout screw, aluminium tea infuser, tin stand, lamp and spirit container. 3 pint, 8/9; 4/6. 2 pint...

SHIRTS

Smart khaki drill hiking shirts fitted with Zipp fastener fronts. These shirts are carefully finished in strong, hard-wearing material; they will give long and faithful service. **5/6** Ditto, in khaki tweed...

SHORTS

Khaki linen hiking shorts, with 2 side and back pockets............. In fine quality drill, 1 back pocket only...

TENTS

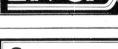

P.ELIABLE TENTS Fron

The Roadster.—A new and exceptionally manufactured specially to our combine; that we might offer a good quality tent at a moderate price. The tent is made from weatherproof hard-wood poles, guys, and in a renowned carrying value. Length 4 ft., height 3 ft. 6 in., walls 6 in., Weight 6½ lbs. Into, when packed, 18 in. x 8 in. wide: to campers in wet weather. Full size 6ft x 3ft. Heavy weight, 9/11; mediam weight, 6 ft. 6 in. x 7 in............

The Scout.—Improved 1933 model. Ground proof. Made from strong closely-woven Complete with three-piece brass metallic poles and metal pegs. Easy to erect, the are attached to the ridge at the tent. Pack in carrying value. This new model for sale at a dual pole (telescopic). Length 7 ft., 6 in., walls 8 ins. Weight 6¼ lbs. In green, 28/-. In white......

The Week-End.—Now used by hikers world. A tent combining strength, lightness and dependability. Ample floor space. packed, 24 ins. x 6 ins. Can be carried upper extreme. Length 4 ft. 6 in., walls 9 ft., walls 18 ins., weight 4¼ lbs. In green.........

Other Tents at 32/9, 39/-, 47/6, 49/6, Bell Tents, Army capitation size......

GROUNDSHEETS

Made from tough (fine ground-sheet twine, proofed with heavy rubber. Launded size, 8 ins. x 6 ins. 6/6 Medium weight, 6/-. **3/3** Featherweight, 4/-. Cape pattern ground sheet, can be used as ground sheet or worn as a cape. Can be used to campers in wet weather. Full size 6ft x 3ft. Heavy weight, 9/6. 8 ft. x mediam weight, 6 ft. 6 in. x 7 in. **7/6**

DON'T FORGET YOUR WEATHERPROOF

Elvery's Litemac.—The ideal coat for the hiker. Weighs only 20 ozs., can be rolled into weatherproof case easily be folded into a very small space and carried in your rucsac or cotta; special flexible proofing, thoroughly waterproof, double-breasted with all-round belt. Available for ladies and men in a number of up-to-date shades. **21/-**

1933 HIKING & TENT LIST (ILLUSTR
SENT POST   FREE ON APPLICAT

Elvery
DUBLIN E

GOLFING *or* HIKING

You'll look your an IRISH S tailored by D LEADING GRADE TAILO IRISH CLOT MODERATE P

IRISH FLANNE
Striped or plain look we they'll be very popular this seas yours early!

O'BEIRNE & O'NEIL

66 Mid. Abbey St., Dublin,

(Just opposite Independent House.)

FEATURE MAGAZINE

... 1, No. 2   MARCH, 1946

...naging Editor   J. J. MURPHY

...ving Editors   LAURENCE HILTON
              MARIE DUDLEY
              PETER RUDDY
              ERIC FORDE

...dvertisement Manager   P. M. OWENS

...lishers   **ABBEY PUBLICATIONS**

Editorial and Advertising Offices :
39 DAWSON STREET, DUBLIN
Telephone 76053
'Grams: "FEATURMAG" Dublin

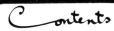 Contents

...our

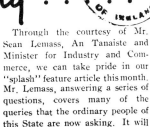

Featuring . . .

RUMOUR, says Shakespeare, is a pipe. It blew a merry tune into this office in the past month. It said the foundation issue of FEATURE was good; it said the issue was fair to middling. It brought warm tributes, many of them from our colleagues in the publishing and printing business; it brought lively criticism, stirring suggestions. It even went the length of jingling in a bar or two about a rival publisher who is supposed to have thumped his desk in rage !

*   *   *

The wise man never acts on rumour, but he never disregards it. We are glad of the congratulations, naturally proud of professional tributes, thankful for the suggestions, prepared to remedy the causes of criticism. As for rumour's story of the enraged publisher, we discount it entirely; FEATURE treads on nobody's corns.

*   *   *

It is a good sign when a man's best critic is himself. As soon as the first issue of FEATURE came off the presses an editorial conference was held in this office. Criticism was merciless; and yet it added up to very little. We ended in general acclamation; we could take honest pride with every justification.

*   *   *

This month again we have made it our object to pack into these pages the widest variety of reading matter, illustrated with action pictures. "Something for everybody" is hard to make in the space at our disposal; matter has to be pared down to the minimum; the photo coverage has to be reduced. Yet, we are making it a first priority to give each member of the family a reading quota.

Through the courtesy of Mr. Sean Lemass, An Tanaiste and Minister for Industry and Commerce, we can take pride in our "splash" feature article this month. Mr. Lemass, answering a series of questions, covers many of the queries that the ordinary people of this State are now asking. It will be interesting to see the public reaction to what he has to say.

*   *   *

In the sports-writing field we have, to judge from readers' letters, made a capture in Peter Ruddy. This month again he features a personality—in fact a whole family of personalities—with a great name in Irish sport. Ruddy's story of the departure of the racing Beasleys is a notable exclusive.

*   *   *

A last word: the presentation with pictures of a great film, "The Bells of St. Mary's," in this issue is an example of FEATURE's policy of going after the kind of material we think our readers want. This film was released in America only last Christmas, and Eric Forde, our film editor, brings you the story in this issue. Eric believes in the direct cable to Hollywood and uses it.

*   *   *

Plans for our April issue are already well in hands. It will bring you the same standard of service, with, I can safely predict, some big surprises.

*   *   *

Watch out for us in April . . . until then . . .

The Editor.

A March 1946 issue of Feature magazine published by Abbey Publications. Its advertisement manager was Peter Owens.

The late Jack Dempsey was promoted from advertisement manager to general manager of the Irish Press in 1946, having seen the newspaper through the advertising difficulties of the Emergency.
Photograph: Irish Press.

In 1949, the Sunday Press held a dinner in Jammet's restaurant to celebrate its launch with the advertising world. Seated around the table, starting left: unknown, unknown, John McConnell, P. J. Dempsey, Michael B. Kenny, Sean Lynch, Frank Padbury, Denis Garvey, Ernie Keogh, Leo O'Farrell (RCN, London), C. J. Furlong, Chris McDonagh, unknown, R. W. Young, T. J. Mangan, T. J. Kelly, Tim O'Neill, J. B. Clancy, unknown. Dempsey's agency, Parker Advertising, handled the advertising for the launch, which included double crown posters for the Horse Show arena, boards outside newsagents and window bills for buses.

Leo Blennerhassett, who after spending some years as Charlie McConnell's right hand man in starting up McConnell's Advertising agency, became first publicity manager and then London manager of Independent Newspapers, had personal recall of the starting up of the new-look *Irish Independent* in 1905. He said that advertising in those days was still regarded as a "vulgar intrusion".

A new man came to head up the newspaper's advertisement department Thomas À Kempis Grehan, who proved a revolutionary influence on the course of newspaper advertising in Ireland. The father of distinguished columnist Ida Grehan, Tom Grehan was from Ballinasloe, Co Galway. When he was 18 years of age, he went to Liverpool to work in the advertising department of Lever Brothers, the soap manufacturers. Then he went to London to work in the well-established agency world.

With years of good English advertising experience behind him, he was ready for the big challenge, when about four years after the launch of the new style *Irish Independent,* he came to Dublin as its advertisement manager. He was full of enthusiasm and vigour, determined to bring a fresh look to the face of Irish newspaper advertising, just as the brash new popular newspapers in London revolutionised advertising concepts there. In his ambition, Tom Grehan was greatly helped by the fortunate coincidence of a technical

WILL THAT BOY NEVER STOP GROWING—
—Master IRISH PRESS in last week's circulation.

By March, 1933, the Irish Press (launched less than two years previously), was claiming big gains in circulation and advertising. It extended its press capacity and brought 100 Irish advertisers to see its new machine that it had recently installed.

In 1948, Melville (Sandy) Miller was appointed advertisement manager of The Irish Times in succession to Michael Clarke. Miller had worked with McConnell's before World War II; during the war, he served with the Royal Artillery. At the time of his death in the Staines air crash in 1972, he was managing director of Rowntree-Mackintosh (Ireland), Dublin.

breakthrough that enabled the presentation of advertisements to be greatly improved. In 1911, the concept of half-tone illustrations for newspapers arrived in Ireland and was immediately taken up by the *Irish Independent*. The use of photographs in advertisements, together with the new styles in typefaces and borders that came in at the same time, enabled the appearance of advertisements to be much improved. Grehan wasted no time in encouraging advertisers to make the most of these new techniques. But he was fighting an uphill battle: when he addressed a lunch meeting of the Dublin Chamber of Commerce in 1911 on the subject of advertising, half the attendance walked out because they thought that the subject was too vulgar to be worth their interest! In Britain, advertisers were much keener to use the new advertising techniques; in Ireland, local firms, even though they were competing for business against these self-same cross-channel advertisers, were far less enthusiastic about the benefits of publicity. As D. P. Moran said in a widely quoted piece in *The Leader* at this time: "Irish manufacturers do not believe in advertising."

At the start of 1946, David Luke joined the advertisement staff of J. J. McCann & Co. of Dame Street, Dublin, shortly afterwards being appointed advertisement manager of the firm's new Radio Review publication.

387

Scale of advertisement charges for the Dublin Evening Mail, 1952. Its front page was available to advertisers for £200.

Terry Spillane, for many years editor and publisher of the Hardware and Allied Trader magazine.

Dublin Evening Mail

8 columns to page, depth 22", (Front page 20¼") width, 2", screen 65, Blocks or Matrics.

TRADE ADVERTS	Per S.C. Inch
Ordinary Position	15/-
All Guaranteed Positions Extra According to Page and Position.	
SOME REGULAR SPECIAL POSITIONS.	
Bottom Right or Left Chief News Page, 8" D.C., Semi-Solus	25/-
Top Right or Left Second News Page, 8" D.C., Semi-Solus	20/-
Title Spaces—Front (1½" S.C. or 1½" D.C.)	17/6
Strip Advertisements exceeding 3 Cols. across foot of page	18/-
Full Page (Front)	£200
Half Page (Front)	£100
Full Page (Inside)	£150
Half Page (Inside)	£75
Advertisements exceeding 15" x 4 Cols., or exceeding 4 Cols. in width, charged at pro rata page rate.	
MISCELLANEOUS.	
Amusement Notices	15/-
Dances and Whist Drives	15/-
Balance Sheets & Financial Announcements	25/-
Company Meeting Reports and Commercial Prospectuses	25/-
Municipal Election Addresses and Notices	33/-
School Notices	15/-
Railway, Shipping and Transport Notices ...	15/-
Auctioneers' Announcements	17/6

	Per S.C. Inch
Public Notices, Appeals and Subscriptions	15/-
Readers and Paragraphs with word " Advt." (2/- line)	24/-
Paragraphs under Radio Programmes (2/6 per line)	30/-
Government and Election Notices (3/6 per line)	42/-
Legal Notices	33/-
Social and Personal Announcements (2/6 per line)	30/-
Sporting Notices	15/-
Bookmakers' Notices (Minimum 10/-) ...	20/-
Draws, Raffles, etc. (1/3 per line) ...	15/-

Births, Marriages and Deaths—Five Lines (six words to the line). Minimum, 2/6. Each additional line, 6d.

"Evening Mail" Popular Prepaids—12 words, 1/- (minimum). Additional words, 1½d. each.

Situations Wanted and Domestics Disengaged, 10 words 1/- (minimum). Additional words, 1d. each.

Trade Prepaids—1/3 per line.

Box Number charged as 2 words, plus 6d. postage (returnable) on replies if required.

No Series Reduction.

When the *Kerryman* newspaper was launched in Tralee in 1904, by Maurice Griffin, Thomas Nolan and Daniel Nolan, there was much emphasis on the editorial and printing sides of the newspaper, little on the advertisement side. The post of advertisement manager simply did not exist. Even 40 and more years later, when Tom Nolan's son, Dan, was managing director, the classified advertising came in of its own accord and looking after display advertising from the agencies was one duty among many for Dan Nolan.

Perhaps the founders of the *Kerryman* should have taken a leaf out of two very different books. In Carrick-on-Shannon, a local optician called Harman started advertising in the *Leitrim Observer* about 1904. His small advertisement appeared in every subsequent issue of the newspaper until he retired, 30 years later. Patrick Pearse, leader of the 1916 Rising displayed an uncharacteristically commercial touch over advertising in a small magazine he was running in 1910. He employed an unnamed advertisement representative and to him he wrote tartly in December, 1910: "We must have the issue on sale before the boys (at

Scoil Eanna, Rathfarnham) go home for vacation. I hope you have made good progress with advts. Hand in copy as you get it to Dollard. Make a great effort this time to have advts up to mark. Last issue would have paid if advts had been anything like they were in first issue. We must make this issue pay. No time is to be lost." Yours, P. H. Pearse.

As a postscript, he suggested trying a grocer in Rathmines Terrace, a baker in Rathfarnham and a furniture removers and ironmongers in Highfield Road. "Try also Horan's, tailor, 63 Dame Street, who has three boys here. Also McCabes, fishmongers, Rathmines Road, and L. Nugent, Irish Creamery, Lr Baggot Street, with whom we deal."

A second letter, dated five days later, showed signs of desperation: "For God's sake, make the best use you can of these two days and have as many advts as possible in by tomorrow night. Try Eastman's, Rathmines and Purcell, cigar merchant, 16 North Earl St. Make a good show. It will be a good number."

Business was better for William Martin Murphy. His new morning paper was going so well that soon 111, Middle Abbey Street became far too cramped and Murphy acquired Carlisle Buildings at the corner of D'Olier Street and Burgh Quay. Part of the building was used to house the commercial sections of Independent Newspapers: one amusing story survives from that time. An opera company from London had arrived in Dublin and was being entertained at a reception in Carlisle Buildings. An Irish KC called Moriarty happened to call to the building, saw the big crowd and blurted out: "Are all these people putting in advertisements?"

John Flynn, the blind publisher, who published the East Coast newspaper before World War II and many consumer and trade magazines after the war.

Spring Show about 1956. From left: Dessie O'Leary, The Irish Times, Peter Finnegan, Independent Newspapers and Sir Raymond Grace, The Irish Times.

389

George F. Crosbie, chairman, Cork Examiner. **He started in the newspaper's advertisement department after World War II. He remembers coming home from Dublin every January with bookings from the Dublin advertising agencies, so many forms that he could hardly carry them.**
Photograph: Cork Examiner.

The *Irish Independent* became the first daily newspaper to achieve serious distribution throughout the country. Other titles like *The Irish Times,* often failed to reach main provincial cities until late in the afternoon of publication. The *Irish Independent* was the first newspaper from Dublin to start arriving in time for breakfast. In addition to Cork, with its *Cork Examiner* (mornings) and *Evening Echo* (afternoons) and also the *Cork Constitution* (mornings), inviolable bastions against any inroads from Dublin, other cities did have daily newspapers, like the *Waterford Evening News,* that were affected by the increasing competition from Dublin. For the first time, under Grehan's influence, the *Irish Independent* had shown the effectiveness of a national advertising medium.

More tremors to disturb the complacency of much of the press in Ireland came with the advent in 1914 of the Great War. Within months, there was rationing of newsprint. Commodity scarcities meant cutbacks in advertising, yet with the shortage of newsprint meaning smaller papers, many newspaper publishers were able to increase substantially their advertisement rates. Some advertisers kept a "black book" of these publishers and exacted revenge after the war; Tom Grehan of the *Irish Independent* was one of the very few advertisement managers who did not seek to exploit his customers in this way, despite his paper being reduced to four pages.

Government advertising in 1916 heralded a momentous event: the Easter Rising. The Rising started on Easter Monday: on the Wednesday, Dublin Castle published in the main newspapers its

Advertisement placed by the Meath Chronicle in the early 1950s.

An advertisement used by the Drogheda Independent in the early 1950s, aimed at auctioneers.

NAVAN

To get results from prosperous Meath, advertise in the Paper that covers the entire County and the adjoining portions of Westmeath and Cavan.

The "Meath Chronicle"

Read by the

COMMERCIAL, AGRICULTURAL, LABOUR AND LANDED CLASSES

EVERY FRIDAY. TWOPENCE.

Rates for Advertising on Application to

The Manager,
MEATH CHRONICLE, LTD., NAVAN
Telephone: Navan, 42

A *MUST* for Auctioneers

Advertising is the most potent weapon of your sales force. Use it to its best advantage—Advertise in

The

Drogheda   Independent

PUBLISHED WEEKLY
ON FRIDAY MORNING.   Price 2d.
A.B.C. AND AUDITOR'S CERTIFIED NETT SALES

16,099 COPIES

Members of Audit Bureau of Circulations. Circulating over the entire Counties of MEATH, LOUTH, NORTH DUBLIN, DUBLIN CITY, NORTH KILDARE and CAVAN.
'Phone—DROGHEDA 58.
Telegrams: "Independent," Drogheda.

POSTER WORK A SPECIALITY.

OFFICES AND WORKS:
9 SHOP STREET, DROGHEDA.
All communications to be addressed to the Managing Director.

In 1955, Independent Newspapers held a lunch in the Shelbourne Hotel to mark the 50th anniversary of the present *Irish Independent*. **Present at the lunch were from left: Ernie Keogh, Dermod Cafferky (both Arrow), Sean Lynch (Lynch Advertising), Joe Clancy (Easons), Brian D. O'Kennedy (O'Kennedy Brindley), Edward Maguire (Independent Newspapers), Denis Garvey (Janus), Peter Owens (Domas), Bill Bergin (Padburys), Desmond B. O'Kennedy (O'Kennedy Brindley), Frank Padbury (Padburys), T. V. Murphy, Frank Geary, John J. Dunne and Mr O'Riordan (all Independent Newspapers) and C. E. McConnell (McConnell's).**
Photograph: Independent Newspapers.

proclamation of martial law in the city and county of Dublin, with attendant restrictions on pub opening hours. In the bombardment of the city centre area by Crown forces later that week, the paper stores of *The Irish Times* in Lower Abbey Street were destroyed by fire. Its main offices at Westmoreland Street escaped unscathed.

The offices of the *Dublin Daily Express* and the *Evening Mail* at the top of Parliament Street, opposite City Hall, were briefly occupied by a unit of the Citizen's Army, but soon 'liberated' by Crown forces. Although the *Irish Independent* was unable to publish for the best part of a week, its premises in Middle Abbey Street were undamaged. After the war of independence was over, William Martin Murphy was able to build the present Independent House on a large site left ruined in the aftermath of 1916. Just at the back of the Independent, the *Freeman's Journal* offices

At the *Irish Independent* **lunch in 1955, from left: Bill Bergin, Mr O'Riordan, Edward Maguire, Desmond B. O'Kennedy, Brian D. O'Kennedy, Frank Geary and Joe Delaney of Domas.**
Photograph: Independent Newspapers.

Victor Salter, for many years advertisement director of the Belfast Telegraph. He died in 1958.
Photograph: Belfast Telegraph.

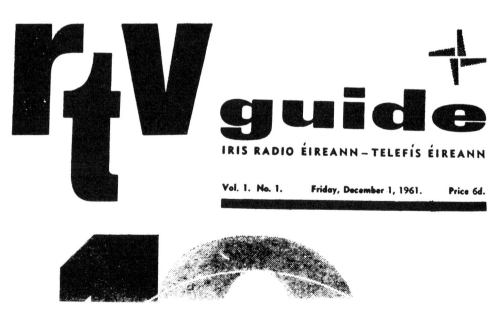

in Princes Street, just at the side of the GPO, were completely destroyed. Also published here were *Sport* and the *Evening Telegraph*. The *Freeman's Journal* moved to new editorial and printing premises in Townsend Street, on the site of the present day Hawkins House, while an advertisement office was opened in Westmoreland Street.

All six columns of the front pages of the *Nenagh Guardian* in this memorable year of 1916 were given over to advertisements, in common with all other provincial newspapers. Most of the advertisements came from Nenagh itself, centre of the newspaper's circulation area.

In 1917, the year following the Easter Rising, a young lad had ambitions of entering the newspaper business. Billy King wanted to write and asked J. P. Rice, the editor of the *Evening Herald*, about his chances. Neither Rice nor William Chapman, the works manager, had anything to offer, but some months later, the ever-reliable Tom Grehan, the *Irish Independent's* advertisement manager did write, offering Billy a post. He accepted with alacrity and enthusiasm, starting work in the advertisement department at Carlisle Buildings, first on the telephone side. The *Irish Independent* was one of the very first Irish newspapers to make use of the telephone in its advertisement department. Then Billy graduated to taking copy in the office, before being promoted to an advertisement representative. He went on to spend the rest of his publishing career on the advertising side. He has long had a keen interest in matters cultural and literary, carrying on a correspondence in the 1930s with George Bernard Shaw.

Jim Furlong, for many years group advertisement manager of the Irish Press group of newspapers. He masterminded the advertising side of the Evening Press launch in 1954.
Photograph: Irish Press.

The masthead of the first issue of the RTV Guide, published on December 1, 1961.

rtV guide +

IRIS RADIO ÉIREANN – TELEFÍS ÉIREANN

Vol. 1. No. 1.   Friday, December 1, 1961.   Price 6d.

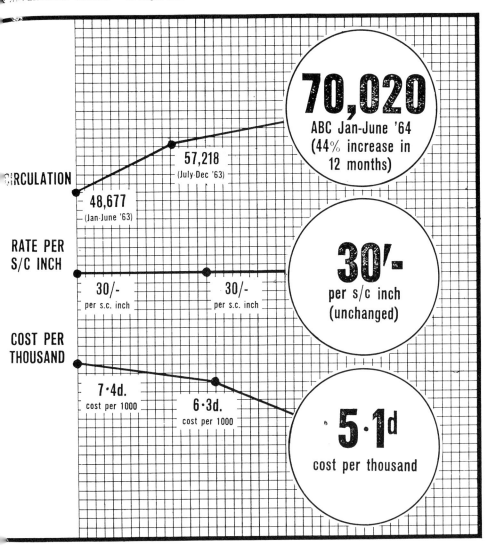

CIRCULATION

70,020
ABC Jan-June '64
(44% increase in
12 months)

57,218
(July-Dec '63)

48,677
(Jan-June '63)

**RATE PER
S/C INCH**

30/-
per s/c inch
(unchanged)

30/-
per s.c. inch

30/-
per s.c. inch

**COST PER
THOUSAND**

5·1ᵈ
cost per thousand

7·4d.
cost per 1000

6·3d.
cost per 1000

Leo Blennerhassett,
who died in August,
1960, aged 75. He was
the first manager of
McConnell's, soon after
the agency was founded
in 1916, then he became
advertising manager at
Brown Thomas. From
there, he joined
Selfridge's, London, in a
similar capacity — in
the late 1920s,
Selfridge's owned
Brown Thomas.
Returning to Dublin, he
worked on the
advertisement side of
the new Irish Press
newspaper from 1931
until 1932. He joined
Independent
Newspapers in the
latter year as publicity
manager, becoming
London manager in
1944, a position he held
until his death. He was
a founder member of
the Publicity Club.

rtv guide

Ireland's
largest-selling weekly publication
sells for you seven days a week!

For details contact: D.W. Mayes Ltd., 69 Fleet St., E.C.4. Tel. FLE 4447 and 4412, or Advertisement Dept., RTV Guide, GPO, Dublin 1. Tel. 42981

A 1964 trade
advertisement for the
RTV Guide, published
by Telefis Eireann.

Woman's Way **was launched by Hugh McLaughlin's Creation group in 1963. Gerry McGuinness, its first advertisement director, invested in a media survey, unknown in the business then. The findings were presented in September, 1964. From then, McGuinness pioneered the idea of magazine presentations to agencies and clients, using available demographics and putting together media packages for clients that included of course the Creation magazines. "There was no independent research then, so we did pioneering work, it was of great value to multinational clients and of benefit to us," recalls McGuinness. In those days,** Woman's Way **cost 1/- and had a 75,000 circulation weekly. Creation also published a monthly magazine called** Creation **and later a back-up to** Woman's Way **called** Women's View, **which became** Woman's Choice. **It and** Woman's Way **were bought by the Smurfit group after the collapse of the Creation group in 1975.** Woman's Way **now has a circulation of 71,000, mainly young housewives; its advertisement manager is Bob McMahon. U magazine launched by JS Publications in 1981 and targetted at the 16-25 age group, has a 28,000 monthly**

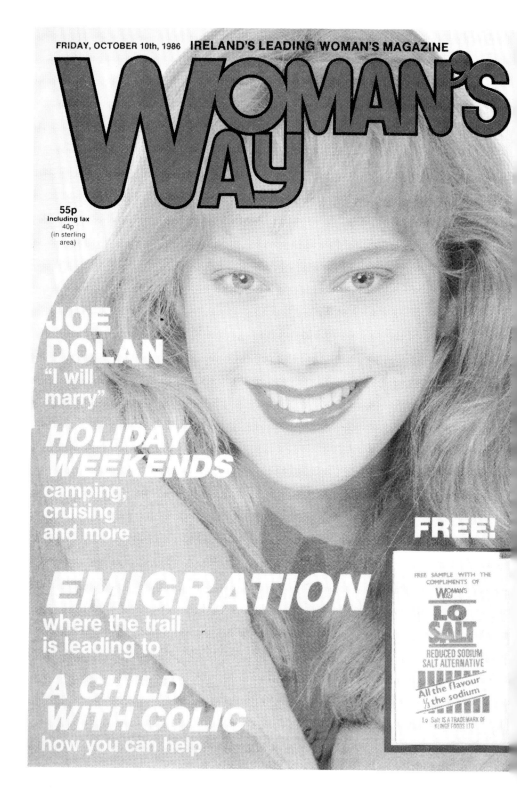

FRIDAY, OCTOBER 10th, 1986 **IRELAND'S LEADING WOMAN'S MAGAZINE**

WOMAN'S WAy

55p
Including tax
40p
(in sterling area)

JOE DOLAN
"I will marry"

HOLIDAY WEEKENDS
camping, cruising and more

EMIGRATION
where the trail is leading to

A CHILD WITH COLIC
how you can help

FREE!

FREE SAMPLE WITH THE COMPLIMENTS OF **Woman's Way**
LO SALT
REDUCED SODIUM
SALT ALTERNATIVE
All the flavour
⅓ the sodium
Lo Salt IS A TRADEMARK OF KLINGE FOODS LTD

A meeting in the Railway Hotel, Athenry, Co Galway on Monday, February 19, 1917, started off the establishment of the Irish Provincial Newspaper Owners' Association, now the Provincial Newspapers' Association of Ireland. Leading the effort at organising the industry was Tom Kenny, founder of the *Connacht Tribune* in 1909. The excessive cost of newsprint and printing materials had spurred the newspapers into collective action. A meeting at Dublin's Mansion House was organised for March 10: the outcome was the first general meeting of the new association, in the same venue, on June 11. W. Copeland Trimble of the *Impartial Reporter,* Enniskillen, was the first president and E. T. Keane, *Kilkenny People,* was treasurer. Tom Kenny of the *Connacht Tribune* was elected secretary. The most pressing problem was the supply of newsprint, priced that June at 4½d a lb. "Free" paper could be obtained at fancy prices.

The first fruits of combination were felt on the advertisement side. During the war, the Department of Agriculture ran extensive publicity campaigns to increase tillage. The Secretary of the Department, T. P. Gill, told a delegation from the new association that arising from the campaign, newspapers had enjoyed a great deal of outside advertising. He also stated that he found posters outside police barracks an effective form of advertising. Subsequently, the Government Advertising Agents (Kenny's), sent out orders to the provincial press for 160 inches of food production advertising at prices ranging from 1/- to 2/6d an inch. The price fixed by the newspapers' association for this type of advertising was a flat rate of 4/6 per inch. Before long, the Government gave way and accepted a reasonable flat rate.

circulation. JS Publications' sales and marketing director is Ciaran Havelin who used to be media manager of Arks.

Tommy Thomas, The Irish Times **(right) with** Tommy Mangan, Irish Press.

An Irish Press grouping. From left: Mrs Kay Mangan, Jack Dempsey, Frank McGouran (who now heads the advertisement sales team at the group) and Tommy Mangan.

Frank Madden, former advertisement director of Checkout set up Today's Grocer in 1985. The magazine's editor is Sarah Coyle who was previously editor of Checkout.

TODAY'S **Grocer**
& CONVENIENCE STORE

60p

INSIDE
- Waterford bitten by recession
- Today's Grocer visits Greece
- Monopoly concerns Noonan?

1986 OCTOBER

In 1967, advertising executives from Dublin and London visited the new Sunday News newspaper in Belfast. The newspaper had been launched in 1965 and Brian A. Croley, then managing director, decided to have a large scale visit to Northern Ireland by the advertising profession. Frank Loughrey, who comes from Belfast, commented: "I look forward to the day when the 32 counties of Ireland are regarded as a viable marketing unit". The photograph shows members of the Dublin party.

WINTER WARMERS

Superb Jacket Offer from Erin Soups.

Erin Soups will be moving off the shelves faster than ever this Winter with an exciting new 'Winter Warmers' promotion. Your customers will be able to pick up a beautiful quilted Irish made jacket – only with Erin Soups. The 'Winter Warmers' promotion will be heavily advertised on TV and in the consumer press. So, order extra stocks of Erin Soups now.

IRELAND

F THE WELCOMES   VOL. 34   NO. 4   JULY-AUGUST 1985

Ireland and the United Kingdom 95p.
(Includes VAT in the Republic of Ireland)
United States and Canada $2.25

CARR CHALADH
51 KILLIMER
CAR FERRY

BÓTHAR COIS FAIRRGE
COAST ROAD

BÓTHAIR NA TRA
LIOS DÚIN BHEARNA
LISDOONVARNA 19
VIA COAST ROAD

AILLWEE CAVE
OPEN TO VISITORS

T LIOS DUIN BHEARNA
69 LISDOONVARNA 10

CEANN BÓIRNE
BLACK HEAD 6 L54

CASTLE HOTEL

IONAD IASCAIREACHTA km
SHORE ANGLING
CENTRE 16

Frank Grennan, managing director of Jemma Publications, which he founded in 1970 with the Irish Licensing World magazine and which is now Ireland's largest trade publishing house. The firm publishes in both Dublin and Belfast, as well as in Glasgow, home of the Scottish Grocer. The firm is also active in trade exhibitions.

Ireland of the Welcomes, **published by Bord Failte, is one of the country's oldest established consumer magazines, founded 33 years ago. It is published bi-monthly. Its ABC circulation is about 111,000, according to publisher Tom Behan. Advertisement sales are contracted out, to McCarthy Advertising Sales, Bray. A full colour page costs £2,140; virtually all advertising originates in Ireland.**

397

Jack Briggs,
advertisement manager
of The Irish Times **from
1958 until his
retirement in 1970. He
died in 1985.**
*Photograph: The Irish
Times.*

**Opposite page:
Colin McClelland
(editor) left and
Michael McCormack
(advertisement and
marketing manager),**
Sunday World.

**Berkeley Vincent, who
retired from the
advertisement
department of** The Irish
Times **in 1966, was a
great favourite with
auctioneers. At the
annual dinner of the
Irish Auctioneers and
Estate Agents'
Association that year, a
special retirement
presentation was made
to him by Frank W.
Meldon, then
association president.
Centre is Mrs Berkeley
Vincent.**
*Photograph: The Irish
Times.*

By the time the first annual general meeting was held, in December, 1917, the new organisation had 75 provincial newspapers in membership, 37 in Ulster, 18 in Leinster, 14 in Munster and six in Connacht.

Offices were secured at Star Buildings, 12/14 College Green, where the next meeting of the executive was held on February 11, 1918. The advertisement rates for Government notices, Food Control advertisements and commercial advertising were all revised. The expertise in advertising often rested with the proprietors or managers of newspapers: few had separate advertisement managers. Con O'Donoghue, formerly with the *Kerryman* in Tralee, joined the *Drogheda Independent* in 1917 and for many years ran the managerial side of the paper with great aplomb. Joachim Casey, who was later to spend just a year as editor of the paper before he dropped dead, referred on more than one occasion to Con O'Donoghue's "expert advertising abilities".

The floating of the National Loan by the Dail in 1919 caused problems for many newspapers. Quickly after the start of the 1916 Easter Rising, many newspapers of nationalistic hue were suppressed by the British authorities: the first to be banned was the *Enniscorthy Echo*. With the decision to raise the £250,000 National Loan, for which publicity was prepared by Sean Lynch, founder of Lynch Advertising, newspapers that carried the advertisements often found themselves in trouble with Dublin Castle. The *Midland Tribune* ran a full page advertisement for the loan in defiant contravention of a British Government order. It was immediately suppressed for a week, by the simple expedient of removing parts of the printing machinery. The

Michael Whelan, for many years advertisement manager of the Munster Express, Waterford, whose editor and publisher is the renowned J. J. Walsh.

Kerryman in Tralee suffered a similar fate. Yet despite the difficulties, more papers were launched. In 1919, John Downey and C. A. Stephens founded the *Donegal Democrat* in Ballyshannon. With the shortage of paper and advertising and the necessity to handset all copy (since a Linotype was wild luxury), the *Donegal Democrat* long remained a small circulation publication in the Ballyshannon area, with advertisements from traders in the town. Now, it has a circulation of nearly 20,000 and it is one of the prime advertising vehicles of the North-West.

The War of Independence grew nastier: in 1920, the advertisement offices of the *Freeman's Journal* in Westmoreland Street were shot up by a gang of unknown identity. After the notorious raid on its main premises in 1922, when much of the machinery was put out of action, the *Freeman's Journal* was on the road to extinction.

The end of the newspaper came in December, 1924, yet for several years before its demise, the paper may have been ailing, but one advertisement representative was doing rather nicely for himself. Seamus Funge, who founded the Elo Press in Dublin in 1929, worked on the *Freeman's Journal,* where one of his main accounts was for Clery's department store. Every Monday, Clery's decided on its advertising programme for the week and Funge was said to have earned so much in commission on Mondays that it nearly amounted to enough to live on for the rest of the week. In the midst of war, some sections of publishing were doing well enough. In 1920, for instance, Wilson Hartnell decided to relaunch its long running magazine, *Lady of the*

B. J. Gillespie, former advertisement manager of the Connaught Telegraph, who died in 1982. He was responsible for shifting advertisements off the front page of the newspaper in the mid-1960s.

Four Guinness drinkers printing the first

𝕷𝖔𝖓𝖌𝖋𝖔𝖗𝖉 𝕷𝖊𝖆𝖉𝖊𝖗

75 years ago, as today, a newspaperman with a
printer's-devil of a thirst slaked it in Guinness.
Like Guinness, the Longford Leader has moved with the times,
and still preserves the high standards it set for itself
when printing its first issue. Congratulations from

GUINNESS

(213 years old)

In 1972, the Longford Leader **celebrated its 75th anniversary with a fine supplement, put together by Derek Cobbe, who now runs the** Longford News **and** Longford Express. **Guinness advertised in the issue.**

P. J. Hennelly, advertisement manager, Connaught Telegraph, **Castlebar.** *Photograph: Tom Tobin.*

House. It was rechristened the *Irish Tatler and Sketch*. For many years subsequently, *The Irish Times'* old front office in Westmoreland Street, where generations of customers handed in their classifieds, was said to have carried a mark of those turbulent times: disfiguring marks on the counter were believed to have been caused by the boots of a Black and Tan soldier.

There was still the odd flash of humour: a farmer and his daughter arrived in the *Derry Journal* offices one day and demanded the name of a matrimonial advertiser in the paper. They were so persistent that they were given the name and set off to find Derry's most confirmed bachelor. Not everyone enjoyed the joke.

In Cork, in the midst of the civil war, the *Cork Examiner* suffered grievously. Not long before, it had been harrassed by the Black and Tans. Now much of its machinery was out of action for three months and every night, escorted by Free State soldiers, the formes of type, including advertisements, set in Guy's old factory just up the road, had to be wheeled down to the Examiner. Advertising revenue in the city slumped, so much so that the paper's main rival, the *Cork Constitution*, went out of business in 1924. Tom O'Neill, the *Cork Examiner's* advertisement manager for many years, was appointed to the post in 1923.

In the early years of his job, O'Neill would come to Dublin regularly and call on the different advertising agencies. Every Monday morning, a list was prepared of the agencies' bookings for that week in the three Examiner publications, the *Cork Examiner*, the *Evening Echo* and the *Weekly*

400

Examiner. All agencies were reminded of the time blocks or matrices were required, for onward dispatch to Cork by train. Working in tandem with Tom O'Neill was Ned Looney, advertisement manager of the *Evening Echo* and the *Weekly Examiner,* although the latter newspaper never had a big throughput of advertising. Looney was described by the famous Miss Lynch as "the kindest person you ever saw".

Brid Lynch was appointed to the Dublin office of the *Cork Examiner* in 1928. For many years, she managed it with great skill, until she retired in 1973. So well-known was she in the business that when the late W. T. Cosgrave retired from public life, she received a letter from him thanking her for her contribution to newspaper publishing. Before being sent up to Dublin, Miss Lynch was given a crash course in advertising by Tom O'Neill. She remembers that he was so dedicated to his job that on one occasion when he was spending a couple of hours between trains in Belfast, he saw a poster advertisement for a firm of oatmeal millers, went to see its publicity manager and came away with a series of advertisements for the *Cork Examiner.* For the 1920s, with the air full of talk of economic boycotts between North and South, it was a formidable achievement.

While the *Cork Examiner* survived the vicissitudes of the civil war, the *Freeman's Journal* did not. Its closure in December, 1924 was the biggest newspaper closure since that of *Saunder's Newsletter,* also in Dublin, nearly 50 years previously. Paddy Montford had joined the *Freeman's Journal* as a boy, becoming assistant editor on the *Sunday Freeman* and then circulation manager. In 1918, he made a strange career switch, becoming advertisement manager of the *Freeman's Journal.* When the paper closed, he went to America for two years before returning to work briefly in McConnell's, then succeeding Percy Gillespie as advertisement manager of *Dublin Opinion.* The magazine had been

Pat Cleary, who has been advertisement and marketing manager of the Clare Champion, Ennis, since 1979. *Photograph: Clare Champion.*

Gerry O'Boyce, who joined the Irish Farmers' Journal 26 years ago. For many years he was advertisement and marketing director of the weekly newspaper, responsible for developing the advertisement side and also for promoting the publication. Gerry joined the paper when Jack Carmody was still there; Gerry is now semi-retired but says that working with the paper, he never knew a bad Monday or any other day of the week.

Diarmuid O Broin, for many years advertisement manager of Management magazine when published by the Irish Management Institute.

Barry McIntyre, of the Regional Newspaper Advertising Bureau in Dublin, who is co-ordinating the input of national advertising into the provincial press. The bureau was set up in 1986; McIntyre was formerly with the Irish Press **group.**

founded shortly after the Treaty by C. K. Kelly and Arthur Booth. Until the early 1950s, it remained one of Ireland's most influential magazines. In its heyday, issues sold over 60,000 copies and advertisement revenue was concurrently strong.

The demise of the *Freeman's Journal* was a big boost for its arch-rival, the *Irish Independent*. In 1926, the *Irish Independent* carried about 250,000 column inches of advertising for the year: no other Irish newspaper could claim to publish as much. The *Irish Independent* fought tenaciously to prevent the *Freeman's Journal* being taken over and restarted. In the end, Independent Newspapers bought the title, but never revived it. Enjoying an increased monopoly position in the daily newspaper market, the *Irish Independent* managed to push its yearly column inch total to around 350,000 by 1931.

The worldwide economic slump that set in during 1929 seemed to matter little as far as the burgeoning fortunes of the Middle Abbey Street newspaper "empire" was concerned. For one country newspaper, there were good times, too. In the late 1920s, two drapery shops in Carrick-on-Shannon anticipated the present day supermarket advertising wars by over 50 years. The two shops advertised cut price offers week in, week out, remembers Gregory Dunne of the *Leitrim Observer*, which benefitted considerably from the two shops' advertising campaigns. An advertisement in the *Co Down Spectator* in 1925 was from a local travel agency, Orr's Travel, which

Sean Colgan, advertisement manager, The Kerryman, Tralee. The newspaper was one of the first provincial titles to designate an advertisement manager.
Photograph: The Kerryman.

offered a passage to Canada for £2. The fare included a guarantee of a job at the other end.

The *Irish Independent* had the Dublin morning newspaper market to itself — with the main exception of *The Irish Times* — for seven years. In 1928, the *Irish Independent* strengthened its grip on advertising by the Murphy family's offer to the public of £200,000's worth of shares. Business people like auctioneers, newsagents, solicitors and undertakers bought the shares and had a vested interest in supporting the paper with their advertising. When the *Irish Press* was launched in September, 1931 (the first brand new national daily newspaper to be launched in Ireland for nearly a century), the first issue was over-subscribed with advertisements. Very unusually for the time, it carried news, not advertisements, on its front page. Leo Blennerhassett, the founding advertisement manager, who never used one word where two would do, was a happy man. The second day's issue was a different matter; few agencies put the new *Irish Press* on their schedules. The Fianna Fail party, destined to come to power in 1932, had a professed policy of building up home industry. The many big British firms who dominated the Irish market then refused to advertise in the *Irish Press*. Firms like Lever Brothers would advertise soap powders in *The Irish Times*, but not in the *Irish Press*.

Opposite page:
The late Dessie O'Leary, who sold property advertisements in The Irish Times **for many years. He was meticulous over servicing clients with proofs and reproofs, vital in auctioneers' advertisements.**
Photograph: The Irish Times.

John Hamilton, advertisement manager of the Southern Star, **Skibbereen, Co Cork.**
Photograph: Southern Star.

In the advertisement department of The Kerryman, **Tralee, supervisor Jimmy Lavin with Margaret Griffin and Mary Lyons.**
Photograph: The Kerryman.

The late Tommy
Mangan, who died in
the summer of 1986. A
former chairman of the
Publicity Club, Tommy
joined the Irish Press
advertisement
department ten days
after the newspaper
began publication in
September, 1931. For
around 30 years, he was
assistant to Jim
Furlong. Tommy also
had the distinction of
retiring twice from the
Irish Press.
Photograph: Irish Press.

Gerry Murphy, managing director, Irish Trade and Technical Publications, Blackrock, Co Dublin. The firm was set up in 1962 and since then, has been a major force in trade publishing, although in recent years, it has become more involved in exhibitions. Gerry Murphy says: "With trade publishing in Ireland, there is always the problem of conveying to some advertising agencies the exact difference between trade and consumer press."

Fergus Farrell, managing director of Tara Publishing, Dublin, which publishes three monthly magazines, two bi-monthlies, including its latest title, Energy Ireland, two quarterlies and a dozen annuals and yearbooks.

When the Sunday
World was launched in
1973, it was the
outcome of well
authenticated research,
claims Gerry
McGuinness (right),
who started the colour
tabloid together with
Hugh McLaughlin.
"The Sunday World was
marketed like a can of
beans," says
McGuinness. Today,
the research continues,
with for instance,
substantial qualitative
research done twice a
year. The paper's
current ABC
circulation figure is
361,622, of which
83,032 copies are sold in
Northern Ireland,
20,000 more than the
Sunday News.
Advertisement sales in
the North are
"disappointing". 30
pages are changed for
the Northern editions.
Until 1975, Gerry
McGuinness oversaw
sales of the
advertisement content
of the paper; then
Michael McCormack,
the present
advertisement/
marketing director,
took over the job. When
it started in 1973, the
Sunday World offered a
full colour page for
£1,000; now, a full
colour page is £8,500.
Since 1982, Sunday
Newspapers has been a
wholly owned
subsidiary of
Independent
Newspapers and Gerry
McGuinness is the
second largest
shareholder in the
group. Before the end of

this year, the Sunday World aims to spend £100,000 on its current promotional campaign. Altogether, it spends about £200,000 a year on promotions and direct advertising, using mainly TV and radio.

The late Charles Hunniford, father of TV star Gloria Hunniford. He was advertisement manager of Morton Newspapers' Ulster Star newspaper, published at Lisburn, from 1958 until 1974. Before joining Mortons, he had worked in design and poster painting. After leaving the Ulster Star, he worked for another Morton title, the Portadown News/Times, until he retired in 1976.

Hugh Hogan, advertisement manager, Business and Finance, **the weekly business publication. He worked in Creation before joining** Business and Finance **in 1976; he is also responsible for advertising in the** Practical Farmer **and** Build **magazines.**

Jim Moraghan, advertisement manager, Institute of Public Administration, responsible for advertisement sales on such publications as the Administration Yearbook and Diary. *Photograph: Lensmen.*

Frequently, the *Irish Press* advertisement canvassers were told: "The paper is only read by penniless raparees. Its policy is not in the best interest of the consumer."

The young advertisement staff were not discouraged. They included Tommy Mangan, who joined the new paper about ten days after its first issue, leaving behind a career in the pharmaceutical trade. Dick Young, later to work in Arks and then to found his own agency, was there too, noted as an imaginative and successful salesman. Jack Dempsey had been a dedicated worker in Kenny's Advertising agency; Tommy Mangan's father Joe, for so long a canvasser on the *Dublin Evening Mail,* often used to see Dempsey working away in Kenny's. Joe Mangan remembered that Dempsey rarely lifted his head from his work, beyond a courteous nod to him. Dempsey joined the *Irish Press* just before it started.

Ironically, Blennerhassett left the *Irish Press* before long, going to Kenny's agency for a while before joining the deadly rival of the *Irish Press,* Independent Newspapers, as publicity manager. The next advertisement manager on the *Irish Press* who had been manager of the American Express office in Paris was Erskine Childers. He died in 1974 while in office as President of Ireland. Remembered Tommy Mangan: "His enthusiasm included an overwhelming interest in publicising Irish goods. To promote them, he organised a nationwide gift scheme in the

Irish Press. The prize fund exceeded many thousands of pounds and the fillip to sales of Irish-made goods had very beneficial effects for the paper." Many of Childers' original ideas were thoroughly exploited, often reaching supplement size. In April, 1933, the paper began publication of a series of Open Air supplements, reflecting another of Erskine Childers' interests. He often worked in his office at Burgh Quay until late at night, telephoning his innumerable contacts to drum up sufficient advertisement revenue for the following day's paper.

Image **magazine, launched by Kevin Kelly ten years ago as a stablemate for** Checkout, **his grocery trade publication.** Image **claims a circulation of 26,000 copies and a total readership of 283,000 an issue. Its full page colour rate is £990. Its advertisement director is Laura McDermott.**

Tony Browne, commercial manager (publications) at the Institute for Industrial Research and Standards. He has worked at the Institute since 1970 and is responsible for the advertisement content of Technology Ireland magazine and other IIRS publications. Before the IIRS, he worked for the National Publishing Group, Dublin.

SEPTEMBER 1986
£1 INC TAX 90p STG IN UK

THE BEST AND
THE BIGGEST

THE NEW WORLD
IMAGE
BUCKS AND BIZZ!

NEW YORK —
NEW GUIDE
IRISH IMMIGRANTS —
NEW CUSTOMS

SAM STEPHENSON
SKYSCRAPER HIGH

ELGY GILLESPIE
WASHINGTONED UP

FINTAN O'TOOLE
BROADWAY ANYWAY

SILVER DOLLAR GALS
DONNA KARAN
THE MAN-MAD GUGGENHEIM

PLUS
TAKING OFF AMERICA —
STYLE WISE

U.S. AND THEN ...

BARRY DEVLIN'S
IN, IN, IN-DEPTH
IRISH SURVEY

ANNE HARRIS'S
DIRTY POSTBAG

MARY MAHER'S
UNMADE BILLS

CLARE BOYLAN
RONAN SHEEHAN
JOHN BANVILLE

Advertising strategies
at Independent
Newspapers have
changed greatly over
the last 20 years,
according to Brendan
McCabe, advertisement
sales manager (right).
At one time, there were
five advertisement
managers in the Dublin
headquarters, with
Peter Finnegan in
overall charge, Jack
Lawrence on the Irish
Independent, Billy King
the features manager,
John Kane on the
Evening Herald and
Willie O'Meara on the
Sunday Independent. In
the late 1960s, Dan
Cotter played a major
rôle in developing sales
from features. From the
1970s through to the
present day, says
McCabe, features have
"gone off the boil" and
the advertisement
operation has become
more marketing
oriented. In the last two
years, there has been a
strong move towards
supplements with high
grade colour printed on
the firm's own gravure
press. The present five
weeks' lead time on
gravure printing gives
plenty of time for
reproofing to ensure
that the job is exactly
right, says McCabe.
In the old days of
advertisement sales at
Independent
Newspapers, canvassers
with much of their
salary stemming from
commission would
often earn more than
managing directors,
especially when clients
like Clery's took the

One of Erskine Childers' most intriguing exploits at the *Irish Press* is remembered by his widow, Mrs Rita Childers. Recalling that his annual salary at the paper was about £125, she tells how he went over to Dunlop in London after the firm had cancelled its advertising contract with the *Irish Press.* Dunlop's advertising director asked if he were related to the author of *The Riddle of the Sands,* which he re-read constantly. On learning that the author was in fact Erskine Childers' father, the contract was promptly reinstated.

Sometimes, events did not turn out quite as planned. On one occasion in the early days of the *Irish Press,* someone in the classified department "lifted" a death notice from the *Irish Independent* and ran it free in the Burgh Quay paper, just to help fill out the death notices' column. Unfortunately, it happened to relate to the death of one of the Murphy family from the Independent and *Irish Press* editor Frank Gallagher had to make a personal apology.

More changes in advertisement staff took place at the *Irish Press.* Erskine Childers left and was succeeded as advertisement manager by Jack Dempsey, who remained in that position until 1946. Dempsey, as a representative, had become friendly with Jim Furlong, then working in O'Kennedy Brindley. When Dempsey was promoted to advertisement manager, he asked Furlong to join the *Irish Press.* Jim Furlong needed little encouragement, since by 1935, the *Irish Press* was able to pay much more than O'Kennedy Brindley, in Furlong's recollection.

As Childers was going from the *Irish Press,* a young man called Peter Finnegan was arriving at Independent Newspapers. He joined in 1934, just as a new departure was being organised at the *Irish Independent:* advertisement features, to try and boost the amount of display advertising carried in the paper. For years, Finnegan and Billy King ran the features department. They had the help of a marvellous layout artist, Jim Creenan, who was full of ideas. Very often, Peter Finnegan travelled the country organising support for advertising features and what's more, often writing the editorial copy too! Finnegan and King were helped in their work by a block clerk called J. P. Heard, who literally knew where everything was.

Up in Belfast, the *Irish News* soon followed the example of the *Irish Press* by banning advertisements from the front page. It took years for the practice to die out altogether: in the early 1950s, the *Dublin Evening Mail* was willing to sell the whole of its front page to a single advertiser.

In the mid-1930s, Kevin Kenny of Kenny's Advertising agency (which always signed its advertisements "KAA") went on record at the Dublin Rotary Club as saying that newspapers were the only reliable method of letting the public know of the goods to be sold. His remarks came just a few months after a leading provincial newspaper, the *Anglo-Celt* of Cavan, sued Kenny's for non-payment. The agency was sued for £1,393.3.10; in court, in November, 1934, Kevin J. Kenny said that his bookkeeper had found that only £124.12.11 was due. John O'Hanlon, managing director of the *Anglo-Celt* said he had no objection

whole front page of the Irish Independent. **Now,** advertisement sales people are much more specialised, covering particular areas like property, jobs and motors, as well as agency sales and service. The specialists sell right across the three titles published in Dublin by Independent Newspapers. One representative in Cork and another in Wexford cover those areas for all three newspapers. In Dublin, apart from the specialists, the group has the city divided up into sales areas following the boundaries of postal districts. In recent times, Brendan McCabe notices a drift back to London in advertisement sales revenue, with brands like Harp shifting to London. The next major step is likely to be an updating of the telephone system used by the 22 full-time tele-ad girls.

to a 15 per cent commission. Kenny's was said to have ordered the publication of advertisements, including Government notices, in the *Anglo-Celt.* Judgment was given for the plaintiff for £1,164.4.4, with costs; it was one of the few occasions when the media successfully sued an agency.

Kenny's lost, but survived. *The Irish Times* lost much revenue because of the Spanish Civil War, which started in July, 1936. Editor R. M. Smyllie took an independent line, as fair as possible to both Republican and Nationalist sides. Many Catholic schools and colleges dropped their advertising from *The Irish Times* as a result. The *Irish Independent* was unashamedly pro-Nationalist, pro-Franco, pro-Church; it lost no advertising revenue. A brief publication in the 1930s was *Ireland Today,* launched in 1936 as a monthly review of the arts, politics and social affairs. It lasted just 22 months: a lack of advertising and pressure on newsagents and book shops not to sell what was termed a "left wing rag" at the time of the Spanish civil war forced its demise.

In Longford, a much more casual approach to advertising was about to be launched. Vincent Gill had been a garda, with no experience whatsoever of newspaper publishing. After losing a prisoner at Limerick Junction, his time in the force was numbered. In 1936, he started the single sheet *Longford News.* His approach to news reporting was decidedly erratic; when his primitive press broke down, he took a sledge hammer to it. Keeping accounts was of no great interest. When people came in with planning permission advertisements, he merely asked them to put what they could afford in the bowl on the ground. When ESB bills came up for payment, Gill did the rounds of big advertisers in the town. They were always touched at Christmas, too, being asked to pay what they thought was appropriate for the season.

Noelle Campbell-Sharp, currently publishing four magazine titles, IT, Success, Social & Personal **and** The Spirit of Ireland (**Ryanair**).

411

Magill magazine, established ten years ago, is Ireland's leading current affairs publication and claims 235,000 readers per issue.

The inimitable Danny Moroney, who retired in 1985 as group advertisement manager, Irish Press. He spent over 20 years with the Burgh Quay organisation and on his retirement his friends in Brindley Advertising presented him with this caricature.

The cover of the tenth anniversary issue of IMJ — Irish Marketing Journal. **The magazine was founded by Norman Barry and first published in April 1974.**

Irish Marketing & Advertising Journal

IMJ

Official Magazine of The Marketing Institute of Ireland   APRIL 1984

A.S.A.I. SHOWS ITS TEETH

During the period July 1983 – March 1984 175 written complaints were received by the Advertising Standards Authority for Ireland. Of these 32 per pursued and investigated.

"The Code of Advertising Standards is becoming better known and fewer contraventions are occurring", according to Kevin O'Doherty, Chief Executive of ASAI. "The ASAI 'Watchdog' advertising campaign is having a good effect. Advertising agencies are using the pre-publication vetting service to a greater extent and monitoring of advertisements by the Authority is continuing". He added that ASAI was not established to protect the advertising industry. The voluntary controls do not have the force of law but are applied speedily when needed.

It is clear that ASAI has teeth. One member was fined £2,000 for breaching the Code and two major advertising campaigns have been withdrawn following the Authority's decision that they were in violation of the Code.

The following are a cross section of the complaints received and the action taken. COMPLAINT: (a) That illustrations used in the magazine advertisement for Roankabin portrayed, inter alia, types of unit not available from the advertiser either new or second-hand. One of the units was no longer in production and another was available from the advertiser only in second-hand condition. (b) That the wording of the press advertisement implied that NEW as well as second-hand Porta-kabin units were available from the advertisers.
FINDING: The Authority regarded the advertisements as misleading and was informed that all advertisements to which reference had been made had been withdrawn and would not re-appear. No further action was deemed necessary on the part of the Authority.
COMPLAINT: Young Advertising Ltd. objected to a radio advertisement for Ilvico throat tablets on the grounds that it carried a reference to the Abbey Theatre, Dublin, no permission having been granted for any such testimonial/endorsement.
FINDING: Complaint upheld. The Authority received confirmation that the unauthorised wording had been cut. No further action was deemed necessary on the part of the Authority.
COMPLAINT: ICL through their Solicitor renewed objections to claims by Brittany Ferries in
Continued back page

Ten Years of Marketing and Advertising in Ireland

TimeWarp 1974·1984

Readers of this issue of IMJ will be forgiven if they get the feeling they're in a time warp - its our 10th. birthday issue and we're celebrating by devoting practically the whole issue to a review of the comings and goings of marketing, advertising and public relations over the past ten years.

The approach we have adopted is to review the period year by year, putting together a nostalgic scrapbook of stories and pictures from past issues of the magazine. This saga begins on page 2 and goes straight through to page 25. We have also invited the four heads of the major organisations involved in the industry at the time we began publishing in 1974 to submit an article giving their impressions of the intervening years. These articles appear from pages 26 to 33.

Its not the complete picture of ten years in Irish advertising and marketing by any means, but hopefully readers will get a general idea of the main issues, trends and personalities in the period 1974-84.

At the April Tuesday Club luncheon of the Marketing Institute were (l/r) Dr. Tim O'Driscoll, Dr. Takeda, Japanese Ambassador, the guest speaker and Phil Flood, Chairman of the Institute.

NEW COMPANY FOR GUARANTEED IRISH

As a result of a ruling by the European Court, the promotion of the Guaranteed Irish scheme can no longer be undertaken by a State agency and its function has been taken over by Guaranteed Irish Ltd. with effect from next June.

Guaranteed Irish Limited is a new independent company formed under the aegis of the Confederation of Irish Industry, to develop and promote the scheme. The activities will be funded, on an annual basis, by manufacturers using the symbol. Directors of the company represent manufacturing, retail and trade union interests. A full time Executive Director will be appointed shortly following which a strong Guaranteed Irish campaign will be undertaken in

support of Irish made products. The new company's plans for Guaranteed Irish include.
– maintenance of a register of member manufacturers and conducting spot checks on the use of the symbol.
– encouragement of all participating manufacturers to use the symbol widely in advertising, promotions and packaging
– to encourage the distributive trades to prominently display products bearing the Guaranteed Irish symbol
– to undertake imaginative consumer campaigns to sell Guaranteed Irish products.

Guaranteed Irish Ltd. are at present advertising for a new Chief Executive.

MARKETING NEWS

THE TUESDAY CLUB

The guest speaker at the Tuesday Club luncheon of the Marketing Institute of Ireland on May 1st. next will be Donal Kinsella of Dublin Gas.

He is often refered to by the press as a financial maverick due to his interest in and activity of buying into sluggish companies like Dublin Gas and Seafield Gentex.

His activities in these areas have shown him to be a particularly aggressive member at board level and his share purchases have proved very profitable.

Donal Kinsella is a hotelier by trade and runs his business affairs from The Grove Hotel, Dunleer.

The Tuesday Club luncheon is held at Jury's Hotel. Booking can be arranged by contacting the Marketing Institute at 685176/684797.

'Marketing News' on page 35 has all the M.I.I. news for this month.

THE BALLYNEETY EXPERIENCE

This year's Case Study - P.36

PMPA CHANGE AGENCY

The PMPA advertising [ ] estimated to be worth £[ ] has been won by Mc[ ] Advertising following a hot[ ] amongst at least four a[ ] who pitched for the b[ ] including O'Sullivan Rya[ ] have handled the accou[ ] number of years.

New Poster Company

Mike Beetlestone has [ ] from Regan Advertising, [ ] door poster company and [ ] up his own company Dist[ ] Services.

The new company h[ ] offices at Leopardstow[ ] Park and intends to trad[ ] area of outdoor advertisin[ ]

We understand that[ ] director of Regan's, [ ] Beetlestone's equity st[ ] been bought out in retu[ ] number of Regan sites [ ] gives the new company a[ ] late holding.

HOTEL & CATERING REVI[ ] BAKERY WORLD

Serving the food and hospitality industries

WANT TO KNOW MOR[ ]
Contact Ian Collie
Advertisement Manager

Jemma

TELEPHONE 886946

dublin opinion

June 1969   The National Humorous Journal of Ireland   2s.

Dublin Opinion **was** founded shortly after the Treaty by C. K. Kelly and Arthur Booth. In its heyday issues sold over 60,000 copies. It was one of Ireland's most influential magazines.

Sneem- c'est moi

415

In the 1930s, Victor Salter, working for the thoroughly organised *Belfast Telegraph* since World War I, when he joined the advertisement staff at the request of Sir Robert Baird, was active as honorary secretary of the Advertising Club in Northern Ireland. He also had lifelong honorary membership of the Poor Richard Club in Philadelphia, one of the largest organisations of advertising people in the world. Salter organised the publicity for the British Empire Weeks that ran in Belfast from 1927 until 1933, was first chairman of the publicity committee of the Ulster Tourist Development Association and a member of the Ulster Savings Council's publicity committee.

Jimmy O'Shea, who worked in the advertisement department of *The Irish Times* for many years until his retirement in 1982, remembers that in the late 1930s, staff in the department often had to work until 8 p.m., with no overtime payments. Benny Greene was about the only person who would willingly work round the clock. Church services were advertised much more extensively in those days, enjoying special nominal rates.

Earl Connolly, the jovial, bow-tied veteran of the *Limerick Leader*, joined the paper in 1937. He had been designing posters for concerts and school film performances as early as 1932, so when he joined the staff of the paper, he was given the task of improving the entertainments pages. Very shortly, he introduced the first ever feature page in the paper on a local carnival, designed cinema advertisements which

The cover of the advertisement rate card for *Cara* magazine.

416

drew favourable comments from both British and American film companies and tackled the advertising of the dance scene: orchestras kept local ballrooms full with patrons. All this "entertainment" type of advertising was built up in the *Limerick Leader,* years before many other newspapers followed suit. Of all the members of staff with the *Limerick Leader* before World War II, Earl Connolly is the only one still there in 1986. Meanwhile, Paddy Montford was preparing to launch his own publishing company. Montford Publications, which he did in 1939, towards the end of his active involvement with *Dublin Opinion.* In 1938, Tom Grehan retired from Independent Newspapers. He was described by P. L. McEvoy, of McEvoy's Advertising Service, as one of the forerunners of modern advertising efficiency. Grehan is also remembered for being a kind, generous man with a big heart, not always a notable attribute of the newspaper world.

With Grehan's retirement, an era was coming to an end. Already Denis Garvey had moved, in 1938, from the *East Coast* newspaper run by John Flynn, where he was a reporter, along with J. J. McCann, founder of the *Radio Review.* Garvey left the newspaper business for good, beginning his long involvement with Janus, the advertising agency. With the advent of World War II in September, 1939, and the beginning of the Emergency, many facets of newspaper life, including advertising, were set to change.

As the war built up, the rationing of newsprint became more and

Seamus McBride, Letterkenny-based advertisement sales representative for the Donegal Democrat. **Recently, the newspaper strengthened its editorial and sales operation in Letterkenny.** *Photograph: Donegal Democrat.*

Cara Advertising Rates 1986

ngus inflight magazine, is published every two months, on
ay of January, March, May, July, September and November.
magazine is placed in the seat pockets on all aircraft for the
the airline's two and a quarter million passengers per year.
flies scheduled, commuter and charter services to over fifty
destinations in Ireland, Britain, Continental Europe,
North Africa and the U.S.A.

CARA

the travel magazine of Aer Lingus Irish Airlines

YOUR
PERSONAL
COPY

418

more stringent. By 1941, it was very severe and while the main Dublin newspapers — all departments, including advertisements — contributed to the formation of an LSF unit, the size of newspapers was drastically cut back. For most of the war, the *Irish Independent* was reduced in size to six or eight pages. Display advertisements normally went in either the A or the B editions, but not both. Classifieds went in both. Similar restrictions applied on all the provincial papers as well; the *Enniscorthy Echo* printed a "pup", a half page insert filled with advertisements. Advertisers weren't keen, since they said it looked too much like a poster. In the *Irish Independent,* big scale advertisement features had to be suspended for the duration. It was a time when advertisers plied advertisement staff with all kinds of favours: bottles of whiskey were often slipped under the counter. It was the last time that advertisers had to beg to get into newspapers. One advertiser told Jim Furlong of the *Irish Press:* "You'll be on your hands and knees when this is over". In 1942, the *Irish Press* made a profit of £16,548. Annie Roycroft, long-time editor of the *Spectator* newspaper in Bangor, Co. Down, remembers that during the war, one trip into Belfast each week by the advertisement manager used up the entire petrol allocation. Further trips had to be made by bicycle.

Before the rationing got too severe, the *Weekly Irish Times* was transformed into the *Times Pictorial,* in 1941, the handiwork of George Burrows and Eddie MacSweeney. The only major newspaper launch during the Emergency was that of the *Argus* in Drogheda, by the Stanleys in 1943. It had been dormant since the late 1930s, but Joe Stanley happened to be a great friend of Eamon de Valera, considered a help when it came to newsprint supplies. Otherwise, newspaper advertising people didn't have much to do: endless rounds of coffee in Bewleys and other city centre restaurants and quite frequent trips to Bundoran. No wonder that people in the business had sufficient time to get the Advertising Press Club off to a flying start in 1942.

In July, 1943, the Advertising Press Club managed to scrounge enough paper to start producing a four page newsletter, which was newsy and gossipy. Sadly, the AP club's publishing stamina was not to last long much beyond the end of the war.

The very first issue informed readers that (Sir) Kenneth Murphy "was taking unto himself a wife", a young lady called Mollie Smith, while Niel O'Kennedy, brother of Desmond O'Kennedy, was reported cartooning for *Dublin Opinion.* Then years later, he was to do the same for *The Irish Times.* In the autumn of that year, it was reported that Victor Salter, advertisement director of the *Belfast Telegraph* was going to give a talk on a "Newspaper in the Emergency". It was a real emergency for his paper, far more than for any of the Dublin newspapers, for in April, 1941, during the great German blitz of Belfast, the offices of the *Belfast Telegraph* were severely damaged. Yet by the following day, the paper was printing its own editions and those of the other three Belfast newspapers, the *Irish News, Newsletter* and

Horace Denham, who died in early 1985. He first joined The Irish Times in December, 1934; he rejoined the newspaper in 1960 after a break of some years when he was with the Irish Press group. At the time of his death, he was London advertisement manager for The Irish Times. *Photograph: The Irish Times.*

Opposite page: Cover of the first issue of Cara magazine, January-March, 1968.

419

John Allen (above) is
administrator of Cara,
the inflight magazine of
Aer Lingus edited by
Bernard Share. The
first issue, edited by
Gordon Clark, was
published in January,
1968; for the previous
two years, it had been
inset into Ireland of the
Welcomes. For the first
ten years of its
existence, Cara was
quarterly. In 1978, it
went bi-monthly. The
first advertisement
manager was Kevin
Dunne, who died
recently. He had to sell
the early issues to
agencies with few back-
up figures. Aer Lingus
was one of the first
airlines in the world to
publish its own inflight
magazine. Now, Cara
has an annual
advertisement revenue
of around £400,000, 90
per cent of which is
generated within
Ireland. 55,000 copies
are produced of each

Northern Whig, all of whose printing presses had been put out of action.

In early 1944, O'Kennedy Brindley managed to book space for itself on the leader page of *The Irish Times,* a 5" single column, in which it rang the copy changes every Saturday — on its own behalf. Said the *AP Newsletter:* "Let's hope its clients don't ask for the same!" Meanwhile, Jim Furlong of the *Irish Press* remarked that "the newspaper representative should be an ambassador of goodwill, whom the advertiser will be glad to see from time to time. All the facts, circulation, reader interest, special articles, area of circulation, can be administered in small doses when a suitable opportunity arises. High pressure salesmanship is out — I know of no business in which it can do more harm than in space selling for a daily newspaper." By April, 1945, there were the first faint signs of the easing of newsprint restrictions: the daily papers were allowed to produce three six page papers a week. The *Irish Independent* carried virtually no display advertising towards the end of the war: by early 1945, it was carrying up to 90 advertisements in a six page issue. Newspapers even had enough space to publish 8" double column advertisements. Other transformations were on the way: for much of the Emergency, Tom Kelly, who ran an advertising agency called Kelly's (Peter Owens was there at the end of the war) also did a very popular magazine called *Barracks Variety.* soon, it reverted to its civilian title, *Passing Variety,* before vanishing for ever.

Paddy Montford, who had taken over the *Leinster Express* in 1943, died in 1947. One of Montford's first acts when he took over the *Leinster Express* in 1943 had been to increase the advertising rates. The linage rate was said to have jumped overnight from 5d to 5/-. Advertisers were outraged; Beecham's Pills, which had a 3" double column every week, eventually cancelled its standing order. The editorial side of the newspaper had been run by his nephew Gordon Clark, himself destined to die tragically young. When Clark first arrived, he was subjected to a barrage of creditors, who sought payment of a great many bills. Under the old regime, traders in Portlaoise had exchanged goods and services for free advertising in the paper. Now, they wanted some of the cash they were also owed. Meanwhile, Terry Spillane was taking the step that marked out the rest of his career. Just before the war, he had worked briefly as editor and advertisement manager on the *Shoe Trades' Journal,* which Harry O'Brien of Arrow had started. Before long, O'Brien sold the magazine to Basil Clancy of *Hibernia* fame. Spillane was then involved in the launch of the *Hardware and Allied Trader* magazine; after doing a successful advertisement feature on the new Galway Technical College for *The Irish Times,* general manager John Dockery asked the young Spillane to join the newspaper. He stayed with it for most of the war. Not long after the return of peace, he became a full partner in the hardware magazine. The editor and co-publisher then was J. G. McCaul. Over the next 40 years, under Spillane's guidance, it turned out to be one of the most consistently successful of all trade magazines in Ireland. Terry Spillane is now

Heralding a great evening

THIS EVENING, we launch the Evening Herald on an exciting new course with the change of format to compact, modern tabloid.

We would like to say a fresh hello to the many thousands of loyal readers who have contributed to the paper's recent upsurge and to welcome the host of new readers who we feel sure will be joining us in the days ahead.

After months of painstaking research and probing, we bring you this evening the sort of newspaper which

BIG NAMES in your Herald tabloid . . . John Feeney, Kevin Marron, John Comyn, Helen Rogers, Ronan Farren and Kerry McCarthy.

you, the readers, have told us you want.

We will continue to bring editorial services on which our recent success has been built—the real difference is that it will be coming to

you in a contemporary, convenient format.

This is the sort of format which will allow us to bring you more.

What you see today—and we're confident that you will like what you see—is just the

beginning.

It is phase one of an exciting programme in the editorial development of the Evening Herald.

We would like you to stay with us. In fact, we are confident that you will.

Evening Herald

LATEST ★

Friday, Oct. 1, 1982, Vol. 91. No. 229. Price 23p

SATELLITE TV COUP BY RTE

By JAMES MORRISSEY

RTE are involved in a massive £200 million deal to launch satellite television in Ireland, Britain and Europe.

'Rape' stars still held

TWO British footballers were still being held by police in Sweden today after a 20-year-old nurse alleged she had been raped by them.

The two Southampton players Steve Moran and Mark Wright who were arrested yesterday at Norrkoping airport as the team prepared to fly home, can be held for up to five days without being charged.

Both players were believed to have gone out for drinks with colleagues after the fifth division 0-0 draw with Southampton's Wednesday.

The girl said she had met them at the Palace nightclub in Norrkoping and later went back to their room at the Esso Motel where she claimed she had been raped by four men.

Chief Insp. Lev. Nattauld said: "We have just started our investigations and we are continuing our interview with the girl.

"She claims that she was raped by four men and has claimed that these two players were among them, after she identified them."

And the Government are to receive a special report on the proposals from the Chairman of the RTE Authority, Mr. Fred O'Donovan, within a matter of weeks.

If the deal is clinched RTE would beat the BBC and ITV to satellite television — and increase their revenue by £18 million a year.

Mr. O'Donovan and RTE's director general, Mr. George Waters, have secured an orbital position and five television channels by international agreement, from the European Broadcasting Union.

Top secret negotiations between RTE's top two executives have been taking place over the past few months and broadcasting bodies in the United States, Soviet Union and England, it was learned today.

Mr. O'Donovan confirmed the details of the project to the Evening Herald. And he also outlined the plan at a meeting of the RTE Authority at Montrose today.

"We have the talents, we have the facilities — what we need now is the money to finance the project," said Mr. O'Donovan. "What we intend to do is to sell four of the television channels and we're already been approached by interests in England, Spain and Portugal".

"We also would hope to sell one of the channels to an Irish-American consortium and we will keep the fifth channel for RTE. In that way the huge project would be completely self-financing without any burden being placed on the taxpayer", Mr. O'Donovan said.

"We believe that we can be first with satellite television our orbital position will have a 'footprint' which will cover Britain, thus giving the RTE satellite channel a potential to reach almost 20 million homes" explained Mr. O'Donovan.

In recent weeks, a special department has been set up at RTE to deal with future planning with satellite television as the top priority for the station.

"Getting an orbital position and television channels like this is like striking oil," declared the RTE Chairman.

It is understood that a consortium of businessmen have approached RTE with a view to buying one of the channels.

Cab man has throat slit

The 16-inch butcher's knife which was used in the attack on Dublin taxidriver, Brendan Losty.

By RAY MANAGH and PAUL THOMAS

A DUBLIN taxi driver was in hospital today with his throat slit — for a mere £20 theft.

Father - of - two, Brendan Losty, came within a millimetre of death when a butcher's knife was drawn across his neck.

Brendan, of The Dingle, Woodfarm Acres, Palmerstown, is recovering in St. James's Hospital following emergency surgery.

Three teenagers who hired him for a short fare turned into potential killers within minutes.

He lifted the youths at the junction of Dolphin Road and Herberton Road on Dublin's southside. They asked him to take them to Bluebell.

But at Davitt Road one of the youths, sitting in the rear, arm-locked the driver and pushed the knife knife against his throat.

He ordered Mr. Losty (24) to stop and hand over his takings . . . amount-

Mrs. Bernadette Losty talks to reporter Ray Managh.

ing to a £5 note and 15 £1 notes.

As the knife-man left the taxi he drew the razor-sharp blade across Mr. Losty's throat, leaving a deep gash.

Miraculously, the knife did not sever any vital artery.

The blood-stained weapon was being fingerprinted at Kilmainham Garda Station. Forensic experts will search the Peugeot taxi for clues.

A hospital spokesman said Mr. Losty was now "quite satisfactory".

Ad Lib—Pages 26 and 27. What's On—Page 18. TV and Radio—28, 29. Sport starts on Page 44.

issue; the largest issue to date contained 128 pages. Competition to the magazine now comes from Visitor, produced quarterly by Donal McAuliffe's Transworld Advertising and The Spirit of Ireland, the Ryanair magazine produced by Noelle Campbell-Sharp.

Since the Evening Herald was changed from broadsheet to tabloid in October, 1982, a major effort has been made in boosting linage revenue, through coupons, special promotions and offers, such as that giving three lines for three nights for £5. Extensive radio advertising, devised by Hunter's, has also played an important part. Before the Evening Herald went tabloid, it had 32 per cent of the Dublin evening newspaper classified market. Now, it claims 52 per cent. About 80 per cent of the Evening Herald's classified revenue comes in by 'phone.

retired; the magazine is run by Jemma Publications, but Spillane is still consultant. Other magazines came and went: Peter Owens was advertisement manager on a publication called Feature, modelled on Life magazine, full of news features and photographs. In 1947, yet another magazine was launched, Air Travel. Priced at 1/-, it was published by CA Publications of 194 Pearse Street and featured extensive use of two colours on its editorial pages. Air travel may have been taking off

Domas placed a full page, full colour advertisement for Chadwicks, the hardware firm, in the first issue of the Daily News, on October 7, 1982. The leader by editor Jim Farrelly promised: "We are here to win". The paper lasted for just 15 issues; it was Hugh McLaughlin's last publishing venture.

after the war, but this magazine belly flopped shortly afterwards. January, 1947, saw J. J. McCann launch *Wit* magazine; its art editor was Niel O'Kennedy. With *Dublin Opinion* still going strong and selling 55,000 copies an issue, the market could not bear another magazine of similar genre.

One of the big successes of the immediate post-war years was *Radio Review*, founded by J. J. McCann in March, 1946. Soon, its circulation climbed to 35,000 a week. David Luke, closely associated with its early advertising and circulation success, said in early 1949 that the magazine could reach the 100,000 circulation mark once paper restrictions had been eased.

Other areas of magazine publishing flourished after the war. The *Irish Catholic* and the *Standard* both flourished, while the *Father Mathew Record* was described by David Luke as having perhaps the widest appeal. Altogether, Ireland boasted some 25 religious magazines, weekly, monthly and quarterly, all good advertising "vehicles". Various

"Digest" publications did well, after the style of the *Reader's Digest*. The short-lived *Woman's Digest* was launched in the summer of 1947, while the main part of the women's magazine market was held by *Woman's Life*.

Surprisingly, the trade press flourished. Trade publishing may seem to have been a new growth in the last ten years, but in 1949, there were no fewer than 49 titles in existence. One of the few to survive in its original title has been the *Hardware and Allied Trader;* others such as *Irish Industry,* published by McEvoy's Publishing, an offshoot of the agency, have long gone. One of the many general interest titles launched just after the war is happily still going in 1986: *Social and Personal,* run by Noelle Campbell-Sharp since late 1984. It came as competition to Wilson Hartnell's *Irish Tatler & Sketch,* described then as "Ireland's premier social monthly". Mick Clarke, in the 1930s, with the *Irish Press* advertisement department and advertisement manager of *The Irish Times* until 1948 (it was the first time the newspaper had an advertisement manager designated as such), became the advertisement manager of the new *Social and Personal* magazine.

Terry Gogan, who started his career with McConnell's, worked on the *Western Daily Press* in Bristol before coming home to work in Irish publishing. Parkside Press and Mellifont Publications were merged to form Castle Publications and Gogan remembers that when he was with Castle, it was handling 39 publications, such as the *Chamber of Commerce Journal* and the BEA guides to Ireland. After four years with Castle, Gogan set up his own firm, Maxwell Publicity, which has several publications, including *Old Moore's Almanac*. Says Terry Gogan: "If a client hasn't got an agency, I love doing the ads for them. Very few of our advertisements are printer's layouts".

At the *Standard* in the late 1940s, May Kneafsey was in charge of the commercial side; in those days, it was rare to find a woman in an executive position in advertising or publishing. The advertisement manager of the *Standard* through the late 1940s and 1950s was Malachy O'Gorman, a tall ranchy Armagh man, with an immaculate knowledge of advertising procedures: he had once been advertising manager at Pims' department store. His assistant was Billy McFeely, also from the northern part of the country (Donegal). The two made quite a pair of characters. One of the best happenings on the *Standard* was in 1951, when Dr Noel Browne was Minister for Health and determined to bring in the Mother and Child scheme. Working on the paper at the time was young Frank Chambers, for so long creator of the limericks for O'Dearest mattresses, who went to the Department of Health to show officials there the rearranged layout he had done of an advertisement they had had in *The Irish Times*. They agreed to run the ad as a half page in the *Standard:* needless to remark, after the advertisement was published, there was an unholy row, since the Catholic Hierarchy was so opposed to the scheme, eventually forcing Browne's resignation.

Anois

Iml. 3　Uimh. 2.　14 M. Fómhair '86　40p CBL air) (30p Stg)

FAISEAN TRÍD AN bPOST

SEAICÉAD leathair, blús i viscos agus triús leathair as catalóg nua Kay Selections, an comhlacht postdíola.

SINN FÉIN AR TÍ SCOILTE

le Seosamh Mac Thomáis

-Tionól Ráth Cairn ina chúliarracht réitigh

TÁ tromlach na gceannairí óga i nGluaiseacht na Poblachta, i mBéal Feirste ach go háirithe, meáite ar sheasamh traidisiúnta Shinn Féin maidir le haitheantas a thabhairt do Dháil Éireann a athrú go bunúsach.

Tabharfaidh siad aghaidh ar sheanfhondúirí an Pháirtí ar mian leo cloí leis an seasamh traidisiúnta baghcait ag Ard-Fheis an Pháirtí an mhí seo chugainn.

Dar le foinsí taobh istigh den ghluaiseacht tá sé cinnte go n-éireoidh leo agus go mbeidh iarrthóirí agus lipéid Shinn Féin á gcaitheamh acu ag seasamh sa chéad toghchán eile sa Phoblacht.

Glacann an cheannasaíocht nua, agus an tUachtarán nua Shinn Féin, Gearóid Mac Adaim, Feisire tofa d'iarthar Bhéal Feirste, gur ga dearcadh nua de chineál éigin a chur chun cinn, má tá Sinn Féin le dul chun cinn i gcúrsaí toghchánaíochta sna 26 chontae.

Níl muintir Shinn Féin ar aon intinn faoin scéal, áfach, go háirithe an dream is mó a raibh baint acu le bunú na heite eite Oifigiúil le polasaí páirtíochta sa Dáil i 1969.

Ó thaobh mhuintir an tuaiscirt de, is iad muintir Shinn Féin sna 26 chontae fein — an dream a mbeifí ag brath orthu le dul mbun an fheachtais urnua atá á lua — is mó atá in aghaidh athraithe.

Tá cuid mhór den dream traidisiúnta seo ag tarraingt na gcos cheana féin mar nach bhfuil siad sásta leis an treo ina bhfuil cúrsaí ag gluaiseacht ó thuaidh.

Meiriceá

Tá siad ag rá nach féidir aon athrú den chineál atá beartaithe a dhéanamh toisc nach mbeadh an lucht taca i Meiriceá sásta leis an athrú agus go dtitfeadh an Ghluaiseacht ar fad

Go Lch. 2

RTÉ FAILLITHEACH GO FÓILL

le Fiach de Paor

Lark mar chlár Gaeilge.

CÉ go bhfuil ceannairí na n-eagras Gaeilge sásta le gné amháin de sceideal teilifíse RTÉ don Fhómhar tá an-mhíshásamh orthu faoin bhfailli atá déanta arís ag RTÉ i solathar clár Gaeilge do pháistí. Agus is bocht leo go n-áiríonn RTÉ *The Mountain*

Tá fáilte á cur roimh an iriscláir nua a bheidh ar siúl i ndiaidh Nuacht a 8 gach oíche ó Mháirt go hAoine le cur le *Súil Thart* an Luain ag an am sásúil céanna.

Ní bheidh aon chlár dá leithéidí á chraoladh De Sathairn ná Dé Domhnaigh.

— rud nach bhfuil ag teacht le ráiteas a thug Stiúrthóir na gClár Teilifíse ar 9 Feabhra nuair a gheall sé clár Gaeilge gach weeknight san Fhómhar.

Tar éis na moille gan leithscéal de thrí bliana cuirfear fáilte roimh Super Ted ina leagan Gaeilge — gheall Muiris Mac Conghail i 1983 go mbeadh an clár úd do pháistí á chraoladh gan mhoill níos deine dúirt sé gur chuir osclaíochtaí teilifíse le nuachláracht an mholta mholta ar an astriúcháil — ag am nuair a bhí an tsraith á craoladh Bhéarlacha eagsúla ar fud an domhain!

Tá Dáin Ó Domhnas le craoladh arís — agus gan ann ach an cúpla nóiméad nach aon chrotromaí iad ar a mbeidh á chraoladh i mBéarla do pháistí. Agus nár chuid de sin beidh leath uair a chloig de Dún Front lar Fein tá Breiefá)

Na FÍRÉIN sa Harcourt Hotel anocht

Cúira an racghrúpa Ghaelaigh agus a gceirnín nua faoi chaibidil ag Ruaidhrí Ó Baille ar Lch 8-9.

Leabhar nua conspóideach chugainn ó

Noel Browne.
Proinsias Mac Aonghuis — Lch 10.

Noel Browne.

An bhfuair do chairde airgead ó Údarás na Gaeltachta anuraidh?

Sonraí iomlána ar Lch 15.

424

THE IRISH TIMES, SATURDAY, MAY 31, 1986 C

Solid Citizens!
The printer with the 2 year guarantee from
GRAFTEL
Graftel Limited, Unit 1 Enterprise Centre, Pearse Street, Dublin 2
Telephone (01) 712344 Telex 90943 GRAF Fax 712352

BIRTHS, MARRIAGES AND DEATHS

...es in this column must be authenticated. Minimum 2 lines per insertion.

BIRTHS

... — May 27, 1986, at the ...e Hospital, to Patience (née ...) and Norman, of Malahide, a ...obin John Charles), a brother ...liam.

...T — May 19, 1986, at ... Carmel Hospital, to Fiona ...McGlone) and Richard, a ...er (Rachel), a sister for ... David and Ruth.

... — May 17, 1986, in the ...e Hospital, to Linda (neé ... and Kevin, a son, David ..., a welcome brother for Paul.

...Y — May 17, 1986, to Ita ...laguire) and John, a daughter ... Clare), a sister for Peter and ... Deo Gratis.

...N—O'MAHONY — May ...86, Breda and Frank are ...ed to announce the birth of ...aughter Carol Ann.

... - May 24, 1986, in Arizona, ...to Patricia (née O'Mahony) ...n, a son (Michael James), a ... for Christopher and Melissa.

...Y — May 5, 1986, at Holles ... to Catherine (née Cooper) ...ack, a daughter (Elaine ...ne Anne), a sister for Sarah ...ara. Deo gratias.

...RICK — May 17, 1986, to ...ny (née Kinlay) and Allan, a ...onathan), a brother for Simon ...ndrew.

...N — May 24, 1986, in Holles ...Hospital, to Paula (née Wiley) ...ive, a son, (David Clive), a ... for Susan.

...NA — May 5, 1986, at ... Medical Centre, The New ...Hospital, New York, to Eavan ...Oliver, a second daughter ...rine Sheelagh). Buiochas le ...

... — May 19, 1986, at St. ... God, Newry, to Gillian (née ...ge) and James, a beautiful ...er (Jane), a pal for Alison. ...ratias.

...VE — May 21, 1986, to ... (née Elliott) and Pat, a baby ...illian). Deo Gratias.

...E-SCHEERDER — May ...86, Worcester, Massachusetts. ...ts and Janpieter, a daughter ...).

...RD-STEVENSON — May ...86, Sydney, Australia, to ... and Gordon, a son (Rowan), ...er for Julia and Daniel, great-...on and grandson of Madame ... Schlumberger, Paris, and Dr ...rs R. D. Stevenson, Dublin.

... — May 28, 1986, to Jackie ...arroll) and Jim, a beautiful ...er (PollyAnna), a sister for ...ain and Lucie (in heaven). ...atias.

...R — May 24, 1986, at St. ...'s, London, to Judith and ..., a daughter (Georgina ...

MARRIAGES

...UR—BERGEN — Judy ...s were married on April 19, ...onton.

...TILSON — The marriage ...ce between Hugh and Patri-... May 2., 1986, in Newcastle-...me.

DEATHS

...LL (Church Street ...non, Co. Clare) — May 2... at Our Lady's Hospice, ...s Cross, Dublin, Ellen, relict ...ael Carroll and daughter of ... Denis and Mary Vaughan; ...regretted by her son, daugh-...er, son-in-law, grandchildren, ...s, nieces, relatives and ... R.I.P. Remains will leave ... after 12 noon Mass in Our ...Hospice Church, this (Satur-...iving Ennistymon Church at ...nately 7.15 o'c. Concele-...Mass tomorrow (Sunday) at ... Funeral afterwards to ...glonane Cemetery. Ameri-...d English papers, please ...

... (Bray) — May 30, 1986 ...lly), at the Richmond Hos-...ublin, Timothy John (Tim), ... eldest son of Frank and ...adly missed by his parents, ... and brothers Michaella, ... Owen, Noreen and Declan, ...rents, family and friends. ...Removal this (Saturday) even-... hospital to the Church of ...st Holy Redeemer, Bray, ... 5.30 o'c. Funeral on Mon-...t, after 11 o'c. Requiem ... Dean's Grange Cemetery.

... (Dublin and Kilrush) — ..., 1986, at his home, Glasnevin ...ohn J. (Jack) (late of E.S.B.), ...nd dearly loved husband and ...deeply regretted by his wife ... daughters Elizabeth and ..., sons-in-law, grandsons, ...sister-in-law, relatives and ... R.I.P. Funeral today (Satur-...after 11 o'c. Mass from ... of Our Lady of Victory, ...an Road, to Balgriffin ...y.

... (Kenmare, Co. Kerry) — ..., 1986, at Mount Carmel ..., Dublin, Liam (retired ...céile ionmhain Shighle (nach ...n); deeply regretted by his ...relatives and friends. R.I.P. ... today (Saturday) to Holy ...hurch, Kenmare, arriving at ... p.m., via Mallow-...e-Kilgarvan. Funeral tomor-...unday) to Old Kenmare, ...y after 11.30 Mass.

... Naas) — May 29, 1986 (after ...llness, bravely borne), in the ...are of the Sisters and staff of ...ady's Hospice, Harold's ...Dr. Mary Ita, 10 Woodlands, ...and late of Athlone and ...); very deeply regretted by ...band Joseph, daughter Ann, ...rmot, Conor and Brendan, ...er Eithne, brother-in-law, ...s-in-law, son-in-law, grand-... relatives and friends. Rest ... Funeral today (Saturday), ... o'c. Mass in Our Lady's ... Chapel, to St. Corban's ..., Naas, arriving at 12.30 ...ox. House private.

...ICK (Dublin) — May 30 ... Dr. Steevens's Hospital, ...early loved wife of John, 18 ...ds Park, Terenure, and ...mum of Arthur, Killian and ...adly mourned by her sister, ... brothers-in-law and sisters-... May she rest in peace ... to Terenure College, ...arriving 5 o'c. this (Satur-...ening. Funeral on Monday ...ter 10 o'c. Mass to ...oreena Cemetery. House ...

... (née Murphy) — May 30, ... The Stiles Road, Clontarf. ... (Kitty), much loved by ...band George, son John, ..., the late June McGrath ...rjorie Tierney, sons-in-law ...nd Michael, daughter-in-law ...nd her 12 grandchildren, all ...ved by her. Rest in peace. ... from Kirwan's Funeral ...Fairview, at 5.15 o'c. today ...ay), to St. Anthony's ... Clontarf, arriving 5.30 o'c. ... Monday next after 10 o'c. ... Dean's Grange Cemetery.

DEATHS

LEWIS (John Street, Kilkenny) — May 29, 1986 (unexpectedly), at St. Luke's Hospital, William C. (Billy), much loved husband of Louie and devoted father of Geraldine; sadly missed by his loving brothers, sisters-in-law, nephews, nieces, neighbours and very many friends. Funeral to St. Kieran's Cemetery, following Service in St. John's Church at 4 o'c. today (Saturday). "Resting where no shadows falls."

McDONNELL (née **Conkley**) (Dublin) — May 29, 1986, at St. Vincent's Private Hospital, Patricia (Patsy), late of Rostrevor Road, Rathgar, beloved wife of Jeff and mother of Bairbre; sadly mourned by her husband, daughter, brother, sister, son-in-law and grandchildren. Rest in peace. Funeral today (Saturday) after 10 o'c. Mass in St Joseph's Church, Terenure, to Templeogue Cemetery. House private.

McVEIGH (Killiney, Co. Dublin) — May 29, 1986 (peacefully), at his home, Beech Court, Eugene, beloved husband of Kathleen and father of Eugene, Brendan, Paul and Claire; deeply mourned by his loving wife, children, mother, brother, sisters-in-law, brothers-in-law, relatives and friends. R.I.P. Funeral today (Saturday), after 11 o'c. Requiem Mass in St. Stephen's Church, Killiney, to Dean's Grange Cemetery.

MULLIGAN (Bray and Swinford, Co. Mayo) — May 29, 1986 (suddenly), at the Presbytery, Queen of Peace, Bray, Rev. John Mary, S.J.; very deeply regretted by his Community, relatives and parishioners. Rest in peace. Funeral today (Saturday), after 11 o'c. Concelebrated Mass in Church of Our Lady Queen of Peace, to Glasnevin Cemetery.

WILSON — May 24, 1986, at The Royal Alexandra Hospital, Edmonton, Alberta, Canada, John, formerly of The Rise, Mount Merrion, Dublin; sadly missed by his wife and family.

SHIELS (Dublin) — May 30, 1986, at St. Joseph's, Kilcroney, Co. Wicklow, Joseph, B.A., H.Dip.Ed. (N.T., former Principal of Star of The Sea N.S., Sandymount); deeply regretted by his only surviving brother Nicholas, relatives and friends. R.I.P. Interment today (Saturday) at Holmpatrick Cemetery, Skerries, Co. Dublin, following 10 o'c. Mass in St. Joseph's, Kilcroney.

ACKNOWLEDGMENTS

MARPER — Mrs Anne Marper wishes to thank all those who sympathised with her on the death of her beloved husband, Ernest, those who attended and took part in the funeral service, those who sent flowers, letters or Mass cards. A special 'thank you' to the doctors and staff of Hampstead Private Hospital, for their kindness and support during the past two years.

RYAN (Dun Laoghaire) — The family of the late Walter M. Ryan wish to thank all those who sympathised with them in their recent bereavement, those who attended the removal of the remains, Mass and funeral, those who sent Mass cards and floral tributes. We trust this will be accepted by all as a token of our appreciation. The Holy Sacrifice of the Mass will be offered for your intentions.

IN MEMORIAM

BATEMAN — With loving thanks to our God-given Mother and Father, from Ken and Beryl.

CULLINANE — Sarah (Sadie), loved and remembered always.
—Helen.

CURLEY (Eleanor Margaret) (Forty-ninth Anniversary) — In ever loving memory of our darling mother.
— Kitty and Nellie.

DONNELLAN Second Anniversary) — In loving memory of Eileen, late of O'Connell Ave., Limerick, who died June 1st, 1984. R.I.P.
—Frances and Frank.

ELLISON (First Anniversary) — Betty, late of Corballis, Rathdrum, died June 1, 1985. Remembered with affection by her husband William, Fiona and John.
"To where you rest, we travel,
it's where we are most near
we place our flowers around you
and whisper we are here."

FINNAMORE (Rev. A.J. (Bart) — June 1, 1984. Always in our thoughts, never forgotten.
—Joan and family.

JOHNSTON (George) — Lovingly remembered.
—Bobbie and Eva.

JORDAN — Treasured and beautiful memories of our only little girl, Alison (aged 12). Second anniversary occurs today. Sadly missed.
—Daddy, Mammy, brothers David and Philip.

LYNCH — In loving memory of Harry Lynch, Lucan, died May 31, 1978. Always remembered by his wife and family.

McCABE (Alasdair) — May 31, 1972, and his wife Norrie, March 27, 1976.
"Love's greatest gift — remembrance."

OWENS — Treasured memories of our Simon.
—Mum, Dad, David, Tim and Aisling.

RICHARDSON — Cherished memories of dear Dad, May 31, 1955.
—Beryl and Jean.

RICHARDSON — Treasured memories of Bertie, May 31, 1955. Philippians 1.3.

PERSONAL

ANYONE FOR TENNIS?

MURPHY'S IRISH STOUT

now being served at

THE LAWNS

BALLYFERMOT

PERSONAL

THE DEER PARK

The Murphy's Irish Stout Season starts here.

THE DEER PARK
CLONSKEAGH

IT'S ARRIVED!

We're proud to announce the arrival of

MURPHY'S IRISH STOUT

at

VAL HATTON'S

DRIMNAGH

EUREKA!

We've just discovered

MURPHY'S IRISH STOUT

at

BELLAMY'S
OF BALLSBRIDGE

MURPHY'S
IRISH STOUT
TRADITION IN THE MAKING.

GET YOUR TALONS ROUND . . .

. . . a pint of

MURPHY'S IRISH STOUT

at . . .

THE KESTREL,

WALKINSTOWN

MURPHY'S IRISH STOUT
Tradition in the making.

PADDY'S DAY?

We're proud to announce the arrival of

MURPHY'S IRISH STOUT

at

PADDY CULLEN'S
BALLSBRIDGE

MURPHY'S IRISH STOUT
Tradition in the making.

LIGHTING UP TIME
IN HAROLD'S CROSS.

THE LANTERN

is aglow with

MURPHY'S IRISH STOUT

MURPHY'S IRISH STOUT
Tradition in the making.

WILD HORSES . . .

. . . couldn't tear a

MURPHY'S IRISH STOUT
man away from

THE COACH HOUSE
BALLINTEER

PERSONAL

IF YOU'VE BEEN
LOOKING FOR IT

WE'VE FOUND IT

MURPHY'S IRISH STOUT

THE FOXHUNTER
LUCAN

NO COUNTY COUNCIL
NECESSARY!

It was a unanimous decision.

MURPHY'S IRISH STOUT

now on tap at

THE COUNTY BAR
DECIES ROAD,
BALLYFERMOT

MURPHY'S
IRISH
STOUT

Tradition in the making.

OPEN ALL HOURS?

THE GATE BAR,

CRUMLIN

MURPHY'S IRISH STOUT

now on sale

MURPHY'S IRISH STOUT
TRADITION IN THE MAKING.

A SURE THING

It's a safe bet.

There's bound to be a pint of
MURPHY'S IRISH STOUT

waiting for you in

JONAH'S BAR
LEOPARDSTOWN

OLD TREE, NEW BEER

MURPHY'S IRISH STOUT

is a new arrival at

THE OLD PINE TREE,

INCHICORE

UNCLE TOM COGLEY
AND ALL . . .

. . . are now enjoying
MURPHYS IRISH STOUT
at
UNCLE TOM'S CABIN
DUNDRUM

THE WORD IS OUT

O'ROURKE'S

OF BLACKROCK

have it!

MURPHY'S IRISH STOUT
Tradition in the making.

PERSONAL

DROP IN . . .

to . . .

THE DROPPING WELL,

DARTRY

MURPHY'S IRISH STOUT

has arrived.

MURPHY'S
IRISH
STOUT

Tradition in the making.

HIT THE ROAD!

For the

HI-WAY

INCHICORE

We've just received

MURPHY'S IRISH STOUT

MURPHY'S IRISH STOUT
Tradition in the making.

WHAT MORE COULD YOU

WISH FOR?

MURPHY'S IRISH STOUT

Now on draught at

THE WISHING WELL,

BLACKROCK

YOU BE THE JUDGE

Try

MURPHY'S IRISH STOUT

yourself at

JURY'S HOTEL
BALLSBRIDGE

MURPHY'S IRISH STOUT

TRADITION IN
THE MAKING.

SOLID AS A ROCK

MURPHY'S IRISH STOUT

is here to stay

at . . .

THE SILVER GRANITE,

PALMERSTOWN

PULL UP . . .

at . . .

THE STEERING WHEEL,

CLONDALKIN

MURPHY'S IRISH STOUT

now on draught

TAP LESSONS . . . !

At the

LAURENCE LOUNGE
INCHICORE

MURPHY'S IRISH STOUT

now on tap.

PERSONAL

IT'S OFFICIAL

GLEESONS HAVE GOT IT

MURPHY'S IRISH STOUT

is now available at

FRANK GLEESON'S

BLACKROCK

SAME AS IT

EVER WAS

THE RATHMINES INN,

as ever is to be found in Rathmines.

But there's a subtle difference now.

MURPHY'S IRISH STOUT

GO WEST
YOUNG MAN

MURPHY'S IRISH STOUT

now at
THE WEST COUNTY BAR
CHAPELIZOD

RIDING THROUGH
THE GLEN?

Stop off for a pint of

MURPHY'S IRISH STOUT

O'DONOGHUE'S
THE GLEN,
INCHICORE

MURPHY'S IRISH STOUT

TRADITION IN THE MAKING.

ROSIE HAS GOT

WHAT IT TAKES

MURPHY'S IRISH STOUT

ROSIE O'GRADY'S

HAROLD'S CROSS

LOOK SHARP!

Leg it down to

BLADES
of
TERENURE.

MURPHY'S IRISH STOUT
now in residence.

MURPHY'S IRISH
STOUT
TRADITION IN THE MAKING.

THERE'S A CERTAIN LUXURY
IN BENTLEY'S

A pint of
MURPHY'S IRISH STOUT

BENTLEY'S
DRIMNAGH ROAD

STONE ME!
They've got

MURPHY'S

here too!

THE THREE ROCK,

RATHFARNHAM

U-BET
U-BiX
U-WIN!
MJ FLOOD
BUSINESS EQUIPMENT TECHNOLOGY
Phone 952701

PERSONAL

YOU NEED A
LOT OF BOTTLE . . .

. . . to avoid having a pint of
MURPHY'S IRISH
STOUT
in
THE BOTTLE
TOWER
CHURCHTOWN

MURPHY'S
IRISH STOUT

TRADITION IN THE MAKING.

THROW AWAY YOUR

BOOKS!

MURPHY'S IRISH STOUT

is here!

U.C.D. STUDENTS' BAR,

BELFIELD

MURPHY'S IRISH
STOUT

Tradition in the making

MURPHY & CO.

MURPHY'S IRISH STOUT

now at

THE COUNTY BAR,

GRANGE CROSS

CALL INN

Draught

MURPHY'S IRISH STOUT

now available

THE MERRION INN,

BALLSBRIDGE

MURPHY'S IRISH
STOUT

Tradition in the making.

CROSS OVER . . .

. . . to

MURPHY'S IRISH STOUT

at

GLEESON'S BRIDGE,

WINDY ARBOUR, DUNDRUM

CLIMB EVERY

MOUNTAIN

And when you get to the top, check out the

MURPHY'S IRISH STOUT

at the

MOUNT MERRION INN

MURPHY'S IRISH STOUT
Tradition in the making.

PERSONAL

DIVE! DIVE! DIVE!

Get down to the

SUBMARINE,
WALKINSTOWN.

MURPHY'S IRISH STOUT

has arrived

MURPHY'S IRISH
STOUT

Tradition in the making.

FLY . . .

. . . down to

THE MAGIC CARPET,

FOXROCK

MURPHY'S IRISH STOUT

now on tap

IRISH COTTAGE?

Irish Stout

MURPHY'S IRISH STOUT

COTTAGE INN,
BLUEBELL

MURPHY'S IRISH STOUT
TRADITION IN THE MAKING.

GERTIE THE GOAT . . .

. . . is proud to announce the arrival of

MURPHY'S IRISH STOUT

at

THE GOAT GRILL,

GOATSTOWN

MURPHY'S
IRISH STOUT

TRADITION IN THE
MAKING.

SO, WHAT'S NEW
IN RANELAGH?

MURPHY'S IRISH STOUT

AT

MURPHY'S
OF RANELAGH

OTHER PERSONAL NOTICES ON PAGE 29

Printed and published in Ireland by The Irish Times Ltd., P.O. Box 74, 11-15 D'Olier Street, Dublin 2.

SATURDAY, MAY 31, 1986

Telephone 792022 main switch line, or 717191, 9.00 - 5.15 Monday - Friday, 9.00 - 12.30 Saturday, for direct line to Classified Advertising Department. Telex 93639

OFFICES AT
2 MacCurtain St., Cork. Telephone Cork (021) 509197, 509248.

Fanum House, Great Victoria Street, Belfast, BT2 7BE. Telephone Belfast 223324.

P.A. Buildings, 85 Fleet Street, London E.C.4 YILB. Telephone (031) 353-8970 or 8981.

On May 31, 1986, the entire back page of classifieds in *The Irish Times* was booked on behalf of one advertiser — Murphy's Stout, Cork.

Opposite page:
Mary Colley, whose husband was the late George Colley, is advertisement manager of *Anois*, the Irish language weekly tabloid. Its circulation is about 6,000 and the paper attracts full colour national brand advertising; it charges £850 for a full page, black and white, with 25 per cent extra for full colour. Firms and organisations advertising in the newspaper include An Bord Gais, the Civil Service Commission, the ESB, the Irish Sugar Company, Lyons Tea, NET, the fertiliser firm, Toyota, Waterford Glass and Wolfhound Press, as well as banks, building societies and insurance companies. *Anois* is the only Irish language weekly and replaced the more literary publication, *Inniu*.

Paddy Meehan, advertisement manager, the Irish News, Belfast. A former advertisement manager of the newspaper, Tommy Wells, was a pioneer on the Belfast advertising agency scene in the 1920s.

Malachy O'Gorman was a great man for stories; one of his best concerned this lady in the snooty Balmoral golf club in Belfast telling about the whores embarking for Korea, to service the soldiers there. The ladies of Balmoral were disgusted and got up to leave. "Don't all rush," O'Gorman had the lady in the story saying, "the boat doesn't leave until tomorrow." Another great stalwart of the magazine field then was Tommy Carroll, advertisement manager of the *Irish Builder and Engineer* for 50 years.

Good fun was had by all in the advertisement department of *The Irish Times*. The circulation of the paper was then around 30,000; display and classified advertising came in more or less of its own volition. Benny Green was there, liaison man between advertising agencies and the paper. He had joined *The Irish Times* in the 1920s and ever since has remained "married" to the paper, devoting all his time to it and even in retirement, coming in daily. Dessie O'Leary was there, too, a great personality who worked with the paper for 50 years, starting in the caseroom but graduating to the advertisement department. He spent his later years in charge of property advertising and with his meticulous attention to detail and service with proofs, did much to build the paper's present eminence in the property advertising market.

Percy Moore, Farming Life advertisement manager.

Cynthia Hudson, group advertisement manager, Century Newspapers.

Cathy Liddy, classified advertisement manager, News Letter.

Sam Sharpe, display advertisement manager, News Letter.

Jack Webb, who joined *The Irish Times* as assistant general manager in 1945 and who became general manager in 1947, remembers that in those early days, he went on the road to sell property advertising. In a year, he built up that advertising from seven columns a week to 32 and *The Irish Times* became known as the "auctioneers' paper". His salary may have been just £4 a week, but with commission, he was soon earning a total of £25 a week. A later and equally popular property advertising man was Berkeley L. Vincent, who retired in 1966. In 1947, Jack Briggs joined *The Irish Times* as an advertisement representative. He was appointed advertisement manager in 1958, a job he held until his retirement in 1970. A keen member of the scout movement, and closely involved in TABS, Briggs who died in 1985, had an outstanding name in the business for honesty and integrity in his business dealings, remembers Noel Hayden.

Nelson Clarke, News Letter.

Dessie O'Leary was also confidant of "Pussy" O'Mahony, who died in early 1948. He was a most extraordinary man, with a colourful past. During and after World War I, he served in the British forces, including the Palestine Gendarmerie. In the mid-1920s, he worked with the advertising and news departments of the *Daily Express* in London,

427

Isobel Wood, classified advertisement manager, Sunday News.

Stephen Carroll, weeklies' advertisement manager, Century Newspapers.

Frank McGouran, advertisement sales manager, the Irish Press **group.**

joining *The Irish Times* in 1928. He worked in all departments there, including editorial and advertising and was made assistant manager in 1940 and manager in 1942. He occupied half a house in Templeogue: the other half was occupied by Joe Delaney, the Domas man. At the time of his death, O'Mahony, one of whose sons is Dave Allen the comedian, was chairman of the Publicity Club. O'Mahony, whose false leg announced his arrival well in advance, used to canvass all the advertisements for *The Irish Times'* annual review — and write all the editorial copy.

Sir Raymond Grace was another great advertising personality at *The Irish Times,* the son of Sir Walter Grace of Monkstown. He had had many jobs in his time, including a spell in Hollywood, doing menial jobs like butler and chauffeur. He came to *The Irish Times* with some fabulous stories, including the time he was arrested in Hollywood for a minor misdemeanour and found himself incarcerated in jail along with the neighbourhood pimps and whores, then had to pay twice as big a fine as they did, because of his posh accent.

In those demarcation-free days, there was good humour, often of a black kind. A woman rang up late one night to have a death notice inserted in the following morning's paper. Sullivan, the night man, whose right hand was largely devoid of fingers, answered the call. He was having some difficulty writing down the details. To his irate tone, the woman replied: "My husband has just died. "Well," said Sullivan, "I didn't kill him". On another day, the 100 copies at the front counter went remarkably quickly: someone had noticed a literal in an estate agent's advertisement. "46 acres" had been transformed, in the caseroom, into "46 arses".

The same year that Jim Furlong was made advertisement manager at the *Irish Press,* 1946, a young Peadar Pierce, now advertisement sales controller at RTE, joined the Burgh Quay organisation. Initially, he worked in the *Irish Press* accounts department and remembers that the advertising ledgers were a "shambles". One day, Eamon de Valera met him carrying two accounts books upstairs and promptly issued an edict forbidding the messenger boys to carry up more than one at a time.

In the late 1940s, when the commercial manager of the *Kilkenny People* was a Dickensian figure called Hugh Keenan, there was consternation over a machinery dealer called Joe Murphy who wanted to take a half page to advertise reconditioned tractors. Would he be able to pay? With great reluctance, Keenan accepted the advertisement. There was such a rush for the tractors that Murphy soon ran out of stock — the advertisement had been much too successful.

Times improved for newspaper advertising. George Crosbie, now chairman of the *Cork Examiner,* started with the family firm in 1946. He remembers that in the years immediately after the war, when the linage rate in the *Cork Examiner* was 2/6d, there were huge amounts of

Three dimensional outdoor poster for the Sunday Tribune.

national and local display advertising, as well as all the classifieds. Many Cork firms such as Woodford Bourne took advertisements on the daily contract rate. "I always remember going to Dublin in the first week of January every year and coming back to Cork with so many agency orders that I could hardly carry them."

In those halycon days, around 60 per cent of the *Cork Examiner's* revenue came from advertising, the rest from cover sales. Now the balance is about half and half. Tom O'Neill, still going strong as advertisement manager in the early 1950s, was a gruff man, with a heart as big as a bucket, remembers George Crosbie. "As long as you put an ad in the Examiner, you couldn't go wrong". There was more than enough leeway for the occasional mishaps and laughs. One regular Cork advertiser sold beds and mattresses; one day, his advertisement featured an upside-down block. Angrily, he demanded a free insertion. In the meantime, all Cork had been talking about his advertisement. Then there was the time that a canvasser from the *Cork Examiner* went in to see a client, a lingerie firm. They wanted to put in an advertisement for a bra, but were unsure of a slogan. The canvasser obliged: "Keep abreast of the times."

So good were the advertising times for newspapers that when it was decided to launch the *Sunday Press* in September, 1949, there was no great problem with advertising content. Jim Furlong, who had been promoted to advertisement manager at Burgh Quay in 1946 when Jack Dempsey was made general manager, remembers that there was a lot of work calling on the agencies — "Frank Padbury even wanted me to join him, but I didn't get on too well with him, he was a very volatile man" — but it was a question of pushing an open door. Agencies were delighted that their reliance on Independent Newspapers was being lessened. Orders poured in for the new *Sunday Press* and the night before the launch, the advertising agency people were regally entertained by the *Sunday Press* in Jammets. The early issues so overflowed with advertising that the footnote on the rate card was applied. Some of the agencies could not even get colour positions because they booked space too late. Parker Advertising — by now run by Jack Dempsey's brother, P. J. — handled the publicity for the launch.

1949 saw the launch of another new paper, the *Mourne Observer* in Newcastle, Co Down. It was founded by David James Hawthorne; the first issue appeared on Friday, October 7, 1949, put together in a room rented in the "Home from Home" guest house in the seaside town. Advertisers in that very first issue included the Palace and Ritz cinemas, Methven Photographic Studios, Donard Dairy, the Newcastle Optical Company and Jack White cycle repairs. The paper was printed by the *Dromore Weekly Times* and news and advertisement copy was sent by train; late copy was 'phoned.

Some provincial papers were not as well organised at this time. After the *Argus* newspaper moved from Drogheda to Dundalk in 1952, the

Barry Connolly, advertisement manager, Sunday Tribune.

Barbara Nugent,
formerly advertisement
manager, Sunday
Tribune, now its
managing director.

The Sunday Tribune, where Vincent Browne is editor and chief executive, has a circulation of 95,835 (latest ABC figures) and a total readership of about 370,000, according to a recent JNMR survey. It has a 60 per cent ABC1 profile. Advertisement revenue is showing a steady volume increase. Barbara Nugent, who was advertisement manager from its relaunch over three years ago and was subsequently promoted to marketing director, is now the newspaper's managing director. Barry Connolly was made advertisement manager earlier this year.

The colour section, printed heatset web offset, offers colour at very competitive cpt rates, £63 per single column inch. It carries a good volume of car and drink colour advertising, as well as food advertising for clients like Kellogg's and Kelkin wholefood products. The first advertising campaign for Ballygowan spring water was run in the colour section, where 6″ x 2 cols colour advertisements ran for three months just after the product was launched nearly three years ago. In the two broadsheet sections of the newspaper, special notices are being built up at £39 a single column inch. Property advertising is

THE SUNDA

28 SEPTEMBER 1986   VOL 6 NO 4

SPORT

Barry and Barney's Beef

GERRY CALLAN on the McGuigan Eastwood feud

PEOPLE

On the Kerry Trail

DEIRDRE PURCELL follows the Sam Maguire to Kerry

GETTING RID OF EDDIE

Did Collins have to go?

Y TRIBUNE

PRICE 65p (incl VAT) 55p in Sterling area

important and with the help of the high technology innovations page, recruitment advertising is being steadily increased.

PROFILE

urrent
ffairs
racker

VIN DAWSON on
s Wonder Woman
via O'Leary

ARTS

Thumping
Theatre
Festival

FINTAN O'TOOLE'S
guide to the Dublin
Theatre Festival

EXCLUSIVE
by VINCENT BROWNE
and FINTAN O'TOOLE

BOB HOBBY

433

The Phoenix **magazine**, with a fortnightly circulation of over 18,000, prints stories that other publications never touch. Its readership is over 120,000; advertisement manager is Pat Moylan. Some major brands, such as cars, cigarettes and drink are using full colour advertising in the magazine, but Pat Moylan admits that the no holds barred editorial policy can be offputting to some potential advertisers. The magazine, which was launched by John Mulcahy in late 1982, often advertises itself, using TV slides, radio and print promotions.

Donie Bolger of the Irish Press group. He has worked on the Evening Press since its inception in 1954.

PHOENIX
THE

VOL. 4, No. 18   SEPTEMBER 26, 1986   PRICE 85p (incl. VAT)

BRITISH SPIES IN IRELAND
PROFILE: JOAN FITZGERALD

quality of its book-keeping declined. Its sole means of recording payments, including those for advertisements, was a tattered case book, which had such entries as "Mrs ---- will pay £2 for her ad next week." At the *Leitrim Observer*, Pat Dunne was often said to have used deadly means of collecting advertisement debts. At the *Dublin Evening Mail*, published in Parliament Street and a favourite of generations of Dublin readers, the traditional approach to advertising prevailed. A man called Sugg was advertisement manager, friendly but formal. In the public office of the *Mail*, beneath the painting of the newsboy announcing the death of Queen Victoria in 1901, was the semi-circular mahogany counter at which members of the public placed classified advertisements. Announced a Mail publicity brochure of the early 1950s: "Some 900 of these are published every day and practically all of them are handed in over the office counter." There was no canvassing for small ads. then. For the public, it was very much a "take it or leave it" attitude.

Jim Furlong always remembers the time he went to put a small ad in the *Evening Mail:* "the girl said to me, one insertion, I suppose". When the *Evening Press* started in September, 1954, under Douglas Gageby's editorship and with David Luke's publicity elephants, Furlong told the ad girls that if they took the same casual, offhand approach to customers, they would be fired. To ensure that there was six weeks' supply of small ads for the start of the *Evening Press*, Furlong wrote to all headmasters in the Dublin area and offered £3 a week for school leavers canvassing small ads door to door. Having analysed the small ads in the *Evening Mail* and found that 75 per cent of them were private, Furlong decided on an unorthodox approach for the new *Evening Press*.

Joe O'Grady, the Cork Examiner's **Dublin manager. He has worked for his entire career in the Cork** Examiner **and in its Dublin office since 1967. He succeeded Bridget Lynch as Dublin manager in 1973. Joe O'Grady was Publicity Club chairman in 1984 and is current TABS chairman.**

Nuala Pollard (right) and Deirdre Feeney, advertisement sales executives, Independent Newspapers, Dublin. Nuala was the first female salesperson to work for the group's newspapers, covering the Dublin 2 area. Deirdre works on the advertising agency side of the newspapers' ad sales department.

Vacant shops were rented in various districts to act as depots for the teams of teenage canvassers. The first issue of the *Evening Press* carried four pages of small ads — the *Evening Herald* had been trying unsuccessfully for the previous 50 years to build up its small ads, says Furlong — and soon people also started flocking to the O'Connell Street offices to place ads, taking advantage of the "3 for 2" offer on classifieds.

"I'm often blamed for the demise of the *Evening Mail* by taking away its small ads, but they only had themselves to blame by failing to develop the market," says Furlong now. Still, the *Evening Mail* managed to survive a further eight years, until 1962. It became the first big casualty of the new television era, as advertising drained away to TE. After the *Dublin Evening Mail* closed, the cream of its advertisement staff stayed with *The Irish Times*. Harry Adcock, one of the old school, would think nothing of cycling down to Wicklow looking for ads when he was in his heyday. Its contract printing division helped its survival. In late 1952, it was awarded the contract to print the *Irish Farmers' Journal.* The blossoming publication enlarged its pagination from eight to 12. Larry Sheedy, then on its editorial staff, remembers the sterling work done on the advertisement side by Jack Carmody. The single column inch rate in the paper at the time was 15/-. Its circulation was 5,000.

Michael Maughan of Wilson Hartnell started off his advertising career selling space. He worked on a hospitals' magazine run by the Parkside Press and has vivid memories of his first sale, persuading HB Ice Cream that hospital patients would be ideal consumers of its products. In 1971, a young man newly returned from London, John Fanning, started in the Dublin advertising business by spending about nine months selling advertisement space at the Institute of Public Administration. He is now managing director of McConnell's Advertising agency.

Working at the *Irish Press* group was a very loyal and dedicated team of advertising men. One of the most colourful characters was John Berryhill Meehan, from Carrickfergus, who worked on features in the *Irish Press,* he wore a bow tie and a beautiful suit and worked at Burgh Quay until past his 80th birthday. The Class of '54 at Burgh Quay contained many other people who rose to greater prominence in the business. Gerry O'Boyce was there: later, he developed the advertising side of the *Irish Farmers' Journal,* helping to place that publication in its present pre-eminent position, Gerry Doherty, the man who later founded G & S Doherty, the advertising agency and Don O'Connell, the man who now runs Doherty Advertising. Ray Kennedy, the public relations man, a most jovial and genial class of man, was there too and still inclined to reminiscence at length, Tommy Bates, who used to do the "Paul Jones" dance column and who was once in big trouble with the management for playing a trumpet in the office. Vincent Blake was there, sometimes regarded as the "father" of the *Irish Press* advertisement department. Ray Kennedy, who worked with David Luke on the launch of the *Evening Press*, was a prime mover of the annual reunions of the Class of '54; it met once a year, for some 16 years, in the snug in Mulligans, for pints and jollifications. Of all that motley medley of talent, only one person is still with the *Irish Press* group: Alan Maxwell, gold medal winner in advertising. There were one or two would-be recruits who never made it: Sir Raymond Grace, who worked for years on the advertisement side of *The Irish Times*, was said to have applied to the *Irish Press* for a job. Jim Furlong felt that the title could have been a drawback.

By the time 1956 came round, the *Irish Press* was ready to celebrate its 25th anniversary. A formal dinner and dance was arranged for the Gresham Hotel on September 5 that year; what most people remember now about the event is Denis Garvey's little joke about how you told the difference between the three Dublin morning newspapers. *The Irish Times* would report a news event as follows: "Dublin man killed by train in London". The *Irish Independent*: "Catholic Irishman killed by London train". *Irish Press:* "Irishman killed by British train". *Irish Press* top management was not altogether amused; Eamon de Valera was heard to say that the paper was fair to everyone. At another national newspaper on one occasion, spoof copy for a birth notice slipped through the control system; the following morning, the birth's column announced that a basset dog had given birth to a litter.

Miss Lynch, Dublin office manager of the *Cork Examiner*, had an extraordinary ability at fixing and arranging: on one occasion, machinery for the paper was stuck in the customs in Dublin. Not even the intervention of Jack Lynch, then Minister for Industry and Commerce, was able to get it freed. Miss Lynch, who had a vast store of closely-guarded telephone numbers, got on the 'phone and was able to announce, ten minutes later, that the machinery was being released. The *Cork Examiner* has always had good relations with all the Dublin agencies: Miss Lynch remembers well all the dealings over many years with Caps, Miss Harrison who looked after the Hospitals Sweepstakes' advertising, Maureen, late wife of Dr Cyril Cusack, the actor, and Bridie O'Rahilly, the agency's principal. Details of the Sweeps' results were a regular feature of newspapers 30 and 40 years ago. Often, Miss Lynch had to arrange for them to be collected from the Sweeps' office in Ballsbridge, put on the train to Cork, while from a second copy, the details were 'phoned to Cork for cross-checking. Some advertisers were not so helpful: when a man came into the *Cork Examiner* office, then in Grafton Street, with ad copy in English and his name and address in Irish, Miss Lynch politely suggested he should put them in English too if he wanted more replies. The would-be advertiser replied: "The *Cork Examiner* is being anti-national as usual. Let them get an interrupter". *Sic.*

Following the sudden death of Tom O'Neill, advertisement manager

Gordon Magee, who joined Morton Newspapers' advertisement department in 1968. From 1970 until 1986, he was advertisement manager of the Lurgan Mail. **He is now with the group's** Farmweek **publication, responsible for circulation promotion.**
Photograph: Morton Newspapers.

of the *Cork Examiner* in 1952, he was succeeded by his son, Billy, who held that post until 1975, when he collapsed and died while playing golf. Both father and son were extraordinarily dedicated to the *Cork Examiner,* says George Crosbie, present chairman. Three years after Tom O'Neill died, so too did Ned Looney, advertisement manager of the *Evening Echo* since 1923. He was succeeded by Dave Lenihan.

In the mid-1950s, the trade and consumer magazine field had been narrowed down by the restricting economic circumstances of the period. Unusually, a new title was launched. The new Irish Management Institute decided to launch its own magazine in 1956. For years, it remained a small publication; not until the arrival of Diarmuid O Broin as advertisement manager in the late 1960s did it begin to develop.

The provincial press continued to go its own way: the *Munster Express,* under the control of J. J. Walsh, veteran of the Bundoran outings and life-long friend of Charlie McConnell. Other papers in Waterford closed down, like the *Waterford Evening News,* which shut in 1957, but the *Munster Express* soldiered on. Even today, when advertising is so difficult, it can count on having 15 or more columns of pre-paid ads per issue. Michael Whelan was advertisement manager of the paper for many years, having joined in 1936. Before the war, he recalled recently, "it was a grand, fair and easy time and there was give and take in all quarters". By the 1950s, the style had changed. "The cost of newsprint rose sharply. Hours of work were shortened, wages were increased, bonuses went into operation and social services charges and income tax went crazy. A clerk could not do what he did before and help a printer and each job became separate."

Some customers who placed advertisements were more difficult than others, especially businessmen who would demand exactness in return for their hard earned money. Michael Whelan recalls one particularly thorny customer and how he managed to outwit him. The advertisement to be placed dealt with a boutique in Waterford. The owner was from Dublin where he had operated a string of such premises. "The man in question was a Jew — but let me hasten to add — that was not held against him! Jew or other his money was as good as any in the land. He was not wanted anywhere because he tried to strike costing bargains that were not only ludicrous but ridiculous. However it fell to me on account of my position to deal with him. I will say this much in his favour — he believed in paying for what he wanted in cash but not until after he had outwitted you to the last $\frac{1}{2}$d. Dealing with him always proved to be a battle of wits. He was a man of fine physique and smoked a pipe which emitted clouds of horrible smoke to the discomfiture of those around. When the deal had been made about size, number of insertions, position in paper and cost, it came to the time for payment. He was very happy when the business was concluded — all in his favour; but then cash customers always get preferential treatment.

"Knowing that I was to be paid in hard cash, my thoughts worked furiously; how was I to even up matters by not alone getting the correct money back but also the discount allowed? I was determined that on account of his meanness I would teach him a lesson he would never forget. Looking furtively about him the customer produced a wad of notes and began thumbing them. Knowing his form I started telling him a story in an effort to distract him from counting the money properly. He soon faltered, falling for the yarn hook, line and sinker. Like the true fisherman I am I knew I had him! The count re-started. There was another long drag on the pipe, and the usual remark 'Where was I...'. After each pause I made the figure of the cost of the ads much smaller. He didn't notice. Eventually he paid the agreed sum and went away. I recounted the money and found out how much he over-paid me. I told my boss about the deal and how things had fared."

"He certainly enjoyed it and we shared a good laugh. We agreed that our business friend would be back after doing a little homework, and of course he was. He tore into our offices, growled that he had been done, but was politely told how objectionable he had been, always looking for more than his pound of flesh and that what had happened was a lesson for him, not to be so aggressive or mean when it came to using the press for publicity. The amount, over and above the agreed sum was handed back immediately to a grateful but deflated and chastened man. Afterwards we became fast friends and there were no more deals made. Instead the proper amounts were charged and paid for".

More papers came on the scene: in 1957, *The Irish Times* launched the *Sunday Review*, but it never took off with advertising agencies, who failed to see the need for it in addition to the *Sunday Independent* and the *Sunday Press*. In Belfast, with the start of transmissions by Ulster Television in 1959, the *TV Post* magazine came into being as the local programme journal, being succeeded eventually by the *TV Times*. In Dublin, the *Radio Review* was coming to the end of its life. Not only had other publications usurped the popularity of its crosswords, but with the start of Telefis Eireann planned for the last day of 1961, TE decided to launch its own programme guide, the *RTV Guide*, with Billy McFeely as advertisement manager. What had been talked about since the inception of the *Radio Review* in 1946 was now a reality. In 1958, Victor Salter, for many years the advertisement director of the *Belfast Telegraph*, died. In 1951, he had been made a director of W & G Baird, publishers of the *Belfast Telegraph*. Later, he became joint managing director. In 1959, the year after the death of Victor Salter, William Cassidy, the *Belfast Telegraph's* advertisement manager for many years, passed away. By the time he had retired from the company, he had had an extraordinary 70 years of service, beginning in 1881, when he answered an advertisement which sought a "smart boy" to assist the advertisement manager. The paper's offices were still in Arthur Street and the *Belfast Telegraph* was a four page, hand-set paper.

Within three years of Cassidy's death, the *Belfast Telegraph* was taken

John Thompson, marketing and sales director, Farmer's Journal, which he joined in 1980 from JS Publications, where he launched U magazine in 1979. Previous media appointments included Independent Newspapers, Creation and the Sunday World, where he was first marketing and sales director. On the agency side, he worked for Arks in the early 1960s; from 1964 until 1970, he was media director of O'Keeffes. The Farmer's Journal has a current weekly circulation of 72,000 and a full colour page rate of £4,400. Thompson claims that advertisement revenue is 8 per cent up this year, thanks to more colour advertising, despite the recession in farming.

Seamus Morahan, advertisement manager of the Leinster Leader, Naas. The photograph was taken when he was chairman of the Junior Chamber of Commerce in the town in 1985.

over by Roy Thomson, founder of the Thomson Organisation, after acrimonious court battles. Thomson had already entered the London and Scottish newspaper markets and to his UK newspapers, he brought brash Canadian selling techniques. Classified advertisement sales were never the same again. Soon, a battery of telephone sales girls was installed at the *Belfast Telegraph*. The innovation was quickly copied elsewhere in the Irish newspaper industry.

At the more staid *Irish News*, a small advertisement department was managed by the late Joseph Nelson. In 1962, a young lad called Paddy Meehan (advertisement manager since 1970) joined the paper as a junior advertisement representative/messenger boy/part-time tea maker.

That same year, 1962, saw Mortons of Lurgan install the first web offset printing press in Ireland. It made newspaper printing not only much quicker, but much cheaper too, with better quality half-tone reproduction and an easy ability to print in several colours, up to full colour. Morton's newspaper in Derry, the *Londonderry Sentinel*, became the first newspaper in Ireland to run full colour advertisements with this new system. However, not until 1971 did Northern Ireland have its first newspaper readership survey. In Dublin, the *Irish Press* was using older printing technology to run advertisements in several colours for a variety of clients, notably for Time beer and Caltex petrol, with acceptable results. In 1962, the *Sunday Independent* put the newly installed gravure press at Middle Abbey Street into action with its colour supplement. It only lasted a short time, having failed to attract sufficient advertising support.

September, 1964 saw a major advance on the magazine front: Hugh McLaughlin, with his newly formed Creation group, which began where his old Fleet Publishing Company left off, decided to start a weekly business magazine, *Business and Finance*. With the business confidence of the country only just starting to lift, it was a major gamble. Nicholas Leonard was recruited as editor. Billy McFeely, formerly of the *Standard*, was advertisement manager. The business sector was not ready for a weekly magazine and within a year, it was on the point of foundering, with accumulated debts of £12,000. McLaughlin had other magazines, notably *Creation*, an upmarket womens' magazine, edited by his wife Nuala and the more downmarket *Woman's Way*. In charge of the advertisement side of these two magazines was a young protege of McLaughlin, Gerry McGuinness, not far removed from his days in the cinema business. The collapse of *Business and Finance* would have brought down McLaughlin's empire, which included the publishing offices in Creation Arcade in Grafton Street and the printing works at South Circular Road. In May, 1965, he brought in an English Cockney character called George S. Harman to run the advertisement side of *Business and Finance*. Harman, a generous but sometimes quarrelsome individual, started doing special reports on the lines of those in the

440

Financial Times. Soon, the level of display advertising built up and the magazine was saved.

Sadly, Harman's alcoholic excesses took their toll. On one occasion, he had a mid-morning quarrel with Nicholas Leonard. After a very liquid lunch, he continued the quarrel, storming in to the editorial room to throw a punch at Leonard. Fortunately, Harman missed, but went sprawling the length of the room. On another occasion, Harman, his wife and his pet dog attended an evening press reception in town: by the time it finished, all three were stretched out, drunk on champagne. Harman ended his publishing days with a venture that

Advertisement run in late 1985 by the National Newspapers of Ireland, as part of its campaign to promote the eleven national titles in the Republic as advertising media. The new organisation is working to encourage advertisers and agencies to make more use of newspapers. Says the NNI: "For years, there has been a clear creative and planning bias in the top Dublin agencies towards TV."

Frank Cullen, co-ordinating director, National Newspapers of Ireland.

New Hibernia **magazine, published by Agricultural Publications, Dun Laoghaire, who also publish** Irish Farmers' Monthly. **David Markey, current chairman of the Advertising Press Club, is advertisement director for both magazines.**

turned out disastrously for him: the *Irish Bystander.*

In the mid-1960s, the dishonest business of Shanahan's Stamp Auctions meant good advertising business for many publications. Every newspaper and magazine in town was after Shanahan's and Dr Paul Singer for advertisements, which he gave quite readily and paid for. Billy King, working on the *Irish Independent,* remembers the time vividly and is glad to say in retrospect that the *Irish Independent* was virtually alone among publications in not taking Shanahan advertisements. Peter Finnegan booked a series of 10″ x 4 column ads in the *Irish Independent* for gold: the client paid with £2,000 in £1 notes, an enormous amount of cash for the time.

Also increasingly active on the magazine publishing front in the late 1960s was the National Publishing Group, an offshoot of Drogheda Printers. It expanded rapidly, taking over *Irishwoman's Journal,* which had been founded in the mid-1960s by Sean O'Sullivan, formerly with Creation. It also took over *Development,* a business magazine founded nearly ten years before by Jim Gilbert. A GAA magazine was published along with *Garda Review* and various trade magazines. The publishing company eventually faded away; in retrospect, perhaps the NPG's most notable achievement was to employ Frank Grennan, founder and managing director of Jemma Publications, as its marketing manager. Other present day notables in the advertising business who had rough edges knocked off in the NPG were Harry McEntee, now a print representative, Tony Browne, for long advertisement manager of *Technology Ireland* magazine published by the Institute for Industrial Research and Standards and Jim Moraghan, now head of advertisement sales at the Institute of Public Administration. Another genial character there was Joe O'Reilly, a Co. Louth solicitor turned adman. The NPG and its titles are long gone and mostly forgotten, but for the participants on its advertisement staff, life there was quite fun, if slightly mad, bedevilled by interminable management meetings to try and boost advertisement revenue.

Also as the 1960s drew to a close, *The Irish Times* began the first properly organised system of selling classified advertising in Dublin. It took a leaf out of the Thomson book at the *Belfast Telegraph* and if it all appeared meticulously organised from outside, the internal workings were slightly more chaotic, sometimes hilarious. Brenda McNiff, who now runs *The Irish Times'* general services division, was instrumental in setting up the telephone sales system for selling classified advertising. Later came the bonus payments scheme. Also closely involved in the early stages was Anne Mallon, trained on the *Belfast Telegraph.* For the first two weeks, until a proper telephone system was installed, the large room in *The Irish Times* where the scheme was put into effect contained a maze of old-fashioned black telephones, whose wires were all entangled. When the 'phone rang, it was a little difficult making out the right instrument. Nevertheless, bright young girls from a variety of backgrounds were brought in to sell advertising by telephone.

Sometimes, they were over-enthusiastic. One girl was overheard by her supervisor selling a series of insertions to an undertaker for a death notice. She pointed out that the man had agreed to the deal and that it would have clinched a bonus payment for her. Perhaps the greatest success of the classified team at *The Irish Times* was in building up the appointments advertising. Gradually, firms were persuaded, with a total advertisement department staff of over 50, into taking display advertisements when they sought staff. Today, the new paper has an undoubted lead in both jobs and property advertising. The new classified system, in which *The Irish Times* played such a pioneering rôle, was successful: as Brenda McNiff points out somewhat ruefully, other papers promptly followed suit. The *Irish Independent* soon developed major sales in appointments and property advertising.

Also in the newspaper field, Peter Finnegan, who had been appointed head of the advertisement department of Independent Newspapers following the death of E. C. Maguire in 1966, made plans for a radical new departure for the morning paper. With Bartle Pitcher, chief executive, he planned a new weekly property supplement for the *Irish Independent.* Its founding editor was Frank Cairns, who just retired recently. The new supplement rapidly became a major earner of advertising; the *Irish Independent* and *The Irish Times* have long had a good reputation as a property advertising medium, while the *Irish Press* has long lost out in this field. Some sources believe the antagonism of property advertisers to the *Irish Press* dates back to the days when it failed to attract any advertisers of pro-Unionist persuasion, although the *Evening Press* gets good revenue from new house advertising. Solid property advertising has long helped fuel the revenues of Independent Newspapers. The *Evening Herald,* has managed to win a bigger share of the classified market since going tabloid three years ago. The *Evening Herald* runs a major property section every Friday, edited by Valerie McGrath, whose father was circulation manager of the *Irish Independent* for many years and whose daughter Jill works in the media department of Bell Advertising.

While the *Galway Observer* was on the count-down to its final closure in October, 1966, P. J. Hennelly of the *Mayo News* in Westport was preparing to make the big move, to the *Connaught Telegraph* in Castlebar, where he has now managed the advertisement department for the past ten years. The late Bernie Gillespie had been advertisement manager for over 30 years — in itself an unusual segregation of duties on a provincial paper at that time. By the mid-1960s, he had moved advertisements from the front page of the *Connaught Telegraph,* a revolutionary move for the time. Bernie Gillespie, who died in 1982, was well-known throughout the newspaper industry in the West of Ireland as a colourful, "bubbling" character. Interestingly, although he was advertisement manager, he was also closely involved with the editorial side and was one of the founding members of the NUJ in the region. Around 1976, he fell into ill health and handed over

A front page of the Impartial Reporter, Enniskillen, the last newspaper in Ireland to devote its front page entirely to advertisements.

management of the advertisement department to P. J. Hennelly, himself a worthy candidate in the "colourful candidate" stakes. Sadly, in Galway, after the Scott family and John Robinson had closed down the *Galway Observer*, in the little house where customers brought in hand-written scraps of paper with advertisements, memories of the old-style publication soon faded. John Robinson went to work with the *Connacht Tribune* and even though he retained ownership of the *Galway Observer* title, its chances of revival faded with each passing year.

Within four years of the passing of the *Galway Observer*, a new dimension in Irish provincial newspaper advertising was launched in the western capital. O'Gorman's had long been respected in the printing and stationery trade, although its printing house closed down in 1986. Nora Barnacle, later to be wife of James Joyce, worked in its bookbinding section at the turn of the century. In 1970, the O'Gorman's took a brave step: they launched the *Galway Advertiser*, a newspaper distributed free of charge in the Galway area and totally dependent for its revenue on advertisements. For the first time in modern Irish newspaper publishing history, a free provincial newspaper had been launched.

The first print run of the *Galway Advertiser* was 7,000: now, it is over 33,000. Its delivery area extends in a 30 mile radius round Galway city. Since door to door deliveries are impossible in rural areas, distribution in these areas is achieved through local shops. Most issues, it runs to 32 pages. It also produces a high standard of editorial content, with Benson and Hedges' awards going to members of its editorial staff over the last three years. Just as the *Galway Advertiser* was being launched in the West of Ireland, so the ever-imaginative Hugh McLaughlin was launching his Dublin city give-away newspaper, the *Dublin Post*. Initially, it was distributed on the affluent southside of the city. It had a certain editorial content; one of its early editors was Michael Keating, now better known as a Progressive Democrat TD and a former Fine Gael junior minister. Chris O'Kelly, who is now a partner in the highly successful Confidential Report Printing firm at Clondalkin was general manager of the *Dublin Post*. He remembers that he did special deals with barmen round town to give him tonic and ice — nothing alcoholic — while he entertained agency people who were more than capable of drinking him under the table. In those far-off, halcyon days, there was no problem about filling the paper with advertisements. "If you were short one or two pages, you simply rang up agency contacts, who regardless of schedules, would fling in an ad or two." He also remembers that Hugh McLaughlin had a peculiar lunchtime habit of doodling one's name on his napkin, then crossing it out. If this happened while one was being entertained by him, it was time to quit. This happened with Chris O'Kelly, who promptly left and went down to Dingle, Co Kerry, where he bought his own trawler.

The idea of free distribution publications dependent entirely on advertisement revenue was also extended to the magazine field. In

1970, Frank Grennan founded Jemma Publications. He bought his first magazine, the *Irish Licensing World,* for £300 from W. J. McFeely, the well-known advertising man, who had worked on the *Standard,* the *RTV Guide* and *Business and Finance,* among other publications. McFeely's son, Diarmuid, was an advertisement manager in Creation at this time and married to rally driver Rosemary Smith.

A major bank strike during the summer of 1970 helped Grennan, because McFeely did not lodge the cheque that paid for the magazine title until after the strike was settled. Frank Grennan was on his way: now his firm has a dozen magazines mostly in Dublin, but some in Belfast and a grocery publication in Glasgow, as well as being active in exhibitions. He is repeating the magazine publishing success enjoyed in a previous era by J. J. McCann. At the end of the 1960s, advertising in paid publications was not always easy. Hugh McLaughlin ran a paid weekly news feature magazine called *This Week,* edited by Joseph O'Malley, now political correspondent of the *Sunday Independent.* Despite high quality editorial and reasonable cover sales, it failed to attract sufficient advertising content. *Nusight* magazine, in which such luminaries as Gordon Colleary, Vincent Browne, John Feeney, Michael Keating and Kevin Myers were involved, lasted for an even shorter time, but proved an eventual forcing ground for Vincent Browne's *Magill* magazine.

Magill and *In Dublin* began almost simultaneously; the latter began on Good Friday, 1976, as a 10p listing of entertainment events. It now has a circulation of around 9,000. In a pioneering move in the Irish media, part of its advertising revenue comes from personal column advertisements of an explicit nature from both the gay and heterosexual communities, as well as from Dublin massage parlours. No other Irish magazine carries this type of advertising. *Magill,* now nearly ten years in existence, has a print run of about 33,000 on each of its 14 issues a year. Revenue comes 50:50 from sales and advertising.

On the women's magazine front, *Woman's Way* where Gerry McGuinness pioneered magazine presentations to agencies, continues its long run, having been bought by the Jefferson Smurfit Group after the collapse of Creation in 1975. Ten years ago, Kevin Kelly, who began his meteoric publishing career with the purchase of *Checkout,* (started by Louis O'Sullivan and which had Billy King as advertisement manager), started *Image* as a modern, up-market equivalent of the old *Creation* magazine. Advertising competition in this area comes from *IT* magazine and *U* magazine, also published by the Smurfit Group.

In the late 1970s, Noelle Campbell-Sharp, who had been contributing editorial features to many newspapers and magazines, including the *Irish Tatler and Sketch,* went into a 50:50 partnership with John Kerry Keane of the *Kilkenny People* on the magazine. She helped a lot of fashion people, who returned that help when she started on her own. After 18 months of joint ownership, she bought out John Kerry

Keane — "dearly". *IT* has continued to be a well-used advertising vehicle. Next came *Success* magazine and more recently, *Social and Personal,* as well as the most recent of all, the Ryanair inflight magazine. She says: "The art of selling advertising is neglected in Ireland. I don't sell space, I sell what to do with it." She believes that magazines will continue to attract good advertising support against continued TV competition.

Diarmuid O Broin, who started work in Easons alongside Brian Cronin and whose first experience in selling space was for the floats in St Patrick's Day parades in Dublin, arrived at the Irish Management Institute in 1967 and was made advertisement manager of its magazine in 1969. The publication was changed to A4 size; its main competition was *Business and Finance* magazine. Other business-type magazines, like *Irish Business, Aspect* and *Success* were still in the future. Up to the 1974 recession, *Management* magazine (now published by Jemma) used to get 30 to 40 pages of advertisements a month. The arrival of the recession also coincided with the institute's move to Sandyford; before then, it was ensconced in what is now the USSR embassy in Orwell Road. In those good old days in Rathgar, Christmas parties for media managers became part of the annual entertainment circuit. Bill Davis of O'Kennedy Brindley made an excellent honorary barman, remembers O Broin. The morning after one such party, a well-known agency man was found asleep in the orchard.

There was the amusing side, too. An English agency sent late ad copy direct to Mount Salus Press, the magazine's printers. In the middle of the night, O Broin had a call from one of the night shift machine men: the late block was on the machine. The wrong ad had been sent: on the press at Mount Salus was an advertisement for a contraceptive vending machine. What should be done? He decided upon a speedy advertisement substitution. Also, O Broin was able to send out letters about advertisement features signed "O Broin, the Baron of Barr-na-Coille". In 1982, one such letter, highlighting the 30th anniversary of the institute, said: "I am excited about the new format of our long established journal. With a new editor, a fresh approach to content and a totally different design and layout, we intend to make our competition look like tired old wastepaper." It was not the first time such stirring words were heard in magazine publishing and hardly the last.

Meanwhile, O Broin noticed another change that coincided with the first great recession, back in 1974. Until then, agencies' personnel and people on the media side had very personal relationships and judgments about individual publications were much more qualitative. Now, computer printouts rule the roost and agency people are only interested in figures, he says.

In the provincial field, the change to web-offset printing began, giving much better half-tone reproduction for readers and better quality for advertisers. The first provincial newspaper in the Republic to go for web-offset was the *Connacht Tribune* in Galway (with its mid-week sister paper, the *Connacht Sentinel).* It was closely followed by the *Kerryman,* which put in a web-offset press in 1972. From the start, both papers, in Galway and Tralee, started offering advertising in full process colour at relatively inexpensive rates. A mainstay full colour advertiser of those early days of web-offset printing was Carroll's cigarettes, but that hoped-for boom in colour advertising for the weeklies has never materialised. The first daily newspaper to go offset, anticipating the Dublin daily newspaper scene by ten years, was the *Cork Examiner,* with its evening paper, the *Evening Echo,* which made the change in 1976. The Cork papers had been first in the Republic to conduct readership surveys, in 1968.

By 1972, the amount of advertising spent with the Creation magazines was enough to warrant publication in magazines like *Business and Finance,* the top ten spending agencies. Even though the top agencies were each spending around £5,000 a month with the group, cumulatively, it was good advertising business. Creation was riding the crest of a wave; in 1973, it launched the *Sunday World* as an aggressively down-market Sunday paper. Quickly, it built up a circulation of 200,000 and a corresponding degree of advertising revenue. Hugh McLaughlin and Gerry McGuinness had commissioned market research which showed that there was a definite place for the new paper. The *Sunday World* was started under the aegis of Creation and when the latter group folded in 1975, with debts of about £1.5 million, many suppliers were left unpaid. Before the crash, the *Sunday World* moved out to the old Terenure Laundry, immune from the Creation debts. Eventually, the *Sunday World* was taken over by Independent Newspapers, which had itself been acquired by Tony O'Reilly in 1974. Gerry McGuinness went on to become the only advertisement director in the history of Irish publishing to become a multi-millionaire on the proceeds. Ironically, the year that O'Reilly took over Independent Newspapers was the year the group turned in its best ever advertising revenue, a figure never since repeated.

The year that O'Reilly acquired Independent Newspapers was also the year that the oil-induced recession hit the Irish economy and important advertising sectors, like property, took a nose dive. *The Irish Times* had a significant reduction in advertising revenue; in its 1975 financial year, it lost nearly £300,000. In 1973, it had 418,000 column inches of advertising. By 1979, that figure had been cut to 367,000. In 1973, *The Irish Times* started a newspaper called the *Education Times,* which lasted until 1977. In one issue of 1975, for instance, it was bereft of advertising. Since those harrowing days, *The Irish Times* has made drastic efforts to improve its advertising revenue. In 1985, it turned over £10.7 million in advertising revenue, about 60 per cent of the paper's total revenue. Rates are dearer and circulation is lower than that of rivals, admits general advertisement manager, Seamus O'Neill. Building societies tend to book solus positions at the beginning of

Billy King has probably been involved in the advertising business longer than anyone else, almost 70 years.
He joined Independent Newspapers in 1917 and spent over 50 years with the paper, before joining Dublin Opinion magazine and later Construction and Property News, from which he retired in 1986.
Photograph: Fergus Bourke.

449

the year, but virtually nothing else comes in of its own accord. Over half the newspaper's advertising revenue comes from the agencies. Now, the paper has about 20 telephone salespeople, handling recruitment and personal advertisements. Other sales teams cover such areas as motor dealers. Presentations to agencies now include videos, unheard of even three or four years ago. Seamus O'Neill believes that with the new press, capable of producing spot and process colour, the paper will become more specialised. Already, advertisement features form a substantial part of revenue. With the new press running, the paper intends to develop a lot of new sections. O'Neill also reckons full colour will benefit non-equine advertisements in the weekly *Irish Field*. Louis O'Neill, *The Irish Times'* deputy chief executive and managing director, admits that newspapers have been slow to keep pace with changes in the marketplace, but says that there is a range of advertisers who want full colour facilities and short lead times. "Some major advertisers have shown great interest in doing full colour advertisements in *The Irish Times*. It's not just a question of winning back lost ground, but developing new ground."

New-style advertisement copy taking at the Cork Examiner. **Copy taken over the 'phone is keyboarded into the direct input photocomposition system and semi-display ads are formatted on screen.** *Photograph: Cork Examiner.*

By the time Billy O'Neill died in 1975, the *Cork Examiner* was well on the way to introducing modern sales techniques into its advertising department. In the early 1960s, the paper put representatives on the road, further strengthening its sales efforts about 1968 by introducing tele-ad sales. Dave Lenihan was *Evening Echo* advertisement manager from 1955 until 1975, when the advertisement manager of the *Cork Examiner,* by then Barry Wood, took responsibility for the evening paper as well.

Joe O'Grady came to the Dublin office of the *Cork Examiner* in 1967; when the ubiquitous Miss Lynch retired in 1973, he took over as Dublin manager. Over 95 per cent of the paper's full colour advertising comes from Dublin agencies, even for Cork-based firms like Murphy's and Beamish and Crawford, the brewery concerns. The paper's full colour advertising is only about 30 per cent more expensive than black and white. O'Grady, who was chairman of the Publicity Club in 1984

The new web offset press with full colour facilities at *The Irish Times.*

and who is current chairman of TABS and on the committee of management of the Advertising Standards Authority, says that the single most important advertising area for the newspaper to crack is food brands, in colour, business that is now going exclusively to TV and magazines. Over the last three or four years, the *Cork Examiner,* with its sister paper, the *Evening Echo,* has been going strong in full colour advertising. In Cork, the papers' new direct input System 6 enables classified advertising to be inputted for setting by the tele-ad girls, at the same time that the whole accounting side of the ad is catered for. Display ads can be formatted on screen. In 1986, the firm has also updated its colour scanner, so that it can produce its own separations for colour advertisements, if necessary, with a very short lead time.

One new Sunday paper came and went, building up huge losses for Joe Moore of the PMPA, who had acquired it soon after its launch in 1979. The *Sunday Journal* closed three years later, despite a display advertisement rate of £9 a single column inch.

The *Sunday Tribune* was launched in 1980, as the old *Hibernia* magazine in new form. John Mulcahy remained as editor, while Hugh McLaughlin financed it. Later, McLaughlin sold out to Smurfits. Eventually the paper was closed down, only to be revived in early 1983, edited by Vincent Browne and largely financed by Tony Ryan of Guinness Peat Aviation. After changes of financing, Browne, by now both editor and owner, has steadied the paper into a 100,000 circulation publication. Its colour supplement attracts much upmarket advertising support, developed by advertisement director, Barbara Nugent, now the paper's managing director.

The *Belfast Telegraph,* which brought in web offset printing in 1985, now offers full colour to advertisers. Before Christmas, 1985, local store groups like Dunne's and Stewarts used extensive full colour in their advertising. In the first seven months of 1985, the *Belfast Telegraph* published 326,470 classified advertisements. Nearly 85,000 were motor ads, 16,500 for property and 12,000 job vacancies. The paper now has a classified sales staff of over 50; one of its classified tele-ad girls, Lorraine Greene, has been featured extensively in the paper's TV advertising for its tele-ads' service.

Outside the *Belfast Telegraph* and its attendant weekly newspapers, the Morton group of Lurgan is Northern Ireland's biggest newspaper grouping. It began with Jim Morton's father, who owned the *Lurgan Mail.* In 1946, the firm bought the *Portadown Times,* while the *Londonderry Sentinel* was taken over in 1950. In addition to its newspaper titles, Mortons launched such publications as *Farmweek* and *Project.* The *Londonderry Sentinel's* present advertisement manager, Robert Tate, notes that over the last three or four years, the amount of advertisements received from agencies has dropped back. More advertisers, particularly from country areas, are coming to the newspaper direct.

Gordon Magee of the Morton Group was not always an ad man. In fact he was a charge-hand engineer living in England and had become bored with his job. He contacted his brother in Northern Ireland who suggested advertising. He said he knew nothing about advertising but then took up a correspondence course and went back to school as it were in the evenings. His brother knew Jim Morton very well and as he was able to see how well Gordon was doing he contacted Jim to see if there were any job prospects for him at Morton's. Morton gave Gordon an interview and obviously liked what he saw of his 'work'. Morton was willing to give him a job but asked him the question "Would there be any time when you would not advertise?" Although giving the answer 'yes', which must have made Morton think again, Gordon explained, "I wouldn't advertise if the product was not any good to the customer." He was taken on 18 years ago. "I was two years ad manager in Lurgan and I have just been placed in charge of developing a new horticultural section inside *Farmweek*" he says.

An interesting fact was that quite a few of the ad managers in Morton's at one time all came from the same area in Lurgan and all went to the same school, such as Ivor Smyth at headquarters who has been responsible for developing the new *Skylines* publication. There was also Drew McConnell who had applied for an ad job in the *Portadown Times* which he didn't get. The person who got the job didn't stay. Gordon recalled that Drew had a job in the swimming pool in the town, spoke to him, Drew took the job and became advertisement manager in the *Portadown Times* and *Lurgan Mail*. There was also Robert Tate who had started with the *Ulster Star* in Lisburn where Ivor Smyth was ad manager. He was offered a move to the *Londonderry Sentinel* and he has been there ever since.

30 years ago there was a very short man, a great character, who

Major T. B. McDowell is chairman of The Irish Times Trust and chairman and chief executive of The Irish Times. **He regards the selling of advertisement space as much more competitive nowadays, for both black and white and full colour: "With our new press, we can offer colour at a sensible price, but while we want to increase colour revenue in the newspaper and in the separate supplements we are now producing, we take great care to ensure that the paper does not lose any of its character." Major McDowell also sees the advent of colour printing as being very beneficial to the weekly** Irish Field.

worked as advertisement manager of the *Ulster Star* in Lisburn. His name was Charlie Hunniford, father of Gloria Hunniford who is today a well-known name on British television and radio.

Elsewhere in the provincial press in Northern Ireland, the *Ballymena Times,* now part of the *Belfast Telegraph,* notes a significant falling off in jobs advertising. The paper's advertising accounts section is now centralised in Belfast. At the *Tyrone Courier,* which carries four or five pages a week of motoring advertisements, there has been a big drop in Government and cigarette advertising. In May of 1985, VAT was imposed on newspaper advertisements for the first time in Northern Ireland, in keeping with Britain. This led to a drop in turnover, at the *Outlook,* Rathfriland, says Vera McDowell, the advertisement manager. Much of the paper's classified advertising is taken over the 'phone, but as much as 25 per cent is never paid for. With the paper's small staff, it is not worthwhile chasing such small amounts.

Jack Cairns was appointed advertisement manager of the *Newtownards Chronicle* on February 9, 1961. "I recall that date however for a very different reason", he admitted, "for my daughter was born on that day." He then reflected back to the way things have changed over the years. "There is certainly no way I would be doing what I am today without the introduction of web-offset. It has also changed the whole aspect of newspapers and its advertising as, with the old Cossar's, we were limited to 16 page editions, whereas of course we are publishing 28/32 page editions.

"Without question advertising has been good to me and Newtownards is perhaps like nowhere else in the country. It has remained very parochial which is not a bad thing. People are very proud of their town and know everything that goes on in it. And the *Chronicle* has continued to be the lifeblood of the local community."

He also recalled trying to prove to a potential advertiser that a classified ad in the *Chronicle* could sell almost anything. And although a little disbelieving he agreed to submit the following "docile donkey very fond of children for sale." The following week the *Chronicle* ran its own plug: "Ten shillings sold one donkey and could have sold five more."

"I was also quick to learn that you don't pay anyone a visit before 10.00 a.m." He was on his first visit to a particular business in the town. The manager hardly glanced up from reading his newspaper as he walked in. "I introduced myself as the new ad rep for the *Chronicle* only to get this reply 'Do you people never sleep?'" "I was responsible for the introduction of the motor pages and now the response from garages in advertising revenue is quite substantial in the *Chronicle* and the *Bangor* and *Newtownards Spectators.*" Jack Cairns died in 1985.

1985 saw the national newspapers of Ireland banding together to promote themselves collectively. The eleven national newspapers, four morning, three evening and four Sunday, have formed the National Newspapers of Ireland, in an attempt to win back advertising revenue for newspapers. RTE television and radio is now getting £40 million worth of advertising revenue a year, while the national newspapers combined get about £25 million worth of national advertising. The National Newspapers' share of the country's advertising "cake" has slipped from 56 per cent in 1979 to 40 per cent in 1985. The new association has been making presentations to both advertisers and agencies to prove the power of the press as an advertising medium. The biggest advertisers in the national press are retail outlets (£4.2 million in 1984), followed by tobacco companies (£3 million in 1984) and the motor trade (same expenditure level) and financial institutions (£2.2 million in 1984). The top 20 advertisers in the national press in 1984 included three building societies, Cadburys, Carroll Industries, ESB, Fords, Gallaher, Guinness, Irish Distillers, Kelloggs, Mars Confectionery, Nissan, Player and Wills, Proctor & Gamble, Quinnsworth, Switzers and Toyota. *The Irish Times* web offset press started printing the newspaper and the *Irish Field* in August, 1986. The first full colour advertisement in *The Irish Times,* printed on its own press was a ½ page for Brown Thomas on August 18, 1986.

The provincial press has combined as well in its efforts to sell advertising at national level. As John Hamilton, advertisement manager of the *Southern Star* since 1964, points out, the paper had much national brand advertising in the early 1960s. In common with all other provincials, that revenue has now largely gone to TV. He recalls that in the "good old days", London agencies would automatically send in series' bookings for ¼ page advertisements for brands like Aspro.

Dermod Cafferky, formerly of Arrow, started an Irish Media Representation Service in 1985, with the aim of representing provincial newspapers to advertising agencies and giving a centralised copy collection, invoicing and voucher system. The scheme failed, but the provincial newspapers' own Dublin-based central advertising bureau, which appointed Barry McIntyre as manager in 1986, seems to be off to a better start.

Over the last few years, individual provincial newspapers have made their own efforts to improve advertisement sales, moves forced on them by the serious decline in advertisement revenue. Willie O'Hanlon of the *Anglo-Celt* admits that the advertising side of the paper was badly neglected. "Until the advent of TV advertising 25 years ago, provincials were the accepted medium and advertisements came in more or less automatically." Only within the last five years has the *Anglo-Celt* had a proper sales structure for its advertisement division.

Likewise at the *Kerryman* in Tralee, Sean Colgan, the present advertisement manager, is the first person to hold that title on the paper. "Dan Nolan used to do all the national advertising, while the classifieds came in by themselves. Now we have a staff taking classifieds and may soon start telephone canvassing. Already, we have three representatives on the road, Jimmy Curtin and John O'Flynn covering Kerry and Christine Lynch based in Cork for the *Corkman.*" At the *Clare Champion* in Ennis, the late Bill Dargan, who died in August, 1985, was the accountant, with a sideline in advertising for a while. He had succeeded Frank McInerney, who had been advertisement manager before leaving for the short-lived *Clare News* in 1979. McInerney is now out of newspaper advertising; he is sales manager for Leadmore Ice Cream in Kilrush. He was succeeded, in 1979, by Pat Cleary, who joined as advertisement and marketing manager. Cleary had much UK experience before returning home; before taking the Ennis job, he spent five years with the *South Wales Argus* group of

Louis O'Neill, deputy chief executive and managing director, The Irish Times. **He says of the newspaper's new web offset press with full colour facilities: "There is a range of advertisers who want full colour with short lead times. We will be developing new ground with our new printing facilities."** *Photograph: The Irish Times.*

456

newspapers, first as classified advertisement and then as display advertisement sales manager. His arrival at the *Clare Champion* has been symptomatic of a growing professionalism in advertisement sales in the provincial press. He is assisted by two representatives, Oliver O'Regan and Pauline Keogh. Before Paul May was appointed advertisement manager of the *Nationalist and Leinster Times* in Carlow in 1974, no-one was really selling advertisements on the paper. Front office staff simply took in ad copy. Now, May, who has worked on the advertisement side of the paper since 1961, has a staff of five. Display advertisements are actively sold, but classifieds still come in of their own accord. The *Donegal Democrat,* which started off at the end of World War I as a small-scale, hand-set paper, now covers most of the north-west. Elizabeth Crawford is advertisement manager based at the Ballyshannon head office, while Seamus McBride heads up the ad sales team at the paper's other office, at Letterkenny in north Donegal. McBride has been with the paper about five years, Crawford for seven. Before them, the paper had no proper advertisement sales structure. 95 per cent of its advertisements are of local origin; of the national advertisements, most are from building societies. Up to the 1960s, advertisements for the *Western People* in Ballina were handled by the office staff; there was no formal structure for advertisement sales. Today, John Reilly, the advertisement manager, Tommy Knight and David Dwan look after feature and general display advertising, while a team of four girls looks after classified. The back page In Memoriam column is one successful source of revenue, while the paper gets two and more pages an issue of entertainments advertising.

Seamus Morahan came into newspaper advertising from trade publishing; he has been with the *Leinster Leader* in Naas since 1981 and was the first advertisement manager as such. Before then, Bill Britton looked after display advertisements and the classifieds came over the counter. Freesheets have grown, such as the *Liffey Valley News* and *Cill Dara,* published by the *Meath Chronicle,* "pirate" radio stations offer cheap ad rates and RTE Radio 2 has very competitive package deals for smaller town traders. Five years ago, up to 80 per cent of advertisements arrived at the paper unsolicited; now the figure is down to about 50 per cent. When Morahan arrived at the paper, advertisers and newspapers stuck to the rate card: now, the norm is to do a deal.

Despite all the problems in the press, humour still abounds. Not long ago, Switzers had an advertisement featuring "fur coats from Chilly".

Mistakes continue to happen from time to time. At the end of 1984, some prominent Dublin journalists and businessmen, including John Feeney of the *Evening Herald* and Kevin Marron of the *Sunday World,* were killed in an air crash at Eastbourne. Several days later, a national daily published a page of photographs taken at the removal of the remains. A 10" by six columns advertisement for British Airways was inserted in too close juxtaposition: the following day, an apology had to be printed. Two years earlier, another daily published an obituary of Joe Walsh, the holiday company man, instead of his father. There were no long-term effects on JWT advertising. In an *Irish Independent* issue in August, 1986, a typesetting error had a jobs advertisement placed by Kildare County Council offering the position of waterworks caretaker at a **weekly** wage of up to £12,371.

The *Nenagh Guardian,* within recent memory, had an advertisement which read: "Mick Foley won't lend his ass to no-one no more". At the *Leinster Leader,* in the remembrance of Bill Britton, a small ad showed a thoroughbred ram for sale under the name of a local man. The man's solicitor was told that his client would appear even more foolish if he pursued the matter in the paper, but for the next six months, every similar pre-paid ad was carefully checked for similar faults. One provincial newspaper once ran an advertisement for a sireing service, complete with photograph of the generously endowed bull. If photographs of defendants in court cases are published, it is with black strips over their faces. The bull's photograph appeared complete with black strip over its head.

In early 1985, one of the stalwarts of the newspaper advertising

Jean Callanan, senior brand manager, Harp lager (left), views the first full colour lager advertisement printed on the new press at The Irish Times, **in August, 1986. Also in the photograph are Dolores McCarthy, Arks Advertising and Seamus O'Neill, general advertisement manager,** The Irish Times.
Photograph: The Irish Times.

industry died: Horace Denham, who worked on the *Evening Press* and *The Irish Times*. His last job was as London display advertisement manager for the latter paper. From 1947 to 1950, he worked on the *Radio Review*. Then followed ten years with the *Irish Press*, where he was much involved in the advertisement side of the new *Evening Press*. In 1960, he rejoined *The Irish Times* as advertisement manager for *Radio Review*. Later, when he was working for *The Irish Times*, he was transferred from London to Dublin. Seven months later, the paper transferred him back to London, where he worked until his death.

Danny Moroney retired as group advertisement manager at the *Irish Press* in 1985, after 15 years in the job. He remembers that while O'Connell Street was a mecca for small ads, it was difficult from a production point of view, since it was separated by several hundred yards from Burgh Quay. The O'Connell Street office has now been sold off. Tele-ads are based in Burgh Quay, there are sales outlets for small ads in the ILAC centre and in College Green and the rest of the sales team, now headed by Frank McGouran, formerly assistant advertisement manager and a member of the project team that brought the *Irish Press* into the computerised phototypesetting era.

While Southside Publications, the big Dublin area free distribution newspaper group started by Andrew Whittaker, a former business editor of *The Irish Times*, nearly ten years ago is now part of the *Irish Press* group, provincial freesheets have continued to expand. One of the most recent has been the *Longford Express*, produced weekly by Derek Cobbe's *Longford News*; 10,000 copies are distributed every Friday in the main urban areas of Co Longford.

In 1986, the *Impartial Reporter* of Enniskillen remains the only provincial newspaper in Ireland to keep all advertisements on its front page. Explains Joan Trimble, owner: "It would be difficult to get good, front page news in our area. Readers like the advertisements and there is much competition for front page space."

CHAPTER EIGHT

Outdoor Advertising

"Guinness is Good For You".

JOHN GILROY POSTER CAMPAIGNS, 1930s

Outdoor advertising is the oldest and youngest medium of all; today's bus shelter advertisements can trace their ancestry back to the outdoor advertising of ancient Rome, 2,000 years ago. Today, outdoor advertising makes use of sophisticated techniques; the message may have changed, but the medium remains the same. In ancient Rome, where there were no printed media for advertising, shopkeepers crafted elaborate displays to put outside their shops. The red and white pole, so traditional outside barbers' shops, traces its origins back to Roman times. In Pompeii, wiped out by the volcanic eruption of AD 79, prostitutes in the town's brothels hung out signs depicting their services. With the collapse of the Roman empire, advertising went into a decline that lasted over 1,000 years. In the Middle Ages, the most common form of outdoor advertising was the town crier, who paraded up and down dung-filled streets shouting his wares, which included slogans for local shops. In the embryonic towns of Ireland, such as Dublin and Cork, the town crier was the only means of advertising.

The invention of printing marked the first stage in the development of poster advertising. The earliest surviving poster produced in Britain was printed by Caxton in 1477 and advertised the Pyes of Salisbury, a set of rules for the clergy relating to offices during the Easter festival that year. The poster measured $5\frac{1}{4}$" × 3" and includes a phrase, which

David Allen (1830-1903), the founder of the poster firm that bears his name.

A billposter at work in Dublin in 1890; he is posting notice of cheap railway excursions to Drogheda, Navan, Kells and Oldcastle. The maximum return fare from Dublin to Drogheda was 4/- (20p).
Photograph: A. V. Henry.

An early outdoor sign on a strawberries and cream eating house somewhere in Ireland about 1900. The exact location is unknown, but judging by the thatch, probably in the midlands.
Photograph: RTE Illustrations library. Restoration by George Morrison.

The building on the right of this watercolour painted by Frank McKelvey, RHA, is believed to have been the original premises in Arthur Square, Belfast, where David Allen started business in 1857.

translated from the Latin, reads: "Pray do not pull down this advertisement". In Elizabethan and Jacobean England, in the 16th and early 17th centuries, broadsheet posters came into vogue, but printing was slow to supplant hand drawing for poster production. A proclamation issued by Francis I of France in 1539 says that royal edicts should be written in large letters on pieces of parchment for display on boards.

Printing in Belfast was started about 1697 by artisans "imported" from Glasgow; they printed public notices, the forerunner of Government advertising and displayed outdoors. By the 18th century, bill posting had become an accepted and widely used form of advertising, including in Ireland, where it was a serious rival to newspaper advertising, started in earnest about 1730.

In Paris and London, specially equipped poster hangers toured towns and cities putting up posters about patent medicines, politics and concerts. The new-fangled coffee houses, which sprung up during the century to promulgate the recently discovered coffee bean, were also advertised by poster.

The invention of lithography by Aloys Senefelder in 1793 created the technical means for the growth of poster production, which reached its zenith in Paris in the 1890s. Merchants and tradesmen of the city used the poster medium extensively. Toulouse Lautrec designed a full colour poster for the Moulin Rouge in 1891 that is widely considered to have given birth to the concept of the modern poster. A cabaret poster painted by Toulouse Lautrec in 1893 sold in Chicago in 1985 for £27,500. The golden age of poster advertising in Paris lasted until 1900.

But before such posters came into vogue, there were many other developments in outdoor advertising. One of the earliest in Ireland was used by an Englishman called Thomas Bish, who promoted lotteries and who was using aerial advertising by 1810. To promote his lotteries in Dublin, people were paid to go aloft in hot air balloons, which floated over the city, causing great excitement and interest. The men in the balloons dropped leaflets, advertising the lotteries, on the crowds below. Bish displayed an ingenuity that anticipated modern outdoor techniques by a century. The next big advance in outdoor advertising did not come until the advent of the railways; Ireland's first railway line, from Westland Row to Kingstown (now Dun Laoghaire) was opened in 1834. The newspaper and advertising agency of J. K. Johnston & Co of Eden Quay had been set up in 1819; it went bankrupt in 1850 and was taken over by W. H. Smith, the London newsagents which was also starting to develop railway advertising. In 1850, some 73 million passenger journeys were made in Britain and Smith's started renting advertising concessions from the railway companies and in turn hired out these sites to advertising contractors. Charles Eason was brought over from Manchester to manage the Smith business in Dublin. He arrived in Dublin in 1856 and the following year, the firm signed its first contract, with the Great Southern Railway. By 1858, the Dublin firm was responsible for placing advertisements at 16 railway stations on the Great Southern system.

By one of those fine historical ironies, the year that Smith's in Dublin started advertising on the railways, a young man called David Allen set up business in Arthur Square, Belfast. Allen, who had served his printing apprenticeship with the *Weekly Vindicator* and who knew Daniel O'Connell, decided to open his own printing house, which later developed into Ireland's biggest poster advertising company. The improved techniques of poster production allied to a growing demand for poster advertising by the theatres, created possibilities for expansion by Allen. At one end of the poster scale, there were the elaborate productions made possible by the use of lithographic colour printing, while at the other, were the bill stickers that appeared on so many urban walls in Ireland in the latter part of the 19th century. In London in 1877, it was estimated that there were some 200 men working as bill posters. Ladder men, working a 12 hour day, could earn up to £1.15s.0d a week. Fly-posters, whose work was supposed to be illegal, earned four shillings a day, but only worked during the summer months. By the 1860s in Ireland, privately rented sites became available for the first time; advertisers could have guaranteed displays for agreed periods of time.

While outdoor advertising in the streets of Ireland was beginning to grow, railway advertising was still in its infancy. By 1864, Smith's was enjoying an annual revenue from railway advertising in Ireland of just £2,083. Just over ten years later, in 1875, that amount had only risen to £4,538. In the late 1870s and early 1880s, a major economic depression

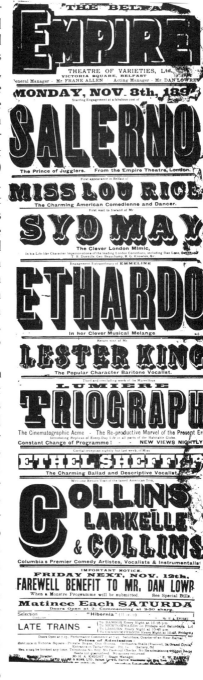

1897 poster for the
Empire Theatre,
Belfast.
Illustration: Alex Findlater.

463

This sign for Rudge Whitworth cycles hung outside a Kilkenny bicycle dealers in 1899.
Photograph: Dick Shackleton.

Trams at Royal Avenue, Belfast, about 1900. Brands advertised include Fry's cocoa, Hudson's soap and Murray's Mellow Mixture tobacco, produced in Belfast.
Photograph: Lawrence Collection.

meant big cuts in advertising expenditure. However, despite the cutbacks, particularly on the Great Northern Railways' station advertising, progress was being made. In 1877, William Russell & Co of Lower Sackville Street, Dublin, was contracted to place 96 railway station advertisements over a period of three years, at a total cost of £60, which included printing charges and the battens for holding the advertisements in place at the stations.

The railway companies were keen to ensure high standards in advertising at stations and on lineside hoardings; by the 1890s, when the railway network was virtually at its zenith and most of the 800 stations throughout Ireland carried advertising posters, the railway firms provided facilities for the poster production companies to visit each station two or three times a year. Free carriage for men and materials was provided. Most of the railway station advertising was literally outdoor — on the platforms, or by the tracks, but some was "indoor" in the waiting rooms. By the 1880s, railway advertising was aimed at the sophisticated and wealthy middle classes; the Dublin and Wicklow line, which ran through Bray and which terminated at Harcourt Street, presented an important "captive" audience. Such firms as Elverys, Prescotts, McBirneys, Clerys and Jacobs all advertised on the railways; there was one payment recorded of £3.15s.0d, to the Dublin photographer Lawrence, for taking photographs of hotels in Co Wicklow for use in railway poster advertisements. Many of the posters for the railway stations were all enamelled; in 1898, Easons, as the firm was known by then, since Charles Eason had acquired control in 1886, went into advertisement production itself. Its factory was at Great Brunswick Street, now Pearse Street. It produced railway posters and survived for a half century. The factory made both the

enamel posters and the printed posters used for shorter duration campaigns. By 1900, Easons was deriving half its profits from railway advertising.

A rival medium came into being in the 1880s: trams. The main cities of Ireland, Dublin, Cork and Belfast, got their own tram services and advertisers were quick to spot the possibilities. Examples of tram advertising in Belfast can be dated back to at least 1885. Very quickly, all available spaces — front, rear, sides and the staircase — were filled with advertisements, which coincided with the start of modern brand advertising in Britain. Products like Neave's Food (for infants) and Wincarnis tonic wine began using tram advertising as an ideal mobile medium.

With the development of tram advertising and the improvement in poster printing techniques, Allens in Belfast decided to extend its printing business into poster display contracting in 1887. This was so successful in the North of Ireland and also in Britain, that by 1895, Allen's had extended this poster display business into Dublin. David Allen & Sons (the title reflected the expansion of this family firm) put up its first multiple poster site on Dublin's North Circular Road in 1895. Some 40 posters, many printed in full colour, were pasted onto a wall space measuring 35 feet by 20 feet. The posters were pasted directly onto the wall; there was no frame, no back panels and no apron. Advertisers included Power's whiskey, Phoenix Dublin-brewed stout, D'Arcy's Dublin stout, cigarettes, cocoa and tea, soap and starch, bicycles and pianos, *The Weekly Irish Times* (for a serial entitled "The Death Mask"), the *Daily Nation* and, incongruously, the *Sheffield Telegraph,* the RDS Horse Show, "Edna" wine ("sold in all respectable bars"), table water and syrup, ladies' made-to-measure corsets,

Thompson's bakery was a household name in Cork for many years and its bread and cakes, produced at MacCurtain Street, were advertised continuously on the Cork trams. This photograph was taken about 1900.
Photograph: Cork Examiner.

The Dublin United Tramways Company (1896), Ltd.

ROUTES   ROUTES.

NELSON'S PILLAR   NELSON'S PILLAR
to   to
DALKEY   HOWTH
to   to
TERENURE   SANDYMOUNT
to   to
SANDYMOUNT   DARTRY ROAD
to   to
PALMERSTON   CLONSKEA
PARK
RATHFARNHAM   DOLPHIN'S BARN
to   to
DRUMCONDRA   GLASNEVIN
to   to
DONNYBROOK   HATCH STREET
to   to
PHOENIX PARK   KINGSBRIDGE
O'CONNELL
BRIDGE   INCHICORE
PARKGATE   WESTLAND ROW
to   to
KENILWORTH   PARK GATE
SQUARE
LANSDOWNE RD.   BALLYBOUGH

THE NELSON PILLAR.
The Centre of Dublin Tramway System.

Directors:
WM. M. MURPHY, J.P., Chairman.
Ald. W. F. COTTON, J.P., D.L., M.P.;   JOSEPH MOONEY, J.P.;
CAPT. C. COLTHURST VESEY, D.L.

Secretary:
R. S. TRESILIAN, A.M.I.C.E.I., F.C.I.S.

Manager:
C. W. GORDON.

Offices: 9 UPPER SACKVILLE STREET, DUBLIN

In the early years of this century, the Dublin tramway network was expanded considerably, thanks to the work of William Martin Murphy, chairman of the tramways company and also owner of Independent Newspapers. The Dublin trams became an important outdoor advertising medium.

McBirney's sale and Todd Burns' department store of Dublin and Paris. David Allen & Sons, which had the poster market more or less to itself, designed, printed and pasted all the posters.

While Allen's was about to move into the Dublin market, Wilson Hartnell was expanding in the outdoor field. In 1893, it signed an agreement for a three year period, at £100 a year, for the advertising rights on the Ha'penny bridge in Dublin. In the agreement, Wilson Hartnell, described as publishers and press agents, undertook to spend the sum of £50 painting and improving the Metal Bridge. They also undertook not to sheet over the railing of the bridge, so as to unduly increase the wind pressure. The use of gas lighting on the bridge was also covered by the agreement.

The full colour outdoor poster was in its heyday in the 1890s; no other advertising medium could offer such possibilities. Two types of advertising lent themselves to the new technical excellence: music hall and touring theatre companies needed considerable quantities of posters, which David Allen & Sons turned out in huge amounts. Large pictorials for theatre shows and personalities were printed by Allen's in Belfast, with space left for overprinting venues, dates and prices. National brand advertising also made full use of the new full colour facilities.

Fred Mullen, for so long associated with Allen's, wrote some of his memorable verse to commemorate those days, nearly a century ago. He described the "stock litho displays, in the Music Hall days, for Robey or Lloyd-Harry Tate". In another verse, he wrote:

In that golden period from the nineties onwards
What clients we had — they conjure up an age;
John Martin Harvey-Tree — and Cyril Maude,
Giants of the music hall and stage.

From music hall and theatre posters developed the cinema posters; Dublin had its first picture showing in 1896 and before World War I, a spate of penny picture houses had mushroomed in Dublin. All used lurid posters to advertise their wares. Theatre and cinema poster advertising had to be completed on time, regardless of the weather, as versifier Fred Mullen wrote:

You had to get out your barrow
and push off to Terenure.
You might be back by Sunday
but you weren't completely sure.
When theatres came in at the last minute,
it was raining like a flood.
You fared out into the weather
to do the best you could.

The other big impetus to poster production in the 1890s came from the development of branded products. Brands, mostly British, like Bovril, Fry's cocoa, but some Irish like Thwaites soda and Downes', bread were all developing and amenable to poster advertising. A typical

466

turn-of-the-century poster campaign, using 5,000 × 16 sheet bills in four colours cost about £1,200, made up of £20 for the artist's sketch (the best-known artists could command up to £100), £300 for the printing, £800 for posting and site rental (calculated at £1 per 100 d/c units a month) and £80 for the agent's services.

Printing posters were important, but for greater durability, enamel ones were used. Brands such as Oxo, Players and Bass all used enamel posters in Ireland. Most of the enamel signs used in Ireland were imported from Britain; the Dublin Japon Works was the only such sign producer known to be operating in the city 85 years ago. Some of the enamel signs advertised local firms and brands, like the Ulster Bank and Murray's Belfast tobacco, but the most elaborate signs were made for the big British brands. Perhaps the best-known of all was the one for Player's cigarettes, showing the bearded sailor from HMS Invincible. The sign was made in sizes up to 3'6" high, with the colours layered on before being heat glazed. From mono dimensional signs grew such masterpieces as the Stephen's Ink thermometer, frequently seen in Ireland until 20 years ago.

By the time the Irish International Exhibition was opened in Herbert Park, Dublin, in 1907, David Allen & Sons was sufficiently well established in the city to issue a handsome book detailing the attractions of Ireland. The album featured over a hundred tinted picture postcards of views of the main towns and cities of Ireland.

80 years ago, breweries were major advertisers on the tram services. A tram with an advertisement for Cairnes' ale, brewed in Drogheda, is seen entering the old Vergemount tram depot at Clonskeagh Road, Dublin.

Early advertising on public transport. This photograph, taken in Eyre Square, Galway, in the 1890s, shows Moon's, the Galway department store, advertising on the Galway-Salthill tram. *Photograph: National Library.*

A Belfast City Tramways' ticket, complete with advertisement.
Photograph: J. M. Maybin.

Allen's stated that each and every town featured in the book "has its own attractions for the visitor and they will all receive a large measure of patronage. Consequently, posters appearing on bill posting stations in both large and small Irish towns during the run of the exhibition will be fruitful canvassers for advertisers." Allen's had its head offices at 18-24 Corporation Street, Belfast. It described itself as a firm of "pictorial placard printers, show card manufacturers and publishers". Allen's was active in Britain: it had 16 offices in Scotland (following a series of take-overs of local poster companies) and 30 branches. In England, it had six offices and a factory. Here in Ireland, the firm had offices at Dublin (40 Great Brunswick Street, now Pearse Street), Belfast (22 William Street South), Derry (5 Richmond Street), Waterford (14 O'Connell Street), Dundalk (Market Street), Portadown (Castle Street) and Ballymena (70 Church Street). In addition, Allen's also had branches at Omagh, Lurgan, Larne, Portstewart, Newtownards, Holywood, Dunmurry, Lisburn, Enniskillen, Dalkey, Kingstown, Strabane, Armagh, Coleraine, Portrush, Bangor, Comber, Carrickfergus, Whitehead, Blackrock, Rathmines and Banbridge. The firm also announced that "it was at Australia".

Simpler, but no less effective, posters continued to be printed for politicians. Firms like Danns of Longford, which has continued to the present, used big wooden type for printing political and other single colour posters, a far cry from the elaborate full colour posters being used in London and Paris at the turn of the century. Just as Allen's had

Poster site at Church Street, Dublin, in the early years of this century.

468

developed posters in the North of Ireland as an offshoot of printing
and publishing, so too did Guys and News Bros in Cork and George
McKern & Sons in Limerick. In 1909, Wilson Hartnell signed an
agreement with the Great Northern Railway Company for
advertising rights on the Howth tramway cars. In June, 1914, it
concluded an advertising rights' agreement with the Royal Dublin
Society.

Fred Mullen remembers the old times in posters:

> When hoardings had ornate skirtings supported by wooden
> stays
> And we had the "stock litho" for Colleen Bawn in the old
> melodrama days,
> When the Bisto Kids were just starting and Johnnie Walker
> was young
> And they loved to hear "Daisy, Daisy", when pops by our
> pops were sung.

Theatre safety curtains have always provided well-used advertising platforms. The photograph shows the safety curtain of the Opera House, Cork, some time in the early years of this century, covered in advertisements from local traders.
Photograph: Cork Examiner.

469

Following the tremendous success of the 1907 international exhibition in what is now Herbert Park, Dublin, an equally impressive civic exhibition was planned for Dublin in 1914. The outbreak of World War I totally overshadowed the event. This poster was printed by the old Dollard printing house, now part of Brindley Dollard.

World War I produced perhaps the most famous poster of all: the Kitchener recruiting poster issued by the British Government in 1915. "Kitchener wants you. Join your Country's Army. God save the King." These recruiting posters were widely displayed in Ireland in the early days of the war.

Theatre posters continued to be elaborately four and five coloured, while the new medium of entertainment, the cinema, provided a new outlet for poster printers. At first, cinema posters advertising forthcoming attractions tended to be masses of type, cramming in as much information as possible. The cinema came into its own in the early 1920s; accordingly, so did its publicity posters blossom, with elaborate use of half-tone reproductions for the first time in Irish posters. Some of the 1920's posters remain works of printing art: so sophisticated had the art of cinema advertising become that distributors, principally London-based, sent out whole packages of advertising material in advance of each new film. While cinema posters were gracing many cinemas, particularly the new, purpose-built ones in Dublin and other cities, cinemas also meant good business for David Allen & Sons. By the mid-1920s, it had a large poster site outside Harcourt Street station in Dublin; the entire hoarding was pasted with posters advertising forthcoming cinema showings in the area. Such was the profusion of cinemas then in just one small area of South Dublin, that the Stella and the Princess were thriving in Rathmines, while the De Luxe and the Camden flourished not far away in Camden Street. Yet the sophistication of cinema poster designs had not penetrated into other types of poster: Bob Milne of CDP, for instance, recalls that in the 1930s, when he was a small boy growing up in West Cork, there was a poster that advertised quite simply "DC Orange". It was his first sight of advertising.

However, Allen's, which had been concentrated in Dublin and the east coast region, decided in the late 1920s to increase its spread throughout Ireland. By 1930, it had display facilities in most Irish towns with populations over 3,000. A rival firm was McConnell-Hartley, set up by Charlie McConnell in 1922.

One of the great tragedies of outdoor advertising in the 1930s was that Guinness in Dublin never sanctioned the kind of poster campaigns that graced British roadsides. Guinness had appointed an advertising manager in London in 1928, closely followed by an agency, Benson's. The first Guinness poster appeared in 1929, using a design that had already been test marketed in Scotland. It showed quite simply, a glass brimful of Guinness, with the slogan: "Guinness is good for you". In the autumn of that year, the "Guinness" reference was dropped, showing how quickly the campaign had taken root in the public consciousness. The work of John Gilroy, the celebrated poster artist, soon brought acclaim to the brand. He had joined the staff of Benson's in 1925. His first humorous poster for Guinness was done in 1930; it showed a series of plaster casts of famous heads, surrounding a glass of Guinness: "famous for its perfect head". In 1931, Guinness advertising in Britain was extended to a neon sign in Piccadilly Circus, London, that flashed the Guinness slogan.

In 1930, Gilroy started designs based on the "Guinness for Strength" theme, which culminated in the 1932 design showing the man with the girder. With the help of his son, who was training to become a civil engineer, Gilroy achieved the illusion of perfect balance in his design. The man carrying the 40 ton girder in the Gilroy poster was so successful that soon, people ordering Guinness in pubs started asking for a "Girder". So strong was the brand awareness created by the poster that people who weren't even born when it was used have an astonishing recall of the design! Jeremy Bullmore of J. Walter Thompson, who reintroduced the girder man in 1976, believes the poster's popularity might be evidence for the existence of pre-natal advertising recall. In 1935, Gilroy brought in the Guinness toucan. The original design shows a pelican, but copywriter Dorothy L. Sayers (later to become famous as a thriller writer) changed it to a toucan. Other creatures featured, too, in pre-war Guinness poster advertising, such as the ostrich and the tortoise, as well as the well-known sea lion. Yet of all the astonishing variety in the Gilroy posters during the 1930s, it is probably the "strength" ones that remain most memorable. David Ogilvy, the advertising "guru", believes these posters have never been excelled anywhere in the world.

While Guinness was erecting neon signs in Piccadilly Circus, this new medium also came to Ireland. McDowell's, the jewellery shop in O'Connell Street, Dublin, claimed to have had the first animated neon sign in Ireland. McDowell's is an old firm, established in 1870;

The poster for the play that never was — the Abbey Theatre was scheduled to put on the first production of T. H. Nally's play, The Spancel of Death, on Tuesday, April 25, 1916. It was cancelled because of the Easter Rising and only performed for the first time in Boston in May, 1986.

The Ha'penny bridge over the River Liffey in Dublin was built in 1816; in the late 19th and early 20th centuries, it carried advertising posters. Wilson Hartnell was advertisement contractor for the bridge for many years.
Photograph: Laurence O'Connor collection.

471

Russell's, the Limerick flour millers, produced this glass sign in three colours for shop use in the 1920s.
Photograph: Nenagh Heritage Centre.

generations of engaged couples have come to it for their rings. The firm moved to what was then Sackville Street in 1904; in 1916, the premises were burned down, but rebuilt soon afterwards, using girders salvaged from the GPO. The firm's owner, Jack McDowell, achieved fame in 1947 when his horse, "Caughoo" won the Grand National at Aintree. On the boat coming home, Jack McDowell and his brother Herbert made the *Guinness Book of Records* by buying everyone on the boat the world's largest round of drinks. McDowell's also had its niche in outdoor advertising history, thanks to its flashing neon sign. Elsewhere in Dublin, electric bulbs were used for the first time to illuminate outdoor posters.

Tram and bus advertising was also coming on. 1937 saw posters

A military recruitment scene outside Cork railway station, about 1917. Outside the railings of the station yard, on the Lower Glanmire Road, there are hoardings. They are advertising Wolsey brand underwear, the Cork Holly Bough, **published once a year by the** Cork Examiner **and to the left of the photograph, Wincarnis tonic wine.**
Photograph: Cork Examiner.

printed on paper used for the first time on the Dublin trams. Previously, all advertisements had to be produced in the form of enamel signs, because of their durability against the elements. After the war, the Dublin tram fleet was broken up with undue haste and little preserved of this excellent means of urban communication. One of the few surviving tram advertisements can be seen on the wall beside Hayes, Conyngham Robinson's chemist shop in Ballsbridge, Dublin. It is a long side panel, once used for advertising the firm on a Dublin tram. Many other household names once used the Dublin trams, such as Downes' bakery and Tyler's boots. In 1936, the trams of Belfast were all lit up — literally — with special slogans and illuminations to commemorate the coronation of King George VI.

But with the advent of motor buses after World War I, a rival advertising medium had sprung up. Many private lines were started, such as the Old Contemptible Bus Company in Dublin, named thus because many of its staff had fought in World War I. "Old Contemptible" was a term of affection for soldiers in that war.

The Irish Omnibus Company was also prominent in the 1930s: it provided a useful sideline for O'Kennedy Brindley. Just as Wilson Hartnell dabbled in outdoor advertising for many years, so too did O'KB. The agency had the franchise for IOC advertising, a lucrative addition to turnover. Jim Furlong, later to work with the *Irish Press* advertisement department, was the executive at the agency responsible for bus advertising. While the buses were motoring their way through the city, often picking up and putting down passengers at unauthorised stopping places, the horse drawn bread cart was still a familiar sight, trotting round its delivery route. Before the war, when so many people still lived in the tenement blocks in Dublin's city centre — the big move out to the suburbs had only just begun — rounds in these districts were of vital importance for bakeries like Kennedys/DBC, Bolands and Johnston, Mooney and O'Brien. The bakeries had their names, plus suitable advertising slogans, painted on the tops of the bread carts, so that customers in the tenement blocks could look down and see which bakery cart had arrived.

There was a delightful kind of anarchy about much advertising in the 1930s; it may not have been very sophisticated, but advertisers did more or less what they wanted, often giving a lot of fun in the process. The Lyons' Tea hobbyhorses were very popular; another sight that caused much interest among the young and not-so-young was aerial advertising. Fragile 'planes, with barely enough space for the pilot, but no passengers, looped the loop, signwriting in the sky. It was a popular form of advertising: not long after, when Hollywood film actress Jane Russell became famous for her 38" breasts, a skywriter made two circles, each with a central dot, over San Francisco. Everyone knew what was being advertised!

Slightly more mundane sky advertising was used in Ireland about 1936 by Keating's flea powders. A 20' drum was made from light

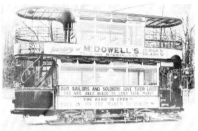

80 year old mirror advertising Boyd's whiskey, Belfast.
Photograph: Irish Distillers' Museum.

A Belfast tram, during World War I, decorated with consumer advertisements and exhortations for the war effort.
Photograph: J. M. Maybin.

materials to resemble a drum of Keating's; the drum was towed behind an aircraft at many locations throughout Ireland.

While some outdoor advertisers were creating good fun — and goodwill for their products — restrictions were looming. The start of the Anglo-Irish economic war in 1933 severely disrupted trade between Britain and the Irish Free State. Poster contractors soon felt the reduction in bookings by British firms selling in Ireland; at least one local firm tried to make up for the shortfall. Independent Newspapers, furious at the arrival of the *Irish Press,* threw tens of thousands of pounds into advertising. By the mid-1930s, it was one of the largest poster users in the country, with hoardings by the side of many main roads proclaiming the virtues of the *Irish Independent.* Some sources believe this rash of poster advertising by Independent Newspapers may have been one of the reasons that prompted the new Fianna Fail government to bring in the 1934 Planning Act. For the first time, poster contractors were under strict scrutiny. The earlier and much more lax local authority building and other by-laws, which gave the poster contractors more or less a free hand, were superseded by far-reaching legislation. This included zoning provisions which sought to exclude poster and sign development from extensive areas and required planning permission for all other new sites for poster and sign

In 1930, Wilson Hartnell was instrumental in having the turret clock erected at the RDS, Dublin. The clockmaker's bill shows that the total cost was £358.10s.

Poster devised by Lynch Advertising for the new Irish Hospitals' Sweep in 1931.

IRISH HOSPITALS SWEEP ON GRAND NATIONAL, 1931.

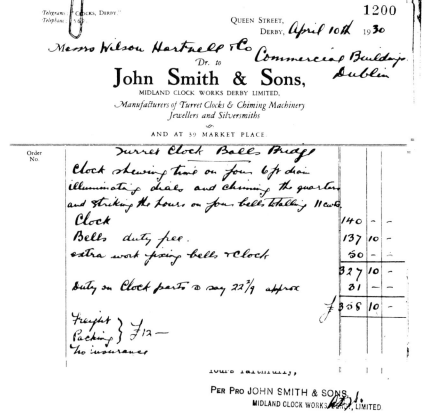

development. Under the new Act, the poster contractors found their activities rigorously curtailed; their reaction to the new Planning Act was similar to that evident when the legislation banning outdoor tobacco products advertising was introduced in 1980. However, some local firms like Becker's Tea, maintained their outdoor advertising. Becker's had a particularly fine window sign in Wicklow Street, Dublin.

In the late 1930s, when the outdoor advertising industry was just starting to recover its ground, another heavy blow fell. Within weeks of the outbreak of World War II in September, 1939, forward bookings of poster space for internationally known branded products fell by 90 per cent. Not only did international brands start disappearing from the local market, but Irish manufacturers soon found that raw material shortages forced a substantial curtailment of advertising.

By 1940, the type of outdoor advertising that was becoming common in Ireland could be seen on the newly-erected air raid shelters at the top of O'Connell Street. These carried posters urging support for the Irish Red Cross. In compensation for the general loss of business, poster firms did report a slight increase in turnover in cinema and theatre posters, although the upturn was not sufficient to deter David Allen & Sons from going ahead with its decision in 1940 to close down the theatre poster side of its operation. That was a sad break with tradition: even more lamentable was the wholesale destruction of stocks. Many theatre posters, some "classics", were thrown out. Today, they would sell for very good prices, a measure of their historical worth.

Before the war, Carroll's, through its advertising agency, McConnell's, had carried out a very successful campaign, an unusual form of "outdoor" advertising. Carroll's electric clocks were installed in many shops and bars; they kept time through the war, and in some instances, until very recently, told Carroll's time. However, Carroll's cigarettes, in common with all other brands, were not always easily available. To circumvent restrictions on outdoor advertising during the war, McConnell's devised a special poster scheme for newsagents and other shops: a poster rack was devised and every week, the poster was changed. The shopkeeper was paid 5/– a week for allowing one of these poster racks to be placed outside his or her premises. McConnell's also devised a scheme of advertising pelmets for shops: different brands could be advertised on them. There was some new poster advertising, however. Consumers' pent-up purchasing power was diverted into investment areas and building society shares. Fred Mullen, then a youthful newcomer at David Allen & Sons, remembers organising the first ever poster campaigns for the Irish Permanent Building Society and the New Ireland Assurance Company. In early 1944, when the Government launched an advertising campaign for Post Office Savings, posters in both Irish and English were used, as well as strips on buses, trains and trams. That year, there was quite a controversy about advertisements on the windows of the Dublin

1920s advertising mirror: "Father loves 'The Baby'" (Powers). The mirror was used by Power's John's Lane distillery, Dublin.
Photograph: Irish Distillers' Museum.

Afton cigarettes enamel sign, made in the 1930s. It still stands outside a newsagent's shop in Grantham Street, off Camden Street, Dublin.
Photograph: Hugh Oram.

United Transport Company's bus fleet. "Writing to the *Mail*" was a popular pastime for people with a grievance and letters came in about the bus window posters obscuring the view. It was a new practice, so much so that when the DUTC started using the front left-hand windows of the buses for advertising posters, complaints from the public forced them to stop. The bus company then started using other window positions, but these too proved unpopular. Some buses were said to have been carrying up to four posters per window. Were advertising men with surplus appropriations to get rid of, to blame for the surfeit of bus window advertising, asked one reader of the Advertising Press Club *Newsletter*.

Just after the war, by which time bus and train transport was being run by the new State-owned company, CIE, the organisation had taken over bus and tram advertising. Bill Maguire, who died in 1985, joined the CIE advertisement department in 1952 at a time when its staff consisted of a manager, two clerks and a typist. He remembered that a side panel on a bus then cost about £20 for a 12 month rental period. Cigarette firms were heavy users of transport advertising. The window stickers in buses remained popular; experiments were conducted with illuminated side panels on buses, but these were not successful. "Dayglo" paints proved a more durable idea.

By about 1950, silk screen printing had come into popular use for poster production in Dublin. Hobson Morris, a large silk screen house, noted that silk screen was ideal for short runs, from 20 to 5,000 copies. The latest development, around 1950, was the production of printed

A Belfast tram decorated for the coronation of King George VI in 1936. The special effects were heightened by the use of electric light bulbs.

transfers, which with the introduction of special extra brilliant transfer inks, quickly became popular. Said Hobson Morris: "They are washable, fast in colour and more durable than the usual small paper bill used in outdoor advertising". Player's Please cigarettes introduced a 12 colour silk screen printed showcard, which included a litho printed stick-on of a cigarette packet. Eamonn P. O'Neill, manager of CIE's outdoor advertisement department at this period, had been manager of Kenny's and had also worked as the Irish manager of Mason's of London, the advertising contractors. In 1949, he advised readers of *Print* magazine that they should commission a commercial artist to produce posters for buses, trams, railway stations and hoardings. He said: "Some artists are very 'touchy' and they should be confided in and treated as a colleague".

A poster for Bushmills whiskey, taken during the 1930s. The vehicle in the centre of the photograph belongs to the outdoor poster contractor and shows ladders strapped to the side.

John Gilroy's Guinness poster, run in the 1930s.

Advertisement for
Easons outdoor
advertising, 1938.

478

ADVERTISING
ON DELIVERY VANS

These small, tidy Delivery Vans may be seen daily in all the principal streets of Dublin and Belfast. Each Van is fitted to carry three Contents Bills, one at the side and two at the back, and a display board on top to carry a Streamer, size 5 ft. 4 ins. x 7½ ins.

RATES for Contents Bills are 5/- each per week, and for Streamer spaces 7/6 each per week, less 15 per cent. discount for three months' order and 20 per cent. for 6 months, or longer.

Only Publishers' advertisements are accepted for these Vans.

EASONS
40-41 L^R O'CONNELL STREET
DUBLIN

BROADCASTS ALL DAY

In the late 1930s, Easons offered mobile advertisements on its fleet of newspaper delivery vans. Rates started at 5/- a week.

479

Trams going across Patrick's Bridge, Cork, just before Christmas, 1927. Brands advertised included Fruitfield jams, "Queen of the West" butter and Thompson's cakes.
Photograph: Cork Examiner.

EVERYWHE

THE LIFFEY. DUBLIN

YOU CAN BE

Shell poster painted by Eve Kirk in 1939.
Photograph: Irish Shell.

E YOU GO

EVE KIRK

IRE OF SHELL

O'Neill concluded by saying: "Of the many and varied methods adopted in placing advertisement matter before the public, few can compare in value with systematised bus, tram, trailway and hoarding publicity. Simply designed and forceful advertising broadcast thus amongst the population is, in effect, the publicity of perpetual motion." McConnell's claimed to be the first agency to develop T-shaped advertisements for buses. CIE had a new advertising medium on offer — its new fleet of long distance vans carried advertising posters on their side panels. Each van had three panels on the offside and two on the nearside; each panel measured 60″ × 40″. In addition, there were two panels at the rear and two in the front. The 60″ × 40″ panels cost £7.16s.0d. annually. While CIE was bringing this new advertising medium to the more remote highways and byways, the Gaelic Athletic Association decided to brighten up the "Railway Wall" at Croke Park. Large-sized posters for such products as Slainte mineral waters, Mick McQuaid tobacco and Packard razor blades were used, with all copy in Irish. Elsewhere in Ireland, a touch of glamour was added to poster advertising, with the large scale displays for Dawn beauty products. Sam McAuley, a go-ahead Northerner, was creating a stir in the cosmetics field with his products; the Irish film star, Maureen O'Hara was launched on her career by winning a Dawn Beauty Queen competition.

A street scene in Cork during the 1930s, showing a poster site for Burton's the tailors.

Opposite page:
An art deco stand designed by Modern Display Artists for clients Carrolls and used in the 1946 RDS Spring Show.

This photograph taken in 1944 on O'Connell Bridge, shows two trams headed southwards. The front vehicle carries advertisements for Tyler's Boots and Powells Lukno sauce, while the rear tram advertises Johnston, Mooney & O'Brien's bread. Both trams were painted in the green and cream livery of the Dublin United Transport Company, introduced two years previously.
Photograph: John Topham Picture Library.

"Come to the ceilidhe" — Inchicore fete advertised on a tram some time during the 1930s.
Photograph: Irish Railway Record Society.

1949 saw two more interesting developments in the outdoor field. First of all, in the publicity campaign prepared by Parker Advertising for the launch of the *Sunday Press*, posters outside newsagents' shops played a prominent part. David Allen & Sons, which did well after the war with the use of outdoor posters on a big scale by motor car, petrol, lubricants, tyres and battery firms, brought in a further innovation in 1949, with its "public information posters", small scale outdoor displays that brought outdoor advertising into previously unexploited locations. In 1950, the firm bought out the poster contracting interests of the local companies in Cork and Limerick and began an overall development programme throughout Munster.

Con Kelleher, advertising manager of Bovril and one of the founding fathers of the Association of Advertisers in Ireland, scored a neat coup for his company. He obtained the rights to place an advertising sign for Bovril at the top of the American Express building in Lower Grafton Street. The lease was long and the rent was said to have been a mere £250 a year. For anyone coming up Grafton Street from the direction of College Green, the sign was a real landmark for many years. No wonder that Con Kelleher had to resist many pleadings from other advertisers who wanted to try and use the site. Outdoor signs employed many novelties in those days; "Don" and "Nelly", the two characters created by Bernard Share, then with O'Kennedy Brindley, appeared in neon form at the D'Olier Street end of O'Connell Bridge. A neon sausage bounced between the two for many years. From the 1920s to the 1980s, the Caltex (later Texaco) sign was prominent on Eason's corner in O'Connell Street. Another Donnelly's gimmick did not work so well, but it created enormous publicity. A huge balloon was fashioned in the shape of a Donnelly's sausage; it was due to be tethered, so that it remained aloft at a

McConnell's stand at the 1947 Dublin Spring Show. The stand had been little changed since its first appearance at the 1936 Horse Show.

reasonable altitude over the city. Overnight, the balloon was filled with gas and moored in the grounds of the old High School at the top of Harcourt Street. Vandals broke in during the night and cut the mooring wires: the sausage drifted up and away, soaring into the airlanes. Eventually, it floated as far as the west coast. An Air Corps 'plane was sent up to intercept the flying sausage, which had to be shot down because of the danger it posed to aircraft. For days afterwards, the papers were full of Donnelly's flying sausage, invaluable publicity for the brand, even if not quite what O'Kennedy Brindley had intended.

In the early 1950s, advertisers in outdoor were keen to exploit new techniques. Some innovations were not quite so successful: staff in McConnell's in the 1950s remember that the agency used litho printing for the first time to print 48 sheet posters for Carroll's cigarettes. The posters looked exceptionally well as they were pasted up around Dublin. Some days later, the posters started to fade and within ten days, they were an unholy mess. McConnell's contractors had to remove them all as quickly as possible, while the agency had to foot the bill for reprinting.

The biggest innovation in Irish poster advertising in the 1950s was without doubt the arrival of More O'Ferrall, in competition to David Allen & Sons. Rory More O'Ferrall, who retired not long ago as the company's chairman, started the company in England in January, 1936. He had worked for Allen's and following a trip to the USA, where he saw that companies were changing from paper posters to painted

A modern advertisement hoarding erected by David Allen & Sons in the Dublin area in the late 1940s. The products advertised included Yardley perfume, Fry's cocoa, Edwards' pickles and Cairnes' ale.

Opposite page: Gaelite Signs erected a sign for Rowntree's on Butt Bridge, Dublin, in the early 1960s.

486

displays, he was convinced that such a development was right for the UK market. He started up in England, providing painted displays. His very first client was the Regent Oil Company, later Caltex and then Texaco. More O'Ferrall opened in Dublin — Rory More O'Ferrall needed little prompting, since he comes from an Irish family. One brother, Roderick, is still active, running a stud farm at Monasterevin. When More O'Ferrall opened for business in Dublin, one of its first clients was the Regent Oil Company. Others soon followed, like Crosse & Blackwell and Pye television. For Donnelly's sausages, the firm did poster sites featuring huge 15' long cut-outs of sausages. The concept of painted signs — More O'Ferrall only changed to the printed variety about 1974 — was widespread. In Belfast, Bernard McLaverty, the noted writer, remembers his father working as a commercial artist for an outdoor poster company.

In Dublin, More O'Ferrall also brought in the concept of bulletin displays measuring 27' by 10', which were hand painted on a series of

Con Kelleher of Bovril. One of his great publicity achievements was the placing of the Bovril sign above the American Express offices in Lower Grafton Street, Dublin, one of the city's prime outdoor sites.

Rory More O'Ferrall,
who founded the More
O'Ferrall outdoor
advertising firm in the
UK in 1936 and in
Dublin in 1953.

Opposite page:
The old Findlater's
building at the corner
of O'Connell Street and
Cathal Brugha Street,
Dublin. The sign above
the third storey
advertised Maxol, Mex
and Kosangas.
Photograph: G. A. Duncan.

metal panels, slotted into the main structure and contained in a frame. Cut-outs were quite popular too, of bottles, cans and television sets, in addition to those famous and tasty sausages. One of the firm's first boards was placed in Newtownmountkennedy, Co Wicklow, for what was by then, Texaco. Planning permission was easier to get in those days and More O'Ferrall erected a huge display featuring a painting of the Vale of Avoca. Less than ten per cent of the design area was occupied by brand advertising — the red Texaco sign was placed discreetly in the top right hand corner. A similar display was erected in Limerick, showing a map of the city.

Cinema posters reached new heights as well, remembers Eddie MacSweeney, then in the film publicity business, now a senior radio producer with RTE. He has a clear recollection of an enormous three dimensional poster created in the 1950s for the showing of *Anthony and Cleopatra* at the old Savoy. The poster required an immense amount of craftsmanship and aroused immense public interest. At the same time, the Abbey Theatre, temporarily housed, (after the fire in Lower Abbey Street), in the since demolished old Queen's Theatre in Pearse Street, was still going strong with its famous black and yellow posters that had become virtually its trademark.

When the *Evening Press* was launched in 1954, bus posters played a big part in the publicity campaign. There was a problem, however. They were all fully booked. Kennedy's, the big Dublin bakery that closed down in 1977, was a big user of bus side advertising in those days — through its agency, Padburys — and David Luke, who handled the publicity for the launch of the new paper, tried unsuccessfully to "borrow" Kennedy's bus sides. Laurence Kennedy was adamant that he would not lend the space. Then something David Luke said reminded Kennedy that Luke's father Charlie had been a driver for the bakery years before. The way was suddenly smoothed, then other clients fell into line.

In 1957, David Allen & Sons celebrated its centenary, a remarkable event for a firm in the publicity business, where companies so often fall prey to changing trends. It is also said to have been the source of TV comedian Dave Allen's stage name. Allen's was still going strong in 1957, as indeed it is today. Elaborate celebrations were staged at the firm's various branches. Fred Mullen, described as the firm's Dublin poet, even composed a special centenary poem. Two verses read as follows:

> It's due to the work of Companies like Allen's
> Without the need for State to intervene,
> That the Poster — good for sales — and good to look at
> Has earned acceptance in the social scene.
> Hence the Poster's power to stimulate the people
> In Selling — Saving — Service to the State;
> If the spirit which accomplished this inspires us
> Then we may not be perturbed about our fate.

To celebrate its centenary, Allen's held a cocktail party in the since - demolished Russell Hotel at St. Stephen's Green, Dublin. 85 people attended, including the Minister for Health, Sean MacEntee, T.D., the Minister for Lands, Erskine Childers, T.D. and Chief Justice Conor Maguire. The guests were received by W. E. D. Allen, chairman of the company and his wife and J. Allen Rogers, joint managing director and his wife. Agency principals attending included Charlie McConnell and Michael Kenny. National advertisers were represented by John McNeill (Players), W. H. Orr (Lever Brothers), Con Kelleher (Bovril), Albert Price (W. D. & H. O. Wills) and W. J. Delaney (Esso). Michael O'Brien, the Dublin planning officer was there as well. Afterwards, guests were unanimous in saying that the party had been one of the best they had attended.

Mullen combined his poster advertising work with his political career. He was a member of Dublin City Council from 1950 until 1974 and chairman of the council in 1973-74, officiating as Lord Mayor. The only other Dublin advertising person who ever attained a key political post was Erskine Childers. While Mullen was working his way up the political ladder, Bob Loughan was climbing the corporate tree at More O'Ferrall. From Belfast, he took a job as development executive with the company's Glasgow office nearly 30 years ago and has been based in Dublin since 1962. He has just recently retired as managing director of the More O'Ferrall/Adshel operation here.

Fred Mullen, for so many years a stalwart of outdoor advertising, through his long association with David Allen & Sons.

In 1935, Jameson's, the Dublin whiskey distillery, used this outdoor painted display near the Stamford Bridge football ground, London.
Photograph: Irish Distillers.

An old-style enamel advertisement, in Irish, for "St Bruno" tobacco. The photograph was taken in Inchigeela, Co Cork, in 1961.
Photo: Bord Failte.

Jameson's whiskey decorated this lorry for the 1955 St Patrick's Day parade in Dublin.
Photograph: Irish Distillers.

In the early stages of its development in Ireland, More O'Ferrall was able to extend the influence and audience of particular advertising campaigns by rotating painted panel sections from site to site. By 1960, both this firm and Allen's were providing floodlit bulletin rotary campaigns for many national advertisers. Other outdoor ideas, like reflectorised treatments and "mobiles", were abandoned because of time and cost constraints.

Another type of outdoor advertising also enjoyed a "vogue" reputation in the late 1950s: aerial banners. Bolands Biscuits, set up in 1957, used this form of advertising, through its agency, Arks. The contractor was Skycraft Services of Dublin. In the summer of 1959, an elaborate sky advertising schedule was drawn up for Bolands. Four routes were used, Dublin-Bray-Greystones; Dublin-Portmarnock-Malahide; Dublin-Rush-Skerries-Donabate and Dublin-Dun Laoghaire-Killiney. The flights took place from July to September and aimed to attract the attention of people enjoying the beaches at weekends. The cost per hour was £12.

With the advent of the 1960s — and Telefis Eireann — outdoor advertising started to take something of a back seat. In the previous decade, much of the advertising innovation went into outdoor posters; in the 1960s, agencies channelled much of their creative energies into the new medium, television. Various efforts were made to drum up business. In one instance, the contractor tied in three clients — Erin Foods, Gouldings and Guinness — on one board, under the "Buy Irish" banner.

Nevertheless, there were more newcomers to the outdoor business, such as Walter Hill & Co (Ireland), described as the first specialist outdoor advertising firm in Ireland. Started in London in 1900, the firm set up in Dublin in the early 1960s; its first general manager was an Englishman called Peter Waddell, who also achieved distinction as an international badminton player. He returned to London in late 1968, but retains his place on the board of the Dublin company. He was succeeded in Dublin by Des Fitzgerald, still managing director. Hill's introduced a number of important innovations into the outdoor market, including the use of 4s and 12s sized posters for national advertisers. These sheet sizes have blossomed to take a considerable share of the outdoor market. Walter Hill & Co (Ireland) has wide experience also in the neon sign end of the outdoor market and handles all the pub and neon sign commitments of Guinness Group Sales: Des Fitzgerald had been the outdoor executive in that firm before joining Hill's. At the same time, Maiden entered the Irish market. The Leeson concern came on the scene, in early 1973, linking the Petrie family — strong in exhibitions — into the outdoor advertising market. Other contracting operations that came into being included Regan and Spectra, the latter specialising in posters for shopping developments.

With the perfecting of the half tone process in silk screen printing in the early 1960s, design techniques in silk screen posters improved

A poster from the
Guinness Light
campaign, 1979, devised
by McConnell's. The
concept was created by
Joe Dobbin and Graham
Stone, copy was by
Graham Stone and
Diedrick Strydom and
art director was Joe
Dobbin.

immeasurably. Good silkscreen enabled advertisers to produce effective advertising campaigns at low cost. Still, as the outdoor industry continued its progress, the planners were not far behind. For many years past, planning departments of local authorities had interpreted the 1934 legislation with reasonable severity in sanctioning planning permission for all new sites. The amended Act of 1963 changed planning appeal procedures from the Minister to Bord Pleanala, but did not materially seek to alter the scope of advertisement planning controls. However, it prompted some contractors to rely on applications to retain structures already built. Most times, this "planning in retrospect" approach worked for the poster contractors. In 1986, the total cost of a planning application for a site, including the appeal, can run to £750.

1970 saw another giant step for outdoor posters: the first piece of audience research. It was sponsored by four companies, David Allen & Sons and Walter Hill on the contracting side and Guinness and Gallaher on the advertisers' side. With audience reaction harder to quantify than with printed media such as newspapers and magazines, poster research proved more difficult to compile, but rewarding nevertheless to both contractors and advertisers. This audience research survey was completed in 1970; the fieldwork had concentrated on recording the daily journey patterns of the sample audience measured

In Galway during the
1954 advertising
conference, from left
Councillor Fred Mullen
(David Allen), Mrs
Gairn, Andrew Gairn
(David Allen) and Mrs
Mullen.
Photograph: G. A. Duncan.

491

against typical campaigns. The subsequent processing of the data was carried out in accordance with the methods and formulae approved by the Institute of Advertising Practitioners in Ireland. The results confirmed that as an urban medium, posters provided opportunities to see at a remarkably low cost, with coverage of up to 90 per cent and weekly repetitions of as much as 20 and more viewings.

That outdoor posters formed a viable medium was evidenced when Adshel negotiated rights to Dublin bus shelters with CIE. Dublin city services manager at the time, Jack Higgins, had seen these shelter advertisements in France and was amenable to their introduction in Dublin. Says Bob Loughan of More O'Ferrall/Adshel: "Getting the Adshel agreement with CIE was my greatest achievement."

Specially designed shelters for O'Connell Street would be the next step forward. In the meantime, around half the Adshel shelters are lighted and over 60 major national advertisers use them on a regular basis, including bakeries, banks, dairy firms, other food firms, the RDS, supermarkets and travel agents. Some of the advertisements have created controversy. As John Boland said in the *Evening Press* in 1984: "In bus shelters all over Dublin these days, you will find large, full colour posters advertising Hickson Holidays. "Hit the Hot Spots" the slogan urges over a picture of a mermaid, her back to the camera, lying on some tropical beach. Last year, the same firm had a poster with the same slogan emblazoned over a girl in a bikini, standing legs spread and unmistakeably presenting her bottom to the viewer." Boland wondered if some people might not find this advertising "sexist"; the

Goulding's Manures used clocks to promote the brand as late as the 1960s. One or two of the clocks can still be found keeping good time in remote country pubs.

A poster site at Kilcock, Co Kildare, in the early 1960s, advertising a long-defunct draught beer.

Opposite page: Belfast trolley buses pictured in the 1970s, complete with bus side advertisements for the Belfast Savings Bank and Schweppes.
Photograph: J. M. Maybin.

Advertising Standards Authority did not. While Adshel was developing its bus shelter poster sites, one traditionally lit advertisement was still going strong in Sligo: the eight feet high mirror in Hargadon's pub in Sligo, advertising Wills' Gold Flake cigarettes at ten for 3d.

The outdoor facilities provided by CIE became increasingly important as the transport organisation exploited the advertising potential of stations, road sites and buses. Energetically developing transport advertising was Dónal O Maolalaí, now CIE's public affairs manager, followed by the present manager of its outdoor advertising, Sean Fox. On the Dublin city buses since 1976, exclusively painted vehicles have been available to advertisers. Among those to avail of this unique bus advertising have been Rowntree-Mackintosh for Smarties, HB for Birds Eye frozen foods and Harrington & Goodlass Wall for Dulux paints. CIE's policy limited the number of such buses to about one per cent of the total bus fleet; in 1976, the first year that the scheme was introduced, the rental charge was £7,000 a year, including

An early outdoor display for Jameson Ten whiskey, on the Sligo road, Carrick-on-Shannon, 1963.
Photograph: Irish Distillers.

charges for painting. Now, CIE has another advertising medium — the DART system, with 12 and 4 sheets available at stations and a certain amount of strip advertising available in the trains. At the same time, a similar development came to Citybus in Belfast, where major "all over" advertisers included the Trustee Savings Bank and Pepsi Cola. Sky panels were also introduced on the Belfast buses.

Through the 1970s, More O'Ferrall introduced back illuminated poster sites into Dublin and Limerick. The displays were painted on PVC material and stretched across a specially made metal box. The illumination was provided by fluorescent tubes installed in the box. The displays were as big as 28' by 14', in the case of those in Limerick. In 1975, More O'Ferrall won the franchise to put advertisements round a number of racecourses, including Leopardstown. Six years later, in 1981, the company was given the advertising rights for the two RDS showgrounds' complex in Dublin. The entire presentation to the RDS was made by Rory More O'Ferrall himself. As the 1970s progressed, the most notable development in outdoor advertising was the introduction of the 50 square feet 12 sheet broadside panel, which brought into effective use many high quality sites not adapted to already established standard sizes. Poster advertising gained a considerable impetus from this development.

A major blow fell on the outdoor advertising industry in 1979 when the then Minister for Health, Mr Haughey, decided to introduce new regulations completely banning cigarette and tobacco advertising from all outdoor sites. The outdoor companies wanted to phase out this type

An early Texaco poster site at Cornelscourt, Co Dublin, in the early 1960s, complete with cut-out of a can.

An early Caltex poster at Ballina, Co Mayo, erected in the early 1960s. A note on the photograph reads: "After storm, replaced 'star' and painted panels".

A neon sign erected by Taylor Signs for Guinness and Harp lager in the early 1960s.

of advertising over a three year period: in the end, they were given just three months. Some sources in the outdoor industry still wonder if there was not a deal done between the Minister and the tobacco companies' association under which the latter organisation got its way over shop signs, while the outdoor contractors had just over three months to eliminate such advertising. The cancellation period in outdoor advertising is normally 13 weeks and that is the time margin within which the outdoor companies had to work. Over the years, the tobacco firms had built up reservations on about 40 per cent of outdoor sites: they were being booked as they were built. Some contractors had 80 per cent T.C. bookings.

The contractors had to diversify out of the one product category on which they had placed so much reliance. In the summer of 1979, when the new regulations were being proposed, sources say that the outdoor industry could have fought them and won. Instead, it did relatively little, until the new regulations came into force. Says Vincent Whelan, who had set up his own specialised company, Outdoor Advertising Services, in 1976: "The big temptation was for contractors to race after clients like Guinness to fill up the spaces left by the tobacco manufacturers. If they had done that, they could have prompted a ban on drink advertising." Whelan's firm ran the Pretty Polly tights campaign on 60 or 70 sites. The design caught the public imagination: the legs shown in the poster generated incredible media coverage. "It was a crossroads for us," remembers Whelan. His firm signed up nine of the main advertising agencies in town, which resulted in a whole new spectrum of poster advertising clients, to fill the vacant 40 per cent of national sheetage, car distributors, food and confectionery firms and financial institutions. Within the next 18 months, many clients who had been anxious to use outdoor advertising, but who could not be accommodated, were fitted in. Many of the sites that were built for and solely used by the tobacco companies, particularly in rural areas and these 12 sheets have still not fully recovered from the blow of the 1980 ban. Questioned in the Dail over the ban, Mr Haughey replied that he had outlawed outdoor tobacco advertisements because they were "compelling and invasive", a back-handed compliment to the outdoor advertising industry. The outcome of the ban, from the industry's point of view, was the development of network selling. More O'Ferrall introduced the idea of networks into Ireland in 1981. These networks consisted of a group of sites, for example, 60 sites with national coverage or a Dublin network with 30 sites, all in prime positions and booked as a package. They are used either for supportive advertising for campaigns in other media or for campaigns in their own right.

Whelan himself has an interesting background in the industry. He joined O'Kennedy Brindley from school in 1965, working in the media department with such people as Bill Davis, Brendan Miller and John Conway. He spent three or four years there before changing to O'Keeffes, where John Thompson (now with the *Irish Farmers' Journal*)

This enamel sign at the top of the side wall of Hayes Conyngham & Robinson's chemist shop at Ballsbridge, Dublin, came from a Dublin tram when the fleet was broken up in the late 1940s.
Photograph: Derek Garvey.

was running the media department. Six months with O'Keeffes was followed by 2½ years under Ken Grace at Wilson Hartnell, then three months as an agency representative in the *Irish Press*, under Donie Bolger. After that, he worked for three years with More O'Ferrall, selling Adshel as a medium. "The industry was very small then and very closed. I was the first outsider, from an advertising agency, to come into it." His own company followed, in 1976. Whelan says that his company offers service and flexibility, making it easy for advertising agencies to buy outdoor space. He claims to have around 50 to 55 per cent of all outdoor spending in the Republic. The firm's turnover is now around £4 million, compared with £½ million in 1980. In 1982, it went into the Northern Ireland market, where it claims to act for all the advertising agencies except one. In September, 1984, Whelan's company bought Poster Publicity in London and Harrogate; that firm now has a staffing level of over 40, compared with about 20 in Dublin and three in Belfast, as at the end of 1985. Whelan claims that his company has the most advanced computer systems in the industry. It has the intention of classifying every site in the Republic. Now, says Vincent Whelan, posters are now part of the multi-media mix. Inventiveness continues to distinguish the medium; in 1985, McConnell's used doors on billboards for Sterling Ronseal, a home decorators' paint preservative. Also last year, Janus Advertising had real wallpaper used on displays for Polycell, located near shopping centres and do-it-yourself stores. In 1983, it had used bus advertising to announce its move to new premises in Raglan Road.

At the opening of David Allen's new poster printing plant in Dublin in February, 1969, were from left Michael Hayes (Arks), Tony O'Sullivan (Hunter's) and Mike Tobin (McConnell's).

Meanwhile, another outdoor company is going into Northern Ireland — More O'Ferrall. A new company is being set up, called More O'Ferrall/Adshel (N.I.), which will sell bus shelters there in the same way as they have been sold in the Republic for the past 15 years.

Figures show how the outdoor industry has grown in recent years. According to Donal Bruton of Outdoor Advertising Services, poster advertising now accounts for about eight per cent of the total advertising market in the Republic, compared with 38 per cent for TV, 12 per cent for radio, 32 per cent for the national press and ten per cent for magazines. In 1979, posters accounted for just four per cent, while national newspapers had a huge 46 per cent.

In 1984, poster advertising was divided as follows: beer, 16 per cent, spirits, 18 per cent, food and confectionery, 17 per cent, financial, ten per cent, motor, nine per cent and others (tourism, clothes, footwear, retail outlets, fuels and soft drinks), 30 per cent. Several trends have become apparent over the last few years as short term campaigns predominate and T.C. bookings fall off: there is much more spending on food and confectionery, up from nine per cent in 1979 to 17 per cent in 1984. The financial sector has grown from two per cent in 1979 to ten per cent in 1984. As a measure of the growth of food spending, when the Dairygold blend product was launched in 1985, most of the advertising expenditure was on posters.

Poster expenditure in 1984/85 showed the following figures, compiled by Walter Hill & Co (Ireland):

Category	£,000 1985	£,000 1984
1. Alcohol — beers	1,471	1,304
2. Alcohol — spirits	1,303	1,300
3. Services*	1,065	376
4. Foodstuffs	595	800
5. Cars and Accessories	558	523
6. Financial	511	575
7. Paints and DIY	303	217
8. Confectionery	282	190
9. Miscellaneous	267	418
10. Shopping outlets	224	172
11. Holidays and Leisure	209	222
12. Home heating	167	217
13. Durables	163	237
14. Clothing	157	314
15. Petroleum Products	136	82
16. Non-alcoholic drink	130	190
17. Transport	121	131
18. TV/Radio/Audio	99	20
19. Newspapers	45	59
Total	7,806	7,347

*Services include advertising by Bord Telecom.

Basil Brindley, chairman, Brindley Advertising, introducing Dublin's Lord Mayor Alderman Eugene Timmons at the launching of the first major anti-litter campaign at the zoological gardens in 1966. The Brindley agency subsequently won the More O'Ferrall trophy for its outdoor advertising contribution to the city's massive cleaning up operation.

Bob Loughan, who recently retired as managing director, More O'Ferrall (Ireland)/Adshel.

From the 1920s until 1984, Texaco and its predecessor brand, Caltex, occupied the prime outdoor site at Easons on the corner of O'Connell Street and Middle Abbey Street, Dublin. This photograph was taken in 1968; in the early 1980s, Texaco incorporated a clock in the design. The site is now occupied by Metrovision.
Photograph: Bord Failte.

As at 1984, there were nearly 7,000 poster sites in the Republic, nearly 60 per cent of them in the Dublin area. Maiden had 2,185 Adshel, 1,394, David Allen, 1,277, CIE 761, More O'Ferrall, 427 and Regan, 138. There were a total of 2,464 48 sheet posters in the Republic, nearly half of them in the Dublin area. Since 1979, there has been over 30 per cent growth in the 48 sheet market. In Northern Ireland, there are 2,500 poster sites, of which 60 per cent are in the Belfast area. There are about 75 12 sheet sites; the 12 sheet size has never developed in the North, in line with the rest of the UK, where they are not popular. Cigarettes and tobacco still hold 14 per cent of the poster market in Northern Ireland, where much poster advertising is placed from Dublin, including Bord Failte, Coca-Cola, Seven-Up, Pretty Polly tights, Bass, Irish Distillers and Cadburys. In the North, Mills and Allen has about 42 per cent of the market, as at 1985, Maiden, 38 per cent, Arrow, a local contractor, ten per cent and George Hughes of Newry, three per cent.

The poster contractors have formed the Poster Advertising Association of Ireland, which deals with standards of conduct and general performance. For the last four years, the association has also organised the successful annual poster awards competition, aimed at improving standards of design work in posters.

The biggest recent deal in outdoor advertising was the takeover of Maiden Poster Sites by David Allen Holdings. The deal was reckoned to have been worth up to £3 million. David Allen is by now a large international group, controlling such companies as Pearl and Dean, the cinema advertising contractors. It is the largest poster company in the UK, while Maiden is the largest privately owned UK poster firm. Maiden had been in Ireland since 1962; Tom Goddard, who was managing director of Maiden in Ireland for some years, sold his shareholding in 1985 and set up his own poster company, Metro Posters. His departure may have influenced the British owner of Maiden, Ian Maiden, to sell out to Allen's. At one stage recently, Maiden had considered a takeover of Allen's interests in Ireland. In recent years, Independent Newspapers and the Smurfit group had tried to buy Allen's. Smurfit has a major holding in Leeson Advertising, now rated about fifth in the outdoor advertising business. The new deal, between Maiden and Allen's, gives the enlarged company about half the poster market in Ireland. One result of the deal is that Peter Smyth, former managing director of Maiden in Ireland is now deputy managing director of More O'Ferrall/Adshel. The chairman of the company, following the retirement of Rory More O'Ferrall, is Vincent Slevin, formerly with D. E. Williams, which owns various soft drinks brands and also the *Leinster Leader* newspaper. Poster Management was set up in the early 1980s by Dave Richards and Gerry O'Donoghue, who had run Pembroke Publicity in Hunter Advertising. Multimedia, run by Tom Power, who is a partner with Brian Davitt in Davitt & Partners, handles sales of all advertising space at Dublin, Cork and Shannon Airports.

The facade of Rice's pub at St Stephen's Green, Dublin, showing an elaborate neon sign for Keiller marmalade. Rice's was demolished in August, 1986, as part of the redevelopment of the west side of the Green.

Pictured at the 1973 launch of Leeson Advertising, the outdoor advertising contractors, were Ken Tyrrell (Guinness), Michael Hayes (Arks) and Denis McDonald (Ogilvy & Mather).

Arks' farewell party to Bob McElheron when he retired from CIE in 1979. Included in the photograph are John Lindsay, Michael Vaughan, Michael Bolger, Michael Hayes, Padraic Guilfoyle, Neil Warnock, Monica Meleady, Pat Ferguson, Bob McElheron, Edith Jacobs, Eric Bannister, Georgina O'Sullivan, Bill Molloy, Jim Nolan and Tom Ring.

The past six years, following the banning of tobacco advertising on posters, has been the most traumatic and swiftly developing in the industry's history. Has the bloodletting stopped? However, the poster industry retains its sense of humour. In 1984, Rory O'Kelly of Action Drain used a series of advertisements on CIE buses. They showed a woman waiting, in obvious pain, outside an "out of order" lavatory. The slogan was "Why wait in pain? Phone Action Drain." The then president of the Institute of Creative Advertising and Design, Frank O'Hare, said that the poster had received a merit award. "It was extremely clever and creatively very good." Following three complaints from members of the public, the Advertising Standards Authority asked CIE to withdraw the poster. During the three months it was used on the buses, Rory O'Kelly claimed business had soared by 37 per cent. After the banning, he enjoyed further massive publicity.

In Cork in 1985, a sandwich board man called Bernard Murphy won a seat on Cork Corporation and brought enormous publicity to the outdoor advertising profession. Murphy had a poor background in Cork and made something of a living from parading up and down with

Illuminated sign for Harp lager, Limerick, early 1980s.

Northern Ireland bus advertising in the 1980s.
Photograph: J. M. Maybin.

his sandwich board, describing himself as an advertising agent. Murphy, the People's Choice, was elected following a bar dare in Cork: bookmakers in the city were said to have lost thousands of pounds on his election, where one of his main aims was the abolition of gas meters. During the successful campaign, the slogan "Murphy, the People's Choice" was superimposed on a photograph of what else, Murphy's stout.

Scannervision, now renamed Metrovision, pioneered a new form of outdoor advertising in Belfast. Using self-focussing tungsten bulbs, the displays not only show news headlines and weather forecasts, but a constant procession of advertisements. The advertisements, aimed at young street audiences under 35 years of age, are created using a video camera and digitiser and are animated at 15 picture frames a second. The first such display sign in Europe was erected at Shaftsbury Square in Belfast; subsequent research claimed that it was reaching over half a million people a week. Recall was said to be 88 per cent. The cheapest rate for a 10 second advertisement worked out at £100 per week; from Belfast, the system expanded into Dublin early in 1986, placed on the site of the old Texaco advertisement that occupied the corner site at Middle Abbey Street/O'Connell Street. Texaco claimed that its display there had been one of the oldest outdoor display advertisements in continuous use in Ireland, since the 1920s. Now, the site has been updated, with videos, digitisers and computer-supplied news and weather details. Soon, the system should be extended in Belfast, as well as to Patrick Street, Cork.

However, the Metrovision concept is not entirely new. In the 1930s, when O'Kennedy Brindley was over the Rainbow Café in Lower O'Connell Street, Brian D. O'Kennedy had an electric newspaper erected on the facade. All went well until a few days after the launch, when an IRA man got into the offices and put a message from the movement on the sign. The authorities promptly closed it down.

Now comes news of more Government restrictions on outdoor advertising, aimed at cutting back cigarette and tobacco promotions. While shopfront advertising escaped the 1980 purge, under new regulations made by Minister for Health, Barry Desmond, T.D., in 1986, from December, 1987, cigarette advertising on shopfronts will be banned, including fascia signs, fixed window advertisements and hanging box designs. Tobacco companies have been supplying complete shopfronts for over a decade. The new regulations mean that even the old-style enamel advertisements for brands like Sweet Afton, Player's Navy Cut and Woodbine will have to be taken down. These are among the last examples in existence of the enamel signs that formed such a dominant advertising medium in Ireland 80 years ago.

Dundalk railway station has Ireland's last displays of enamel railway signs; included are these three signs for Virol, at least 60 years old.
Photograph: Derek Garvey.

Opposite page:
The O'Brien family of Display Contracts/Riverside Exhibition and Conference Centre, pictured from left: Paula, administrator, Riverside Centre, Jim designer, Jim (snr), the firm's founder and managing director, Tony, administration and Adrienne, accounts executive. Jim O'Brien set up his company in 1959. He had started at the age of 16 with Dunfoy Displays, before joining the Artel Group. His company, Display Contracts, is now one of Ireland's foremost display and exhibition contractors. Over the last twenty seven years Display Contracts have undertaken assignments in all the major exhibition centres both at home and abroad.

CHAPTER NINE

Radio

"If you feel like singing, do sing an Irish song"
— WALTON'S PROGRAMME

The Irish School of Wireless was advertising for boys and girls to learn the art of wireless telegraphy as early as 1916.

GET—YOUR—BOYS—AND GIRLS—TO

LEARN WIRELESS

Splendid positions await qualified Wireless Telegraphists. We are now making a feature of Special Quick Courses for Students preparing for Marconi and Navy.

Write for Prospectus to-day to

IRISH SCHOOL OF WIRELESS,
11 Lr. SACKVILLE STREET, DUBLIN.

EVERY SATURDAY AFTERNOON at 1.45 p.m., following the lunchtime news on Radio Eireann, the immaculately enunciated tones of Dublin music teacher Leo Maguire entranced the country. For just short of 30 years, his words, spoken "live" and woven deftly around the music from the Glenside Label discs produced by Walton's of North Frederick Street, made one of the great "monuments" of the week in nearly every Irish home. The Walton's programme spanned the golden years of sponsored radio; fittingly, the very last sponsored programme to be transmitted was the one for Walton's that went out on January 3, 1981.

Sponsored programmes as a means of bringing in advertising revenue to the radio service developed with considerable hesitancy in the decade before World War II — the Radio Eireann authorities of the time had a deeply engrained suspicion, bordering on downright disapproval, of the business of advertising. The sponsored shows resumed in 1946 and came to a glorious crescendo in the years between 1950 and 1970. They faded away in a medley of forgettable showband programmes before being killed off in favour of all spot advertising.

Radio broadcasting in Ireland began in the early 1920s, with 2RN, the Dublin station, coming on the air on January 1, 1926, but it took a further decade for advertising to make any serious impression on the

CAN YOU CUT OUT DUBLIN ?

We Can for 25/-!

AT

GRAFTON RADIO

And ELECTRICAL SUPPLY CO.

(At Leechman's)

40 Grafton St., Dublin

A Dublin wireless supply company advertised sets in 1926 for 25/-.

In 1924, Dixon & Hempenstall imported this wireless advertising van. Programmes from various BBC stations, including Belfast, were broadcast to enthusiastic crowds, first in Dublin, then in country towns, from the loudspeakers on the roof.

Photograph: Irish Radio Journal/National Library/RTE.

"Hello the Free State! — Dublin Calling!"

are **You** ready for the **Big Day**?

ANY day now broadcasting will start in the Saorstat under the auspices of a most sympathetic P.M.G. when the permission of the Dail has been secured. Don't be left waiting in the rush for sets, loudspeakers, telephones, components, etc.—place your order to-day.

Ericsson 3 Valve Set minimum range 750 miles **£18 15 0**

This advertisement for wireless sets was published just before 2RN came on the air for the first time on January 1, 1926.

medium. One of the very first public examples of the new medium had been given in 1923 and created an immediate, but quickly forgotten, sensation.

During the Horse Show at the Royal Dublin Society showgrounds in Ballsbridge, a receiving loudspeaker transmitted primitive programmes from the Royal Marine Hotel, Kingstown (now Dun Laoghaire). In the hotel, before the Marconi microphone, an assortment of artistes performed every morning and afternoon. In addition, for the afternoon show, the *Dublin Evening Mail* supplied three minutes of Stop Press news. Members of the public attending the Horse Show were amazed to hear the sounds of singing coming from high up on a wall at the RDS. The following year, 1924, Dixon & Hempenstall of Suffolk Street, Dublin, imported a wireless advertising van, which travelled first around Dublin and later main country centres, relaying programmes from the new BBC station in Belfast, 2BE, opened in October, 1924, as well as from BBC stations in Britain, through loudspeakers on the top of the vehicle. Street audiences were most enthusiastic, so that by the time the Dublin station came on the air, the idea of wireless broadcasting was well accepted in the public mind. In October, 1925, the *Dundalk Democrat* newspaper published its first wireless advertisement, which

NIGHTS OF PLEASURE!

There is no better or cheaper entertainment than a———— **Wireless Installation** in your home. Opera, Dance Music, Songs, Lectures, and the Last News at your command every night. I can Supply and Last any make of Set, including Gecophone, Sterling, A.J.S., Marconi, also Loud Speakers, Browns, Amplion, Claritone, etc.

If you already have a set why not have it thoroughly overhauled for the coming winter.

Quotations, Catalogues and Advice Free.   Accumulators Re-charged

EDGAR ARNOTT,
Wireless Engineer,
Francis Street, DUNDALK

Edgar Arnott, a Dundalk wireless engineer, promised "Nights of Pleasure" in his local newspaper advertisements, about 1924.

504

promised "nights of pleasure — with a wireless installation".

Political squabbles delayed the start of the new station. As early as November, 1923, the Government had proposed the setting up of an Irish broadcasting service, transmitting from Dublin and including 15 minutes of advertising daily. Over two years slipped by before 2RN did come on the air, from makeshift studios rigged up over the employment exchange in Little Denmark Street. The Cork station, 6CK, started the following year, 1927, in even more rudimentary studios, in a disused jail at Sunday's Well, the door of which was opened by a foot long key! "Lash-ups" characterised the formative years of Irish radio and there was no better example than 6CK.

In April, 1927, the Minister for Posts and Telegraphs, J. J. Walsh, had an advertisement published in the Dublin newspapers. It read:

"Broadcasting Station.

Advertising of Irish Industries, etc.

The Minister for Posts and Telegraphs has arranged to have a period of five minutes allocated, in the nightly programmes, on payment of a moderate fee, for the delivery of lectures Advertising particular Irish industries or National Concerns or Undertakings.

Applications from intending Advertisers should be addressed to the Secretary, Department of Posts and Telegraphs, Dublin."

The aim of the Department was to confine advertising to Irish Free State concerns and to firms from outside the newly-founded state that did not compete with local organisations. Local advertisers were to pay a £5 fee for every five minute broadcast, while those from outside the state were to pay double that amount. A later concession allowed short announcements of forthcoming functions at a guinea a minute.

O'Kennedy Brindley, then a very newly formed advertising agency, booked the first five minute advertising spot, for Olhausen's sausages. 30 years later, the same agency did the noted sponsored

The first authorised public service broadcast in Ireland originated in the Royal Marine Hotel, Dun Laoghaire, on August 14, 1923.

J. J. Walsh, Minister for Posts and Telegraphs, who sought to encourage advertising on 2RN in April, 1927.

Noel Hartnell of Wilson Hartnell speaking at an Advertising Press Club debate on sponsored radio in 1944. Right in the photograph is Denis Garvey of Janus.

shows for Donnelly's sausages, with the *Mexican Hat Dance* jingle.

This first attempt to bring in radio advertising was less than successful; in July, 1927, Mr Walsh, moving the Wireless Broadcasting Estimate for 1927-28 in the Dail, announced that up to March 31 that year, advertising had brought in precisely £200. Import duties on wireless sets were bringing in twice as much revenue as licence fees and advertising combined. In November, 1927, P. S. O'Hegarty, secretary of the Department of Posts and Telegraphs, said that advertising on radio should be allowed to die a natural death. Seamus Clandillon, the station's first director, said: "From a programme point of view, they (the advertisements) are a nuisance and are regarded by listeners as an impertinence." Yet despite this official indifference to advertising, 2RN broadcast its very first sponsored programme on the very last day of 1927, an hour-long show on behalf of Euthymol toothpaste, which began at 9.30 p.m. on December 31.

The following year, 1928, provided two highlights in the history of Irish radio broadcasting. In October, station personnel started moving into the newly provided studios at the General Post Office building in central Dublin. For nearly 50 years, Henry Street was to be the official address of the main Irish radio studios. That year also provided a total advertising revenue of just £28, so that in practice, if not in theory, 2RN was not far removed from the BBC position in Britain and Northern Ireland. From its inception, the BBC had been forbidden to accept any form of advertising and had to depend entirely on licence fee revenue.

In a Dail debate in May, 1930, a young T.D. called Sean Lemass said that since advertising had only brought in £50 revenue in 1929, it should be banned or developed properly. Ironically, given his responsibility, during his period as Taoiseach, for the tremendous economic development of Ireland in the 1960s, he preferred to see advertising banned from radio. The Government of the day seemed equally lukewarm about radio advertising, for the Dail reply to Deputy Lemass was: "We are not expecting to get revenue to any appreciable extent from advertising."

But the move towards more sponsored programmes was already underway, inspired by Continental examples which could be heard in Ireland. Radio Hilversum began in 1928 and Radio Toulouse the following year; both stations made heavy use of sponsored shows. During a radio publicity week in Dublin at this time, one advertiser made a show of himself by putting on a programme and using it to advertise himself "in the most blatant and irregular fashion." In October, 1930, a London firm, Radio Publicity, won the concession for sponsored programmes on an experimental basis, using McConnell's Advertising agency as the local organiser.

Radio Publicity leased time on 2RN and sub-let it to individual firms. No doubt the scheme had a particular appeal for Charlie

Wet (right) and dry batteries were a hallmark of the earlier years of radio listening in Ireland.

ANOTHER RELIABLE PRECAUTION

to ensure against monotony during the long dark nights of the

BLACKOUT

is to consult us about that PHILCO, PILOT OR MURPHY RADIO

NOW

These are the Sets. that Rule the Waves—Long, Medium and Short They are the Best All-round Value for Money, and can be had for Cash or on Hire Purchase, but locally only from

The Radio Depot

(Hall and Mulhern)
10, Jocelyn St., Dundalk

The oldest established and only local firm dealing exclusively in Radio

During the Emergency, radio dealers advertised sets that would beat the monotony of the blackout.

Advertisement for Pye radio sets, 1948.

Advertisement for the Dublin Wireless Exhibition, which took place in the Mansion House eleven months after 2RN came on the air.

The studios of 6CK at Sunday's Well, Cork. The station went on the air in 1927.

McConnell, founder of McConnell's, for he had begun his advertising career early in the century by using exactly the same principle as a newspaper space broker. The Radio Publicity fee was £5 per programme slot of 15 minutes, which defined the standard programme length for the duration of sponsored programmes. In addition to that fee, advertisers had to pay all programming costs, so that a show could cost in total the grand sum of £25! Among the very first advertisers to take advantage of this new scheme for sponsored radio programming were Carrolls (for its Sweet Afton cigarettes, then newly launched on the Irish market), Findlaters the grocery firm whose headquarters was at Upper O'Connell Street, Dublin, and Independent Newspapers, today, ironically, the largest single advertiser on RTE Radio (£380,000 in 1985).

The Irish Hospitals' Trust, newly founded and highly controversial, came to the rescue of radio advertising; its first sponsored show went out on October 1, 1930 and for the next 30 years, the Sweeps programme was a mainstay of sponsored radio and a vital source of revenue for the station. In countless Irish homes, the show's signature tune, "When You Wish Upon a Star", was prelude to bedtime.

In November, 1930, came the first Sweeps' draw and the client insisted that the speeches at the celebratory dinner in the Gresham Hotel had to be relayed to 2RN listeners. Moreover, they had to hear the full results of the draw: it took Mairead Ni Ghrada in the Henry Street studios 90 minutes to complete the task. When it was over, she was revived by a bottle of Veuve Clicquot champagne sent over by one of the diners in the Gresham, sympathetic to her plight.

Early programmes for the Hospitals' Trust were rudimentary indeed, with no continuity, except for the titles of the 78 rpm discs that were being played. Then not long after Jack Tate joined the new Dublin advertising agency of Arks, in 1931, he won the Sweeps' account and the programme's sophistication was greatly improved. The more ambitious programmes were bought in as a package from London production studios, but in 1935, Arks set up its own radio department, headed by Ian Priestley Mitchell. Deputy Dick Corish of Wexford, father of Brendan Corish, complained that the Hospitals' Sweepstakes' programme was being compered "by an Englishman, or Englishmen". His facts were not entirely accurate; Priestley Mitchell came from Caithness in the far north of Scotland. The Gaelic League protested strongly about the content of the new sponsored programmes, yet listeners seemed to take to them, a reflection on the large amounts of money — an average £30 an hour — being spent on programme content, far more than the station itself was spending.

Yet the early sponsored shows had their ups and downs. By January, 1931, they were cut back to four nights a week, while the following month, after just four months in the job, Radio Publicity of

508

CROSSE & BLACKWELL
MAKERS OF FINE QUALITY FOODS
PRESENT

" CAUGHT IN THE ACT ! "

Master sleuth, ex-Chief Superintendent Fabian, pauses outside London Sessions Lower Criminal Court to reminisce with Mr. J. R. Gillespie, Director of Crosse and Blackwell (Ireland) Ltd.

'FABIAN of the YARD'
Introduced by Noelle Middleton

In an exciting new series of thrilling! true ! detection stories:

Listen to-day to Radio Eireann at 2.15 p.m. and hear

'MARITA and the COUNT'

Another absorbing episode specially selected from the personal records of Ex-Superintendent Robert Fabian of Scotland Yard

EXCLUSIVE TO
CROSSE & BLACKWELL

Joe Lynch as a young actor. He remembers vividly the time he was having a cup of tea in Clery's restaurant, forgetting that he was supposed to be doing a "live" sponsored show across the road in Radio Eireann's Henry Street studios.
Photograph: RTE Illustrations Library.

Leo Maguire, photographed as a young man. He scripted and presented the Walton's programme from its start in 1951 until it ended in January, 1981, when it was the very last sponsored show broadcast by RTE.

In 1954, Crosse & Blackwell started a new sponsored radio series, Fabian of the Yard, introduced by Noelle Middleton. The programme was produced by Brendan Smith of Radio Publicity, the McConnell's subsidiary. This advertisement was taken from Radio Review.

509

London dropped out in favour of the Irish Publicity Company, whose tenure was even shorter — three months. An advisory committee looked at the question of sponsored programmes and recommended that they should be produced by 2RN staff, with the station director responsible for booking the artistes.

To the surprise of station staff and a certain disappointment on the part of advertising agencies like Arks and McConnell's, the committee's recommendations were accepted.

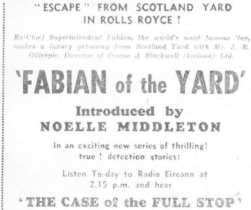

CROSSE & BLACKWELL
MAKERS OF FINE QUALITY FOODS
PRESENT

"ESCAPE" FROM SCOTLAND YARD IN ROLLS ROYCE !

Ex-Chief Superintendent Fabian, the world's most famous 'tec, makes a luxury get-away from Scotland Yard with Mr. J. R. Gillespie, Director of Crosse & Blackwell (Ireland) Ltd.

'FABIAN of the YARD'
Introduced by
NOELLE MIDDLETON

In an exciting new series of thrilling! true ! detection stories:

Listen To-day to Radio Eireann at 2.15 p.m. and hear

'THE CASE of the FULL STOP'

Another absorbing episode specially selected from the personal records of Ex-Superintendent Robert Fabian of Scotland Yard

EXCLUSIVE TO
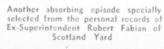
CROSSE & BLACKWELL

"Din Joe", Denis Fitzgibbon, the man who brought Irish dancing to radio and also compered such sponsored radio programmes as that for the Smithfield Motor Company.
Photograph: RTE Illustrations Library.

Ian Priestley-Mitchell, for many years compere of the Irish Hospitals' Sweepstakes' programme on Radio Eireann.
Photograph: RTE Illustrations Library.

This Crosse and Blackwell advertisement appeared in the Radio Review **on January 8, 1954 to promote the food firm's new sponsored programme,** Fabian of the Yard. **The series was produced by Brendan Smith.**

A major problem soon surfaced in Henry Street. Often, the station orchestra, set up in 1927, had to be augmented for sponsored shows. Its leader at the time, Terry O'Connor, was frequently apprehensive when the extra players slipped out of the studio for refreshments during the intervals. She never knew when or in what condition the extra musicians would return. The Tower Bar directly across the road from the GPO came to be known as "Studio Six" and the switchboard girl knew the bar's number by heart.

Denis Brennan, the actor with the dark brown velvet voice, compered many sponsored programmes. He is seen here in 1959, discussing a radio programme with P.P. O'Reilly.
Photograph: The Irish Times.

Joe Linnane, popular sponsored shows compere.
Photograph: RTE Illustrations Library.

The Gaelic League made recurrent attacks on the content of sponsored shows; in some quarters, jazz was seen as highly decadent and morally subversive. But by the time serious planning began for the new Athlone transmitter, public appreciation of the sponsored programmes was considerable and advertising had come to be seen as a vital component of the station's revenue. One event alone convinced the general public of the merits of wireless broadcasting: the Eucharistic Congress held in Dublin in June, 1932.

Listeners heard the voice of the Pope himself relayed, while Count John McCormack sang the *Panis Angelicus* during the High Mass in the Phoenix Park. The achievement of radio broadcasting came to be recognised. The new transmitter at Athlone was temporarily commissioned so that it could broadcast the religious events of that June, then it went off the air, not being officially opened as Radio Ath Luain by Eamon de Valera, president of the Executive Council, until February, 1933. With the arrival of the new transmitter, virtually the whole of Ireland could receive the station clearly, with the exception of seaboard fringe reception areas in counties Donegal and Kerry.

With this new nationwide coverage, the broadcasting authorities took seriously the idea of properly organised sponsored programmes, with a little inspiration perhaps from the English-language service of Radio Luxembourg, which went on the air for the first time in 1933. It used an unauthorised wavelength — the first of the "pirates".

As the Athlone transmitter came on the air, the contract to supply sponsored programmes was awarded to Athlone Radio Publicity. The new company booked one hour a night, six nights a week, at £60 an hour, with an extra £1 10s for copyright fees. The amount of advertising was limited to 100 words per programme, or about five per cent of airtime. Sponsored programmes under the new system began on April 24, 1933, but soon the company was complaining about technical shortcomings, particularly about poor reception in the London area and breaks in transmission. Although these breaks only amounted to $20\frac{1}{2}$ minutes in 90 hours of sponsored programmes, a rebate of £1,000 was offered on payments for the year, the first

Marie Kean, stalwart of the Kennedys of Castleross, **the twice weekly serial sponsored by Fry-Cadbury (Ireland).**
Photograph: RTE Illustrations Library.

512

Leo Maguire, composer of A Dublin Saunter, pictured strolling through St Stephen's Green. For 30 years, he presented the Walton's radio programme.

Willie Styles, the RTE producer, who was the driving force behind the Kennedys of Castleross for nearly all the serial's 15 years' run.
Photograph: RTE.

In the 1950s, Radio Publicity, McConnell's radio production subsidiary, produced several series of *Fabian of the Yard* thrillers for Crosse & Blackwell, the soup firm. Pictured here about 1956 were from left: Bob Fabian of Scotland Yard, Jimmy Gillespie (C & B's sales director), J. F. Kearney (recently retired as Willwood's managing director) and Terry Balfe.

Time	Sponsors	Type of Programme
Monday 8.15 a.m.	May Roberts (Tape (Vaseline)	"Sports Parade" by Mícheál Ó Hehir Compere: W. Styles Programme the same as previous year
8.30 a.m.	Gael-Linn (live)	Draw Results. Irish songs and band music Compere: P. Ó Raghallaigh
8.45 a.m.	Ed Ryan	Programme of popular records, introduced by Noel Andrews No change
1.00 p.m.	Fruitfield (tape)	"Information Desk" in which listeners queries on housekeeping cookery gardening etc. are answered by "Tom" and "Peggy" Also a "Fruitfield" question asked which is answered the following week Compere: Godfrey Quigley with Pauline Delaney This programme is running now for about 10 months.
1.15 p.m.	Mitchelstown (tape)	Programme of Irish music mainly by Jim Cameron and his Band. Guest artist each week - e.g. Richard Cooper, Seán Ryan Compere: Ita Little No change
1.45 p.m.	Radio Review (tape)	Programme of popular records introduced by Roy Croft. No change.
2.00 p.m.	Colgate Palmolive (live)	Programme of popular records. Comperes: Frank Purcell and Beryll Fagan
2.15 p.m.	Gael-Linn (tape)	At the moment playing music of other countries - some programmes are folk music and some classical. Compere: P. Ó Raghallaigh
2.30 p.m.	Mansion Polish (tape)	"Mrs. Maguire" and her daughter "Maura" introduce mixed records (popular and light classical). Commercial in Dialogue form. Compere: Beryll Fagan
2.45 p.m.	Burtons (tape)	"Meet Maestro Mantovani". Programme of music played by Mantovani and his orchestra Bing Crosby as guest star. Compere: Pat Layde.

The following six pages
show a week's sponsored
shows' schedule in 1959.

Time	Sponsors	Type of Programme
Tuesday 8.15 a.m.	Gala (on disc)	Programme of light melodies - mainly orchestral. Compere: Patrick Begley No change in the last 12 month
8.30 a.m.	Castle Hosiery	Programme of music and light script introduced by an Irish singer, e.g. Bridie Gallagher, Brendan O'Dowda, Patrick O'Hagan at the moment. Each singer does a series of 10 or 12 programmes. Compere: Denis Brennan.
8.45 a.m.	Brookfield Sweets	A new programme, Commenced in September. Musical recipe consisting of "slipped", "snipped", "flipped", "chipped" and "should be nipped" records. Contains an interview in which the interviewee is asked to name what disc he thinks should be taken off the air. The disc is played once again and for his pains the listener gets a box of Brookfield sweets. Compere: Harry Thuillier
1.00 p.m.	Fry-Cadbury	"The Kennedys of Castleross". Dramatic serial. Compere: Godfrey Quigley. Actors: Mainly Abbey Theatre.
1.15 p.m.	Birds	Popular records Comperes: Joe Linnane and Cecil Barror. No change in past 12 months.
1.45 p.m.	Batchelors	"Transatlantic Call": Irish people in America or Canada. 3 interviews per prog. and a record played for each interviewee. Compere: Pat Layde No change in past 12 months.
2.00 p.m.	Irel	"Hall of Fame": information and music of some well-known artiste each week. Compere: Denis Brennan. No change in past 12 months.
2.15 p.m.	E.S.B.	Maura Laverty in a weekly miscellany of "Music and Musings". Compere: Pat Layde No change in past 12 months.
		x "Slipped" - One that has fallen from favour. "Snipped" - from a sound-track recording "flipped" - other side of a hit record "chipped" - an old recording

515

Time	Sponsors	Type of Programme
Tuesday (cont.)		
2.30 p.m.	Carlsberg Lager	"The Carlsberg Casebook". Famous mystery stories, scripted by Hugh Leonard and read by Denis Brennan.
2.45 p.m.	Tayto	New programme. "Leisure Time", in which listeners are invited "take it easy with Tayto" and Harry Thuillier introduces records designed for relaxed listening.
Wednesday		
8.15 a.m.	Macleans	Continuous music programme. Compere: Joe Linnane. No change in past 12 months.
8.30 a.m.	Silvikrin	A programme of tunes which have some "common denominator" and listeners are requested to "Spot the Link" and forward replies. Names of first three correct entrants are announced in following week's prog. Compere: Cecil Barror.
8.45 a.m.	T.P. Whelehan	New programme. Designed for the farmer's interest. Described as a magazine for country folk through which members of farming and rural organisations give news of topics and interesting problems of the farming industry in Ireland. Speakers: Peter Murphy Sheila Hughes Louis Moran.

Time	Sponsors	Type of Programme
8.15 a.m.	Sunbeam Wolsey	New programme of light music on records. Introduced by Derek Young for the first few weeks. Changed to Fred Cogley last week (15/10/59).
8.30 a.m.	Golden Vale	New prog. in which "Uncle Dan, the rambling man" talks to two children, and introduces records. Philip O'Flynn as Uncle Dan.
8.45 a.m.	Philips	Humorous script with records read by Denis Brennan. (No change).
1.00 p.m.	Fry-Cadbury	Same as 1.00 p.m. on Tuesdays
1.15 p.m.	Prescotts	Popular records. Compere: Ronnie Walsh. Once a month interviews with customers in various Prescott branches, done by Joe Linnane. (No change)
1.45 p.m.	Birds	Same as Tuesday, 1.15 p.m.
2.00 p.m.	Colgate Palmolive	Same as Monday, 2.00 p.m.
2.15 p.m.	Bradmola	Popular records: Compere: Ronnie Walsh.
2.30 p.m.	Hovis	Prog. slightly altered since they got afternoon time. Listeners invited to send in stories of incidents under the following headings: (1) The most honest deed (2) The bravest deed (3) The most intelligent animal story (4) Favourite story about children. Some of these are read in the prog. Portion of time still reserved for Harry Thuillier on sport. Compere: Niall Boden.
2.45 p.m.	Moore Street Traders	New prog. of popular discs with short script. Compere: Noel Andrews The prog. is presented by "The Green Star" Shops in Moore St. and this is mentioned in the prog.

	Sponsors	Type of Programme
8.15 a.m.	Clarks	"Jacqueline": dramatic serial mainly of interest to children. (same as last year). Over summer months had a prog. called "Stargazing with Eamonn Andrews" in which each week information was given on some particular "star" in the music world and his records played. Compere: Pat Layde or Denis Brennan.
8.30 a.m.	Goodbodys	New programme - commenced in May. Records and light script. Compere: Joe Lynch.
8.45 a.m.	Irish Shell	At the moment, a prog. of continuous music (light) played by Jack Gregory and his quintet with singers, Tommy Nolan and Patricia Conlon (sometimes Betty Impey). Compere: Frank Purcell.
1.00 p.m.	Chivers	Music from the sound-tracks of two film Compere: Niall Boden. (No change).
1.15 p.m.	Imco	Popular records. Compere: Terry O'Sullivan. (No change).
1.45 p.m.	P.O. Savings	Prog. of music - often light classical or operatic music. Compere: Eddie Golden.
2.00 p.m.	E.S.B.	"Ladies Journal": a magazine for women with interviews by Maxwell Sweeney (No change). For the summer months they had short plays each Friday - called the series "Summer Playhouse". Compere: Pat Layde.
2.15 p.m.	Science Polish	Light orchestral music introduced by Godfrey Quigley.
2.30 p.m.	Bear Brand.	New Prog. based on names of brands of stockings, e.g. "Las Vegas", "Ohio", "Oklahoma", etc. a little information given about the place & appropriate music played. One programme devoted to each name. Compere: Noel Andrews.
2.45 p.m.	Korona Watches	New programme. Popular records introduced by Harry Thuillier.

	Sponsors	Type of Programme
8.15 a.m.	Hercules	Light music. Usually one LP record per prog. Compere: Harry Thuillier
8.30 a.m.	Bulmers	Humorous script with records. Actors: Denis Brennan and Pat Layde. Commercial in humorous vein also.
8.45 a.m.	Murrays' Car Rentals	Popular Records. Sometimes an interview with a customer and the customer's choice of records played. Compere: Harry Thuillier.
1.00 p.m.	Urney	"The Planet Man". A spaceship serial on disc running since July. Compere: Gay Byrne
1.15 p.m.	Donnellys	Popular records. Compere: Niall Boden (No change)
1.45 p.m.	Birds	Same as on Tuesdays (1.15 p.m.)
2.00 - 2.30 p.m.	Gateaux	"The Dalys of Honeydew Farm", dramatic serial. Main participants: Harry Brogan, Ita Little, Paddy McGowan. Compere: Ita Little (No change)
2.30 p.m.	Waltons	Programme of Irish music introduced by Leo Maguire. (No change)
2.45 p.m.	Dubtex	New prog. Up-to-the-minute information on sporting events by Harry Thuillier.

The Hospitals Trust programme (everynight, 11 - 11.30 p.m.) broadcast a racing commentary, of 5 to 7 minutes duration, and then a programme of records and linking script for the remainder of their period They cover all kinds of music - classical, operatic, light orchestral music, "pops", etc. etc.

advertising rebate in the history of Irish broadcasting. However, Athlone Radio Publicity was short lived; the New Ireland Assurance Company, which had guaranteed its payments until the end of 1933, took over the remaining time and appointed the International Broadcasting Company's Irish subsidiary as its agent.

Selling time at the full rate on Radio Athlone proved difficult, so programme fare on the sponsored shows was of poor quality, often using outdated discs. Manufacturers of patent medicines and cosmetics were the principal sponsors. Only Arks, on behalf of the Sweepstakes, produced good quality programming. The competition from abroad, particularly from the new Radio Luxembourg, intensified. After the Athlone transmitter had been on the air for a year, the Department of Posts and Telegraphs was sufficiently disenchanted with sponsored programmes to want to drop them, with the exception of those for the sweepstake. By 1934, its programmes had developed into a national institution, firmly ensconced in the public affection. Sweepstakes were illegal in Britain, with no newspaper or other advertising for them allowed there (the British editions of Irish newspapers had to omit Sweepstakes' advertisements), so the Hospitals' Trust used the Athlone transmitter to reach Britain. So too did a toothpaste manufacturer. Reception was best in Wales and north-west England.

Radio Athlone was not entirely suitable for this purpose, since it was poorly received in the south of England, so when Radio Normandy, set up by the aptly named Captain Plugge, went on the air in 1930 from studios in Fécamp converted from a hayloft, the Hospitals' Trust was an early and enthusiastic advertiser. A young announcer, Roy

Niall Boden, who produced and compered many of the top sponsored radio shows while he worked for O'Kennedy Brindley. One of the best known was the Donnelly's Sausages' show, with its Mexican hat dance jingle.
Photograph: RTE Illustrations library.

Louis Spiro's Imco cleaning firm became a household name through its sponsored programmes. These featured the two characters invented by Spiro, "Spotless" and "Stainless". The Imco building at Merrion Road, Dublin, was a noted landmark.

Plomley, later famous for his long-running "Desert Island Discs" programme on BBC radio, and who died in the early summer of 1985, often introduced the Sweeps' programme on the northern French station. So successful was Radio Normandy that in 1937, it bought land in Co. Wexford with the intention of building a transmitter there, but the plan never came to anything. Radio Luxembourg was also getting into its stride, with sponsored shows for advertisers like Horlicks and Ovaltine.

In Ireland, the sponsored programmes started coming into their own. In 1934, the practice was abandoned of using the Customs duty collected on imported wireless sets to partially fund the radio service, so advertising revenue became much more important. In 1932-33, radio advertising yielded just £220, but by 1933-34, that figure had shot up to £22,827. Complaints continued about the content of sponsored shows. Musical purists said that too many jazz records were being played, while Deputy Corish complained that the National Anthem at the end of the day's broadcasting was being played in jazz time, from an old American record. The Government decided, meanwhile, against making Radio Athlone an international service along the lines of the Continental commercial stations, despite considerable pressure from private interests who wanted to sell advertising aimed at an international audience.

For the three years until 1938, the Hospitals' Trust remained the mainstay of the sponsored programmes, taking a half-hour or hour nightly. In 1938, the broadcasting service from Dublin, Cork and Athlone became Radio Eireann.

Living with Lynch **was a memorable radio series, still fondly remembered 20 years after its demise. This photograph shows the people connected with the series; several have close connections with radio and TV commercials' production.**

Front row, left to right: Ronnie Walsh, Charlie Byrne, Joe Lynch, Dermot Doolan (scriptwriter) and Gerry Duffy, office manager with Eamonn Andrews Studios. Back row, left to right: Tommy Ellis (bass), Sean Wilkinson (drums), Pamela Duncan (actress), Joe Coughlan (alto sax and clarinet) and the late Richie Burbridge (piano).

Harry Thuillier pictured in 1962: during the 1960s, he was one of the best-known presenters of sponsored radio programmes.

During 1938, the Government agreed to a scheme for national advertisers, which came into effect on October 1, 1939, less than a month after World War II was declared. There were just 150,000 licensed sets. Under this scheme, one hour a day of airtime on what was now known as Radio Eireann was allocated to sponsored programmes, divided into 15 minute slots between 1.30 p.m. and 2.30 p.m. Rates varied from £15 for a weekday slot taken on a long contract to £55 for a Sunday slot. Advertising was to be restricted to Irish products and services and all commercials had to be read by station announcers.

In the end, only three firms took time. They were all Irish subsidiaries of British companies; one dropped out after six months. Irish newspapers were vehemently opposed to the scheme, fearing that the radio service would take advertising revenue from them. The newspapers refused to sell space to advertisers who wanted to draw attention to their programmes and in the newspapers' listing of radio programmes the afternoon schedules containing the sponsored shows mysteriously disappeared. As an agency man remarked at the time, you had to be on very friendly terms with a journalist or else there had to be an accident involving a participant in a sponsored show to ensure any kind of mention of the taboo topic in the newspapers.

The Director of Broadcasting, Dr T. J. Kiernan, appointed in May, 1935, made strenuous and largely unsuccessful efforts to persuade advertisers to go for "quality", using artistes of the calibre of Margaret Burke Sheridan and Sir Hamilton Harty in place of jazz musicians and crooners. Advertisers resisted; they and their audiences clearly preferred the crooners, so that after the first $4\frac{1}{2}$ hours of airtime a week had been sold, the Government called a halt to the scheme. The Emergency did what else was needed to kill sponsored programmes for the duration of the war.

With the growing shortages of consumer goods, advertising started to fall away; there was no point in firms advertising goods they could no longer supply. Even the Sweepstakes decided to go off the air, for a

Tom Hardiman (far left), then RTE director-general, turning the first sod for the new radio centre at Donnybrook, 1969.
Photograph: RTE.

substantial proportion of the Emergency; the dropping of the Sweepstakes' show cost the station £23,000 a year. When the first year's contracts for sponsored programmes started to run out in September, 1940, the Government took advantage of the situation to revise the format of sponsored programmes, in order to make newspapers more amenable. All retail and distributive trades, patent medicines, cosmetics and alcohol were banned from advertising on radio. The prohibition on non-Irish advertisers remained in force, so only Irish manufacturing firms, tourist interests and the newspapers themselves were allowed to advertise. There was a daily maximum limit of two hours' sponsored programmes and none at all between 5.30 p.m. and 11 p.m. St Patrick's Day, Ash Wednesday, Holy Thursday, Good Friday and Christmas Day were all placed beyond the reach of advertisers. Strangely enough, RTE Radio still has vestiges of those early decisions; there is no advertising on Radio 1 between 7 p.m. and 11 p.m., while Sunday advertising on the same channel was only permitted in October, 1985, although Radio 2 has had Sunday advertising since its 1979 inception. Also in the 1940 regulations, jazz was officially discouraged. These stringent restrictions were of more theoretical than practical value — for the duration of the Emergency, radio's advertising revenue never rose above £4,000, despite the intense demand for advertising space in the daily and weekly newspapers. At one point, in the autumn of 1943, there were no sponsored programmes at all.

Dick Young, who left Arks to found R. Wilson Young Advertising in 1943, and his client, Eric Williams of Bird's the custard and jelly makers, claimed that in 1946 they had been instrumental in persuading the Radio Eireann authorities to start up the sponsored programmes again, once the Emergency was over.

Bird's was the first such show back on the air, in May, 1946, quickly followed by Donnelly's sausages. The first Bird's shows were compered by Liam Gaffney, the actor; soon after, when he got work in films in England, he handed over the job to Cecil Barror. From 1947, Barror compered the Bird's shows continuously, up until 1969. He did two and sometimes three shows a week, scripting them, selecting the discs and presenting the programmes. Although Barror was a professional actor, working in the Abbey for ten years from 1938, his full-time job was in the ESB in Fleet Street. Not long after Young had set up his advertising agency in 1943, he moved offices from Grafton Street to Fleet Street, very handy for Cecil Barror. The Bird's custard and jellies' slogan "After all, you *do* want the best, don't you," — became a national catchphrase as early as 1947, used in variety shows and pulpits alike.

Growing competition to the Radio Eireann sponsored programmes came from Radio Luxembourg, back on the air in 1946, after being used for Nazi propaganda purposes during World War II. In 1948, the station started its "Top Twenty" show, based on sheet music sales, a major innovation in popular music broadcasting that eventually permeated the civil service ways of Radio Eireann.

After RE's sponsored programmes returned in 1946, it took a further three years for them to blossom. The Hospitals' Trust played a major role in that expansion, for it returned to radio advertising. By Radio Eireann's 1949-50 financial year, its advertising revenue was up to the healthy sum of £47,000, 85 per cent of which came from the Sweeps' shows. The Hospitals' Trust became the only radio advertiser to have its own production studios, nicknamed the "Red House", in a corner of its huge site at Ballsbridge, Dublin. In 1945, north Dublin listeners enjoyed music from what was claimed as Ireland's first "pirate" station, Radio Galaxy, run by disc enthusiast Tony Boylan. Soon, north Dublin listeners were provided with a second transient alternative — an embryonic "pirate" station called the "Killeen Road Home Service", which broadcast from the Santry area but carried no advertising.

John McDonagh, who had been production director of Radio Eireann for ten years, joined the Hospitals' Trust radio production unit. Among the personalities appearing on the nightly show in the late 1940s was Frankie Byrne's father, Mick, the well-known newspaper racing correspondent, who gave astute information and tips to his many fans. Dell Allen, who wrote early O'Dearest mattress limericks, composed the linking verses.

In May, 1949, the Government decided to lift many of the restrictions placed on sponsored radio shows. The newspapers were still short of space for advertisement requirements and the advertising agencies were clamouring for greater access to Radio Eireann. Under the easing of restrictions, advertising on radio was still confined to firms registered in Ireland, but the ban on cosmetics' advertising was dropped. That on patent medicines was retained. In 1949, a total of 266 hours of sponsored programmes were broadcast. In 1950, the Hospitals' Trust dealt a crushing blow to Radio Eireann's advertising revenue: it cut back its broadcasting time from an hour a night to just half an hour, at a week night rate of £90. The decision cost Radio Eireann £26,000 a year, but sponsored programmes still accounted for ten per cent of the station's total hours.

Erskine Childers, by this time Minister for Posts and Telegraphs, wanted a more liberal approach to sponsored programmes on Radio Eireann, as a means of improving the station's finances. The big Dublin newspaper strike of 1952 was a great indirect help, for the station began broadcasting a news bulletin at 8 a.m., to make up for the absence of the Dublin morning newspapers and sponsored programmes were brought in to fill the gap between the news bulletins of 8 a.m. and 9 a.m. That same year, Radio Eireann was allowed to take advertising for products sold by Irish firms, even if they were not made in Ireland, but all-Irish firms selling Irish-made products started to enjoy a one-third reduction in rates in addition to

Martin Giblin, managing director, T. P. Whelehan Son & Co, Dublin. The firm produced its own sponsored radio programmes until 15 years ago, when it changed to spot advertising.

Brendan Smith, who headed McConnell's Radio Publicity subsidiary and who gave a young Mike Murphy his start in radio — on the production side.
Photograph: RTE Illustrations Library.

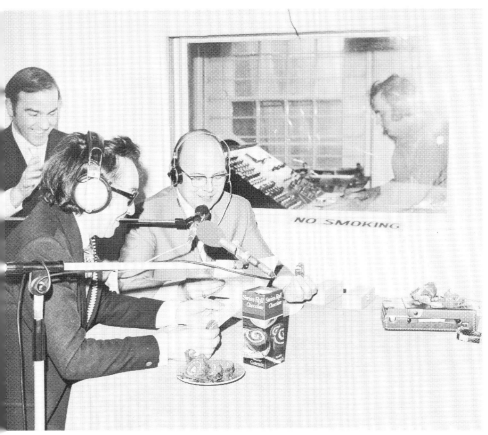

Hal Roach and Pat Quinn making one of their famous series of radio commercials at Tommy Ellis Studios during the early 1970s. Directing operations is Donald Brindley of Brindley Advertising, which handled the Quinnsworth account in those exciting days.

525

series discount. The advertising of patent medicines remained banned. The full rate stayed unchanged at £42 for 15 minutes between 1 p.m. and 2.30 p.m. on weekdays. One of Childers' other ideas did not come to fruition until 1961, however. He wanted Radio Eireann to publish its own programme journal, replacing the privately-owned *Radio Review* which had been set up just after the end of the emergency.

The tone of sponsored programme content remained conservative. Radio Eireann even insisted on contracts for these shows being sealed with wax! The *Standard* newspaper had its own show in the early 1950s, compered by Terry O'Sullivan, who later became noted as the *Evening Press* diarist. The *Standard* show, which had voice-overs by Frank Chambers, was opened by a roll of bells from St Peter's in Rome. No wonder then that when O'Kennedy Brindley did a show in 1955 with a rock n' roll theme, Niall Boden, the presenter and the influential figure in sponsored radio, along with his brother Eric, on both production and presentation sides, received the adulation of hundreds of youngsters crammed into Henry Street. Pop stars of the 1970s and 1980s frequently received this treatment, but for a sponsored show presenter in 1955, it was a novelty. In the remembrance of Anthony Kennedy, now retired from O'Kennedy Brindley, inspiration for the show came from an American record of Bill Haley and the Comets.

Only a short while before this rock n' roll show, Radio Eireann banned the record, "Thank Heaven for Little Girls", because it was considered licentious! Surprisingly, a listener from Annagassan, Co. Louth, writing in to the Brookfield Sweets' information desk, was told in reply to his query: "If done to excess, it can affect you badly in later life." The practice was not explained.

The longest running of all the sponsored radio shows, outlasting even the Bird's programme, was that for Walton's, the music firm. Leo Maguire, a choral music teacher, who ended his teaching career at the Dublin College of Music, was a great friend of Martin Walton, the man who founded the firm back in 1924. Between them, they hit upon the idea of a show devoted to Irish music. At first, the detractors were out in force. When the first shows went out in late 1951, they said that there would never be enough demand for such a programme. In the event. Leo Maguire's famous phrase, "If you feel like singing, do sing an Irish song" became a nationally known and used catchphrase.

Leo, who was born in the Liberties of Dublin in July, 1903 and who died at the end of 1985, started his broadcasting career on 2RN back in 1927. When Martin Walton and himself decided on the Walton's show, Leo soon settled into his ideal type of broadcasting. The show was usually done "live", since Leo believed this gave the sound engineers less chance to "mess". All the records used in the show were Irish, many of them on Walton's own Glenside label, launched in 1952. They were recorded at the Peter Hunt Studios in St Stephen's Green, Dublin, and pressed, "not always very well", in Leo's remembrance, by HMV in Waterford. Firm favourites on the show were songs by Delia

Mike Murphy ... began
his broadcasting career
on the production side
of Radio Publicity, run
by Brendan Smith.
Photograph: RTE.

Gene Martin, the radio
producer who worked
with Peter Hunt Studios
in the 1950s, before
returning to RTE for the
rest of his broadcasting
career. He retired in
1986.
Photograph: RTE.

Radio Centre, RTE,
Donnybrook, Dublin.
Photograph: RTE.

527

Murphy, wife of Dr Kiernan, the immediate pre-war Director of Broadcasting, and the *Whistling Gypsy* by Joe Lynch. Martin Walton and Leo Maguire picked the discs for the show, while Leo also wrote the script and timed the production. Leo also wrote over a hundred songs himself, of which he regarded the *Whistling Gypsy* as the least interesting. His best-known composition, *A Dublin Saunter,* sometimes entitled *Dublin Can Be Heaven,* came about through a chance meeting one day in 1953 with his friend Noel Purcell, the actor. The two men met up in Walton's old shop in Camden Street, Dublin; Noel was doing an inaugural programme for An Tostal, the great festival of the 1950s that started that year, and was looking in vain for a suitable song. Leo Maguire went home to Frankfort Avenue, Rathgar, and locking himself away in his study, wrote the lyrics and score in just two hours. An everlasting "hit" was created.

Three years after the Walton's programme began, another show took to the airwaves, at first tentatively, then becoming the most popular programme on radio. The *Kennedys of Castleross* was loathed at the time by Gay Byrne, who also disliked Urney Chocolates' imported sci-fi series, *The Planet Man,* which he compered, but soon the twice weekly serial became so popular that most factories round the country changed their lunch arrangements so that staff could tune in to this everyday story of village life in "Castleross".

Mark Grantham (real name Marvin Gross) was an American studying for his PhD at Trinity College, Dublin. At home in the USA, soap operas — so called because Procter and Gamble sponsored many of the radio serials — occupied much airtime. Intrigued that Irish radio had no such serials, Grantham drafted a couple of scripts and sent them in to Arks, which with its own radio production studios, had a major interest in sponsored shows. Arks was impressed and sold the idea to a client, Fry-Cadbury (Ireland), which much later came to regret its backing, since the programme became so popular that listeners forgot about the sponsor's involvement. The serial was set in a fictional Irish village and was cast largely from the Abbey Theatre. Marie Kean played Mrs Kennedy, Aideen O'Kelly was Ellen Kennedy and Norman Rodway transformed himself into the village doctor, Dr John Carrigan. Others in the cast included Pauline Delany, Philip O'Flynn Jim Norton, Angela Newman, Jim Fitzgerald, Vincent Dowling and Barbara McCaughey. Within a week or two, listeners' letters started to deluge Radio Eireann: the programme was an instant success. Not long after it began, the *News of the World* did a series on the show, with which it launched its Irish edition, after it had been permitted to circulate in the Republic.

The first scripts were written by Mark Grantham in conjunction with Bill Nugent. Its first producers were Godfrey Quigley and Alan Tate. Grantham is remembered for having a perfect ear for Irish dialogue, despite being American: his scripts were always totally accurate. Then Joe Dillon, later of public relations' fame, took over and did a sizeable stint on scriptwriting for the show. Over a 2½ year period, Hugh Leonard wrote some 300 scripts, at eight guineas a time; he says that the experience knocked the clichés out of him. He recalls that up to eight episodes were recorded in one session, the cast having been sent script copies a few days previously.

Sadly for posterity, unauthorised lines slipped into the script were snipped from the tapes before the broadcasts were out, although in another sponsored programme transmitted in the late 1950s, a reference was made on air to a fish often caught in the West of Ireland and known as a "little bollox". Kennedy's bread did a sponsored show and on one occasion, the product was referred to on air, in Desmond O'Kennedy's recollection, as "the breast in bed".

For 13 out of the 15 years that the *Kennedys of Castleross* ran, its producer was Willie Styles, a New Zealand-born actor who is now a distinguished RTE radio producer, noted for such works as the 1982 marathon reading of Joyce's *Ulysses*. Often, when Marie Kean was performing in London, he would have to fly over there and record her lines in her hotel bedroom for splicing into the tape. There were certain peculiarities about the show inflicted upon it by the client. It never had a pub scene and Mrs Kennedy was always having a cup of something warm, never anything as specific as a tea. Hugh Leonard claims that the client was sometimes mean: one occasion saw Marie Kean and himself visiting children at an orphanage. The firm, according to Leonard, refused point blank to send over a suitable box of chocolates.

In 1964, ten years after the show started, Jack W. Tate, the then chairman of Arks, complimented all concerned on the production. On Tuesdays at 1 p.m., it attracted 796,000 listeners, while 777,000 people tuned in to the Thursday edition.

Just as the *Kennedys of Castleross* was getting into its peak, however, Radio Eireann suffered a serious setback with the sponsored shows, with the abandonment of radio by the Hospitals' Trust. In 1959, the middle of the day sponsored shows were given another half an hour of airtime, between 2.30 p.m. and 3 p.m.

The Hospitals' Trust changed the time of its evening programme from 10.30 p.m. to 11 p.m. in the hope of attracting more listeners. Then it decided to change back, but the Radio Eireann authorities, having already altered their evening programme format, were reluctant to fall in with the Hospitals' Trust request. The late Donal Stanley was sponsored programmes officer at the time. In September, 1959, Radio Eireann and the Trust agreed that its programmes should be continued on a day-to-day basis. The following year, 1960, the Hospitals' Trust gave up radio advertising, signing off for the last time on April 1 that year, almost exactly 30 years since it had started its sponsored show on the old 2RN. Val Joyce, who began his broadcasting career as a junior in the Hospital Trust's studio, moved on to Radio Luxembourg. The familiar voices of Bart Bastable — who went to live in Florida in 1978 — and Ian Priestley Mitchell, faded from the trust's show. No longer were listeners wished "health, happiness and good fortune" on the show by Ian Priestley Mitchell, who went on to compere *Town Hall Tonight* and who died in 1969. Although Radio Eireann feared the dip in revenue, most of the shortfall was made up from other sources.

Sponsored programmes gave much work, however, to both performers and production people. Peter Hunt had recording studios that were kept constantly busy, through the 1950s, 1960s and into the 1970s. Gene Martin, the RTE radio producer, started with the station nearly 40 years ago as an effects man, also responsible for playing discs. In 1951, Peter Hunt, asked him to work for his studios on a part-time basis. Amazingly, Radio Eireann, then firmly part of the civil service, allowed Martin to take this work, which soon developed into a full-time job. Gene Martin did so well with sponsored programmes' production in the early 1950s that he was earning around £40 a week — an enormous sum in those days — and he was one of the few people in Ireland able to afford a new car. Sean O Riada, the musician and composer, would record with no-one other than Gene Martin.

A youngster who started in radio production at the age of 16 and who is still going strong in the business is Brian Halford, who recently left Youngs, where he was head of radio and TV to start his own production company. He began his radio career as a trainee disc operator in the Eamonn Andrews studios, moving after a year to RTE as a disc operator. From RTE, he went to Youngs to replace Gene Martin.

Another newcomer to the production side of the business in the mid-1950s was Fred O'Donovan, more recently chairman of the RTE authority and of the National Concert Hall. He had served in the RAF and after a year spent in Switzerland recuperating from TB, he came home to Dublin in 1954. He had had radio production experience abroad and was very keen to get into radio here; Maura Fox, now with McConnell's, then in charge of the radio department in Janus, gave Fred O'Donovan his start with the production of the Irel coffee programme. Within two years, he was producing something like 26 shows a week; from this work blossomed his own recording studios, Broadcast and Theatrical Productions. His production workload was only equalled by Niall Boden. O'Donovan's brothers Dick and Bill also did well in sponsored radio production, Dick developing a masterful talent for writing humorous scripts, while Bill ended up running the production side of the company. Later, Fred O'Donovan was managing director of Eamonn Andrews Studios and also ran the Gaiety. Eamonn Andrews had set up his studios in 1948 with Dermod Cafferky. Andrews and O'Donovan were to part company after the latter fell ill with a heart condition. Brendan Smith, the man behind the Dublin Theatre Festival for so many years, also ran McConnell's production studios, Radio Publicity. One of Smith's earliest productions was *Fabian of the Yard*, for Crosse & Blackwell. Ciarán

Breathnach who joined Arks when the *Kennedys of Castleross* was at episode 150 and who stayed with the show until it was eventually taken over by RTE, after a period in Willie Styles' own production company, now runs Avondale Studios. Like the other outside radio production people, Breathnach now does radio commercials rather than the sponsored programmes that were once the mainstay of such studios, as do other noted production people like Tommy Ellis.

The production of sponsored programmes gave opportunities to many immensely talented young people now prominent in broadcasting. Colin Morrison, the RTE radio producer, started his career with the Eamonn Andrews Studios. The young Gay Byrne, in his own words, had been "nibbling at the edges of radio for a long time". He was working, by day, for the Guardian Insurance company, then based in Kildare Street.

One day, Desmond O'Kennedy of O'Kennedy Brindley asked him to do one performance on the Urney's chocolate programme, as Pat Layde was going on a short tour with the Abbey Theatre. The show was produced in the CIE hall in Marlborough Street and also featured Joe Lynch and Norman Metcalf on the organ. Gay Byrne was an instant success; one week stretched into two and then three. He ended up doing the show for nine years. Before long, his insurance company boss put the inevitable question to him: "Show business or insurance?" Very fortunately for the listening and viewing public, Gay Byrne had absolutely no hesitation in choosing the former.

Eventually, Gay Byrne also got involved in the production side of radio. John Young, son of Dick Young, was looking for someone to run the radio department in his agency, which was responsible for producing ten or twelve shows a week for such clients as Bradmola Mills, Brittain's (the car assemblers) and Prescott's, the cleaners and dyers. Some of the shows were recorded at the Peter Hunt Studios (a good improviser and an immaculate man for coiling his microphone leads, recalls Gene Martin, who retired from RTE radio in May, 1986), while others were done "live" in the Henry Street studios, with the young Gay Byrne doing the discs.

One of Gay's favourite sponsored programmes was that for Prescott's. About once a month, Joe Linnane and himself would do a lightning tour to meet customers in some of the 80 shops in the chain. Joe was a great man for chatting up people, harmless old banter and blather, recalls Gay Byrne, looking back on those times with much affection. He would come back to town with lashings of tape from these shop visits and edit it down to fit the 15 minute programme slot. In those days, tape was still a comparative novelty, for it had only replaced the old-fashioned and cumbersome disc recording in Radio Eireann as recently as 1949. Another firm of cleaners, incidentally, also sponsored regular shows: Imco. Terry O'Sullivan compered many. Louis Spiro, amiably nicknamed "Stainless", was a fine singer and broadcaster and often wrote scripts for the show himself. The two

Terry O'Sullivan, who compered many sponsored radio shows. In his later career, he became better known as the *Evening Press* diarist.
Photograph: The Irish Times.

radio characters he created, "Stainless" and "Spotless", became quite popular with listeners. In some of the early shows, Spiro and Eamonn Andrews acted them. As a result of the radio publicity, the Imco tower on Dublin's Merrion Road became a noted south city landmark.

After some time, Gay Byrne started commuting to Manchester to work for Granada television during the week, coming home to do sponsored shows on Fridays and Saturdays. His leaving Wilson Young Advertising gave a good chance to Gene Martin, who had been doing five or six programmes a week on a freelance basis. One day, John Young was said to have told him: "For the money I'm paying you, I could have a full-time man." The job went initially to Gay Byrne, but when Gay left for Granada a couple of years later, Gene Martin took over.

Larry Gogan — given his first radio break, as a teenager, by Maura Fox, then with Janus.
Photograph: RTE.

Maura Fox gave the young Hugh Leonard, real name John Keyes Byrne, his first scriptwriting break. He was still working as an anonymous clerk in the Land Commission, which he hated; his first scripts were for the *Carlsberg Casebook,* a mystery series read by Denis Brennan, whose deep brown velvet voice, much missed now, was ideal for the part. Leonard, in retrospect, was not entirely enamoured of Janus Advertising, which handled the Carlsberg account, claiming that the agency had a somewhat cavalier attitude to its scriptwriters. "They wanted a lot of work, including research, for not much money." On the other hand, Fred O'Donovan, who made such a success of the National Concert Hall, says that Janus was excellent for not interfering. However, the combination of Maura Fox and Janus did enable Leonard to give up his job in the Land Commission. Maura Fox remembers him

Pat Harkin, sales manager of Sunshine Radio.

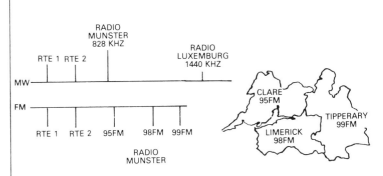

Press advertisement for "Pirate" station in Limerick.

Tommy Ellis, pictured right at the control console, is the best-known sound recording man in the advertising business. The Tommy Ellis Recording Studios at 30 Upper Mount Street, Dublin, set up in 1970, are widely regarded as the best equipped in the business. 80 per cent of the work in the three studios (seven Studer recording machines) is for radio production, with the remainder for TV sound tracks. The studios have full video voice-to-picture facilities and film dubbing as well as the most extensive music and sound effects library in commercial recording in Ireland.

A one-time pupil of Synge Street, Tommy went straight from school into the professional music business. He studied violin and double bass at the Dublin College of Music and worked with many top bands such as Peggy Dell's, Tommy O'Brien (Crystel and Cleary's), Joe Coughlan (Ballerina), The Viscounts, and as musical director at the Green Isle hotel. He finds his musical experience invaluable in the recording business; his break into commercial radio production came when he joined ACT studios in 1964. The studios were run by Proinsias MacAonghusa, its director of commercial radio was Harry

coming to her one day and explaining that if she could give him a couple more programmes to write, he could throw up the civil service. Soon, he had quadrupled his six guineas a week wages from the Land Commission.

Another young hopeful scriptwriter at this time was Bobby Gahan, now assistant director-general of RTE. As a sideline, he wrote for such shows as Murray's Car Rentals and Tayto Crisps, delivering the scripts on his bicycle.

Top Radio 2 disc jockey Larry Gogan also owes his start to Maura Fox. Immersed in the pop music sounds of Radio Luxembourg since his childhood, Larry had a burning ambition to get on the air himself. The Gogan family ran a newsagency in Dublin's Fairview; Maura Fox was a regular customer, so one day, the youthful Larry gathered enough courage to ask about getting into radio. He was training for the stage, so she gave him a part in a serial called District Nurse, sponsored by Johnson Bros. Angela Newman was Nurse Carmichael and Eddie Golden played the doctor. Larry Gogan's first sponsored show of his own, as a disc jockey, was a half-hour programme for the Astoria Ballroom in Bundoran. Later on, he became well-known for the Saturday afternoon Television Club Show.

Mike Murphy was terrified the first time he did a broadcast. He started with Brendan Smith in Radio Publicity writing up the logs for the shows. Adrian Cronin — more recently the Late, Late Show director — was in charge of production, remembers Mike. When Adrian Cronin eventually left to join RTE, Mike Murphy took over — "I used to be quite nifty with the controls". He used to get three guineas a show, producing programmes for such sponsors as Colgate Palmolive, Lemons and Willwood. Featuring in some of the shows was Brendan Smith's wife, Beryl Fagan, the actress. One day, a presenter was too sick to do a programme, so Mike had to take over. "Every word in the show was scripted and I only had to do a few lines of dialogue, but I was terrified," he remembers. After his four years with Brendan Smith, Mike Murphy started compering sponsored programmes himself, for advertisers like Stewarts' cash stores and Winstons. He ad libbed on the Stewarts' show, even though Radio Eireann, through the then sponsored programmes officer, Donal Stanley, kept a strict check on what was broadcast. Also doing a little ad libbing was a young Terry Wogan, who did Take it from Terry for International Artists. Mike Murphy also met his wife, Eileen, through the sponsored shows. She was working with the Eamonn Andrews Studios and Mike remembers that neither Fred O'Donovan nor Brendan Smith was particularly happy about the association, for professional reasons.

The sponsored shows produced many humorous incidents. On one occasion, Maura Fox got stuck in the very antiquated lift in the Henry Street Studios, complete with script and discs for a "live" show. The lift kept going up and down as transmission time edged ever nearer; fortunately, the lift came to a halt on the ground floor, just minutes

534

Thuillier and Vincent Corcoran was director of film production. As studio manager in ATC, Tommy's first big jingle (the first of numerous successes) was for Squadron Shoes. He remembers studio time being booked, in his own studios in 1972, to record a jingle for the Irish Permanent; the singer was Joseph Locke and the accompanist the late Albert Healy. The studio cost was £34 and the resultant jingle was used on radio and TV for five years.

before the show went on air. Another time, when the presenter fainted on a "live" show, she had to take over the microphone. Larry Gogan was presenting a "live" programme on one occasion when the cleaning lady in the Henry Street studios failed to see the red light, meaning that the show was in transmission, breezed in and started dusting round him! Luckily, she never opened her mouth.

Some of Eamonn Andrews' early radio broadcasting was in sponsored shows; his first major programme in this *genre* was for Kavanagh's pure food products, with its signature tune, "You Are My Sunshine". The first time Andrews introduced the show, he said: "Kavanagh's, makers of *poor* food products." Paddy Kavanagh, the firm's owner, said nothing, but for weeks afterwards, every time he entered his golf club, he was hooted at. Like Gay Byrne, Eamonn Andrews had started in the insurance business and he feared, needlessly, that he might be set for a quick return.

Once, Bing Crosby was turned away from the O'Donovan studios in Henry Street. The firm made recordings for sponsored shows at 40 Henry Street and band recordings at No. 4. Finding the studios at Number 40, up several flights of stairs, was not easy and Bing was given the complicated set of directions, which made little sense to him. He got well and truly lost, asking in shops to the utter amazement of the shop assistants. The legend goes that he found the right place eventually, but never turned up for the recording. When questions were asked, the young man on the reception desk was reported to have said: "There was an oul' fella in alright, but I fecked him out." The truth was slightly more prosaic. The young man in question, Tony Hogan, who now works with Tommy Ellis Studios, in fact told Bing Crosby: "You're not booked in here" and directed him to the other set

535

of studios at 4 Henry Street. No wonder that when Harry Thuillier interviewed Spike Milligan for a sponsored show and said to Spike: "Welcome to Ireland", Spike replied: "You're welcome to it, too."

Fred O'Donovan was accused of having a quirky sense of humour when Dr Tom Dooley, the medical missionary, died in 1968. A pre-recorded programme that went out immediately after the 1.30 p.m. news bulletin that announced Dr Dooley's death, used a disc entitled *Hang down your head, Tom Dooley.* Another time, the death of a Pope was announced, followed straight away on a sponsored show by a disc called *Arrivederci Roma.*

Fortunately, Radio Eireann's sponsored programmes officer then, Paddy Geoghegan, had a good sense of humour. Joe Lynch, who compered countless programmes for different sponsors, says that he found Paddy a real gentleman, very charming, with a great sense of humour. Even though the rules had to be obeyed, Joe Lynch found this period in broadcasting very open and great fun. Some of the fun was against himself, as on the occasion he was in Clery's when he should have been doing a "live" show. He survived the episode, as did Terry O'Sullivan when he was similarly forgetful on one occasion. Joe Lynch, incidentally, claims to have been the first disc jockey to have recorded the chat between discs; his voice was recorded on discs, dropped in manually during the course of the programme.

In the autumn of 1959, a new series started for Korona watches. The script called for regular time checks, using of course the client's clocks in studio. The show was "live", but the compere was said to have made so many errors reading the time that the programme was dropped after only six of the 13 shows planned had gone out. Harry Thuillier had great fun when he was doing sponsored shows; once, when he was due to make a "live" broadcast from Henry Street, he left his house on Dublin's northside, but could not start his car, so he hitched a lift from a passing ambulance. When he was doing the Lucozade *This Is Your Town* show, he paid a man in Kilkenny 2/6d to confirm stories about the ghost in the castle. Listener reaction was strong! Many of the best "fluffs" never go on air, a shame in retrospect! One time, Gene Martin was playing a tape in the control room of a commercial recording studio while Denis Brennan was rehearsing at the microphone. Suddenly, Gene burst out laughing. Denis thought he had been slighted, until he received the explanation. On the tape, made by another presenter, the advertising slogan came across as "If you want a decent suit, go to Premier Dairies." Clark's shoes in Dundalk used to have a regular sponsored show, presented by Eamonn Andrews. After listening to the recording of one show, the representative from Clark's wanted a remake; Eamonn Andrews had gone abroad and was not available to re-record the show, as the client wanted, so Noel Andrews stood in. The client was said never to have noticed the difference. During the Tayto Crisps' show, contestants piled up coins. What they didn't know was that a string attached to the table leg was pulled now and again so the coin pile didn't get too high!

Some clients were very touchy. Bill O'Donovan remembers one Cork advertiser who insisted that the production people came down to Cork. He would never go to Dublin to meet them. Once, O'Donovan was in Cork with this client when he noticed some packaging that contained a serious misprint, necessitating a large volume reprint. He pointed this out to the client with a certain undisguised glee! Other programmes were great fun to make. In the early 1970s, Pat Quinn

Brian Halford set up his own company, Halford Productions, in 1985. He was formerly head of television and radio at Young Advertising. Halford joined Young's sixteen years ago from Telefis Eireann where he started in the drama and sound effects department. He wrote and produced sponsored programmes while at the station, before moving to Young's where he developed their television and radio department. His most notable work at the agency was for The Irish Times.

Ivan Tinman, managing director of Downtown Radio, Newtownards — now expanding into Derry and the north-west.

537

Kieran Boyle, head of advertisement sales at Downtown Radio.

and his supermarkets, which he later sold out to the Westons to form Quinnsworth, was Brindley's largest client. The sponsored shows done by Pat Quinn with Hal Roach, with background assistance from Basil and Donald Brindley, were hilarious recording sessions. Equal fun was had then by Frank Kelly and his co-scriptwriter on the *Glen Abbey Show,* David Hanly, now co-presenter of the *Morning Ireland* programme.

A typing error annoyed a client, who was Jewish. A script for his firm's show had been handwritten in its first draft. A reference to a "jem in America" turned out as a "Jew in America", which caused considerable embarrassment until the client was shown the original draft.

Still the shows went on, the output of a considerable band of broadcasting talent. Harry Thuillier did his famous show, *Come Fly With Me,* done in conjunction with Aer Lingus and Jacobs. The programme started in 1960 and ran for eight years, during which time Harry reckoned he travelled 100,000 miles round the world. Flying into the airport for Lourdes, he announced into his microphone: "We are now coming into Lourdes. "Then he did the same intro all over again, minutes later, for another show on Rome. Nearby passengers who heard were thrown into a state of confusion. Another time, he met a travel agent in Beirut with a 26 syllable Arabic name ending in "Ali". Said Harry Thuillier: "Hi, Ali". Eventually, Harry Thuillier went to the USA to try his luck there and when he came home, he found all doors in RTE closed to him. At one stage, he was director of commercial radio for Proinsias MacAonghusa's ACT studios. Thuillier now runs his own company producing tapes for supermarkets. One Radio Eireann announcer, Patrick Begley, lost his job because his accent was said to have been too Anglicised. He transferred to sponsored shows and presented the Gala cosmetics shows on Tuesday and Thursday mornings.

Fred O'Donovan, who was producing about 25 sponsored radio shows a week in the late 1950s and early 1960s. Until 1985, he was chairman of the RTE Authority.
Photograph: RTE.

The *Come Fly With Me* show carried advertisements for Jacobs and Aer Lingus. When it ended, Frankie Byrne continued the Jacob's radio advertising tradition through her *Women's Page* programme, complete with Sinatra discs. A typical question was: "Dear Frankie, I'm a 19 year old girl. I know a man of 40 with a good business. How can I get him to ask me out?" One of the few other programmes with shared sponsors was *Sixpence A Second* with Michael O'Hehir, from Rowntrees and *Radio Review*.

Niall Boden ran the Donnelly's sausage programme, with its double meaning sign-off: "Bye now". His nickname was "Niall of the Nine Sausages". Boden claims that he gave Val Doonican his first big break; the young man was singing with a group on the front in Bray and asked Niall Boden for a chance. Val turned up at the recording studios a few days later, complete with guitar, and was given something to do on the show. He became one of the Donnelly's Music Makers' group.

Donnelly's was also famous for its theme song, to the tune of the *Mexican Hat Dance:*

> So the next time you visit your grocer,
> Tell him no other sausage will do.
> To his other suggestions, say no, sir —
> It's Donnelly's sausages for you.

Din Joe introduced Irish dancing to radio, a seemingly contradictory feat. When Denis Fitzgibbon, now with Toyota, the car firm, was sales manager of the Smithfield Motor Company, he did a 15 minute show for the firm, which ran every Saturday morning for four or five years. He also featured in a number of other sponsored show programmes, including the K & S Sunshine Food's show, a programme that also gave Roy Croft his first break in sponsored radio. Later, he did such shows as *Tune Time with Teresa Duffy* for Scott's Foods. Established actor Harry Brogan did heart-rending monologues at the end of *The Dalys of Honeydew Farm* sponsored by Gateaux. When Gateaux went on strike and the programme was suspended, sales of all cake brands went down.

Broadcasting was a much more casual affair in those far-off days in the 1950s. Gay Byrne, who lived with his mother on the South Circular Road at Rialto, often used to finish his lunch at 1.30 p.m. and drive into the Henry Street studios in time for a "live" programme at 1.45 p.m. When Cecil Barror was doing a "live" show in Henry Street in the early afternoon, he would stroll from the ESB in Fleet Street to have his lunch in the old Metropole. In those easy-going days, it came as a surprise when Philips, the electrical products' firm, sanctioned a humorous approach by scriptwriter Dick O'Donovan, Philips was said to have been the first radio advertiser to poke fun at itself. Denis Brennan, in reading the commercials for Philip's electric razors, made a great joke out of saying he never used one, since he had a beard. Brennan also did the *Bulmer's Cider Show.*

There was even the odd sponsored programme produced in Dublin, but never heard in Ireland until years later, when it had a certain curiosity value, like the St Patrick's Eve show done in the Phoenix Hall 1960 for Schaefer's beer in America, featuring the Artane Boys' Band and compered by the Irish-American singer, John Feeney. Radio Eireann's total advertising revenue that year was £76,000. October, 1960, saw the station start "spot" advertising in earnest, sold by Niall Boden and Jimmy Shields.

Most of the sponsored programmes related to national brands, although for one series, the Moore Street traders banded together to have a programme extolling their shopping virtues. Agricultural programmes were somewhat rarer, despite Radio Eireann's country-wide listenership. The *Farmer's Journal* had a show of its own and received special permission from the Radio Eireann authorities for scripts to be cleared the day before transmission, because of their topicality. The usual procedure in the station was for a week-long clearance period. Every week, the producers of the *Farmer's Journal* programme would feature a different county and use a person said to have been from that county, who would pretend to be an avid reader of the paper.

The producers didn't know until the day before transmission which county was going to be featured, so a variety of passers-by were roped in from Henry Street: barmen, guards, civil servants, teachers, even Jack Plant the stuntman on one occasion. The pay was good — two guineas for 30 seconds' work. After the show, there were always prolonged celebrations in a nearby pub. One solicitor who featured on the show said that the next time he did it, he would accept no pay, since he had just had to spend £15 on drinks! Improvisation was elevated to

Robbie Robinson, managing director of Sunshine Radio. He broadcasts under the name of Robbie Dale.

Stella Robinson, head of advertising at Sunshine Radio.

an art form in those days. Bill O'Donovan, then working for Eamonn Andrews Studios, remembers that the ceiling in the studios at 40 Henry Street was made from egg boxes, which gave a fine acoustical effect. Alleged long distance calls were faked by presenters talking into a teacup. When Julie Andrews was interviewed from Hollywood for a sponsored show, the line was so clear that distortion had to be added for the benefit of listeners! After one of Harry Thuillier's famous shows, the late Donal Stanley, then sponsored programmes officer at RTE, is said to have complimented Thuillier. Then he said, out of the corner of his mouth: "I've a funny idea the Killarney jarvey was really Jimmy Magee." Now widely known for his sports reporting, Magee worked closely with Harry Thuillier on the production side of his shows, together with Bobby Gahan.

Whelehan's of Finglas was one of the very first companies to use radio to advertise agricultural chemicals. Says Martin Giblin, the firm's managing director: "Radio was a great way of introducing our reps. Radio was a very good calling card and we heard of many instances of customers waiting for shops to open at 9.30 a.m., once they had heard the Whelehan's programme."

The cock crowing to introduce the programme became quite famous: as one source in the broadcasting business was heard to remark, "the Whelehan's crowing cock was open to various interpretations". Whelehan's was unusual in another respect: the show was largely put together by its own staff, rather than by broadcasting production personnel. Noel McMahon, who worked for the firm and who was keenly interested in amateur dramatics, produced the show. Martin Giblin, then sales manager, now managing director, wrote the scripts and read some of the commercials on air. Peter Murphy was the presenter. Remembers Martin Giblin: "The early productions were a pantomime. It took a whole morning to record one show of 15 minutes duration but we enjoyed it immensely." Martin travelled the whole country and through his intimate knowledge of the farming community, knew exactly how the scripts should sound. Domas used to book the time, but Whelehan's did all the production work, for around £60 per show. The time cost £100, so it was inexpensive advertising. After the sponsored programme was dropped, 15 years ago, Whelehan's continued to use spot advertisements on RTE Radio. Martin Giblin again: "We have always been convinced of the power of radio. It's amazing how many people still remember our sponsored shows after all this time."

Through the early 1960s, the radio service suffered in the cause of television. As Kieran Sheedy, now head of drama in RTE Radio, remembers, there was a big drain of resources and people from the radio service, still based in Henry Street, to the new television centre in Donnybrook. But in 1966, two developments took place that were to signal major expansions of radio broadcasting in Ireland. First of all, RTE started transmitting on the FM frequencies, which give much higher quality reception, free of interference. The main drawback of FM is lack of range: transmissions are line of sight and so cover a much smaller area than AM broadcasts, which also suffer from severe interference at night time.

By now, the entire RTE FM network is virtually completed, giving RTE much more flexible programme scheduling, as with the FM3 classical music and speech programming on weekday afternoons and at weekends. In time, RTE intends FM to be its main means of radio transmission, with AM a secondary service. 1966 saw another radio news event, the first of the "serious" unlicensed or "pirate" stations.

Ronan O'Rahilly was running Radio Caroline from a ship in the North Sea and it was proving quite successful: soon, a Dublin broadcasting enthusiast called Eamon Cooke was inspired to start his own station. So in 1966, Eamon Cooke, later christened "Captain" Cooke by one of his disc jockeys, Don Moore, about 1975, began Radio Dublin in a very small way, broadcasting at first only on Sunday afternoons from Inchicore in Dublin. It took nine years before Eamon Cooke had the resources to launch 24 hour broadcasting from his station. Now he says that advertising is "rolling in", with many major brands using the station. On one occasion, the FCA used Radio Dublin to advertise for recruits, a decision that provoked a storm of controversy, since unlicensed stations are illegal under the law.

Radio Dublin transmits on AM, which reaches listeners up to 40 miles away. The station is also on FM and interestingly, used a 1 kilowatt shortwave transmitter that according to Eamon Cooke, can be picked up in America and Australia. In 1939, Radio Eireann began transmitting all its programmes, except the sponsored shows, on a $1\frac{1}{2}$ kilowatt shortwave transmitter. The shortwave experiment was abandoned for the duration of the war and started again in 1947, soon afterwards being closed down for good. "Captain" Cooke's station remains the only one in Ireland to transmit on shortwave.

In 1968, two years after Radio Dublin came on the air, Radio Eireann closed the gap in transmissions that had long existed in mornings and afternoons. All day programming was introduced that year. It was also the start of the present "troubles" in the North, which prompted much greater news feature coverage.

Even in the 1950s, the News at 1.30 p.m. was the most popular programme on radio, listened to by 45 per cent of the entire adult population. In those days, most people had their midday meal at home, which helped listening figures, but even today, when people's life styles have changed so much, the *News at 1.30* is still the most popular programme on Irish radio, attracting one third of all adults, or 775,000 listeners, almost as many as the *Kennedys of Castleross* in its heyday. By the time this book is published, that peak news programme could have been shifted forward and rechristened *News at One*.

During the 1970s, radio continued to claw back listeners. A major move came in 1975, when the radio service finally moved from the rather decrepit studios in Henry Street, often compared to a public lavatory, with their tiled corridors, to the brand new, custom-built radio centre in Donnybrook. It has eleven studios, including one for the RTE Symphony Orchestra and RTE Concert Orchestra and another for the RTE Players and their drama productions. Engineering standards in the new centre are regarded as among the best in the world. Output from regional studios is fed into the network. Not long ago, the Belfast studios were substantially upgraded, so that they are capable of handling virtually any type of programme. Centres like Castlebar, Galway, Letterkenny, Limerick, Sligo and Waterford have their own studios with "live" input facilities to the national network. The Cork studios were the first purpose built ones in the Republic when they opened in 1958. There are special studio facilities to cover Leinster House and a small studio in the Meteorological Office, from where the all-important weather forecast is broadcast several times a day.

While RTE brought the radio centre on stream in 1975, preparations were going ahead for Ireland's first, and so far, only commercial, licensed local radio station, Downtown Radio. In Britain, local commercial radio has failed to have the impact as an advertising medium that RTE radio has had here in Ireland. In the UK, commercial radio accounts for just two per cent of national advertising expenditure, while in Ireland, RTE radio will have had about eleven per cent, or £14 million in 1986.

Val Joyce ... started his broadcasting career with the Irish Hospitals' Sweepstakes.
Photograph: RTE.

Downtown Radio went on the air on March 16, 1976; the very first advertisement was for Cookstown sausages, with the theme of the "Cookstown sizzle". The advertisement was placed by Belfast Progressive Advertising. The very first advertising spot on 2RN in Dublin, almost 50 years previously, had also been for sausages! Downtown occupied the first purpose built commercial radio station in the UK; it began with £400,000 capital and according to managing director Ivan Tinman, who until his promotion to managing director in 1978, was Downtown's first advertisement sales manager, it has never failed to pay a dividend.

Operating under franchise from the Independent Broadcasting Authority in London, Downtown broadcasts on AM and FM stereo, covering most of Northern Ireland, as far west as Limavady and Enniskillen. The population in its transmission area is about 87 per cent of the Ulster Television area population. Out of the total radio audience in Northern Ireland of 801,000. Downtown claims to have a cumulative weekly audience of 541,000. By the end of 1986, the station plans to extend its coverage to Derry and the North-West. 185,000 people in the Derry, Coleraine and Limavady areas will be served by the first FM transmitters there. When coverage is extended to the Omagh and Enniskillen areas, a further 75,000 people will be brought within range of Downtown. At present, from its Newtownards studios, Downtown Radio broadcasts 21 hours a day, Monday to Friday, an hour less on Saturdays and Sundays. During the day,

Recently, McConnell's became the first advertising agency to spend more than IR£1 million on radio advertising with RTE. Between radio and television, McConnell's spent over IR£5 million with RTE in 1985. At a celebratory reception in RTE were Brian Pierce (left), head of radio sales, RTE, Nicky Cornick, media buyer, McConnell's and Mike Tobin, media director, McConnell's.

545

programming is mostly music, with such well-known presenters as June Nightingale and Lynda Jane. In the evenings, more minority interests are catered for, with such programmes as Alfred Burrowes' classical music show and the Downtown book programme. Peak listening is between 8 a.m. and 9 a.m., with the greatest average half hour audience on Sundays between 9 a.m. and 3 p.m. — 119,000. The station is allowed to broadcast a maximum of nine minutes of advertisements in any one hour; rates vary from £5 for 30 seconds between midnight and 7 a.m. and £105 for peak Saturday and Sunday listening. 85 per cent of advertisements on the station are produced in the Downtown studios, according to Kieran Boyle, present advertisement sales manager.

Downtown Radio's two production studios have been designed to cope with all aspects of recording work, from voice only to multi-track techniques. Studio One can hold up to 30 musicians, while Studio Two can take up to five musicians and is also used for voice-overs and over-dubbing. Says Ivan Tinman: "We must target our advertising to be of a similar quality to the music we broadcast." 65 per cent of the station's advertising originates in Ireland, the rest comes from Britain. Of the local advertising, 40 per cent is from Belfast agencies, 24 per cent is from Dublin agencies and 36 per cent is placed direct. While the Belfast agencies were not as well equipped technically as the Dublin agencies when Downtown started, they were positive and responsive to the new medium. There have been few occasions when commercials went wrong, but Ivan Tinman and Kieran Boyle remembered the time a London agency sent in a tape containing the advertisement slogan "Well worth shopping at Woolworth", unaware that Wellworth is the name of a large supermarket group in Northern Ireland.

Ten years on, Downtown Radio is a very successful and profitable commercial station, employing just 58 permanent staff. It attracts over 43 per cent of total radio listening in its area, an impressive figure considering that listeners have a choice of eight other licensed channels, including five from the BBC and Radio Luxembourg. Downtown Radio remains the kind of local, commercial station that would be set up in the major population centres of the Republic, if the long-awaited Radio Bill is presented to the Dail and the ten year long argument over local radio is finally brought to a conclusion.

While Downtown Radio in the North represented the legal development of commercial radio there, in the Republic, illegal commercial radio flourished. This year, these illegal stations will carry an estimated IR£3 millions' worth of advertisements. An often repeated tale in Dublin puts the start of "pirate" radio down to the Dubliners' song, *Seven Drunken Nights*. It was banned by both RTE and the BBC for its alleged bawdiness and this banning was said to have provided encouragement for the spread of illegal stations. The real explanation of the "pirate" stations' growth is not quite so simple, according to Robbie Robinson, managing director of Sunshine Radio.

He points out that illegal broadcasting here was flourishing long before the Dubliners cut that disc. According to the European Broadcasting Union, quoted by Robinson, Vatican Radio was using unauthorised wavelengths into the 1970s. The first major "pirate" stations, however, were Swedish and started transmitting in 1962. Radio Nord was ship-based off the Danish coast, while Radio Sud transmitted from off the Swedish coast. The Stockholm Government acted swiftly, closing down both stations the following year, but the seeds of illegal broadcasting had been sown. Ronan O'Rahilly, regarded as the Grand Old Man of "pirate" broadcasting, was in London. He recorded a group called the "Blue Flames" whose lead singer was Georgie Fame. The BBC and Radio Luxembourg declined to play the disc, so O'Rahilly and an Australian man, Alan Crawford, decided to set up their own station. Two ships were bought, the MV *Mi Amigo* and the MV *Frederick* and fitted out at Greenore, Co. Louth. O'Rahilly then went alone in the venture and had the MV *Frederick* sailed to the Essex coast off south-east England. He rechristened the ship *Caroline* after the daughter of the late American president, John F. Kennedy. It started broadcasting at Easter, 1964, thereby starting a revolution in radio in these islands. Later, O'Rahilly and Crawford came together again and launched a second ship-borne station, Caroline 2, which broadcast to all of Britain and Ireland from Ramsey Bay in the Isle of Man.

The British Marine Offences Act, which came into effect in 1967, made it a criminal offence to supply "pirate" broadcasting ships. Radio Caroline moved out of British jurisdiction and its head office was transferred to Amsterdam. In 1968, it was put off the air by unpaid bills but returned in 1970 and broadcast, under new ownership, from off the south-east coast of England until the ship sank in 1980. By the time Ronan O'Rahilly ended his involvement with Radio Caroline in the late 1960s, Radio Dublin, run by Eamon Cooke, had been going strongly for several years.

ARD was set up in Cabra in 1970 and remained in its first studios, a council house, until early 1978, when it moved to a Georgian house in Belvedere Place, off Mountjoy Square, on Dublin's northside. Bernard Llewellyn, who took over the running of the station at that time, said that Downtown Radio had inspired him to run a local commercial radio station. On January 23, 1978, many politicians and media personalities attended the lavish launch of the new-look ARD in a Dublin nightclub. On February 1, it covered the Dail debate on the Budget, using the newly recruited Howard Kinlay (now with *The Irish Times*). Other well-known journalists, such as Brian Trench (now on the *Sunday Tribune*) joined the station. Llewellyn said that he made a point of employing NUJ journalists and using the same professional standards of broadcasting as local radio stations in Britain. On ARD, all kinds of broadcasting innovations were carried out, such as extensive coverage of the June 1979 local government and European elections and a series of programmes in which the late Noel Purcell reminisced about the

Dublin he knew. In October, 1978, ARD brought a new transmitter on the air and claimed that its signal rivalled that of RTE's Tullamore 500 kilowatt transmitter, opened in 1975.

Bernard Llewellyn claimed he broke new ground by hiring a professional recording studio to produce the advertisements for the station. Many people in the broadcasting industry thought it less than coincidental that shortly after ARD beefed up its image and listening appeal, RTE launched Radio 2 in May, 1979 as a primarily music station aimed at a young listenership. Cathal McCabe, controller of programmes on Radio 2, vehemently denies this and says that RTE's plans for the new station had been in the pipeline for several years previously, awaiting Government approval.

In the event, ARD ceased transmissions on January 1, 1980, in the hope that local commercial radio would be legalised and that it would win a licence. To date, that Government approval has not been given. Other stations came and went with similarly unfulfilled ambitions. Radio Leinster was set up in a location near Lamb Doyle's in Sandyford, south Co. Dublin, in 1981 and closed down two years later in anticipation of the legislation that never happened. Other Dublin stations thrived for a while, such as Big D, based in Chapel Lane off Parnell Street from 1980 to 1981 and Southside Radio, which was on the air from the Hotel Victor in Rochestown Avenue in Dun Laoghaire from 1979 to 1981. Other Dublin stations included Radio City, which lasted from 1979 to 1982 and TTTR, which came on the air in 1981 as the city's only specialised music station, broadcasting all country and western music. Outside, stations included Radio Carousel in Dundalk, started in 1979 and Boyneside in Drogheda. Cork had South Coast, which closed down, leaving the present Cork "pirate" ERI going strong. Limerick has Radio Luimni and Waterford has two stations. Many cross-channel disc jockeys arrived on the scene. So similar was their mode of dress that they were known as "The Anoraks".

1980 saw the launch of the so-called "super pirates", beginning with Sunshine Radio, which went on the air in September that year from studios at Sands Hotel, Portmarnock, in north Co. Dublin. The station was started by Robbie Robinson and Chris Cary but the business relationship broke up the following year when Cary went off to start his own radio station, Radio Nova. Robinson had previously worked in Radio Caroline first as a disc jockey and then as station manager.

Robbie Robinson remembers that for the first few months, all the advertisement spots came from local traders in north Co. Dublin. Lawless Brothers, the Malahide TV and radio retailers, were among the first advertisers to give good support to the new station. Just before Christmas that year, came Sunshine's first agency advertisement, from Gaffney McHugh, for a pre-Christmas campaign for the Northside shopping centre. Shortly afterwards, Aer Lingus took to the Sunshine airwaves, using the station to broadcast for the very first time its famous "Look up, it's Aer Lingus" jingle. However, it took some time for the agencies to take serious interest in the new station. Jerry Brannelly (then with Brian Cronin's, now with DDFH & B) was as interested in radio as his then managing director, Brian Cronin. In the late spring of 1981, Robinson's Dutch-born wife, Stella joined Sunshine and started making presentations to agencies, nervous in the face of alleged pressure from RTE. Sunshine obtained counsel's opinion that advertising on the station would not constitute an offence. Major companies took counsel's opinion to reach the same verdict. Big advertisers, such as Beechams, Clerys, Independent Newspapers, the Irish Permanent Building Society and Switzers, all started advertising on Sunshine, in Robbie Robinson's recollection. Now 60 per cent of the station's business comes from advertising agencies.

Sunshine claims to have been the first unlicensed station to have been run professionally — there are now some 60 on the air — with traffic logs and royalty payments, for instance. Sunshine transmits on AM and FM from Portmarnock, where it uses two broadcast studios and a production studio in the grounds of Sands Hotel. Its transmission area is most of Leinster, although it can be heard strongly as far away as Yorkshire. Today, Sunshine employs about 30 full-time staff and its advertising revenue this year is likely to be just short of £1/2 million.

Robbie Robinson's main unlicensed competitor was Radio Nova, which was started by his one-time associate, Chris Cary, from studios in Herbert Street. The station later moved to Rathfarnham and went into receivership in March, 1986, following a protracted dispute with the NUJ over the dismissal last year of eight journalists working for the station, because they were in the union, Chris Cary, the colourful character behind the five year run of Radio Nova, claimed that the station had cost him £150,000. "How many times do you have to tell people that they won't make money out of pirate radio?" At its peak, Radio Nova was bringing in £30,000 in spot ads weekly. Soon after Nova closed down, ZOOM 103 went on the air; Cary said he had no involvement in the new station, a claim hotly disputed by the NUJ.

Mike Hogan, who had worked for both Sunshine Radio and Radio Nova, left the latter station in March 1984 and has been working for Q102 since January last year. The main shareholder in the station is Dublin nightclub owner Pierre Doyle. The station is totally music — "you don't make money on talk shows", says Hogan, who gained publicity in 1986 for broadcasting traffic reports from a helicopter for work-bound listeners. The broadcasts were sponsored by Fiat Ireland; Mike Hogan's reports were transmitted to Q102's studios in the Mount Street area of Dublin. Such helicopter reporting is common with US radio stations, but had never been tried in Ireland before.

Bray Local Broadcasting has been on the air for the past seven years, forming, with 14 other stations, such as those in Arklow, Cavan,

**Brian Pierce, RTE's head
of radio sales.**
Photo: RTE.

Kilkenny, Tipperary and north Dublin, an unusual variant on the
unlicensed station theme. Bray, like the other stations, is community
owned and non-profit making. A management committee is elected by
such groups as the churches, business interests and voluntary
organisations. The Bray station has three studios and broadcasts
between 6 a.m. and 2 a.m. the following day. It has much speech

programming, such as the lunchtime magazine programme, a two hour show for senior citizens once a week and community council programmes. 30 seconds' advertising at peak time costs £15, while the cheapest rate is £8 for 30 seconds after 5 p.m.

Most of its advertisement revenue comes from local traders, says advertisement sales manager Liam de Siún, with the spots made by a privately owned recording studio in Bray. Some national brands, like Avonmore milk, use the station. BLB's transmission area, on AM and FM, covers from Ashford in the south to Naas in the west and Malahide in the north.

RTE's Community Radio has been developed, legally, over the last ten years. Under the aegis of manager Paddy O'Neill, the mobile studio visits a number of different localities each year, producing a week of programmes in each area based entirely on the local community. Sometimes, local advertising content is broadcast. In 1985, when RTE Community Radio visited Dun Laoghaire, the full allocation of time for local advertisements was quickly taken up.

Cork Local Radio operates from the RTE studios at Union Quay in the city, the Republic's first purpose-built broadcasting studios when they were built in 1958. The Cork station is the only licensed local station in the Republic; it has a very high and loyal listenership and brings in advertising valued at between £1/4 million and £300,000 a year. The station is an opt-out from the RTE Radio 1 network on both AM and FM and to the frustration of its staff, is restricted to about three hours' output a day. RTE's other community-type radio broadcasting, Radio na Gaeltachta, has been on the air for the past 14 years. The nationally broadcast Irish language service is on the air daily from 8 a.m. until 1.30 p.m. and from 5 p.m. until 8 p.m. It carries no advertising.

In contrast to the "pirate" stations, the entirely legal and more respectably sedate world of RTE radio has seen notable advances made during the last decade, recapturing much of the high ground lost to television in the 1960s. In 1968, Radio Luxembourg made a significant move, not unnoticed here in Ireland. It dropped its sponsored programmes and settled instead for all "spot" advertising. In RTE Radio, the move began, away from the old format used since before the war, of 15 minute programme segments, in favour of "strip" programming in hour long slots. *Morning Ireland*, which began hesitatingly in early 1985 amid much speculation inside and outside the station as to how long it would last, now has a daily listenership of 650,000. The morning programme hosted by Gay Byrne, which started in 1973, has had the biggest increase in listening figures of any RTE radio show; during the twelve months from early 1985 to early 1986, listenership has gone up by 30 per cent. The show, which now runs for 1¾ hours, attracts 44 per cent of all housewives in the country and pulls in over £1 million's worth of advertising revenue a year.

RTE's Sligo studios provide regional news and feature coverage for both radio and TV. Recently appointed to the Sligo team was Tommy Burke, responsible for TV and radio advertisement sales in the region. Photograph shows Jerry Murray (left) and Jim Gartlan, both studio technicians. Background, broadcasting, is Tommie Gorman, regional correspondent.
Photograph: RTE.

552

Mike Hogan, former general manager, Radio Nova, now managing Q102.
Photograph: Robert Allen/The Irish Times.

Radio 1, which in the words of Michael Carroll, director of programmes, Radio, has the immensely complex task of pleasing all listeners all the time, both majority and minority interests. So important is Radio I's morning and lunchtime audience that 75 per cent of the channel's advertising is transmitted between 7.30 a.m. and 1 p.m. The top agency spender on radio is McConnell's (£1,113,000 in 1985), followed by Wilson Hartnell (£721,000 in 1985), Hunter Advertising (£719,000 in 1985) and Brian Cronin & Associates (£648,000 in 1985).

Afternoon listening on RTE Radio 1 falls off, but a recent success has been Marian Finucane's *Live Line*, bringing in 240,000 listeners. No advertising is carried on Radio I between 7 p.m. and 11 p.m., partly because programmes like symphony concerts do not lend themselves to breaks. Yet a symphony concert by the RTE Symphony Orchestra will attract an audience of 50,000 — 50 times as many people as can hear it in the National Concert Hall.

A late evening programme like the *Late Date* show, hosted until recently by Liam Nolan, can attract a big audience of up to 350,000. Michael Carroll's only ambition for Radio I's transmission hours is for the channel to stay on the air until 1 a.m. Radio 2 stays on the air until 1.50 a.m. and its head, Cathal McCabe, would dearly like it to become a 24 hour station. Its programming is aimed at an under-25 audience, with a mixture of pop music, news and sport. In that category, Radio 2 claims to have 54 per cent of all possible listeners, yet in the under-35 category, it still has 48 per cent. In contrast to Radio I, Radio 2's peak listenership comes in the afternoon and from 10 p.m. until close-down. The full-time staff of Radio 2 is just over 25. With fine irony, the station does many tie-ups with outside organisations, such as the *Evening Herald* newspaper for the evening *Hit List* show. Other newspapers like *The Irish Times* have had tie-ups with Radio 2, as have banks and building societies. Sponsorship has returned to radio in a very different form to its original format.

Present advertising revenue on RTE radio has nearly reached £13 million from under £5 million in 1979. The head of radio sales, Brian Pierce, says however that he would like to see more creativity in advertisements, citing such examples as the "Bollards for Libya" campaign prepared by Gaffney, McHugh and Brindley's "Get your TD on the job — Tetra Delta" campaign. In the longer term, RTE plans to open up a long wave channel aimed at the British market, as well as extensions of the FM3 quality programming. The long wave station, a joint venture with Radio Luxembourg, is due to go on the air in two years' time, from a transmitter on the east coast of Ireland. It is likely to be called Radio Tara. When Leo Maguire signed off the very last sponsored programme on RTE radio, the Walton's show that went out on Saturday, January 3, 1981, with an appropriate party to follow, it was not just the end of an era, and the loss of IR£190,000 a year revenue, but the start of a new beginning for radio in Ireland. The last sponsored programmes officer, Maura Clarke, is now an RTE radio producer and film critic on *The Gay Byrne Show*.

Maura Clarke of RTE, the station's last sponsored programmes officer. Before joining RTE for the second time in her career, she was an account executive with O'Kennedy Brindley. Now she is a radio producer, as well as film critic on The Gay Byrne Show.
Photograph: RTE.

Gay Byrne.

CHAPTER TEN

Film and Television

"Moving pictures, a scientific curiosity, no commercial future".
ANTOINE LUMIÈRE, 1895.

L ITTLE DID THE Lumière brothers of Paris know what they
were starting when they screened their first moving pictures in the
French capital in December, 1895. It was the first time in history
that a public projection of moving pictures had taken place; still
photography had been used for some 60 years previously, but now,
audiences could see moving images. From those first faltering cinema
pictures came the development of the cinema industry and then,
television. Cinema in Ireland has never been a mainstream advertising
medium in terms of spending, but in the 25 years since RTE television
started, TV has become the most powerful and persuasive medium of
all.

Auguste and Louis Lumière were not the first to project images on a
screen; Edison, among others, had done previous work on motion
picture development, but the Lumières were the first to show moving
images in public. A wooden sign with the word "Cinématographe" was
placed on the pavement outside the Grand Café at 14 boulevard des
Capucines, pointing to the basement. George Méliès, the magician and
director of the Théâtre Robert Houdini in Paris, remembered: "A still
photograph of the place Bellecour in Lyon appeared on the screen. A
bit surprised, I scarcely had the time to say to my neighbour, 'So it's for
projections they bothered us. I've been doing them for ten years'. I had
hardly finished my sentence when a horse-drawn cart moved towards

Cette image de « L'Arrivée d'un train en gare » effraya les premiers spectateurs du cinématographe.

A scene from the first film made by the Lumière Brothers, in 1895. Entitled The Arrival of a Train at the Station, it frightened the audience, which thought the train was charging straight at them.
Photograph: France-Soir, Paris.

The world's first cinema poster — it was in full colour and advertised the cinema shows organised in Paris in 1895 by the Lumière Brothers.
Photograph: Liam O'Leary Film Archives.

557

The world's first
cinema, opened by the
Lumière Brothers at 6,
boulevard Saint-Denis,
Paris, in 1896.
*Photograph: France-Soir,
Paris.*

The Volta cinema in
Mary Street, Dublin,
which James Joyce
managed. It opened for
business in December,
1909.
*Photograph: Liam O'Leary
Film Archives.*

us, followed by other vehicles and pedestrians. We stared flabbergasted at this sight, stupified and surprised beyond all expression. At the end of the show, there was complete chaos. Méliès and other showmen offered huge sums of money to buy the new moving pictures process, but the Lumière Brothers' father, Antoine, a manufacturer of photographic products, said: "My sons' invention is not for sale. It would ruin you. It can be exploited for a short while as a scientific curiosity. Beyond that, it has no commercial future."

The arrival of moving pictures was the technological triumph of the age; within a year of that first Paris showing, 200 cinematographes had been set up throughout the world. Dublin was among the first cities of the world to demonstrate the new system; the first cinema show in Ireland took place in the Olympia Theatre on April 20, 1896. Cinema advanced fast, with picture houses being set up in great profusion in Dublin and to a lesser extent, country towns, before the advent of World War 1. Surprisingly, for a medium that attracted so much public interest and enthusiasm, there was little effort made in developing cinema as an advertising medium. Cinema advertising did not begin serious development in Ireland until the 1930s, yet paradoxically, cinemas soon became proficient at advertising themselves.

James Joyce may have been less than successful at running the Volta in Mary Street, for which he obtained financial backing from a group of businessmen in Trieste, but other early cinemas flourished. As early as 1912, films were being shown at the Rotunda, on the site of the present day Ambassador. Most of its programme consisted of American-made "shorts", for the film industry in the USA had quickly blossomed into life. The Rotunda used remarkable posters outside the premises to advertise present and forthcoming attractions. Very often, these posters were hand printed with wooden type and showed a remarkable ingenuity of design. Quickly, the notion of cinemas using posters to advertise their wares quickly caught on, yet no-one seemed to realise the potential of cinemas as an advertising medium. In film as in many other aspects of the advertising and publicity business, Charlie McConnell was the pioneer.

As early as 1922, McConnell, his agency just six years old, signalled his first interest in films. With a partner from London called Hartley, he set up a company called McConnell-Hartley in 1922. It produced outdoor advertising, but also developed film production in a modest way; later, McConnell's film interests traded under the name of Irish Photoplays. Four years after McConnell-Hartley was set up, it was christened with a subtitle, "Advertising in Film", for in 1926, Charlie McConnell had his first film made. Black and white stock was used and in some sections of it, each frame was hand tinted, to give a coloured effect that was regarded at the time as being daring, but of acceptable quality. The film was editorial in content, featuring the Ardnacrusha hydro-electric scheme then under construction on the Shannon and the scenic delights of Gougane Barra in west Cork. Charlie McConnell

¶ TO-DAY,
FRIDAY AND SATURDAY.

SCREEN ADAPTATION OF THE POWERFUL
NOVEL BY BULWER LYTTON IN FOUR PARTS

'EUGENE ARAM'

FEW stories are more intensely dramatic or more closely
packed with thrilling situations than Bulwer Lytton's great
story "Eugene Aram." From the first scene in which
Eugene Aram is led by his ambition to take a false step
until the thrilling climax, in which he is seen on the
gallows expiating a crime he did not commit, the
interest is fully maintained.

The Picture House

Orchestral
Music

Grafton Street. Dublin.

Dublin cinema
advertisement, 1916.

had anticipated by 20 years the famous Fitzpatrick travelogues that became such an established part of Irish cinema-going. That same year three experimental commercials were made, for Hayes Conyngham & Robinson, the chemists, Lemons Sweets and Persil.

In the early 1930s, Charlie McConnell had another advertising film made, in another pioneering venture. Independent Newspapers, concerned about the arrival of the brash new *Irish Press,* founded in September, 1931, decided to spend heavily on publicity. Outdoor poster sites benefitted enormously and so too did the cinemas of Ireland. It was the first time in Ireland that the new medium of cinema had been used to promote the old medium, newspapers. This advertising film made for Independent Newspapers featured John McConnell, then a teenager, Shelagh Richards and Jimmy O'Dea. John McConnell remembers another early film epic, made by McConnell-Hartley for Mackintosh's toffee, which in those days, had its own factory at Rathmines, Dublin. The firm has been merged into Rowntrees, to form Rowntree-Mackintosh (Ireland), for over 20 years. Each frame in the film for Mackintosh's toffee had to be hand tinted, producing an effect remarkably similar, says John McConnell, to the recent series of television commercials for Quality Street chocolates made by Rowntree-Mackintosh.

An early Irish film production, Willy Reilly and his Colleen Bawn, produced in 1920 by the Film Company of Ireland. The poster was printed by David Allen and Sons.
Photograph: Liam O'Leary Film Archives.

ROTUNDA

ROUND ROOM.

6.45 TWICE **9**
NIGHTLY
Matinee Daily at 3

IRISH ANIMATED PICTURE CO.'s
POPULAR

Picture & Vaudeville

SEASON

IRISH LADIES' STRING ORCHESTRA

SPECIAL FEATURES.

MONDAY, TUESDAY & WEDNESDAY
OCTOBER 21, 22 & 23:

THE BAD MAN
OF THE RANGES

A Gripping Wild Western Drama.

BUNCH OF VIOLETS | EYES THAT SEE NOT!

Absorbing Vitagraph Drama. Dramatic Subject.

JIM, THE BOXER!

FREE FROM SUSPICION!
Very Fine Dramatic Subject.

HER OLD SWEETHEART
The Old Maid Mistakes a Burglar for Her Sweetheart.

A FOOTWEAR SEARCH!
Very Funny

PATHE GAZETTE
Of Current Events. Historical, Sporting, &c.

THE BATTLE
OF TRAFALGAR
Picture Story of this Terrific Battle at Sea.
AND NUMEROUS OTHER SUBJECTS.

SPECIAL ENGAGEMENT of the NEW IRISH BARITONE, MR.

LEONARD SHEA
In Illustrated Song.

ADMISSION: 3d., 6d., 9d., 1/- & 1/6

Two early posters for local cinemas. Above is a handbill produced for the Rotunda Round Room, Dublin, in 1912, while on the right is a poster advertising Edison's speaking pictures at the Coliseum in Cork.
Photograph: Liam O'Leary Film Archives.

COLISEUM
KING STREET CORK.

Proprietors .... Southern Coliseums Ltd.
Manager .... Mr M. J TIGHE.

THREE TIMES DAILY
AT 3 - 7 9.

We are pleased to announce to our Patrons that we have secured the
exclusive rights for Cork of the

KINETOPHONE
(EDISON'S SPEAKING PICTURES)

Monday	**Thursday**
Mr. T. A. Edison Lectures	" After College Days "
" Faust "	" Musical Blacksmiths "
"Few Shamrocks from Ireland"	" Edison Minstrels "

Picture Programme

Monday	**Thursday**
" A Daughter of Belgium "	" The Coward "
Thrilling War Drama	Two-part Drama
" The Hold Up "	" Bombs and Bangs "
Western Drama.	Keystone Comic
Etc., etc. etc.	Etc., etc. etc.

GRAND ORCHESTRAL MUSIC AT EACH PERFORMANCE

Admission. 1s., 6d. & 3d.
CHILDREN HALF-PRICE.

Persil was the first washing powder to use visual advertising in Ireland. McConnell-Hartley made an experimental advertising film for the brand in 1926. In 1943, the firm made the first film commercial in Ireland using colour stock, a cartoon for Persil. The powder had been invented in Germany early this century and was introduced in Ireland about 1907. Persil Automatic was marketed from 1968.
Photograph: The Robert Opie Collection, Gloucester.

Despite the very slow progress of cinema as an advertising medium, the film making and distribution companies proved adept at advertising their wares, particularly when "talkies" were introduced about 1930. Liam O'Leary, the film archivist, has samples of some of the publicity packs produced by London film distributors in the 1920s for use in Ireland. These publicity packs featured full colour posters to be displayed outside cinemas and in the foyer, reprints of press features about the stars and hints on other means of generating publicity. As early as the mid-1920s, the cinema publicists needed to learn remarkably little about modern publicity techniques. During the 1930s, the cinema business in Ireland built up to its peak, with some 350 cinemas scattered the length and breadth of the country. Dublin had many fine picture houses, long since gone, like the Princess on Lower Rathmines Road and the Phoenix on Ellis Quay, as well as the Grand Central in Lower O'Connell Street (now occupied by the Bank of Ireland), opposite the then offices of O'Kennedy Brindley. For country audiences out of reach of cinemas, there were travelling cinemas doing the rounds. These too produced impressive posters.

Into this promising situation came a solicitor called Peter Rackow, who started Cinema and General Publicity in 1936. His offices were in Middle Abbey Street and he rented films and sold advertising time. About three years after the establishment of the firm, it suffered a serious setback when the offices were burned out. For some six months, Rackow's firm had to operate from offices borrowed from a rival renter. Fergus Flynn, who is now a director of the firm, joined it as a teenager not long after it had started; he recalls that in those days,

Until comparatively recently, travelling cinemas brought films and advertisements to rural audiences. This poster was used in 1933 to advertise a travelling cinema in Co Cork; "perfect projection and perfect sound" was promised. Adult admission was 9d, while children under 12 got in for 4d.
Photograph: Liam O'Leary Film Archives.

Reach the Irish Public

through the Irish SCREEN

CINEMA & GENERAL PUBLICITY LIMITED
MEMBERS OF THE SCREEN ADVERTISING GROUP OF THE I.A.P.

35 Upper Abbey Street, Dublin
LONDON OFFICE: 15 Clarges Street, London, W.1. Tel.: Gros. 3316.

Opposite page:
The first Irish advertisement to make use of the television idea — in 1935! The BBC was about to start an experimental TV service at Alexandra Palace, London, and Chivers & Sons (Ireland) used the theme to advertise its jellies, lemonade crystals and custard powder to the local grocery trade. The promotional leaflet stated: "1935 gives promise of being the year of television — people will be looking in as well as listening in on a scale which even a short time ago seemed impossible". Chivers' sales office was headed by Bill Cavanagh at 11 Burgh Quay, Dublin.

Cinema & General Publicity used this trade advertisement for its cinema advertising services in the late 1940s. Advertisers mentioned included Aspro, Gillette and Vick.

565

glass slides were the main means of advertising to cinema audiences. Some slides were professionally drawn and lettered, but others were merely scratched on the glass and appeared decidedly amateurish.

Maurice Clarke-Barry, who worked with Columbia Pictures in Ireland for 39 years, remembers that often the projectionists themselves would write the slides. The old Pillar cinema in O'Connell Street, near the site of the present day CIE offices, had wide seats at the back that were much used by courting couples. The cinema also had a projectionist called "Dinny" Byrne, well-known in the business, who was expert at drawing advertising slides freehand. Often, slides were cracked in transit, and projectionists had to be skilled in patching them together with film cement.

Not until the late 1930s did Cinema and General Publicity start using black and white film for advertisers. Very often, the footage was from the library, the only local touch being the name and address of the supplier whose goods or services the film was advertising. Although the "talkies" became popular in the early 1930s, very few of these first advertising films shown in Irish cinemas had soundtracks. If there was any audio accompaniment, it came from rather scratchy 78 rpm gramophone discs. The rates were remarkably cheap by today's standards. It cost just 2/6d to have a glass slide shown at every performance in a cinema for a week; no-one was prepared to say how many people attended those performances, but since cinema going was such a popular leisure time activity in the 1930s, advertisers were not concerned about such research data.

A Swastika laundry van of the 1940s; the striking insignia featured in a major advertising film premiered in the late 1940s.
Photograph: Paddy Clarke.

Guard precious
whiteness against
decay with **IRIUM**
exclusive to
Pepsodent
TOOTHPASTE

A glass slide cinema ad,
produced in the late
1930s and advertising
Pepsodent toothpaste.
*Photograph: Liam O'Leary
Film Archives.*

Inside
TeleVision

By

Gordon Duffield

LOOK forward to the big-
money quiz game pro-
ducers taking a keen interest
in Ulster. An Ulster con-
testant has already been
chosen for "SPOT THE
TUNE," others will appear on
"CONCENTRATION."

I prophesy that very soon the
other prize-winning shows like
"DOUBLE YOUR MONEY,"
"DOTTO" and "BEAT THE CLOCK"
will be searching for likely Ulster
people.

Burly bearded Scot,
BILL KELLIE, who spent
two days in Belfast chos-

Gordon Duffield, who
now runs his own
public relations
company, was Ulster
Television's first public
relations man when the
station started in 1959.
He made this
contribution to the first
issue of TV Post on
October 29, 1959.

Early days of film sound recording: at Ardmore Studios in 1958, Liam Saurin, sound mixer (right) is pictured with sound engineer, Brendan Redmond. They are using a Leevers Rich ¼" tape recorder for location work.

Basil Lapworth — later with UTV — was lucky to get into cinema advertising at the outset when in the 1930s he joined a company which was the first to produce and distribute a five minute advertising film, which featured Raymond Glendinning commentating on cricket. He talked for something like 4½ minutes and then at the end the viewer realised it was an advertisement for Player's cigarettes. The film was made in England but widely shown in the North of Ireland, where cinema attendances were much higher than anywhere else in the UK. There was a "queue at all times" situation, no "on or off" times. By 1936/7, Lapworth joined a company called Granada as a trainee manager. War came and he joined the army and was away for the duration; while he was stationed in the North, he met and married his wife.

The same year that Cinema and General Publicity started up, so too did the world's first television service, launched by the BBC from

Some of Ulster Television's earliest technical equipment, about 1960.
Photograph: Ulster Television.

Alexandra Palace in London. Its technical standards were primitive and all programmes had to be produced "live", but up to the start of World War II, a daily programme schedule was transmitted. The first documentary ever produced by BBC television, in 1938, was produced by S. E. Reynolds, who later became the first programme controller of Ulster Television when it went on the air in 1959.

Ulster Television advertised itself as it was going on the air for the first time in October, 1959. 60 seconds cost £80.

Probably the first time an Irish advertiser mentioned "television" was in 1935. Chivers, the jam manufacturers, had started up its own factory in Dublin three years previously. Its sales manager, Bill Cavanagh, a founding member of the Association of Advertisers in Ireland, ran trade advertisements that year featuring Chivers' "Jellyvision", using the theme of the new television service that had just started in London. Although there was some interest by Irish newspapers in what the BBC was doing, no-one conceived of a time when there would be an Irish television service. For the duration of the war, the BBC's television service was suspended. In Ireland, cinemas were subjected to severe restrictions, partly due to the need to save electricity and partly to the difficulties in getting adequate supplies of new films into the country. The only major advertising development came in 1943, when McConnell-Hartley performed an incredible feat: the firm managed to acquire some of the newly invented colour film stock. Just as Persil provided a "first" for the firm back in 1926, the same brand was the subject of McConnell-Hartley's 1943 production, a colour cartoon production.

Fergus Flynn was practising his running: in 1939, he had won the famous Tramway 100 at Croke Park. Over the next few years, he won many sprint championships. He was so proficient at winning in record times that he was dubbed the "Dublin Flash" and "Boy Wonder". After the end of the Emergency, the cinema business continued to expand: no-one could foresee how close was the emergence of television in Ireland. The Ellimans, who owned the Theatre Royal, where ciné-variety shows (films plus "live" variety and quizzes) were very popular, also built new cinemas, such as those at Whitehall and Cabra, to cater for the residents of these newer suburbs. Most of these new cinemas have now been converted to other uses, for instance, the Rialto is now car showrooms, while the Leinster was turned into an ice skating rink.

After the war, Basil Lapworth saw the opportunity to come back and get into the entertainment industry for although the cinemas were plentiful, they were not well run. George Lodge who owned the Opera House, purchased the Hippodrome from Guy Birch. He had a lovely Victorian building making no money except for the circus held every year; the place was badly run. George had been told that Lapworth was available. In 1950, he was invited over and met him in the Opera House. He saw the takings were £700 per week, minus tax. He took the job and built it into a very prosperous theatre before becoming publicity director for the whole group which included the Opera House, Imperial and the Royal cinema. Lodge then took over the Curran group which included the Astoria on the Newtownards Road, Regal on Lisburn Road and the Tonic in Bangor, before purchasing a group called Irish Theatres which included all the intermediate cinemas and spread into the country areas with cinemas like the Regal in Enniskillen. This totalled around 45 cinemas in all.

Lapworth then had a call from a colleague from what was to become the Rank Organisation asking if he would like to open up cinema advertising in the North, which they considered had tremendous potential. To do this he had to change his then great interest in the entertainment industry and go back into advertising. He went over to London to talk to them and realised that there was great potential in the idea, for Northern Ireland had a dull, insipid approach to advertising relying almost entirely on David Allen's poster sites (there were a few of More-O'Ferrall's), bus and tram sides and the press. Cinema stood a very good chance of winning a battle bearing in mind

An advertisement for TV sets, placed in the TV Post on October 29, 1959, to coincide with the opening of Ulster Television.

Basil Lapworth, who pioneered advertisement sales on Ulster Television.
Photograph: Ulster Television.

the tremendous potential. One of the last things he did with George Lodge was to book the tram coming up High Street to celebrate the final days of tramways; they had both sides of the tram advertising the first cinemascope film called *The Robe.*

The more he considered the potential of cinema advertising the more he was amazed at its prospects, even down to two little cinemas in Cookstown. Wherever you went there was an opportunity. He gave the local advertiser moving pictures of 15/30/60 seconds based on the size of the cinema and its potential, for example Holywood was able to sell ordinary 15 seconds commercials for £39 per annum — not a great deal of money considering they were getting constant coverage in that cinema twice a night. Every cinema without exception showed a weekly budget reel. Reels were changed every week for national advertisers. In terms of revenue, in 1955 the Classic in Castle Lane, Belfast was taking £800 a year, Holywood £40 a year. On top of this there were the national reels of one minute films. When he was looking for advertisements for the cinema, some potential clients would claim that "surely with the ads between the feature film and the news, most people get up and go to the toilet?" He always responded: "But how many can get into the average cinema toilet?"

There were 40 cinemas in Belfast; in nearly every town there was one, perhaps two — even Dromore in both Co Tyrone and Co Down each had a cinema, Enniskillen had three, Cookstown three, Bangor three and Portrush two. Their demise started in with the advent of UTV. While cinemas throughout Ireland continued to enjoy fair prosperity during the 1950s, the medium was under renewed threat from television. The BBC had restarted its service in London in 1946. Within a few years, the service started spreading to the rest of Britain: the Holme Moss transmitter serving north-west England, began transmissions in 1951. Two years later, transmissions began from Belfast. Those early Holme Moss transmissions were picked up in Ireland; one enthusiast in Co Meath built his own television set. The coronation in 1953 of Queen Elizabeth II drew huge television audiences; the new medium came of age.

In 1948, veteran film maker and archivist Liam O'Leary made a publicity film for Clann na Poblachta called *Our Country*. It focussed on the poor social conditions then widely prevalent in Ireland and had a powerful impact: it was said to have played a key part in ousting De Valera and the Fianna Fail party from power. In the late 1940s, the Swastika Laundry of Ballsbridge, Dublin, created quite a sensation when its new advertising film was premiered at the old Carlton cinema. When patrons came out of the cinema, young teenage boys, dressed entirely in white and looking suitably angelic, handed them leaflets detailing the Swastika's services. Sadly, like all the other early advertising films made in Ireland, all the original stock, plus copies, have been lost.

A rare boost to film production came from Dr Noel Browne when he was Minister for Health. *Voyage to Recovery* was made in 1952 as part of the anti-TB campaign. The film was made by Gerard Healy and featured Joe Lynch as the young man who had caught TB and Marie Kean as the visiting relative. This film and other publicity films of the 1950s feature in Kieran Hickey's new film, *Short Story*, which covers film making in Ireland between 1945 and 1958. Other Government financed publicity films made in the 1950s covered such topics as road safety, hygiene and health. One "short" on agriculture was shot on colour stock, very unusual for the time.

An early Ulster
Television programme,
Seven Degrees West,
**featuring Murray
Moore and Peter
Tomelty.**
*Photograph: Ulster
Television.*

Telephone No. 72654

RADIO ÉIREANN—IRISH TELEVISION

ADVERTISEMENT SALES DIVISION: 34-37 Clarendon Street, Dublin 2.

**CONFIRMATION
BOOKING**

No. .... *One*

McConnell's Advertising Service,
Publicity House,
10, Pearse Street,
Dublin, 2.

WHITE—ADVERTISER
GREEN—EXECUTIVE
PINK—ACCOUNTS.
YELLOW—TRAFFIC.

Dear Sirs,
We have pleasure in accepting your Order No. *42443*

dated... *31st May, 1961* (subject to the Conditions
published in our Rate Card), details of which are set out below.

Date.... 5th June,

Yours faithfully,
RADIO ÉIREANN—IRISH TELEVISION.

Niall Sheridan Advertisement Sales Manager.

CLIENT : Carrolls of Dundalk   PRODUCT : SWEET AFTON   AGENT : McConnell's Adverti

No. of Spots	Length (seconds)	Time Segment	Rate	Surcharges	Discount	Total Cost	Day	Month and Dates
								1962
2	60	A	293			£196. *	Sunday	April 22nd.
								December 23rd.

S=Spot Advertisement.   FXS=Fixed Break.   FP=Fixed Position.   M=Advertising Magazines.   F=Flash or Short Adve

T. P. GALLAGHER. .... Sales

**The first time order for
Telefis Eireann-booked
by McConnell's in June,
1961, for Carroll's
Sweet Afton cigarettes.**

In the early 1950s, Niel O'Kennedy, brother of Desmond O'Kennedy, who has a strong interest in the visual media and who drew the famous "NOK" front page cartoons for *The Irish Times* in the mid-1950s, produced a film for Urney's chocolates in the early 1950s. Pat O'Rorke, who joined the agency in 1946 and became one of its copywriters in a career with the one agency of remarkable longevity, remembers devising the slogan "Any time is Urney time", which was used in the film, among other campaigns. It won acclaim as one of the most ambitious advertising films of the era. In the late 1950s, a cartoon commercial widely screened in Dublin cinemas, advertising Johnston, Mooney & O'Brien, the Dublin bakery, was a firm favourite. The bakery film, complete with catchy jingle, still produces good recall among older cinema goers. Its jingle went as follows:

> Johnston, Mooney & O'Brien
> Make the best bread,
> Bread you can rely on.
> Johnston, Mooney & O'Brien
> For your favourite family pan.

While the idea of an Irish television service seemed just a wild idea for agency lunches in the early 1950s, the new medium came into its own in the USA, presenting advertisers with the most powerful medium ever known. In America, it was an economic golden age, with the average citizen in 1955 having six times as much discretionary income as he had in 1940. Inflation was one per cent, energy was cheap and unemployment barely existed. Millions of Americans joined the newly affluent middle classes, all keen to shop in the new supermarkets. The big American networks, such as NBC and CBS, blossomed as advertisers poured millions upon millions of dollars into TV advertising. One American advertising man, Rosser Reeves, developed a new technique for TV advertising that has remained of paramount importance to the present day, the concept of the unique selling proposition. During the 1950s, his idea of the USP came to the forefront in American TV advertising and Reeves used his technique to sell everything from confectionery to Bic ballpoint pens. In the USA in the 1950s, the fiercest marketing battle of all, fought out almost exclusively on television, was between Crest and Colgate toothpastes. Reeves created "Gardol", the invisible protective shield, for the Colgate brand. TV commercials showed a player hitting a baseball towards the screen; it was stopped by a clear plastic wall. The presenter, a well-known sports commentator, then drew the analogy with Colgate's Gardol. The TV campaign persuaded millions of Americans to switch to Colgate. For the first time ever, the 1952 American presidential election saw Madison Avenue in action with TV campaigns. Rosser Reeves "sold" the Republican candidate, Dwight D. Eisenhower, like a tube of toothpaste. Many of the selling techniques used on American television in the 1950s, in black and white, spread first to Britain and then Ireland in the succeeding decade. The 1977 general election in

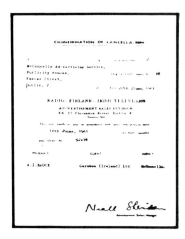

The first advertisement cancellation for Irish television.

Pictured on a "Jim Figgerty" commercial shoot in Spain are, amongst others, Jim Hoblyn, Jacob's, Mack Kile, Irish International and Theo Hogers, Cinevision.

Pictured in the late 1950s on a shoot in Belfast for an Aspro commercial are: John Devis, cameraman, standing immediate left of Devis is Paddy Barron, director of photography and producer, and sitting, the late Joseph Tomelty. The commercial was shot on location in Dublin, Belfast, London, Paris and Rome, by Irish International Films.

RATES FOR SPOT ADVERTISEMENTS

CLASS			15 Seconds	30 Seconds	45 Seconds	60 Seconds
A 7.30 p.m. — 10.30 p.m.	**MONDAY/SATURDAY**	Standard	£33	£53	£73	£93
		Preferential	£30	£48	£66	£84
	SUNDAY	Standard	£37	£59	£81	£99
		Preferential	£33	£53	£73	£93
B Before 7.30 p.m. and after 10.30 p.m.	**MONDAY/SATURDAY**	Standard	£25	£40	£55	£70
		Preferential	£23	£36	£50	£63
	SUNDAY	Standard	£28	£44	£61	£77
		Preferential	£25	£40	£55	£70

Preferential rates shown above will apply to Irish advertisers, as defined in the " General Terms and Conditions of Contract " overleaf.

OTHER RATES AND CONDITIONS

FLASHES :
Slides with announcer's voice over, transmitted at the most favourable time available. Five-seconds. Eight pounds each.

SHORT ADVERTISEMENTS :
Seven-second spots, transmitted at the most favourable time available. Ten pounds each.

FIXED SPOTS :
Subject to availability, spots may be fixed within a preferred break at a surcharge of 10%. Fixed positions within preferred breaks may be purchased at an additional surcharge of 5%.

SPECIAL DISCOUNT :
Discount of 20% will apply to Irish-language advertisements.

SPONSORSHIP :
Special programmes of a high s t a n d a r d may, exceptionally, be considered for sponsorship on terms and conditions to be arranged.

STATION FACILITIES :
Charges and conditions for Live and Video Tape Commercials, participation in Advertising Magazines, and for the preparation of slides will be published later.

VOLUME DISCOUNTS :
The following scale will apply :—

£10,000 ... 1½		£15,000 ... 2%	
£25,000 ... 3½		£50,000 ... 5%	

These discounts will be allowed on the total gross expenditure for a 52-week period, the commencement of which must be indicated in advance by the advertiser. Not less than ⅛th of the expenditure in any 52-week period must be allocated during July and August.

The appropriate discount will become payable at the end of the 52-week period.

RADIO EIREANN—IRISH TELEVISION
Advertisement Sales Department, 34-37 Clarendon Street, Dublin.   Phone : 72654

The first rate card for
Telefis Eireann, 1961.

Ireland was the first to make extensive use of television for marketing the two main political parties.

In Britain, commercial television started in 1955. Two years previously, the Conservative Government had decided to break the BBC's monopoly on television broadcasting by allowing a second channel to be set up, funded entirely by advertising. The Television Act of 1954 set up the Independent Television Authority, which had the task of creating a network of 14 regions, each run by a contractor.

Unlike the USA, advertisers in Britain were not allowed to sponsor programmes, only advertise in programme breaks, a practice followed when the Irish television service was set up. The first commercial TV transmitter came on the air in September, 1955, at Croydon, covering the London area, for which the contractor was Rediffusion. By November, 1956, the new ITV network covered the Midlands, Lancashire and Yorkshire. 60 per cent of the UK population was within reach of these four transmitters; licence numbers grew from three million in 1954 to eight million in 1958. By 1968, the number of TV licences was 15 million. From the start, television advertising in Britain was highly successful. Many agency production personnel had been weaned on advertisement production for printed media, so many of the early TV commercials looked and sounded like adaptations of

In the television sales department of RTE, from left: Aidan Burns (administration manager), Dominic O'Reilly (traffic manager) and Colm Brophy (sales executive).

newspaper advertisements. Agencies brought in many American TV producers, who by this stage had had ten years' experience of the new medium, just as when Telefis Eireann started, many of the TV commercials' producers for Dublin agencies were imported from London.

By the end of 1959, commercial television came to Belfast. Two main groups battled it out for the contract, which was won by the one that included the Belfast *News Letter* as a principal shareholder. The first offices for Ulster Television, long before the new station went on the air, were in a corner of the *News Letter* building, in Lower Donegall Street. Gordon Duffield was the public relations man and Dave Dark of McConnell's, remembers ringing up one of his clients, a carpet firm, to beg some carpeting for Gordon's office. Basil Lapworth, who had had much experience in cinema advertising, was a "natural" for setting up the advertisement side of the new TV station. He joined Ulster Television in February, 1959, as sales manager. He was also one of the early shareholders, a holding he still retains.

Lapworth remembers well the Hendersons, Bill McQuitty and Lord Antrim forming the company and starting work from those offices in Lower Donegall Street. Basil Lapworth had a major job to do, educating advertisers in the brand new medium. In the mid-1950s,

In November, 1960, Bill Cavanagh (right), chairman of the Association of Advertisers in Ireland addressed a meeting of the Incorporated Sales' Managers Association in the Metropole, Dublin, on the advertising possibilities offered by the forthcoming Irish television service. Also in the photograph is W. D. Fraser, chairman, ISMA.
Photograph: Irish Press.

Belfast had just two agencies, both space placers rather than originators of creative work.

A. V. Browne was in Donegall Street and had one member of staff, a secretary, in addition to Val Browne. Tommy Wells ran Wells Advertising on the Limestone Road. Then McConnell's and Osborne Peacock opened up in Belfast. While Lapworth was selling the idea of television advertising to potential clients in Northern Ireland and London, work was progressing on the conversion of an empty warehouse on the Ormeau Road, last used by a clothing firm, into Havelock House, the headquarters of Ulster Television. Tom Singleton, then an executive with ABC television in London, advised UTV in those early days. He remembers walking through the near-derelict three floors of the warehouse in company with Bill McQuitty, the creative genius of the new station, deciding upon the layout. Cast iron pillars supporting the floors determined the layout of the studio space in the complex. R. B. "Brum" Henderson had just been appointed general manager.

When UTV came on the air on Hallowe'en night, October 31, 1959, the critics were out in force. It was the tenth ITV station to come on the air and many armchair critics in cross-channel television said that UTV was too small to be viable. Just before the new station came on the air for the first time, the total set count in Northern Ireland was 50,000, a figure which was virtually doubled by Hallowe'en night, thanks to an intensive publicity campaign-in the printed media. Today, the Northern Ireland set count is 460,000. The night that UTV opened, it had just one studio, two Vidicon cameras and three telecine units for screening films, including commercials, all on film stock. Today, UTV has two big production studios and an outside broadcast unit and advertisers can have their commercials produced either in the studio or on location with the OB unit.

The very first advertisement transmitted on UTV was for Gibbs SR toothpaste. During that first night's transmission, a total of three live commercials were produced, including one for Brands & Norman, the Belfast store.

In those early days of selling advertising time on UTV, Basil Lapworth had few personnel resources to draw upon, one assistant and two secretaries. In the London office, a staff of 14 sold to the London ad agencies, for in the first year of UTV, all but £100,000 of a total advertisement revenue of £870,000 came from national UK advertising. By 1984, that total revenue figure had risen to £14 million. To encourage local advertisers to increase that local spend of £100,000, Basil Lapworth devised a simple sales slogan: "You can be on the air for £1 a second, or £5 for five seconds." He wanted to encourage local traders to take airtime and to this end, even appeared in "house" commercials himself. The rate was keenly priced against the newspaper competition — a 4" double column in one of the Belfast daily newspapers in late 1959 cost around £10. An early performer in

Niall Sheridan, first advertisement sales manager with Telefís Eireann. From advertising, he moved to head up the station's public relations function. He is pictured here speaking at a ceremony outside the Blackrock, Co Dublin, home of his life-long associate, Brian O Nualláin, otherwise Myles na Gopaleen. *Photograph: Peter Thursfield, The Irish Times.*

581

UTV commercials was an up-and-coming comedian called Frank Carson. One of his early "takes" for the Belfast Savings Bank had him saying: "Will ye take a cheque." It quickly passed into local folklore.

By encouraging national manufacturers to advertise on UTV, not alone did Basil Lapworth bring in more big brand advertising, but he also helped encourage those firms to bring in new products to Northern Ireland. He found many products, such as Old Spice, which were distributed and advertised in Britain, but not in Northern Ireland, so by getting firms like Beechams and Crosse & Blackwell to advertise on UTV, he also ensured that many more new products were launched in the province. There was great fun educating clients in the use of the new medium, like the Belfast Rope Works, which wanted to advertise baler twine on TV, but knew nothing of how the new medium worked. Other potential advertisers were sceptical because they had been oversold on press advertising, which sometimes produced poor sales returns, so trust in TV advertising had to be built. One of the first local advertisers to appreciate the new medium and the opportunities it offered was Harold McCausland, big in the car hire business. He became an early and enthusiastic client. To coincide with the start of UTV, a new programme guide was launched, *TV Post,* in which the new station was the major shareholder; it was later replaced by the Ulster edition of the *TV Times.*

Once UTV began transmissions, pressure mounted for an Irish television service in Dublin. From 1951, transmissions from the BBC in Lancashire had been picked up in parts of the north-east of the Republic by a handful of enthusiasts. In 1952, George Hussey, for 20 years editor of the Co Louth-based *Argus* newspaper, claimed to have seen one of the very first TV pictures in Ireland. A Co Meath man called Shane McNamee had built his own TV set to pick up Holme

A drunk is ejected from the Gresham hotel, Dublin, during the launch of Telefis Eireann on December 31, 1961.
Photograph: Lensmen.

582

Moss transmissions. That early flicker of interest in television quickened to a torrent in late 1959 when UTV went on the air. Pressure built up quickly for the Government in Dublin to give the go-ahead for an Irish service. In 1960, just over six months after UTV went on the air for the first time, the Government set up the Radio Eireann Authority with the responsibility of inaugurating a television service. Its chairman was Eamonn Andrews, by then a well-known TV presenter with the BBC in London, who had started his career with Radio Eireann just over ten years previously. Besides the chairman, eight other members were appointed, Edward B. McManus, Commander George Crosbie, Dr T. W. Moody, Fintan Kennedy, Earnan Uasal de Blagd, James Fanning, Charles Brennan and Aine Uasal Ní Cheannain.

The advertisement sales department was set up at 34-37 Clarendon Street in the centre of Dublin; Niall Sheridan was the first advertisement sales manager. He was responsible to John Irvine, the deputy director-general; Irvine was later succeeded by Bobby Gahan. Assisting Sheridan on sales were Tom Gallagher, who had joined from O'Keeffes Advertising agency and Conor McGrath. Both left before the new station came on the air; McGrath is now the Aer Lingus manager in Britain. Bobby Gahan became the sales administration manager. He put the department on the right course with the help of ABC, Granada, STV and UTV. In April, 1961, he spent ten days in London learning systems and came home to set up the sales booking operation, which included copy control and transmission arrangements. Only recently has this booking system been computerised. After Gallagher and McGrath left, Gahan was promoted to sales; he was joined by a newcomer, Peadar Pierce, who is now advertisement sales controller. Other youngsters in at the start of the department were

Michael O'Hehir addressing the camera at the official opening of Telefis Eireann in the Gresham hotel, Dublin, on December 31, 1961.
Photo: RTE Illustrations Library.

Reception area of the
Kippure transmitter
when it opened 25
years ago.

250 micro V/m contour line.

▲ Transmitter

With acknowledgments
Telefis Eireann and
Geographia Limited.

584

Aidan Burns (now administration manager) and Dominic O'Reilly, who is now traffic manager. Staffing in the advertisement sales department of RTE has shown remarkable continuity since those very early days before the TV service came on the air.

The advertisement department, which was in Clarendon Street until March, 1963, was modelled on those well tried with the ITV contractors in the UK. From Clarendon Street, the department moved to Montrose, then to Hawkins House about 1964, then back to Montrose, permanently. The very first commercial to be booked for the new TV service came from McConnell's. The agency's order was dated May 31, 1961, and was for 60 seconds in time segments at a rate of £93 for two Sunday transmissions in 1962. The client was Carroll's. McConnell's also made the first cancellation; on June 14, 1961, it wrote the very first cancellation order for AI sauce made by Cerebos (Ireland). Charlie McConnell was justifiably proud of his agency's "firsts" with the new television service, since his agency had been a pioneer in so many other aspects of Irish advertising, including cinema advertising and sponsored radio programmes. McConnell had also played a leading role in the development of aviation in Ireland; his agency held the Aer Lingus account when the national airline started

Early Irish TAM report on Telefis Eireann audiences.

TELEFIS EIREANN – IRISH TELEVISION

SIZE & NATURE OF TV AUDIENCES
(KIPPURE TRANSMISSION AREA)

TABLE 1-ANALYSIS OF HOUSEHOLDS

TYPE OF HOUSEHOLD	TOTAL HOUSEHOLDS No.	%	HOUSEHOLDS RECEIVING TELEFIS EIREANN No.	%	HOUSEHOLDS NOT RECEIVING TELEFIS EIREANN No.	%
ALL HOUSEHOLDS	290 (100%)	100	95 (33%)	100	195 (67%)	
CLASS						
URBAN – WHITE COLLAR	87		39		48	
NON-WHITE COLLAR	94		35		59	
RURAL	109		21		88	
AGE OF HOUSEWIFE (or other person performing housekeeping duties— 12)						
Under 35 yrs.	58		22		36	
35—49 yrs.	102		39		63	
50 yrs. and over	130		34		96	
SIZE OF HOUSEHOLD						
1 and 2 persons	89		15		74	
3 and 4 persons	103		34		69	
5 and 6 persons	55		28		27	
7 and 8 persons	26		12		14	
9 persons and over	17		6		11	
CHILDREN						
with	126		58		68	
without	164		37		127	

TABLE 2-ANALYSIS OF INDIVIDUALS

INDIVIDUALS	IN ALL HOUSEHOLDS No.	%	IN HOUSEHOLDS RECEIVING TELEFIS EIREANN No.	%	IN HOUSEHOLDS NOT RECEIVING TELEFIS EIREANN No.	%
ALL INDIVIDUALS	1166 (100%)	100	451 (39%)	100	715 (61%)	100
MALES—TOTAL	561	48	216	48	345	48
Aged under 15 yrs.	181	16	79	18	102	14
15-24 yrs.	84	7	35	8	49	7
25-34 yrs.	63	5	25	6	38	5
35-49 yrs.	100	9	38	8	62	9
50 yrs. & over	133	11	39	9	94	13
FEMALES—TOTAL	605	52	235	52	370	52
Aged under 15 yrs.	183	16	81	18	102	14
15-24 yrs.	87	7	35	8	52	7
25-34 yrs.	73	6	33	7	40	6
35-49 yrs.	114	10	44	10	70	10
50 yrs. & over	148	13	42	9	106	15
CHILDREN under 15 yrs.	364	31	160	35	204	29
ADULT MALES	380	33	137	30	243	34
ADULT FEMALES	422	36	154	34	268	37
HOUSEWIVES	278	24	94	21	184	26
AVERAGE SIZE OF HOUSEHOLD	4.02		4.75		3.67	

TABLE 3-RECEPTION

	TOTAL HOUSEHOLDS RECEIVING TELEFIS EIREANN	HOUSEHOLDS RECEIVING TELEFIS EIREANN ONLY	HOUSEHOLDS RECEIVING TELEFIS EIREANN AND OTHER TV
No	95	19	76
%	100	20	80

TABLE 4-QUALITY OF RECEPTION

HOUSEHOLDS		WITH BAND III SETS	USUALLY RECEIVING TELEFIS EIREANN TRANSMISSIONS				NOT RECEIVING TELEFIS EIREANN TRANSMISSIONS		
			TOTAL	GOOD	POOR	SET TEMPORARILY OUT OF ORDER	TOTAL	SET IN ORDER	SET OUT OF ORDER
TOTAL	No	99	95	90	3	2	4	4	-
	%		96	91	3	2	4	4	-

IRISH TAM LIMITED

up in 1936, but of course all its early advertising was confined to press.

While the advertisement sales department of Telefis Eireann was being set up in Clarendon Street and the first issue of the *RTV Guide* was in planning, to replace *Radio Review,* and first advertisement manager Billy McFeely was selling space for the new publication, work was going ahead on the new broadcasting studios at Montrose. The new centre was designed by Ronald Tallon of Michael Scott & Associates as the first phase in a complete broadcasting centre for both radio and television. The TV centre was built first, taking into account that only ten per cent of studio time was productive, the other 90 per cent being used for pre-setting, lighting and rehearsing. The whole building was designed on a modular system, separating functions such as telecine from studio areas and allowing for future expansion. To construct the new centre meant laying 40 miles of cable. Late in 1961, it became clear that the main studio would not be finished in time for the opening of the service on December 31, so emergency measures had to be taken.

TE management decided to concentrate on bringing into production at Montrose studio 3, the master control room and the telecine facilities, used for transmitting films and commercials. Studio 3 at Montrose had 600 sq.ft. of space and two vidicon cameras. At the Abbey Studios in Upper Abbey Street (run by Eamonn Andrews' father-in-law), a second studio was opened. It was being built by the

Gay Byrne, producer and host of The Late Late Show, which started on July 6, 1962. The initial series was of 13 programmes, which grew to be a mainstay of RTE programme schedules.

Group photograph taken at the first Jacob's television awards in December, 1962. The presentations were made in Jacob's Bishop Street factory, Dublin; the awards were presented by the then Taoiseach, the late Sean Lemass, T.D. Award winners from left: Proinsias MacAonghusa, Irish programmes, for the Fear agus a Sceal series, Michael O'Hehir, head of sport, for Telefis Eireann sports coverage, the late Jack White, head of current affairs, for his department's programmes, particularly the Broadsheet series, Charles Mitchel, news reader, who received the individual award, Burt Budin, then in the sports department, now with Yorkshire Television, who won the producer's award, the late Hilton Edwards for his Self Portrait series and an unnamed BBC producer on behalf of the late Tony Hancock, star of Hancock's Half Hour. Front are (left), Marie Lynch (Mrs Joe Lynch) representing Joe Lynch, best actor and the late Eileen Crowe, best actress award.

Strand Electric Company and used the cameras and other equipment earmarked for studio 2 at Montrose. This city centre studio with an area of 200 sq.ft. had three 4½" image orthicon cameras; pictures and sound were transmitted by cable to the top of Jervis Street Hospital, from where they were beamed to the master control centre at Montrose. There, programmes emanating from Abbey Studios were either video taped or re-transmitted to Kippure for "live" broadcast. This sophisticated "lash-up" reminded older hands of what happened when the Cork radio station went on the air for the first time in 1927. The temporary arrangement with the Abbey Studios lasted until May, 1962, when TE was able to move all television production to Montrose. During this initial period, about 22 hours of programmes a week were produced in Dublin, almost half the total transmissions.

The new studio 1 had an area of 4,000 sq.ft., a vast improvement in facilities. During the summer of 1962, studio 2 was completed, opening on October 1 that year. Further major studio accommodation did not come into use until 1986. Also in 1962, the station changed over to 625 line working. It had opened with one transmitter, at Kippure, transmitting on 405 lines. By January, 1963, it was reported that TE had five transmitters, covering most of the Republic, Kippure, Mullaghanish (serving Cork), Maghera (covering Co Galway), Mount Leinster (serving the south-east) and Truskmore, covering Sligo and much of the north-west and the only other dual standard transmitter, besides Kippure, on both 405 and 625 lines.

For the gala launch of the Telefis Eireann service on the night of December 31, 1961, hundreds of formally dressed guests of TE, including many advertisers and agency people, packed into the ballroom of the Gresham Hotel in O'Connell Street. It had taken two

Line-up at the 1962 Jacob's awards, from left: Mrs E. C. Bewley, E. C. Bewley, chairman and joint managing director, Jacob's, Mrs Sean Lemass and An Taoiseach, Sean Lemass, T.D.

Fergus Flynn, director of Cinema & General Publicity, with whom he has spent his working life of over 50 years.

days to plan the seating arrangements of the "do". Amid a snowstorm, guests arrived at the Gresham; some sources reckon that the first ever "commercial" ever seen on TE, unofficially, was a bus side on a CIE bus that slid past the camera outside the hotel. The set count in Leinster, served by the Kippure transmitter up on the Dublin mountains, was about 80,000. That gala banquet was transmitted "live"; the first day's programming began at tea time the following day, January 1, 1962. There was intense competition between the agencies as to who would have the first commercial on the new service, so a draw was held. The honours fell to O'Keeffes, for client Sunbeam Wolsey; the five second commercial went out at 5.35 p.m. that day. It was followed by Brillo, Cuticura, Mobil Oil, Clery's and a range of products we don't hear about today, including Rosedale Lanospray, Askit, Robert Usher towels and Tot Quicksuds.

The breaks either side of the news were highly prized on that night, as they are today, and Philips Electrical gained the prime position of last advertisement before the news, with Sunbeam getting the first break — after the 9 p.m. News. The other commercials involved in those two breaks were Imperial Tobacco Company, Guinness stout, Irish Permanent Building Society, Radox, Harp lager, Constellation sheets, Esso Blue, Kelloggs and Clarnico Murray. Other major Irish advertisers featured on that first night were Ford Motor Company, Irish Dunlop, Urney chocolates, Donnelly's sausages, Cerebos, Irish Shell, Carroll's cigarettes, Denny's, Lever Brothers, W. C. McDonnell, Unidare, Butlin's and Williams and Woods. Kenny's Advertising agency was the one advertising agency to have thought of including an advertisement for itself on that first night!

One charming story concerns the owner of a well-known food firm, who had been an early, if slightly reluctant, convert to television

At the 1962 Jacob's television awards (later extended to include radio), from left: Gordon Lambert (then Jacob's marketing director), Jimmy O'Keeffe (Lord Mayor of Dublin) and Mrs J. B. Jenkins, wife of the then joint managing director of Jacobs.

advertising. He thought initially that he would take five or ten minutes, before realising this wasn't feasible; for the first night, his agency booked a five second slide costing all of £8. He brought all his friends to his house to watch the great event, when his firm advertised on television for the first time. The story goes that he was passing round the sweets when the commercial came on and he only caught the most fleeting glance.

The new service quickly took off, just as Ulster Television had done in the North. UTV had pioneered many programme developments, such as the early evening news magazine called *Roundabout,* presented by Ivor Mills and Anne Gregg. 22-year-old Adrienne McGuill was the very popular first announcer and first Miss Romper Room, while Tommy James introduced *Teatime with Tommy.* Val Doonican, who had been given his first radio "break" in Dublin by Niall Boden, had his first appearances on Ulster Television.

In many ways, 1962 was a crucially important year for the new Telefis Eireann service. On the programme front, the biggest impact came from a new show called *The Late Late Show,* which went out for the first time on July 6, 1962, hosted by a presenter previously well-known for his sponsored radio work, Gay Byrne. Although the initial series made a good impression with viewers, no-one guessed that it would turn out to be the world's longest running programme of its type. The late Tom McGrath said about the new experiment, in January, 1963: "*The Late Late Show,* which ran for a 13 week period during the summer of last year was an experiment which could easily have ended "on the rocks", but fortunately did the opposite. It was considered to be the first show of its kind on this side of the Atlantic."

Also to honour the programme makers, Gordon Lambert of Jacob's

the biscuit makers, was instrumental in starting up the Television Awards scheme, later to be extended to include radio. The first awards were presented at a banquet in Dublin in 1962: principal guest was Taoiseach, Sean Lemass, compère was Harry Thuillier. Later the sponsor said that the event was to be made an annual event. The awards were selected by a panel of national newspaper critics; they went to Eileen Crowe (best actress), Joe Lynch (best actor), Burt Budin (best producer), *Hancock's Half Hour* (best imported programme), *Broadsheet* (best home produced programme), Proinsias MacAonghusa (best contribution to the Irish language), *Self Portrait* (most original contribution to television), the TE sports department (best outside broadcast) and Charles Mitchel, Telefis Eireann's chief newsreader (best individual award).

From the beginning, there was pressure on Telefis Eireann to provide an audience research service and a contract was entered into with Irish TAM, a company specially set up for the purpose by the Attwood Group and A. C. Nielsen. The first report covered the three weeks ended April 29, 1962, when television homes were estimated at 104,600, all in the Kippure transmission area and representing a penetration of about 35 per cent. Of these television homes, over 80 per cent were multi-channel, since many had television in advance of Telefis Eireann to receive BBC and UTV programmes.

Then, as now, news was very popular, with ratings over 60 per cent for the main news at 9 p.m. Other programmes to show up in this first report were the popular magazine and current affairs programme, *Broadsheet, Pick of the Post, My Job and I, Showcase, For Moderns, Jackpot, The School Around the Corner* and *At Home with O'Hagan.* Among the imported programmes, the most popular were *Bachelor Father, Dragnet, Checkmate, Mr. District Attorney, Have Gun Will Travel, World Championship Golf, Medic, The Twilight Zone, The Honeymooners* and *The Flintstones.* TAM manager John Watchorn said that since at the start of Telefis Eireann transmissions, Kippure was the only transmitter, the area it served was the universe until other transmitters began operations. Irish TAM's first step was to select 1,000 homes in the Kippure transmission area and find out whether TV sets could receive just Telefis Eireann or BBC and UTV as well.

A device called a Recordimeter was attached to each set in the sample homes and diaries given to panel members to record the viewing habits of households. Watchorn reported that there were high viewing figures between 6.15 p.m. and 6.45 p.m., with the evening peak reached between 9 p.m. and 10 p.m. The first TAM report appeared in May, 1962 and showed that Telefis Eireann had held the majority audience, despite the competition from the BBC and UTV. During the

Opposite page: Robin Morton (left), Telefis Eireann's first London manager and Peadar Pierce, now advertisement sales controller. The photograph was taken about 1962.

Pictured at the 1962 presentation of TE's autumn TV schedule were Michael Hayes, Peter Bolt, Alan Tate (all Arks) and Capt. Oliver Walsh (IAPI).

Bill Stapleton, founder of Stapleton Studios in Bray, later Silverpine.

LIST OF COMMERCIALS TRANSMITTED
DURING OPENING WEEK OF
TELEFIS EIREANN

MONDAY, JANUARY 1st. 1962

Time	Item	Duration
5.35	Sunbeam (FxP First)	00.15
	Brillo	00.30
	Mobil Oil	00.07
	Cuticura	00.07
	Rosedale Lanospray	00.07
	Askit	00.07
	Robert Homer Tomato	00.05
	Clery's	00.05
	Tot Quickmade	00.05
6.11	First Nat. Bld. Soc.	00.15
	Urney	00.07
	Time Beer (fxd.)	00.45
	O'Dearest	00.07
	Ryans Car Sales	00.05
	Williams	00.05
	Winstons	00.05
6.25	Joyce Floral (Fxd.)	00.45
	Bulmers	00.30
	Clery's	00.05
	Bantime Baby Powder	00.05
	Williams Super Market	00.05
6.40	Ford Motor Co. (Fxd.)	00.60
	Irish Dunlop (Fxd.)	00.60
7.12	Friendship Flour (Fxd.)	00.15
	Donnelly's (Fxd.)	00.30
	Chivers (Fxd.)	00.30
	Royco Soups (pf.)	00.15
	Sunbeam	00.07
	Mobil Oil	00.07
	Roches Stores	00.05
	Ryans Car Sales	00.05
	Tot Quickmade	00.05
7.40	Afton	00.60
	Irel Coffee	00.15
	A.1 Sauce	00.15
	Players Cigarettes (Pref.)	00.30
	Irish Shell Oil	00.45
	Carlsberg Lager (Pf.)	00.15
7.55	Cerebos Bisto	00.30
	Speedicook Oats	00.15
	Denny's	00.15
	Kelloggs	00.30
	Cadbury's Dairy Box (Pf.)	00.30
	Surf (Pf.)	00.30
	Stork (Pf.)	00.30

summer of 1962, TE reported no falling off in viewing figures, a factor attributed to the poor weather that summer, as well as to the strong programming, such as the new *Late Late Show.* Concluded Anthony D. Suttle, TE research officer: "After a year's operation, it has been generally indicated by the TAM reports that Telefis Eireann in being consistently viewed by the majority of its audience is fulfilling its aims as the national television service."

On the sales front, the first advertisement sales manager, Niall Sheridan, later to become TE's director of public relations, said that the new service had been well supported by advertisers. In its first year of operation, TE transmitted over 30,000 commercials for over 700 advertisers. He said that many of the advertisement sales success stories were of the type that made money, rather than headlines. Dealers for a well-established medicinal product found that six weeks' stock sold out in one week. Household aerosols advertised on TE during its first three months' transmissions achieved an 800 per cent sales increase. The production line for one consumer product broke down trying to meet the sudden increase in demand. Towards the end of 1962, Niall Sheridan was succeeded as sales manager of the television service by John Talbot, who joined from the TV copy clearance authority in London and who stayed with TE for two years. When he left, he was succeeded in turn by Bobby Gahan.

In October, 1962, Telefis Eireann opened its London office at Beulah House, 257-261 Oxford Street. The first London manager was Robin D. Morton; the second and present incumbent is Des O'Connell Redmond. Back in 1962, Morton said that the competition in the Irish television market, with TE battling for audience loyalty against two

Time	Item	Duration
8.10	Maltan Tobacco	00.15
	Bolands Bread	00.15
	Swift Carpet Cleaner	00.45
	Sweet Afton	00.15
	Bovril	00.30
	Phoenix Ale (Pf.)	00.30
8.27	Bush (Pf.)	00.15
	C.W.S. Soap	00.15
	Peartex (Pf.)	00.30
	Rinso (Pf.)	00.30
	Smarties	00.20
	Roches Stores	00.05
	W.&.T. Hanlon	00.05
8.55	Imperial Tobacco Co. (Pf.)	00.60
	Guinness Stout (Pf.)	00.45
	Sunbeam (Fxd.)	00.15
	Irish Perm. Bldg. Soc. (Fxd.)	00.15
	Madox (A. Nicholas) (Fx.)	00.30
	Philips (FxP Last)	00.15
9.12	Sunbeam (FxP First)	00.15
	Harp Lager (Fxd.)	00.30
	Constellation Sheets (Pf.)	00.30
	Esso Blue (Fxd.)	00.15
	Kelloggs	00.30
	Clarnico Murray (Pf.)	00.30
9.27	Clarks Shoes (Pf.)	00.30
	Healthex (Fxd.)	00.15
	Afton	00.30
	Canada Dry (Pf.)	00.15
	Zip Firelighters (Pf.)	00.15
	Irish Bakeries	00.05
	Menswear	00.05
	Winstons	00.05
9.45	Sunbeam (FxP First)	00.15
	Loxene Hair Cream (Pf.)	00.30
	Lux Soap (Pf.)	00.30
	Anadin (Pf.)	00.30
	Daidore Hosiery (Pf.)	00.15
	Butlins	00.60
10.00	Williams & Woods Marmalade	00.15
	Aspro Nicholas	00.30
	Sweet Afton	00.15
	Babycham	00.15
	Brown & Polson (Pf.)	00.30
	Lyons Tea	00.15
	Brylcreem	00.15
	Bolands Biscuits	00.15
	Shell Oil	00.15
	Clery's	00.05
	Kenny's A.A.	00.05
	W.&.T. Hanlon	00.05

Time	Item	Duration
10.27	C.W.S. Soap	00.15
	Broadlook Oats	00.30
	Even Industries (Pf.)	00.15
	Magee & Co. (Pf.)	00.15
	O.I.S. (Pf.)	00.30
	Lyons Tea	00.15
	Williams & Woods Marmalade	00.15
10.55	Shell Petrol	00.60
	Aer Lingus (Pf.)	00.15
	First Nat. Bldg. Soc.	00.15
	Askit	00.30
	Robert Usher	00.05
	Tot Quickauds	00.05
	Ryans Car Sales	00.05
	Roches Stores	00.05
11.08	Pretty Quick (Pf.)	00.15
	Kosangas	00.15
	Sunbeam	00.30
	Irishmade Stationery	00.07
	Clery's	00.05
	Tillium Supermarket	00.05
	Winstons	00.05

Commercials transmitted on Telefis Eireann on Monday, January 1, 1962, the first full day's schedule on the new station.

other channels, was unique in Europe. One London agency executive claimed that with the opening of TE, he had been done out of a trip to the USA to study multi-channel competition. Also in early 1963, Morton claimed that there was a possibility that TE would start transmitting advertising magazines, similar to *Jim's Inn* produced by Rediffusion in London. This hope never materialised, for TE decided that such magazine type programmes were unsuited to the Irish market. So well did the new medium succeed that for its financial year ended March 31, 1963, television advertising on the station amounted to £699,878.

To provide the new medium with commercials, a whole host of new production companies sprang up; some radio studios, like those owned by Eamonn Andrews, also went into TV. Many early efforts at TV commercials' production were poor, because few people had much experience of the new medium. The Eamonn Andrews Studios filmed a series of commercials for Kilmaine Clothes, a client of Janus. The series was filmed on location at Gormanstown Castle, near Balbriggan. The production cost just £500 and the quality is remembered to this day by people who worked in Janus at the time as having been "abysmal". Guinness was an early user of the medium, having been converted to the idea of any kind of serious advertising expenditure in Ireland only in 1959. Guinness rushed into television with the enthusiasm of the convert, but some of its early commercials, shot in pubs and attempting humour, are recalled now, even by Guinness executives, as having been extremely embarrassing.

Some of the agencies geared up for television production before the start of Telefis Eireann. Janus for instance, then a top rated

TELEFIS EIREANN—CARD RATE COSTS
PER THOUSAND HOMES AND ADULTS REACHED
DAY MONDAYS

START OF 15 MINUTE PERIOD	TAM RATING	HOMES VIEWING 000's	ADULTS VIEWING 000's	STANDARD RATE			PREFERENTIAL RATE		
				CARD RATE COST	COST/000 Sh		CARD RATE COST	COST/000 Sh	
					HOMES	ADULTS		HOMES	ADULTS
12.00									
15									
30									
45									
1.00									
15									
30									
45									
2.00									
15									
30									
45									
3.00									
15									
30									
45									
4.00									
15									
30									
45									
5.00	28	29	33		28	24		25	22
15	33	34	38		24	21		21	19
30	30	31	38	B	26	21	B	23	19
45	33	34	45	15 SECS £25 / 30 SECS £40 / 60 SECS £70	24	18	15 SECS £23 / 30 SECS £36 / 60 SECS £63	21	16
6.00	49	51	76		16	11		14	9
15	56	58	101		14	8		12	7
30	55	57	99		14	8		13	7
45	52	54	94		15	9		13	8
7.00	52	54	93		15	9		13	8
15	57	59	111		14	7		12	6
30	51	53	104		20	10		18	9
45	52	54	106		20	10		18	9
8.00	53	55	111		19	10		17	9
15	52	54	112		20	9		18	9
30	56	58	121	A	18	9	A	17	8
45	57	59	122	15 SECS £33 / 30 SECS £53 / 60 SECS £93	18	9	15 SECS £30 / 30 SECS £48 / 60 SECS £84	16	8
9.00	61	63	130		17	8		15	7
15	55	57	120		19	9		17	8
30	57	59	129		18	8		16	7
45	58	60	132		18	8		16	7
10.00	34	35	81		30	13		27	12
15	30	31	75		34	14		31	13
30	33	34	78	B	24	10	B	21	9
45	32	33	75	15 SECS £25 / 30 SECS £40 / 60 SECS £70	24	11	15 SECS £23 / 30 SECS £36 / 60 SECS £63	22	10
11.00	16	17	33		47	24		42	22
15	8	8	15		100	53		90	48
30									
45									

IRISH TAM LIMITED

Rate card costs, Telefis Eireann, 1962.

agency for print media work, started preparing for television in 1960, when Denis Garvey, perceptively, sent Bernard Share and Bill Bolger, his top creative team, to London to study the art of producing commercials. Janus also brought in an outside TV expert to run its new television department; he was said to have caused much friction in the agency. O'Kennedy Brindley brought over Don Cresswell from London to run its television department. Niel O'Kennedy, who had long been interested in films, remembers that the agency was one of the first to put in projection facilities. Cresswell advised the agency on equipment installation. At the start, remembers O'Kennedy, because few people in Dublin had the necessary production experience, commercials were shot in England. "Then we started making commercials in Ireland, using imported British technicians. Very quickly, local talent — lighting cameramen, make-up people and so on — came to the fore and we started using them as quickly as possible." Processing and finishing still had to be done in England.

A list of the film production companies established in Dublin by January, 1963, makes interesting reading. The Abbey Studios was based at 30 Upper Abbey Street, while ACT, run by Proinsias MacAonghusa, was at 2 Upper Mount Street and Ardmore Studios was flourishing at Bray. Celtic Film Productions of 44 Lower Leeson Street produced over 100 commercials for showing on TE in 1962; it claimed to be one of the few all-Irish production companies. Other film production firms included Dolphin Studios in Earlsfort Terrace (an offshoot of Sun Advertising), the Peter Hunt Recording Studios at 130 St Stephen's Green (sound only), Bob Monks of Bray, Munster House Productions, also of Bray, Rex Roberts Studios of Appian Way, Shaw Films of 25 Upper Pembroke Street, Stapleton Studios of Merrion Court, Merrion Row, Toonder Films (Ireland) of Upper Abbey Street and R. Bestick Williams of Frankfort Avenue, Rathgar. A total of 28 agencies were recognised by Telefis Eireann. While Ardmore was flourishing, it attracted a nucleus of production companies to the area, like Bill Stapleton's Silverpine Studios and Gunther Wulff, who set up animation studios and later went into film processing. Bill Stapleton is remembered by cameraman Vincent Corcoran as having been a brilliant technician, but someone who tried to do too much. Corcoran himself has spent the last 25 years working round the world for the big Hollywood film companies — he has a world-class reputation that has been rarely used in Ireland in recent years. Gunther Wulff is a long time established in Bray: in 1964, he was delegated by the film studios in Bonn, West Germany, for which he then worked, to look after six students from Limerick who had come over to Germany to study film making. That started his interest in Ireland and soon afterwards, the head of the Bonn studios decided to open up a subsidiary company in Dublin. After the death of his boss, Gunther bought the equipment used by the Dublin firm and set up his own production company in Bray, in premises adjoining the Ardmore film studios. He says of those times: "Big budget commercials always went to London in the 1960s. People in the business used to say 'If you haven't any money, go to Gunther's because my firm specialised in small and medium budget productions'."

Early into TV, some of the building societies came on air. The Educational Building Society was the leading society in terms of assets when Telefis Eireann first came on the air, but the Irish Permanent Building Society — then, as now, a client of O'Keeffes Advertising — came into TV and started spending heavily. Sources in the industry reckon that of all the factors that propelled the Irish Permanent to the top of the building society tree, the use of television was perhaps the prime influence.

The first commercial ever taken off Irish television after viewer complaints happened two years after Telefis Eireann went on the air. A commercial for ICI Bri-Nylon featured Anthony and Cleopatra in a cartoon: several viewers rang up to complain it was lewd and lascivious

Two scenes from Dublin Corporation's television advertisement, showing (top) the goldfish swimming comfortably before the water level drops and the fish floundering at the bottom of a almost empty bowl.

Two scenes from the TV commercial made in 1974 to persuade Dublin consumers to use less water during the great drought of that year. The film was produced by GPA Films for Wilson Hartnell, the client was Dublin Corporation. Script was by Brian Martin, camera work was by Sean Corcoran and the director was Brian de Salvo.

and the commercial was promptly withdrawn.

The station was bringing in about £2½ millions' worth of TV advertising a year.

The Irish Advertising Awards Festival has now been going since the early 1960s; the recent event was the 24th to be held. Kinsale still tries hard to live down its original image of non-stop boozing, but it has proved extremely useful for the creative side of Irish advertising. Each festival attracts about 700 entries from all over the world, as well as judges of the calibre of Jerry Della Femina and Bill Bernbach; judges mingle with the delegates and creative standards benefit. But the boozy image lives on. One advertising man got so drunk at one festival that he came to in a corridor of Acton's hotel early one morning wearing nothing except for a paper hat.

One of the most influential people in film production was Brendan Redmond, now chairman of McConnell's. He did his training in electronics at Kevin Street College of Technology and then went to work for Philips, the electrical appliances firm. Then followed a long stint with the overseas projects division of the Decca Navigation Company, installing and maintaining navigational equipment, mainly for aircraft and shipping. Then one day in the late 1950s, he received a letter from his mother, who wrote from the family home in Bray with the news that new film studios were being set up nearby. He wrote to Emmet Dalton, who was a prime mover in the Ardmore project. Says Redmond: "Dalton and I became firm friends. He was very interested in Irish industrial development, as was Louis Elliman." So the young Redmond joined the new studios, becoming the firm's first technical employee, looking after sound recording and equipment maintenance. Eventually, he became head of sound, spending a total of six years there. One of the technicians he worked with there was Tom Curran,

This photograph was taken about 1963 when Telefis Eireann launched a new season's rate card. From left: Tom Milner (Lever Bros), Dermot Jordan (advertising manager, Esso) and Brendan Byrne (O'Kennedy Brindley).

now involved with Anner Communications. Another "graduate" of Ardmore was Stuart Hetherington, the RTE cameraman.

When Telefis Eireann started up in 1962, there was an obvious need for expertise in the production of commercials. Arks, for instance, produced a silent film for experimental purposes long before the television service opened transmissions. Frank Sheerin scripted it, remembers Vincent Corcoran, and a youthful John Allen (now with Aer Lingus) was also involved in its production. Corcoran also recalls that another agency in town even equipped a stills photographer of its acquaintance with movie equipment. The man had had no previous experience of film making, so naturally enough, the experiment was disastrous and ended swiftly. Against this background and with up to ten UK-based production companies setting up subsidiary production firms in Dublin, there was a great need for locally controlled film making facilities. John McConnell invited Brendan Redmond to come in on a joint venture he had in mind. McConnell wanted to set up a joint production company in which McConnell's, Arks and O'Kennedy Brindley would be involved. At that time, there were no dubbing facilities in Dublin — all dubbing had to go to London. Talks went on between the three agencies for six months, but in the end, nothing came of the idea.

Instead, John McConnell offered Brendan Redmond a job with the McConnell agency. Its first TV man had been John Devis, invited in by Charlie McConnell shortly before Telefis Eireann went on the air. Devis commuted from London, because he had his own production company there. It was not an entirely satisfactory state of affairs for either McConnell's or Devis, who now quips that he must have been the only person to have turned down the inducement of a pay rise from Charlie McConnell! In those far off black and white days,

Peadar Pierce, RTE's advertisement sales controller.
Photograph: RTE.

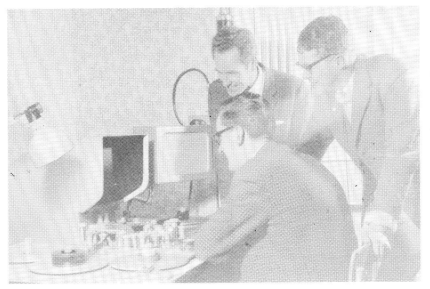

The first 35mm Steenbeck editing machine in Ireland, 1965. Inspecting their work on it are Larry Hogan (sitting), Gunther Wulff (standing, rear) and John Banim. Gunther Wulff says that the sound track has only half the width of the 35mm picture, the German method of saving some costs in film production.

This map (re-published by kind permission of the Editor of " The Irish Radio & Electrical Journal ") shows in colour the original anticipated contours within which a strong signal of at least 500 microvolts would be received around each of the five transmitters. In practice, it has been found that the areas of good reception extend well beyond these limits.

Transmission coverage of the five main Telefis Eireann TV transmitters, as shown in January, 1963.

☐ Kippure
☐ Mt. Leinster
☐ Mullaghanish
☐ Truskmore
   Maghera

The 625-line and 405-line transmitters at Kippure and Truskmore, as well as the 625-line transmitters at Mullaghanish and Mt. Leinster, were supplied by Pye. The 625-line transmitter at Maghera was supplied by Marconi.

Shooting a recent TV commercial under the shadow of the gasometer, Ringsend, Dublin.

remembers Devis, it was all trial and error. No-one in Dublin had much experience of commercials' production, so it all had to be made up as the production technicians went along. Another early name in TV production at McConnell's was Brendan O'Reilly. In 1964, therefore, McConnell's set up the first inhouse TV production unit in a Dublin agency. Pan International was in existence before most of the Irish production companies, says Redmond, and has always employed Irish labour. To a large extent, Pan has contributed to the development of the commercials' production industry in Ireland and says Redmond, the firm is as determined as ever to keep the work here in Ireland. He was managing director of Pan International and also television executive of the agency. He then became deputy managing director of the agency in 1969, managing director in 1971 — a post he held for ten years — and is now chairman.

In his time at Pan International, perhaps the best-known commercial produced for McConnell's was the Lyons tea "Minstrels". In 1970, McConnell's and Lyons wanted to produce an animated commercial for the brand. Gunther Wulff was asked to produce two storyboards, one featuring a lion. Both were turned down. Then he produced a storyboard with the Minstrels theme and he remembers that both client and agency were ecstatic. Wulff says that he did not like the theme himself at that stage, but since that was what McConnell's and Lyons wanted, it went into production. Someone from a Dublin dance school did the routine, which was filmed. Then from the film, Wulff used a Rotoscope to draw out the cartoon sequences. These drawings were then used to form the basis of the cartoons. The jingle was composed by Johnny Johnson. The combination of cartoon and jingle was highly effective, so much so that sources in the advertising industry today claim that all subsequent Lyons tea advertising, since the account left McConnell's after a long stay there, has been little more than derivative from that 1970 commercial.

Pictured during the shoot of a TV commercial at Ardmore Studios in 1978 are from left: Michael Healy (CDP), Seamus Corcoran, unnamed, Sean Corcoran, Paddy Keogh, unnamed, Brian de Salvo, unnamed, Brendan Maguire, unnamed and Brendan O Broin (CDP).

it's a **TV** world

and the Republic of Ireland has enlarged this world with the completion of its first year in television. In terms of revenue and as an attractive new medium for Irish advertisers, it has been a successful year. At Royds, in Dublin, we, modestly claim a share of this success; for, on behalf of our various clients, most of whom use television, we create TV commercials that sell, yet don't cost the earth. We do our own scripting, casting and take productions onto the floor. Royds TV advertising, created in Dublin, works for our clients in several markets, helping to make a TV world for products like Brickcrem, Denny Bacon and Sausages, Jacob's Biscuits, Lucozade, Urney Chocolates—to name a few.

If you would like to know more about Royds TV advertising, or how we operate in any advertising or marketing world, write to:

Royds
ADVERTISING AND MARKETING LIMITED, 7 DAWSON STREET, DUBLIN 2 · TELEPHONE 70715

A Royd's advertisement placed in the London advertising trade press in 1963.

This photograph was taken at the Fischerkoesen film studio at 7 Northumberland Road, Dublin, in 1965 during the filming of a commercial for the Educational Building Society. From left: Roisin Daly (now Roisin Hogan, an art teacher at Dun Laoghaire School of Art), Gunther Wulff, John Banim (now in banking) and putting the final touches to the artwork, Larry Hogan. Later, Roisin Daly claimed a major creative input into the Lyons Tea Minstrels.

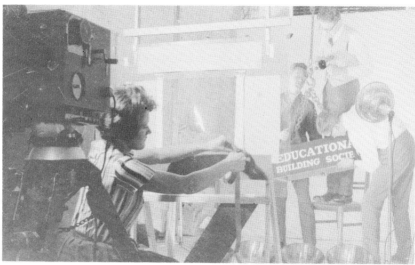

Back in the 1960s, remembers Brendan Redmond, the film technology, particularly on the sound side, was very primitive compared with that used today. Sound recording then was not even linked to the camera; the Nagra recorder was a big step forward. Inventiveness was often the order of the day; Peter Hunt, for instance, had a great reputation for improvisation and invented his own loop system.

Pan International has been responsible for developing some of the outstanding talent in the commercials' production business. Harry Ellis, who now runs Primrose Pictures, began at Pan. Peter Brady, now a Windmill Lane director, started his career at 18 with Pan, while the company was also responsible for giving Tiernan MacBride a place in the Dublin industry, after his return from the USA. Later, MacBride left Pan to set up his own production firm.

In those first years of Telefis Eireann — it became RTE in 1966 — when Pan International was starting to develop its techniques, it used Ardmore extensively, for all its dubbing and mixing work. Track laying was done at the Tommy Ellis recording studios. While McConnell's was developing the TV production side so extensively through Pan International, Arks was following in a similar direction. In the 1960s, while some agencies like Janus did not adapt altogether successfully to the new television age, Arks managed to bring the creative brilliance it had shown in print media work during the latter part of the 1950s and early 1960s into the television arena. Arks' creative team on the TV side included Jim Strathern, Eamonn O'Flaherty (art director), Frank Sheerin (copy chief) and Catherine Donnelly. Remembers Michael Algar, now chief executive of the Irish Film Board, who joined Arks' TV department in 1966, it was a very intensive time, with many commercials being produced for big spending clients like Guinness, Harp lager and Player's cigarettes. Like McConnell's, Arks also

John Talbot, who succeeded Niall Sheridan as advertisement sales manager at Telefis Eireann.

Robin Morton, Telefis Eireann's first London advertisement manager.

produced an award winning tea commercial, for Capital tea. It was directed by Charles Creighton, a veteran English director who worked on many Ealing films in the 1950s and whose best-known film was the *Lavender Hill Mob.*

From 1976 until he joined the Irish Film Board in 1982, Algar was managing director of Pan International, responsible for TV productions. During his time at Pan, the company also produced a totally independent film, the *Ballad of the Irish Horse.* Rory O'Farrell directed it, Michael Algar was the producer. Con Houlihan of the *Evening Press* wrote the script, Niall Tobin did the voiceover and music was by the Chieftains. The 60 minute documentary cost about £20,000 to produce, with Pan contributing nearly 50 per cent. A small contribution came from Bord na gCapall (the Irish Horse Board) and the rest was put up by the Irish Hospital Sweepstakes.

Also closely involved in commercials' production from the agency side in those early days was Niel O'Kennedy, brother of Desmond O'Kennedy. Niel had a long-established reputation on the graphics side of the business and also a keen interest in films. He was actively involved in O'Kennedy Brindley from about 1958 onwards and recalls clearly how it set up its TV side.

When Telefis Eireann started, O'Kennedy Brindley brought in Don Cresswell, a very experienced English TV producer to run its TV department. He advised the agency on which equipment to put in; it became one of the first agencies to install its own projection facilities. As soon as local talent came on stream, recalls O'Kennedy, the agency started using it. "We were in the forefront of using Irish film technicians," he claims. But the big drawback was that even though more local film making talent came to the fore, all processing and finishing had to go to London. Still, despite that drawback, interesting commercials were shot in those days, including many for Independent

Newspapers, for which commercials had to be scripted on Wednesdays, shot on Thursdays, edited on Fridays and screened on Saturdays. The speed with which this advertising for the *Sunday Independent* was produced in the 1960s never ceased to amaze the rest of the local film production industry.

Don Cresswell stayed with O'Kennedy Brindley about six years, then set up his own independent production company and eventually went back to England, where he died about five years ago. After Cresswell left O'Kennedy Brindley, Niel O'Kennedy took over his job at the agency. From the time Telefis Eireann started, he had been closely involved in the TV side, scripting, account handling and going on some shoots. Then he ran the TV side until he retired from the agency in 1982. O'Kennedy remembers another early product launch which depended heavily on TV: Erin Foods, the subsidiary of the Irish Sugar Company set up in the early 1960s to process foods for the home and export markets. Tony O'Reilly, then just 30 years of age, joined the Irish Sugar Company in 1966 and was closely involved with the first of the product launches for Erin Foods. In May, 1969, O'Reilly moved on to become managing director of H. J. Heinz in the UK, although he retained for a time his position as joint managing director of Heinz-Erin, the jointly owned company set up by the international and Irish food firms.

Frozen foods were starting to be marketed in Ireland in the mid-1960s, principally Birds Eye and Findus. Clarence Birdseye first sold frozen foods in Massachusetts, USA, in 1930. Birds Eye frozen vegetables arrived in Britain in the late 1940s and fish fingers were launched there in 1955. It took a further ten years for the frozen food concept to arrive in Ireland, with Birds Eye playing a key rôle in their development here, helped by television, as well as other, now forgotten brands, such as Hardy's. In retrospect, the use of accelerated freeze drying by Erin Foods on a variety of vegetables was not an entirely wise market move seen over the long term. Such products now have a small market share compared with frozen foods. However, in 1966, Erin Foods was ready to launch its new range and did so mainly on TV. The firm's vegetables were launched first, then came the soup varieties. Its Hot Cup instant soup brand was launched entirely on TV, remembers O'Kennedy. Not all television launches were successful. Corsair was the new cigarette launched in 1968 by Player Wills and featuring a poker game. As soon as it was launched, pressure was put on the firm to ban the game and by the following Christmas, the brand had disappeared from the shelves, but not before some £200,000 had been spent by O'Kennedy Brindley on television time for the new brand.

An interesting facit of the ESB's corporate campaigns in the 1960s was the production of documentary films. Most of these were written by Michael Colley and produced by George Fleischmann and they covered such areas as the design and construction of new power

602

Pictured during filming
of a Bank of Ireland
commercial were
Brendan O Broin
(second from right)
CDP and Pat White (far
right) Bank of Ireland.

603

1965: Larry Hogan talks to an important client while Mary Lacey is delighted to send out the invoice for that "chain job".

Gerry Poulson has directed many award-winning commercials for Irish agencies; he is seen here (right) with Roy Galloway, Poulson's recent shoots in Ireland include Guinness Logo, Stag, Bulmer's Cider, Harp lager, Erin Foods, the National Dairy Council and the ESB, through his production company, GPA Films (Ireland). The firm also operates in London and Amsterdam.
Poulson started with the Rank Organisation, editing at Pinewood Studios before directing documentaries. To date, he has directed over 3,000 commercials throughout the world and has won over 100 international awards.

facilities — for instance the Turlough Hill pump storage project and the Poolbeg and Aghada power stations and also such new activities of the ESB as consultancy in the Middle East. All of these films were accepted for distribution by 20th Century Fox and went on the cinema circuits and some also appeared on RTE. One early commercial shot by Vincent Corcoran was for the ESB; filming took place at the Monaloe Estate in Cornelscourt, then under construction. The male half of the "married" couple was a young Frank Delaney.

John Devis, who has worked in commercials' production in Ireland for so long that he can remember the days 20 years ago when total production costs on a film would be no more than £2,000, remembers also doing an Andrews Liver Salts film for O'Donnell Earl when it was being run by Bill Walshe. He said to me: "What do you think of when you hear the tune 'The Continental'. I replied: 'Something really refreshing', so I went off and shot the Andrews' commercial with that theme." He says that in those far-off days of film production, directors had a much freer hand, there was none of the present day market research. When the Satzenbrau commercial was being shot not long ago, market research even dictated what the actors in the film should look like and what they should wear.

Until 1973, RTE had little car advertising on television: manufacturers always plumped for print media advertising. One of the first "breaks" into car advertising on television came with the

launch of the Fiat 126 Bambino. A Cork dealer had complained about Fiat's system of using numbers to designate models: the firm acted on his suggestion and started naming its cars. The Bambino was the first such Fiat model and it was launched to the all-important dealers in the studios of RTE. One source in RTE claims that while the Bambino campaign was launched in the daily press, the name did not really register with the motoring public until the TV campaign started. By now, around seven per cent of RTE's television advertising revenue comes from motor advertising, equal to the volume of alcohol advertising. The development of car advertising counter-balanced the withdrawal of cigarette advertising. RTE was the first media organisation to phase out cigarette advertising: the last cigarette commercial was for Carroll's Major brand and went out on March, 31, 1973. Cigarettes had represented eleven per cent of RTE's total advertisement revenue.

He has directed many episodes of the TV series Black Beauty **and** Dick Turpin **for London Weekend Television and has completed** The Legendary Story of Dick Turpin **feature film for RKO Pictures.**

Brian de Salvo, TV commercials' director, pictured in 1978.

One of the most memorable advertisements of the 1970s was also one of the simplest. In 1974, a prolonged drought meant severe water rationing throughout the country. For Dublin Corporation, Wilson Hartnell produced a famous water saving commercial, which showed water draining out of a goldfish bowl and the fish floundering. The campaign cost the corporation £30,000. The goldfish belonged to four year old Gareth, son of a Wilson Hartnell copywriter, now a director, Brian Martin, and the filming was done so the goldfish suffered no cruelty. However, it generated an enormous amount of public controversy and interest and the campaign certainly proved effective, for over the period of its showing, there was a huge improvement in the water consumption levels. The film was borrowed for showing in the North and also for use in the Wessex Water Authority area in southern England, where the drought was equally bad.

By 1972, McConnell's had a TV/radio studio with a new video system which included complete videotape recording studio with full black and white and colour facilities with three TV cameras, telecine unit, special effects, sound and vision mixing and three mobile monitors.

In the 1970s, the standard of television commercials became much more sophisticated. In some cases, bastardised commercials were made, to save costs. Today, making an original TV commercial can cost at least £50,000, sometimes double that figure. Some agency sources claim the most expensive commercial ever produced for RTE was a corporate image one for Irish Shell, made two years ago by the KMMD, now Momentum, agency. Brian Cronin's agency made a memorable campaign for Barton and Guestier wines, then distributed by Seagrams, at low cost, for it was assembled from various commercials made in Canada and the USA, some on 16mm film. The impressively expensive looking campaign highlighted "Monsieur Barton and the French connection". Another similar device was produced for Ribena, where the local manufacturers, Beecham, could not justify the huge costs of original TV production, so the agency assembled a "bastard" commercial from a variety of film and video sources. There were hilarious times, too. Once, the distributors of Mateus Rosé wine were persuaded that the TV commercial really needed shooting on location in the northern Portuguese vineyards. A crew went there from Dublin, but found the lighting unsatisfactory, so they came home and found the perfect location — on the banks of the river Dargle near Bray.

There has been the odd calamity with TV advertising on RTE, such as the occasion when a Harp commercial was followed by one for Harpic, the lavatory cleaner. Not so long ago, an advertisement for a haemorrhoids' preparation was followed by one for Perri crisps, with the copy line "Bags to drive you Perrinoid". In another drinks commercial, the actor was seen taking a sip from his glass; immediately after the commercial, RTE returned to the world title fight in question and a shot of the boxer spitting out. Such occurrences are few and far between. One time "live" on Ulster Television, an announcer lifted a box of Blue Max soap powder: the bottom fell out. In the 25 years of RTE television, there has never been a "live" commercial, apart, of course, from the slides with voice-overs. The closest to that was when a commercial for Esso featuring a price reduction coming into effect the following day, was recorded just 30 minutes before transmission. RTE never suffered the same fate as the TV station in north-east England which put out a "live" commercial for Berger non-drip paints. The model tipped the can of paint upside down, to demonstrate its non-drip quality. What no-one realised was that the heat of the studio lights had melted the paint and the ensuing flood of paint over the studio floor was the last "live" commercial ever shown in the UK.

Shooting commercials produces stories of the ones that got away. In

THERE WAS NO QUIET ON THE WESTERN FRONT FOR THE HEROES AND COWARDS WHO FLEW TO THEIR RENDEZVOUS WITH HELL!

THE BLUE MAX

20th CENTURY FOX Presents

GEORGE PEPPARD · JAMES MASON · URSULA ANDRESS in "THE BLUE MAX"

Also Starring JEREMY KEMP · KARL MICHAEL VOGLER · ANTON DIFFRING Produced by CHRISTIAN FERRY Executive Producer ELMO WILLIAMS Directed by JOHN GUILLERMIN

Adaptation by BEN BARZMAN and BASILIO FRANCHINA Screenplay by DAVID PURSALL and JACK SEDDON and GERALD HANLEY

1967, a film crew went to the Scilly Isles, off the coast of Cornwall, to shoot footage with daffodils for a new Cadbury's commercial. It was March, so the journey was necessary. On the way back from the islands, the crew, complete with all their film gear, flew by helicopter over the newly-wrecked Torrey Canyon oil tanker. They did not know at the time that the wreck lay directly beneath their flight path, so the chance of tremendous footage was lost.

Colour came to RTE 15 years ago. When Ireland staged the Eurovision song contest in the Gaiety Theatre, Dublin, in 1971, following Dana's win the previous year in the Netherlands, RTE was catapulted into colour, because so many of the European networks that took the relay were already transmitting in colour. Some viewers in Ireland saw the programme in colour. It took until the end of 1972 to gear up the technical systems for transmission of colour commercials; just as with the opening of Telefis Eireann on December, 31, 1961, a

Poster for The Blue Max film shot at Ardmore and on location in Co Wicklow in 1966; one of the Army officers taking part in the film, as an extra, was Captain Jack Phelan, now managing director, GPA Films. Vincent Corcoran introduced him to the world of film production.

draw was held for the first colour commercial to be shown on RTE. As had happened so many times in advertising developments, McConnell's came first, winning the draw on behalf of one of its clients, VG, the grocery voluntary group. The commercial's theme was "VG pop in and shop". However, only now has colour set coverage risen to 80 per cent.

The arrival of colour was a wonderful boost for food advertising, remarks Niel O'Kennedy. He is backed in his comments by Peadar Pierce, RTE advertisement sales controller, who says that TV, apart from being the most powerful medium for selling products, is equally powerful in building brand image.

Although the arrival of colour created more problems — such as the need to blend set and costume colours much more carefully — some advertisers deliberately use black and white for effect. Holsten Pils used clips from old black and white movies to create atmosphere, while two years ago, the Russian theme TV and cinema commercials produced for Levi jeans and placed here by Peter Owens, and later Arks, also used black and white, to recreate the drab settings of the USSR.

Interesting statistics were published for the years 1970, 1971 and 1972 for agency volumes with RTE television, just as colour was coming in. If the British agency, Lintas, had been included, it would have been placed fourth in both sets of statistics.

The figures below are after allowing for the agency discount.

Opposite page:
In the mid-1960s, Carrolls used three minute cinema filmlets to promote its cigarettes. They were filmed in many locations throughout Ireland; the score was written by Manfred Mann. Seen here trying an experimental double shot with two Ariflex 35mm cameras (the effect is now easily obtained electronically) are from left: Brendan Redmond, Seamus Corcoran and Sean Corcoran. The photograph was taken about 1965.

		1971/72	1970/71
1	McConnell's	268,336	310,960 (1)
2	O'Kennedy Brindley	262,288	270,960 (3)
3	Arks	226,388	279,690 (2)
4	Kenny's	190,496	119,560 (7)
5	O'Keeffes	172,732	189,910 (4)
6	P. Owens	166,935	168,420 (6)
7	Irish International	162,947	188,950 (5)
8	Young Advertising	121,403	100,320 (9)
9	Wilson Hartnell	107,133	77,840 (11)
10	O'Donnell-Earl	104,011	109,650 (8)

One of the big developments in film production came in the early 1970s, when the business became unionised. Vincent Corcoran recalls that not long after he had finished shooting the Supertrain commercials for CIE and Arks (Michael Algar was the director), he got wind of news that Arks was bringing in an all-British crew to film a commercial for Allied Irish Banks. *The Irish Times* reported the development and AIB ordered Arks to stop work on the commercial. At the time, commercials were being shot in England for Guinness: Ed Browne of the Irish Transport & General Workers' Union told Guinness that the commercial would not be allowed through. The union stand in 1974 has increased the work being done here by local production companies and only one or two directors from outside the country now have tickets here.

While the production business was unionised, Ardmore Studios were being phased out. Mike Curley of Wilson Hartnell believes however that the loss of the Ardmore studios at Bray has not been a big loss to the advertising business. "It's very sad that we lost this industry, but as far as advertising production is concerned, it is not a major deprivation." Ardmore had four sound stages; C stage was used most often for filming commercials, but nowadays, if a set has to be built, a facilities firm like Film Lighting Facilities, which has its own studios at Stillorgan, Co Dublin, fits the bill perfectly well. With present day film facilities and crew flexibility, there is no reason why a building like a church hall cannot be hired for a day and used for shooting commercials. Niel O'Kennedy says of Ardmore: "In its day, it was a wonderful facility, with all the technical equipment and expertise we wanted. We could not have operated without it then, but if it reopened now, there would have to be a substantial updating of its equipment." Ardmore has now reopened under new American ownership (MTM). It may become a major commercials production facility again.

A very famous series of commercials directed by John Devis was that in 1977 for Guinness, the "Island" series, which won over a dozen awards worldwide. Arks' commercial was scripted by Frank Sheerin, with art direction by Eamonn O'Flaherty. The small west of Ireland bar was built at Ardmore, using a Connemara backdrop. The currach scenes were shot on location, from a helicopter. The shoot had one amusing side story: the three champion rowers in the boat could not understand English, so the walkie-talkies were of little use. These location sequences were shot first, then the pub ones. Production costs were around £12,000. The closing sequences were particularly memorable: the rowers deliver the Guinness. In the pub, there is silence except for the ticking of the clock, until the door opens. Then the first Guinness is poured and the people in the bar all start chattering away — in Irish — and the closing caption comes up in Irish. Interestingly, nearly ten years later, Sheerin has been used by Guinness to create the equally memorable advertisements for Fürstenberg German lager, imported specially into Ireland, for which a powerful, thirst inducing brand image has been built up. It now has 3.8 per cent of the lager market. After he left Arks, he set up his own company, Frank Sheerin Associates. He still maintains a close relationship with Guinness.

The next major opening by RTE was that of the second TV channel in November, 1978. The programming was scheduled to complement that of RTE 1, and the first rate card was launched in the expectation that most of the country would be able to receive RTE 2 and that there would be a significant erosion of RTE 1 viewing figures. This did not happen and in May, 1979, the rate card had to be adjusted accordingly. For the first few years, audience growth on the second channel was slow, but now RTE claims that there is very little difference between the two channels. It issues revenue figures for the two channels combined, with no division between the two. This year, RTE's total revenue from TV advertising is expected to top £38 million. 84 per cent of that figure comes from Irish advertising agencies, with London agencies and local advertising placed direct accounting for the rest. Input from the Belfast agencies is small. RTE's revenue position is in direct contrast to that of Ulster Television, where about 75 per cent of its revenue comes from London agencies and the rest from local sources, including Belfast and Dublin agencies.

Wilson Hartnell is a major TV user: about 60 per cent of the agency's work is in TV. In 1978, the agency decided to set up its own TV production company, Arena Productions. Harry Ellis, nephew of Tommy Ellis, was TV producer with the agency at the time. After Ellis came Peter Finnegan; the current incumbent is Jimmy Ellis. As Mike Curley, a creative director of the agency, points out, the bigger the agency, the more need for an inhouse production company. "We hire in everything, but if we are not happy with a set, for instance, we can change it." With the cost of TV production so high, such close control is essential. A day's shooting can cost around £25,000; weather insurance is a particular bane of agency production schedules. One day's cover against wet weather costs around £6,000 and many clients cannot

Watching the filming of the Player's Country Life cigarette commercials in 1968, from left: Ray O'Keeffe (O'Keeffes Advertising), Roger Byers (marketing manager, John Player & Sons (Ireland) and Paul Moy (account executive, O'Keeffes Advertising).

This photographic sequence shows TV commercials being filmed at Chiswick House, London, in the late 1960s, for Player's

afford that kind of "extra". Another problem faced in producing TV commercials here is the imbalance between the cost of the media campaign and the cost of production. As Mike Curley points out, in the UK ten per cent of a budget can be allocated for production. A £½ million campaign there allows a reasonable margin for production, whereas here in Ireland, production costs can sometimes equal and even surpass the media costs. "There is no solution to the problem. You cannot produce a cheap commercial — viewers now, particularly younger audiences, are so sophisticated that they can spot the flaws in

Country Life brand. The main artist (wearing the hat) was mime specialist Julian Joy-Chagrin. Country Life and another brand, Shannon, were especially tailored for the Irish market by Players: both were unmitigated disasters.

611

Proinsias
MacAonghusa, whose
ACT commercials'
production company,
located at Upper Mount
Street, Dublin, was one
of the first locally based
firms to produce
commercials for the
new Telefis Eireann
service. It also produced
radio commercials.

cheap productions," says Curley. He reckons that there are about seven production companies active in TV commercials' production, including those run by Michael McGarry, Harry Ellis, John Devis, Tiernan MacBride, Jack Phelan and Brian Halford.

A big plus for video is the ease it gives for editing. Film can be transferred to video for editing. Instant dissolves can be produced at the press of a button: with film, they used to take three or four days. Many titles and other opticals, including graphic tricks, can be produced easily on video. Says Mike Curley: "Video is a marvellous editing tool, yet for the foreseeable future, commercials, will continue to be shot on 35mm film and finished on video."

TV facilities have advanced far from the days when not alone did all opticals have to be sent to London, but even film processing had to be done there. Perhaps the biggest factor in the improvement of production facilities here has been the advent of Windmill Lane. "It's been a tremendous boon for the industry," is Niel O'Kennedy's view, widely echoed throughout the advertising business.

Windmill Lane's origins date back to the mid-1970s, when James Morris, a film editor, set up his own editing company. In 1978, he was joined by Russ Russell, a scriptwriter who had scripted such commercials as those for the Health Education Bureau, directed by Tiernan MacBride, and Meiert Avis, now a leading director in the pop promo market, to form Morris Russell Avis. From Herbert Lane, where there were cutting and other facilities, the new firm moved to Merrion Square, employing 12 people and offering more extended video and audio facilities, both for commercials' production and music recording. With the start of video, the firm became the third off-line facility in Europe and agencies in Dublin started putting their showreels on tape. Then in 1979, the firm moved to Windmill Lane, joining with Windmill Lane Recording Studios run by Brian Masterson where it had a film cutting room and a 24 track sound studio. Now the firm has a variety of broadcast suites, as well as two studios. A third studio is planned for the next few months, as Windmill Lane expands. It does a lot of "pop" promotional videos, as well as working for most of the Dublin agencies. In 1985, production on commercials brought in £800,000 worth of revenue. With new mobile video facilities, Windmill Lane can now do special effects on location.

Says Russ Russell: "With field video cameras improving all the time in mobility and quality, more and more production will be done on tape, but I can't see tape taking over completely from film until the quality of the new medium is guaranteed." The high definition revolution could ensure this transition: already a Paris facility is shooting and post-producing commercials on 1,125 line systems that offer as good a quality as 35mm film. The Paris facility is still very much at the prototype stage, says Russell and it could be another ten or 15 years before 1,125 lines becomes the norm for transmission standards.

On the sound side, Windmill Lane has equipped its edit suites with the very best in equipment. On the visual side, it can add a full range of opticals and titles, including computer graphic effects. Once, all opticals for Irish commercials had to be done in London: no longer. With Windmill's 3D computer graphics package, there is very little limit to what effects can be created here at home.

Also on the board of the holding company are Peter Brady, who had been a producer in Pan International, Tim Morris, the chief editor and Jim Butler, the chief engineer. Brian Cash also joined the firm, having been a competitor in the film editing area. The firm is now investing over £2 million in a new wholly owned subsidiary, Hanover Street Production Centre, which will have full service TV facilities.

Video started coming into use in the late 1970s and early 1980s. Production firms still shoot up to 80 per cent of commercials on 35mm film, but the resultant film is then transferred to video tape for transmission. RTE phased out the use of film in 1985. Tapes arrive at RTE in 1″ C format K spools; in a three stage process, RTE transfers incoming tapes to ¾″ high band continuous Sony tape. RTE says that there is no loss of sound or vision quality in this transfer process, but some outside sources say that not only is RTE the only TV station in these islands to use such a process, but that it does sometimes mean a slight loss of quality. It is not a major problem, say these agency sources, but they claim that UK stations transmit from 1″ C format spools.

A total of ten per cent of broadcast time can be allocated to commercials, or six minutes in every hour. RTE can however take up to 7½ minutes in every clock hour accumulating time and using it later so as not to break into particular programmes that need to run without interruption. The longest commercials ever to run have been of six minutes duration. One, in late 1962, was for Vauxhall Viva when it was launched here. It featured Peter West, the recently retired BBC commentator. Peadar Pierce saw the commercial on UTV one night, then next morning went to the late Tommy McCairns of McCairns Motors and persuaded him to run the commercial on TE, through Domas. Local titles were added: the commercial started at 7.57 p.m. to overcome the time restrictions. The second commercial of similar duration to be shown featured Ford trucks: it was only screened twice, but research showed that many viewers thought they had seen it four or five times. Once Peter Owens placed a commercial for showing after the Nine O'Clock News; the target audience for the ICI Fibres' film was just 20 people in the trade. McConnell's did a clever "broken" commercial for Zip firelighters; before the news, the firelighter was lit. After the news, the second part of the commercial was screened, showing the firelighter still burning.

Although RTE has six regionally-based sales people based in Cork, Galway, Limerick, Sligo and the Midlands, selling time on its radio and television services, it does not regionalise its TV advertising. RTE says

Ken Hamilton, Northern Ireland sales manager, Ulster Television.
Photograph: Ulster Television.

Pictured at an RTE
reception in the late
1960s, from left: Pat
Ferguson (later to
become chairman and
managing director of
Arks), Niall O Nualláin
of CPC Ireland (brother
of Brian O'Nolan, alias
Myles na Gopaleen),
Alan Tate (Arks) and
Peadar Pierce (RTE).

The former Rialto
cinema, Nenagh, Co
Tipperary, which closed
down 20 years ago. It is
now a hardware store.

that there is no great demand for it at the moment, but the facilities are there and could be developed in the longer term. However, there are regional rates and local advertisers are canvassed to take advertising time during coverage of local events being shown on the national network, as happens for instance with coverage of Galway's major race meeting at the end of the summer. RTE claims that in these cases, local advertisers reach much bigger audiences than they could through local newspapers and that the regional TV time rates are cheaper than many local newspaper rates.

In 1983, RTE had to write off £300,000 after the collapse of Arrow Advertising. After the debacle, credit control procedures within the station were considerably tightened.

Many sales conferences are held in the RTE studios; the first was for Lever Brothers, the next one was for Carling Black Label. The biggest ever held was a joint one between three companies, Kelloggs, CPC (Ireland) and Willwoods, featuring breakfast products. On another occasion, the whole of studio 1 was taken over by Philips.

In its 1983/84 financial year, Ulster Television brought in advertising revenue worth £13.3 million. With the advent of Channel Four, many new advertisers have been drawn to television, who had previously only advertised in the press. A main growth area for TV advertising in Northern Ireland since 1980 has been cars. Says Ken Hamilton, UTV's sales manager: "This advertising used to be very

In 1966, McConnell's produced TV commercials for the Sunday Mirror newspaper. David Niven (centre) is seen here on location, with film director Brendan Redmond.

615

Harry Ellis started his career with ACT Studios, specialising in sponsored radio production, before moving to McConnell's where he spent 10 years in Pan International, following which he became a freelance producer and then a freelance director with Advertising on Film. He set up his own production company, Primrose Pictures, in 1985.

press oriented because of the detail newspapers can give. But TV is a great image seller for cars, styling and appearance. We get a lot of commercials for expensive cars like Mercedes and BMW." Other growing areas for UTV include banking, supermarkets, children's products, such as sugar confectionery, estate agents and publishers. In some other ITV areas, estate agents have used TV extensively for image building campaigns. Des Bingham of the RMB agency in Belfast points out useful statistics about the Northern Ireland television market. UTV now has a potential audience of 92 per cent of homes, 462,000. Channel Four is useful in targeting spots to particular audiences, for instance, teenagers, due to the style of programming. TV AM offers a new regionalised dimension. Newcomers to TV advertising in the North have included accountants. In 1985, following the lifting of restrictions on accountants advertising, Coopers & Lybrand became the first accountancy practice to advertise on TV in Ireland, taking time on UTV and Channel Four.

The North has a certain amount of production facilities; the most recent issue of the Ulster Television marketing guide to Northern Ireland lists ten audio visual and film production companies, including A.E.L. Video of Belfast, The Design and Production Company, Belfast, Middleton Film Productions of Belfast, Screencraft Video Presentations of Belfast, T.E.S. Video of Belfast and H.E.TV of Belfast.

By now, RTE television signals can be clearly received throughout Ireland, except for some small pockets in north Co Antrim. While no official research has been done into RTE viewing figures in the North, there would appear to be a substantial audience there for its programmes. Cross-border viewing is reciprocated, since Ulster Television can be received in about half the television homes of the Republic, slightly more than the total UTV set count in Northern Ireland. In certain areas of the east and south coasts, Welsh commercial television can be received. Channel Four is also available for many viewers in the north and east of the Republic. These multi-channel figures are carefully monitored, useful preparation for the start of satellite broadcasting.

Lever Brothers is a typical multi-brand company highly dependent on TV advertising. It has around 40 brands, but not all of them are supported by heavy advertising. It competes in markets worth about £100 million, for cleaning and hygienic products, both personal and household. The firm spent about £1 million on advertising in 1985, according to Shane Molloy, its marketing director. Of that expenditure, TV took 92 per cent, with most of the rest going on radio and magazines. Much of its advertising material originates in the UK, but it also uses campaign material originated in Germany, Sweden, France and Australia. All the media buying of the Unilever companies in Ireland, which include Lever Brothers, W & C McDonnell, Birds Eye, John West and Brooke Bond Oxo, is done through the media department of SSC & B:Lintas, London, which works alongside the

David Kelly the actor (right) on location for a Pan International commercial for McConnell's in 1968. Left is Brendan Redmond, who directed the film. The advertising link continues: Kelly's son, also David, is an art director with Irish International Advertising and Marketing.

Director John Devis (left), then of Ocean Films, during the shooting of a TV commercial for Crackerjack firelighters at Ardmore Studios, Bray, in June, 1969. On the right are Michael Algar, producer and Eamonn O'Flaherty, art director, Arks Advertising.

617

The RTE site at
Montrose, Dublin,
pictured in the early
1970s, before the
construction of the
radio centre. The
television studios are to
the right of the mast,
the administration
block to the left.
Photograph: RTE.

Noel Cautley about to "knife" Herman van Eelen, the Henri Winterman man, during the shoot for a Winterman's commercial by Cinevision for O'Keeffes.

agencies used by Unilever. In Ireland, it uses six agencies, of which only one, Arks, is Dublin-based. When it reduced TV spending in 1984 on Persil Automatic, its housewife television ratings showed a 30 per cent decline over the previous year. So for this brand in 1985, Lever Brothers decided to maximise ratings and frequency on TV, within a tightly defined budget that was increased by about 17 per cent. Ratings went up by one-third. The brand recovered strongly.

John Devis directed the new campaign for the First National Building Society. For the Harp lager commercials, scripted by Frank Sheerin, and featuring "Sally O'Brien", the desert was recreated at Ardmore Studios. The set included oilfields painted in perspective. The mechanics were fairly straight-forward. Not quite so with the recent FNBS commercial for the Innovation Group. The original script called for a cast of 200, which Devis realised was quite impractical. So he had a four sided set built of which three sides were mirrors. The mirrors, each measuring 14' by 10' were front silvered to give a true image. The mirrors were specially made by A. C. Taylor and when the set was built at Film Lighting Facilities' studio, the nine people reflected perfectly to make 200. A 40 second version was shot on 35mm film and transferred to video for editing; a cut-down version lasting 30 seconds was also made.

Among the famous commercials produced by Pan International was the series to launch Guinness Light, the new formulation drink from St James's Gate that foundered in 1981. The launch cost around £2 million in advertising and other marketing costs. The commercials were directed by Michael Algar and were universally acclaimed. The commercials included footage from NASA in the USA, showing the take-off of an American space rocket.

Some advertising sectors present remarkably similar commercials. In one recent piece of research, a client was shown the tape of one building society commercial, dubbed with the soundtrack from a rival's commercial. He did not spot the anomaly.

Other memorable commercials over the years have included the Barney and Beany cartoons for Batchelors, devised by Brian Cronin's agency. Cronin himself takes credit for transforming the characters from two rather dull packside characters into fully-blown television commercial "personalities". In the early 1980s, Des O'Meara and Partners created enormous public interest in a series of TV commercials shot with Sean Doherty, the then Minister for Justice, in a £165,000 campaign. A TV commercial done by Frank Chambers was the modest TV slide announcing the winner of the Mater Hospitals' pools, which went out on RTE every Saturday night between the end of the nine o'clock news and the start of the *Late Late Show*.

In recent years, 3-Hands washing-up liquid advertising has helped to add humour and entertainment to a household chore not renowned as a housewife's favourite pastime. The key to this consumer appeal and parallel sales success has been that all the fun of the advertising has emanated directly from and revolved around the brand name and the product image.

When Nokia planned the re-launch of 3-Hands in the autumn of 1983 with a product improvement of 33 per cent extra strength, a key consideration in the strategy and planning was whether or not this high impact campaign treatment should be continued.

Exceptional brand and advertising recall has always been achieved by the individual 3-Hands commercials. How could Wilson Hartnell ensure that the "33 per cent stronger" message would not be lost in the "entertainment context" of the new TV commercials? They were made by GPA Films.

Experience with "3-Hands" has underlined the fact that in creative terms the obvious can be the ideal. The mutant 3-handed presenter on TV has scored heavily on branding and recall, so he was a natural (if that word can be used in the circumstances) choice when it came to re-launch the product. This time, however, it was decided to use three different presenters in three separate 10-second commercials.

The message presented was a simple one — "3-Hands is now 33 per cent stronger". Or, in the parlance of Brendan Grace, "33 per cent more powerfuller!" In addition to Brendan, former TV newsreader, Maurice O'Doherty presented "some good news for a change", and Frank Kelly appeared as the campaign progressed.

Once again the video tape Ultimatt technique worked its magic by hiding the owner of the "other hand" — M.R.A. being the ones who saved the expensive and bothersome surgery! Put Maurice, Brendan

Opposite page:
Theo Hogers, a Dutchman, who worked with the Toonder company in Holland, came to Ireland in 1961 to join Martin Toonder in helping to establish a similar studios here, specialising in animation and table top. Subsequently setting up a firm of his own, Cinevision, his productions included the Jacob's Jim Figgerty ads for Irish International shot in Spain, which was the first commercial series, six in total, ever produced for television here. The character Figgerty went to 'Figgeria' to sort out a revolution and to ensure Ireland would get all the figs it wanted. He returned to Dublin with a train of camels and donkeys ladened with figs. In fact, it was Swansea because Dublin could not supply the camels. Cinevision has produced commercials for Rothmans, Consulate, Henri Winterman's, Jacob's Cream Crackers, Schweppes and CIE Expressway.

Ken Tyrrell of Guinness draws the first colour commercial for RTE television in 1971. Also in the photograph, from left: Tom Hardiman, director general, Bill Cavanagh (Association of Advertisers in Ireland), Bobby Gahan and Oliver Walsh (IAPI).

During a sales
conference at RTE,
Peadar Pierce is
pictured on the stairs.
Jack Downey, then
with Janus, commented:
"Religious service at
RTE".

Enjoying a Kinsale
advertising film festival
in the 1970s: Bob
Gahan (RTE), Eileen
Ball (Johnson Bros) and
Peadar Pierce (RTE).

At a Kinsale advertising film festival in the early 1970s, from left: Mr and Mrs Brian Doyle (Player-Wills), Ray O'Keeffe (O'Keeffes), Mr and Mrs Norman McConnell (Aspro-Nicholas), Peadar Pierce (RTE) and Mr and Mrs Noel Cautley (O'Keeffes).

At the Irish Advertising Awards Festival at Dun Laoghaire in September, 1979, New York advertising executive Jerry Della Femina presented awards for Zip firelighters' "Coal Party" TV commercial. In the photograph, from left: Jimmy Murakami (director), with the delegates' award, Frances Swift (producer) with the category award, Michael Algar (managing director, Pan International Films) with the Irish Grand Prix and Jerry Della Femina.

Niel O'Kennedy was in charge of the TV department at O'Kennedy Brindley until his retirement from the agency in 1982.
Photograph: The Irish Times.

Denis Price, star of many horror movies, came to Dublin in 1971 to shoot a TV commercial for Aubrey Fogarty Associates. He is pictured here (right) with Aubrey Fogarty.

In 1986, Johnston, Mooney & O'Brien, the Dublin bakery dating back to 1835, has been updating its image, with the help of its new advertising agency, QMP. As part of the bakery's new promotional drive, it spent £250,000 on advertising its family pan. QMP devised three baker characters, used on all the bakery's

and Frank on the same shoot and a lively day is guaranteed. The out-takes are now collectors' items!

On the technical side, Mike Curley of Wilson Hartnell would like to see a more flexible attitude to crewing on commercials. He is not suggesting for a moment that this in itself will significantly reduce costs on commercials, but it would help. Another area is the degree to which agencies concentrate on technical expertise. A strong idea, reasonably executed, will communicate far more effectively than a complicated or routine idea that has been immaculately executed. How often have production personnel been on shoots where an excessively tricky pack shot, that will occupy the last two seconds of a commercial, involves the production company, agency and client in an inordinate amount of overtime.

Brian Martin of Wilson Hartnell explains how a product doesn't exist in the public mind unless it is advertised on TV. "When we got the Aer Lingus account in 1980, we put the airline on TV and the campaign evolved into the 'Green Bird' theme. With the Chrysler car commercials, the copy line, 'Nice car, Mr Chrysler' became something of a catch phrase. "Not all TV advertising works: Cadburys launched a product called Scrumble, which was a disastrous flop.

The question of women in TV advertising has come to the fore in recent years, perhaps most forcibly with the Glen Abbey episode in 1984. A commercial was prepared by QMP which showed a woman in tights, in a cage. The video had cost about £20,000 to produce, and it passed all the normal copy clearance channels to reach the screen. Nell McCafferty says that there was "a storm of protest" when the commercial was screened. Sources in RTE and the agency world claim that the protests were rather less than a storm, but vociferous, from a well-organised protest lobby. The Campaign Against Sex Exploitation swung into action and protested to RTE, the Advertising Standards Authority and to Glen Abbey. The advertisement was withdrawn by RTE and Anne O'Donnell and two colleagues from the Rape Crisis Centre met with Glen Abbey and QMP representatives. O'Donnell said later that she had not had such a good time since Irishwomen United occupied the offices of the Federated Union of Employers in the mid-1970s.

While RTE admits that the changing role of women in society is being reflected in TV commercials, some women's organisations want still more done to correct what they see as an imbalance. Kate O'Shanahan of the Dublin Women's Centre said in 1985 that male voice-overs were used in most RTE TV commercials. She said: "Women are being told what to buy by an anonymous male voice in almost all station advertisements." The female equivalent of Bill Goulding or Jonathan Ryan has yet to emerge in the Irish commercials' production industry. Ms O'Shanahan also complained about the way women were employed to drape themselves over cars in order to attract male buyers.

packaging and in its advertising; they can be seen here on the set of the TV commercial. Jimmy Murakami was the director. In the photograph are Chris Tiernan (left), the bakery's marketing manager and Terry Pattison, creative director of QMP.

Maurice Pratt, the man in the Quinnsworth TV commercials produced by Des O'Meara & Partners. Pratt, who is now Quinnsworth's marketing manager, used to work in the media department of O'Meara's where he was pictured (below) about 1973.

Basil Singleton, former Ulster Television marketing manager, later managing director, A. V. Browne.

In 1985, there were calls for a women to be appointed to the copy clearance panel at RTE, which examines all RTE advertisement copy for possible infringements of the Code of Standards. The team is made up of Aidan Burns, Peadar Pierce and Brian Pierce. At a 1985 hearing of the Oireachtas Joint Committee on Women's Rights, Madeleine Taylor-Quinn, a Fine Gael deputy for Clare, said that the offensively sexist attitudes of the advertising business had made the hearing necessary. Monica Barnes, a Fine Gael deputy for Dun Laoghaire, said that it was striking that no woman held an executive position in the copy clearance department of RTE. However, she added that the copy clearance team had made a very positive input with its response to the committee. Aidan Burns said the hearing was stimulating and useful.

Sponsorship has returned to broadcasting, in a new format. For instance, *Murphy's Micro Quiz-M,* presented by Mike Murphy, has had much support from the Ford Motor Company. So far, the motor firm has donated cars to the show, for prizes, worth well over £100,000, but it reckons it has got good publicity value for its money. The biggest response ever seen on an RTE TV show was last year, when JWT holidays celebrated its 25th anniversary. In conjunction with RTE a special competition was offered on the *Late Late Show,* with a hefty prize of a free holiday every year for 25 years, worth around £50,000. It drew 900,000 postal entries from 1.2 million viewers.

In 1985, clever media buying by Janus resulted in massive coverage for clients Arnotts. An Ireland-USSR soccer match was being played in Moscow. £500 was spent buying a site at the Lenin Stadium in Moscow. The TV cameras picked up the poster, which was relayed to a huge audience at home in Ireland. Further publicity came when Martyn Turner, *The Irish Times'* cartoonist drew a "special" on the topic for the Saturday supplement in the newspaper. As Michael Nesbitt, Arnott's managing director, said, it was remarkably good advertising value.

The next major challenge to be faced by RTE will be direct broadcasting by satellite. By 1989, when Ireland's direct broadcast satellite is placed in orbit, Irish viewers with dish receivers could be able to receive up to 32 channels. Low powered channels would be received through communal cable links, while high powered transmissions would be received directly. An extensive cabling system, using these transmissions, is planned for the Belfast area and is likely to start in 1987/88. The first channel to be broadcast to European viewers has been Sky Channel, which is received in four million homes and which has over 100 advertisers. RTE reckons it is well placed to cope with the new competition: it has operated against multi-channel competition since its TV service began 25 years ago. Since the early 1970s, cable television has operated in Ireland, making it one of the most cabled countries in Europe. RTE owns the cable operators. At the moment, up to 16 satellite channels can be received here, and the spread of DBS will make the whole country multi-channel. The main drawback is the poor programme content of much satellite broadcasting.

Cinema still plods along, handicapped by the fact that a film has to be prepared for each cinema, whereas one video tape suffices for television. Cinema advertising has held up remarkably well, particularly advertising aimed at the 15-34 age group. The Republic still has 110 cinemas mainly twinned, so the number of screens in use is now about 160. Cinema and General Publicity remains the main cinema advertising contractor in the Republic.

Cinema remains unsurpassed in reaching young up-market adults. The impact of the cinema screen still creates a greater awareness of advertising and as a medium targetted to the elusive young audience it is unrivalled, according to Rank Screen Advertising. Due to the modernisation of many sites, multi-screen cinemas are now well established in the new image of cinema.

The cinemagoer of today remains firmly in the 15-24 age group and has become increasingly selective in the type of films they see. A developing facility for special effects and advanced camera techniques has given the film industry the opportunity to 'reach out' into new dimensions. Films such as *Superman, E.T.* and more recently *2010* and *Return To Oz* show the current expertise and future possibilities for the continued excellence of the 'Big Screen'.

Although the Government does not publish admissions statistics for the Republic, the JNMR Survey data enables the industry to estimate the number of admissions. Based on the 1983/84 survey, there are

A still from the first Lyons' Tea commercials, produced 15 years ago. Agency was McConnell's; the animation was done by Gunther Wulff Studios in Bray. The jingle was composed by Johnny Johnson.

627

A typical satellite in orbit; by the end of this decade, satellite transmissions may have made the whole of Ireland multi-channel.

about nine million admissions per annum (including children). Comparison with other northern European countries show a high cinemagoing population and continued high calibre film product will ensure large audiences for the future.

The cinema audience is centred around the urban areas, and particularly Co. Dublin which, although only 29 per cent of adults live there, has 41 per cent of the cinema audience. Dublin itself is a key market for many goods and services — accounting for a much higher proportion of sales than the population figures would suggest.

A cinema advertising campaign in the Dublin area will cover young people very thoroughly. A 13-week campaign with a 30 second commercial achieves a 51 per cent coverage of the 15-24s, and a 26-week campaign will increase the coverage to 63 per cent. During the same 13-week period, the cinemagoer would average over three visits and the 26-week campaign will raise this figure to almost six visits.

Little did the Lumière Brothers know what they were starting 91 years ago. The cinema may not have developed as a major advertising medium, but television, used in Ireland for the last 25 years, has become the most dominant and persuasive advertising medium the country has ever known. The whole brand marketing strategy of the modern consumer society depends on television, advertisements beamed into almost every home in the country. The Republic now has 918,000 sets, of which 740,000 are colour.

By now, TV has become the most important advertising medium in Ireland; RTE's television revenue in its current financial year will be around £38 million. Adding in the UTV contribution, the spend on TV advertising in Ireland this year will be well over £50 million.

Maurice O'Doherty, the former RTE newsreader, featured in the 1983 TV campaign for 3 Hands washing up liquid, produced by Wilson Hartnell for Nokia.

1978 treatment of 3 Hands washing up liquid commercial by Wilson Hartnell.

CLIENT

Jeyes Limited

PRODUCT/SERVICE

'3-Hands' Washing-Up Liquid

OBJECTIVES

Very strong branding operation for keenly-priced Jeyes contender in highly competitive market.

SPECIAL FACTORS

Product, prior to theme advertising, regarded by housewives as being in the "own brand" spectrum of the market. Need for very distinctive treatment in competition with 'Fairy', 'Quix', etc.

CONCEPT

Unusual 'presenter' approach featuring a three-handed presenter washing up and punching across the product message. Concept derived from the existing brand name. Budget area £11,000 (3 different versions).

COMMENT

Humour plays directly to the br name and the nature of the prod Product now vying for No. 1 spo market.

John Devis, director of many prize-winning TV commercials, including Harp's "Sally O'Brien".

In 1982, Sean Doherty, then Minister for Justice, announced an anti-crime publicity campaign, featuring himself, which had a media spend of around £164,000. Des O'Meara of Des O'Meara and Partners is seen here on the set (left) with Sean Doherty. O'Meara makes no apologies for the campaign in retrospect, which he says was "very justifiable and useful".

Bobby Gahan, assistant director general, RTE. When Telefis Eireann began 25 years ago, he set up the traffic system in the advertisement sales department. *Photograph: RTE.*

The first colour television commercial, in 1971, was for VG, the voluntary group grocery stores. Celebrating another first for McConnell's were from left: Bobby Gahan (RTE), Jill Wagner (then with McConnell's) and Bruce Carswell of VG.

Robert Hardy (centre), the star of All Creatures Great and Small, during the shooting of a TV commercial for ICI Nilverm in 1981. Left is Paul Myers, then a copywriter with McConnell's and Michael Algar, then producer, Pan International Films.

Sometimes, black and white film stock is used for creative impact, as in this commercial filmed in 1984 by Bartle Bogle Hegarty, London, for Levi jeans. The commercial recreated life in the Soviet Union; the campaign was handled in Ireland by Peter Owens and shown on RTE television as well as in cinemas.

Margaret Jennings, now production manager, Ardmore Studios. She has been 25 years in film production.

Mike Curley (centre) of Wilson Hartnell is seen during the set-up of a TV commercial at a local racecourse.

A scene from the Ritz commercials produced in Paris by Young's.

A group from Ulster Television on a visit to Dublin in 1978, from left: Jim Creagh, Bobby Gahan (RTE), Brendan O'Regan (Co-operation North), Mike Hutchinson (UTV sales controller, London) and R. B. "Brum" Henderson (then managing director, now chairman).

Pictured at a recent *Late Late Show,* **two ex-**Synge Street pupils, Gay Byrne and Tommy Ellis.

Opposite page:
The computer graphics' facilities at Windmill Lane Pictures.

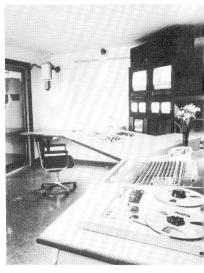

J. R. Ewing (Larry Hagman) on a "shoot" for a Department of Agriculture commercial in September, 1985, with the late Brendan Byrne, producer (left) and Don O'Connell, Doherty Advertising (centre). During that visit to Ireland, he also starred in an anti-smoking commercial for the Health Education Bureau.

Cork multi-channel TV televised many events during the Cork 800 celebrations in 1985. Its production team is seen in action here at a City Hall event. The network carries a limited amount of local advertising. Some BBC shows relayed by it are punctuated by commercials. Its managing director is Jim O'Shea, whose previous media experience included the Sunday World and the Sunday Tribune mark one.

Jimmy Murakami is one of the best-known commercials' directors in Ireland. He started his career in the USA, where he worked for United Productions of America, which made the Mr Magoo cartoons. From there, he worked on documentaries and commercials in Europe. His first experience of Ireland was 15 years ago, when he worked on the shooting of The Red Baron film. His first experience of commercials' production in Ireland was with Bob Nealon of Padbury's on a campaign for Youghal Carpets. Then came other agencies, such as CDP (Bank of Ireland), Cronins (Bass and Toyota), Doherty's (Dairyland and Sadolin), Hunter's (Knorr) and O'Connor O'Sullivan (Carlsberg). In 1985, he directed the award-winning 'Dogs and Sheep' commercial for Doherty's on behalf of the Department of Agriculture. He likes humorous commercials, such as the Hamlet series, a preference dating back to his time in animation, when the themes were slanted towards fun.

634

Stills from Levi Strauss
"Russian" commercial.

635

Martyn Turner cartoon published in The Irish Times on October 19, 1985, inspired by the Arnott's site placed at the Lenin Stadium, Moscow, for an Ireland-USSR televised football match. Janus booked the space to reach Irish TV viewers for a mere £500.

James Morris (left) and Russ Russell editing at Windmill Lane.

Maxwell House is a classic instance of a brand built on television. The instant coffee was launched in Ireland in 1957 and was advertised on Telefis Eireann on the first full day of transmission, January 1, 1962. In those days, the product was only available in tins. The two stills (left) are from 1962 commercials, which highlighted the American origins of the brand. Some early Maxwell House commercials, with outstanding jingles, had the copy line: "sniffable, whiffable, oh so get withable." The third commercial, used about 1967, featured Bruce Forsyth, the comedian. The brand went colour on RTE in 1972. Then the brand used a Brazilian theme, The Maxwell House "Shake", (overleaf) to show the coffee's origins. In the early 1970s, Personality was brought back to the advertising in the shape of David Niven. For the last three years, the advertising has featured Pauline Collins and John Alderton; only pack shots were changed for Ireland. According to Isobel Rankine, the account executive at Wilson Hartnell responsible for the brand, the new campaign starting about now will be the first produced entirely in Ireland for Maxwell House, According to Sean Murray, in charge of marketing in Ireland for Maxwell House, the instant coffee market here is worth £15 million a year, mostly branded. Maxwell House, with its warm, family image, claims about 40 per cent. Earlier this year, Alfred Bird & Sons Ireland (part of General Foods) launched the Master Blend range of instant coffee, which in a unique production process, captures pieces of ground coffee in the granules. The firm also markets Café HAG decaffeinated coffee; according to Murray, this market represents 6 per cent of the overall coffee sector, but is growing fast. Overall, the firm spends over £400,000 a year promoting all its coffee brands.

Photographs: Wilson Hartnell.

Channel 4 began transmissions in Northern Ireland in 1982; although only a small number of potential viewers in the North cannot yet receive the channel, complete coverage will be attained by 1987. Although Channel 4 is funded by subscription through the IBA, with UTV contributing some programme content, the Ulster Television sales team sells advertising time on the channel. Audiences on Channel 4 are younger and more specialised; the separate rate card reflects its smaller rating. Channel 4 has proved a useful and inexpensive means of introducing new local advertisers to television. A 10 second slot can cost as little as £26, while the current peak rate for 60 seconds is £1,200.

639

Postscript

FORECASTING THE FUTURE is fun, but dangerous. How many predictions will come true and in what precise form? The future of advertising and communications exercises many minds in the industry, for everyone is keen to know how the future is going to be scheduled. Forty years ago, few people in the industry forecast the huge growth in broadcasting, radio and television. No one imagined Ireland's entry into the European Economic Community, with the vast impact that single event has had not alone on advertising and marketing, but on social mores and the very structure of society.

The advertising industry in Ireland is small by comparison with that in other, larger industrialised countries in the Western economic system. Globally, the advertising industry currently turns over $160 billion; in Ireland, the advertising business turns over somewhere in the region of £100 million, a minute fraction of the worldwide spend. Yet Ireland is as receptive to new trends as any other country and the pace of change in years to come will be no less hectic. One future aphorism seems likely to come true: as the nature of work changes so rapidly (witness the growth of flexitime) and computer enables more people to work at home, leisure time activities will become more dominant. In 15 years' time, the 30 hour week could become the norm and if it does, advertising of many extra leisure pursuits could become more significant. Holidays, travel, sport, home improvements, all could be even bigger areas for advertising spending than now. More working people with more leisure time could become a big bonus to the advertising industry, but on the reverse, what about the seemingly unreducible pool of unemployment? Quarter of a million are effectively removed from the consumer society and are of little use as a catchment area for advertisers. Will their situation change, or will technological change mean simply bigger dole queues, with advertisers selling to fewer potential customers?

The advent of mini-computers is important: 60 and 70 years ago, the introduction of the motor car was considered elitist. Few people could afford to own cars and using these new-fangled machines was thought beyond the ability or concern of most people. Today, everyone takes the motor car for granted, like running water. A world without cars is considered the ultimate horror, just as a world without the horse buggy was unthinkable less than a century ago. In a decade or two to come, everyone will use computer terminals with as much ease as people today use cars. A terminal in every home could mean many different types of work being done at home: the already dissolving divide between home and office/factory will break down much more. Shopping patterns, too, could change. Home terminals could soon allow people to do exactly what kind of shopping they want at home. There are suggestions that in the not too distant future, holography will be used to "show" people larger goods, like pieces of furniture, in the comfort of their sitting rooms. Will the large, multi-unit shopping unit of today become obsolete?

Arm-in-arm with the development in computer technology goes the advance of television. Already, satellite television is with us and viewers with reception dishes can pick up some 20 channels from Europe and the USA. More does not mean better: the biggest drawback in satellite broadcasting is the poor quality of nearly all programming. This lack of quality could make satellite TV as much of a passing phase as the video recorder. Two years ago, video recorders were the passion of the moment: now, the enthusiasm has waned, although videos still have their uses. In five years' time, will satellite TV be well entrenched, or have become just another passing fad? Local radio could become "live" in the next few years. With the speed of today's communications, trends are changing faster than ever before in history. Before television, fashion trends, could last ten years; now, they are lucky to last ten weeks.

Some experts in the industry believe that with the continued development of television and its impact on a generation that have, for the first time, been weaned since infancy on it, people raised in the non-linear style are going out of the habit of reading. Images and sounds are what count, the stronger the better. Will the written word be banished in less than a century? The pessimists estimate that at the present rate of "progress", newspapers, books and other forms of printed media will be almost extinct. Copywriters will cater only for the spoken word: preparing copy for print reproduction will be a task of the past. Or will the present vehicles for the printed word be transmuted into new variations not as yet invented?

As Nick van Vliet of Wilson Hartnell forecast in that firm's centenary booklet in 1979, flawless and comprehensive communications will have been established. Anyone will be able to have aural and visual contact with anyone else, anywhere in the world. The drive to promote more widespread means of advertising communication will mean a drive to produce more and more semi-global brands using multi-market advertising. More mega brands will be produced, with less individuality for each national market, yet this push towards pan-European or even pan-Global advertising and marketing may throw up a reverse effect: more regional individuality. Ballygowan spring water is a very Irish product that has ousted a multi-national product from market leadership. With more internationalism in advertising, will there be greater incentives for more such individually Irish brands?

Consumers are likely to be far more critical of advertising and products. The present demand for "pure" food is symptomatic of this critical trend: it seems unlikely to revert into the old-style bad eating

641

habits. Will consumers react less positively to exhortations to buy, strident and blasting into the home? Will the subtlety of Japanese advertising become a norm for the industry? Rather than following the American ways of cajoling consumers, Japanese advertisers approach consumers with kanjo (feeling) and go for entertaining, soft sell tactics, so that Japanese television viewers rush to view the commercials, rather than zap them.

On the home front, the trend of recent years for the biggest advertising appropriations to come from within the State sector seems unlikely to be reversed. The State now plays too central a rôle in the structure of the economy for that influence to readily fade: State influence on and control over the advertising industry has assumed proportions that would have been dismissed as absurd 20 years ago. Even the main media, radio and television, are largely State controlled. This influence and regulation may make it harder for agencies to be creative and for marketing managers to encourage originality. Brand successes, with the opportunities those successes offer to the advertising industry, may happen more in export markets than at home. Perhaps the biggest new brand success in the commercial economy over the last 20 years has been Bailey's Irish Cream: the scale of that success was simply impossible on the home market. Like the monks of old, taking their learning to Europe, Irish advertising may find its true outlet in foreign markets, as brand managers and export managers enjoy rewarding rôle mingling-abroad.

Restrictions on the local advertising industry take their toll. As Peter O'Keeffe of CDP has pointed out, the shortfall in numbers of young people being trained into the industry must have its effects. He believes that the lack of new, young trained people in advertising will work to the benefit of foreign-created campaigns. Already, some 60 per cent of advertisement material used on RTE is produced outside the country: will that figure increase as the cost and creative advantages fall more and more to the multi-national agency working in tandem with multi-national brand managers? Will there be a reaction against the growing internationalism? Will the small, highly creative hot shop suddenly come back into fashion?

Whatever happens, discovering the future as the industry heads into a new century — provided someone, somewhere doesn't press the wrong nuclear button — will be fun. Look how much the industry has changed in the last two decades. The next two cannot fail to be as exciting and momentous.

Sources

Personal recollections provided much of the research material for this book. Advertisers, advertising agencies and many sections of the media, both print and electronic, provided much material from their own archives. The National Library, Dublin, was a useful source of information, while many illustrations of newspaper advertisements were supplied by the Newspaper Library, Colindale, London. The following printed sources were consulted.

Advertiser's ABC. London, 1897.
Advertising. Gillian Preston. London, 1971.
Advertising in Britain. T. R. Nevett. London, 1977.
Advertising inside out. Philip Kleinman. London, 1977.
Blessings in Disguise. Alec Guinness. London, 1985.
Cigarette Pack Art. Chris Mullen. London, 1979.
Dictionary of Irish Biography. Henry Boylan. Dublin, 1978.
Dundalk in the Emergency. Victor Whitmarsh. Dundalk, 1980.
History of Advertising from the Earliest Times. Henry Sampson. London, 1874.
History of the Irish Newspaper, 1685-1760. Robert Munter. Cambridge, 1967.
ICAD volumes. Dublin. 1979, 1980, 1982.
Ireland from old photographs. Maurice Gorham. London, 1971.
Irish Marketing Journal, Dublin.
Leopold Bloom, a biography. Peter Costello. Dublin, 1981.
Lost Dublin. Frederick Dwyer. Dublin, 1981.
Lost Ireland. Laurence O'Connor. Dublin, 1984.
Marketing Opinion, Dublin.
The Book of Guinness Advertising. Brian Sibley. London, 1985.
The Complete Guide to Advertising. Torin Douglas. London, 1984.
The Image Makers. William Myers. London, 1984.
The Mirror Makers. Stephen Fox. New York, 1985.
The Newspaper Book. Hugh Oram. Dublin, 1983.
The Press in Ireland. Stephen J. M. Brown. Dublin, 1937.
This is My Life. Eamonn Andrews. London, 1968.
Ulster Tatler. Ron Chapman profile by Kevin Magee. December, 1984.
Wheels and Deals. John O'Donovan. Dublin, 1983.
World Advertising Review, 1985. Ed. Philip Kleinman. London, 1985.

Statistics on Advertising

1958

The following statement sets out the results of a statistical inquiry covering the advertising business handled by Irish advertising agencies in the year 1958. Receipts and expenses connected with any ancillary business activity such as publishing have been excluded. In all, 20 establishments were covered by the inquiry.

Individual returns were completed for the business year most nearly conforming to the calendar year 1958, i.e. business years ending between July 1, 1958 and June 30, 1959. Over 90 per cent of the total business relates to accounting years ending in the period December 31, 1958 - March 31, 1959 inclusive.

Gross amounts charged to clients, including any service fees	Amount 1958
	£000
(A) **Space etc.**	
(i) Press	1,723
(ii) Billposting, including transport advertising	76
(iii) Radio time	57
(iv) Film screen time	45
(v) Printing	80
(vi) Other	38
(B) **Production**	
(i) Radio programme production	56
(ii) Other production work (e.g. typesetting, blockmaking, artwork, films, etc.)	157
(C) **Other**	
Other work (e.g. research) not shown above	5
Total amount charged to clients	**2,237**
Remuneration	
Total payments of wages and salaries during the year, including fees to directors working in the business	199

Persons engaged in April, including those sick or on leave	Number 1958
Proprietors (including directors) working in business	45
Paid employees working in business:	
(i) full-time	321
(ii) part-time	21
Total number of persons working business in April	**387**

Figures were not published for 1959.

1960, 1961, 1962

The following statement sets out the results of a statistical inquiry covering the advertising business handled by Irish advertising agencies in the year 1962. Receipts and expenses connected with any ancillary business activity such as publishing have been excluded. In all, 26 establishments were covered by the inquiry.

Individual returns were completed for the business year most nearly conforming to the calendar year in question, i.e. business year ending in the period July 1, 1962-June 30, 1963. About 77 per cent of the total business relates to accounting years ending in the period December 31-March 31 inclusive.

The results of previous similar inquiries for the years 1960 and 1961 have been included for purposes of comparison. The figures for 1962 include particulars for a few establishments which carried on business in 1960 and 1961 but which did not furnish returns at the inquiries for those years. A small part of the expansion in the business as shown by the 1962 figures is due to this cause.

Gross amounts charged to clients, including any service fees	Amount		
	1960	1961	1962
	£000		
(A) Space etc.			
(i) Press	2,195	2,409	2,693
(ii) Billposting, including transport advertising	87	101	153
(iii) Radio time	88	130	146
(iv) Television time	13	46	691
(v) Film screen time	60	49	35
(vi) Printing	145	149	183
(vii) Other	57	64	42
(B) Production			
(i) Radio programme production	59	66	112
(ii) Television and other film production fees including artistes' fees and use fees ...	2	59	150
(iii) Other production work (e.g. typesetting, blockmaking, artwork, films, etc.)	242	274	307
(C) Other			
Other work (e.g. research) not shown above	26	26	67
Total amount charged to clients	**2,972**	**3,372**	**4,580**

Remuneration			
Total payments of wages and salaries during the year, including fees to directors working in the business	264	313	412

Persons engaged in April, including those sick or on leave	Number		
	1960	1961	1962
Proprietors (including directors) working in business	52	53	64
Paid employees working in business:			
(i) full-time	393	424	523
(ii) part-time	29	52	58
Total number of persons working business in April	**474**	**529**	**645**

1963

The following statement sets out the results of a statistical inquiry covering the advertising business handled by Irish advertising agencies in the year 1963. Receipts and expenses connected with any ancillary business activity such as publishing have been excluded. In all, 27 establishments were covered by the inquiry.

Individual returns were completed for the business year most nearly conforming to the calendar year in question, i.e. business year ending in the period July 1, 1963 - June 30, 1964. About 89 per cent of the total business relates to accounting years ending in the period December 31, - March 31 inclusive.

Gross amounts charged to clients, including any service fees	Amount 1963
	£000
(A) Space etc.	
(i) Press … … … … … … … … … … … …	3,011
(ii) Billposting, including transport advertising … … … …	152
(iii) Radio time … … … … … … … … … …	156
(iv) Television time … … … … … … … … …	1,031
(v) Film screen time … … … … … … … … …	22
(vi) Printing … … … … … … … … … … …	192
(vii) Other … … … … … … … … … … …	50
(B) Production	
(i) Radio programme production … … … … … …	106
(ii) Television and other film production fees including artistes' fees and use fees … … … … …	189
(iii) Other production work (e.g. typesetting, blockmaking, artwork, films, etc.) … … … … …	311
(C) Other	
Other work (e.g. research) not shown above	91
Total amount charged to clients	**5,311**

Remuneration	
Total payments of wages and salaries during the year, including fees to directors working in the business … … … … … … … … … … …	490

Persons engaged in April, including those sick or on leave	Number 1963
Proprietors (including directors) working in business … … … … … … … … … … …	71
Paid employees working in business:	
(i) full-time … … … … … … … … … …	567
(ii) part-time … … … … … … … … … …	64
Total number of persons working business in April	**702**

1964, 1965

The following statement sets out the results of a statistical inquiry covering the advertising business handled by Irish advertising agencies in the year 1965. Receipts and expenses connected with any ancillary business activity such as publishing have been excluded. In all, 28 establishments were covered by the inquiry.

Individual returns were completed for the business year most nearly conforming to the calendar year in question, i.e. business year ending in the period July, 1965 - June 30, 1966. About 86 per cent of the total business relates to accounting years ending in the period December 31 - March 31 inclusive.

Gross amounts charged to clients, including any service fees	Amount	
	1964	1965
	£000	
(A) Space etc.		
(i) Press	3,386	3,554
(ii) Billposting, including transport advertising	139	148
(iii) Radio time	174	165
(iv) Television time	1,519	1,730
(v) Film screen time	27	31
(vi) Printing	310	339
(vii) Other	82	72
(B) Production		
(i) Radio programme production	101	100
(ii) Television and other film production fees including artistes' fees and use fees	201	281
(iv) Other production work (e.g. typesetting, blockmaking, artwork, films, etc.)	402	497
(C) Other		
Other work (e.g. research) not shown above	54	66
Total amount charged to clients	**6,394**	**6,985**
Remuneration		
Total payments of wages and salaries during the year, including fees to directors working in the business	627*	719

Persons engaged in April, including those sick or on leave	Number	
	1964	1965
Proprietors (including directors) working in business	73*	82
Paid employees working in business:		
(i) full-time	634	713
(ii) part-time	55	22
Total number of persons working business in April	**762***	**817**

*Revised

1966

The following statement sets out the results of a statistical inquiry covering the advertising business handled by Irish advertising agencies in the year 1966. Receipts and expenses connected with any ancillary business activity such as publishing have been excluded. In all, 28 establishments were covered by the inquiry.

Individual returns were completed for the business year most nearly conforming to the calendar year in question, i.e. business year ending in the period July 1, 1966 - June 30, 1967. About 90 per cent of the total business relates to accounting years ending in the period December 31 - March 31 inclusive.

	Amount 1966
Gross amounts charged to clients, including any service fees	
	£000
(A) **Space etc.**	
(i) Press	3,825
(ii) Billposting, including transport advertising	147
(iii) Radio time	218
(iv) Television time	2,010
(v) Film screen time	39
(vi) Printing	486
(vii) Other	104
(B) **Production**	
(i) Radio programme production	88
(ii) Television and other film production fees including artistes' fees and use fees	305
(iii) Other production work (e.g. typesetting, blockmaking, artwork, films, etc.)	492
(C) **Other**	
Other work (e.g. research) not shown above	85
Total amount charged to clients	**7,797**
Remuneration	
Total payments of wages and salaries during the year, including fees to directors working in the business	875

	Number 1966
Persons engaged in April, including those sick or on leave	
Proprietors (including directors) working in business	87
Paid employees working in business:	
(i) full-time	752
(ii) part-time	20
Total number of persons working business in April	**859**

1967, 1968

The following statement sets out the results of a statistical inquiry covering the advertising business handled by Irish advertising agencies in the year 1968. Receipts and expenses connected with any ancillary business activity such as publishing have been excluded. In all, 29 establishments were covered by the inquiry.

Individual returns were completed for the business year most nearly conforming to the calendar year in question, i.e. business year ending within the period July, 1968 - June 30, 1969. About 85 per cent of the total business relates to accounting years ending in the period December 31 - March 31 inclusive.

	Amount	
Gross amounts charged to clients, including any service fees	1967	1968
	£000	
(A) Space etc.		
(i) Press	3,777	4,276
(ii) Billposting, including transport advertising	190	236
(iii) Radio time	244	317
(iv) Television time	2,404	2,692
(v) Film screen time	100	78
(vi) Printing	515	675
(vii) Other	139	190
(B) Production		
(i) Radio programme production	106	110
(ii) Television and other film production fees including artistes' fees and use fees	342	395
(iv) Other production work (e.g. typesetting, blockmaking, artwork, films, etc.)	499	610
(C) Other		
Other work (e.g. research) not shown above	86	134
Total amount charged to clients	**8,401**	**9,714**
Remuneration		
Total payments of wages and salaries during the year, including fees to directors working in the business	976	1,087

	Number	
Persons engaged in April, including those sick or on leave	1967	1968
Proprietors (including directors) working in business	89	90
Paid employees working in business:		
(i) full-time	774	825
(ii) part-time	24	21
Total number of persons working business in April	**887**	**936**

1969, 1970, 1971

The following statement sets out the results of a statistical inquiry covering the advertising business handled by Irish advertising agencies in the year 1971. Receipts and expenses connected with any ancillary business activity such as publishing have been excluded. In all, 34 establishments were covered by the inquiry.

Individual returns were completed for the business year most nearly conforming to the calendar year in question, i.e. business year ending in the period July 1, 1971-June 30, 1972. About 76 per cent of the total business relates to accounting years ending in the period December 31-March 31 inclusive.

Gross amounts charged to clients, including any service fees	Amount		
	1969	1970	1971
	£000		
(A) Space etc.			
(i) Press	4,828	5,523	5,852
(ii) Billposting, including transport advertising	260	241	302
(iii) Radio time	415	513	691
(iv) Television time	2,908	3,022	3,091
(v) Film screen time	84	88	111
(vi) Other	234	152	95
(B) Production			
(i) Radio programme production	128	131	177
(ii) Television and other film production fees including artistes' fees and use fees ...	607	663	598
(iii) Printing	635	643	729
(iv) Other production work (e.g. typesetting, blockmaking, artwork, films, etc.)	706	1,018	1,039
(C) Other			
Other work (e.g. research) not shown above	127	157	157
Total amount charged to clients	**10,932**	**12,150**	**12,845**
Remuneration			
Total payments of wages and salaries during the year, including fees to directors working in the business	1,260	1,432	1,554

Persons engaged in April, including those sick or on leave	Number		
	1969	1970	1971
Proprietors (including directors) working in business	97	103	100
Paid employees working in business:			
(i) full-time	846	881	875
(ii) part-time	13	16	15
Total number of persons working business in April	**956**	**1,000**	**990**

1972

The following statement sets out the results of a statistical inquiry covering the advertising business handled by Irish advertising agencies in the year 1972. Receipts and expenses connected with any ancillary business activity such as publishing have been excluded. In all, 34 establishments were covered by the inquiry.

Individual returns were completed for the business year most nearly conforming to the calendar year in question, i.e. business year ending within the period July 1, 1972 - June 30, 1973. About 79 per cent of the total business relates to accounting years ending in the period December 31 - March 31 inclusive.

	Amount 1972 £000
Gross amounts charged to clients, including any service fees	
(A) **Space etc.**	
(i) Press	6,885
(ii) Billposting, including transport advertising	375
(iii) Radio time	885
(iv) Television time	3,742
(v) Film screen time	144
(vi) Other	51
(B) **Production**	
(i) Radio programme production	141
(ii) Television and other film production fees including artistes' fees and use fees	688
(iii) Printing	864
(iv) Other production work (e.g. typesetting, blockmaking, artwork, films, etc.)	1,339
(C) **Other**	
Other work (e.g. research) not shown above	353
Total amount charged to clients	**15,468**
Remuneration	
Total payments of wages and salaries during the year, including fees to directors working in the business	1,658

	Number 1972
Persons engaged in April, including those sick or on leave	
Proprietors (including directors) working in business	107
Paid employees working in business:	
(i) full-time	837
(ii) part-time	22
Total number of persons working business in April	**966**

1973

The following statement sets out the results of a statistical inquiry covering the advertising business handled by Irish advertising agencies in the year 1973. Receipts and expenses connected with any ancillary business activity such as publishing are excluded. In all, 34 establishments were covered by this 1973 inquiry.

Individual returns were completed for the business year most nearly conforming to the calendar year in question, i.e. business year ending within the period July 1, 1973 - June 30, 1974. About 74 per cent of the total business relates to accounting years ending in the period December 31 - March 31 inclusive.

	Amount 1973
Gross amounts charged to clients, including any service fees	£000
(A) **Space etc.**	
(i) Press … … … … … … … … … … … …	8,322
(ii) Billposting, including transport advertising … … … …	441
(iii) Radio time … … … … … … … … … …	1,172
(iv) Television time … … … … … … … … …	4,426
(v) Film screen time … … … … … … … …	144
(vi) Other … … … … … … … … … … …	96
(B) **Production**	
(i) Radio programme production … … … … … …	246
(ii) Television and other film production fees including artistes' fees and use fees … … … … … …	831
(iii) Printing … … … … … … … … … …	900
(iv) Other production work (e.g. typesetting, blockmaking, artwork, films, etc.) … … … … …	1,306
(C) **Other**	
Other work (e.g. research, promotions) not shown above … …	345
Total amount charged to clients	**18,228**
Remuneration	
Total payments of wages and salaries during the year, including fees to directors working in the business … … … … … … … … … … … …	1,969

	Number 1973
Persons engaged in April, including those sick or on leave	
Proprietors (including directors) working in business … … … … … … … … … … …	90
Paid employees working in business:	
(i) full-time … … … … … … … … … …	850
(ii) part-time … … … … … … … … …	17
Total number of persons working business in April	**957**

1974

The following statement sets out the results of a statistical inquiry covering the advertising business handled by Irish advertising agencies in the year 1974. Receipts and expenses connected with any ancillary business activity such as publishing are excluded. In all, 33 establishments were covered by this 1974 inquiry.

Individual returns were completed for the business year most nearly conforming to the calendar year in question, i.e. business year ending within the period July 1, 1974 - June 30, 1975. About 78 per cent of the total business relates to accounting years ending in the period December 31 - March 31 inclusive.

		Amount 1974
Gross amounts charged to clients, including any service fees		£000
(A)	**Space etc.**	
	(i) Press	9,342
	(ii) Billposting, including transport advertising	547
	(iii) Radio time	1,301
	(iv) Television time	4,895
	(v) Film screen time	180
	(vi) Other	16
(B)	**Production**	
	(i) Radio programme production	232
	(ii) Television and other film production fees including artistes' fees and use fees	957
	(iii) Printing	1,283
	(iv) Other production work (e.g. typesetting, blockmaking, artwork, films, etc.)	1,480
(C)	**Other**	
	Other work (e.g. research, promotions) not shown above	314
	Total amount charged to clients	**20,546**

	Amount 1974 £000
Remuneration	
Total payments of wages and salaries during the year, including fees to directors working in the business	2,273

	Number 1974
Persons engaged in April, including those sick or on leave	
Proprietors (including directors) working in business	104
Paid employees working in business:	
(i) full-time	796
(ii) part-time	23
Total number of persons working business in April	**923**

1975

The following statement sets out the results of a statistical inquiry covering the advertising business handled by Irish advertising agencies in the year 1975. Receipts and expenses connected with any ancillary business activity such as publishing are excluded. In all, 33 establishments were covered by this 1975 inquiry.

Individual returns were completed for the business year most nearly conforming to the calendar year in question, i.e. business year ending within the period July 1, 1975 - June 30, 1976. About 76 per cent of the total business relates to accounting years ending in the period December 31 - March 31 inclusive.

	Amount 1975 £000
Gross amounts charged to clients, including any service fees	
(A) Space etc.	
(i) Press	10,143
(ii) Billposting, including transport advertising	717
(iii) Radio time	1,745
(iv) Television time	5,529
(v) Film screen time	198
(vi) Other	101
(B) Production	
(i) Radio programme production	231
(ii) Television and other film production fees including artistes' fees and use fees	1,525
(iii) Printing	1,198
(iv) Other production work (e.g. typesetting, blockmaking, artwork, films, etc.)	1,339
(C) Other	
Other work (e.g. research, promotions) not shown above	242
Total amount charged to clients	**22,968**
Remuneration	
Total payments of wages and salaries during the year, including fees to directors working in the business	2,462

	Number 1975
Persons engaged in April, including those sick or on leave	
Proprietors (including directors) working in business	112
Paid employees working in business:	
(i) full-time	728
(ii) part-time	21
Total number of persons working business in April	**861**

1976

The following statement sets out the results of a statistical inquiry covering the advertising business handled by Irish advertising agencies in the year 1976. Receipts and expenses connected with any ancillary business activity such as publishing are excluded. In all, 33 establishments were covered by this 1976 inquiry.

Individual returns were completed for the business year most nearly conforming to the calendar year in question, i.e. business year ending within the period July 1, 1976 - June 30, 1977. About 89 per cent of the total business relates to accounting years ending in the period December 31 - March 31, inclusive.

		Amount
Gross amounts charged to clients, including any service fees		1976
		£000
(A) **Space etc.**		
(i)	Press	12,540
(ii)	Billposting, including transport advertising	1,062
(iii)	Radio time	1,919
(iv)	Television time	7,542
(v)	Film screen time	201
(vi)	Other	23
(B) **Production**		
(i)	Radio programme production	241
(ii)	Television and other film production fees including artistes' fees and use fees	1,803
(iii)	Printing	1,244
(iv)	Other production work (e.g. typesetting, blockmaking, artwork, films, etc.)	1,817
(C) **Other**		
	Other work (e.g. research, promotions) not shown above	695
	Total gross amount charged to clients	**29,088**
	Remuneration	
	Total payments of wages and salaries during the year, including fees to directors working in the business	2,897

	Number
Persons engaged in April, including those sick or on leave	1976
Proprietors (including directors) working in business	112
Paid employees working in business:	
(i) full-time	730
(ii) part-time	28
Total number of persons working business in April	**870**

1977

The following statement sets out the results of a statistical inquiry covering the advertising business handled by Irish advertising agencies in the year 1977. Receipts and expenses connected with any ancillary business activity such as publishing are excluded. A total of 37 agencies were covered in the 1977 inquiry.

Individual returns were completed for the accounting year closest to the calendar year 1977, i.e. accounting years ending between July 1, 1977 - June 30, 1978. About 83 per cent of the total gross amount charged to clients relates to accounting years ending in the period December 31, 1977 - March 31, 1978 inclusive.

		Amount 1977 £000
Gross amounts charged to clients, including any service fees		
(A)	**Space etc.**	
	(i) Press	15,862
	(ii) Billposting, including transport advertising	1,382
	(iii) Radio time	2,856
	(iv) Television time	9,263
	(v) Film screen time	403
	(vi) Other	158
(B)	**Production**	
	(i) Radio programme production	483
	(ii) Television and other film production fees including artistes' fees and use fees	1,933
	(iii) Printing	2,125
	(iv) Other production work (e.g. typesetting, blockmaking, artwork, films, etc.)	2,715
(C)	**Other**	
	Other work (e.g. research, promotions) not shown above	834
	Total gross amount charged to clients	**38,014**

	Amount £000
Remuneration	
Total payments of wages and salaries during the year, including fees to directors working in the business	3,608

	Number 1977
Persons engaged in April, including those sick or on leave	
Proprietors (including directors) working in business	118
Paid employees working in business:	
(i) full-time	760
(ii) part-time	17
Total number of persons working business in April	**895**

1978

The following statement sets out the results of a statistical inquiry covering the advertising business handled by Irish advertising agencies in the year 1978. Receipts and expenses connected with any ancillary business activity such as publishing are excluded. A total of 31 agencies were covered in the 1978 inquiry.

Individual returns were completed for the accounting year closest to the calendar year 1978. About 84 per cent of the total gross amount charged to clients relates to accounting years ending in the period December 31 1978 and March 31 1979 inclusive.

		Amount 1978 £000
Gross amounts charged to clients, including any service fees		
(A)	**Space etc.**	
	(i) Press	20,076
	(ii) Billposting, including transport advertising	2,294
	(iii) Radio time	3,422
	(iv) Television time	12,226
	(v) Film screen time	308
	(vi) Other	67
(B)	**Production**	
	(i) Radio programme production	383
	(ii) Television and other film production fees including artistes' fees and use fees	2,501
	(iii) Printing	2,709
	(iv) Other production work (e.g. typesetting, blockmaking, artwork, films, etc.)	3,520
(C)	**Other**	
	Other work (e.g. research) not shown above	855
	Total amount charged to clients	**48,362**
	Remuneration	
	Total payments of wages and salaries during the year, including fees to directors working in the business	4,845

	Number 1978
Persons engaged in April, including those sick or on leave	
Proprietors (including directors) working in business	133
Paid employees working in business:	
(i) full-time	766
(ii) part-time	34
Total number of persons working business in April	**933**

1979

The following statement sets out the results of a statistical inquiry covering the advertising business handled by Irish advertising agencies in the year 1979. Receipts and expenses connected with any ancillary business activity such as publishing are excluded. In all, 33 agencies were covered in the 1979 inquiry.

Individual returns were completed for the accounting year closest to the calendar year 1979. About 84 per cent of the total gross amount charged relates to accounting years ending between December 31, 1979 - March 31, 1980 inclusive.

	Amount 1979
Gross amounts charged to clients, including any service fees	£000
(A) **Space etc.**	
(i) Press	26,410
(ii) Billposting, including transport advertising	2,698
(iii) Radio time	4,724
(iv) Television time	15,542
(v) Film screen time	250
(vi) Other	27
(B) **Production**	
(i) Radio programme production	595
(ii) Television and other film production fees including artistes' fees and use fees	2,993
(iii) Printing	3,509
(iv) Other production work (e.g. typesetting, blockmaking, artwork, films, etc.)	4,693
(C) **Other**	
Other work (e.g. research, promotions) not shown above	1,586
Total gross amount charged to clients	**63,027**
Remuneration	
Total payments of wages and salaries during the year, including fees to directors working in the business	6,099

	Number 1979
Persons engaged in April, including those sick or on leave	
Proprietors (including directors) working in business	144
Paid employees working in business:	
(i) full-time	858
(ii) part-time	19
Total number of persons working business in April	**1,021**

1980

The following statement sets out the results of a statistical inquiry covering the advertising business handled by Irish advertising agencies in the year 1980. Receipts and expenses connected with any ancillary business activity such as publishing are excluded. The 1980 results cover 34 agencies which have responded to date.

Individual returns were completed for the accounting year closest to the calendar year 1980. About 83 per cent of the total gross amount charged to clients relates to accounting years ending between December 31, 1980 - March 31, 1981 inclusive.

	Amount 1980
Gross amounts charged to clients, including any service fees	£000
(A) **Space etc.**	
(i) Press	29,860
(ii) Billposting, including transport advertising	2,775
(iii) Radio time	5,863
(iv) Television time	17,911
(v) Film screen time	344
(vi) Other	144
(B) **Production**	
(i) Radio programme production	680
(ii) Television and other film production fees including artistes' fees and use fees	3,754
(iii) Printing	3,772
(iv) Other production work (e.g. typesetting, blockmaking, artwork, films, etc.)	5,496
(C) **Other**	
Other work (e.g. research, promotions) not shown above	1,031
Total gross amount charged to clients	**71,631**
Remuneration	
Total payments of wages and salaries during the year, including fees to directors working in the business	7,011

	Number 1980
Persons engaged in April, including those sick or on leave	
Proprietors (including directors) working in business	135
Paid employees working in business:	
(i) full-time	846
(ii) part-time	14
Total number of persons working business in April	**995**

1981

The following statement sets out the results of a statistical inquiry covering the advertising business handled by Irish advertising agencies in the year 1981. Receipts and expenses connected with any ancillary business activity such as publishing are excluded. The 1981 results cover 32 agencies which have responded to-date out of the total number of 52 known to have been operating in that year.

Individual returns were completed for the accounting year closest to the calendar year 1981. About 83 per cent of the total gross amount charged to clients relates to accounting years ending between December 31, 1981 and March 31, 1982 inclusive.

			Amount 1981
Gross amounts charged to clients, including any service fees			£000
(A)	**Space etc.**		
	(i)	Press	29,679
	(ii)	Billposting, including transport advertising	3,469
	(iii)	Radio time	7,216
	(iv)	Television time	20,496
	(v)	Film screen time	298
	(vi)	Other	129
(B)	**Production**		
	(i)	Radio programme production	850
	(ii)	Television and other film production fees including artistes' fees and use fees	4,189
	(iii)	Printing	4,054
	(iv)	Other production work (e.g. typesetting, blockmaking, artwork, films, etc.)	6,817
(C)	**Other**		
		Other work (e.g. research, promotions) not shown above	871
	Total gross amount charged to clients		78,068
	Remuneration		
	Total payments of wages and salaries during the year, including fees to directors working in the business		7,769

	Number 1981
Persons engaged in April, including those sick or on leave	
Proprietors (including directors) working in business	132
Paid employees working in business:	
(i) full-time	788
(ii) part-time	20
Total number of persons working business in April	940

660

1982, 1983

The following statement sets out the results of a statistical inquiry covering the advertising business handled by Irish advertising agencies in the year 1983. Receipts and expenses connected with any ancillary business activity such as publishing are been excluded. The 1983 results cover 30 agencies which have responded to date out of the total number of 47 known to have been operating in that year.

Individual returns were completed for the accounting year closest to the calendar year 1983. About 83 per cent of the total gross amount charged to clients relates to accounting years ending between December 31 1983 and March 31 1984 inclusive.

		Amount	
Gross amounts charged to clients, including any service fees		1982	1983
		£000	
(A) **Space etc.**			
(i)	Press	32,645	31,663
(ii)	Billposting, including transport advertising	4,303	4,809
(iii)	Radio time	8,420	10,278
(iv)	Television time	25,728	25,219
(v)	Film screen time	181	248
(vi)	Other	76	108
(B) **Production**			
(i)	Radio programme production	736	759
(ii)	Television and other film production fees including artistes' fees and use fees	4,401	4,022
(iii)	Printing	4,855	4,891
(iv)	Other production work (e.g. typesetting, blockmaking, artwork, films, etc.)	7,730	7,776
(C) **Other**			
	Other work (e.g. research, promotions) not shown above	565	487
Total amount charged to clients		**89,640**	**90,259**

		Amount	
Remuneration Total payments of wages and salaries during the year, including fees to directors working in the business		8,474	8,688

	Number	
Persons engaged in April, including those sick or on leave	1982	1983
Proprietors (including directors) working in business	131	124
Paid employees working in business:		
(i) full-time	705	640
(ii) part-time	10	12
Total number of persons working business in April	**846**	**776**

1984

The following statement sets out the results of a statistical inquiry covering the advertising business handled by Irish advertising agencies in the year 1984. Receipts and expenses connected with any ancillary business activity such as publishing have been excluded as far as possible. The 1984 results cover 33 agencies which have responded to date out of the total number of 42 known to have been operating in that year.

Individual returns were completed for the business year closest to the calendar year 1984. About 77 per cent of the total gross amount charged to clients relates to accounting years ending in the period December 31 1984 and March 31 1985 inclusive.

Gross amounts charged to clients, including VAT and any service fees	Amount	
	1983	1984
	£000	
(A) Space etc.		
(i) Press	33,941	37,657
(ii) Billposting, including transport advertising	5,278	6,666
(iii) Radio time	11,112	12,800
(iv) Television time	26,565	34,943
(v) Film screen time	254	248
(vi) Other	124	134
(B) Production		
(i) Radio programme production	811	1,124
(ii) Television and other film production fees including artistes' fees and use fees	4,255	5,870
(iii) Printing	5,642	6,874
(iv) Other production work (e.g. typesetting, blockmaking, artwork, films, etc.)	8,330	10,069
(C) Other		
Other work (e.g. research, promotions) not shown above	511	572
Total amount charged to clients	**96,823**	**116,957**
Remuneration Total payments of wages and salaries during the year, including fees to directors working in the business	8,688	9,708

Persons engaged in April, including those sick or on leave	Number	
	1983	1984
Proprietors (including directors) working in business	124	147
Paid employees working in business:		
(i) full-time	640	636
(ii) part-time	12	21
Total number of persons working business in April	**776**	**804**

Top 20 Advertisers on RTE Television, 1985

		£000's
1.	Guinness Group Sales	1,871
2.	Unilever	1,767
3.	Master Foods	970
4.	Kellogg Co. of Ireland	922
5.	Reckitts (Irl.)	867
6.	Albright & Wilson	853
7.	Beecham of Ireland	701
8.	Rowntree-Mackintosh	609
9.	Cadbury (Irl.)	583
10.	Quinnsworth	550
11.	Willwood Group	465
12.	Johnson Bros.	444
13.	Irish Permanent Building Society	413
14.	J. Lyons & Co.	408
15.	A. Bird & Sons	399
16.	General Motors	382
17.	Coca-Cola	367
18.	CPC Ireland	357
19.	Henry Ford & Son	326
20.	Educational Building Society	310

RTE television advertising income, 1962-1986

Year	Amount
1962	£206,345
1963	£699,878
1964	£1,047,316
1965	£1,564,953
1966	£1,796,265
1967	£2,061,745
1968	£2,345,909
1969	£2,629,231
1970	£2,833,117
1971	£2,750,560
1972	£2,871,212
1973	£3,499,111
1974	£3,847,416
1975	£4,633,164
1976	£5,582,959
1977	£7,203,908
1978	£9,198,115
1979	£11,561,838
1980	£14,245,267
1981	£16,739,163
1982	£19,848,826
1983	£20,471,836
1984	£24,167,645
1985	£26,351,606
1986 (estimated)	£38,000,000

N.B.: Before 1975, RTE's financial year ended in April.
After 1975, it ends in September. 1975 figures reflect
the changeover.

Advertising Organisations

Advertising Press Club of Ireland
Chairmen

1943	D. J. Fogarty	Inks' representative
1944	B. D. O'Kennedy	O'Kennedy Brindley
1945	J. H. Webb	The Irish Times
1946	D. J. Fogarty	Inks' representative
1947	W. G. King	Independent Newspapers
1948	D. J. Garvey	Janus Advertising
1949	J. H. Webb	The Irish Times
1950	W. G. King	Independent Newspapers
1951	F. W. Padbury	Padbury Advertising
1952	Gordon Clark	Montford Publications
1953	H. C. Denham	Irish Press group
1954	A. R. Thomas	The Irish Times
1955	Albert Price	W. D. & H. O. Wills
1956	M. B. Kenny	Kenny's Advertising
1957	M. J. O'Connor	Mount Salus Press
1958	H. C. Denham	Irish Press Group
1959	W. G. King	Independent Newspapers
1960	Jim Nolan	Arks
1961	Tom Milner	Lever Bros.
1962	Eileen Ball	Johnson Bros.
1963	Neil Renton	McConnell's Advertising
1964	Fred Mullen	David Allen & Sons
1965	Winnifred Stacey	Cerebos
1966	Harry Byers	Janus Advertising
1967	Robert K. Gahan	RTE
1968	Michael Hayes	Arks
1969	J. A. Cleary	Irish Ropes
1970	Danny Moroney	Irish Press group
1971	Stuart Kenny	Kenny's Advertising
1972	Jack McGouran	Kenny's Advertising
1973	Frank Grennan	Jemma Publications
1974	Frank Grennan	Jemma Publications
1975	Roger Wornell	Kenny's Advertising
1976	Colm Brangan	Brangan Luhmann Knight
1977-84	Frank Grennan	Jemma Publications
1984-86	Shay Keany	Hunter's Advertising
1986	David Markey	New Hibernia/ Irish Farmers' Monthly

Albert Price Communications Award
(presented by Publicity Club of Ireland)

1984	Douglas Gageby	The Irish Times
1985	Bob Geldof	Live Aid
1986	Gay Byrne	RTE

Association of Advertisers in Ireland
Presidents

1951/52/53/54	J. O'Sheehan	Irish Hospitals Trust (1940
1955	A. E. Snow	W. & R. Jacob & Co.
1956/57	W. S. Douglas	Lamb Bros. (Dublin)
1958/59	W. P. Cavanagh	Chivers & Sons (I)
1960/61	C. P. Kelleher	Bovril (Eire)
1962/63	J. C. Bigger	Hammond Lane Foundry Co
1964	J. M. McNeill	John Player & Sons
1965	J. F. Kearney	Williams & Woods
1966/67	F. C. Palmer	Reckitts (Ireland)
1968	N. McConnell	Aspro-Nicholas of Ireland
1969/70	B. Doyle	Player & Wills (Ireland)
1971/72, 1972/73	E. S. Cooke	Irish Biscuits
1973/74, 1974/75	K. E. J. Tyrell	Guinness Group Sales (I)
1975/76, 1976/77	G. E. Nairn	Lamb Bros. (Dublin)
1977	R. P. Knight	CPC Ireland
1977/78, 1978/79	J. P. Fitzpatrick	Irish Dunlop Co.
1979/80, 1980/81	F. P. Hayden	Temana Ireland
1981/82	B. R. George	Albright & Wilson (I)
1982/83, 1983/84	B. P. Walsh	W. & C. McDonnell
1984/85, 1985/86	L. M. Hughes	P. J. Carroll & Co.

Marketing Institute of Ireland
Chairmen

1962/63	B. M. Murphy	Hammond Lane Industries
1963/64	N. McConnell	Aspro Nicholas
1964/65	H. V. Woods	Mart-Woods Ltd.
1965/66	H. V. Woods	Mart-Woods Ltd.
1966/67	J. C. Bigger	Hammond Lane Ironfounders
1967/68	A. N. Fogarty	Fogarty Advt. Ltd.
1968/69	G. F. Maher	Reming Rand Irl. Ltd.
1969/70	L. C. Thorn	Metlex
1970/71	W. D. Fraser	Jeyes Irl. Ltd.
1971/72	H. A. Wyer	Armstrong Cork
1972/73	John D. Carroll	Carroll Catering Ltd.
1973/74	D. J. Fitzgibbon	Motor Distributors
1974 (July-Dec.)	J. C. McGough	Bord Bainne
1975	J. C. McGough	Bord Bainne
1976	A. J. Neville	E. K. O'Brien Ltd.
1977	R. E. Reid	EMR Enterprises Ltd.
1978	Dr. P. Kehoe	Kehoe & Associates
1979	P. J. Nolan	Twinnings
1980	J. B. O'Reilly	Sales Placement Ltd.
1981	M. D. Shields	NIHE
1982	J. S. Burns	Biotex
1983	J. Downey	Janus
1984	P. R. Flood	College of Marketing & Design
1985	W. Ambrose	Belenos Publications
1986	B. Weafer	NBST

Marketing Society
Chairmen

1970-71	J. M. Lepere	P.J. Carroll & Co.
1971-72	J. M. Lepere	P.J. Carroll & Co.
1972/73	Peter M. Owens	Peter Owens Advertising & Marketing
1973-74	T. J. Garvey	Coras Trachtala
1974-75	John F. Meagher	Irish Marketing Surveys
1975-76	J. V. Liston	United Drug Co.
1976-77	Finbar Costello	Irish International Advertising
1977-78	Archie Cook	Irish Distillers
1978-79	Denis N. Henderson	Irish Biscuits
1979-80	Frank J. Young	Wilson Hartnell Advertising
1980-81	P. J. McKenna	Guinness Group Sales
1981-82	John Fanning	McConnell's Advertising
1982-83	M. J. MacNulty	Irish Dunlop
1983-84	A. P. McCarthy	Coras Trachtala
1984-85	Colm Lyons	Sterling Winthrop
1985-86	Graham Wilkinson	

McConnell Award Winners
(presented by Advertising Press Club)

1952	William G. King	Independent Newspapers
1954	Charles E. McConnell	McConnell's Advertising
1955	Denis Garvey	Janus Advertising
1956	Denis Swords	McConnell's Advertising
1962	Brian D. O'Kennedy	O'Kennedy Brindley Advertising
1963	Albert Price	W. D. & H. O. Wills
1964	John Tate	Arks Advertising
1966	Luke Mahon	Arks Advertising
1967	John Lepere	P. J. Carroll & Co.
1968	F. C. Palmer	Reckitt's (Ireland)
1969	Jarlath Hayes	O'Kennedy Brindley Advertising
1970	Daniel Nolan	Kerryman
1971	Capt. Oliver Walsh	Institute of Advertising Practitioners in Ireland
1972	J. C. Dempsey	Irish Press Group
1974	James Nolan	Arks Advertising
1975	K. E. J. Tyrrell	Guinness
1976	Robert K. Gahan	RTE
1977	George Gracie	Guinness
1979	Noel Cautley	O'Keeffes Advertising
1983	John Fanning	McConnell's Advertising

Publicity Association of Northern Ireland — Chairmen

1958	Robin Kinahan	Ulster Bank
1959/60	Brum Henderson	Ulster Television
1961	Ron Chapman	McConnell's, Belfast
1962	Fred Binks	Nicholson & Bass
1963	John Williams	Northern Ireland Tourist Board
1964	Gerry Gilmore	McConnell's, Belfast
1965	Ted Jerram	Wells Advertising
1966	John Caughey	Public Relations Advisers
1967	Norah Byrne	Wells Advertising
1968	Brian Boyd	Alexander Boyd Displays
1969	Basil Singleton	A. V. Browne
1970	George Miskimmins	Irish Press
1971	Harold Beattie	Government Information Service
1972	John McCann	Nicholson & Bass
1973	Mrs Doreen Francis	Dairy Council for Northern Ireland
1974	Bob McCammond	Ross Poultry
1975	Dave Dark	McConnell's, Belfast
1976	Ken Hamilton	Ulster Television
1977	Rex McKane	Belfast Progressive Advertising
1978	Bill Jeffrey	Arrow Poster Sites
1979	Pat Meehan	Irish News
1980	Hugh McWilliams	Century Newspapers
1981	Stanley Anderson	Trustee Savings Bank
1982	Mrs Hillary Rafferty	Anderson & McAuley
1983	Kieran Boyle	Downtown Radio
1984	Brian Chambers	Ulster Television
1985	Eleanor Turkington	Belfast Telegraph
1986	John McQuiston	RMB Advertising

Publicity Club of Ireland — Chairmen

1923/24	Dr Lombard Murphy	Independent Newspapers
1924/25/26	Sir Thomas Robinson	
1926/27	A. L. Canavan	
1927/28	F. W. Summerfield	
1928/29	Rose Waldron	
1929/30	Charlie McConnell	McConnell's
1930/31	T. A. Grehan	Independent Newspapers
1931/32	P. T. Montford	Dublin Opinion
1939/44	Charlie McConnell	McConnell's
1944/45	Jack O'Sheehan	Irish Hospitals' Sweepstake
1945/46	Brian O'Kennedy	O'Kennedy Brindley
1946/47	Albert Price	W. D. & H. O. Wills
1947/48	C. T. Tynan O'Mahony	The Irish Times
1948/49	George Childs	New Ireland Assurance
1949/50	M. J. Clarke	Social & Personal

1950/51	Eddie MacSweeney	Odeon Cinemas	1967/68	J. C. Bigger	Hammond Lane
1951/52	G. Sutton Kelly		1968/69	Dermod Cafferky	Arrow
1952/53	Victor Woods	Williams & Woods	1969/70	Bart Bastable	Irish Hospitals' Sweepstake
1953/54	David Luke	Irish Press Group	1970/71	Aubrey Fogarty	Fogarty Advertising
1954/55	Liam Boyd	TWA	1971/72	Eileen Ball	Johnson Bros.
1955/56	Melville (Sandy) Miller	The Irish Times	1972/73	Tommy Mangan	Irish Press Group
1956/57	Fergus O'Sheehan	FOS	1974/75	Brian Doyle	Player-Wills
1957/58	W. S. Douglas	Lamb Bros.	1975	Paddy Neilan	Independent Newspapers
1958/59	Michael B. Kenny	Kenny's	1976/77	Eileen Wickstone	Linguaphone
1959/60	John McNeill	John Player & Sons	1978/79	Tim Dennehy	Tim Dennehy PR
1960/61	Andrew Gairn	David Allen & Sons	1980	Niall O'Flynn	Player-Wills
1961/62	Oonagh McWhirter	Odeon Cinemas	1981	John Culleton	Philips
1962/63	Arthur Thomas		1982	Joe O'Grady	Cork Examiner
1963/64	Eileen Ball	Johnson Bros.	1983	Donal O Maolalai	CIE
1964/65	Billy King	Independent Newspapers	1984	Bill Tyndall	Tyndall Advertising
1965/66	Bob McElheron	CIE	1985	Bill McHugh	Irish Press Cuttings
1966/67	Terry Spillane	Hardware & Allied Trader	1986	Frank Fitzpatrick	PF Marketing

Index

Index — Text

Index — Illustrations

Index — Colour Section

IRISH MANAGEMENT
LIBRARY
★ INSTITUTE ★